The Compleat Victory

James T. Patterson
Brown v. Board of Education: A Civil Rights Milestone and Its Troubled Legacy

Maury Klein
Rainbow's End: The Crash of 1929

James McPherson
Crossroads of Freedom: The Battle of Antietam

Glenn C. Altschuler
All Shook Up: How Rock 'n' Roll Changed America

David Hackett Fischer
Washington's Crossing

John Ferling
Adams vs. Jefferson: The Tumultuous Election of 1800

Joel H. Silbey
Storm over Texas: The Annexation Controversy and the Road to Civil War

Raymond Arsenault
Freedom Riders: 1961 and the Struggle for Racial Justice

Colin G. Calloway
The Scratch of a Pen: 1763 and the Transformation of North America

Richard Labunski
James Madison and the Struggle for the Bill of Rights

Sally G. McMillen
Seneca Falls and the Origins of the Women's Rights Movement

Howard Jones
The Bay of Pigs

Lynn Parsons
The Birth of Modern Politics: Andrew Jackson, John Quincy Adams, and the Election of 1828

Elliott West
The Last Indian War: The Nez Perce Story

Glenn C. Altschuler and Stuart M. Blumin
The GI Bill: A New Deal for Veterans

Richard Archer
As If an Enemy's Country: The British Occupation of Boston and the Origins of Revolution

Thomas Kessner
The Flight of the Century: Charles Lindbergh and the Rise of American Aviation

Craig L. Symonds
The Battle of Midway

Richard Moe
Roosevelt's Second Act: The Election of 1940 and the Politics of War

Emerson W. Baker
A Storm of Witchcraft: The Salem Trials and the American Experience

Louis P. Masur
Lincoln's Last Speech: Wartime Reconstruction and the Crisis of Reunion

David L. Preston
Braddock's Defeat: The Battle of the Monongahela and the Road to Revolution

Michael A. Cohen
American Maelstrom: The 1968 Election and the Politics of Division

Marc Gallicchio
Unconditional: The Japanese Surrender in World War II

The Compleat Victory

SARATOGA AND THE AMERICAN REVOLUTION

Kevin J. Weddle

OXFORD
UNIVERSITY PRESS

OXFORD
UNIVERSITY PRESS

Oxford University Press is a department of the University of Oxford. It furthers the University's objective of excellence in research, scholarship, and education by publishing worldwide. Oxford is a registered trade mark of Oxford University Press in the UK and certain other countries.

Published in the United States of America by Oxford University Press
198 Madison Avenue, New York, NY 10016, United States of America.

First issued as an Oxford University paperback, 2024

Library of Congress Cataloging-in-Publication Data
Names: Weddle, Kevin John, author.
Title: The compleat victory : Saratoga and the American Revolution / by Kevin J. Weddle.
Other titles: Battle of Saratoga and the American Revolution
Description: New York, NY : Oxford University Press, [2021] |
Series: Pivotal moments in American history |
Includes bibliographical references and index.
Identifiers: LCCN 2020041604 (print) | LCCN 2020041605 (ebook) |
ISBN 9780195331400 (hardback) | ISBN 9780197695166 (paperback) |
ISBN 9780199912537 (epub) | ISBN 9780199715992 (epdf) |
ISBN 9780197549445 (ebook other)
Subjects: LCSH: Saratoga Campaign, N.Y., 1777. | Burgoyne's Invasion, 1777.
United States—History—Revolution, 1775–1783—Campaigns. |
New York (State)— History—Revolution, 1775–1783.
Classification: LCC E241.S2 W43 2021 (print) |
LCC E241.S2 (ebook) | DDC 973.3/33—dc23
LC record available at https://lccn.loc.gov/2020041604
LC ebook record available at https://lccn.loc.gov/2020041605

Paperback printed by Marquis Book Printing, Canada

MIX
Paper from responsible sources
FSC® C103567
FSC
www.fsc.org

For Jeanie

CONTENTS

LIST OF MAPS

EDITORS' NOTE

Most historians of the American War for Independence agree that Saratoga was a pivotal moment in that long struggle. The victory of American citizen-soldiers and the surrender of an entire British army caused Europe's leading military power to intervene in support of the American cause. When France entered the war, other European states followed. The fighting spread from America to Europe, Africa, and Asia. A colonial rebellion became a world war. Great Britain suffered the worst defeat in its modern history, and the new United States won their independence.

That understanding of Saratoga's importance is widely shared by scholars. But precisely how and why it happened is a more difficult and complex question. Saratoga was not a single battle. It came as the climax of a long campaign, after many other events that drew in a diversity of American Continentals, State militia, British regulars, Canadian troops, German mercenaries, and Indian warriors. Their commanders had different traditions of leadership, and the many men who served with them had profoundly different ideas of why they were there.

These events have drawn the attention of Kevin Weddle, an historian who has distinguished himself in two professional careers. He is a graduate of West Point who, like other leading graduates of that great institution, joined the Army Corps of Engineers. His long military career has spanned a broad range of assignments, including as battalion commander, as well as service in Operations Desert Storm and Enduring Freedom. At the same time, Weddle actively pursued another career as a professional historian. He earned a doctorate in American history at Princeton, published a major dissertation on the American Civil War, and produced other important works of scholarship. And he brought his two professional careers together as a professor at the Army War College, where he rapidly rose to become its Deputy Dean.

We invited Weddle to contribute a volume to the Pivotal Moments in American History series at Oxford, on a subject of his own choosing.

He selected the Saratoga campaign, which had first drawn his attention when he began to study it as a cadet. His continuing interest in the campaign centered on problems of leadership. For many years, the study of leaders had been at the heart of much historical scholarship. More recent generations of scholars have shifted their primary inquiries to other questions of high importance in social, economic, demographic, cultural, and intellectual history. Much was gained by this enlargement of historical research, but something important has been lost.

In recent years, we in the United States have suffered a decline in the quality of leadership in high elective offices of our American Republic. The primary cause is not only a pattern of failure in our leaders themselves, but in those of us who choose them. Our culture on many levels has tended to move away from the vital task of preparing Americans for their primary civic responsibilities in the choice of those who should lead in a free and open society.

In consequence, historians are returning to the study of leadership. Weddle's book on Saratoga centers not merely on a few at the top. It is broadly conceived to include a diversity of people who functioned in many prominent roles in a world-historical event and who made a difference, both positive and negative, in its outcome. It studies a broad array of leaders, senior and junior, civilian and military, who functioned in the thirteen American states, in Britain's constitutional monarchy, in French and British Canada, in German professional forces, and within American Indian nations. Some have given rise to an historical literature that is large and often deeply divided. Weddle, who commands a large range of primary and secondary materials and whose inquiries draw on his own personal experience and background, comes to his own balanced conclusions. His inquiries combine the precise thinking of a professional soldier with a scholar's concern for the evidence. At the same time, he has written a fluent, graceful, and engaging book that brings out the drama of pivotal moments.

The Saratoga campaign occurred in a flow of events that began in 1775 and continued to 1777 and beyond. Each of its battles featured different sets of commanding officers and supporting leaders. Weddle's book takes the form of a braided narrative, centering on several sequences of leaders who made choices, choices that made a difference in the world. Military history can be confusing to the nonprofessional reader, especially when it involves so many characters operating over such a wide geographic area. Weddle's skill keeps

the story of Saratoga moving forward with a clarity that conquers confusion.

More than any other book on its subject, Weddle's narrative studies the central role of an American leader who was not present on the field at Saratoga—George Washington, who was learning by trial and error to master his role as commander-in-chief of the Continental army and as a leader in the American cause. Washington began with a near-fatal failure to perceive the vital importance of events on the distant northern frontier. Then, through a process of learning and growth, he worked constructively with individual military commanders and civilian leaders in the Saratoga campaign, sending some of his most able officers and best fighting units from his own forces. Weddle reconstructs a pattern of change and growth in the man and the event. Altogether it enlarges and refines our understanding of the man, the event, and problems of leadership in a long sequence of critical moments.

Weddle does something similar for major leaders on every side and is always very careful, creative, and independent in his judgments. In that way he makes fresh and original contributions to our understanding of a number of individual leaders on the American side, including St. Clair at Ticonderoga; Gansevoort at Stanwix; Herkimer at Oriskany; Stark at Bennington; Morgan and Dearborn at Freemans Farm; Gates and Learned and Arnold at Bemis Heights; and British, Hessian, Canadian, and American Indian leaders in equal measure.

In this book, Weddle reflects on general models of leadership, such as Bernard Montgomery's idea of "grip." And through it all, he also gives particular attention to forms of effective leadership in open systems. All of us can put his knowledge and judgment to work, when we choose our own leaders or when we find ourselves chosen to lead in a free society.

David Hackett Fischer
James M. McPherson

ACKNOWLEDGMENTS

No one can complete a book that takes more than ten years to research and write without being indebted to many people. First and foremost, David Hackett Fischer not only brought me into the project, but he went above and beyond the call of duty by reading at least two full drafts of the book and many other versions of important sections. His feedback and suggestions were instrumental in fleshing out key themes, and he enthusiastically endorsed my focus on strategy and leadership. David is an exceptional historian and a national treasure, and I am fortunate to call him a mentor and a friend. Jim McPherson, another mentor and friend, provided helpful feedback and support.

Eric Schnitzer, chief historian at the Saratoga National Historical Park, cheerfully offered his time and considerable expertise. He not only shared his own research, he also reviewed and provided timely expert feedback on major portions of the book. He patiently answered all my queries, which was especially critical to my understanding of how the two major battles unfolded and the details of the often-confusing orders of battle. His deep knowledge of the campaign, the sources, and the period came to my rescue time and time again.

My colleagues at the United States Army War College have been encouraging and helpful at every stage. My boss, Dr. Clay Chun, was an enthusiastic supporter. Several of my good friends and fellow faculty members read and provided invaluable feedback on early drafts, including Pete Haas, Chris Bolan, Joel Hillison, Bill Johnsen, and John Paterson. The book is much better because of their generous efforts.

I spent many days exploring the various sites associated with the Saratoga campaign. I profited from numerous discussions and correspondence with park rangers and other staff members at the Fort Ticonderoga Museum, the Mount Independence State (Vermont) Historic Site, the Hubbardton Battlefield State (Vermont) Historic Site, the Fort Stanwix National Monument, the Oriskany Battlefield

State (New York) Historic Site, and the Saratoga National Historical Park. They all enthusiastically responded to my many questions.

While serving as the William L. Garwood Visiting Professor at Princeton University in 2019, I taught a course on World War II strategy and leadership, which helped crystalize my thinking about the two topics that figure so prominently in this book. I owe many thanks to Robbie George and Brad Wilson of the James Madison Program for offering me the appointment, the Army War College's leadership for approving it, my hardworking and supportive preceptor, Mark O'Brien, and last but never least, my wonderful students.

I am indebted to the extremely helpful staffs at all the archives and libraries I physically and virtually visited during my research. Librarians and archivists at the British Library, the Library of Congress, Ellen McCallister Clark and Rebecca Cooper at the Society of the Cincinnati Library, Miranda Peters and Christopher D. Fox at the Fort Ticonderoga Museum, and April Miller at the Firestone Library at Princeton University, promptly responded to my many requests. Also, the Interlibrary Loan staff at the Army War College Library was extremely efficient and always cheerful. Three institutions, at which I spent many weeks researching the book, and their staffs deserve special mention: the William L. Clements Library at the University of Michigan, the Army Heritage and Education Center (AHEC), and the David Library of the American Revolution (DLAR). Terese Austin and Valarie Proehl helped me negotiate the marvelous collection of the papers of British senior leaders at the Clements Library. AHEC, a part of the Army War College, was invaluable for its extensive collection of secondary sources and published primary material as well as the microfilm collection of Horatio Gates's papers. Finally, I spent the most time at the DLAR (now the David Center for the American Revolution at the American Philosophical Society in Philadelphia), which was one of the most user-friendly places to conduct research I have ever visited. Its librarian, Kathy Ludwig, has an encyclopedic knowledge of the DLAR's unsurpassed collection of material—British and American—related to the American Revolution, and I benefitted many times from her wise counsel and suggestions.

I was very fortunate to receive a Society of the Cincinnati Scholar's Grant and a United States Military Academy Omar N. Bradley Research Fellowship, which helped defray the cost of travel and research. Many thanks to Ellen McCallister Clark, Clifford Rogers, and Lee Johnston.

My editor, Tim Bent, and the entire staff at the Oxford University Press were always professional, encouraging, and responsive. Tim did a superb job of editing, counseling me to let the story unfold, to keep things moving, to cut extraneous detail, and, whenever possible, to show not tell. Not only that, but Tim displayed almost infinite patience with me when the project was delayed for an extended period due to a serious family health crisis. I will be forever grateful for his support. Joellyn Ausanka carefully and skillfully shepherded the project through to competition. Joellyn and her team were a joy to work with.

Finally, my wonderful wife, Jeanie, has cheerfully allowed Saratoga to live with us for more than a decade. She also patiently and with great forbearance listened to me for hours as I read major portions of the book out loud to her, and she offered many useful critiques and suggestions. Jeanie's support was essential, and her courage while successfully fighting a terrible disease was inspirational. This project would have never reached a conclusion without her.

The Compleat Victory

Introduction: Fatal Ambition

THE QUEEN'S HOUSE WAS modest as royal palaces went in eighteenth-century England. In 1761, King George III purchased the former country home of the Duke of Buckingham for his young wife, Princess Charlotte of Mecklenburg-Strelitz. This unpretentious retreat for the royal family—later expanded substantially—would one day be known as Buckingham Palace. A family home, only a few steps from St. James Palace, the official royal residence, the Queen's House provided the king and queen with some respite from their official duties.

It was there, in late August 1777, that the king received a message. It so thrilled him that he burst into his wife's chambers, waving the paper in the air, exclaiming, "I have beat them! I have beat the Americans!"[1] The message informed His Majesty that British Lieutenant General John Burgoyne had captured Fort Ticonderoga, the strategically important American fortress located on the southern narrows of Lake Champlain. Achieved with minimal casualties, the victory convinced the king and his ministers that the military strategy they had put in place that spring was unfolding according to plan.[2]

In October 1777, two months after the king's impromptu celebration and three months after taking Ticonderoga, Burgoyne surrendered his entire army of almost six thousand officers and men to an American force of Continental soldiers and militia under the command of Major General Horatio Gates at a place called Saratoga.

Only one year earlier, the American Revolution looked to be on its last legs. The Americans had been forced out of New York, and the rebel army was slowly evaporating. However, the Americans were able to stave off their seemingly inevitable defeat by winning at Trenton and Princeton in late 1776 and early 1777. After these surprising

setbacks, the British were determined to end the war once and for all. They devised a complicated plan. Three different British armies would converge on Albany, New York, take control of the Hudson River, and split the newly self-proclaimed independent nation in two. Burgoyne would command the army from Canada; the main army, under the British commander-in-chief, General Sir William Howe, was to first seize Philadelphia, then support Burgoyne by moving up the Hudson. The strategy miscarried badly.

When word of Burgoyne's surrender reached London on the evening of December 2, 1777, the country was stunned. Everyone had been led to believe that victory over the upstart American colonists was just around the corner. Politicians, newspapers, and the public clamored for blame to be assigned. Opposition members in Parliament demanded the resignation of key ministers. Senior military officers were embarrassed.[3] The American victory at Saratoga was a major military setback for the British. It profoundly affected the course of events over the next five years, not least because it led directly to France's decision to enter the war on the Patriot side, which changed the entire character of the American Revolution, from a colonial rebellion to a world war.

Given that the focus of this series about pivotal moments in American history is on historical contingency, it would be unthinkable to omit the Saratoga campaign. The planning and execution of the campaign are replete with critical decisions by leaders on both sides, and chance played a major role, as it always does in war. This book covers the entire campaign in all its complexity, including its origins, execution, and aftermath, and a more dramatic and consequential American story is hard to find.

I first became interested in the American Revolution and the Saratoga campaign while a cadet at the United States Military Academy at West Point, located 130 miles south of the main battlefield. Throughout a long military career, I have been fortunate to lead hundreds of staff rides and battlefield tours to sites in the United States and Europe, ranging from the Battle of Agincourt to Saratoga to Waterloo to Gettysburg to Gallipoli to the D-Day landings in Normandy. These trips, combined with two combat deployments, command of a battalion, and teaching posts at West Point and the US Army War College, sharpened my interest in leadership and military strategy, which are the two major themes that run through this book.

Essential to understanding the Saratoga campaign's outcome is an appreciation of the origins of the strategy that drove the military

operations and of the leaders whose decisons drove the British and American forces to their final clashes along the Hudson River.

Who was to blame for Britain's ignominious defeat? Most have assigned the lion's share of the responsibility to Lord George Germain, Secretary of State for the Colonies, and the minister responsible for British military operations in North America. Howe is also blamed for wasting time and resources on other campaigns when he should have been assisting the army from Canada. Yet I argue that it was the strategy itself that was ultimately responsible. The foundations for the British defeat at Saratoga were laid in London, New York, and Quebec, where the strategy was devised in the winter and spring of 1777.

Indeed, responsibility for the loss at Saratoga spreads wide. Germain tried to micromanage the war from a continent away and failed to ensure that all the British commanders in North America, especially Burgoyne and Howe, coordinated their efforts. By the summer of 1777, Howe understood that the only way to win the war was to destroy the American Army under the command of General George Washington. However, he did not move quickly or synchronize his actions with those of Burgoyne's army to make this happen. Finally, Burgoyne, the man who surrendered to Gates, proved to be simply out of his depth. Despite being an experienced and popular commander, Burgoyne never understood until it was too late just how challenging the American environment would be for moving and supplying and fighting with a large European army.

Despite their ultimate victory, the Americans were not immune to failures of leadership during the Saratoga campaign. Major General Arthur St. Clair, commanding Fort Ticonderoga, committed a series of blunders that led directly to the fortress' evacuation and ensured that Burgoyne's invasion got off to a fast start with a major success. For the most part, Major General Philip Schuyler, commander of the Northern Department, made decisions that helped lay the groundwork for ultimate American success. Still, his wildly pessimistic reports to Congress and General Washington caused his superiors to lose confidence in his ability to stem Burgoyne's seemingly inexorable advance south toward Albany.[4]

Schuyler's replacement was Horatio Gates, who built on the foundation that Schuyler had already laid. Later in the war, events would demonstrate just how fortunate Gates had been in August 1777 to inherit a situation in which his talents meshed with the circumstances. Major General Benjamin Lincoln, Gates's second-in-command late in the campaign, proved invaluable to his superiors in handling

the sometimes unreliable militia units from the New England states and in the substantive reinforcement of the Northern Army when it mattered the most. The Americans also had a depth of strong leadership in many outstanding field officers and junior general officers who performed admirably during the campaign. Brigadier General John Stark led his troops to victory at the Battle of Bennington, an engagement that proved the beginning of the end for Burgoyne and his army. Though heavily outnumbered, Colonel Peter Gansevoort successfully defended Fort Stanwix. Colonel Daniel Morgan led his riflemen at the Battle of Freeman's Farm and the Battle of Bemis Heights. All of these American senior leaders—and many more besides—contributed to the victory at Saratoga.

Perhaps the most dynamic combat leader on either side was Major General Benedict Arnold. From the moment he joined the Northern Army, he made a difference—helping to restore morale, managing militia, conducting reconnaissance missions and raids, and personally leading the final assault at the Battle of Bemis Heights. There is no doubt that Arnold's role was central to the American success at Saratoga, even though he was volatile and easily took offense. But the advantages Gates derived from having Arnold as one of his combat commanders far outweighed the disadvantages.

The Americans in the Northern Department were also fortunate that their commander-in-chief was George Washington, even though he was almost 300 miles away to the south and distracted by the challenge of facing Howe's main British Army. Washington underestimated the threat to and the readiness of the Northern Department in the winter and spring of 1777. Nonetheless, he more than made up for his earlier inattention to the theater after the loss of Ticonderoga in July. Washington patiently counseled and mentored the anxious Schuyler and provided sound advice. He also appealed to New England governors and assemblies to muster and dispatch militia forces to join the Northern Army, hurried significant reinforcements northward, and, perhaps most importantly, assigned Benedict Arnold and Benjamin Lincoln to report to Schuyler. Washington's contributions to the Saratoga campaign are generally glossed over, but they were essential for American victory. Washington could have neglected or even ignored the Northern Army while he faced General Howe, but he did not. He continued setting priorities and allocating his resources accordingly.

While preparing one of my Army War College courses, I encountered British Field Marshal Sir Bernard Montgomery's notion of "grip," a term he used to describe a commander who was

able to manage a battle or campaign by personally scrutinizing and supervising all elements of a military operation.[5] These attributes are essential elements of leadership. However, I wanted to take the concept a step farther. For this book, I have expanded on Montgomery's definition of grip to include the ability to anticipate how operations might unfold and how to react to change, something closer to what Carl von Clausewitz called "genius."[6] "Grip" results when superior leadership combines with experience and expertise. According to my formulation, Alexander the Great, Napoleon, Lord Nelson, Ulysses S. Grant, Robert E. Lee, and (closer to Montgomery's own time) General George Patton all had "grip," in their ability to sense how a battle or maneuver was unfolding, how the overall engagement was playing out, and when to take the right action, even in uncertain environments and in the absence of critical information. Montgomery's definition mainly concerned tactical actions on the battlefield. My concept of grip can equally be applied at the operational and strategic levels of war.[7] Simply put, the Saratoga campaign turned out the way it did because American leaders displayed more grip—at all levels of war—than their British counterparts.

In war, geography is everything. The Saratoga campaign was epic in both its scope and its impact. Few operations in American history—with exceptions in the Civil War and World War II—took place over such vast distances in such forbidding terrain. It ranged across thousands of square miles and involved dozens of separate battles, engagements, sieges, and maneuvers, some relatively minor, but others pivotal.

To understand this reality and make sense of a very complex campaign, I spent many days walking the sites. The beauty of the Lake Champlain region and the Mohawk River valley in central and western New York made this a very pleasurable experience. It also drove home just how challenging it would have been for eighteenth-century armies to manage operations over such rugged terrain. The experience increased the respect I already had for those on both sides who marched through these woods, across these rivers and creeks, and over these hills and mountains from June through October 1777.

Native Americans played a major role in the Saratoga campaign, and they participated on both sides of the conflict. I use the terms *Native* and *Native American* frequently in the book, but for the most part employ *Indian or Indians,* as most people, Indian and non-Indian, did at the time.

I have relied on many earlier works on the Saratoga campaign, including those by Hoffman Nickerson, John Elting, Richard Ketchum, Brendon Morrissey, John Luzader, and others. This book benefits from and, I hope, complements theirs, while at the same time, I have made my own interpretations and conclusions. As much as possible, I have tried to let the participants tell the story and have also addressed some errors and misunderstandings about the operation that sometimes have made for a good story if not for good history.

Saratoga changed the American Revolution. The campaign's outcome reverberated everywhere—in Quebec, New York, Philadelphia, Boston, York, London, and Paris. It has become almost a cliché to describe Saratoga as a turning point in the war, but this should not diminish the fact that Saratoga was decisive. It was, as one of the campaign's participants labeled it, "The Compleat Victory."

CHAPTER 1

Opening Moves

WHEN THE ROYAL NAVY frigate HMS *Cerberus* arrived in Boston harbor on May 25, 1775, she was carrying three British Army major generals—William Howe, Henry Clinton, and John Burgoyne. One London wit seized on the occasion to create one of the most memorable rhymes of the war: "Behold the *Cerberus*, the Atlantic plough, Her precious cargo, Burgoyne, Clinton, Howe, Bow, wow, wow!"[1] Seldom had so much military experience and expertise been concentrated in one (appropriately named) vessel. Only two years after they arrived in America, all three would be involved in arguably the most significant campaign of the American Revolution. They were sent from England to reinforce a British army trying to control the increasingly unruly colonists in Massachusetts and its neighboring provinces. War had already broken out in Lexington and Concord with the retreat of British soldiers back into Boston, and a ragtag American army was now besieging the city. Howe commanded four thousand reinforcements, intended to bring General Thomas Gage's small army there up to a total of about nine thousand redcoats, and, although the senior general among the three, was assigned to serve as Gage's second-in-command.

To break the siege, the generals conducted a frontal assault on entrenched American positions on Bunker Hill and Breed's Hill on June 17, 1775. The attack was led by Howe, with Clinton in a supporting role. Howe's action resulted in a pyrrhic victory. Clinton reportedly wrote after the battle that Bunker Hill was a "dear-bought

victory; another such would have ruined us."[2] Howe, writing to another officer, called the battle "this unhappy day" and "I freely confess to you, when I look at the consequences of it, in the loss of so many brave officers, I do it with horror."[3] Howe soon replaced the unfortunate Gage and became the commander-in-chief of the British Army in America in October 1775.

Howe's counterpart, George Washington, named the American commander-in-chief three days before Bunker Hill, arrived in Boston several weeks after the battle. The fledgling Continental Army was formed by an act of Congress on June 14, 1775, the day before Washington received his commission. Two weeks later, Congress directed that the state militias be incorporated into the Continental Army.

After Bunker Hill, both sides settled down to a siege that lasted for months. While the two sides eyed each other from their fortifications, General Howe (promoted to full general in January 1776, as befitted his position as commander-in-chief) delayed conducting any major operations and was content to hunker down in the city. Burgoyne, who was unable to secure a meaningful position in the army at Boston, returned to Britain to seek new opportunities.

While the siege of Boston dragged on, Clinton, now Howe's second-in-command, became increasingly disenchanted with his boss, and the feeling was mutual. Clinton thought that a part of his job was to provide military advice and counsel to the commander-in-chief. Howe did not see it that way. He believed Clinton should accomplish the tasks assigned to him and keep his mouth shut. Where Clinton was outspoken, if introverted, Howe was amiable and easygoing. It was almost inevitable that they would clash, and they were simply unable to reach a meeting of minds, especially involving the proper strategy to fight the Americans.[4] The relationship between Howe and Clinton was emblematic of one of the major problems facing the British in America: disagreements among the senior political and military leadership.

The siege of Boston finally ended in the midwinter of 1776. The Americans were able to mount heavy cannon, dragged overland from Fort Ticonderoga, which had been seized without difficulty by Patriots under Ethan Allen and Benedict Arnold on May 10, 1775, under the supervision of Colonel Henry Knox. They placed the artillery on Dorchester Heights, overlooking the town and the harbor. Although Howe thought about attacking the heights, memories of Bunker Hill were fresh in his mind, and he decided to evacuate Boston. On March 17, 1776, British troops and their equipment were

embarked on ships and sailed for Halifax, Nova Scotia. By the end of March, there were no British troops in the American Colonies.

Howe's frustration with Clinton, newly promoted to lieutenant general, came to a head in January 1776, when the commander-in-chief sent his second-in-command on an expedition to the Southern colonies to explore possible military operations in North or South Carolina.[5] Most British leaders thought that the Southern colonies were home to large numbers of Loyalists who were being oppressed by the rebels. Supported by the presence of British troops, they would be instrumental in putting down the rebellion and securing territory. Howe both wanted to explore this opportunity and rid himself of his talented but annoying subordinate, at least for a while.

Further, Howe sought to take advantage of the unsurpassed mobility that the Royal Navy gave him. Howe's older brother, Vice Admiral Lord Richard Howe, was the commander-in-chief of the naval forces in America, ensuring that much of the service parochialism that typically hamstrings joint operations between naval and ground forces would not be a problem. Clinton's southern expedition involved only about fifteen hundred troops and never had much of a chance to accomplish any meaningful objectives. The joint operation between Clinton and Commodore Sir Peter Parker in June 1776 went badly when a landing of the troops and a naval bombardment at Charleston, South Carolina, failed to dent the American coastal defenses. Horace Walpole, the famous British man of letters, called the Charleston raid "a disgraceful miscarriage."[6] Clinton's troops rejoined Howe's army in Halifax; the British would not return to the Carolinas again until late in 1778.

After the British Army evacuated Boston in March 1776, Washington surmised that Howe would return in short order. He also guessed that Howe would not try to retake Boston, but would instead try to seize the greatest port city in North America: New York. Consequently, Washington moved the nineteen-thousand-man Continental Army, augmented by militia units, from Boston to New York, stationing his troops in forward positions on Brooklyn Heights on Long Island against an invasion by sea. Major General Charles Lee, one of Washington's key leaders, gauged the massive British advantage as the Americans prepared to defend the city: "What to do with the city, I own puzzles me; it is so encircl'd with deep navigable water, that whoever commands the sea must command the town."[7] This would be an advantage that the British would enjoy for much of the war.

On July 2, 1776, Howe landed nine thousand troops unopposed on Staten Island, but he delayed the offensive operation he believed would end the rebellion until reinforcements and naval transports arrived. Over the next several weeks, thousands of British and German mercenary troops joined the army until it grew to almost thirty-two thousand well-trained soldiers. Finally, on August 22, 1776, twenty thousand of them landed on Long Island. Still studiously avoiding a frontal attack after Bunker Hill, Howe outmaneuvered and routed the Americans. Washington was able to save his army only by retreating across the East River into Manhattan, mainly due to the skill and courage of Colonel John Glover's Massachusetts regiment, made up largely of fishermen who were able to improvise a Dunkirk-like evacuation.[8]

Two weeks later, Howe renewed his offensive against the hastily prepared American positions on Manhattan, using the Royal Navy to land forces near Kip's Bay. The landing was accompanied by an overwhelming naval bombardment that shocked militia units, which broke and ran despite Washington's efforts to stop them. Howe failed to trap the Continental Army, however, and the campaign settled into a month-long standoff when the American troops were able to retreat into fortifications on Harlem Heights. Howe finally broke things open in October, when he landed another force in Washington's rear at Pell's Point, forcing another evacuation, this time of Manhattan itself, with the exceptions of Forts Washington and Lee in the northern end of the island. Washington hoped that these forts would deny the British ships access to the upper part of the Hudson River and, ultimately, the Hudson Highlands. With Washington trying to keep the Continental Army intact and avoid direct combat, Howe was able to capture Fort Washington and its three-thousand-man garrison on November 16, and the Americans were forced to evacuate Fort Lee, a dual disaster.[9]

In the space of two and a half months, Howe had completely turned the tables on the Americans, who had celebrated the departure of the last British soldier from Boston only a short time before. By mid-November 1776, Washington's army was a shadow of its former self and beginning a slow retreat across New Jersey; New York and its magnificent harbor were now in the hands of the British Army, and the river route up the Hudson was open.[10]

Washington was widely criticized after the multiple defeats on Long Island and Manhattan and the loss of Fort Washington. Charles Lee wrote to his friend Major General Horatio Gates in December, complaining that its loss "completely unhinged the goodly fabric

we have been building." It was a devastating blow and "*entre nous*," Lee confided to Gates, "a certain great man is most damnably deficient."[11] Washington himself was disheartened by the multiple debacles, writing to John Hancock, president of the Continental Congress, that the loss of soldiers and officers would be "severely felt."[12]

Over the next few weeks, the demoralized Continental Army and even the cause of independence itself suffered what were probably their worst moments. As it made its way westward, the army hemorrhaged soldiers—through desertions, illness, and the expiration of short-term enlistments. For his part, Howe leisurely followed its retreat. Clinton repeatedly urged his superior to crush Washington and his rapidly evaporating army, and, as he always did, peppered Howe with advice on how to fight the rebels. Howe, who sympathized on many levels with the Americans, preferred instead to overawe them, hoping they would disperse and come back to their senses and to the Crown.[13] It was not the first time Howe would underestimate American resolve.

As the days grew shorter, Washington was forced into a steady retreat through New Jersey, a state with a significant Tory population. Although the army continued to shrink, the commander-in-chief tried to put the best face on the situation. At the end of November, Washington learned that Howe wanted to seize Philadelphia and assured his erstwhile critic, Charles Lee, that the British general would not be successful: "Should they now really risk this undertaking then there is a great possibility that they will pay dearly for it and I shall continue to retreat before them so as to lull them into security."[14] Washington was also beginning to formulate a new strategy, one that had been suggested by Major General Nathanael Greene back in September. The strategy involved neither holding terrain nor fighting pitched battles against the British Army, which was superior in numbers, equipment, and training. Instead, Washington would wait for the opportunity to strike only when the Americans had a marked advantage.[15]

The battles of Long Island and Manhattan had demonstrated that fighting set-piece battles, or luring the British to attack defended positions, a war of posts against one of the best armies on the planet, was simply not feasible, at least not in the fall of 1776. The New York campaign also confirmed to Washington the advantages and disadvantages of the militia. Militia was usually a short-term force. Unless the enemy threat was particularly grave and imminent, it was difficult to muster units during planting and harvest seasons, prime

campaigning periods for eighteenth-century armies. While militia tended to do well when defending their own homes, towns, or state, and when behind stout fortifications, without capable leadership they were apt to melt rapidly away in dicey situations. Asking militia to fight regular troops in a standup battle was asking too much.

Washington had argued from almost the beginning that the Continental Army enlistments had to be long-term, preferably for the duration of the war, and not merely for a few months.[16] A well-trained army that was supplemented by properly employed and led militia was essential to the implementation of the new strategy. While this strategy was, in part, forced on him by circumstances, Washington recognized its necessity and implemented it despite his critics. It almost guaranteed that the war would be a protracted one and would try the patience of the American people.

Several months after Washington abandoned the war of posts and embraced the new strategy, his young aide, Lieutenant Colonel Alexander Hamilton, observed that the "Fabian conduct"—referring to the Roman general who avoided giving battle and patiently waited for the enemy to wear down—would be "imputed either to cowardice or to weakness" but that the "more discerning" would realize that "it proceeds from the truest policy." Because the British could expect few if any reinforcements from Europe, Hamilton argued, it was "Howe's business" to take advantage of the situation, given that the enemy's "only hope lies in fighting us and giving a general defeat at one blow." He acknowledged some of the disadvantages of the strategy, such as leaving "a part of the inhabitants a prey to [British] depredations," but Americans must take the long view; "a part must be sacrificed to the whole, and passion must give way to reason."[17] Whether it worked or not, the strategy was not in the short term going to halt the inexorable advance of Howe and his army or the desultory retreat of Washington's deteriorating army.

Washington's strategy was, in fact, a modified Fabian strategy. Maintaining the army was paramount, but Washington and his senior commanders were also constantly on the alert for targets of opportunity. These limited offensive operations were essential to maintain the will of the American leaders and people to continue the war.

In late December 1776, an opportunity for just such a strike presented itself. Earlier in the month, the Continental Army made its way into Trenton, on the banks of the Delaware River, with fewer than four thousand soldiers.[18] In the space of four months, Washington had lost almost 80 percent of his original force. On December 8, the army started crossing the river into Pennsylvania—a maneuver that

took five days to complete—to prepare for Howe's onslaught. Two days later, a despairing Washington wrote his cousin that so far they had prevented an enemy crossing, "but how long we shall be able to do it God only knows, as they [the enemy] are still hovering about the river."[19]

Washington began a campaign to keep what was left of the army together. A year earlier, Thomas Paine had published *Common Sense*, which argued eloquently for the independence of the American colonies from Great Britain. Now in December 1776, Paine, a British-born writer who accompanied the Americans during their retreat through New Jersey, wrote *The American Crisis*, which urged his new countrymen to do their bit for the war, and appealed to the troops already serving to stay on. Washington was so impressed that he not only ordered Paine's tract printed and distributed but read aloud to the troops: "These are the times that try men's souls. The summer soldier and the sunshine Patriot will, in this crisis, shrink from the service of their country; but he that stands it *now* deserves the love and thanks of man and woman."[20] Whether Paine's plea accomplished its objective is debatable. What's not in doubt is the fact that Washington, the army, and the newly formed United States of America were at rock bottom in late December 1776.

While Washington and his army were clinging to their defensive positions on the west bank of the Delaware, Howe ended his pursuit. The British commander-in-chief sent Clinton and a small force to take Newport, Rhode Island, and then ordered the garrisoning of several outposts throughout New Jersey, including New Brunswick, Princeton, and Trenton. Howe evidently thought Washington's ragtag forces would disperse and go back home as their enlistments expired on January 1, 1777. Congress, reacting to the threat of Howe's approach, left Philadelphia for Baltimore.

On December 20, Washington wrote Congress to ask that since Howe was about to take Philadelphia and "ten days more will put an end to the existence of our Army," that he be given the authority to take charge of the recruitment of soldiers and the raising of regiments. Were these issues "to be referred to Congress, at the distance of 130 or 40 miles, so much time must necessarily elapse as to defeat the end in view." Washington reminded Congress of his repeated warnings "that short inlistments, and a mistaken dependence on the Militia, have been the Origin of all our misfortunes. . . . I can only add, that desperate diseases, require desperate remedies, and with truth declare, that I have no lust for power."[21] Congress reluctantly agreed a few days later. Given Washington's understanding of

the necessity for healthy civil-military relations in the newly formed republic, only a crisis of the magnitude that faced the Americans in late December 1776 would have forced him to seek this authority.

Taking advantage of Howe's army entering winter quarters, Washington devised an operation to attack the enemy outposts. He was able to scrape together almost seven thousand men, including two thousand soldiers under Major General John Sullivan and another eight hundred under Major General Gates, joining Washington's force from New Jersey and Fort Ticonderoga, respectively. Gates himself begged off the upcoming action due to illness and promptly decamped for Baltimore.[22]

On Christmas Day, Washington crossed the Delaware with three columns and attacked the enemy garrisons, a brigade of Hessian soldiers, stationed at Trenton and Bordentown. Two of his columns were forced to abort the crossing because of heavy ice on the river. Only about twenty-five hundred troops, under Washington's personal command, made it across the river in a driving snowstorm. Once again, John Glover's Massachusetts fishermen led the effort to cross the Delaware—this time toward instead of away from the enemy. After a march through snow and sleet, during which two men died of exposure, Washington's detachment arrived on the outskirts of Trenton early on the morning of December 26, 1776.

With volleys of musketry, skillful use of artillery, and a well-timed bayonet attack, the Americans overpowered the enemy troops. The battle was over in an hour. Only two Americans were killed (the ones lost on the march) and five were wounded in action. Twenty-two Hessians were killed in action, including their commander, eighty-three wounded in action, and between nine hundred and one thousand men captured.[23] The day after the battle, now safely back on the Pennsylvania side of the river with his catch of Hessian prisoners, Washington wrote Hancock praising the soldiers under his command, something he had seldom been able to do before Trenton. "In justice to the Officers and Men, I must add, that their Behavior upon this occasion, reflects the highest honor upon them."[24]

In his first report of Trenton to Lord Germain, Secretary of State for the Colonies, Howe attempted to downplay the defeat, but the royal governor of New York, William Tryon, recognized Trenton for what it was: a disaster for the British that breathed new life into the American cause. "The moment was critical, and I believe the Rebel chiefs were conscious if some stroke was not struck that would give life to their sinking cause, they should not raise another Army."[25]

Tryon was right. Howe tried to pass off the loss at Trenton as nothing more than a skirmish, of little importance to the overall war effort. A month later, he admitted that Trenton might be more critical "than what was at first apprehended."[26]

Having achieved the first real victory of American arms since the siege of Boston and knowing that the British would react strongly to the Trenton defeat, Washington followed up with another offensive action. With the additional emergency powers granted to him by Congress, he used the victory, and a ten-dollar bounty, to convince soldiers to stay on past the January 1 expiration of their enlistments. Washington was able to field a force of about five thousand men to cross the Delaware and again take the war to the enemy.

This time there would be no surprise. Howe ordered Lieutenant General Lord Charles Cornwallis in New York to gather a force of about nine thousand men, march to Trenton, and confront Washington should he dare to attack. Washington and his small force crossed the Delaware on New Year's Eve day and marched to Trenton. On January 2, 1777, Cornwallis attacked at Assunpink Creek. Three times his troops attacked the American positions, and each time they were driven back. Nightfall convinced Cornwallis to reconvene the battle the next day. During the evening and into the early morning hours of January 3, Washington led his men around Cornwallis's positions, heading toward the town of Princeton, where he knew the British had a small detachment.

The resulting Battle of Princeton saw heavy fighting in and around Nassau Hall, the main building of the College of New Jersey, now Princeton University. Washington attacked as the British force was getting ready to join Cornwallis at Trenton. This time instead of facing sleepy Hessian mercenaries, his men faced British regulars. After a short, sharp fight, the outnumbered and outgunned British fled Princeton, leaving behind nearly five hundred casualties, including dozens killed in action, and almost three hundred prisoners. American casualties were less than half that, though Washington grieved the loss of two key officers, Brigadier General Hugh Mercer and Colonel John Haslet.[27]

Hoping to encounter another isolated British or German detachment, Washington wanted to push on to New Brunswick but ultimately decided against it. As he explained to Hancock two days after the battle, the risk "of losing the advantage we had gained by aiming at too much induced me by the advice of my Officers to relinquish the attempt."[28] Instead, he moved the army into winter quarters at Morristown, New Jersey.

For their part, the British also decided to end active operations and consolidated their outposts at New Brunswick and Perth Amboy to better defend themselves against American raids. They had been impressed by Washington's attacks. Horace Walpole noted that after the news reached London, it was "now the fashion to cry up the manoeuver of General Washington in this action," noting that the campaign to defeat the colonists "has by no means been wound up."[29]

While Washington's audacious operations at Trenton and Princeton were expertly carried out, he was undoubtedly aided by Howe's desire to capture and hold territory instead of destroying the American Army. The British Army was overextended, and the isolated detachments of British and Hessian soldiers made them vulnerable. Howe's strategy, one that began with so much promise after the succession of British victories on Long Island and Manhattan, would have to change if the British were to subdue the rebellion.

Trenton and Princeton not only renewed and galvanized support for the war, they also ensured that Washington would be able to maintain the army, and indeed increase its size. They also convinced Howe that he could no longer hope to beat the Americans by simply intimidating them. He had to adjust his overall strategy. Washington's triumphs at Trenton and Princeton, while not sufficient for ultimate victory, were enough to ensure that the fight would continue.

Eighteen months before Trenton and Princeton, while Washington and his army surrounded Boston, Congress had begun to consider an invasion of Canada, which would form a vital element of the strategy for both sides. Colonial Americans had long coveted Canada. Indeed, since the French and Indian War (a separate North American theater of the larger Seven Years War), many Americans served in Canada alongside and in the British Army. They had been impressed by the vast lands, teeming with game and rich in resources. On June 27, 1775, two months after Lexington and Concord, Congress directed Philip Schuyler, then a newly commissioned major general, in charge of the forces in New York, that if he "finds it practicable," to seize as much Canadian territory as possible, "which may have a tendency to promote peace and security of these Colonies."[30] Congress hoped the French-Canadians would join their efforts, assuming that British occupation since their defeat in the French and Indian War had disaffected them. The Americans also wanted to strike preemptively, since they had heard that General Sir Guy Carleton, the British governor of Canada, had very few available troops and was actively recruiting Indians to help put down the rebellion.[31]

By June 1775, Carleton was a thirty-three-year veteran of the British Army. The most well-known portrait of him gives him aristocratic bearing, belying his modest beginnings in life. Born in Ireland to Scotch-Irish middle-class parents, he joined the British Army at age seventeen and served over three decades before finally reaching the rank of full general by the outbreak of the rebellion. He served during the Jacobite Rebellion, an effort to regain the English throne for the Stuarts, during which he became friends with fellow officer, James Wolfe. He also served in the War of Austrian Succession in 1747, the Europe-wide war over the rightful heir to the Habsburg monarchy. He fought in America for the first time during the French and Indian War, serving with Major General Jeffrey Amherst when the British captured the French fort of Louisbourg in present-day Nova Scotia in 1758. He was then asked by Wolfe, now a major general, to act as quartermaster general for his upcoming expedition to take Quebec. Carleton happily agreed, and he proved invaluable both to Wolfe and the army. He was not only responsible for securing provisions for the army, he also acted as a military engineer and led a battalion of grenadiers during the campaign. Carleton was wounded during the final and successful assault on the French-held city.[32] The oldest city in Canada, Quebec was founded by French explorer Samuel de Champlain in 1608 and had long been the most important settlement in the province. During the French and Indian War, the city was taken by British forces under General Wolfe on September 13, 1759 (Wolfe was killed in the battle and immortalized in Benjamin West's famous painting). Sixteen years later, Quebec was still central to the defense of Canada.

Carleton was wounded again in 1761 during operations off the coast of France (as part of the larger Seven Years War). In 1766, after the war ended, Carleton returned to Canada as the lieutenant governor of Quebec. Later, he was appointed captain general and governor of the province of Quebec. During his two tours of duty in Canada, he developed skills in dealing with the French-Canadian population as well as with British and British-American colonists. Returning to England, he was promoted to major general. He provided advice to Parliament as it debated the 1774 Quebec Act, which outlined how the newly won province would be governed. Carleton argued that the province's French heritage made it unique and that it could not be managed merely as a British colony.[33] He favored allowing the Canadian population to retain many of their customs, laws, and the free practice of Catholicism within the province, which

was adopted along with other provisions such as partially restoring French civil law. While this liberal and humane policy seems eminently sensible today, the program was often cited as one of the great British crimes against the American colonists, who viewed the Quebec Act as facilitating the resurgence of the defeated French enemy right on their doorstep. Carleton returned to Canada in 1774 to help implement the provisions of the act, which he found challenging. The British community hated some provisions of the act, and the French population hated others. In any case, he soon found himself dealing with more important issues as the American rebellion broke out, and with it came the threat of invasion.[34]

Carleton's counterpart on the American side was Philip Schuyler. Schuyler came from a long line of Dutch settlers, the Schuylers being one of New York's most prominent and wealthy families.[35] He spoke French and Mohawk, the latter from traveling widely throughout the western part of the colony, now upstate New York. Schuyler served as a militia captain in the French and Indian War. He proved adept at handling transportation and supply missions for various expeditions; the lessons he learned about overcoming the logistical challenges inherent in conducting operations in the northern wilderness would serve him well. In 1768 he was elected to the New York Assembly, then named a delegate to the Second Continental Congress because of his opposition to the Crown's increasingly restrictive measures. Not long afterward, at the urging of the New York Provincial Congress, he was appointed a major general, and later was among the first four major generals of the Continental Army.

Schuyler was the same height as Washington (6 feet, 2 inches) and looked every bit the soldier. Almost every description of Schuyler from contemporary observers is that of a patrician who demanded esteem and obedience. He developed a good relationship with Washington and was the obvious choice to command the Northern Department. As an Albany native, he was already intimately familiar with the region, and with the challenges involved in conducting operations there.[36]

Congress had given Schuyler an almost impossible mission. An invasion of Canada—which is essentially what it was—would not be easy. Although the Americans had seized Fort Ticonderoga and now had possession of Crown Point (located 10 miles north of Ticonderoga), Schuyler had very few troops, provisions, and transports with which to conduct offensive operations. Throughout the summer of 1775, he was only able to scrape together a little more than one thousand men from various militia units. Placing Brigadier General Richard

Montgomery in command of them, he sent them north, planning to join them once he had completed all logistical preparations for the campaign.[37]

While Schuyler worked to prepare a force that could invade Canada, Benedict Arnold resigned in a huff over who was to command Fort Ticonderoga. This was the first of many times that Arnold would react to actual or perceived slights. Arnold was born in Norwich, Connecticut, in January 1741 to a well-to-do and influential family. His early life was almost idyllic. However, during young adulthood, his father fell on hard times due to failing business ventures. Arnold apprenticed to an apothecary for a few years and then set up his own business in New Haven. He briefly served in the Norwich militia during the French and Indian War but saw no active service. The life of a simple merchant did not satisfy his ambition, and, captivated by the sea, he invested in several merchant ships. Soon he had gained enough experience to become a ship's master himself. In 1767, he married Margaret Mansfield, the daughter of a prominent New Haven citizen, and they had three sons in quick succession.

Because of his new profession, which had made him wealthy, Arnold became involved with other merchants and ship owners who started to push back against what they viewed as overly restrictive British mercantilism. The step to becoming a radical was a short one. As a prosperous and prominent member of the community and with obvious and instinctive leadership talents, Arnold was the natural choice to command a company of local militia. News of the outbreak of hostilities in Massachusetts in 1775 made its way to New Haven. Despite opposition from local leaders, Arnold and his militia company joined the Patriot army surrounding Boston.[38]

Knowing that the new army had very little artillery, Arnold proposed that an attempt be made to capture Fort Ticonderoga, then of course still in British hands, where he knew there were many heavy cannons. Fort Ticonderoga was crucial for controlling the Lake Champlain–Hudson River invasion corridor to and from Canada, and though it has already been introduced in this account, to appreciate its significance to the story of Saratoga (since, for the first three years of the American Revolution, both the British and American forces would focus much of their attention on Ticonderoga), we need to more fully address its construction and situation. First built by the French in 1755 during the French and Indian War, and named Fort Carillon, Fort Ticonderoga adopted the classic star shape popularized by the famous late-seventeenth- and early-eighteenth-century French military engineer Sébastien

Le Prestre de Vauban. The stone fortress itself was dominated by Rattlesnake Hill (later renamed "Mount Independence" by the Americans) on the eastern shore of Lake Champlain directly across from the fort to the southeast, and Sugar Loaf Hill (called "Rattlesnake Mountain" by the French and later renamed "Mount Defiance" by the Americans), located southwest of the fort across from the mouth of the La Chute River.

Arnold persuaded the Massachusetts Committee of Safety, the colony's revolutionary government, to assign him the mission to capture the fort and set out with a small force of newly recruited Massachusetts soldiers. On his way west, he discovered that Connecticut had also sent an expedition under Ethan Allen to seize Ticonderoga. This was mainly due to information about the fort that Arnold had unwittingly passed on to another officer. The two men fought over who was to command the expedition. In the end, the Massachusetts Committee of Safety, Congress, and Washington choose Allen—he had the larger force—and Arnold essentially went along for the ride.

As we've seen, the capture of the fort and its artillery and other valuable military stores was easier than anyone anticipated, but resolving the conflict between Arnold and Allen was not. Their disagreements induced Arnold to resign his commission and return home. His wife, Margaret, had died while he was gone, and his sister had assumed care of his three boys. Arnold stayed in New Haven for a short time then traveled back to Massachusetts to petition the Committee of Safety to reimburse him for his out-of-pocket expenses from the Ticonderoga expedition.[39]

While he was in Massachusetts, Arnold convinced Washington—still managing the siege of Boston—to give him command of a detachment to conduct a supporting attack against Quebec. Thus, when Montgomery began his journey from Fort Ticonderoga via Lake Champlain to Montreal on August 25, 1775, with about twelve hundred troops, Arnold, with a new commission as a Continental Army colonel, was leading his supporting detachment of one thousand men up the Kennebec River.

Shortly after sending Arnold off on his expedition to Canada, Washington reminded him that "You are intrusted with a Command of the utmost Consequence to the Interests & Liberties of America." This was a campaign to win hearts and minds.[40] Washington sent a proclamation with the expedition to be distributed among Canadians by Arnold in the hope of enticing them to join the American cause.[41] Meanwhile, Schuyler, who was away from the army negotiating

with Indian tribes, caught up with Montgomery and his troops as they moved northward. However, illness soon forced his return to Ticonderoga, leaving Montgomery and Arnold to conduct the first American invasion of Canada.[42]

When Washington agreed to send Arnold on his expedition to Canada, he was still adjusting to the responsibilities of being the American commander-in-chief. As he would throughout the war, he now had to deal with Congress's desire to direct military operations, especially those of the Northern Department. Not willing to interfere with his civilian masters, Washington had to tread lightly when dealing with issues surrounding that department. Early in the war he contented himself with prodding and coaxing and mentoring Schuyler. On August 2, Schuyler wrote Washington that he hoped to hear from him soon regarding Canada and what was happening. "I am extreamly Anxious to hear from your part of the world, reports prevail that a body of [British] troops have left Boston and are Gone to Canada."[43] Washington allayed Schuyler's fears, assuring him that "no Troops have been detached from Boston to Canada or elsewhere."[44] Washington had to wonder about Schuyler's lack of confidence.

Arnold departed Cambridge, Massachusetts—then headquarters of the Continental Army—on September 11, 1775, with his small force of one thousand men. With the assistance of Abenaki warriors, he led his men through almost 400 miles of trackless wilderness crisscrossed with nearly unnavigable watercourses, through challenging portages and poor weather. Arnold later praised his men and described the march as "not to be paralleled in history." Despite all the challenges, the officers and men, "inspired and fired with the love of liberty and their country, pushed on with a fortitude superior to every obstacle."[45] Arnold had led through his personal example sharing the hardships with his men and would continue to demonstrate superior leadership skills in the months and years to come. The thrust toward Quebec through the wilderness of present-day Maine was one of the most memorable and epic military expeditions in American history.

On November 14, Arnold and six hundred survivors from the grueling march climbed the bluffs and arrived on the Plains of Abraham, outside the walled city of Quebec. Arnold's weakened force could not hope to take the city by themselves, so it was compelled to fall back to Point aux Trembles (*trembles* are aspen), west of the city.[46] There he awaited the arrival of Montgomery and his army.

Montgomery's advance "down" Lake Champlain (Lake Champlain drains northward) might have been less memorable than Arnold's through the Maine wilderness, but it was not without its own challenges. Montgomery departed Fort Ticonderoga on August 25, 1775, and arrived on September 4 at Île aux Noix, an island in the Richelieu River, which runs from the north shore of Lake Champlain to the Saint Lawrence River. The Americans moved downriver to Fort Saint-Jean (known to the Americans as Fort Saint Johns), a fortification first constructed by the French in 1666 and which guarded the approaches to Montreal. After several false starts and a few indecisive skirmishes against British forces, Montgomery settled into a siege of the fort, one that lasted from September 17 until the garrison surrendered on November 3. One American officer wrote that the fall of the fort would be "a most fatal stab to the hellish machinations of the foes of freedom, as it will facilitate the reduction of Canada and secure the Canadians in our favour."[47] Actually, the seven-week delay would have rather different consequences. After Fort Saint-Jean fell, Montgomery quickly moved to Montreal and occupied the town almost without a shot after General Carleton decided he could not possibly defend it.[48]

Carleton had seen holding Fort Saint-Jean as his best chance to defend the province from an American offensive from Fort Ticonderoga. Now that the fort was lost and Montreal occupied, only Quebec remained. After a daring escape, Carleton traveled northeast down the Saint Lawrence River to Quebec to direct the city's defense, arriving on November 19. While the American forces invading Canada were small even by the standards of the day, the British defenses were even thinner. Carlton had been forced to send several regiments to join the siege at Boston and had only a few militia and about eight hundred regulars to defend the entire province. Immediately upon his arrival in Quebec, Carleton moved to strengthen the defenses and to augment his meager force. He directed that all civilian men of military age take up arms to supplement his small force, and he strengthened the city's defenses with additional earthworks and obstacles. Quebec became the last line of defense.[49]

Once he occupied Montreal, Montgomery traveled northeast with about five hundred men, hot on Carleton's heels, and arrived outside Quebec on December 2, 1775, when he linked up with Arnold's surviving force. Montgomery informed Schuyler of the union of the two small armies on December 5, expressing optimism over their chances to take the imposing citadel. Carleton, according to

Montgomery, was only putting on a "show of defence." Still, he added, "The works of Quebeck are extremely extensive, and very incapable of being defended." Montgomery also had a very favorable impression of the New England troops and their commander: "There is a style of discipline among them much superior to what I have been used to see this campaign." He found Arnold "active, intelligent and enterprising." Montgomery planned to take Quebec by beginning a traditional siege that would mask a frontal attack against the "lower town, which is the weaker part. . . . I do think there is a fair prospect of success."[50]

Twice Montgomery demanded that Carleton surrender the city and the garrison; twice the British general refused. Although Montgomery tried bombarding the fortifications with the few cannons he had on hand, the result was disappointing. He found himself facing the same dilemma that would later confront Washington: the imminent expiration of short-term enlistments of many of his troops. Thus, Montgomery and Arnold were forced to hurry the assault on Carleton's defenses before their small army melted away. Several attacks were planned and canceled.

Finally, on December 30, conditions were deemed favorable, and the Americans attacked the lower town the next morning in the middle of a blizzard. Both American commanders led their men forward. Montgomery was killed, Arnold was severely wounded in the leg, and their forces were repulsed. In a letter written a week later to his sister, a convalescing Arnold described Montgomery's death as the deciding factor. Had he not been killed, "the town would have been ours."[51] Whether or not this was true, the assault failed, with the Americans losing approximately fifty men killed in action, more than thirty wounded, and more than four hundred captured. Carleton reported only five killed (although the actual number was probably higher) and fourteen wounded.[52]

Although now heavily outnumbered, Arnold decided to continue the siege as newly recruited units had augmented his force throughout the winter. But there were never enough troops for the Americans to resume offensive operations. If Carleton's superior forces sitting behind the walls of the city, a mere cannon shot from his tent, was not enough, Arnold also had to deal with a shortage of provisions and an outbreak of smallpox.

For his part, Carleton decided to wait for reinforcements that he knew were on the way before venturing out of the city. Finally, on May 6, 1776, they began to arrive by sea on the newly ice-free Saint Lawrence River "to the inconceivable joy of all the garrison," and the

American Army, diminished and devastated by illness, began to pull back.[53] Over the next month, almost nine thousand British troops arrived under General Burgoyne, who became Carleton's second-in-command, and four thousand German mercenaries, mostly from Brunswick, under the command of Major General Friedrich Adolf Riedesel.[54] When the news arrived in London that Carleton had withstood the American siege, Horace Walpole wrote that it "greatly raised the spirits of the King and Court, who now talked of nothing but reducing the Americans to a state of never rebelling again."[55]

CHAPTER 2

The First Invasion

CARLETON HAD TO HAVE been very pleased with the situation in June 1776. The Americans had attacked from two directions, down Lake Champlain to the Richelieu River, to Fort Saint-Jean to Montreal, and directly through the Maine wilderness to Quebec. With only a handful of troops, Carleton had delayed their main body at Fort Saint-Jean, repelled a direct attack by their combined force on Quebec, and withstood a six-month siege. And he accomplished all of that with only a handful of troops. Now that Burgoyne had arrived with significant combat power, he could finally think about going on the offensive. Carleton's first goal would be to recapture all the Canadian terrain still held by the Americans. His second was to conduct a campaign south up the Richelieu and Lake Champlain, ultimately retaking Crown Point and Fort Ticonderoga.

Arriving on the ship along with the first reinforcements on May 6 came the news that he had been promoted to full general and commander-in-chief of British forces in Canada in addition to his post of governor. Also arriving were instructions from Secretary of State for the Colonies, Lord Germain. Germain directed Carlton to use the reinforcements along with his existing troops, totaling almost ten thousand soldiers, to expel the Americans from Canada and then conduct an offensive up Lake Champlain, the goal being to link up with General Howe's army in New York. Like Carleton, Germain believed that an army operating from Canada would be instrumental in crushing the rebellion.[1]

Late in May, Carleton took the first steps toward retaking the rest of the province from the rebels. He dispatched ships transporting two regiments to Trois-Rivières on the Saint Lawrence River, southwest of Quebec, which guarded the approaches to Montreal. The Americans attempted to make a stand on June 8 but were quickly routed by the fresh British troops supported by the guns of Royal Navy ships in the river. The Americans suffered almost three hundred casualties, compared with fewer than twenty British losses. Carleton nonetheless didn't press his advantage and passed on an opportunity to cut off the American retreat from the battlefield.[2]

Despite his rapid movements in early June, after the Battle of Trois-Rivières, Carleton seemed reluctant to close with and destroy the shattered remnants of the invading American Army. Over the next two weeks, he pushed the dispirited and smallpox-riddled American troops all the way back to Fort Saint-Jean, and on at least two occasions, had a chance to cut off their retreat south. The first was after retaking Montreal without a fight. On June 19, the Americans destroyed Fort Saint-Jean as they abandoned it and embarked on boats and sailed up Lake Champlain for Fort Ticonderoga. Again, the British forces didn't engage. One of the last Americans to board the waiting boats was Benedict Arnold, who shot his horse just before stepping off the shore, ensuring nothing would be left behind to help the British, who were advancing under Burgoyne's command.[3]

Canada was now free of American occupation. The attempt to take possession of the province had started out with much promise as the two American columns, Montgomery's and Arnold's, pushed Carleton's small army back into the walls of Quebec. However, the Americans were ultimately defeated by the short enlistment policy, poor planning, scanty provisions, too few troops, the Canadian weather, illness, and Carleton's spirited defense.[4]

Standing on the ashes of Fort Saint-Jean in June 1776, Carleton was now confronted with a new series of challenges. First, he had to organize his forces into a coherent army, one capable of conducting extended offensive operations. Second, he had to start preparations for an operation up Lake Champlain and beyond, as directed by Lord Germain. Third, he had to construct a fleet—both warships and transports—capable of securing Lake Champlain and the approaches to Fort Ticonderoga, 120 miles south of Fort Saint-Jean. Finally, Carleton was still governor general of Canada, and much of his day was consumed by political and administrative tasks. He nonetheless learned that he had been appointed a Knight of the Bath for his service in defending Quebec and was being called the "Savior of

Canada." This was over the objection of Lord Germain, who thought Carleton should have accomplished more against the Americans in the spring and early summer of 1776.[5]

Carleton had anticipated the need for vessels suitable for Lake Champlain and had requested they be sent to him, but the government was unable to provide more than a handful of craft, which meant that he would have to build or procure locally almost all the shipping he might need. He assigned Major General William Phillips, a career artillery officer who had arrived with Burgoyne and the other replacements in June, to supervise the shipbuilding effort at Fort Saint-Jean, and he dismissed from active duty all the militia that had been mobilized. He also repaired and rebuilt the Fort Saint-Jean fortifications and the associated shipyard, directing that all useable vessels on the Saint Lawrence River that could be used on Lake Champlain be dismantled and hauled up the Richelieu River (requiring a 10-mile portage). Finally, all available soldiers not otherwise engaged in the province's defense were put to work shipbuilding and preparing for the campaign. Of all the myriad tasks he carried out throughout the summer, there was one mission that Carleton did not undertake, or even attempt: to gather intelligence about the Americans.[6]

Germain's objections over the honors being bestowed Carleton were not new. Throughout the winter of 1776, while Carleton withstood the American siege of Quebec, he had sent numerous missives from London to Canada. Due to the harsh Canadian winter and ice on the Saint Lawrence River, Carleton received none of these letters until the reinforcements arrived in early May. Thus, Carleton had no idea that Germain was his new boss until a full eight months after the appointment. While early on, their relationship was professional and correct, each man soon grew to hate the other. Delays in communications didn't help matters. Letters took at least six weeks to cross the Atlantic, and sometimes twice that time, depending on the weather. An order and the response could take two months or more, and if the addressee was on an active campaign, the time lag was even longer. These were not circumstances conducive to maintaining good relationships among senior leaders and ensuring that everyone understood written intentions. Here was a major source of the tensions between Carleton and Germain that began in the summer of 1776.[7]

The first hint of conflict began when Germain responded to Carleton's May 14, 1776, report recounting the lifting of the siege of Quebec. Germain answered on June 21 with congratulations but

noted with regret that the general had omitted any report on "the actual force of the Rebels." The lack of information meant Germain could not offer useful instructions.[8] Carleton was not happy with the censure, and that was clear in his September 28 reply, in which he noted that "expulsion of the rebels" had been his main objective and that it had been "happily executed long before I could profit by any instructions your lordship might think necessary to favour me with." Carleton explained at length that he now had to build a fleet for Lake Champlain before he could possibly embark on any extensive operations against the rebels to the south.[9]

Other issues exacerbated the growing discord between Carleton and Germain, such as the use of Indians to fight the Americans. Germain thought that all means available should be used to suppress the rebellion, and this included employing Indian tribes friendly to the Crown. Carleton disagreed. Having served in North America during the French and Indian War and having had extensive experience with Indians as part of his duties as governor, he saw too many downsides. While they could certainly instill terror in the Americans and excelled at some military missions, the Native populations were extremely difficult to control. They tended, for one thing, not to discriminate between combatants and noncombatants. Carleton thought that their actions could very well backfire, hardening American resolve instead of breaking it. Second, like many senior British officers, including the Howe brothers, Carleton believed that most Americans did not want to separate from the Crown.[10] Thus, he favored conciliatory policies, such as treating American prisoners of war with compassion, and even released them after he had expelled the Americans from Canada in May and June of 1776. Germain advocated harsh, aggressive measures.

Germain's insistence on these aggressive measures doubtless stemmed from his background and personal history. Few civilian leaders in British history have had a greater impact on events. Born George Sackville on June 26, 1716, the third son of Elizabeth and Lionel Sackville, first Duke of Dorset, he was raised in the family seat of Knole, one of the finest houses in England. Educated in both London and Ireland, he joined the army as a captain in his early twenties, and promotions came rapidly, probably due to his family connections. His military career had several fits and starts, for he took a number of long leaves of absence from his regiment to act as secretary to his father, who in 1731 had been appointed Lord Lieutenant of Ireland. In 1741 he was promoted to lieutenant colonel and was named one of King George II's aides-de-camp.

Sackville distinguished himself at the Battle of Fontenoy during the War of Austrian Succession in 1745 when he led his cavalry regiment in a charge deep into the French lines, where he was wounded and captured. Shortly after his release, he was promoted to colonel and served with the Duke of Cumberland, the son of George II, in Scotland during the Jacobite Rebellion. Soon after, he left the army again to serve in both the English and Irish Parliaments and once again as his father's secretary, becoming allied with William Pitt, who would soon serve as prime minister. He returned to duty on the outbreak of the Seven Years War and served as the third Duke of Marlborough's second-in-command during a failed raid on Saint-Malo, France. Immediately after the action, rumors circulated that Sackville had not attacked with energy and had withdrawn prematurely.[11] Walpole observed that some said that "Lord George Sackville was not among the first to court danger."[12] While there were no official inquiries, rumors spread throughout the army and in government.

Even if untrue, these reports would set the stage for the next act in Sackville's life. During the planning and execution of the Saint Malo raid, he became acquainted with the Howe brothers, and almost immediately, the two siblings developed a strong dislike for their superior. Walpole noted in a letter to a friend that "Howe and Lord George are upon the worst terms."[13] Not long after the raid, through the intervention of his political friend Pitt, Sackville rejoined the main allied army in Germany. The British Army was placed under the command of Duke Ferdinand of Brunswick, and, after the death of Marlborough in October 1758, Sackville assumed command of the British contingent and became Ferdinand's second-in-command.[14]

One of the pivotal battles of the Seven Years War occurred on August 1, 1759, near Minden, where the German-British allied army faced a French force. During the course of the battle, the French launched four separate attacks against the allied army's center, without success. After the last attack, Duke Ferdinand ordered a general advance, which broke the weakened French lines. At this critical part of the battle, Ferdinand ordered Sackville to launch the British cavalry to finish off the confused enemy. There was no response from the British commander. Several more messages, each more frantic than the last, were sent to Sackville. Finally, after a delay of more than half an hour, the British cavalry advanced, by which point the bulk of the French soldiers had already retreated into their fortifications. The battle was over, and the allies lost an opportunity to destroy the French army.[15]

Although it was still a major victory for the allies, Sackville's reputation was now indelibly tarnished, given that what had happened reinforced the earlier rumors. He was immediately accused of ignoring repeated orders from his superior officer, and worse, by implication, of cowardice. Sackville argued that the duke's orders were confusing and contradictory. Thus, as he put it, "I was puzzled what to do," and so he had to personally seek out clarification, thus accounting for the delay in sending in the cavalry. Sackville offered to resign and demanded a court-martial to review his conduct. The government accepted his resignation but refused to grant a court martial. Most of his political friends, including Pitt, turned their backs on him. Finally, in January 1760, after Sackville's repeated requests, the king authorized a court martial, which was convened on March 7, 1760, and lasted about four weeks. Public opinion was arrayed against him, and the outcome was never really in doubt.[16] The court found that Sackville had "disobeyed the order of Prince Ferdinand of Brunswick when he was, by his Commission and Instructions, directed to obey him as commander-in-chief, according to the rules of war."[17]

Although the death penalty was possible and many in power wanted the ultimate punishment, Sackville was spared. He was also shut out of any government and military positions. Some were surprised that Sackville had gotten off so lightly. "Lord George's sentence," Walpole wrote a friend, "is . . . very moderate in comparison of what was intended and desired, and truly not very severe, considering what was proved."[18] Sackville suffered further humiliation when the king banned him from court and ordered that the court martial results be read aloud to every unit in the British Army.[19] His disgrace was complete.

But Sackville was nothing if not a survivor. The successful conclusion of the Seven Years War enabled him to start a steady reintegration into public life, ultimately being reinstated to the Privy Council by King George III in 1765. He was constantly reminded of Minden, however. Indeed, he fought an inconclusive duel in December 1770 with a fellow Member of Parliament after being insulted in the House of Commons, a common occurrence throughout Sackville's political career[20]—a political career that soon underwent a significant transformation.

Sackville had been involved with the Rockingham Whigs, which included such figures as Edmund Burke. However, since he saw little chance of their gaining real power, he started aligning himself with the Tory administration of Frederick North, second Earl of Guilford (known as Lord North), who had risen to prime minister on the

eve of the American Revolution. North favored taking a hard line against the Americans and saw the potential loss of the colonies as a disaster for Great Britain and its place in the world. Now known as Lord George Germain, Sackville's rehabilitation was complete when in November 1775, only months after the American troubles had escalated into armed conflict, the king appointed him Secretary of State for the Colonies.[21] Many in Britain were surprised. Walpole wrote that the Sackville's appointment as minister was "a proof at least of his political courage."[22] Germain was now the man responsible for formulating, planning, and directing military strategy against the American rebels.

Germain not only had to live down Minden and the mistrust and suspicion that it created but also develop strong relationships with the senior military officers he directed, as well as key leaders in and out of government. Most of the generals with whom he had to serve had participated in the Seven Years War in some capacity or another and were intimately familiar with the Minden controversy. To many of these generals, Germain was a man without honor and thus not deserving of respect. There were two other challenges facing him. First, although he was married and had fathered five children, he was almost certainly gay. This was more or less an open secret and exposed him to behind-the-scenes ridicule and diminished him in the eyes of his superiors, subordinates, and peers.[23] The second was his temperament. Germain did not suffer fools gladly and could be painfully direct and sharp-tongued.[24] None of these attributes were conducive to developing close ties with his general officers.

On the other hand, Germain was very good at his job. He was dedicated, energetic, capable, loyal, smart, and he endeavored as much as possible to support his generals in the field. Still, it was almost preordained that there would be problems, misunderstandings, and hurt feelings when Germain attempted to direct and coordinate a war that was arguably the most challenging in British history, and to do so from more than 3,000 miles away.[25]

His relationship with Carleton was a case in point. In his letters, Germain offered both effusive congratulations to Carleton over expelling the Americans from Canada, and sharp criticism. In late August 1776, Germain sent instructions that would have come as a shock to Carleton had he received them in a timely manner. Because Carleton had so many administrative tasks to perform as governor, Germain directed that he "return to Quebec, detaching Lieut.-General Burgoyne or such other officer as you shall think most proper, with that part of your forces which can be spared from the

immediate defence of your province, to carry on such operations as shall be most conducive to the success of the army acting on the side of New York."[26] In essence, Germain ordered the commander-in-chief of the forces in Canada to relinquish that part of his duties to his subordinate. Germain may have been trying to force Carleton's resignation by a demotion that was particularly repugnant, but it may have simply been another example of the secretary's blunt manner and casual disregard for anyone's feelings.[27] Whatever the case, it was fortunate for Carleton's peace of mind that he did not receive a copy of Germain's letter until the late spring of 1777, fully eight months after it was written.

As the summer months melted away, and with them the year's best campaigning weather, Carleton's shipbuilding continued.[28] By September 1776, Carleton's forces were still not ready to move against the Americans. Carleton explained the delay to Germain by complaining that he had not received the vessels he had requested, and the Americans had a "considerable naval force" at the entrance to the lake, and moreover had fortified Crown Point and Ticonderoga. Given all these difficulties, he doubted he could accomplish much in 1776 other than draw off enemy attention from Howe's forces.[29]

Finally, on October 4, 1776, Carleton's small fleet and army were ready to embark on their mission to gain control of Lake Champlain and the American fortifications at the south end of the lake.[30] Carleton's forces included almost ten thousand British and German soldiers, commanded by Burgoyne, and a fleet consisting of twenty gunboats mounting twenty 24- and 9-pounder guns, two gondolas with seven 9-pounders, and two captured American schooners with 6-pounder guns. Carleton also had at his disposal the 180-ton frigate *Inflexible,* mounting eighteen 12-pounders, and the *Thunderer,* basically a large barge mounting six 24-pounders and six 12-pounders.[31]

In addition to the warships, Carleton's men had constructed dozens of transports for provisions and troops. Most of these boats were known as bateaux—flat-bottomed and double-ended vessels that were ubiquitous in the region and originated with the fur trade but became essential for the conduct of military operations. Although they came in many sizes, the basic bateau was about 30 feet long and 6 feet wide with a shallow draft of about 2 feet. Sails could be rigged and used with great effect when they were deployed on large bodies of water such as Lake Champlain, though more often they were rowed. These highly versatile craft could carry up to 2 tons of cargo or twenty-three men, or a combination of both.[32] They were

relatively simple to build, and their dimensions made them useful on both lakes and rivers.

The naval firepower available to Carleton was impressive, and his force vastly outgunned and outnumbered the Americans. In fact, arguably, his forces were too large, based on the assumption that he faced twenty thousand American troops and a large fleet.[33] Had he settled for a warship fleet half the size, he might have been able to begin his campaign much earlier than October, but Carleton insisted on overwhelming firepower.

While Carleton and his men were preparing for movement to the south to clear Lake Champlain and capture Crown Point and Fort Ticonderoga, the Americans were not idle. On June 17, 1776, Congress directed Washington to detach Horatio Gates from his staff and send him to Canada, "to take the command of the forces in that province," upon the death of the previous commander from smallpox.[34] Washington's follow-on order to Gates directed him to take command of "the Troops of the United Colonies in Canada" and consult with Schuyler in Albany to receive "such Advice & Information respecting the Operations of the Campaign as may be useful & necessary."[35]

By the time Gates arrived in New York in late June 1776, the remnants of the American Canadian army had stumbled back to the protection of the outposts at the south end of Lake Champlain. Gates wrote John Adams that "Where, or in what Condition I shall find the Army, I have no conception! The Prospect is too much Clouded to distinguish Clearly."[36] Gates was essentially a commander without a command. This resulted in the first of several conflicts over who should command the Northern Department and, indeed, what elements exactly comprised the department. This confusion and controversy would plague the Americans for the next fifteen months.

When Gates reached Albany, he met with Schuyler, still officially the commander of the Northern Department. While Gates thought he was the rightful commander of the army that had retreated from Canada, Schuyler thought he should command them. Gates had been clearly ordered to command the army *in* Canada. Now that the army was back in New York at Crown Point, Schuyler argued, command should fall to him. Gates contended that its current physical location should not matter. Both men had reasonable arguments. On July 1, Schuyler asked Washington for clarification—so that the "Line be clearly drawn"—and warning about the "Dangers and Evils that may arise from a Disputed Command."[37]

At Washington's urging, Congress addressed the dispute on July 8 and basically split the difference between the two men, confirming that they had no intention to vest Gates "with a superior command to General Schuyler" and that it was "the intention of Congress to give [Gates] the command of the troops whilst in Canada." While confirming Schuyler's precedence in command, Congress encouraged the two generals to "carry on the military operations with harmony, and in such a manner as shall best promote the public service."[38] Both men acknowledged the directive and resolved to cooperate with each other, though the seeds of discord were sown. Part of the problem was that New England politicians and the citizenry tended to support Gates, who had endeared himself to them during his assignment to Boston early in the war, and Schuyler enjoyed the backing of New York politicians and citizens. John Adams explained the political context in his autobiography, noting that all this "Occasioned a Contest Competition" whose consequences were "not yet spent."[39]

Schuyler sent Gates and Arnold, newly promoted from colonel to brigadier general, to take charge of the forces in and around Fort Ticonderoga. At the same time, he concentrated on maintaining Indian neutrality and preparing for the impending British offensive. On July 7, the three generals met at Crown Point to consider the overall situation.

Located about 10 miles north of Fort Ticonderoga, Crown Point was an old French fortification originally built in the 1740s and called Fort St.-Frédéric. It stood on the western shore of Lake Champlain, situated on a peninsula that overlooked one of the narrowest points on the lake, protecting the approaches to Fort Ticonderoga. The fort featured thick stone walls, remarkable considering the remoteness of the location. General Jeffrey Amherst, who destroyed the original fort in 1759, during the French and Indian War, improved the works. Crown Point's star-shaped main stone fort was augmented with additional earthen and timber fortifications.[40] But like most military installations, it suffered from neglect during peacetime and was easily captured by Patriot forces in May 1775. In the summer of 1776, Crown Point was a mere shadow of its former greatness. To repair and defend Crown Point would consume a considerable amount of resources in time, men, and building material, none of which the Americans could spare. Plus, the smallpox epidemic that originated when the American Army was besieging Quebec was now in evidence there. Ticonderoga, on the other hand, was free of disease. Consequently, the three men agreed that they would

concentrate their defensive efforts on Fort Ticonderoga. They could still use Crown Point as a field hospital to isolate the smallpox cases until they could control the disease.[41]

The decision to abandon Crown Point and concentrate resources and efforts on defending Fort Ticonderoga was controversial. New England officers in the Northern Army and politicians from those states were worried that evacuating Crown Point would open their states to the British invasion. While dealing with his own troubles as he labored to defend New York City, Washington expressed "exceeding great concern" to Gates over the decision. The commander-in-chief explained that an evacuation of Crown Point could prove dangerous, as it would provide the British "uninterrupted passage into the three New England Governments for Invasion." Washington noted that many of his senior officers urged him to order Schuyler and Gates to hold Crown Point despite the results of their council of war. He had also heard that many of Gates's and Schuyler's subordinates wanted to defend the post. Washington hoped that "the measure could yet be changed with Propriety."[42] Washington did everything but give Gates a direct order to hold Crown Point, undoubtedly hoping the power of suggestion would suffice.

Gates defended their decision in a letter to Washington that reveals that the relationship between the two men had begun to fray. He was surprised to hear that any field officer disagreed with them because everyone was "Unanimous in Adopting" Schuyler's thoughts, "which were in my Opinion founded in Reason, & Good Sense." "As to the Field Officers being All of a Contrary Opinion," continued Gates, "whoever gave your Excellency that intelligence, was the Author of an Assertion Contrary to Fact." The rest of the letter outlined the reasons behind their assessment—the deteriorated state of the fortifications, the condition of the men, and the fact that the threat to New England was the same whether or not they kept Crown Point.[43]

Gates also addressed the critical need to build a fleet capable of holding the lake. "General Arnold," Gates wrote, has just returned from Skenesborough "where he has been exerting his Utmost diligence, in forwarding the Vessels Constructing there." The little American fleet was now being fitted out, and, once that happened, they would sail to Crown Point where they would link up with their crews consisting of "Three hundred Men and Officers . . . One half Seamen, the Other to Act as Marines."[44]

Finally, Gates informed Washington that he had designated the former merchant seaman Arnold to command the American fleet, which would face Carleton's flotilla as soon as it was ready. Arnold

had "a perfect knowledge in Maritime Affairs, and is besides a most deserving, and Gallant Officer."[45] To Hancock, Gates added that Arnold "will thereby add to that brilliant reputation he has so deservedly acquired."[46] For his part, Arnold was equally delighted to serve under Gates. After all, Gates had supported his expedition to Canada and he had told Washington that he was "happy to hear" about Gates's appointment to the Northern Department.[47] All of the key American decisions—evacuating Crown Point, building the American fleet, and placing Arnold in command of the fleet on Lake Champlain—would have far-reaching impact.

Gates's July 29 letter did little to mollify Washington, who daily watched more and more British ships and troops arrive on Staten Island, troops he would soon face in battle. He rebuked Gates for his implied insults about the intelligence he had received. Losing Crown Point "occasioned much anxiety to all who heard It being almost universally believed, that It was a post of the last Importance, and the only One, to give us in conjunction with our Naval force, a Superiority over the Lake and for preventing the Enemy penetrating into this and the Eastern Governments." Washington closed by assuring Gates that there would be no censure of the northern generals and that he assumed "those who determined that the post ought to be Abandoned, conceived It would but promote the Interest of the Great cause we are engaged in."[48]

Not unlike Germain, Horatio Gates's career would be marked by controversy. He has enjoyed little respect from posterity, primarily due to his involvement in the so-called Conway Cabal that attempted to undermine Washington's command in late 1777 and early 1778, and his defeat at the Battle of Camden in August 1780. But in the summer of 1776, Gates still enjoyed a solid reputation. He was one of several former British Army officers to join the American cause. Born in 1728 in Essex, England, to middle-class parents, Gates joined the British Army in 1745. Like so many of his contemporaries, he participated in the War of Austrian Succession and later in the French and Indian War, in which he served with General Edward Braddock on his expedition into Pennsylvania. He was seriously wounded during that campaign at the Battle of the Monongahela. During this campaign, Gates became acquainted with many American officers with whom he would later serve during the Revolution, including Washington, Charles Lee, and Daniel Morgan. After he recovered from his wounds, he accompanied the expedition to capture the French island of Martinique and was promoted to major. It would be his last promotion in the British Army.[49]

As a brigade major, Gates was responsible for handling the minute administrative details that were essential for the successful operation of a large military unit. Many were unsuited for this kind of detailed work; Gates excelled at it. It was this aptitude that made him a highly proficient staff officer, and his experience in the Seven Years War built on his natural ability. Seeing little chance for advancement after the war, Gates sold off his commission, purchased a modest Virginia estate called Traveler's Rest, and moved his family to America.[50]

Although Gates was about the same age as many of his contemporaries, he looked older. His long, grayish-white hair hung in wisps, and he certainly cut much less an impressive figure than Washington. He often had to wear spectacles, which did nothing to enhance a first impression, though contrary to many accounts, there is no convincing evidence of his being called "Granny Gates."[51] Despite his unimposing physical appearance, Gates was proud and vain. He loved drinking and socializing and used obscenities with reckless abandon. One observer wrote that Gates's speech was often so coarse that it makes "a New Englandman's hair almost stand on end."[52]

Immediately after the beginning of the Revolution, the ambitious Gates offered his services to the Patriot cause and was quickly appointed a brigadier general in the Continental Army, assuming the position of adjutant general, on the recommendation of his old comrade from the Braddock campaign, Washington. Gates performed well in this administrative position and did yeoman's work for Washington as the commander-in-chief struggled to recruit, organize, and train a new army. Washington was thrilled to have Gates on his staff. There were many officers available with plentiful militia experience, but few with Gates's professional military background.[53] Nonetheless, Gates wanted to command in the field. Probably due to his experience with American militia, he favored defensive operations against the British professionals and soon became known for his reluctance to take the offensive. He believed, as did Washington later in the war, that the inexperienced and poorly trained and equipped Americans should only attack when they enjoyed a distinct advantage.

Although cautious, Gates impressed the New Englanders, especially John and Samuel Adams and John Hancock, probably because of his strong support for independence. While his relationships with New England politicians were excellent, his bond with Washington deteriorated. When it began is uncertain—perhaps when Gates counseled against courses of action that Washington

ultimately adopted—but something happened shortly before he received the Canadian army appointment in June 1776. Writing many years later, Washington wrote that he had "discovered very early in the war symptoms of coldness and restraint in General Gates's behavior to me." This attitude "increased as he rose into greater consequence."[54]

While Schuyler and Gates wrestled with the chain of command issues, the spirits of the Northern Army were raised when news of the Declaration of Independence reached Ticonderoga in late July. The document was read out to the troops on July 28, when, Gates reported, "Independence has been received by this Army with . . . applause."[55] Schuyler soon left Gates in command of the forward American defenses at Fort Ticonderoga, Crown Point, and Lake Champlain, while he returned to his home and headquarters at Albany. Gates faced the challenges of defending the lake and the key American fortifications as Schuyler focused his efforts on logistical preparations for the upcoming campaign.

Knowing that there was no useable north-south road network in and around Lake Champlain and that the enemy would have to approach via water, Gates and Schuyler embarked on what was essentially a naval arms race with Carleton hundreds of miles from the sea. As Carleton's men labored to build their fleet at Fort Saint-Jean, the Americans frantically poured men and building materials into Skenesborough (present-day Whitehall, New York), located at the very southern tip of Lake Champlain, about 23 miles from Fort Ticonderoga, where they would build vessels to counter the British threat.[56] Arnold had long recognized the vital importance of maintaining control of the lake. In late June, immediately after returning from Canada, he wrote Washington that "It now appears to me of the Utmost Importance, that the lake be emediately secured by a large Number of (at least Twenty or |thirty) Gundaloes Row Gallies & floating Batteries." It was possible that the British had as many as a hundred, and that this would make them "masters of the lake, unless Every nerve on our part is Strained to exceed them in a Naval Armament."[57]

Arnold traveled to Skenesborough to take personal charge of the building efforts. His seemingly boundless energy, and his experience as a ship's captain, served him well, though it was anything but easy, as one officer explained in a letter to his father. "How we shall maintain our naval superiority I must confess myself much at a loss. . . . 'Tis true we build a thing *called* a gondola, perhaps as much as one in a week, but where is the rigging for them, where our guns?" The

enemy, on the other hand, "have, no doubt, everything ready to their hands . . . [and] I fear they have the advantage of us."[58]

Building the actual ships, the hulls, the masts, and so on, was labor-intensive if straightforward, provided that carpenters with a basic knowledge of boat and shipbuilding could be found. The fitting out of these vessels—rigging, sails, oars, and guns and their mounts—was just as challenging, if not more so. The process required additional specialized knowledge, materials, and equipment. All these tasks could be dangerous for the inexperienced soldier, as the soldiers-turned-sailors learned when one of the new crewmen was killed in a cannon accident on one of the gondolas fitting out at Fort Ticonderoga. The unfortunate soldier was "blown to many pieces & scattered on the water."[59] Fortunately, these incidents were rare.

After prodigious efforts on the part of Arnold and his crew, the Americans were able to build a credible naval presence on Lake Champlain. By early October 1776, the fleet of sixteen ships was complete, consisting of the *Royal Savage*, a two-masted schooner mounting six 6-pounders, four 4-pounders, and twelve swivel guns (small cannon mounted on stands or the ship's railings used primarily as anti-personnel weapons); the *Revenge*, a smaller schooner with eight 4-pounder cannon and ten swivel guns; the *Liberty*, another small schooner with two 4-pounders, six 2-pounders, and six swivel guns; and the *Enterprise*, a sloop with ten 4-pounders and twelve swivel guns.[60]

Arnold also commanded four row galleys, the *Congress*, Arnold's flagship, and the *Lee*, *Trumbull*, and *Washington*, each mounting one 18-pounder, one 12-pounder, two 9-pounders, and six 6-pounders. Finally, the fleet included eight gondolas—the *Boston*, *Connecticut*, *Jersey*, *New Haven*, *New York*, *Philadelphia*, *Providence*, and *Spitfire* with one bow-mounted 12-pounder.[61] All of these ships were manned mainly by untrained, or poorly trained, soldiers based at Crown Point, rather than seamen. Arnold lamented in a letter to Gates that "We have a wretched motley crew in the fleet, the marines the refuse of every regiment and the seamen, few of them ever wet with sea water."[62] The British, on the other hand, manned their ships with experienced Royal Navy officers and men.[63]

On August 7, as the building effort ramped up, Gates provided Arnold with what would be called today among active military his "commander's intent" for the upcoming campaign. First, he reminded Arnold that he must always keep in mind that "Preventing the Enemys invasion of our Country, is the ultimate End of the important Command, with which you are now intrusted." Knowing

that his aggressive subordinate was known for taking chances—just as he, Gates, was known for caution—he reminded Arnold that it "is a defensive War we are carrying on; therefore no wanton risque, or unnecessary Display of the Power of the Fleet, is at any Time, to influence your Conduct." However, he continued, should the British try to make their way up the lake and "force their way through," he was to give them "reason to repent their temerity." If the British fleet was simply too large to stop, on the other hand, he was to "retire" to Fort Ticonderoga.[64]

Gates was clear: Arnold's charge was to stop Carleton and prevent his fleet from forcing the narrows at Crown Point. If that failed, he must at least do his best to slow them down. He also had to safeguard the fleet. If Arnold succeeded, the Americans might just save Ticonderoga and force Carleton into making a premature go-or-no-go decision as the severe northern New York winter approached. Gates had faith in his second-in-command and dismissed those who tried to discredit him as "men of little merit, are ever jealous of those who have a great deal."[65] He had handed Arnold a difficult mission, but Arnold was used to seemingly impossible tasks. He had already helped capture Fort Ticonderoga at the beginning of the war; he had led his small army through the Maine wilderness to besiege and almost capture Quebec; he had sustained the siege of Quebec throughout the bitter Canadian winter through the force of his personality and leadership; and he had been stalwart during the retreat to Crown Point.

While Arnold pushed the shipbuilding effort at Skenesborough, Gates organized his army in and around Fort Ticonderoga. His mission was almost as difficult as Arnold's. Ticonderoga, like Crown Point, was in poor repair, though at least it was smallpox-free. Still, in the summer of 1776, the situation at Ticonderoga was dire. One observer described his first impressions of the fort "which presented but a sorry sight. The glories of Ti were rather on the wane. . . . Its ditches were nearly filled with rubbish, and its ramparts were dismantled and ruinous."[66] John Trumbull, one of Gates's aides and the son of the Connecticut governor, found at Ticonderoga, as he wrote his father, "not an army, but a mob, the shattered remains of twelve or fifteen very fine battalions, ruined by sickness, fatigue and desertions and void of every idea of discipline or subordination." The situation left Ticonderoga vulnerable, and the fort may well have proved impossible to hold, in Trumbull's opinion, "without a naval superiority on the lakes," and significant reinforcements.[67]

Fort Ticonderoga's importance in the summer of 1776 was measured by its location rather than its strength. It lay astride the great invasion route to and from Canada and overlooked the narrowest point on Lake Champlain. Both Lake George and the branch of Lake Champlain south of Ticonderoga, in turn, provided access to the Hudson River, and thus New York. A short distance northwest of the great stone fort was a series of field fortifications called the "Old French Lines," so named because they were first constructed during the British siege and capture of the fort during the French and Indian War. A little farther northwest lay the small wooded hill called Mount Hope, upon which the Americans constructed additional fortifications in 1776. Both Mount Independence and Mount Hope were within easy cannon shot of the fort.[68]

Although the generals had decided to abandon Crown Point, Gates stationed a small detachment of New Hampshire troops there to act as an outer screen for Ticonderoga. He informed the commander, Lieutenant Colonel Thomas Hartley, that since his job was "meant more as an advanced guard than a post to be defended to the last extremity, you are carefully to keep your retreat open to the batteaus."[69] Hartley was also to keep Gates informed of enemy movements and—above all—to keep his force intact.

By the end of July 1776, Gates's concept of operations for facing the imminent British offensive was clear: He had established a small detachment at Crown Point as a conduit for intelligence gathering and to act as a speed bump; he had repaired and improved the fortifications at Ticonderoga, including new posts on the newly renamed Mount Independence; and he had built and manned a fleet to counter Carleton's naval force. Given the early onset of winter in the region, prospects for delaying Carleton's advance were good.

Gates made sure that his troops at Ticonderoga did not sit idle. With the arrival on July 8 of Colonel Jeduthan Baldwin, an engineer from Massachusetts, Gates put the men to work on the fortifications. He directed Baldwin to "acquaint the commanding officer of each brigade with the work expected to be done by each brigade, and the General is confident a spirit of emulation will animate each brigade to finish the task assign'd them."[70] Throughout the summer and into the fall, the troops at Ticonderoga worked twelve-hour days, repairing the old works and building new ones, directed by Baldwin and supervised by Gates and Arnold who, commanding the fleet and a brigade at Ticonderoga, split his time between Ticonderoga, Crown Point, and Skenesborough.

While not a formally trained military engineer, Baldwin did have some experience working on fortifications during the French and Indian War, and was involved in the Revolutionary War from the outset, rendering good service during the siege of Boston, laying out the Patriot fortifications.[71] He would serve a series of commanders over the next eighteen months and generally oversee repairing, designing, building, and maintaining the fortifications at Fort Ticonderoga and the adjacent Mount Independence. Baldwin often did double duty as the army's quartermaster general and paymaster while also directing "all the fatiguing parties."[72]

While Baldwin was a hard worker, he did not have a particularly good eye for terrain. Concentrating his efforts on the stone fort, the field fortifications in front of the main works, and Mount Independence, he ignored Sugar Loaf (Mount Defiance), which at 853 feet dominated the main fort by more than 600 feet, believing that heavy artillery could not be dragged up this rugged and tree-covered hill. Colonel Trumbull disagreed, writing in a journal entry that he was of the "heretical opinion" that not fortifying the hill made the Americans vulnerable, and "I was ridiculed for advancing such an extravagant idea." Trumbull asked Gates for permission to confirm his view, and, using artillery firing from Ticonderoga, proved that shot could reach the top of the hill, thus proving that the reverse would certainly be true. Trumbull's experiment did not impress those who argued that even if artillery on Sugar Loaf could reach the fort, the "summit was inaccessible to the enemy." The persistent young officer was not to be denied, and soon he and Arnold and "several other active officers" took a boat to the foot of the mountain and "clambered to the summit in a short time." "The ascent was difficult and laborious, but not impracticable, and when we looked down upon the outlet of Lake George [mouth of the La Chute River], it was obvious to all that there would be no difficulty in driving up a loaded carriage." Trumbull concluded that they would never have enough men to man the extensive fortifications at Ticonderoga and Mount Independence properly (most estimates called for at least ten thousand troops), but that a "small but strong post" at the summit of Mount Defiance "would be a more effectual and essentially a less expensive defense of this pass, than all our present extended lines."[73] Trumbull advocated a classic economy of force operation; a small force on Mount Defiance would have a huge impact.

Trumbull's efforts to convince the officers at Fort Ticonderoga to fortify Mount Defiance were in vain, most likely because his

recommendation was lost among their other pressing responsibilities. Baldwin knew of Trumbull's concern, and as chief engineer the post's vulnerability should have been obvious to him. Instead, he and the other senior officers concentrated on Mount Independence and the other works in and around the original stone fort.

The region between Fort Saint-Jean and Albany encompasses some of the most forbidding and beautiful terrain in North America. As Carleton started his campaign south, he had to deal with a virtually trackless wilderness, with countless watercourses of all sizes and shapes, swift and treacherous rivers and streams, bleak, rocky shorelines, and seemingly impenetrable forests, populated by strange birds and animals, and, in the summer, with clouds of biting insects. Some of the more senior officers had served in North American during the French and Indian War two decades before, and so had at least some familiarity with the area and its flora and fauna. For most of the soldiers and sailors in Carleton's expedition, however, the land around Lake Champlain was entirely alien.

After weeks and months of delays—again, caused by Carleton's desire to create a fleet that would overwhelm the American vessels—the British armada was finally ready to sail from Fort Saint-Jean on the Richelieu River and lower Lake Champlain in late September. On October 4, Carleton boarded the flagship *Maria* accompanied by General Riedesel.[74] That same day he wrote General Howe and his brother Vice Admiral Howe, informing them that he was ready to go and "shall proceed to endeavor to clear the Lake of Rebels, who are upon it with a considerable naval force."[75] He gave no indication that he would be able to penetrate all the way to Albany, or that he would even try.

Even before the British force started south and proceeded up the lake, Arnold had moved his flotilla of sixteen small warships well north of Crown Point, wanting to face Carleton's superior force as far forward as possible. Arnold's and Gates's intelligence was faulty. Both had sent scouting parties north to try to determine the enemy's intentions, but the results were mixed and therefore misleading. Gates was convinced that the British had already gone into winter quarters. Moreover, some American scouting parties had been captured and were providing Carleton with valuable information on Arnold and the American fleet.[76] Part of Arnold's reasoning for advancing so far down the lake was to conduct a reconnaissance in force—his whole force—to determine what Carleton was up to. As Arnold sailed north in early September, he began to encounter Indian and British Army scouting parties.

Lake Champlain is studded with islands—in addition to bays, inlets, rocky peninsulas, and outcroppings—and Valcour Island, about 2 miles long and a mile wide, is one of the largest. This is where Arnold decided to confront Carleton's fleet. Separated from the western shore of the lake by a half-mile-wide channel, Valcour is almost 50 miles north of Crown Point, and roughly halfway between Crown Point and the mouth of the Richelieu River. As he often did, Arnold went beyond the strict letter of his orders and decided to face Carleton much farther north than Gates ever envisioned. Arnold reasoned that he could delay Carleton—trading space for time, time for Gates to continue his defensive preparations, and for winter weather to arrive. If Arnold could fight and fall back, and fight again, and fall back again, he could slow the British down while inflicting as much damage as possible. He had initially determined to push all the way to Isle La Motte, located just a few miles south of where Lake Champlain empties into the Richelieu River, and, in fact, had sailed the flotilla to that point. Once there, however, he wisely realized that this was simply too far forward, and in the event of a disaster, he would not be able to get his force back to safety. Arnold explained his decision in a letter to Gates dated September 15: "I design making a remove to the island Valcour," because the island featured "a good harbor, and if the enemy venture up the lake, it will be impossible for them to take advantage of our situation."[77] Gates approved Arnold's forward deployment a few weeks later, setting the stage for a major naval clash.

With almost no intelligence concerning Carleton's fleet, Arnold deployed his ships across the channel between Valcour Island and the western shore. He rigged the ships with anchors and cables, so the vessels could be turned broadside when ready to fire and parallel to the shore while reloading to reduce their vulnerability to enemy fire.[78] His first indication that the British were indeed coming up the lake was early on the morning of October 11, when the schooner *Revenge*, which Arnold had stationed north of the island, reported that Carleton's large fleet was in sight in the lake's main channel. Finally, Arnold had firsthand evidence that Carleton's fleet greatly outnumbered his own. One of his senior officers counseled retreat. Arnold refused, and the American crews—made up of citizen soldiers, farmers, craftsmen, and laborers—readied themselves to face trained Royal Navy seamen.[79]

The British fleet, under the operational command of Captain Thomas Pringle, co-located with Carleton on the *Maria*, swept down the east side of Valcour Island, and did not spot the Americans until

they passed the south end of the island. Although a small force of soldiers accompanied the British fleet, the majority of Burgoyne's eight-thousand-strong army component of Carleton's force waited, along with their transports, to be called forward once the American fleet was destroyed.[80]

The battle was joined shortly after Arnold sent the *Royal Savage* around the southern end of Valcour Island, revealing the American fleet's location. The decoy worked. Captain Pringle turned the British fleet back north and into the constricted channel west of the island. As the *Royal Savage* tried to get back into line, her crew's inexperience was evident, and she ran aground on the southwest shore of the island, attracting the attention of enemy gunners. She was quickly put out of action and later captured and destroyed. Arnold had already lost one a ship in a matter of minutes. Late in the morning, the *Carleton* pushed forward toward the Americans, who focused their fire on the British ship, which was quickly disabled. The action degenerated into a general melee at very close quarters, with ships only yards apart firing into their opponents at point-blank range. During the nine-hour battle, the decks of ships on both sides became slippery with blood. Arnold reported the next day, "They continued a very hot fire with round and grape-shot until five o'clock, when they thought proper to retire to about six or seven hundred yards distance, and continued the fire until night."[81]

The Americans fought well, with Arnold personally directing the *Congress*'s guns, managing to sink three British gunboats, and almost destroying the *Carleton*, but the British advantages in experience, numbers, and weight of shot soon took their toll. As Arnold described twenty-four hours after the battle, "The *Congress* and *Washington* have suffered greatly; the latter lost her first lieutenant killed, captain and master wounded. The *New-York* lost all her officers, except her captain. The *Philadelphia* was hulled in so many places that she sank about one hour after the engagement was over. The whole killed and wounded amounts to about sixty."[82] By the time the sun sank below the horizon, the battered American fleet lay at the mercy of Carleton's warships, floating only a few hundred yards to the south.

After nightfall, the British pulled back and decided to wait south of the island until dawn on the 12th to complete the destruction of the American flotilla. Surveying the extensive damage to his ships, Arnold determined that they could not possibly survive another head-to-head slugging match against Carleton's superior ships and decided to escape south to Crown Point. Under cover of darkness and fog, the Americans managed to maneuver the damaged ships

into a single file, hugging the New York shoreline and successfully slipping by the British warships, which were badly positioned. One British officer offered grudging praise, writing, "This retreat did great honor to Gen'l Arnold, who acted as Admiral to the Rebel Fleet on this occasion."[83]

Pringle's pursuit was slowed by a southerly wind, though the same breeze hampered Arnold's efforts to pull away from the British. Halting their retreat on Schuyler's Island, about 10 miles south, Arnold rested his men and reassessed their situation. They were in poor shape, but he put the best face on it in a report to Schuyler: "On the whole, I think we have had a very fortunate escape and have great reason to return our humble and hearty thanks to Almighty God."[84]

Arnold's thanks were premature, as the chase resumed, and Pringle and his ships soon closed the distance on the Americans. The wind shifted to the north, and Pringle finally caught up with Arnold early in the afternoon of October 13, just off Split Rock, 18 miles south of Schuyler's Island. Arnold selected the *Congress* and *Washington* to hold off the British, so the rest of the fleet could escape south. The two ships were quickly overwhelmed, the *Washington* surrendering and the *Congress* suffering crippling damage. In desperation, Arnold ordered the remaining ships into a shallow cove (present-day Arnold Bay) about 2 miles south of Buttonmould Bay, just south of Split Rock on the eastern shore of the lake and about 10 miles north of Crown Point. As one eyewitness observed, Arnold ordered all the ships set on fire "but ordered the colours not struck, and as they grounded, the marines were directed to jump overboard . . . Arnold being the last man who debarked."[85] As his ships burned to their waterlines, Arnold led the surviving crewmembers to Crown Point through the wilderness, hauling their wounded and dodging Indian ambushes.

Twelve American ships were destroyed or captured, and two hundred men killed or wounded. The British lost three gunboats and forty casualties. It was an overwhelming British victory. When he arrived at Crown Point with his exhausted men—they had gone 72 hours with almost no sleep or food—Arnold discovered that four of his ships—the *Enterprise, New York, Revenge,* and *Trumbull*—had escaped and were lying just offshore. Conferring with Colonel Hartley, the garrison commander, Arnold decided to abandon the post, destroy anything that Carleton's forces might find useful, and the small force journeyed to Ticonderoga with the enemy following close behind.[86]

Arnold had inflicted damage to Carleton's superior force, and he led his surviving men to safety. But he had also lost the painstakingly

constructed fleet and had caused the enemy only a short delay.[87] Indeed, many expressed shock at Arnold's recklessness. One general officer complained sarcastically that Arnold, "with a good deal of industry, got us clear of all our fine fleet," which was a "pretty piece of admiralship."[88]

The British were very pleased with their success. Carleton, writing from the *Maria* off Crown Point on October 14—arriving only hours after Arnold, Hartley, the post's garrison, and the survivors of the naval battles, had escaped back to Ticonderoga—informed Germain that "the rebel fleet upon Lake Champlain has been entirely defeated in two actions."[89] By mid-October, Carleton had cleared the lake of American naval power and opened the way south. One big push before the first snow might just pave the way to Albany. Burgoyne, commanding the ground force, issued a general order on October 17 to the troops, celebrating the naval action and his boss. The victory, Burgoyne declared, was "obtained by the commander in chief in person" and the "importance of the conquest is not greater to the national cause, than is the glory achieved to his majesty's arms." He then urged the army to emulate the navy's efforts in the action they were sure was coming.[90]

The question now facing Carleton at Crown Point was whether to push on to Ticonderoga, as Germain and many of his officers certainly expected, or bypass Ticonderoga and strike directly toward Albany. Or, given the lateness of the season, he could garrison Crown Point, overwinter only a few miles north of Ticonderoga, and resume the offensive in the spring. Gates certainly expected Carleton to attack, as he reported to Schuyler on October 24 from Fort Ticonderoga: "Carleton keeps very close to Crown Point . . . I apprehend . . . this stillness will be succeeded by a grand attack."[91]

The "stillness" would be replaced with frantic British activity, but to the north, not the south, for Carleton in the end chose none of these options, explaining to Germain, "The season is so far advanced that I cannot yet pretend to inform your lordship whether anything farther can be done this year."[92] Although the situation called for a quick decision, Carleton delayed for thirteen days after he seized Crown Point, at which point he sent a small force to test the Ticonderoga defenses. Gates's prodigious efforts to improve the defenses in and around Fort Ticonderoga paid off when the detachment commander reported to Carleton that the American defenses were very formidable. Burgoyne nonetheless argued for an immediate attack. Carleton balked, and instead, on October 23, he decided to pull his entire force back to Canada. In a few weeks, all the

British forces had returned down the lake to Fort Saint-Jean and beyond. Fort Ticonderoga, Albany, and the upper Hudson Valley were secure, and the British expedition that began with so much promise, and despite winning a crushing naval victory, ended in a retreat.

Burgoyne was furious. He saw Carleton's decision as a betrayal to all they had accomplished and the blood that had been spilled. To pull back to Canada meant they would give up control of the lake and all their hard-won gains. Also, the withdrawal meant that they would just have to do everything over again in 1777. Carleton's decision, Burgoyne wrote, "jeopardized the fruits of our summer's labor and autumn victory."[93]

Burgoyne was not the only officer disgusted at Carleton's decision. Lieutenant Colonel Gabriel Christie, a Germain confidant, wrote a scathing letter to the secretary in late October. "The whole army," wrote Christie, "is in amazement and the Country dejected as all hopes of opening the Communication is at an end between this province and New York." Christie declared that Carleton was "totally unfit for such a command and must ruin his Majesty's affairs and those of England."[94] This most certainly did nothing to enhance Germain's assessment of Carleton. Indeed, Christie's letter seemed to reinforce all the doubts Germain had had about the governor of Canada.

Of the Battle of Valcour Island, the great American naval theorist, strategist, and historian, Alfred Thayer Mahan, wrote elegiacally, "The little American navy on Champlain was wiped out; but never had any force, big or small, lived to better purpose or died more gloriously."[95] Mahan's basic assessment has been echoed by generations of historians. However, the battle had very little impact on Carleton's decision-making, as he made clear in his correspondence.[96] Royal Navy Captain Charles Douglas, who had commanded the squadron that relieved Quebec earlier that year and who was instrumental in building Carleton's Lake Champlain fleet, mentioned only the naval victory in his report to the Admiralty. "Our reward," for weeks of hard work building the fleet, was "the destruction of almost the whole of the rebel fleet," the captain wrote. Indeed, he reported, they had "outdone them [the rebels] in working as in fighting."[97] At best, the British invasion force was delayed by two to three days—hardly a significant period in a campaign that took weeks. Arnold had disregarded Gates's initial orders to position the fleet much farther south than he did. Instead of hitting and falling back, Arnold allowed himself to become decisively engaged, and so he lost most of the fleet. Arnold's aggressiveness and that of his ships and crews

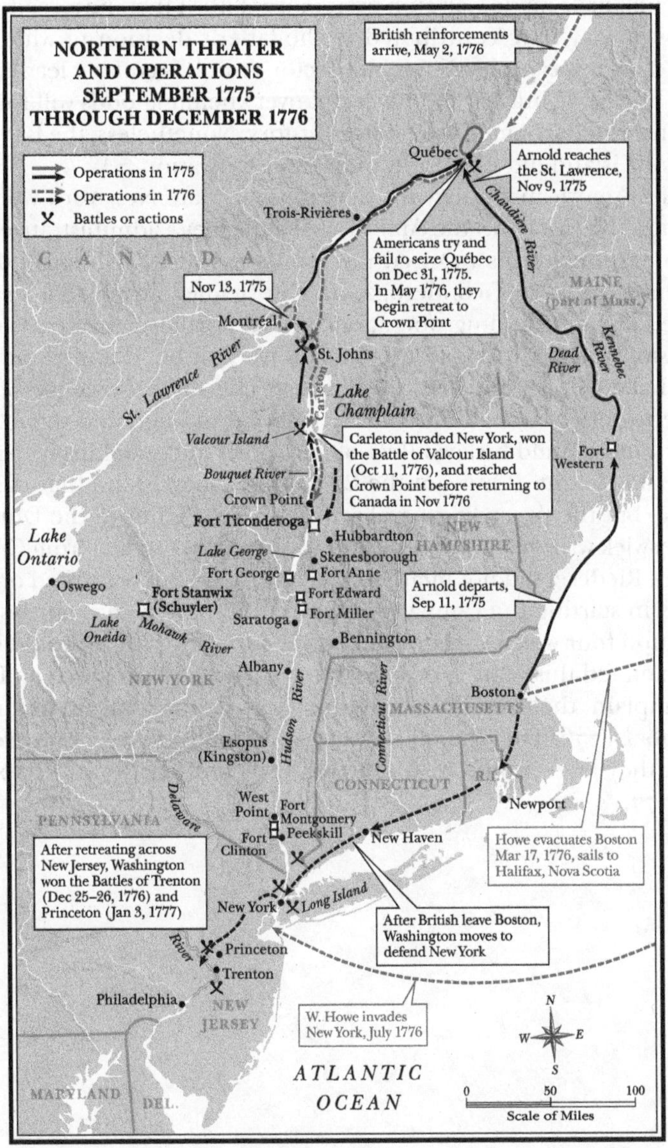

Map 1 Northern Theater of Operations, September 1775 through December 1776

may well have made Carleton even more skittish than he already was. Thus, it may have contributed to the latter's decision to withdraw, but, if so, it was probably a minor factor. Arnold's combat leadership and his crews' bravery in the face of overwhelming odds will forever be enshrined in American military history. Nonetheless, the Battle of Valcour Island did little to stop the British invasion.

The American strategy for defending upstate New York worked, though the price was the American fleet. Gates's administrative and organizational skills restored the army's morale and improved the defenses of Fort Ticonderoga, and he gained invaluable experience in understanding operations in the northern theater. Gates's decision to assign Arnold the mission to both build and command the Lake Champlain fleet proved key. The mere existence of the American fleet forced Carleton to respond in kind, and the time it took him to build his own fleet of transports and warships became a crucial element. It was not the Battle of Valcour Island that was decisive, but the preceding naval arms race. In a letter to the Duke of Brunswick written a few weeks after returning to Canada from Crown Point, Riedesel did not mention Valcour Island but remarked on the delay in starting the campaign: "If we could have begun our last expedition four weeks earlier, I am satisfied that everything would have been ended this year."[98] Despite losing their naval presence on Lake Champlain, the Americans had won a significant strategic victory in October 1776. The fruit of this victory was time—time to prepare for what they knew would be a renewed British offensive in the spring of 1777.

CHAPTER 3

A New British Strategy

ON OCTOBER 24, 1776, Lieutenant General Burgoyne boarded the captured American row galley, *Washington*, on the waters of Lake Champlain off Crown Point. By all accounts, he was in a foul mood. He and Major General William Phillips, the British artillery commander, had tried to convince Carleton to attack the Americans at Fort Ticonderoga after their victories on October 11 and 13. Burgoyne was livid at Carleton's refusal, but all the more determined to press the British advantage. The anticipated attack on Fort Ticonderoga in the spring and summer of 1777 would be his chance to distinguish himself in the American war. As he wrote his friend Henry Clinton, "A secondary station in a secondary army is at no time agreeable."[1] Burgoyne knew that first he would have to convince senior figures in the British government to give him an independent command. Now, in late October, with Carleton's permission, he was on his way back to Quebec and then to England, ostensibly to carry Carleton's report to Germain and deal with personal affairs—his wife had died while he was overseas. On November 9, Burgoyne boarded the 50-gun, fourth-rate Royal Navy warship HMS *Isis*, in Quebec for the voyage home, barely escaping before the Saint Lawrence River iced up.

Burgoyne's passage was comparatively swift, taking only a month; the strong, late-autumn westerly winds swept the *Isis* across the

North Atlantic. By December 9 he was back in London and seeking meetings with the king and Lord Germain. He was not received with universal acclaim. Walpole confided to his journal that Burgoyne "now pretended grief for his wife's death, which was laughed at."[2] His ambition for top command was well known in London.

Burgoyne had brought a memo from Carleton to Germain that he took to Germain's offices in Whitehall, located on the west bank of the Thames. As a Member of Parliament, Burgoyne was intimately familiar with this part of the city. Over the past century, London had expanded west along the river to distance itself from the noxious smoke and odors that emanated from the more industrial and poorer parts of the city to the east and south of the Thames. Government offices and the city's wealthiest inhabitants gradually moved west as well. Germain himself lived on Pall Mall, one of the most fashionable addresses in London, then and now.[3]

In his memorandum, Carleton asked for four thousand reinforcements to resume the offensive up Lake Champlain in the spring, maintain the security of Canada during the operation, and so that they might also "operate upon the Mohawk River." In addition, Carleton suggested that another force could "penetrate the Connecticut River."[4] His plan was not really a plan at all, more a vague concept for a southward offensive.[5] However, it did start a process by which the key British senior leaders in London—primarily the king, Prime Minister Lord North, Germain, Burgoyne, and William Howe in America—formulated strategy for 1777.

By the late autumn of 1776, it was obvious to British decision-makers that the war would extend into 1777, at least. Still, it might be won were an army from Canada to move south, secure control of Lake Champlain and Lake George, reduce Fort Ticonderoga, and link up with the main British Army coming north up the Hudson River. This would separate the more rebellious New England colonies from those provinces containing a large population of Loyalists. This was, of course, the strategy Germain had advocated in 1776, and it formed the basic template for 1777. For many, but not all, of these leaders, it was an article of faith.[6]

Burgoyne, like Germain, believed in the efficacy of the invasion from Canada, but he added his own spin on Carleton's concept. Although there is no direct evidence, Germain or someone in the Colonial Office told Burgoyne about the August 22 letter Germain had written to Carleton—the letter Carleton would not see until the spring of 1777—that relieved the governor of his military responsibilities. Burgoyne desperately wanted Carleton's command

and thought that if he played his cards right, he could secure it by impressing Germain and the king.[7] Burgoyne met with the secretary on December 10 to deliver Carleton's report. Germain told the king later that day that Burgoyne had been "strongly" against abandoning Crown Point.[8]

Three days later, Burgoyne arranged an audience with the monarch at the Queen's House. According to the account of the meeting the king gave to Lord North, Burgoyne made him aware of the animosity between Germain and Carleton, so much so that "it would be idle to say more than that it is a fact." The king concluded that Carleton's shortcomings "may make it advisable to have the part of the Canadian Army which must attempt to join Gen. Howe led by a more enterprising Commander." Burgoyne took the opportunity to put himself forward as just the "enterprising commander" the king was looking for.[9]

In any case, the king agreed to Carleton's request for an additional four thousand troops so that at least three thousand would be available for the defense of the province when operations were resumed in the spring. He provided an outline of these operations, which were essentially based on Carleton's ideas—but with Burgoyne's additions: "Part of the Army must proceed on the lakes to Ticondaroga and another by the Mohawk River." He further suggested that "Burgoyne may command the Corps to be sent from Canada to Albany."[10] Clearly, Burgoyne had impressed the king.

As his letter to Lord North suggests, George III was fully invested in the war. He had risen to the throne in the middle of the Seven Years War in October 1760 with the death of his grandfather George II and became the third British Hanoverian king. A year later, he married Princess Charlotte Mecklenberg-Strelitz, whom he had never met but grew to love; the union produced fifteen children. George III was intellectually curious and, throughout his early reign, had been well served by several prime ministers, including his favorite, Lord Bute (1762–1763), and William Pitt the Elder (1766–1768). Pitt was the architect of the strategy that won the Seven Years War and, in the process, greatly expanding the British Empire. However, by the time Lord North assumed the post in January 1770, the entire government was consumed with the growing crisis in America. Both the king and North wanted to pursue a diplomatic resolution of the disputes with the Americans. After the Boston Tea Party, however, the king hardened his positions. Once shots were fired at the Battles of Lexington and Concord, he was convinced only force would bring the Americans back to their senses.[11] Despite dispatching a large

army, one led by some of the country's best military talent, they had still not subdued the rebels a year and a half later. By late 1776, the king was getting impatient.

On his doctor's orders, Burgoyne left London for Bath on New Year's Day 1777, though not before informing Germain that if needed for information "upon the affairs of Canada, I shall be ready to obey your summons upon one day's notice." Burgoyne made it clear that he sought the Canada command and hoped for "your patronage in this pursuit."[12] In three short weeks in London, Burgoyne had expertly maneuvered himself into gaining a major independent command.

In a portrait by Joshua Reynolds, the leading painter of the period, Burgoyne certainly looks the part of the patrician British officer. In fact, he was born to middle-class parents in 1722 (although there is some evidence to suggest that he was the illegitimate son of Lord Bingley, a key advisor to Queen Anne).[13] Educated at the Westminster School in London, Burgoyne became acquainted with others with whom he would serve in the army or in politics. At sixteen, he joined the British Army as an officer in the prestigious Horse Guards. With his regiment based in London, he was able to cultivate the relationships and patronage of well-known members of society and government. One was Lord Derby, and in 1751 Burgoyne married Derby's daughter, thirteen years his junior—against her father's wishes. Derby renounced the couple for years but was eventually convinced to accept Burgoyne after the birth of a daughter. In the meantime, Burgoyne had bought and sold two commissions in the army to raise cash for paying off gambling debts he had incurred in London.[14]

Moving in and out of the army was not a particularly unusual practice for young officers of the period. When war broke out in 1756, Burgoyne reentered the army with the 11th Dragoons and served with distinction in the raids on Saint-Malo and Cherbourg, in which Germain (then Sackville) had also been involved. During these operations, he served with three men who would have a major impact on his future: Germain, of course, and the Howe brothers. His successes on the coast of France led to relatively rapid advancement. He was promoted to lieutenant colonel and assumed command of the 16th Dragoons, a newly formed regiment of light cavalry that became known as "Burgoyne's Light Horse."[15] After Spain declared war in 1762 on Portugal, a staunch British ally, Burgoyne was promoted to colonel and commander of a combined force of multinational units that captured a key fortified Spanish border town, and he later

personally led a successful cavalry charge. These actions enhanced Burgoyne's reputation as an aggressive, capable commander, and an impressive horseman.

After his return from overseas, Burgoyne's cavalry was often involved in royal reviews throughout the 1760s, catching the eye of the young King George III; he quickly became one of the sovereign's favorite army officers. In the mid-1760s, Burgoyne and his wife moved at the highest levels of British society, and thus, he was able to secure a prestigious assignment in Europe to conduct an inspection tour of the Continent's major powers. Burgoyne not only distinguished himself on the battlefield but proved himself an excellent leader. Unlike many of the senior British officers of the period, he encouraged initiative from his subordinates and opposed the harsh discipline to which British soldiers were too often subjected. During his trip to Europe, he compared the British Army and its soldiers with those of other countries and came to the conclusion that instead of the almost sadistic discipline practiced by the Prussians, or the French method of entreating soldiers to do their duty through personal and national honor and the glory of battle, the British officer "should instead appeal to their [soldiers'] reason, their patriotism, and their comaraderie."[16] He treated his men well, and his esteem and warmth were reciprocated.[17]

Like many ambitious and well-connected British officers of the time, Burgoyne pursued a political career while also serving as a professional army officer. He first served in Parliament in 1762 after returning from Portugal. He later was elected as MP in 1766 and held that post until his death in 1792. His career in the Commons was mostly undistinguished, though he was known as a hardliner throughout the period of increasing tensions with America, voting against the repeal of the Stamp Act, for example. In a 1774 speech, he compared America to a "child, which I think we have already spoiled by too much indulgence."[18] Generally, Burgoyne supported the government's policies. Still, he was no reflexive Tory, often opposing policies that he saw as detrimental to the military.

Burgoyne was fond of the arts and counted among his closest friends Joshua Reynolds and the actor David Garrick. He also was a playwright and achieved some success with his comedies about British society. In an era known for rhetorical flamboyance, Burgoyne had a reputation for grandiosity in speech and manner. Walpole called him "Burgoyne the Pompous."[19] His fondness for the gaming table was also well known, and he was widely thought to be a risk-taker and a "fortunate gamester."[20] His promotion to major general in

1772 made it inevitable that Burgoyne would be sent to America at the outbreak of armed rebellion, and, along with fellow major generals William Howe and Henry Clinton, he arrived in Boston in May 1775.

Burgoyne and Carleton were not the only senior officers thinking about the 1777 campaign. While Carleton's fleet was preparing to meet the Americans on Lake Champlain, Germain wrote to William Howe, congratulating him on his successful joint operations with the Royal Navy and the victory at the Battle of Long Island."[21] A week later, Germain wrote Howe again, urging him to continue to press Washington, expel all rebel forces from Manhattan, and perhaps "pay a visit to Philadelphia before the Campaign ends."[22] Howe received Germain's letters in the fall of 1776, after he had captured Fort Washington, pushed the rebel army out of Manhattan, and settled into his slow pursuit of Washington across New Jersey. As winter approached, Howe, too, came to realize that the war would inevitably extend into 1777, and as the commander-in-chief in the American colonies, he would have to devise a plan for the coming year.

Howe seemed like the perfect choice to head the most important command in the British Empire. Born into an aristocratic family with close ties to the royal family, William and his two older brothers entered the military—he and George into the army and the other, Richard, as we've seen, into the Royal Navy—and all three had illustrious careers. William entered the army at the age of seventeen and served on active campaigns on the Continent in 1747–1748. During the French and Indian War, he served in America, where he distinguished himself at the capture of Quebec with his friend James Wolfe.

During this period, he got to know the colonies and, unlike some of his contemporaries, admired and respected many of the Americans he encountered. His feelings were shared by George, who was killed in an attempt to take Fort Ticonderoga in July 1758, and by Richard, who inherited the family title as the third Viscount Howe. By the end of the war, William had established himself as one of the army's rising stars. Not only an accomplished leader, he was also interested in improving the training and professionalism of the army. He served in several administrative posts, and, like many of his fellow officers, secured a seat in Parliament. On the eve of the American Revolution he had reached the rank of major general, and that was why he was aboard the HMS *Cerberus*, together with Clinton and Burgoyne, on his way to Boston to help suppress the troublesome rebels.[23]

At the end of November 1776, Howe sent *his* plan for 1777 in a letter to Germain. Howe proposed a three-phase campaign. First, he recommended that Clinton command a ten-thousand-man army to seize Providence, and then, if possible, move north to Boston. Second, another army of ten thousand men would move up the Hudson River from New York to Albany, leaving behind five thousand men to defend the city. Finally, a third army of eight thousand men would "cover Jersey" and keep Washington's army in check by threatening "Philadelphia, which I would propose to attack in autumn, as well as Virginia."[24] Howe's plan focused on pacification and holding territory rather than on attacking Washington's army. Like Carleton's, it did not really establish what he hoped to accomplish, other than the vague suggestion of retaking lost ground and expanding the territory controlled by British forces.

Three weeks later, in December 1776, Howe had a change of heart. In a new proposal to Germain, he wrote that he was now convinced that the Americans were so awed by the British Army and its pursuit of Washington that they would fold if Philadelphia was captured. Howe was also convinced that his "army should act offensively on that side where the enemy's chief strength will certainly be collected." He proposed two major objectives for 1777: capture Philadelphia with his army to degrade American will, which was already low, and defeat Washington's army, which would surely try to defend the seat of Congress. One of the virtues of the new plan, Howe argued, was it required many fewer troops than the first: two thousand men to hold Rhode Island, seven thousand men to secure New York City and Long Island, and ten thousand to mount the offensive on Philadelphia. Howe did not mention any direct cooperation with Carleton's army in Canada, as he did not think the northern force would "reach Albany before the middle of September."[25] In other words, Howe suggested Carleton's force would have no major strategic impact in 1777.

Days after sending his Philadelphia plan to Germain, Howe informed the secretary of Washington's Christmas Day raid on the Hessian outpost at Trenton. The rebels' "success will probably produce another campaign," he noted tersely.[26] He did not tell Germain how Washington's victory and the consequent surge in rebel optimism might affect his plan for 1777, which had been premised in part on low American morale.

In London, at least, morale was high. In early 1777, before news of Trenton and Princeton reached the capital, everyone was confident that the war was going well, and why not? Carleton had destroyed

the American fleet, and Howe had chased the rebel army across New Jersey. This was reflected by the press. On January 6, 1777, the *Morning Post* reported that "[T]he Court has been full of Congratulations, and felicitations; the king never was in higher spirits; Administration plume themselves on the success of their measures."[27] News of a new campaign for 1777 was spreading, prompting one newspaper to opine that the new plan would surely "bring about a speedy resolution" of the conflict "in favour of his Majesty's Government."[28]

Howe wrote, yet again, on January 20 with a third plan (a modification of his second plan), one devised after he had a chance to reconsider the impact of Washington's twin victories at Trenton and Princeton, which had "thrown us farther back than was first apprehended, from the great encouragement it has given to the rebels." No longer could he hope to defeat the rebellion by intimidating the Americans with British military might. "I do not now see a prospect of terminating the war but by general action." However, this was easier said than done, added Howe, because "the enemy moves with so much more celerity than we possibly can." To end the war, he had to destroy Washington's army, and Philadelphia was "now the principal object" to act as the bait. He proposed launching a two-pronged attack toward Philadelphia, one part by sea and the other across New Jersey.[29] Howe's January letter demonstrates the evolution of his thinking. Philadelphia was clearly his primary focus. Everything else was secondary.

Before a board of inquiry two years later, Howe would argue that he had four main reasons for going to Philadelphia: to capture the capital city of Pennsylvania and the seat of Congress; to draw the main American Amy away from the operations of the British Army in Canada; to negate the city's role as the rebellion's primary logistical base; and, most importantly, to force Washington into a major and perhaps decisive engagement. "I do not think there was one object, which would have tempted General Washington to risk a general action, so much as the fear of losing the Capital of Pennsylvania."[30]

While Howe's plans were getting sorted out, British leaders discussed the delicate issue of senior officer assignments. The king wrote to Lord North on February 24 that Germain was about to "propose Gen. Clinton for Canada, and Burgoyne to join Howe." The king approved the assignments, adding that Germain also wanted to fire Carleton, "but I have thrown cold water on that."[31] In the end, however, the government dismissed these proposals, and on February 25, 1777, the ministers recommended to the king

that "Lieutenant General Burgoyne should be again employed in Canada."[32] Burgoyne was now at the pinnacle of his career.

While Germain was trying to determine strategy for 1777, he had to endure personal attacks in the Commons, particularly after the news of the Trenton and Princeton setbacks reached London in mid-February. The shadow of Minden was never far away. On February 13, during a debate over the conduct of the war, the radical Whig politician John Wilkes said, according to Walpole, that Lord North, "like a true *dictator*, had chosen for his *Master of the Horse* the noble lord near him (Lord George Germaine)," referring to Germain's command of British cavalry at Minden and his failure to lead them into battle.[33] Germain tolerated the insult in silence. During his entire term, he endured many similarly personal attacks in Parliament, and as the war went on, these became more frequent and vicious. This did little to enhance his relationship with senior British generals serving in America.

Having secured his command, Burgoyne submitted his own plan in late February in a long memo entitled "Thoughts for Conducting the War from the Side of Canada." His detailed blueprint impressed the secretary and the king. In his paper, he proposed that the government provide Carleton with all the reinforcements he requested, an army of eight thousand, plus "a thousand or more savages" to conduct an offensive south up Lake Champlain, to Crown Point, Ticonderoga, and on to Albany. Burgoyne further called for a smaller expedition down Lake Ontario to Oswego and the Mohawk River, as a diversion, "to facilitate" the main body's movement. The overall objective of the main army from Canada was to "effect a junction with General Howe" who would come up the Hudson River with his main army.[34]

Neither Burgoyne nor Germain looked beyond the "junction" of the two armies. Burgoyne suggested that "all the New England provinces will be reduced by their operations." This was little more than wishful thinking.[35] There was some discussion in Burgoyne's memorandum of expeditions toward the Connecticut River and Massachusetts, but these were at best nebulous. Thus, a military maneuver—the linking of the army from Canada and Howe's main army—constituted the main objective of the British military strategy for 1777. This was clearly meant to be Burgoyne's, and later Germain's, ultimate goal. Burgoyne, Germain, and the king were so obsessed with the Canada–Lake Champlain–Hudson River concept they did not consider the much more difficult task of planning and conducting follow-on operations. They simply took it as an act

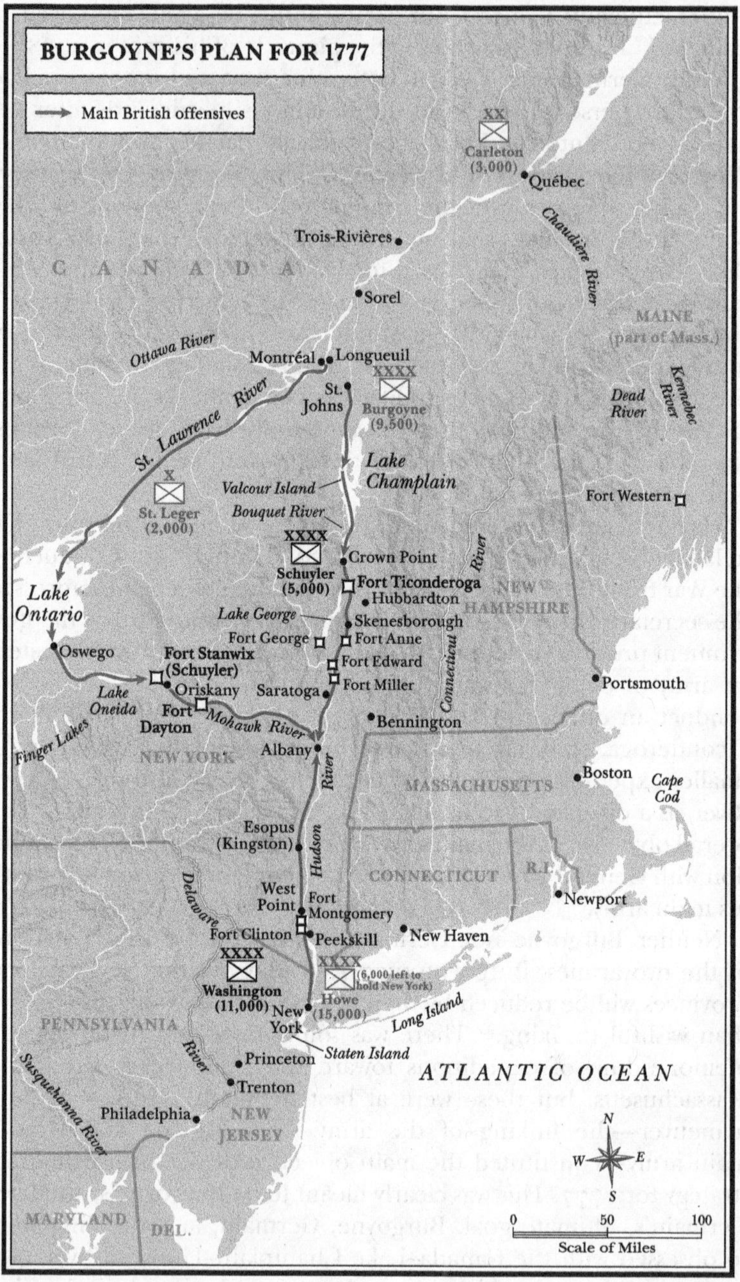

Map 2 Burgoyne's Plan for 1777

of faith that good things would happen when the armies united at Albany.

Like Howe, Burgoyne assumed that the British should have little difficulty all the way to Crown Point. However, he noted, "I will suppose the enemy in great force at Ticonderoga." In addition, Burgoyne knew that the enemy would block the way from Ticonderoga to Albany by cutting down trees and destroying bridges. Nonetheless, he was certain the Americans would give way.[36]

Key to the success of this operation from Canada was for Carleton to exhibit, in Burgoyne's words, "peremptory powers, warm zeal, and consonant opinion," in preparing the expedition from Canada. In addition, Carleton would also be responsible for "the assembly of the savages." Because the governor's role was so important in the logistical arrangements for the campaign, Burgoyne argued, the actual commanding general of the army should be held blameless if sufficient supplies were not gathered prior to departure.[37]

Burgoyne also asked for Lieutenant Colonel Barrimore "Barry" St. Leger to lead the Mohawk River diversion. If he was given the proper support, Burgoyne was certain that Ticonderoga would be "reduced early in the summer." The next phase of the campaign would depend on what the Americans did. Burgoyne might have to take "immediate possession of Lake George" as the "most expeditious and most commodious route to Albany." If this were not possible due to an American naval presence on that lake, the expedition would march south from Skenesborough, placing a premium on large quantities of wagons and animals.[38]

Burgoyne did not argue that the movement of Howe's army up the Hudson was a prerequisite for the plan's success or to enable the northern army's movement to reach Albany. Indeed, he offered two alternative courses of action. First, the army from Canada could move from Ticonderoga to the Connecticut River instead of down the Hudson, and there cooperate with the British troops in Rhode Island. The Connecticut River runs north to south about 60 miles east of Ticonderoga, and if the two armies could meet there, "it would end the war in New England."[39] This option at least included a concrete objective, though he may have offered it to the secretary knowing it would be rejected.

Second, the army in Canada could always be embarked on ships at Quebec to "effect a junction with General Howe by sea." This alternative should be pursued only as a last resort, or if Howe suffered unforeseen losses during the winter months. It would not be nearly as effective as an invasion from Canada.[40] Both of these alternative

courses of action were clearly afterthoughts, sketched out in just a few sentences of the long memo.

Burgoyne's memo must have seemed like a gift from heaven to the king, Lord North, and Germain. Here was a commander who had clearly thought through the complex offensive operation from Canada. He had considered the force required, its size, some of its logistical requirements, and its initial maneuvers, with specificity. He had also predicted the enemy dispositions, their level of readiness, and how they might react to British movements. Perhaps most importantly, Burgoyne promised that if his proposal was accepted, there was a good chance it would "close the war." It was dogma in 1776 that splitting the rebellious colonies in two by gaining control of the Hudson River would hasten the end of hostilities. Burgoyne's memo provided a design for doing just that.

As welcome as Burgoyne's plan may have been, it had shortcomings. First, it was extremely complex, calling for three separate and unsupported columns, each of them out of effective communications with the other or higher headquarters, to move hundreds of miles through enemy-controlled, often wilderness terrain. These columns had to somehow form a junction—not necessarily physically, but in close enough proximity that they could cooperate with each other—and then conduct follow-on operations. Executing such an operation would be difficult for modern militaries, let alone an eighteenth-century army.

Second, Burgoyne's plan, like Howe's, assumed that Loyalists would come out in large numbers to support the British Army as it moved through New York. He therefore discounted the potential combat power that the state militias could provide to augment the small American Northern Army. Burgoyne was also overly optimistic about the numbers of Indians who could be recruited to join the main army and the Mohawk River expedition, and their effectiveness. While he addressed some of the transportation challenges, he was sure that he, and Carleton, would secure whatever was required. Finally, he was certain he could overcome any American efforts to hamper his progress.[41]

Germain and the king were pleased with Burgoyne's plan. Among the papers of George III are notes on the proposal from an unknown author, though probably written by Germain a few days after receipt of Burgoyne's paper. The author tells the king that Burgoyne's plan is "Founded on a Proper Foundation," but doubted if "above 7,000" troops could be allocated to the expedition from Canada. Moreover, the use of Indians would make up for manpower shortages. Very

specific instructions must be sent to the "Respective Commanders, as will putt them out of Doubt, as to what measures are to be taken." Carleton must also be instructed to provide all the assistance required by the "General who advances with the army." To meet the timelines Burgoyne proposed, the reinforcements and other resources that come from England had to set sail by the end of March to reach Quebec to coincide with the ice melt and the opening of the Saint Lawrence River to navigation.[42] At this point, George III and his advisors approved Burgoyne's plan and clearly expected Howe to execute his part of the plan.

If Howe had to move his army up the Hudson, what of his plan to capture Philadelphia and his desire to engage Washington in a decisive battle? What happened next led to strategic incoherence. "I am now commanded," Germain wrote Howe on March 3, "to acquaint you that the King entirely approves of your proposed deviation from the plan which you formerly suggested, being of opinion that the reasons which have induced you to recommend this change in your operations are solid and decisive."[43] Although Philadelphia was never even mentioned in Germain's letter, it was the centerpiece of the plan approved by both the secretary and the king. And yet, at the same time Germain was preparing this letter of approval to Howe, the king and his secretary were commenting favorably on Burgoyne's plan that called for Howe to move his army up the Hudson River. Germain, for one, made no mention of Burgoyne's plan or any offensive from Canada in his March 3 letter to Howe.

As the Secretary of State for America, Germain was charged with reconciling and coordinating these competing plans. Burgoyne was readily available in London and could be easily consulted and questioned about the upcoming campaigns. Howe was thousands of miles away, with communications limited to infrequent and irregularly delivered written missives. Germain had to figure out a way to synchronize all his subordinate commanders to ensure that they worked together and not at cross purposes.

The strategic situation facing the British was daunting: fighting a combination of insurgency and conventional war; a war at sea; a war conducted over vast distances and imposing terrain; a war fought with only three major bases, New York, Quebec, and Halifax; a war in which the French covertly supporting the enemy; and, as we will see, a war against which there was an increasingly vocal domestic political opposition. The key to success in these circumstances was to appoint capable commanders, commanders able to use their initiative and make decisions with minimal guidance based on the circumstances on the

ground, and then provide them with basic guidance on proposed operations and strategic objectives and supply them with the resources they need to achieve their missions. During the winter and spring of 1777, the British learned that they needed either to have all the key players in America or all the key players in London. A split ensured confusion.

Germain was determined to do his best. On March 26, 1777, at the very start of the campaign season, he wrote two letters to Carleton with guidance for the operations from Canada. Carleton received both letters on May 6 with the arrival at Quebec of the HMS *Apollo*, a 32-gun Royal Navy frigate. Personally delivering these messages was none other than Burgoyne, the man who would, of course, replace Carleton as the commander of the British Army in Canada. The first message directed Carleton, in no uncertain terms, to recruit and employ Indians against the rebels. "[I]t is His Majesty's resolution," Germain declared, "that the most vigorous efforts should be made and every means employed that Providence has put into His Majesty's hands for crushing the rebellion and restoring the Constitution." Not only were these Indians to be used on Burgoyne's campaign, but also for "making a diversion and exciting an alarm upon the frontiers of Virginia and Pennsylvania."[44] Germain wanted to ratchet up the pressure on the Americans.

The second letter included the contents of his message from the previous August, the one Carleton had never received, which relieved him of his command of the army in Canada and limited his duties to that of governor only. Given his obvious disdain for Carleton, Germain could not resist following that bad news with reprimanding him for his failure in October 1776: "Since I wrote that [August 22] letter I have had the mortification to learn that upon your repassing Lake Champlain a very considerable number of the insurgents . . . immediately marched from thence and joined the rebel forces in the provinces of New York and Jersey." These reinforcements, he argued, were responsible for Washington's successes at Trenton and Princeton.[45]

Until this point, Carleton was understandably under the impression that he was both the governor of the province and the commander of the army stationed there. Accordingly, he had been preparing for the spring offensive that he had outlined in his mid-October 1776 memo, the one which Burgoyne had hand-delivered to Germain. Now, as he read Germain's letters, he could see that the plan described in Germain's letter was not his. To defeat the rebels as soon as possible, wrote Germain, "it is become highly necessary that the most speedy junction of the two armies [Howe's army and the

northern army] should be effected." Carleton was to stay in Canada with three thousand men and the rest of the army under Burgoyne was to make his way to Albany, while Lieutenant Colonel St. Leger was to make a "diversion" on the Mohawk River. The plan was almost a direct lift from Burgoyne's "Thoughts for Conducting the War from the Side of Canada." Germain further informed Carleton that when Burgoyne arrived at Quebec, he was to consult with him and "adjust the plan as you both shall think most conducive to His Majesty's service."[46]

Germain's letter was a huge blow to Carleton. He had saved Quebec, repulsed the Americans from Canada, and swept the rebel fleet from Lake Champlain, and now he was directed to turn his army over to his former second-in-command.

The penultimate paragraph would be the source of endless debate and controversy during and after the campaign, and deserves examination in its entirety:

> I shall write to Sir William Howe from hence by the first packet; but you will nevertheless endeavour to give him the earliest intelligence of this measure and also direct Lieutenant-General Burgoyne and Lieutenant-Colonel S Leger to neglect no opportunity of doing the same, that they must receive instructions from Sir William Howe. You will at the same time inform them that until they shall have received orders from Sir William Howe, it is His Majesty's pleasure that they shall act as exigencies may require and in such a manner as they shall judge most proper for making an impression on the rebels and bringing them to obedience, but that in so doing they must never lose view of their intended junctions with Sir William Howe as their principal objects.[47]

Germain informed Carleton that he would be sending Howe similar orders, but he never did. Some have explained this seeming oversight by recounting a story told much later by Undersecretary William Knox, one of the secretary's subordinates. Knox claimed that as the staff feverishly prepared Howe's orders, Germain, impatient to leave London for his country house, departed before it was ready, and thus, the critical order was never sent.[48] This story does not ring true. Germain had many faults, but inattention to detail and neglect of his duty were not among them. Instead, he probably and mistakenly thought that sending a copy of Carleton's orders to Howe was sufficient. The copy sent to Howe contained no specific instructions for the commander-in-chief to move his army up the Hudson, though Germain doubtless assumed that his implied intent contained in Carleton's orders would be plain to Howe. It may

well have been, except that Howe chose to ignore the meaning and claimed later that he had not received a direct written order to go up the Hudson.[49] At any rate, Howe had already received approval to conduct his Philadelphia campaign. Like Burgoyne, Germain and Howe likely believed that the army from Canada would have little difficulty getting to Albany.

Germain also directed Burgoyne and Carleton to coordinate with Howe. While Howe initiated some communication with Carleton, Burgoyne made no effort to reach out to Howe throughout the early phases of the campaign, except to provide updates on the northern army's preparations. If the junction of the two armies at or near Albany was the primary objective for the campaign, it would have been imperative that the two commanders coordinate how the campaign should unfold, which never happened. Also, the order directed that Howe was to take command of Burgoyne and St. Leger at some point, though no other details were provided. The orders do state that once Burgoyne reached Albany, he was to "put himself under the command of Sir William Howe," but Albany was almost 100 miles south of Fort Ticonderoga.[50] Did that mean that Carleton was responsible for Burgoyne until he reached New York or Albany? None of these details were clearly defined. Germain probably expected the two generals in Canada to coordinate these details with Howe, but this was not done.

When Germain wrote that it was "His Majesty's pleasure that they act as exigencies may require and in such a manner as they shall judge most proper," he was simply stating the obvious—in the absence of orders or direction from higher, Carleton, Burgoyne, and St. Leger must always use their initiative. No military plan, especially one written 3,000 miles from the area of operations, unfolds as its creators anticipate. Finally, Germain's orders to Carleton provided no guidance, either to him, Burgoyne, or Howe, as to what the two armies were supposed to do after their linkup, except to remind the commanders of the forces from Canada that they must never forget "their intended junctions with Sir William Howe as their principal objects." In other words, the secretary was saying that the campaign's political-military strategic objective was the junction itself. However, his admonition to the officers to use their initiative based on the situation on the ground was secondary to the objective. This was precisely what Burgoyne would argue during and after the campaign: that the objective of reaching Albany and joining with Howe superseded his basic responsibility as a senior leader.[51]

In New York in late March, meanwhile, Howe received a letter from Germain dated January 14, expressing regret that the secretary

could not guarantee the reinforcements Sir William wanted. Howe replied on April 2 that without the extra troops, he would have to modify his plan once again. To avoid the challenges of an overland march to Philadelphia, Howe wrote, he now intended to attack from the sea; that meant abandoning "the Jerseys, which by the former plan would not have been the case."[52] Moving the entire army by sea had its advantages and disadvantages. On the one hand, they were at the mercy of the elements. On the other, having the powerful Royal Navy at his operational disposal, Howe enjoyed flexibility and mobility unavailable to the Americans. The decision to move the army by sea would frustrate Washington later that summer. It would also mean that Howe was unable to support Burgoyne in any meaningful way. Howe cautioned Germain that the Philadelphia campaign might get off to a slow start because of the vagaries of the weather. He assured the secretary, however, that "the operations will be forwarded as expeditiously as the nature of the service will admit."[53]

Having lowered expectations, Howe provided a bleak strategic assessment that must have come as a blow to London. "Restricted as I am from entering upon more extensive operations by the want of force," he wrote, "my hopes of terminating the war this year are vanished." He nonetheless predicted that they would "be in possession of the provinces of New York, the Jerseys and Pennsylvania"—which acknowledged that this depended upon "the successes of the northern army."[54] He still wanted to destroy Washington's army.

Germain's January 14 letter not only persuaded Howe to move his army by sea in his campaign to capture Philadelphia, it suggested the northern army would get to Albany sooner than expected.[55] Concerned that his plan to capture Philadelphia might be derailed by the government's expectations that he cooperate with the army from Canada, Howe wrote what was perhaps the most important letter of the campaign. Dated April 5, and addressed to Carleton, the letter (a copy of which was sent to Germain) should have established for both Burgoyne and Germain what Howe's role in the upcoming campaign would be and what support he would be able to provide to the northern army. Howe informed Carleton that since he was heading to Philadelphia, he had no intention of moving his main army up the Hudson River. He simply didn't have the men, and given that he would most likely be unable to communicate with the commanding officer—meaning Burgoyne—"so soon as I could wish," it would be up to Burgoyne to "pursue such measures as may from circumstances be judged most conducive to the advancement

Map 3 Howe's Final Plan for 1777

of His Majesty's service consistently with your Excellency's orders for his conduct." Like Germain, Howe was reminding Burgoyne that he must use his initiative when he moved south.[56]

Howe was thus fully committed to the Philadelphia campaign. Whoever commanded the northern army would have to depend on his own resourcefulness. Like Burgoyne in his "Thoughts" memorandum, Howe expressed confidence that the northern army would have little difficulty making their way to Albany and "had every reason to expect" that the abundant Loyalists in northern New York would provide material support. Still, despite his preoccupation with the upcoming Philadelphia campaign, Howe promised that he would leave a force upon the lower part of Hudson's River, "sufficient to open the communication for shipping through the Highlands." He noted that it was at present "obstructed by several forts erected by the rebels for that purpose," and that the troops he left would help the northern army deal with them. That was the most he would do.[57]

Howe's letter to Carleton arrived in Quebec shortly before the HMS *Apollo*, with Burgoyne aboard, dropped anchor on May 6. The governor provided a copy to Burgoyne, who was apparently unruffled by Howe's news.[58] Months after the fact, Burgoyne would argue that because Howe's April 5 letter predated the delivery of those from Germain, it "never weighed upon my mind."[59] After all, Howe could not yet know about the grand design that Burgoyne had carried across the Atlantic. Moreover, Germain had said he would send Howe orders consistent with Carleton's. Burgoyne assumed, given the date of Howe's letter, that Germain would set the commander-in-chief straight.

In addition to all that, neither Burgoyne's "Thoughts" nor Germain's March 26 orders for Carleton required Howe to move up the Hudson to facilitate Burgoyne's operations to Albany. In his testimony to the House of Commons in 1779, when he was asked to explain his actions, Burgoyne did not mention this inconvenient fact, arguing that it was critical that Howe cooperated with him to ensure that the northern army could reach Albany, and that even Howe's April 5 letter did not remove the "expectation of co-operation."[60] This was simply not true. The "junction" of the two armies was to facilitate follow-on operations to secure the neighboring provinces and cut off New England from the middle and southern colonies. It was not to help Burgoyne get to Albany. Howe's letter should have given Burgoyne pause.

Long after the fact, Burgoyne revealed that he had written two letters to Howe during this period, one just before he departed from Plymouth on the HMS *Apollo*, and the other upon his arrival in Quebec. In his 1779 statement to the House of Commons, he claimed that he had told Howe "that my orders were to force a junction with his excellency." He also noted in one of those letters, "I wish that a latitude had been left me for a diversion toward Connecticut," but that he had assured Howe that "I should really have no view but that of joining" the commander-in-chief.[61] It is noteworthy that Burgoyne did not reproduce these letters in his self-published *State of the Expedition*, and only quoted a small excerpt, so it is reasonable to assume that in neither of these letters did Burgoyne challenge Howe's April 5 declaration that he would not be joining Burgoyne at or near Albany. Burgoyne did not reproduce them in his post-campaign book because the full text of these letters did nothing to further his cause. He could simply have asked Howe to clarify or to confirm that his Philadelphia campaign had been superseded by Germain's orders to cooperate with Burgoyne up the Hudson.[62] The communications lag was much less from Quebec to New York than it was from Quebec to London. Burgoyne could certainly have received an answer from Howe before he advanced with the northern army toward Ticonderoga.[63]

Burgoyne had his reasons, and they were allied with his ambition. He had just arrived in Canada with the enthusiastic support of his sovereign and Lord Germain. He was about to take command of one of only two British armies in North America, and he was charged to conduct a major campaign that had been touted as a war-winner. He was at the very apex of his career and held a position second only to Howe's in importance. It was only human for him to ignore, or rationalize, or relegate to the deepest recesses of his mind, anything that might derail his success.

Even in Burgoyne's next letter to Germain, written on May 15, 1777, and his first after his arrival in Canada, he made no mention whatever of Howe's letter. Indeed, Burgoyne did not even mention Howe's name. Instead, the newly appointed commander of the northern army updated Germain on the preparations for the upcoming campaign. He told the secretary that though he was technically under Carleton, he would report directly to Lord George, and that while his force "will fall short of the strength computed in England," he was "confident in the prospect of overcoming difficulties and disappointments." He also went out of his way to praise Carleton for his cooperation and the preparations that had already been accomplished.[64]

Perhaps second in importance to Howe's April 5 letter in this series of critical messages back and forth from London to America and Canada, was the letter written by Germain on May 18. Ten days earlier, and almost a month before Howe received a copy of Carleton's March 26 orders, the commander-in-chief had, as noted, obtained approval for his Philadelphia campaign, dated March 3. As the most crucial campaign of the war was about to begin, the senior general officers were operating at cross purposes. The May 18 letter muddled things even more. George III had approved Howe's modified Philadelphia plan that called for the army to move by sea, "trusting however that whatever you may meditate it will be executed in time for you to cooperate with the army ordered to proceed from Canada and put itself under your command." Germain expected that Howe should easily capture Philadelphia and, hopefully, defeat Washington and the rebel army, and still have plenty of time to shift back to the Hudson River.[65]

Germain had underestimated the impact of the American victories at Trenton and Princeton, and the degree to which they had reinvigorated the Americans' war effort. The Philadelphia campaign would not be the cakewalk the secretary and the king thought it would be.[66] While there were no direct orders to that effect, Howe could not ignore the fact that Germain fully expected him to cooperate with Burgoyne; yet, more importantly to Howe, the secretary also approved the Philadelphia campaign. Indeed, in the last line of his missive to Howe, Germain had penned: "I have the pleasure to acquaint you that His Majesty approves of your [April 5] letter to Sir Guy Carleton."[67] The letter not only repeated the March 3 basic approval of Howe's Philadelphia expedition, but it also endorsed the movement by sea of the main British Army in America. Finally, and perhaps most critically. Germain's May 18 letter included the king's approval of Howe's April 5 letter that clearly stated that Burgoyne was on his own, or at least until he arrived at Albany. To Howe, Germain and the king had given an unambiguous green light for the Philadelphia operation, and that trumped everything else.

Howe would not receive this May letter until August 16 as his army was still at sea aboard Richard Howe's ships, and nine days before they landed.[68] By the time Howe saw the letter, Burgoyne's army was already encountering problems as they headed for Albany. Howe was in no position to assist them and would not be for quite some time.

Thus, despite months of communications intent on developing a winning military strategy for 1777, all the main actors—King

George III, Germain, Carleton, Howe, and Burgoyne—were talking past each other. The confusion of letters, commands, and orders, exacerbated by distance and time, plagued British strategy formulation, yet no one questioned the conflicting contents of these letters. No one bothered to seek clarification—not even Burgoyne or Carleton. Howe, at least, tried to make sure everyone understood his intent. No one, least of all Burgoyne, thought the army from Canada would have any difficulty getting to Albany. Every senior British leader underestimated their enemy.

Howe also learned to his dismay that Henry Clinton, who had been on leave in England, was returning to America and his old position. Clinton was determined to convince Howe to abandon the Philadelphia expedition and concentrate his efforts on getting the army up the Hudson River and link with Burgoyne.[69] Howe, meanwhile, was preparing to conduct a campaign to capture Philadelphia and force a decisive battle against Washington's army. Meanwhile, Carleton, humiliated by the loss of his military command, and harboring a burning resentment for Germain, was striving to overcome his disappointment and do his best to prepare the northern army for success. Burgoyne had finally secured a major independent command and was looking forward to the laurels that would accompany a war-winning general.

Germain and George III believed they had put into motion a plan that would end the American rebellion. As the 1777 campaign season fast approached, British commanders planned and executed two separate and distinct campaigns, neither supporting the other. While the British Army and their German allies were experienced, well-trained, well-equipped, and for the most part, well-led, and could stand in battle against any army in the world, tactical virtuosity could not overcome an inadequate military strategy.

CHAPTER 4

A Question of American Command

AS LORD GERMAIN ATTEMPTED in vain to coordinate British military strategy for 1777, following the raids on Trenton and Princeton, the American Army went into winter quarters at Morristown, New Jersey. As we've seen, while others tried to downplay these small victories, Howe recognized their importance when on January 20, he wrote Germain, "I do not now see a prospect of terminating the war but by a general action."[1] Howe knew that final victory was unlikely unless he could win a decisive battle against Washington's main army. Of all the senior British leaders, only Howe seemed to understand that the key to the American rebellion was Washington's army. Defeat it, and the rebellion was finished.

As Washington struggled to maintain the Continental Army throughout the winter and spring of 1776–77, command issues in the Northern Department became a dominant concern. In addition, Washington was forced to deal with a fractured and disorganized Congress. He believed strongly in civilian control of the military and always ensured that his officers deferred to congressional authority, though their interference with purely military affairs was frustrating.[2]

Despite these challenges, Washington and Congress still operated at a distinct advantage over the British when it came to strategy formulation. For the most part, Congress deferred to Washington on how the war should be fought. Washington had to resist calls to defend every city and town on the one hand or to retreat into the interior and rely on a guerrilla campaign on the other. However,

because responsibility for nearly everything rested primarily with him, American strategy tended to be more coherent.

Second, the strategic environment was less complex for the Americans. The British had to operate over hundreds of miles of largely unfamiliar territory and thousands of miles from their main logistical bases. For most of the war, the Americans also benefited from interior lines. Interior lines meant that they were able to move, reinforce, supply, and communicate quicker than the enemy because of their geographical central position.[3] They did not always have this advantage during battles and engagements, but they almost always did at the operational and strategic level, despite the mobility enjoyed by the British through their naval supremacy.

Even more importantly, the Americans had the benefit of what might be called psychological interior lines. Because Washington and Congress could pass messages quickly to each other and with other commands, such as the Northern Department, the Americans almost always had better and timelier information. Whereas Germain might have to wait two months or more to get a response to an order or a question from Howe or Carleton, Washington and Congress could expect an answer in hours, days, or a week, two at the most. This allowed them to get ahead and stay ahead of British strategic decision-making, which was particularly evident during the 1777 campaign in northern New York.[4]

In addition, the overarching American objective was simple: maintain their independence and complete the break from Great Britain. While the objective was straightforward, the ways and means to obtain it were more complex. When Washington gradually switched his strategic approach to the modified Fabian military strategy, he realized that he needed to exhaust not only the British Army but also the will of British decision-makers.[5] Gathering the resources necessary to maintain the armies, the main army and that of the Northern Department, and to conduct limited offensive operations when opportunities presented themselves, posed a formidable challenge to Washington, his generals, and Congress.

Nonetheless, Washington acted as commander-in-chief of the entire American war effort. His responsibilities (despite Congress's special interest in that department) included the Northern Department, commanded by Schuyler. Howe, on the other hand, tended to pay scant attention to operations in and from Canada and made little effort to coordinate with the commanders in that province. His focus was on the main British Army and its operations. The failure of the British expedition from Canada can be traced, at least in part, to

the fact that no commander stepped up to take charge and coordinate the efforts of two very different campaigns—different in terms of terrain, objectives, and operations.[6] In many ways, what happened at Saratoga in 1777 was due largely to Washington's role as overall commander-in-chief.

Meanwhile, Schuyler was in command of the other major American army and, along with Arnold and Gates, enjoyed some success in influencing Carleton's decision to abandon Crown Point and withdraw into Canada in October 1776. Schuyler had played an important but supporting role. In 1777, he would be at the forefront of American efforts to counter Burgoyne's offensive.

Schuyler was still dealing with discord in the ranks. With the repulse of the Americans at Quebec and the disastrous retreat from Canada, he had endured a number of attacks against his character, competence, and courage. Nor was he popular among or respected by some of the troops he commanded, especially those from New England, who remained suspicious of his patrician New York roots and his support of New York's position in its boundary dispute with New Hampshire and Massachusetts.[7] This resentment grew worse when Schuyler decided to abandon Crown Point. At one point during the 1776 campaign, the personal attacks grew intolerable to him, and he submitted his resignation, demanding a court-martial to clear his name.[8] Congress refused, and this unhappy episode illustrated the fragile state of the command situation in the Northern Department.

After Carleton returned to Canada with his army in November 1776, Schuyler focused on maintaining the army over the winter and into the spring of 1777. Schuyler confronted the same issues Washington was facing 200 miles to the south: logistics, morale, short and expiring enlistments, and militia returning to their homes. He had learned through his intelligence sources that Carleton would undoubtedly attempt another offensive south up Lake Champlain in the spring, one with a supporting operation down the Mohawk River. Writing to Washington in late January, Schuyler reported that he was certain that Carleton would attack and "therefore the Army ought to be at Tyonderoga" as well as at Fort Schuyler (also known as Fort Stanwix) and the "other posts on the Mohawks River." He asked Washington to send him troops from regions other than New England, troops who might have what he called a "greater Spirit of Discipline and Subordination."[9] Unfortunately for Schuyler, he would never gain the respect of the New England troops—or their local and congressional politicians, for that matter.

Throughout the winter, Schuyler bombarded Washington with messages lamenting the dire situation in the Northern Department. He also kept up a lively correspondence with the governors and committees of safety of the surrounding states, asking for support. Washington, beset with his own difficulties, did his best to get the resources Schuyler needed to defend the region.[10] On February 9, he assured Schuyler that since "the Defence & security of our Posts in that Quarter is an Object of the first Importance," he had urgently appealed to the nearby states to provide more troops. He also informed Schuyler that soldiers other than New Englanders would not be sent to the Northern Department. The distances were simply too great, and "Prejudices and Jealousies" made mixing troops from different regions just too difficult.[11] Many soldiers did not yet think of themselves as soldiers of the United States of America.

Schuyler was particularly concerned with the manning of Fort Ticonderoga, which would obviously be Carleton's primary objective and the key to the American defenses. Schuyler forwarded a pessimistic report from Colonel Anthony Wayne, the fort's commander, to Washington in mid-February, prompting Washington to reply that troops from Massachusetts and New Hampshire would soon reinforce the garrison at Ticonderoga. He assured Schuyler that Carleton would certainly not arrive before the spring and that if the reinforcements were not enough, Schuyler could always "receive some Aid from the Militia."[12]

Despite Washington's efforts on the Northern Army's behalf, however, his focus was on the main army and determining Howe's objectives for the upcoming campaigning season. This was evident in a March 12 letter in which he provided Schuyler with his assessment of what the British might do in the spring and how the Patriot commanders should station their troops. He argued that a large body of troops should be garrisoned in the centrally located Hudson Highlands area near Peekskill, New York, from where they could quickly move in several directions to face an enemy offensive. In addition, Washington predicted that Philadelphia would be Howe's "Object in View" for the spring, and the army in Canada might move by sea to join them. Thus, if the Americans placed too many troops at Ticonderoga and other similar areas, they would be out of place: "It will signify Nothing to have our Frontiers strongly guarded, While the Enemy are ranging at large in the Heart of the Country."[13] Schuyler replied with an ominous warning of the consequences if Ticonderoga fell before the soldiers stationed at Peekskill could respond.[14] As it turned out, Washington was right about Howe's

intentions to capture Philadelphia but wrong about downplaying the threat from Canada.

On March 26, a day after sending off his last letter to Washington, Schuyler left Albany to address Congress.[15] To strengthen his hold on the command, Schuyler had wanted to visit Philadelphia for some time. He hoped to clear his name once and for all in the wake of all the allegations leveled at him during the last campaign and, more recently, by members of Congress. Plus, he had recently been elected a delegate himself. After speaking with Schuyler, General Nathanael Greene wrote John Adams, "General Schuyler is going to Congress armed with the imperial Cohorts of N. York to support the Assertion that the Northern Operations depend entirely upon his being continued in the command." Dismissing Schuyler's claim, Greene assured Adams that the "Salvation of America [doesn't] Depend on the political sentiments of Albany County." Greene also reported that Schuyler thought it would be "difficult if not to say impossible for the Enemy to penetrate the Country by the way of Ticonderoga."[16] This was certainly a far more optimistic assessment than Schuyler had expressed to Washington. Schuyler's departure from his command, an action for which he did not seek approval from Washington, left a vacuum of senior leadership in the Northern Department.

Into this void stepped Horatio Gates, who arrived in Albany after the moderately successful outcome of the 1776 campaign in northern New York. Gates had left Ticonderoga in December 1776 with eight regiments to join Washington's army, then desperate for reinforcements. He had arrived in Washington's camp outside Philadelphia on December 22, just in time for the troops to participate in the raid on Trenton. Gates himself had not participated in the operation, claiming ill health, and left Philadelphia to meet with Congress in Baltimore. It is curious that such a senior and experienced commander as Gates did not join the commander-in-chief while the army and the cause itself were hanging in the balance. The fact that Washington did not insist on his participation in the Trenton (and Princeton) operations speaks volumes about his relationship with Gates.[17]

The New England delegates to Congress had welcomed Gates with open arms upon his arrival in Baltimore. Samuel Adams informed his cousin John that Gates was there and asked, "How shall we make him the Head of that Army?"[18] Adams's fond feelings toward Gates were shared by almost the entire Congressional delegation from New England, and this would pay dividends for Gates in the future. In late February 1777, he was ultimately offered his old

position of adjutant general of the army, responsible for administrative tasks on behalf of the commander-in-chief. While this was an important staff post, Gates wanted a field command and complained to Hancock that it was a step down and that he deserved a more important assignment. He also expressed surprise that Washington had not personally offered him the post and that he would take it if the commander-in-chief so desired.[19] A few days later, Washington asked Gates to report to headquarters as adjutant general. The fact that Washington did not congratulate Gates, nor did Gates express pleasure over the new assignment, seems noteworthy. The underlying tension between the two men was evident in Gates's cranky reply on March 7 when he pointed out that Hancock's offer "was not preceded by One upon the same Subject from Your Excellency."[20]

Recognizing that the strain between the two men might derail their efforts, Washington moved quickly to assure Gates that he was indeed wanted. "You cannot conceive the pleasure I feel," wrote Washington, that you " 'will with cheerfulness and Alacrity proceed' " to headquarters.[21] If Gates thought his grumbling would convince Hancock and Washington to give him an important command, he was mistaken. Gates still coveted the command of the Northern Department and lobbied hard for it with friendly congressional delegates, particularly those from New England.[22] He had extensive experience up there—and had had some success. To Gates and his allies in Congress, that was where he belonged, not at headquarters, cooling his heels.

Before Gates could assume his new position on Washington's staff, he received another order from Congress, one that would create more problems than it would solve. On March 25, responding to Schuyler's request for senior officers to help relieve his burdens, and his warnings that Ticonderoga was not ready to face the anticipated enemy spring offensive, Congress ordered Gates to report immediately to Fort Ticonderoga "and take the Command of the Army in that Department."[23] When Hancock informed Washington of Gates's new assignment, the commander-in-chief did not even mention the news in his reply.[24]

It was the clear intent of Congress that Gates report to Ticonderoga to take command of the soldiers defending that post, yet he had not been appointed to command the Northern Department. Nonetheless, Gates made his headquarters not at Ticonderoga as ordered but at Albany, and assumed de facto command of the entire department in Schuyler's absence.[25] This action threw the Northern Department and the surrounding states into confusion. Who actually

commanded the Northern Department? Was it Gates, who occupied the headquarters at Albany, or Schuyler, who was in Philadelphia but who had not been relieved of his command? Clearly, with Schuyler away and as the senior officer in the department, Gates was the acting commander in any case. Still, by staying at Albany, he violated Congress's clear intent to report to Ticonderoga to prepare for the anticipated enemy offensive. Congress undoubtedly wanted Gates to reprise his excellent work at Ticonderoga in 1776. Gates wanted more. He wanted department command, and this was his chance.

Even Schuyler was confused about Gates's position. Writing to one of his staff officers, he observed that Congress had put itself in a bind. On the one hand, the congressional committee charged with evaluating his previous performance wanted him to retain his command. On the other, they had "already appointed (or at least implicatively so) Gen. Gates to the command of the Northern department." Congress might be conflicted, but he, Schuyler, would not "serve at Albany on those conditions."[26] At around the same time, a Massachusetts delegate and friend of Gates mocked the very idea that he was only to command at Fort Ticonderoga and not the entire department: "It is nonsense to give you command of the northern army at Tyconderoga and confine you to the fort."[27]

By appointing Gates to command at Ticonderoga, Congress had violated unity of command, which dictates that there should never be two commanders, nor should there ever be confusion over who is in overall command. Congress had muddled the command situation in the Northern Department, a state of affairs that lasted through late May. As a result, preparations for an enemy invasion were ignored or mishandled, and the senior-level leadership that the department needed was in disarray.

It seems easy to see what should have happened. Congress and Washington should have stepped in to address the command issue. Congress should have ordered Schuyler back to Albany and Gates to Ticonderoga to take charge of that critical post. Washington was reluctant to get involved in personnel assignments in the Northern Department due to the political tensions between the New York and New England Congressional delegations. Perhaps he did not intercede because of the growing rift between him and Gates. Nonetheless, Washington should have intervened directly or insisted that Congress clarify the command arrangements.

Gates threw himself into his new job, legitimate or not. The leaders in the New England states were thrilled to hear that Gates was again in the Northern Department. They congratulated him on

his new position, treating him as the department's commander.[28] Gates tried to cultivate members of the New York delegation to Congress, a group that tended to support Schuyler. On May 9, he wrote John Jay, forwarding a copy of his strategic assessment for the upcoming campaigns, warning Jay to "show it to no living soul but yourself."[29] Like Schuyler before him, Gates showered both Washington and Hancock with letters listing weaknesses in the department. In a message dated April 19, Gates sent Washington a long list of the deficiencies and shortages, and he outlined the mismanagement he had uncovered.[30] Washington replied respectfully to Gates's requests, assuring him that he would do his best to help, while at the same time gently reminding him that ultimately his success "must depend much upon your own activity."[31] Washington was right. If Gates was the acting commander of the Northern Department, he needed to get to work rather than cast aspersions on his predecessor. Washington was reminding his subordinate of one of the most basic leadership lessons: when in charge, take charge.

Gates also took time out from his duties at Albany to lecture Hancock on the strategy for the upcoming campaign, arguing that the British objective was "the entire conquest of the State of New York." Howe would move toward New Jersey or Philadelphia because by taking the Hudson Highlands, he would "prevent General Washington from passing the river."[32] Gates forwarded a copy to Washington and his friend, James Lovell, a delegate to Congress from Massachusetts. To Lovell, Gates added that Philadelphia would be safe in 1777, and even if the British seemed to move toward the city, it would be a feint. He urged Washington to move the main army to the Hudson Highlands immediately.[33]

Fortunately for the United States, Washington ignored Gates's advice, which was based on his estimate on what Howe might do instead of what he could do. In the intelligence game, trying to divine enemy intentions—what they plan to do—is very difficult. There are countless instances of military leaders led astray by focusing on intentions rather than capabilities—what they actually can do. In the absence of excellent intelligence, a commander should determine enemy capabilities. Washington tried to figure out Howe's intentions, but he never lost sight of what the British could do, especially given their great advantage in naval mobility.

Congress addressed the needs of the Northern Department in late April. They directed Washington to reinforce Ticonderoga with New England regiments and authorized Gates to abandon the western

part of the fortress if he found he did not have enough troops to man all its defenses. Congress also ordered Major General Arthur St. Clair to report to Ticonderoga.[34] Writing Major General William Heath in Boston, Massachusetts, Washington urged him to hurry all the men he could get to New York. Carleton was surely getting ready to "pass the Lake and attack Ticonderoga."[35] Gates, still in Albany, hadn't even visited Ticonderoga.

As the favorable spring weather arrived, Americans were surprised that the British had yet to make a move. Nathanael Greene told John Adams, "General Howe has lost the most favorable opportunity this Spring of distressing us, perhaps that he will ever have."[36] Howe was nothing if not a very conventional and deliberate British Army officer; he had to have everything in place before embarking on any operation.

Unfortunately, however, the Americans did not take full advantage of the extra time. A particular bone of contention between the Northern and Southern Departments was the availability of tents. Writing to Washington on May 13, Gates accused him of ignoring or downplaying the department's requirements. He had heard that Washington was hoarding tents for the main army. "Refusing This Army, what you have not in your power to bestow, is one thing," wrote Gates, "but saying This Army has not the same Necessities, or does not require the same Comforts, as the Southern Armies, is another."[37] It was a remarkable letter for a subordinate to write to his commander-in-chief.

Washington responded to Gates's letter on the 19th: "Can you suppose, if there had been an ample supply of Tents for the whole Army, that I would have hesitated one moment in complying with your demand?" Washington reminded Gates that he had to prioritize scarce resources and assured him that the "Northern Army is, and ever has been, as much the object of my Care and Attention as the one immediately under my command."[38] The letter was as extraordinary as Gates's—for its restraint.

Gates vented his frustration with Washington in a letter to Lovell. Despite his inability to get Washington to pay attention to his command, Gates lamented that either he was "exceedingly dull or unreasonably jealous" to expect anything from his superior.[39] The tents episode further illustrates the bad blood between Gates and Washington. Gates thought he was more capable than Washington and chafed at having to serve under him, preferring instead to go directly to Congress. For his part, Washington was, by this point, exasperated by Gates's arrogance and condescension.

While Gates and Washington sparred, Schuyler remained in Philadelphia. Assuming some nominal military duties, he also held on to his seat in Congress. He continued to monitor Gates's actions from Philadelphia through the reports of staff members who remained behind in Albany.[40] Schuyler's acting as both general and delegate to Congress shocked some observers, including Nathanael Greene. He saw the New Yorker's merging of military and civilian authority as anathema to the principles upon which the new nation was founded. Writing to John Adams, Greene protested: "I have no objections to General Schuyler as a General, neither have I to his being President of the Congress, if he is thought to be the most suitable person for that important trust; But he must cease to be a General, before he commences a member of Congress." Greene declared that the combination was "incompatible with the Safety of a free people."[41] Greene's statement is one of the earliest expressions of what would become one of the key principles of American civil-military relations: distinct and separate military and civilian spheres, with clear civilian supremacy. What Washington thought of Schuyler's holding two positions is not known, but he most certainly agreed in principle with Greene. He was not particularly upset when a frustrated Schuyler wrote that he would soon "resign my Commission."[42] If Schuyler thought Washington would try to talk him out of it, he was mistaken. Washington's reply—"You are the best judge of the Line of Conduct"—was hardly a vote of confidence.[43]

Schuyler was not the only key leader threatening resignation. Hearing of Schuyler's attempts to regain his command in Albany, Gates wrote Hancock in early May that he had heard that "some change is likely to take place in the Command of the Northern Army." If this was the case, Gates added plaintively, "I beg Sir you will request the Congress to give me an Honorable Dismission from their Service."[44]

With both Schuyler and Gates threatening to resign their commissions, Congress finally acted to clarify the Northern Department's command situation. On May 15, it took up Schuyler's case and his role as commander of the Northern Department. Schuyler's actions and reputation were finally vindicated after a vigorous week-long debate that ended in a five-to-four vote in Schuyler's favor. On May 22, Congress resolved: "That Major General Schuyler be directed forthwith to proceed to the northern department and take upon him the command there." In addition, finally resolving an issue that had been another source of confusion, Congress also established the Northern Department's geographic extent, which

now officially consisted of "Albany, Ticonderoga, Fort Stanwix [on the Mohawk River], and their dependencies."[45] Gates was offered the army's adjutant general position or second-in-command of the Northern Department.[46] This was a bitter pill indeed for Gates. He could either command at Ticonderoga or he could take the staff job he had already rejected.

This time Congress's order was crystal clear: Schuyler commanded the Northern Department, and Gates would be his subordinate, should he desire to stay. After almost eight weeks of confusion and uncertainty, unity of command was reestablished. Whether or not Schuyler was the right man for the job remained to be seen, but at least everyone knew who was in charge. Nonetheless, all the confusion of the previous two months took its toll on the department's readiness.

Gates learned of his fate through a May 22 letter from Lovell, who broke the bad news of Schuyler's reappointment. He also reported that he and others had argued that Gates should have an independent command at Ticonderoga, one not subordinate to anyone at Albany, but that this argument had not prevailed. While the result was not as he had hoped, Lovell assured Gates that he still enjoyed considerable support in Congress. Despite his obvious affection and respect for Gates, Lovell pointed out that the general had not helped his own cause by failing to visit Ticonderoga and staying in Albany.[47] John Trumbull also wrote to Gates, telling him that "all possible opposition has been made by your friends but in vain."[48] Two weeks later, Lovell wrote again, urging Gates to work with Schuyler for the good of the country: "I can only say at large I hope the army at Ty [Fort Ticonderoga] will not be ruined by any misunderstandings of its Leaders."[49]

Schuyler's friends in Congress were overjoyed that they were able to reinstate New York's favorite son. William Duer happily apprised a fellow delegate that "we have got General Schuyler's conduct fully justified," though it had been a tough fight. "There was never I believe a more difficult card to play." Gates was mostly to blame for the controversy over the New York general, Duer grumbled. He had "the wretchedness to poison the minds of most with prejudices against General Schuyler."[50] Certainly Gates had been a vocal critic of the state of the department upon his arrival in Albany, and he had conducted extensive correspondence with congressional delegates from New England. However, Schuyler had done himself no favors by leaving his post in late March to plead his case in Philadelphia and by his constant complaints about ill treatment. Gates and Schuyler,

Congress, and the commander-in-chief share the blame for this sorry episode. The American soldiers in the Northern Department would pay the price for their mistakes.

Schuyler arrived in Albany in early June and, on the 4th, wrote Gates, forwarding Congress's resolutions and requesting a meeting and copies of all orders issued in his absence.[51] Not surprisingly, the meeting between the two men was unproductive. Despite Schuyler's request that Gates take the Ticonderoga position, Gates declined and requested leave, which Schuyler approved, and on June 9, he departed for Philadelphia.[52] Given the deterioration of their relationship, Schuyler was probably happy to see Gates go. For the second time in a little more than two months, an unhappy senior officer from the Northern Department would be pleading his case to Congress. Gates's departure from the department, and his refusal to take the command at Fort Ticonderoga, delivered a major blow to the Americans' ability to defend it.

As Gates prepared to leave Albany for Philadelphia, one of his staff officers, Colonel James Wilkinson (who would later turn out to be one of the great rogues in American history), wrote him from Ticonderoga to say that the New England troops at the fort were furious that Gates had been replaced. They, like their representatives in Congress, expressed "Mortification and dissatisfaction" at the news of Schuyler's return. This was clear evidence, Wilkinson claimed, of their "Judgment and Gratitude" for Gates.[53] Warmed and encouraged by the many expressions of support he received in the days and weeks after Schuyler's reinstatement, Gates prepared to press his case to Congress.

When Gates reached Philadelphia, he secured an interview with Congress, ostensibly to report on the situation in the Northern Department. The delegates would soon regret their decision to allow him into the chamber. When Gates arrived at the Pennsylvania State House (now Independence Hall), home of the Congress, he seemed "discomposed, chagreend and Angry."[54] The general adopted a "Cavalier Posture," which did not go over well with the delegates.[55] He started his address by describing all that he had accomplished in the Northern Department. He then regaled the Congress with, as Duer noted in a letter to Schuyler, "a narrative of his Birth, Parentage, and Education Life Character, and Behavior."[56] Although he had sacrificed for the "Liberties of America," and had been appointed to command the Northern Department, "he was in a most disgraceful manner superseded in his Command."[57]

Had Gates left it at that, he might have garnered some sympathy from the delegates. However, as one witness noted, Gates's speech then became heated as he made "malicious insinuations" against a New York delegate.[58] Trying to explain why he made his headquarters at Albany and not Ticonderoga, Gates argued that he could better address the fortress's problems from Albany.[59] He also openly criticized Schuyler and other delegates in Congress who were against him.[60] This was a serious breach of decorum, and several delegates called for his removal. After a noisy debate, Congress dismissed Gates and determined that he should "not again be admitted on the Floor," but that he could submit items in writing. Gates was escorted out of the chamber. The episode was not "to his credit or advantage." Indeed, wrote Duer, Gates's performance was "ungracious, and totally devoid of dignity."[61] On July 8 Congress ordered Gates to "repair to head quarters, and follow the directions of General Washington."[62] Gates must have wondered whether his career was over. He had embarrassed himself in front of Congress, he was without a command, and he was not endeared to the commander-in-chief. Fortunately for Gates, the vicissitudes of war would very soon provide him with another chance.

CHAPTER 5

Laying the Groundwork

WHILE THE AMERICANS UNTANGLED the Northern Department's command situation, the British army in Canada was preparing for its upcoming campaign. A milder-than-normal winter helped fuel the optimism of the British troops as they prepared to resume their campaign against the Americans.[1] During the winter and early spring, they were kept busy repairing the ships they had used during the 1776 campaign and building new ones for the next operation. By late spring, Carleton was able to report to Germain that the condition of the British fleet was good and that it was ready to transport Burgoyne's armies south.[2]

Commanding the Braunschweig troops, Major General Riedesel believed that the campaign ahead would "finish the war."[3] The use of German troops was controversial. Members of Parliament, such as Edmund Burke in the House of Commons and Lord Chatham (the elder William Pitt) in the House of Lords, questioned the government's decision to use mercenaries. In a May 1777 speech, Chatham complained that the Germans were simply not working out, particularly after the defeat at Trenton, despite government's "ransack" of "every corner of Lower Saxony."[4] In the Commons, John Wilkes condemned the use of "Hanovarians and Hessians" against the Americans.[5] While the politicians debated in London, the British and German troops in Canada had developed an uneasy working relationship.

One German artillery officer noted with some bitterness that only English officers commanded his men during certain gunnery drills. He attributed this to "National pride and arrogant conduct."[6] In addition to the problem of command, the officer argued, there should be healthy competition between the two bodies of soldiers, but instead, there was "enmity."[7] More than likely, the antagonism the young officer referred to was due partly to the fact that the troops had been cooped up in winter quarters for months and by the spring were anxious to go. British officers also tended to treat their German allies condescendingly.[8]

Still, both sides tried to make the relationship work, especially at the lower levels. One junior officer noted just before the campaign started that he was "endeavoring to maintain and foster with the greatest care and particularity" cooperation in the ranks, and while there were incidents between the two nationalities, the Braunschweig and British troops developed a grudging respect for each other's bravery and general military competence. Nonetheless, their leaders felt strongly that their troops were more reliable than the other. This was certainly the opinion of the commanding general. Burgoyne would declare after the campaign that for the Germans, campaigning in North America "was entirely new to them," and that once they had embarked on the expedition, "temptations to desert were in themselves great." Still, Burgoyne maintained that things would have been worse had the German troops not been commanded by Riedesel, whose "frank, spirited, and honourable character" ensured his soldiers' the proper employment.[9]

Far more controversial than the use of German troops was the employment of Indians against the Americans. John Wilkes dramatically protested their use in the House of Commons: "Merciful Heaven! Thousands of Indian savages let loose, by the command of a British general, against our brethren in America!"[10] Carleton, for one, never favored the use of Native Americans on campaign. He wanted their friendship, or at least their neutrality, and he saw their value on campaign, but he had his own views about their shortcomings: they could be unreliable, difficult to control, and undisciplined. They did not recognize the European rules of warfare, and it took officers with specialized skills and experience to lead them. Germain, on the other hand, was certain that using the Indians would pay huge dividends for the British, writing in February 1777 that "all the Indians upon the Continent are united in solemn League . . . in support of His Majesty's Government."[11] Carleton warned the secretary that "there is always an uncertainty as to the force of the Indians."[12]

In any case, by the time Burgoyne was ready to depart on his campaign, more than four hundred Indians from various tribes and settlements had joined the army. This was many fewer than Germain and Burgoyne expected or thought necessary.

While the use of Indians was a contentious matter of policy in both London and Quebec, it was equally so in the rank and file. Both British and Braunschweig troops were skeptical about using Indians against the Americans. Most soldiers and officers were wary of their failure to discriminate between soldiers, civilians, and friendlies, and the inability of anyone to control them. One British soldier declared that the Indians were unpredictable, and although "extremely brave" also "extremely unbridled" and therefore they "must be interlarded with English and Canadian officers."[13] An officer opined incorrectly that Burgoyne had the Indians forced on him by the government and that while he "certainly wished to conquer the revolted Americans, yet he did not wish to exterminate them."[14] Fully aware of these concerns, Burgoyne viewed the Indians as a necessary evil.[15] He reasoned that if the British did not use them, the Americans certainly would. To Burgoyne's credit, he did invest a lot of time and effort into organizing and controlling the Native Americans who accompanied his army into New York. Controversial or not, they were part of the force preparing to head out.

One British officer confided to his diary that despite the challenges in North America, the troops of the Canada army "were all in the greatest health and much improved since their sailing from Great Britain [in 1776]." The army made a "good appearance."[16] The army that Burgoyne would command on his expedition up Lake Champlain to Ticonderoga, and then on to Albany, was indeed in reasonable health and enjoyed good morale, due in no small part to Carleton's leadership over the winter and early spring.

On May 6, 1777, Burgoyne arrived in Quebec on the HMS *Apollo*, the first ship to take advantage of the spring thaw. The 32-gun frigate carried the general and the news that Carleton had been relieved of his military command. To the proud long-serving officer, this came as a shock. Despite his disappointment and embarrassment over losing his military command to an officer junior to himself, Carleton staged a review for Burgoyne on May 9 and a gala welcome dinner.[17] To his great credit, Carlton did not take out his frustrations on Burgoyne—the man who had maneuvered him out of a job—but instead did his best to follow Germain's orders to prepare the army and recruit Indians.[18] The troops were just as shocked as Carleton over the command situation, and his plight was "widely discussed,"

as a British officer, reflecting on the change of command and how it was received by the army, recalled.[19] With the benefit of hindsight, another officer remarked that while Burgoyne "possessed bravery, and some military knowledge," Carleton was "better qualified for this important expedition."[20]

Over the next two weeks, the shock of his relief wore off and Carleton's disappointment turned to deep bitterness. While he tried to be professional, others could sense his distress. Writing to a fellow general officer, Burgoyne praised Carleton for his positive attitude. He also observed that the governor "thinks he has some cause of resentment for the general tenor of treatment he has received from some ministers."[21] There was no doubt which "minister" Burgoyne was referring to. Despite his pressing duties, Carleton composed a letter to Germain in which he both defended his actions in 1776 and accused his superior of duplicity in giving the command to Burgoyne. The animosity between the two men, which always lay just under the surface, now emerged into outright hostility and borderline insubordination. Carleton wrote that he would not have abandoned Crown Point had he known that Germain wanted him to stay there throughout the winter. He had used his best judgment in the matter. "I imputed to an opinion, pretty general, that any officer entrusted with the supreme command ought upon the spot to see what was most expedient to be done better than a great general at three thousand miles distance."[22]

Reminding Germain of his many accomplishments as governor, such as holding Quebec against the American invasion and expelling the rebels from Canada, he was nonetheless "severely censured" and his command taken away. Despite the injustice done to him, Carleton assured Germain that Burgoyne and his army "shall have every assistance in my power."[23] Carleton's letter further soured the relationship between the two men. Few things are more conducive to strategic failure than bad blood between senior leaders. By May 1777, just as the final preparations were being made for Burgoyne's expedition, Carleton and Germain's relationship had hit rock bottom.

Two days after his blistering May 20 letter, Carleton wrote again to Germain, complaining that after supplying all the troops to Burgoyne specified in the secretary's March 26 orders, it was his view that the defense of Canada would be in a "feeble state." They might even be forced to depend on General Howe for "the protection of this province." The acrimony continued as Carleton addressed the damage inflicted on his reputation by Germain's litany of "every

kind of slight, disregard, and censure, occasion and events might render plausible." Therefore, argued Carleton, how could he, as governor of Canada, possibly be effective in his job after the secretary's baseless and unfair attacks, which had become common knowledge throughout the province?[24] This letter was followed by another to Lord North submitting his resignation.[25] Although Carleton's letters were over the top, they were an understandable reaction to the loss of his command, coupled with Germain's insults, both direct and implied, real and imagined. The 3,000-mile expanse between the two men did not help. By this time, however, the chasm between them was as much emotional as it was geographical. In neither of Carleton's two letters to Germain did he mention Howe's news, which was that the main army was heading for Philadelphia and thus would be unable to move up the Hudson.

At around the same time that Carleton was composing his letters to Germain, Burgoyne penned a letter to the secretary, his second since his arrival in Canada. He advised that he had received intelligence that the Americans would "dispute Ticonderoga vigorously." After taking the rebel fort, he planned to feint toward the Connecticut River, by which, if successful, "I may gain a start that may much expedite and facilitate my progress to Albany."[26] Written on May 19, the letter never mentioned Howe's April 5 message about linking up at Albany. Clearly, Burgoyne was unconcerned about Howe's intentions. He was going to get to Albany and would not need help to do so.

In addition to refurbishing the 1776 fleet, Carleton and Burgoyne oversaw other logistical arrangements. Preparing a European army for active operations in the wilderness was a difficult task. Commanders and staffs not only had to arrange for supplies—food, clothing, ammunition, accruements, and fodder for animals—but the transportation of said provisions. In addition, the logistical planning also included the maintenance of the troops' equipment, including watercraft, wagons, carts, and artillery. Finally, they had to plan for care for the wounded and sick. All these needs were extremely complex. While Carleton had made sure most were adequately addressed, there were two major deficiencies in the British logistical preparations for the 1777 campaign: transportation and medical support.[27]

As early as January 1777, Carleton's chief commissary officer, Nathaniel Day, had reported to the governor that there were insufficient wagons and carts to move the army overland beyond Fort Ticonderoga. This report was overlooked, and little was done

to procure the needed transport. Carleton and Burgoyne concentrated their efforts on watercraft, recruiting Indians, and gathering supplies. In June, Major General William Phillips, a veteran artilleryman who had been designated Burgoyne's second-in-command, complained about the shortage of transport for his guns and ammunition, setting off a wild scramble to procure additional wagons, carts, and the animals to pull them. Army quartermasters immediately contracted for four hundred horses and five hundred carts, but these were not ready to go by the time the army departed, and, in any case, were well short of what was needed. Indeed, the additional transport did not join Burgoyne's army until mid-July, which was mid-campaign, and even then arrived only in fits and starts. This was a stunning oversight by both Carleton and Burgoyne.[28]

The transport shortage was most likely due to the fact that Carleton and Burgoyne were focused on one thing, and one thing only: the capture of Fort Ticonderoga. They saw the American fortress as the major obstacle to getting the army to Albany; thus, all their efforts were concentrated on that post. It is understandable that a commander would direct his energy on what he considers the most formidable barrier to success. It is also bad strategy. Ironically, had the capture of Ticonderoga turned out to be a drawn-out affair, the transport problem would have been mitigated somewhat because the horses and carts might have arrived in time to do some good.[29] A long siege of Ticonderoga would have also presented Burgoyne with a different set of logistical and operational problems. The British simply did not devote enough command and staff attention to the army's logistical support.

The other major shortfall, inadequate medical support, was less critical, at least immediately. Many of the participants noted the army's general good health as it prepared to march south, though some ominous signs started to appear in late May: One Braunschweig company commander noted that he rarely had all his men fit for duty "having, at times, from 10 to 12 men sick at the barracks with the bad, and in this country, the ever prevalent diarrhea."[30] Just as he had throughout the spring and early summer, Carleton did as much as he could to help Burgoyne, including giving up almost all of his own medical personnel. Burgoyne incurred Carleton's ire by taking the only surgeon working in the hospital in Canada and four of his helpers for his army, essentially leaving the governor without any medical support.[31] The army's hospital was run by a physician who supervised two or three surgeons, two apothecaries, and fourteen mates, or assistants. An additional seven surgeons and seven

assistants were assigned to various regiments in the army. For the most part, the medical personnel who accompanied Burgoyne's army into New York were well-qualified and adequate by the standards of the day, with one trained medical officer per one hundred soldiers.[32]

For actual hospital facilities, the British used existing structures when available or when the army was stationary for an extended period. While on the march, medical personnel relied on tents to shelter the sick and wounded, making it extremely difficult for them to treat their patients; indeed, toward the very end of the campaign, Burgoyne abandoned his sick and wounded, counting on the Americans to give them proper medical care. He and Carleton may have believed that they had supplied the army with medical support that would be up to the challenges of the upcoming campaign, but they were wrong. The conditions Burgoyne and his army faced from July through October 1777 overwhelmed their medical resources, reducing the number of effective soldiers at Burgoyne's disposal as he tried to push his way to Albany.[33]

Burgoyne decided to organize his army with two wings of infantry, one commanded by Phillips, and the left wing composed of German troops under Riedesel's command. In addition to the two wings, an advanced corps was deployed while the army was on the move, composed of troops selected from the right wing commanded by Brigadier General Simon Fraser, a professional soldier with extensive combat experience.

Burgoyne's army was a bit of a mixed bag. Although many of the more senior officers had combat experience, most of their soldiers had very little. A good number of the troops in Burgoyne's army had participated in Carleton's aborted 1776 invasion into New York. Still, while that expedition provided good training, it was no substitute for battle or extended operations in hostile territory. On paper, the army heading south from Canada seemed impressive. The vast majority of the soldiers were well-equipped and trained, and they were led by European regulars. The British troops wore the ubiquitous red coats, although by the time of Burgoyne's campaign they had been cut down a bit to reduce weight and ease marching. Soldier's headgear varied depending on the units and could either be made of bearskin, felt, or other materials and was adorned by the regimental crest or other symbol according to the unit or branch of the wearer. The average infantryman carried up to 60 pounds of equipment, including musket, cartridge box, knapsack, powder horn, tomahawk, and a 16-inch bayonet. The German soldiers' uniforms varied as well, but most soldiers wore a blue coat with different facings and hats

depending on the unit. The notable exceptions were the soldiers of the German Jäger (elite light infantry) unit, who wore green coats with red facings.[34]

The Land Pattern Musket, more commonly known as the "Brown Bess," was the standard firearm of the British soldier. The .75 caliber flintlock, muzzle-loading weapon fired a loose-fitting 1-ounce ball and had a maximum effective range of between 50 and 100 yards. A well-trained soldier could load and fire three to four rounds a minute. Under the stress of combat, however, the rate of fire and the effective range could vary wildly. The musket weighed a little more than 10 pounds, and a bayonet could be affixed to the end of the barrel with a lug and socket arrangement. Canadians and Loyalists often provided their own weapons or were issued surplus muskets, most of them obsolete. Burgoyne's Indian allies were equipped not only with their traditional weapons of tomahawks, war clubs, and scalping knives but also armed with "a kind of a light Musquet which they used very skillfully." as Lieutenant James Hadden noted in his journal.[35] The German muskets were a little cruder and heavier than their British counterparts, and they were not always of the best quality. The Jäger battalion, however, was equipped with a muzzle-loading rifle that was accurate up to 300 yards. It featured an extremely low rate of fire because a closely fitting ball had to be rammed into the barrel to grip spiral groves, called rifling.[36] The wide variety of weapons and other equipment used by units of Burgoyne's army complicated an already strained logistical system.

The tactics used by Burgoyne's army were modified from the standard infantry maneuvers used by all late-eighteenth-century European professional armies and were designed to maximize two things: firepower and shock. The armies marched in column formation while traveling from one point to another when contact with the enemy was unlikely. Once battle was joined or was imminent, the unit deployed into the standard formation, consisting of three lines of infantry with the men spaced about a foot and a half apart. As one German officer observed, the formation used in North America, however, "departs utterly from our [usual] system" due to the woods, brush, and other difficult terrain.[37] In other words, there were two lines rather than three. The line formation was still difficult to maneuver, which made routine drill very important. Nonetheless, its purpose remained to maximize firepower directed at the enemy. These tactics used two lines, producing a very long formation, forcing the junior officers to take on more responsibility for command and control than in Europe.[38]

The two lines allowed for successive volleys of musket fire directed at the enemy, ideally only about 50 yards away. Aiming individual muskets was not as important as maximizing the firepower by the entire formation; careful aiming tended to reduce the rate of fire. Officers and noncommissioned officers in combat would often direct their soldiers to simply level their muskets in the direction of the enemy and fire on command. Using the terrain to their advantage, officers tried to maneuver their units—whether in column or line formation, depending on the circumstances—to attack an enemy's vulnerable flank.[39]

As Burgoyne's army penetrated deeper into the American wilderness—a much more challenging environment than faced by Howe's army in New Jersey and Pennsylvania—the officers continued to adjust their tactics to suit the situation. While on the march, they posted companies of troops ahead and to the sides of the columns to provide security against ambush. Riedesel trained his men to advance through the woods in open order, using trees for cover and skirmishers leading the way to flush out Americans who might be lying in wait. Burgoyne and his officers sought battle in open areas where their superior training and discipline would give them an advantage. No matter what formation they used, the objective was to maximize firepower with powerful and effective volleys of musketry. Once the commander sensed that the enemy was faltering, he would order a bayonet attack, which, against untrained or inexperienced American troops, could be very successful. This was not always the case. If they maintained fire discipline, the Americans could turn back the assault.[40]

Burgoyne also had the advantage of the advanced corps, which formed the army's vanguard as it penetrated deeper into enemy territory. Composed of General Fraser's own 24th Regiment, along with a corps of marksmen, the grenadier battalion, and a light infantry battalion, it represented the cream of the army. The other advanced corps units were made up of hand-picked men from the rest of the army. These were the biggest, tallest, most experienced, best disciplined, and best trained soldiers, all of whom were able to operate in the woods on equal or at least near-equal terms with the Americans.[41] Often attached to the advanced corps for specialized missions were Burgoyne's Indian allies and the Canadian and Loyalist units.

In late May, Burgoyne provided Germain with another status report. Although he made clear that he still had challenges to overcome, such as rampant desertion among the Canadian troops Carleton had collected for him, Burgoyne assured the secretary that

he saw "no impediment to all my force being very near the point of their embarkation by the end of this week," meaning June 1.[42] But transport shortages continued to plague the army, and the departure date from Montreal came and went. Burgoyne complained to Carleton that he would be short on tents and wagons to carry the army's numerous bateaux from Lake George to the Hudson River, and the five hundred carts he had on hand "will barely carry fourteen days provisions at a time." However, itching to depart, Burgoyne decided to start south despite the transport shortfall. To save "the publick expense," as he put it, Burgoyne reasoned to Carleton, he would "trust the resources of the expedition with the rest." Thus, on the very eve of his departure to Ticonderoga and Albany, Burgoyne had persuaded himself that he would be able to find enough carts, wagons, and horses while on the march in enemy territory.[43] Like the other planning assumptions contained in Burgoyne's initial concept and the March 26 orders from Germain, this would turn out to be incorrect.

Carleton traveled to Montreal and joined Burgoyne on June 10 in time to see him off and wish him luck. While in Montreal, Carleton formally provided Burgoyne with all the correspondence he had received from Germain and Howe concerning the campaign, including copies of Germain's March 26 letter to Carleton and Howe's April 5 letter, both of which Burgoyne had already seen. In a cover letter transmitting these documents to Burgoyne, Carleton noted that he had enclosed "for your private information" a copy of a letter dated April 5, 1777, in which Howe had written Carleton that he wished Burgoyne "a happy and a successful campaign."[44] While it is true that Howe did pass on his best wishes to Burgoyne and his army, the commander-in-chief's main point was to make clear that he would be on active campaign in Pennsylvania and not be coming up the Hudson to Albany. If Burgoyne did not know that he was on his own before, he did now. Burgoyne "must therefore pursue such measures as may from circumstances be judged."[45] As he was making his last-minute preparations for the campaign, Burgoyne had been told twice—once by Germain and again by Howe—to use his initiative based on the situation on the ground.

Burgoyne's soldiers were unaware of Howe's letter, and most were as confident of success as their commander. At Fort Saint-Jean, where they had fought the Americans the year before, the army paraded in Carleton's honor, and the governor bade them farewell. The army then marched overland or traveled by boat to Nut Island, or Île aux Noix, at the very northern end of Lake Champlain. One company

surgeon who had traveled through the area during the 1776 campaign marveled that the little settlement had been transformed into an armed camp. He also observed with dismay that the army was being tormented by insects: "The flies and mosquitos . . . have almost devoured us; everybody has bumps on hands and face from their poisonous stings."[46] The good doctor was not alone. Almost every first-hand account of Burgoyne's campaign made a note of the troops' suffering from the swarms of biting insects that are ever-present in the region during the summer. This was a new phenomenon for these soldiers. The 1776 campaign had gotten such a late start that the insects had largely disappeared by the time the British soldiers reached Lake Champlain. The soldiers not only had to deal with the insects, the weather was also uncooperative. Violent thunderstorms turned the area's primitive roads into quagmires. One officer wrote that since the army was "incumber'd with many Carts &c . . . our march was much retarded by the badness of the Roads, which were uncommonly so."[47] From Nut Island the army marched overland 30 miles to Cumberland Head, a point of land on the west bank of Lake Champlain, near present-day Plattsburgh, New York. By June 18, the army was all together for the first time. On the 19th, the men were issued ammunition and flour instead of bread, sure signs that they were nearing the enemy and that, as one officer noted, "the affair is becoming serious."[48]

It was indeed becoming serious, but the soldiers took the time to appreciate the countryside that was so different from home. After complaining about the ubiquitous mosquitoes, one soldier marveled at the variety of wildlife near the shores of Lake Champlain: "We came upon an astounding number of wild pigeons here," and the huge frogs made the noise "our bitterns make but these were even stronger and coarser than ours." He also described with pleasure the vistas they encountered on the lake, noting that the "terrain and countryside are superb here."[49] A British officer noted the splendor of the countryside, "the *Lake* affording many beautiful prospects." Despite the splendid views, the constant rain was "a very considerable inconvenience." The men had to jury-rig awnings on the bateaux from sailcloth and oars, "which proved a sufficient defence against most Rains."[50]

The next day, June 20, the army embarked and set sail up the turbulent lake as yet another thunderstorm swept in from the west. "Who in the world ever saw anything more unusual than a small army riding in more than 300 batteaux," wrote one participant, "each one

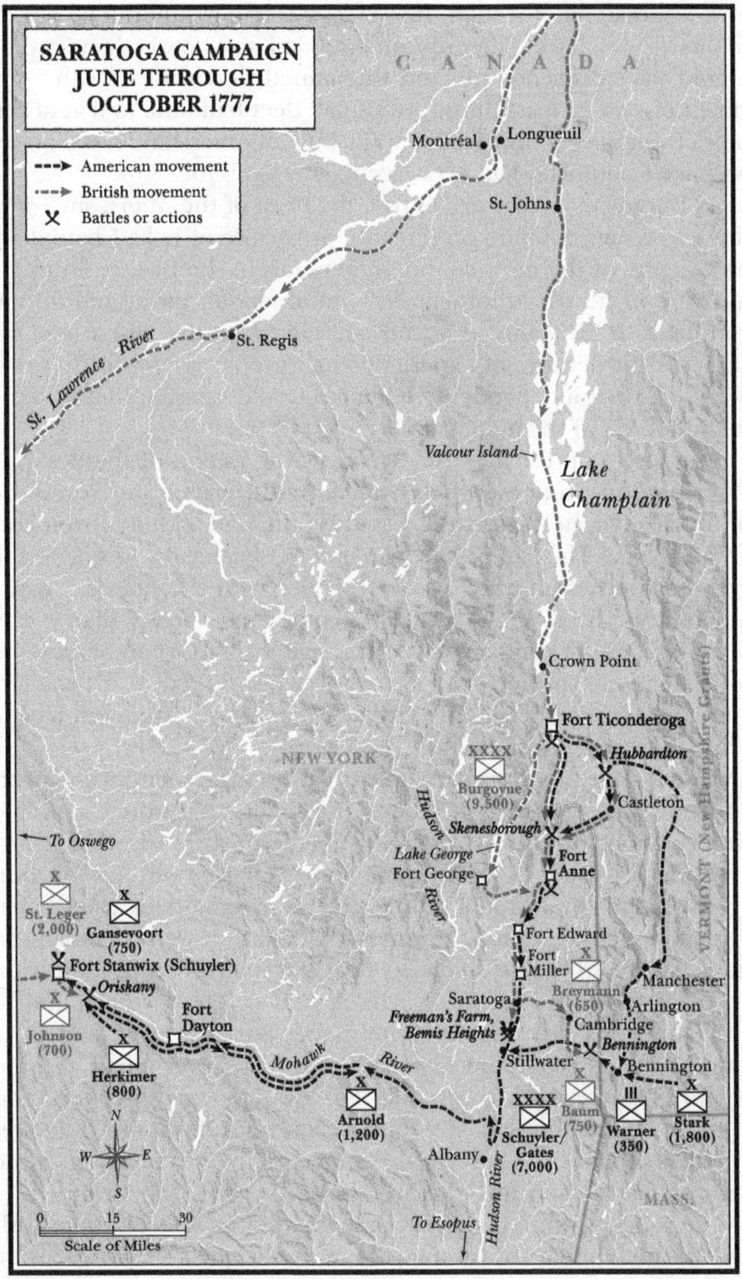

Map 4 Saratoga Campaign, June through October 1777

with a spread sail, through the waves of storm weather? The beauty of this sight is beyond description but I do know how I felt every time a bold wave drenched me and threatened to devour us with a terrible noise."[51] At least Burgoyne's small fleet had little to fear at this point from the enemy, given that the bulk of Americans' naval power on Lake Champlain had been swept away in 1776.

As Burgoyne led the army from the deck of the *Maria*, surveying the sea of sails bobbing on the choppy surface of Lake Champlain, he was one of the most confident generals in the British Army. He was sure of his nine-thousand-five-hundred-man force, and he was confident in his ability to lead them. He was at the pinnacle of his career. Four decades of experience had prepared him for this moment. His first independent command would catapult him into the highest levels of the military and the government.

The next stop for the army was near the mouth of the Bouquet River, about 50 miles south of Cumberland Head on the west shore of the lake, 35 miles north of Crown Point, and 45 miles from Fort Ticonderoga. The trip up the lake had not been easy, "owing to the great tediousness of bringing over Artillery and other stores," wrote one weary officer, but at least the weather was warmer than it had been on the last campaign.[52] At this camp, Burgoyne composed a proclamation that he then printed and distributed to his soldiers and to hostile and friendly civilians throughout the countryside while the army moved south.[53]

Even in an era of florid and theatrical language, Burgoyne's proclamation was over the top. He was practicing what would be called "information warfare" today, an attempt to win over proverbial hearts and minds. To the Loyalist population, Burgoyne offered "encouragement and employment" and urged them to help his army defeat this "unnatural rebellion." At the very least, they were to remain in their houses, where his soldiers would not interfere with their lives. To these friends of the Crown he appealed for provisions and to keep the roads clear. On the other hand, Burgoyne threatened the Patriots. If they continue to resist the British government, "I have but to give stretch to the Indian Forces under my direction, and they amount to thousands," and they will track down the "Enemies of Great Britain . . . wherever they may lurk."[54] This played into the fears of many Americans who lived on the fringes of the frontier.

The proclamation might have had the desired effect if the British had been commanded by someone else. Burgoyne, talented to be sure, was also arrogant, pompous, and self-confident, and his decree instead produced exactly the opposite effect. It was met largely with

derision and ridicule on both sides of the Atlantic. Although having a generally good opinion of Burgoyne, Horace Walpole observed that even the government "laughed at his pomp." The general's flamboyant boasts "would expose him to derision if he failed, and would diminish the lustre of his success if he obtained any."[55] Another British observer called Burgoyne's proclamation a "most ill-judged policy." His Indian allies would "butcher those who continued hostile to the mother-country."[56] The press was split on the value of Burgoyne's declaration. The *London Chronicle*, the official government newspaper, was supportive. Much of the independent press was not. The *Edinburgh Advertiser* claimed that the proclamation had "inflamed the minds of the colonists; and giving them fresh cause for disgust."[57] The *London Evening Post* was particularly critical of Burgoyne's threatening the Americans with Indian depredations.[58]

Burgoyne's proclamation also opened him up to American ridicule. Writing for the *Independent Chronicle* in Boston, one Patriot declared the edict "the most bombasting and gasconading proclamation that British insolence has hitherto exhibited."[59] On July 1, James Thacher, a surgeon with the American army at Fort Ticonderoga, wrote, "We are now assailed by a proclamation of a very extraordinary nature from General Burgoyne." Thacher noted with disgust that the "British ministry, not satisfied with the disgraceful expedient of hiring foreign mercenaries, resort also to savages of the wilderness for aid in the glorious cause of tyranny."[60] Another American soldier at the fort wrote that it was a "pompous proclamation, which is probably intended to frighten us into desertion or surrender."[61]

Long after the campaign had ended, Burgoyne tried to defend his proclamation in the House of Commons. He admitted that the decree had been intended "to excite obedience, first by encouragement, and next by the dread . . . to speak daggers, but use none." He denied that it had been counterproductive.[62] Burgoyne's proclamation was emblematic of how little he understood the enemy he was fighting—their culture, their ideals, and the reasons for their rebellion against the Crown. It is hard to imagine Howe, Clinton, or Carleton issuing a similar decree. While it is difficult to determine precisely how much it hurt Burgoyne's campaign—boosting morale and motivating and helping mobilize the militia—what is certain is that it did not yield dividends for Burgoyne and the army.[63]

At the camp near the Bouquet River, Burgoyne reviewed the troops and updated Germain on the army's progress. Despite the challenges they had faced, "I am nevertheless within two or three movements of Ticonderoga where the enemy at present make

demonstration of standing a siege." He had learned through Fraser's interview of a Loyalist spy that General St. Clair's Ticonderoga garrison consisted of "four thousand five hundred men," then reported that he had assembled more than five hundred Indians and "a larger number daily are expected," to collect intelligence, attack American lines of communication, and cut off their retreat routes to the east and south. Finally, Burgoyne again described the army's shortages in land transport, explaining that contracts he and General Carleton had negotiated concerning the required horses and carts would make up his shortfall. He thought he would have no trouble getting the army safely to Ticonderoga. Even with these few challenges, Burgoyne assured the secretary that the "health and zeal of the army afford a fair promise of compensating all difficulties."[64]

Burgoyne saw a major victory in his future and was relatively unconcerned by the issues he faced. None of the obstacles could stop the expedition. Most of the dispatch to Germain focused on Ticonderoga. His attention was fixed solely on the fortress and not what lay beyond.[65] Burgoyne once again made no reference to Howe or his army, probably because he simply didn't care whether he was coming or not. Burgoyne was going to get to Albany, and he did not need Howe's help. Burgoyne, of course, expected that sooner or later, Howe would get orders to come up the Hudson to facilitate follow-on operations with the northern army, but that was in the distant future.[66]

While still at the Bouquet River camp, Burgoyne called an assembly by a waterfall about a mile and a half up the river from the lake, near present-day Willsboro, New York. The gathering included most of his generals, including Riedesel and Fraser, as well as all the Native forces he had collected. The latter sat in a circle surrounding Burgoyne, who was seated under a decorative arbor of greenery that had been constructed especially for the occasion. The theatrical setting suited the playwright-general perfectly. Burgoyne then stood and delivered his prepared remarks to the five hundred warriors whom he hoped would play a significant role in the upcoming campaign. Burgoyne's speech was only a little less ostentatious than his June 20 proclamation, and an attempt both to incite the Indians and keep indiscriminate violence in check. He explained first that the rebels had violated the king's trust and threatened the Indian tribes. "Warriors, you are Free—Go forth in might of your valour and your cause—strike at the common enemies of Great Britain and America—Disturbers of public order, peace and Happiness—destroyers of Commerce; Parricides of the State." Grandly gesturing

toward the British and German generals behind him, Burgoyne assured the assembled braves that "the Chiefs of His Majesty's European forces . . . esteem you as Brothers in war." He then switched gears and reminded them that many loyal citizens lived in the rebels' midst. Therefore, insisted the general, "I positively forbid bloodshed when you are not opposed in Arms. Aged Men, Women, Children and Prisoners must be held sacred from the Knife or Hatchet." In addition, Burgoyne warned, "on no account, or pretence, or subtlety, or prevarication, are [scalps] to be taken from the wounded," nor are wounded or captives to be harmed. However, should the enemy "dare to countenance acts of Barbarity toward those who fall into their hands it shall be yours also to retaliate." A senior Iroquois chief responded to Burgoyne's speech by telling the general and the assembled crowd, "We receive You as our Father because when you speak We hear the Voice of our great Father beyond the Great Lake." All the chiefs then rose and shook hands with Burgoyne, pledging their fidelity to the Crown and promising to persuade the rest of their tribes to join the British. With that, the formalities of the great assembly ended, and a lavish feast followed, lasting throughout the day. Burgoyne was pleased with the conference and believed that he had succeeded in imposing his will on the Indians.[67]

Not everyone was as sanguine about the effectiveness of Burgoyne's speech. When Edmund Burke learned about it several months later, he mocked the general in the House of Commons for encouraging the Indians to attack the American rebels while at the same time making a plea for humanity.[68] One German officer noted approvingly that Burgoyne had "admonished [the Indians] in most urgent terms and ordering them not to scalp anyone anymore."[69] Another officer believed that while Burgoyne had asserted control over the warriors and instilled discipline and respect for the rules of warfare, the general "gave them full power to scalp the Dead, and Destroy, wherever opposition was made."[70] The distinction is subtle, but the Indians probably viewed Burgoyne's speech much as this officer did: the emphasis was on attack and kill, and not on restraint.

Whatever the case, in the commanding general's view, the campaign was getting off to a very promising start.

CHAPTER 6

The Fall of Fort Ticonderoga

BURGOYNE MAY HAVE BELIEVED that Fort Ticonderoga would present his biggest obstacle, but the great fortress was not in the best shape and did not reflect the same state of readiness it did only nine months earlier. By late June 1777, the fort was still not ready to face the enemy. During that period, a succession of American commanders had squandered opportunities to improve the defenses of the main fort and its surrounding works.

Ticonderoga could have used Gates's experienced leadership that spring. He had, after all, done an effective job of preparing for Carleton's 1776 offensive. However, Gates remained in Albany after he assumed command of the Northern Department in Schuyler's absence. While he had sent aides to the fort to provide him with status reports, Gates should have known that there is no substitute for a commander's firsthand inspection.

Upon his arrival in Albany, Gates was appalled at what he found. He complained in a letter to Robert Morris that he discovered "everything so backward" and that if his requests to Congress and General Washington for resources were not met, "all is at Risque."[1] While Gates tried to collect additional troops, he received a discouraging account from newly promoted Brigadier General Anthony Wayne, Ticonderoga's commander. Wayne had served at Fort Ticonderoga and the Northern Army before and distinguished himself during the American retreat from Canada. He had also served with Gates during the 1776 campaign. Despite his naturally optimistic nature, the young general (he was 32) reported gloomily, "Our whole force . . . don't

amount to 1900 men, one fourth of whom are destitute of arms." Wayne further told Gates that since he did not expect any additional Continental troops for some time, militia reinforcements "are absolutely necessary." Despite the challenges the Ticonderoga garrison faced, Wayne was determined that "in case of an attack . . . this place will not be carried without the expense of much blood."[2]

As noted, Ticonderoga sits astride the main line of communication from Canada to New York via the Hudson River. Almost any route used by an invading army to or from the eastern part of Canada had to pass through or near Ticonderoga. One historian called it "the back gate to the Atlantic colonies."[3] The old stone fort itself is 193 feet above sea level. Mount Independence, where the Americans focused most of their engineering efforts, is 306 feet above sea level, and so it dominated the old fort. The Americans had improved the defenses to the northwest of the fort, where the terrain gently rises to a height of about 240 feet on the wooded summit of Mount Hope. This small rise commanded the link between Lake Champlain and Lake George. Finally, less than a mile to the southwest lay Mount Defiance, also known as Sugar Loaf Hill or Mountain. Steep, rugged, and wooded, it was marked "inaccessible" in a British map from 1758 and looked down on Fort Ticonderoga from a commanding height of 853 feet.[4]

In June 1777, as we've seen, the only way to reach the top of Mount Defiance was to climb through the undergrowth and the rocky wooded slopes. Today the summit of Mount Defiance can be reached by walking up a narrow, steep road. The road rises more than 500 feet in elevation over its three-quarter-mile length, so even for the modern climber, the ascent is not a particularly easy one, and most people will be winded when they gain the summit. Once there, the views are stunning. Looking northeast, one can see the beautiful and expansive waters of Lake Champlain curve their way toward Canada. To the east, the Green Mountains extend northward.

Farther north and off to the west, the Adirondack Mountains rise to the horizon. To the south is the narrow northern end of Lake George, which drains into Lake Champlain just south of the fort through the La Chute River. Still looking south, with a slight turn to the left, one discovers the south bay of Lake Champlain, which narrows to river width and terminates at present-day Whitehall, New York, known as Skenesborough during Revolutionary times. Looking down from the summit while facing north, one views the entire footprint of Fort Ticonderoga, 650 feet below. Turning to the right, Mount Defiance also commands Mount Independence,

located across a 400-yard-wide narrows on the east side of the lake immediately opposite the fort and almost 350 feet below the summit. The main fort, much of its supporting entrenchments and blockhouses, and large portions of Mount Independence—the key parts of the American defenses—were all within cannon range from Mount Defiance. To occupy Mount Defiance, either for observation or as an artillery site, or both, was to seize a significant advantage. In the spring of 1777, two men knew this; unfortunately for the Americans, both were ignored.

Throughout the spring, the garrison worked to improve the fort. The chief engineer, Colonel Jeduthan Baldwin, directed his efforts toward constructing field fortifications on Mount Hope and Mount Independence. To connect the main fortifications to Mount Independence, Baldwin constructed a bridge and a log and chain boom a few yards to the north.[5] This boom was designed to block British warships from continuing up the lake into South Bay and on to Skenesborough. At Skenesborough, the Americans had considerable stores and that valuable shipyard. By late April, the commander at Ticonderoga, Anthony Wayne, could report that the boom had been completed "in such a manner as will effectually prevent the Enemy's shipping from forcing into our rear."[6] The Americans were justifiably proud of this project, "a strong work," as one participant called it, one that took many weeks and countless hours to build.[7] They called the structure the Great Bridge, and the enemy agreed. One German officer exclaimed that the bridge and boom "must have taken an unbelievable amount of work."[8] Unfortunately, much of the work was misplaced.

On May 12, a young military engineer arrived at Ticonderoga to assist Baldwin and report on the fort's defenses. Colonel Thaddeus Kosciuszko, a thirty-one-year-old Polish officer, would play a major role in the coming campaign. Kosciuszko offered his services to the cause of the newly independent country in the summer of 1776. Before the war, Kosciuszko had been a junior artillery officer in the Lithuanian-Polish army but fled after a civil war broke out. He learned about the Patriot cause and, as a strong supporter of liberty, set sail for America along with other European officers. His talents were soon recognized, and he was promoted to colonel in the Continental Army. Kosciuszko was assigned to the Northern Department in May 1777 and immediately impressed Gates, who promptly sent him to Ticonderoga along with Colonel Wilkinson.[9] Gates directed the two men to make a thorough assessment of the fort and its state of readiness. Writing to Brigadier General John Paterson, who had

temporarily replaced General Wayne at Ticonderoga, Gates called the young Pole "an able engineer," and asked Paterson and Baldwin to give their "countenance and protection to this Gentleman, for he is meant to serve not supersede."[10]

Kosciuszko immediately inspected the entire complex with Baldwin. Baldwin was only human and bristled when the young foreign engineer questioned his fondness for blockhouses as well as some of the other work on which the older engineer had already spent so much time and effort. Kosciuszko was astonished that Baldwin had not fortified Mount Defiance. He scaled the rocky hill and declared that guns mounted on the summit could easily range all the major approaches to the forts below.[11]

A few days later, Kosciuszko warned that although his opinion may be "dangerous," much of Baldwin's work was wasted effort. One blockhouse that was supposed to cover the water obstacle was, he said, "very bad for stopping the passage of shipping, more particularly as heavy cannon cannot be mounted on it." This was a fundamental error, as all military obstacles should be covered by fire. Kosciuszko wanted to make several changes to Baldwin's defensive scheme, but as the junior officer, he was reluctant to step in until Gates showed up in person.[12] Until that time, Kosciuszko continued to serve under Baldwin and worked on the bridge from Ticonderoga to Mount Independence and on other redoubts.[13]

Hancock and the delegates of Congress were not the only ones who thought Gates should be at Ticonderoga; James Wilkinson thought so too. General Wayne had departed for a new assignment, and General St. Clair had not yet arrived to take command, leaving the fort essentially rudderless at a critical moment. "I wish to heaven," Wilkinson implored Gates, "either yourself or Genl. St. Clair was here for a few days—Col. Kosciuszko is timidly modest; Baldwin is inclosing the lines on a plan of his own." The generals who were there—Enoch Poor and Paterson—were, he thought, "very ineffectual."[14] In other words, Baldwin was ignoring Kosciuszko's suggestions, and there was no one to step in and correct the faulty work.

From Albany, Gates ordered General Paterson, the fort's acting commander, to execute Kosciuszko's plan "immediately," starting with "the most defensible parts."[15] This was sound advice: allocate limited resources to their best advantage. Even though Gates reacted quickly to the alarming reports on the state of Ticonderoga, this was still no substitute for a firsthand inspection.

Kosciuszko was that rare military engineer who had all the qualities to make a major contribution: an eye for terrain, an understanding

of the ranges and capabilities of the available weaponry, the ability to prioritize the use of resources, and the understanding that fortifications had to be mutually supporting and integrated into the existing terrain. He could identify key terrain at a glance, as he did with Mount Defiance. Baldwin was devoted to the cause, but he was not a skilled military engineer. Despite Gates's clear intent, Baldwin continued to direct the work at Ticonderoga.

Even after Gates's May 23 letter to Paterson, not much changed at Ticonderoga. There was little direction and no sense of urgency. Wilkinson reported to Gates again in late May with a growing sense of dread. "The Adjutants," Wilkinson complained, "generally speaking, are stupid blockheads and two of the Brigade Majors are totally ignorant of their duty." Wilkinson had also determined that Baldwin was "truly the most important nothing I ever saw." Wilkinson repeated his plea for Gates to personally take charge at the fort, or at least to hurry St. Clair forward. He predicted disaster if the fort's garrison continued to plod along without direction because "there is no disposition of defence made in case of attack."[16]

While Wilkinson pleaded with Gates to impose order on Ticonderoga, the commanding general was urging Baldwin to defer to Kosciuszko and told General Poor to employ every able-bodied man in the preparation of the fort's defenses. Gates reminded them that "every moment industrially made use of now, may save their Country, their Honour, and their Lives."[17] As the days grew longer and the weather warmer, an increasingly desperate Wilkinson appealed once more on the last day of May, reporting that despite Gates's clear intent, Baldwin's plan was still being implemented. "For God's sake," Wilkinson begged Gates to give Kosciuszko "proper authority" to take change of the fort's improvements.[18] Despite Poor's assurance to Gates on June 2 that he would direct Baldwin to adopt Kosciuszko's plans, there is no evidence that this ever happened.[19] More than likely, Gates's orders were forgotten when St. Clair finally arrived at Ticonderoga, and Schuyler reassumed overall command.

Major General Arthur St. Clair (pronounced "Sinclair"), the new commander at Ticonderoga, was one of many Continental Army officers with previous British military experience. Born in Scotland, he had served in the French and Indian War, after which he settled in Pennsylvania and became a prosperous landowner. He was a colonel of the Pennsylvania militia at the start of the war and soon after was awarded a colonel's commission in the Continental Army. Assigned to the Northern Department, he led a regiment in the retreat from Canada, served with Gates during the 1776 campaign,

and was promoted to brigadier general in August of that year. St. Clair joined the main army and participated in the Trenton and Princeton campaigns. Promoted to major general in February 1777, he was appointed to command Ticonderoga by Congress on April 1, finally arriving at the fort after several long delays on June 12. The handsome, energetic St. Clair seemed like the perfect choice to command Ticonderoga. He would also soon be put to the test. Although St. Clair could not know it, the day after he arrived at the fort, Burgoyne's army started to move south. The Ticonderoga garrison and its new commander did not have much time.[20]

One of Gates's last acts as the presumptive commander of the Northern Department was to offer St. Clair some advice: "I entreat you to call lustily for aid of all kinds—men, arms, ammunition, and provision." This was easy for Gates to say since he was about to leave for Philadelphia and would not have to listen to St. Clair's demands. Nonetheless, the most important piece of advice he offered St. Clair was to focus his attention on Mount Defiance—"the occupation of which decides the fate of your campaign." Gates blamed Schuyler for refusing to allow the occupation of Mount Defiance in 1776, and he urged St. Clair to rectify this error.[21]

As Burgoyne and his army began their march to Ticonderoga, the fort and its small garrison were still in disarray. A succession of commanders at the fortress, turbulence in the Northern Department itself, and the confusion and inertia of the command situation had compromised readiness. The three months between April and June that should have been characterized by focused preparations to receive the British invasion were instead marred by confusion and wasted effort.

Immediately after Schuyler returned to Albany to reassume command of the Northern Department, he appealed directly to Washington for reinforcements from Peekskill. He knew that if Ticonderoga fell, they would be vulnerable to the British.[22] While the Ticonderoga garrison was probably sufficient to hold it, if a British force tried to cut off the fort by a thrust down the Mohawk River, Schuyler would have little to stop them. He also assailed Gates for his "Inattention in this Department," while he, Schuyler, was in Philadelphia.[23] As Schuyler deluged Washington with increasingly frantic pleas for reinforcements, the commander-in-chief was trying to figure out what General Howe was going to do. Because of this uncertainty, Washington could not afford to send Peekskill troops to Schuyler.[24] From his central position at Middlebrook, New Jersey, Washington could react to Howe's movements. If Howe moved up

the Hudson to join with the army from Canada, Washington could move the main American army to the Hudson Highlands. He could also shift the army to counter British threats to Philadelphia. About the only British course of action that Washington could not respond to in a timely manner was a move to New England by sea. In mid-June, Washington admitted to Major General Israel Putnam, commanding American troops in the Hudson Highlands, that "The Enemy's designs and movements are [truly m]ysterious."[25]

St. Clair was dismayed by the condition of the fort and the troops stationed there when he arrived on June 12. To congressional delegate and friend James Wilson, St. Clair wrote, "I am much disappointed in the strength of the Garrison and the state of the fortifications at this place." He saw very few improvements since the winter and insufficient troops to man the new works. None of this would matter much if the British Army had "no design on us," but intelligence indicated that the enemy was already on the march. Still, despite all these issues, St. Clair was confident that if the enemy "should not be repulsed, I hope to see him [Burgoyne] so crippled as not to be able to continue their journey." Parties of Indians were starting to appear, threatening work parties and patrols—indeed, on June 18, one man was killed and two others captured within sight of the fort—a clear indication that the British were on the move. Despite this, he did not "dare" to use the militia because of the shortage of provisions. Finally, the commander told Wilson that "if you should not hear from me again . . . remember that I have given you this account of our situation."[26] St. Clair made sure he was getting his concerns on the record with a congressional delegate, laying the groundwork for defending himself against the disaster he saw coming.

As St. Clair bemoaned the situation at Fort Ticonderoga, Lieutenant Colonel Richard Varick, mustering officer for the Northern Department, wrote a message to Schuyler that echoed Kosciuszko's May report: the fort was not ready to receive the enemy, and while much work was being done, it was to little effect. Baldwin had prepared fortifications for a huge garrison, not the much smaller one they actually had. The commander at Ticonderoga did not have enough troops to man "such extensive, ill-planned works." He also explained that the garrison's morale also suffered a blow when they learned that Schuyler had replaced Gates.[27]

Schuyler immediately traveled to Ticonderoga to assess the situation for himself. He arrived at the fort on June 19 and stayed three days. His letters to Washington and Congress up to this point had been reasonably optimistic, but what he saw was not encouraging.

He inspected the works, both completed and still under construction, near the main fort and across the lake at Mount Independence, where Baldwin had just begun construction of three additional entrenchments. While Schuyler was at the fort, an Indian raiding party attacked a group of American soldiers along the road from the fort to the Lake George landing, killing and scalping two and capturing one.[28] Time was running out.

Many years later, Wilkinson, who had been at Ticonderoga during Schuyler's visit, recalled that the New York general was not well liked among the officers and men. Schuyler tended to stand aloof from his troops, and American troops expected a more personal touch from their leaders. Schuyler's interaction with the soldiers "was so circumscribed, that he was little known." Indeed, "although he was a perfect gentleman . . . he was far from being a favorite."[29]

On Friday evening, June 20, the same day that Burgoyne issued his grandiose proclamation on the shores of Lake Champlain, Schuyler presided over a meeting of all the general officers at the fort, a council of war. This conference included St. Clair, Paterson, Poor, and Brigadier General Roche de Fermoy, one of the French officers forced on Washington by Congress. The generals concluded that the fort's twenty-five-hundred-man garrison (it was actually much larger) was too small to man all of the fortifications and wholly unsuited to defend the fort against the British. They agreed that both the main fort and Mount Independence must be "maintained as long as possible," and if they must abandon part of the works, "that it ought to be the Ticonderoga side." In other words, if required, the garrison would abandon the main fort and defend their position from Mount Independence until relief arrived. The group also agreed that the water obstacle was key "to prevent the enemy's naval force from getting in our rear." Finally, they appealed to Washington for reinforcements and declared that with only "thirty nine days' provisions . . . . it is prudent to provide for a retreat."[30] However, Ticonderoga would get no additional support from the commander-in-chief, and although the group could not know it, on that same day, Washington wrote to Schuyler that he thought "the Garrison of Ticonderoga is sufficient to hold it against any attack."[31]

A council of war can be an effective way to solicit multiple points of view. It can also lead to a herd mentality that can steer a commander down a dangerous path. The latter was the case on June 20 at Fort Ticonderoga. The five generals had taken counsel of their fears or had been influenced by one or more of their colleagues. The primary result of the meeting was a list of excuses before the

fact. The minutes reveal that during the council of war the generals deliberated over what they could not do and what they did not have, not what they should and could do to hold the fort with the resources at hand. The only clear-cut decision was to prepare for a retreat.

While all options were considered, fighting was given short shrift. Burgoyne's army outnumbered St. Clair's force by two to one.[32] However, a two-to-one advantage is not an unfavorable force ratio when the smaller unit is fighting behind prepared positions.[33] Had St. Clair (and his predecessors) consolidated and shortened their lines, and manned the key terrain as Kosciuszko recommended, the Ticonderoga garrison might have held the fort for an extended period. However, defeatism and despair dominated the council of war. A decisive leader might have turned the tide, but no such leader was present at Fort Ticonderoga in late June 1777.[34] Working long hours in ever-changing weather, swarms of biting insects, rattlesnakes, the ever-present fear of Indian attacks, and the backbreaking effort to maintain and improve the fort's defenses had taken their toll on the Patriots.

Schuyler left the fort by boat for Albany, traveling up the south bay of Lake Champlain on June 23. What should have been a short and easy journey became a nightmare as a storm hit.[35] Schuyler and his travel companions were lucky to make it to Skenesborough alive. The dark, boiling sky and raging tempest must have seemed like omens.

St. Clair's state of mind was no less dark, as was evident from a long letter he wrote to Gates a week after the council of war. If only he had at his disposal the same number of troops that Gates had enjoyed at Ticonderoga in 1776, he might give Burgoyne—now reported to be as close as Crown Point—a good fight. "[B]ut now I find myself able to make but a very feeble resistance." He claimed that he had only two thousand men fit for duty, which did not match his own official returns. With the enemy almost at his doorstep, "I have no Prospect of doing much service to my country and have Captivity or Death before my eyes—however, we will do the best we can."[36]

Indian activity started picking up as the British Army moved south. The Ticonderoga garrison had already suffered losses from sporadic Indian raids over the previous weeks, sometimes within sight of the fort. During the early days of the campaign, Burgoyne's Indian allies proved their value. The British used them for three main missions: raids on isolated outposts, patrols, convoys, and working parties; gathering intelligence (although often with suspect accuracy); and screening the movements of the British Army from American intelligence-gathering efforts. Burgoyne was able

to use them like cavalry, and their operations struck terror into the Patriots and those living in the surrounding countryside. Any resupply convoy or patrol or working party venturing outside the Ticonderoga fortifications had to include a large armed guard. While the American losses to the Indian raids were low, they affected the morale of the garrison. St. Clair was desperate for intelligence on the British army that he knew was approaching, and he sent out numerous patrols. Burgoyne's Native allies held them at bay, however, concealing British strength and movements and keeping the Americans in the dark.[37]

St. Clair continued to send Schuyler plaintive requests for reinforcements and other resources. On June 25, he reported that he was considering calling out the Berkshire militia.[38] In the end, St. Clair never did. He only had seven weeks of provisions at the fort. If they brought in hundreds of militia troops, Wilkinson, for one, believed that "immediate *starvation* is the consequence."[39] This revelation was astounding. A succession of commanders had ample opportunity to stockpile several months of provisions at the fort, yet somehow they failed to do so. Had they doubled their numbers with a militia reinforcement, they might have held out for at least three to four weeks, plenty of time for Schuyler to rush more supplies to the fort.

St. Clair and Wilkinson claimed only seven weeks' provisions were available at Ticonderoga. Yet on June 25, Schuyler wrote to Congress stating that he had pushed more provisions forward to the fort so that they now had "near sixty days provisions of the meat kind at Ticonderoga, and flour for near double that time."[40] Who was right? Given the confusion that took place during and after the evacuation of the fort, it is impossible to know for sure, but even if St. Clair was forced to reduce rations, he had the resources to maintain increased troop levels for at least four to six weeks. There is no doubt that he was in a tough fix. Not taking advantage of all available resources, including the Berkshire militia, made things much worse.

And what about the soldiers he did have? St. Clair's garrison was composed of both Continental and militia regiments, some of which had served in Boston, New York, and the 1776 campaign in Canada. Although Burgoyne's army consisted of European regulars, many American soldiers and their officers had more experience with combat and active campaigning. The tactics used by the American units were similar to those employed by their British and German counterparts: column formations for ease and speed of movement, and line formations to maximize firepower. The only major tactical

difference was that the Americans were typically untrained in the use of the bayonet. Moreover, training among American units was generally inconsistent at best and depended entirely on the diligence of the commanding officer and the other unit leaders. As the war progressed, competence in drill and weapons proficiency improved. Militiamen, while their training was even spottier, could provide additional combat power. Asking militia units to go toe-to-toe with British regulars typically met with disaster. However, militia could be used to great effect behind prepared defenses and when operating in close cooperation with better-trained, better-led, and better-disciplined Continental units. Militia also was useful when employed as irregular forces and in defense of their own and neighboring states.[41]

Americans' equipment varied as much as their training. In 1777, uniforms for both Continental and militia troops were far from standardized. Some of the wealthier militia units had matching uniforms, but most tended to wear whatever clothes they had available. Congress had specified brown as the coat color for Continental troops. Not all soldiers were so equipped, however, and those who were lucky enough to be issued uniforms found that they soon wore out. Ultimately the army moved toward blue as the standard coat color. The American troops that participated in the 1777 campaign wore a wide assortment of uniforms or parts of uniforms. They were also outfitted with a great variety of equipment and weapons. Militia troops often supplied their own personal weapons from home. Continental troops were issued British Brown Bess muskets captured on the battlefield, French Charleville muskets, captured German weapons, and anything else that came to hand. The drill for loading and firing a smoothbore musket was complex. Soldiers had to constantly practice if they were to maintain a rate of fire (three to four rounds a minute under ideal conditions) equal to that of the enemy.[42]

As always, discipline and leadership mattered more than uniforms and equipment, and the Americans would need plenty of both if they were to defeat Burgoyne.

After a two-day stay at the Bouquet River, the British Army once again embarked on their fleet of bateaux and set sail up the lake.[43] On June 24, lead elements of the army arrived at Crown Point, which they had abandoned nine months before. With its fortifications in ruins, Crown Point was not a hospitable place, but Burgoyne's soldiers erected their tents and a makeshift hospital on the rubble and made final preparations to lay siege to the American fortress 10 miles to the south.[44] They confronted the same challenges as the

Americans. They not only arrived at Crown Point during a heat wave with temperatures well into the high 80s and low 90s, but they also encountered other adversaries. One German officer described the suffering of the men who "day and night are tortured by insects." After encountering his first rattlesnake on the journey south along the lake, one officer echoed the sentiments of his comrades when he wrote in his journal, "I cannot describe how afraid, even terrified, I have been of them."[45]

Six days later, Simon Fraser, perhaps the most capable of Burgoyne's general officers, led the advance corps to the eponymous Three Mile Point, named for the distance from Ticonderoga, with the rest of the army close behind.[46] They made final preparations for the investment of the fort, mindful of Burgoyne's order of the day: "THIS ARMY MUST NOT RETREAT."[47] Burgoyne's gunboats also sailed up the lake and anchored just beyond the range of the American guns facing the northern water approaches to the fort. Each side eyed the other warily. British Lieutenant Digby wryly observed, "With our glasses we could distinguish every thing they were about in the Fort . . . and viewing with their glasses our situation." Indian raids succeeded in capturing several American soldiers who assured their captors "that they intended to make a vigorous defense."[48] Burgoyne landed a force of about three hundred men who probed the west shore defense near the bridge/boom and were driven back. The British then lashed the gunboats together across the lake to block any American attempt to push north down the lake, an action which "made a formidable appearance."[49]

From Albany, Schuyler continued his steady stream of melancholy letters to Washington about the situation in Ticonderoga. Schuyler enclosed the latest update from St. Clair, dated June 25, which predicted that he would have to abandon the main fort and concentrate his defenses on Mount Independence, though he was certain he would soon be forced off that post as well.[50]

Schuyler received a report from an officer on St. Clair's staff on June 30 that did little to ease his mind. Lieutenant Colonel Henry Livingston related that enemy Indians had blocked "all communication between Ticonderoga and Lake George." The troops were itching for a fight, but, reported Livingston, St. Clair "chooses to act on the [defensive] and to risque nothing." As he was writing this report, Livingston observed two more British ships approach the fort from the north. Nonetheless, as he put it, the "Spirits of the Men seem to increase in proportion to the number of the Enemy," and despite their problems, he confidently predicted a great victory.[51]

Even St. Clair seemed optimistic on that sunny Monday, informing Schuyler that the garrison will give a "good account of the enemy, should they think it proper to attack us."[52]

Washington finally relented in the face of Schuyler's appeals and ordered a brigade under Brigadier General John Nixon to Ticonderoga instead of to Peekskill. The commander-in-chief tried to calm Schuyler. "I see no Reason for apprehending that [Ticonderoga] can possibly fall into the Hands of the Enemy in a short Time, even were they to bring their whole Force to a point." Indeed, if Burgoyne should split his force, St. Clair could even go on the offensive, advice that Washington would repeat several times over the next few weeks.[53]

On July 1, Burgoyne deployed his army for the siege of Ticonderoga. The right wing, which was under General Phillips and led by Fraser's advanced corps, advanced on the west side of the lake, and General Riedesel's left wing did the same on the eastern shore. Both forces were amply supported by the guns of the British vessels blocking the narrows just north of the fort.[54] All of these maneuvers were executed in full view of the Americans. Both wings soon came within artillery range of the American works, which the British began to shell, to little effect. The next day the British right wing moved even closer, this time all the way to the wooded heights of Mount Hope, that low hill a little more than 1,000 yards to the northwest of the main fort.

Quickly taking possession of the hill, the British troops probed the American outer lines of defense, killing an officer and four privates and wounding eleven others. The enemy is "all around us & very bold," reported Colonel Baldwin.[55] The British troops and their Indian warriors also neared the blockhouse located between the main fort and Mount Hope, which the Americans promptly abandoned on St. Clair's order.

Over the next two days, both sides exchanged cannon fire, though casualties were light. Anticipating an extended siege, the British cut roads through the woods, linking their separated units.[56] St. Clair responded to Burgoyne's moves by trying to "animate the troops," as it became increasingly obvious that Burgoyne would attack the garrison.[57]

The noose was tightening around Ticonderoga. Burgoyne desperately wanted to close off all escape routes, a desire that General Fraser attributed to his fear that the capture of Ticonderoga would not be "sufficiently brilliant" without "great number of prisoners."[58] After Phillips and Fraser seized Mount Hope, a number of small posts were set up near Lake George to keep them from using it to retreat.

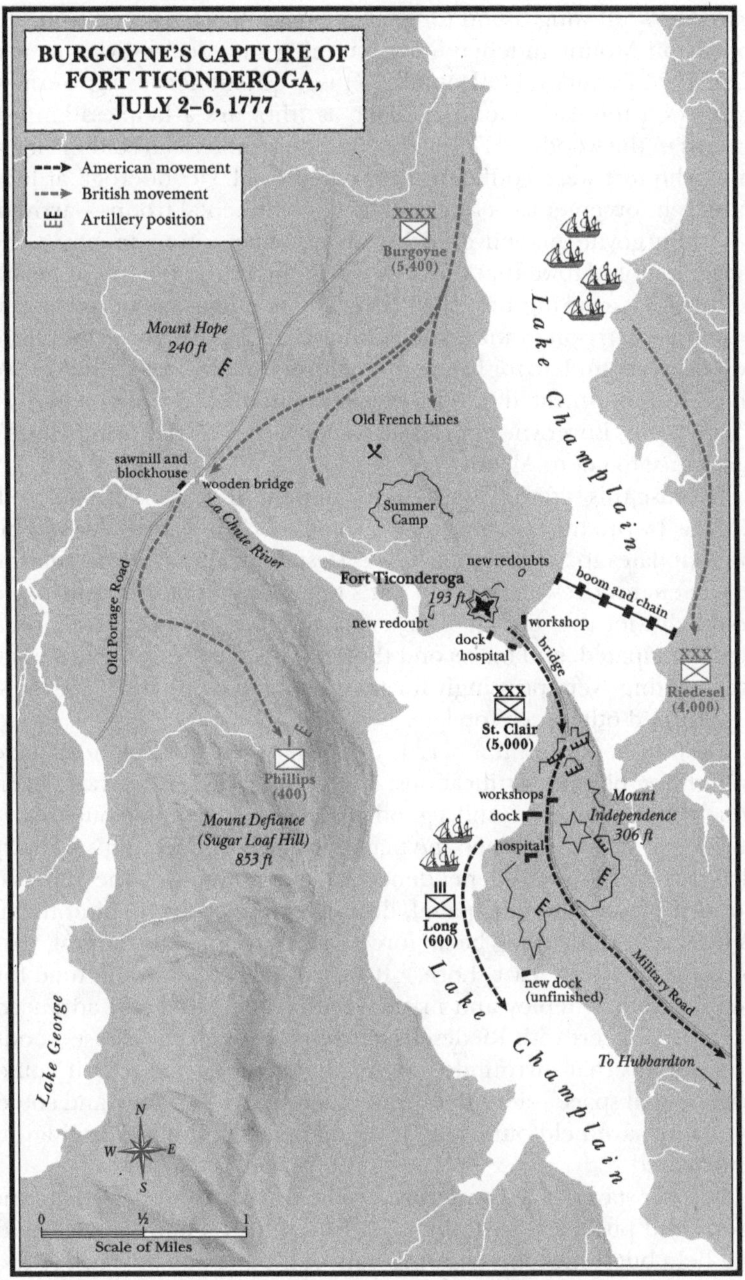

Map 5 Burgoyne's Capture of Fort Ticonderoga, July 2–6, 1777

Riedesel's left wing found tougher going as they advanced from the north on Mount Independence, running into "large Swamps and Creeks of considerable Depth."[59] Fraser questioned using German troops on the east side of the lake as "they are a helpless kind of troops in the woods."[60] Despite all this, most American soldiers manning the fort were confident they could hold Ticonderoga at least until reinforcements—either militia or Continental troops—arrived.

As Burgoyne maneuvered his army into position to begin the siege, he told Howe that the "army is in the fullest powers of health and spirit," assuring him that once Ticonderoga was seized that it would be garrisoned with troops from Canada. "My force therefore will be left complete for future operations," and he would "follow the ideas I communicated to your excellency in my [previous] letters."[61] Once again, Burgoyne expressed no concern over requiring Howe's assistance to get to Albany.

"Excuse this scrawl. I am so much in want of sleep, that I am nodding as I write this," wrote an exhausted St. Clair as he delivered his final updates to Schuyler on July 3. Despite his previous pessimism, as the enemy drew closer, St. Clair's tone became more positive. He told Schuyler that the enemy seemed to have fewer troops than he had anticipated, and on second thought, decided to call out the militia, writing "very pressingly for the people to come in."[62] This was, as it turned out, much too late.

Despite being outnumbered, the Americans had the advantage of fighting behind fortifications, and even had the force ratio been much worse, there was still a good chance for a favorable outcome.[63] If St. Clair had abandoned the main fort and conducted his primary defense on Mount Independence, as the generals at the June 20 council of war had anticipated, destroying the bridge behind them, Burgoyne would have been forced to transport the largest part of his army to the east shore.[64] It would have taken some time for Burgoyne to redeploy and maneuver the right wing and advanced corps in concert with Riedesel's left wing through the dense woods and swamps that surrounded Mount Independence. St. Clair could have traded space—admittedly not much space—for time and could probably have held out for an extended period, just as Washington anticipated.

St. Clair stayed in Ticonderoga. As the British troops seized Mount Hope and pushed toward the main fort on July 3 and 4, they could not help but notice the towering bulk of Mount Defiance just to the south of the La Chute River. With Mount Hope in their possession, the route to Mount Defiance was open. When Burgoyne, Phillips,

Fraser, and the army's chief engineer, Lieutenant William Twiss, saw the hill, they immediately recognized that it was the key to Fort Ticonderoga. Indeed, Fraser observed that the hill "seemed to command everything."[65] In other words, the British officers recognized the same thing that Trumbull, Gates, and Kosciuszko had discovered before them. Artillery mounted on Mount Defiance could not only hit the main fort and parts of Mount Independence, but men posted on the hill could also see everything the Americans did.

Fraser immediately sent 40 light infantrymen and a few Indians to "reconnoiter the hill." After receiving a favorable report, he decided to examine the terrain himself and set out with Lieutenant Twiss to climb the rugged slope. When he reached the summit, he "found this mountain commanded at Ticonderoga and on Mount Independence." One of Fraser's Indian allies asked if the "great father of the sun had created it lately," because that was the only explanation for why "it never occurred to any person to occupy it before we did."[66] Twiss and Fraser reported to Burgoyne that although it would be difficult, a track could be slashed through the woods, and artillery could be hauled to the top. If they did, they could dominate the entire area.

General Phillips was charged with getting guns to the top of Mount Defiance. Phillips, a veteran of the Seven Years War and a graduate of Woolwich, the British military school for engineers and artillerymen, was a highly capable officer with a keen eye for terrain and where his ordnance should be placed to gain the best advantage. He immediately organized a work party and was said to have countered a staff officer's objection that only a mountain goat could climb Mount Defiance by replying: "Where a goat can go, a man can go, and where a man can go he can drag a gun."[67]

Throughout the morning of July 4, the first anniversary of American Independence, British soldiers supervised by Lieutenant Twiss labored in the stifling heat, hacking a path through the woods. By the end of the day, they had succeeded in cutting a trail to the top, and by the end of the following day, two medium 12-pounder artillery pieces were "entirely commanding the Forts of Ticonderoga & Mount Independence."[68]

Burgoyne's men were surprised but delighted that the Americans had overlooked Mount Defiance. "It was a post of great consequence," explained Lieutenant Digby, "as it commanded . . . Ticonderoga, all their vessels, and likewise afforded us a means of cutting off their communication with Mount Independent, a place also of great strength and the works very extensive."[69]

British resourcefulness and audacity stunned the Americans. Colonel Baldwin noted simply that "the Enemy appeared on the Mount above on the S.W. opening a battery."[70] James Thacher, a surgeon, seemed to have a much better appreciation for their predicament: "It is with astonishment that we find the enemy have taken possession of an eminence called *Sugar-loaf Hill.*" He added that many believed that the hill should have been fortified and wondered why it hadn't been. In his final journal entry for July 5, Thacher wrote: "The situation of our garrison is viewed as critical and alarming; a few days, it is expected, will decide our fate. We have reason to apprehend the most fatal effects from their battery on Sugar-loaf Hill."[71]

The Americans tried to dislodge the British from the summit with an artillery barrage, but because they did not sufficiently elevate their guns, their efforts to dislodge the British were unsuccessful.[72] Other than the ineffective artillery barrage, St. Clair made no effort to take back Mount Defiance. One option would have been to land a force on the south side of the hill. This also went untried.

Burgoyne could not believe his good fortune. "The manner of taking up the ground at Ticonderoga, convinces me that they have no men of military science," he wrote. Not only had the Americans failed to recognize the importance of Mount Defiance, but they had also "expended great treasure and the unwearied labor of more than a year to fortify, upon the supposition that we should only attack them upon the point where they were best prepared to resist."[73]

The appearance of British gunners on Mount Defiance seemed to break what remained of St. Clair's fighting spirit, and on the afternoon of July 5, he called for another council of war. The generals gathered in the main fort shortly after noon and, in a matter of minutes, decided to evacuate Ticonderoga after offering up only the most token resistance. From the available evidence, it is doubtful that they considered any attempt to defend the fort or to counter any of Burgoyne's maneuvers. Except for Schuyler, the attendees at the St. Clair's July 5 council of war were the same as on June 20, plus Colonel Pierse Long, militiaman and garrison commandant. St. Clair reviewed their situation: the "Batteries of the Enemy are ready to open upon the Tyconderoga Side, and that the Camp is very much exposed to their Fire, and to be enfiladed on all Quarters"; a simultaneous attack on both the east and west shores seemed imminent, and they were heavily outnumbered. Given these dire circumstances, retreat was a foregone conclusion. They also rejected consolidating the garrison at Mount Independence, "as the Enemy have already

nearly surrounded us."[74] The generals decided to abandon the main fort that night, moving the troops under cover of darkness to Mount Independence, and from there to depart for Skenesborough before first light on July 6.

Even without the loss of Mount Defiance, St. Clair would have most likely made the same decision. The officers attending the July 5 Council of War gave the stamp of approval to St. Clair's inclination to retreat and provided political cover. As one officer recalled, St. Clair said that he viewed his decision as a choice between honor and duty: "If he remained there, he would save his character and lose the army," but if he "went off, he would save the army and lose his character; the last of which he was determined to sacrifice to the cause in which he was engaged."[75] There is little doubt St. Clair believed this. The command responsibilities at Ticonderoga were simply beyond his capabilities.

The decision to evacuate the fort was quickly arrived at, as the council's minutes reveal, but pulling it off would be a different thing entirely. The meeting ended at 3:00 p.m., yet it was several hours before many of the key leaders and soldiers received word of the evacuation, and thus, planning and preparation were poorly executed. A withdrawal under fire or in close proximity of the enemy is one of the most difficult and dangerous operations to execute, and this one was incompetently managed. One senior officer only learned of the retreat decision at 7:00 p.m. on the night of the 5th. Colonel Baldwin found out about the evacuation at 9:00 p.m.; Kosciuszko never received the official word of the evacuation.[76] Many precious daylight hours were wasted.

Those who did hear about the order found it difficult to complete all the tasks necessary to execute the evacuation under the noses of the encircling British and German forces. The first was to move the soldiers and provisions from the main fort and the associated works across the bridge to Mount Independence. The larger artillery pieces had to be spiked and rendered unusable. The wounded and sick and the supplies, powder, guns, and ammunition had to be loaded on vessels and transported to Skenesborough at the southern end of the lake. This was overseen by Colonel Long. St. Clair would lead the rest of the army southeast out of Mount Independence on the only land route still open: the road to Skenesborough via Castleton, Vermont.[77]

There was simply not enough time to do everything. The northwest wind hampered American efforts to move their vessels from the south side of Mount Independence, where they were moored out of

British artillery range, back up to the fort to load the stores. As a result, a number of vital supplies, guns, ammunition, and powder were left behind to be seized by the grateful British.[78] Surgeon Thacher was rudely shaken awake at midnight and told that he had only two hours to load all the sick and wounded on bateaux to be sent up the lake to Skenesborough. "[I] could scarcely believe that my informant was in earnest," he recalled, "but the confusion and bustle soon convinced me that it was really true." In the chaos and darkness, four sick soldiers were left behind. Finally, at around 3:00 a.m., a small American flotilla, consisting of five armed galleys, sloops, and schooners as well as two hundred bateaux and boats, all laden with cannon, tents, provisions, sick soldiers, and women, sailed south away from the fort.[79] Once they had arrived at Skenesborough, Long was to unload the vessels and wait for St. Clair to join him with the rest of the army. The reunited force would then march 20 miles south to join Schuyler at Fort Edward, where he had moved with the rest of his small army.[80]

After St. Clair was satisfied that his small fleet was safely away, he turned his attention to the preparations on Mount Independence and was shocked to discover much frantic activity to no useful purpose. The moonless night, although good for concealing their movements, only exacerbated the commotion.[81] General Fermoy was responsible for Mount Independence, but he soon lost control, and discipline collapsed. After the bateaux departed, some soldiers began looting.[82] St. Clair had prudently ordered a complete blackout to conceal their intentions from Burgoyne. However, light discipline was destroyed when Fermoy set fire to his own quarters, throwing the men assembling on Mount Independence into further disarray. With Burgoyne potentially alerted to their actions, the pressure mounted on St. Clair and his men to wrap up their preparations and get on the road.[83]

Although St. Clair designated a rear guard to cover the garrison's retreat and destroy the bridge across the narrows to the old fort, this was not done, nor was the bridge and boom obstacle covered by fire. Lieutenant Digby was shocked at this tactical blunder. The young British officer remarked that had the Americans left a battery to cover the bridge, "they would, in all probability, have destroyed all or most of us on the Boom."[84] Instead, when the British discovered the American evacuation, they simply marched across the bridge unopposed.

Some have perpetuated the myth—based on one unreliable source—that St. Clair left four volunteers behind to cover the bridge

and prevent the British from crossing the lake or dismantling the boom, but they had gotten drunk instead and left the way open for an easy British pursuit.[85] Even if true, it would still be a leadership failure. Four men without officer supervision were hardly enough to man a battery or cover a major obstacle. Plus, according to Digby and Fraser, both known as reliable sources, there were no American units, drunk or otherwise, left behind to cover the bridge and the boom.

In the early morning hours of Sunday, July 6, the Americans began their retreat and set out along the road leading out of Mount Independence, with Poor's brigade leading the way, followed by the small militia detachment, then Paterson and Fermoy's brigades. St. Clair and his officers found it almost impossible to impose discipline on the march. As one officer recalled, the retreat was conducted "without order or regularity," and the commanding general's attempts to reassert authority "were directly disobeyed." The militia refused to halt and reform their ranks and "pushed on, and drew after them many of the continental troops."[86] The retreat from Ticonderoga was quickly threatening to turn into a rout.

As dawn approached and the last American walked out of the fortress, they had handed Burgoyne a victory that he expected would cost him considerable blood and treasure. As noted, Burgoyne saw Ticonderoga as the most significant obstacle to his ultimate goal of reaching Albany and St. Clair, the former British Army officer, had served it to him on a platter. It was a signal failure of leadership on St. Clair's part. He had failed to instill a fighting spirit in his fellow senior officers that would carry them through the difficult times to come. While admittedly St. Clair had only a short time to develop relationships with his brigadiers and colonels, he had not done so. He could only see his force's vulnerabilities instead of its capabilities, and defeatism had infected his command.

There is no doubt that St. Clair had considered evacuating the fort for quite some time, and so his failure to prepare for an orderly retreat was perhaps his worst mistake. St. Clair and his generals were handed a tough mission. Still, the American soldiers at Fort Ticonderoga deserved better.[87]

Certainly, Congress and Washington did not provide much assistance to St. Clair and Schuyler.[88] Washington sent reinforcements only after it was too late. As the commander-in-chief, he had to balance the needs of both theaters of war—the main theater in New Jersey and vicinity and the Northern Department—and prioritize the allocation of scarce resources. Plus, Washington had received mixed messages from a succession of commanders and assumed that

Ticonderoga was properly manned and led. He had focused most of his attention on what he saw as the most dangerous threat constituted by Howe's main army. Nonetheless, both he and Congress badly neglected the Northern Department in the spring and early summer of 1777.

St. Clair's leadership shortcomings, combined with Congress's and Washington's mismanagement of the command of the Northern Department, Gates's failure to personally oversee the defenses at Ticonderoga, and Schuyler's inability to properly supervise St. Clair and inculcate in him the proper sense of urgency, led to the shocking result: Ticonderoga fell, almost without a shot. The road was now open between Burgoyne and Albany, with little standing in his way except St. Clair's demoralized garrison and the rest of Schuyler's small and scattered Northern Army. On July 6, 1777, the prospects for Burgoyne and his army looked bright indeed. A vigorous follow-up was all that was needed to ensure British success.

CHAPTER 7

Defeat, Retreat, Disgrace

AT 3:00 A.M. ON July 6, General Fraser woke to learn from deserters that, as he put it the "Enemy were abandoning Ticonteroga, and the works on Mount Independence." Wary of a trap, Fraser sent the news to Burgoyne on the *Royal George* and cautiously ordered an advance toward the American lines with his units. He soon learned that the deserters had told the truth and that the Americans had fled "by land towards Castletown, & by water to Skenesborough, leaving all their Cannon, and a great quantity of provisions and ammunition, destroying nothing," except for a half-hearted and failed attempt to burn the bridge across the lake's narrows. It took only minutes for Fraser's men to lay planks across the bridge supports, and they quickly crossed to Mount Independence.[1] As dawn broke on that warm, humid Sunday morning, Burgoyne's troops captured the entire fortified complex without firing a shot. Anticipating a long, bloody siege, the victors could hardly believe their luck. Four and a half months earlier, Burgoyne had calculated that to stay on his timeline, he had to capture Ticonderoga by early summer.[2] He had done just that.

British soldiers were put to work dismantling the log-and-chain boom blocking the water route to the south bay of Lake Champlain and Skenesborough that the Americans had built so laboriously. The Americans were shocked later to learn that the enemy had dismantled the bridge and boom in under an hour. But without soldiers left behind to cover the bridge with musket or artillery fire, it was a simple

matter for Burgoyne's men to negotiate the boom and bridge and pass their ships into the south bay.

Not losing a moment, Burgoyne ordered an immediate pursuit of the American flotilla that had evacuated the supplies and the sick and wounded up the lake. By 8:00 a.m., the British had dismantled the boom, and their warships and transports slipped gingerly between the bridge's stone and timber pilings, sailing south after the American vessels. As the British soldiers occupied Mount Independence, some began to plunder the abandoned American supplies, but Fraser and his officers quickly restored discipline. Believing that the American rear elements were only a few miles ahead of him, he immediately reorganized his advanced corps and put 850 men—two companies of the 24th Regiment under Major Robert Grant, the light infantry battalion commanded by Major Alexander Lindsay, Lord Balcarres, and the grenadier battalion under Major John Acland—on the road in pursuit of St. Clair's retreating garrison. Fraser sent word for Burgoyne to hurry along the rest of his corps as soon as possible. He took advantage of the gift the Americans had given him.[3]

It was an impressive performance. Burgoyne and his men had seized the initiative by capturing Mount Hope and Mount Defiance, forcing St. Clair's hand. Fraser had quickly occupied the fort and immediately began the pursuit. When handed a victory, commanders will sometimes miss opportunities to exploit it. Despite some disappointment at not achieving the total victory he coveted—the capture of the entire American garrison—Burgoyne did not make this same mistake.

One Braunschweig officer was amazed at the amount of stores the Americans had left behind at Ticonderoga. Indeed, he wrote, "If they had been formally beaten and by force dislodged from their entrenched positions, they could not have left more." Forty artillery pieces were found on Mount Independence and another fourteen cannons at the main fort, many of them useful 12- and 18-pounders. Only a few guns had been completely disabled; many more were only "lightly spiked" and could be repaired. In addition to the artillery, the British soldiers discovered "extraordinarily large supplies of ammunition both for heavy artillery and the infantry." One officer marveled, "They had also left behind several thousand muskets, very many tents . . . and pieces of clothing, provisions, especially much rice, coffee and sugar."[4] The fact that muskets were left behind is particularly troubling, given that St. Clair and his predecessors had complained on numerous occasions that many of the soldiers were without arms. Getting their first close-up look at the fortifications,

one officer exclaimed, "If the enemy had made a truly determined effort to defend the post, we could not have taken it."[5] For his part, Lieutenant Digby could not resist the opportunity to mock the Americans for "all their pretended boastings of holding out to the last."[6]

From the time he left Ticonderoga on June 24, Schuyler had concentrated all his energy on stopping Burgoyne's offensive. Moving between his headquarters at Albany and other key locations, such as Fort Edward and Saratoga (present-day Schuylerville, New York), Schuyler forwarded needed supplies to Ticonderoga and kept Washington and Congress apprised of the situation while at the same time appealing to nearby states for additional reinforcements and provisions. As commander-in-chief of the Northern Department, Schuyler's responsibilities included not only Ticonderoga but other key installations, including Fort Stanwix (also known to the Americans as Fort Schuyler) about 100 miles west of Albany near present-day Rome, New York; Fort George at the southern end of Lake George; Fort Anne, located about 10 miles southwest of Skenesborough; Fort Edward, on the east bank of the Hudson River and 12 miles southwest of Fort Anne; and Fort Miller, 8 miles south of Fort Edward, also on the east bank of the Hudson. The vital route between Fort Anne, at the head of Wood Creek, and Fort Edward was a major portage between the Hudson and Lake George.

Schuyler first learned of the disaster at Ticonderoga on July 7 and immediately informed Washington, renewing his pleas for additional troops and supplies. As commander of a secondary theater, Schuyler often had to plead for resources, appeals that soon took on a dark and desperate tone. More than once, Washington had to calm the jittery New Yorker. After the fall of Ticonderoga, Schuyler's letters to Washington and Congress grew increasingly despairing. With Ticonderoga and Mount Independence now in Burgoyne's hands, Schuyler warned, "They may do what they please, as I have not above 700 Continental Troops to oppose them with, and, I fear, not above twice that Number of Militia." All of northern New York "will soon be in their power, unless we are speedily and largely reinforced." Washington's heart must have sunk when he read Schuyler's conclusion: "I shall do every Thing that is left in my power to do, and hope the best."[7]

Later the same day, Schuyler was able to provide the commander-in-chief with more details, including the evacuation of the American vessels to Skenesborough and the overland march. Still, he had no idea where St. Clair was or the garrison's route of march. The

prospect of preventing the British from moving south "is not much," lamented Schuyler, "They have an Army flushed with Victory, plentifully provided with provisions Cannon and every Warlike Store—Our Army . . . is weak in Numbers, dispirited, naked, in a Manner, destitute of provisions." Although Washington had sent General John Nixon's brigade of Massachusetts Continentals to the north, it was not nearly enough. Schuyler needed more men.[8] The generals at Ticonderoga had "ruined our Affairs in this Quarter," Schuyler moaned. "God only knows" what could have induced them to evacuate the fort. Finally, the harassed and traumatized general enclosed a copy of Burgoyne's June 20 proclamation, which had been disseminated everywhere, and reported that it would have "the most evil Consequences to us."[9] The edict that had already garnered so much ridicule from American troops and newspapers had spooked the dispirited Schuyler.

For his part, St. Clair was pleased with himself. "It was morally impossible we could maintain the post with a handful of troops," he wrote during the retreat. Besides, the decision to evacuate had been determined by a council of war. Unfortunately, he explained, the retreat's execution did not go well "owing to the confusion that naturally attends operations in the night."[10] What St. Clair conveniently left out was that most of the "confusion" was due to the lack of leadership and planning. St. Clair was content with not losing his men. "I account myself very happy in effecting this Retreat," he told Schuyler.[11]

The news about Ticonderoga shook Washington deeply. Schuyler and St. Clair had assured him that they would be able to defend the fort, at least for a period of time. If the news was true, Washington told Hancock, they would now need their militias to stop Burgoyne. There were simply not enough Continental troops to go around. However, to engage the militias the Northern Department needed "an Active—spirited Officer to conduct and lead them on." Concerned about Schuyler's state of mind, Washington dispatched Major General Benedict Arnold to the Northern Department. While he wished he could keep Arnold with the main army, Washington explained to Hancock that he was an "Officer in whom the Militia will repose great confidence" and better acquainted with the terrain than almost anyone else.[12] Of all the key decisions made during the entire 1777 campaign, a campaign replete with momentous choices, Washington's determination to send Arnold to the Northern Department ranks as one of the most important.

The nine months between the Battle of Valcour Island and the fall of Ticonderoga was not a happy time for Arnold. He was widely criticized for the loss of the Lake Champlain fleet, and Congress passed him over when they promoted five junior brigadier generals to major general. This was primarily due to the number of Continental generals authorized from each state, but Arnold was deeply insulted. Washington was sympathetic and pushed for Arnold's promotion, which finally went through after he helped turn back a British raid on Danbury, Connecticut. His gallant conduct convinced Congress to promote him to major general, but they failed to restore his seniority. Typical of Arnold, he could not let well enough alone and submitted his resignation to Congress on July 11, 1777, the same day Hancock received Washington's request to reassign the difficult but brilliant major general to the Northern Department.[13] Congress approved Washington's request and ignored Arnold's resignation.[14] Arnold set off for Albany, and for the time being at least, put country before self.

Washington responded to Schuyler on July 12, expressing his astonishment over the loss of Fort Ticonderoga, which was "altogether unaccountable." "I will suspend my Opinion upon the propriety of this every extraordinary and sudden Evacuation," he added, "until I hear something from General St. Clair." He also assured Schuyler that in addition to Nixon's brigade, he was also sending Brigadier General John Glover's brigade of Massachusetts troops and as much artillery and supplies that could be spared.[15] Washington's frustration over not yet hearing from St. Clair was palpable: "It even baffles Conjecture."[16]

To Schuyler's credit, he tirelessly worked to impede Burgoyne's progress with the resources he did have. On July 9, he ordered Brigadier General John Fellows, commanding about five hundred Massachusetts militia at Fort Edward, to march north to Fort Anne and gather food and "whatever carriages may be found." Most importantly, Fellows was to cut down trees to block roads and destroy bridges.[17] Schuyler sent similar orders to Brigadier General Abraham Ten Broeck, who commanded a large contingent of New York militia at Fort Edward.[18] This reflected Schuyler's deep knowledge of the region's roads, rivers, creeks, settlements, and other key terrain, which was proving invaluable in developing a scheme to impede Burgoyne's advance. Given his local familiarity and the Northern Department's situation, Schuyler was the right man in the right place at the right time. Unfortunately for the New Yorker, this was not at all obvious to Washington, nor to many in Congress.

At his temporary Fort Edward headquarters, Schuyler finally learned of St. Clair's whereabouts on July 9. Amazingly, St. Clair was "about fifty Miles East of me" and trying to make his way back to Fort Edward. Desertion was rampant now that St. Clair was "nearing the inhabited part of the Country," which proved to be too much of a temptation for many in the demoralized army to withstand. Consequently, reported Schuyler to Washington, he expected St. Clair to arrive with little more than one thousand men. Schuyler also informed the commander-in-chief that he had put his militia to work and was doing everything he could to slow Burgoyne's advance.[19] Just how St. Clair ended up 50 miles from Fort Edward was anyone's guess.

When he marched his dejected garrison out of Mount Independence in the early morning hours of Sunday, July 6, St. Clair intended to head toward Castleton, about 30 miles southeast of Ticonderoga, and then travel the 14 miles back east to Skenesborough. There they would rejoin Colonel Long with the supplies and sick that had been evacuated by water. The dejected Americans retreated along the primitive military road running out of Mount Independence. The route was dictated by the available roads that had not already been cut off by Burgoyne's army. As the sun rose, the temperature quickly soared, and St. Clair's exhausted and demoralized men suffered from the intense heat, humidity, and the ubiquitous insects, not to mention anxiety, knowing that the enemy was nipping at their heels.

The British pursuit came quicker than anyone expected. Fraser had immediately put elements of his advance corps on the road to chase the fleeing Americans. To support Fraser, Burgoyne ordered General Riedesel and his men to follow Fraser and support them in case of an attack. The fleet and the rest of the army were to make their way to Skenesborough by water and attack the Americans' fleet.[20] British warships were soon closing in on Colonel Long's vessels, and British troops were already following St. Clair and the main body. General Riedesel quickly gathered up his forces and put several of his units in motion behind the advanced corps. In the meantime, Fraser had pushed his men so hard that in six hours, they had closed to within a few miles of St. Clair's rear guard, comprised of the 11th Massachusetts Regiment of Continentals and men from other units commanded by Colonel Ebenezer Francis.[21]

The Americans were exhausted. Most of the officers and men had slept very little since Burgoyne's army appeared at Three Mile Point six days earlier, and few had eaten in the prior 24 hours. Convinced

that he had put many miles between his army and Burgoyne's, St. Clair called the main body to a halt at noon near the tiny settlement of Hubbardton, about 20 miles southeast of Mount Independence. Surrounded by five hills to the north and west, Hubbardton lay where the road intersected the Crown Point road, which ran to the north and ultimately ended on Lake Champlain's east bank across from the ruined fortress. The settlement of nine households, the inhabitants of which had fled south with the British approach, was surrounded by "fields of stumps" and partially cleared woods. About a mile north of the intersection was Sargent Hill. The road ran through a saddle on the southwest slope and crossed the Sucker Brook, a small stream running from the northeast to southwest just west of the hamlet. East of the Sucker Brook and 50 feet above the road was high ground known today as Monument Hill. Still farther to the east, across the Crown Point road, was the Pittsford Ridge. Just south of Monument Hill lay a jagged, rocky eminence soaring well over 1,000 feet high called Mount Zion, which featured a north-facing, mostly bare clifftop.[22]

The spent troops lay in the shade along the road, most too tired to eat. St. Clair had received reports of Loyalist activity to the north, and, because Crown Point was held by the British, the Americans could not afford to linger at Hubbardton. Fearing an attack from two directions, St. Clair decided to continue the march to Castleton, leaving behind Colonel Seth Warner and his regiment, along with Colonel Nathan Hale's 2nd New Hampshire Regiment, to take command of the rear guard when Colonel Francis and his men arrived. As soon as Warner and Francis linked up, they were to follow the rest of the main body to Castleton. St. Clair got the rest of his men back on the road and set out for Castleton and from there to Skenesborough. The main body had gone only a short distance when several officers, including Poor, begged St. Clair to allow the New Hampshire troops to reinforce the rear guard, arguing that they would be quickly overrun if Burgoyne had started a vigorous pursuit. The commanding general refused. After a few minutes march, they asked again, "but without effect."[23]

By 4:00 p.m. on July 6, Riedesel's detachment of about a thousand men finally caught up with Fraser's force. Riedesel told Fraser that Burgoyne had ordered him to support the advanced corps and then continue to Skenesborough. Fraser was angry that Burgoyne had sent the Germans and not the rest of his own men. Plus, the commanding general had not sent food or ammunition or extra surgeons.[24] The aggressive brigadier wanted to keep the pressure on

the Americans, but the German general demanded that they halt the pursuit and make camp. Fraser reluctantly agreed though he understood that opportunities to inflict serious damage on a demoralized enemy were rare. Burgoyne had given Fraser "discretionary powers to attack the Enemy where-ever I could come up with them." He told Riedesel that he intended to do just that, so before halting, the advanced corps units moved 2 miles closer to the enemy, roughly 3 miles west of Hubbardton. The generals agreed that the allies would move at 3:00 a.m. with Fraser's advanced corps in the lead and Riedesel's Germans in support. During the short night, the British and German soldiers slept fully clothed on the ground and with their weapons close at hand.[25]

While Fraser and Riedesel formulated their plan for the next day, the American Colonels Warner and Hale waited at Hubbardton until Colonel Francis's regiment and the sick and stragglers finally appeared late in the afternoon of the 6th. Instead of moving immediately toward Castleton and staying close to the main body, as St. Clair directed, the three colonels met at the cabin owned by farmer John Selleck and decided that their men were too spent to continue their retreat after marching almost nonstop for sixteen hours in the hot and oppressive weather. Plus, they reasoned, while the British were surely following them, they were undoubtedly far behind. They posted sentries along the road, directed the construction of hasty obstacles along the Sucker Brook, and then finally retired for the evening.[26]

Fraser formed up his troops and started down the road at 3:00 a.m. as planned and set off toward Hubbardton. The American sentries arrayed west of the Sucker Brook detected Fraser's approach at about 5:00 a.m. as they moved through the saddle of Sargent Hill, fired one volley at close range, and then withdrew to rejoin their units. For many of the British soldiers, it was their first time under fire. "I must own," recalled one young officer, "when we received orders to prime and load, which we had barely time to do before we received a heavy fire, the idea of perhaps a few moments conveying me before the presence of my Creator had its force."[27]

The rapid approach of Fraser's men surprised Warner. He had placed the bulk of his men on or near Monument Hill with Francis's troops and elements of Hale's regiment occupying forward positions along Sucker Brook. Warner had not been planning for a fight. He had instead been preparing to move his men to Castleton to join the main body. Once the battle began, however, the Americans took

advantage of the natural cover provided by felled trees and brush, which were plentiful in the area.[28]

Fraser quickly deployed his units with the advanced guard under Major Robert Grant in the center, supported by the light infantry under Lord Balcarres on the left, with Acland's grenadiers in reserve. Fraser accompanied Grant as they fought the Americans, who were "aided by logs and trees."[29] Hale's New Hampshire regiment bore the brunt of the British attack and fell back shortly after the first shots were fired, but not before one of their volleys killed Grant.[30] Fraser personally led the light infantry and attacked Francis's men on Monument Hill, and the fighting soon became a contest for the

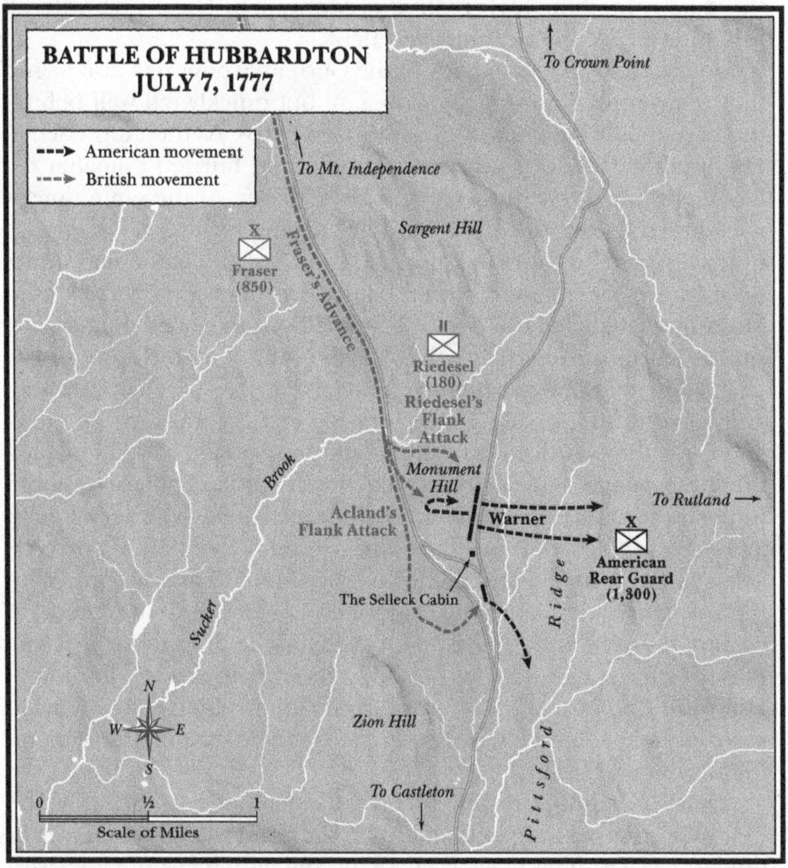

Map 6 Battle of Hubbardton, July 7, 1777

high ground. Acland moved to assist the hard-pressed companies of the 24th Foot along the Sucker Brook. They succeeded in pushing the American defenders back, and Fraser then ordered Acland's grenadiers to maneuver around the American left and cut off the Castleton road and the most direct route to St. Clair and the main body. Despite being outmaneuvered by Fraser, the Americans fought well and hard under Warner's and Francis's leadership.[31]

After multiple attacks on Monument Hill, Fraser finally succeeded in pushing the Americans back to a lower hill a couple of hundred yards to the east just across the Castleton road. There Warner set up another defense along a log fence, and the Americans poured volley after volley into the British soldiers on the crest of Monument Hill. Warner sensed that Fraser's units were in some disarray even though they had gained the high ground of Monument Hill, so he ordered a counterattack on the British left flank.[32]

Riedesel and the main body of the German troops had also begun their march that morning at 3:00 a.m. but quickly fell well behind the hard-marching units of the advanced corps. As they approached Hubbardton, Riedesel heard musket fire and hurried a smaller detachment of his troops forward to assist Fraser. At the same time, a messenger arrived from the brigadier urging his colleague to rush to his aid. As the German troops approached the battlefield unnoticed by the Americans, Colonel Francis led his regiment back onto Monument Hill to turn Fraser's left. The tough New Englanders succeeded in pushing back the British main line consisting of the 24th Foot and the Light Infantry. Fraser's left was soon hard pressed, and it began to look like the American forces might turn the flank and force the British to fall back. Fraser immediately dispatched another messenger to Riedesel, urging him on. Just as Francis was about to push his momentary advantage, Riedesel's 180-man detachment arrived on the road. It was 8:30 a.m. He immediately and correctly assessed the situation and identified the threat to Fraser's left. With the German band playing martial tunes, Riedesel sent into the fight each of his units as they arrived on the battlefield. At the same time, Fraser ordered Balcarres and his light infantry to retake Monument Hill with the bayonet and Acland's grenadiers along with a detachment of light infantry, having completed their flanking movement, hit Warner on his left.[33]

Francis continued to stubbornly hold his position, but now the weight of numbers began to tell. With the combination of Riedesel's timely arrival with his Jäger, grenadiers, and light infantry, along with Balcarres's bayonet attack, the Americans were finally forced to fall

back, a retreat that quickly turned into a rout. One Braunschweig officer recalled that many of the "retreating enemy discarded his weapons and equipment, an occurrence that afforded certain of our men a large quantity of booty."[34] Warner, having successfully faced Acland's flank attack, was soon forced to withdraw to the east. The German attack was so successful that the Americans withdrew before the rest of Riedesel's force could join the engagement. Riedesel had arrived just in time, and his fortuitous deployment of the light infantry and grenadiers defeated the Americans relieving Fraser's hard-pressed advanced corps. By 10:00 a.m., the fighting had ended.[35]

As the Americans retreated to the east over the Pittsford Ridge, they left behind more than 130 killed and wounded, including Colonel Francis, who died while trying to reform his fleeing troops after the German attack. More than two hundred Americans were captured, including Colonel Hale, and to the Germans looked "more like bandits than soldiers."[36] The allied detachment suffered more than 150 casualties, including Major Grant killed in action and the wounding of both Acland and Balcarres. Warner's regiment retreated east and reformed at Manchester along with other survivors of the battle. The rest of the surviving rear guard rejoined St. Clair and the main body.

The first real battle of the campaign was over, and the casualties were high in proportion to the numbers engaged.[37] Both sides had fought well. The professionalism of the British was telling in the way they deployed and outmaneuvered the Americans. Still, the American troops stood up to the regulars for most of the battle, only giving way with the surprise arrival of Riedesel's infantry and grenadiers. Francis and Warner had done their job well, though at a very high cost. Fraser and Riedesel both agreed that they were in no condition to follow up their success by continuing the pursuit.

On July 8, two days after the fall of Ticonderoga, heavy rain fell all day and all night, which did little to cool the intense summer heat and made "it very difficult to start fires and keep them alight," as one British officer wrote in his journal.[38] Both sides huddled miserably throughout the night without shelter, during which the wounded suffered unimaginable hardships. In accordance with his orders, Riedesel's detachment marched to Castleton and Skenesborough, leaving a disgruntled Fraser to take care of the prisoners, wounded, and dead, deep in "the most disaffected part of America, every person a Spy."[39] The next day, Fraser sent his prisoners to Ticonderoga and marched to Skenesborough. St. Clair had long since departed Castleton for Rutland after hearing news of the battle.[40]

The Americans had inflicted great damage on the British, especially on the elite troops of Fraser's advanced corps. The corps had lost a considerable number of men, and particularly troubling was the death of key leaders such as Major Grant. Some 25 percent of Fraser's force became casualties at Hubbardton, casualties that Fraser could not replace. The Americans, on the other hand, would make good their losses. Only a very small part of the American Army was employed at the Battle of Hubbardton. The battle's importance to the cause was out of proportion to its size. The spirited stand of the Americans on Monument Hill had enabled St. Clair's beleaguered force to escape. One historian has even called the battle "the rear guard action that saved America."[41]

The British had expected little more than a demoralized rabble on the road from Mount Independence after the chaotic scenes they had witnessed at Ticonderoga. Instead, they observed American officers leading from the front and soldiers, poorly equipped and many clothed in nothing resembling a military uniform, standing up to some of the world's best troops. Testifying in the House of Commons two years later, Lord Balcarres was asked to assess the Americans' behavior during the battle, responding that despite the fact that they were "an army very hard pressed in their retreat, they certainly behaved with great gallantry."[42] Lieutenant Digby, who was present at the battle, wrote that the enemy fought "with great obstinacy."[43]

Others, such as Lieutenant Hadden, cautioned against overhyping the victory, noting that the battle unnecessarily delayed their advance and that Fraser's units "certainly discover'd that neither they were invincible, nor the Rebels all Poltroons."[44] At Hubbardton, Hadden feared, "We gained nothing but honor."[45] To many British and German officers, it was clear that not all American leaders were as feckless as those who made the decisions at Fort Ticonderoga.

While the American rear guard successfully enabled the main army to march to Castleton and then Rutland, escaping its pursuers, the effort to evacuate troops, provisions, sick, wounded, and the small American fleet to Skenesborough met with a very different fate. The vessels under Colonel Long's command had, as noted, headed south from Ticonderoga into Lake Champlain's South Bay early on the morning of Sunday, July 6.[46] Almost all of Ticonderoga's evacuated stores were aboard. If Schuyler was going to delay Burgoyne, he would need those supplies.

The motley American fleet consisted mainly of the ships that had survived the action on Lake Champlain the year before, along with numerous bateaux and other boats. The ships consisted of the galleys

Trumbull and *Gates*, the schooner *Revenge*, and the sloops *Liberty* and *Enterprise*. These were equipped with varied ordinance ranging from 18- and 12-pounders to 9-, 6-, and 4-pounders, to swivel guns meant to repel boarders or as anti-personnel weapons in a close ship-to-ship fight.[47]

While Long's force was small, it was certainly capable of giving a good account of itself against Burgoyne's warships. When they sailed up the lake at 3:00 a.m., they were secure in the knowledge that the chain and log boom between Ticonderoga and Mount Independence would cut off any British water pursuit. There was, therefore, little sense of urgency, and the officers and men relaxed. The sun rose "with uncommon lustre," James Thacher recalled, and "the day was fine, the water surface serene and unruffled." Even as the harried passengers congratulated themselves on their narrow escape and pondered the hardships to come, they did what they could to raise their spirits. Military musicians "afforded us a favorite music," and several soldiers happily discovered wine in the cargo and "breaking off the necks we cheered our hearts with the nectareous contents."[48] Just how many soldiers were thoroughly "cheered" by the time the ships reached Skenesborough at about 3:00 p.m. on that hot, humid Sunday afternoon, Thacher did not say.

Skenesborough, in July 1777, was not the same bustling shipyard that had built Benedict Arnold's Valcour Island fleet only ten months earlier. By the time Colonel Long and his fellow Ticonderoga refugees arrived at the settlement, the town had diminished in importance. However, it was still a major supply center, boasting valuable mills and storehouses. The settlement was founded by former British Army officer and Loyalist Phillip Skene, who served in the area during the French and Indian War. Skene left the army, secured a land grant of 29,000 acres, and in the years leading up to the start of the American Revolution, turned the area into one of the most prosperous settlements in the region. He had become acquainted with Burgoyne in England, who gave him the honorary rank of colonel and brought him along on the 1777 campaign because of his local knowledge.[49]

Once Generals Fraser and Riedesel had set off in pursuit of St. Clair, Burgoyne turned his attention to the pursuit by water, sending his fastest warships after the Americans, accompanied by the 9th, 20th and 21st Regiments in bateaux. The commanding general himself followed in the *Royal George*, accompanied by the *Inflexible*. The ships made good time, and when the Americans landed at Skenesborough, Burgoyne and his fleet were only 2 miles behind.[50]

Surgeon Thacher recalled that they thought their immediate worries were over once they had landed at Skenesborough and were stunned to learn that the British fleet was right behind. The Americans had made no effort to establish a rear guard against a pursuit. One row galley, posted a few miles behind the rest of the flotilla to simply watch for the enemy, could have bought the Americans an hour or more. Because the channel approaching Skenesborough was so narrow, Lieutenant Hadden observed that the Americans "might have done great execution by leaving a Detachment on the shore to harass" any pursuers.[51]

Burgoyne landed his three regiments and a small group of Indians short of town. This small force then made its way through the woods over a high hill to the northeast of the town, intending to swing south of Skenesborough, blocking an American retreat to Fort Anne. As the Americans started to unload their ships, unaware of the rapidly approaching danger, the British infantry maneuvered their way around the settlement. They were spotted at almost the same instant Burgoyne's warships hove into sight. Recalled Thacher, "we were unsuspicious of danger, but behold! Burgoyne himself was at our heels." Some of the American troops kept their heads and "having previously prepared combustible materials, set fire to the fort, mills, storehouses, bateaux etc." Others panicked, and soon it was every man for himself. A few officers tried to rally the men but failed. Troops "were seen to fly in every direction," Thacher wrote, and officers gave up any idea of fighting and instead tried to rescue their personal effects, but with screaming Indians in hot pursuit, they dropped their belongings to save themselves.[52] The action lasted only 30 minutes, and casualties were light on both sides, but it was a humiliating defeat.

The Skenesborough action was hugely damaging to the Americans.[53] *Liberty* and the *Revenge*, both loaded with tons of critically needed gunpowder, were destroyed. The *Enterprise*, filled with provisions and baggage, was burned to the waterline. The other vessels and bateaux were either captured or destroyed, and their cargos seized. To make matters worse, twenty-eight more artillery pieces were captured, adding to the impressive quantities of ordnance taken at Ticonderoga.[54] "All our cannon, provisions, and the bulk of our baggage, with several invalids, fell into the enemy's hands," wrote Thacher.[55] Supplies sufficient to sustain the American Northern Army for weeks were now either destroyed or seized by the enemy.

The truth is that St. Clair's actions in the early morning hours of July 6 had laid the groundwork for Skenesborough. Since the

water evacuation was critically important, he should have sent more troops to guard the ships and to secure the cargo once they arrived at Skensborough. He should have sent one of his three general officers to take charge of the Lake Champlain retreat and to prepare Skenesborough to receive the main body. Burgoyne and his warships would not have been able to catch the American fleet had the Ticonderoga bridge and boom been covered with fire while the main body escaped. Long and the other American officers should have used their own initiative to protect the ships and cargo, both material and human, during their evacuation and upon landing at Skenesborough. In short, the action at Skenesborough exhibited a breakdown of leadership at every level. There was plenty of blame to go around.

As the Americans at Skenesborough fled south to Fort Anne, they were pursued by the 9th Regiment of Foot, commanded by Lieutenant Colonel John Hill. The headlong retreat, much of it in darkness, was a nightmarish experience for those who lived through it. The road to Fort Anne was little more than a rough country lane through deep woods crisscrossed with small streams, surrounded by heavy brush and tangled heaps of fallen trees. Fortunately for some survivors, a few of the smaller bateaux could navigate the meandering Wood Creek, which started near Fort Anne and emptied into Lake Champlain at Skenesborough and ran next to the Skenesborough-Fort Anne road. Those on foot were less lucky. They "were so closely pressed by the pursuing enemy, that we frequently heard calls from the rear to 'March on, the Indians are at our heels.'"[56] The survivors finally stumbled into Fort Anne at around 5:00 a.m. on July 7. The post, however, offered little in the way of sanctuary for the beleaguered Americans. One recalled that it was nothing more than a "mere block-house surrounded by palisades."[57] It seemed likely that the demoralized Americans would be incapable of defending themselves, let alone the fort.

Fortunately for the Americans at Fort Anne, Schuyler had sent a detachment of New York militia under Colonel Henry K. Van Rensselaer to reinforce the Skenesborough survivors. As Hill's Redcoats approached Fort Anne, the British commander reported to Burgoyne that the dispirited Americans were huddled at the fort and were ripe for the picking. Upon receipt of Hill's note, Burgoyne sent two regiments in support. Before they could arrive, however, Colonel Long regrouped his men and, using the terrain to their advantage, ambushed the British and Indian troops along the narrow road. The Americans heavily outnumbered the British and quickly

gained the upper hand. Hill, surrounded and preparing to pull back, was saved by two events: the Americans had begun to run out of ammunition, and a resourceful British officer faked a blood-curdling Indian war whoop, which induced the Americans "to give way and retreat," as Thacher later wrote.[58] Hill and his 9th Regiment had also had enough and promptly retreated all the way back to Skenesborough.

In this skirmish, the British lost thirteen killed, including one officer and a surgeon, and fifteen officers and soldiers wounded or captured. The American losses are uncertain, though Burgoyne reported that Hill captured "about thirty prisoners, some stores and baggage, and the colours of the second New Hampshire regiment."[59] Total American losses probably amounted to about two hundred killed, wounded, captured, and missing. After defeating Hill's little force, the Americans burned Fort Anne and retreated 15 miles farther south to Fort Edward on the Hudson River to join Schuyler and the rest of the army.

Burgoyne's decision to send only one regiment, particularly one that was understrength, to pursue the Skenesborough survivors did not escape criticism. Lieutenant Digby thought that Burgoyne should have sent in the 47th and 53rd Regiments, which were then at Skenesborough, to support Hill's 9th. Digby, who had seen how well-led Americans could fight at Hubbardton, was astonished at Burgoyne's overconfidence, which played into the hands of the enemy: "It has always been the wish of the Americans to avoid a general engagement, except when they have a great superiority, and to surround small parties of our Troops."[60] Although this was a fairly accurate assessment of American operational inclinations, the lieutenant was unfair to Burgoyne. He had seen firsthand all the confusion, panic, and total disarray among the Americans after being surprised at Skenesborough. The 9th Regiment had been available, and to seize the opportunity, Burgoyne immediately got them moving on the road to Fort Anne. Still, a larger force may well have been able to catch and destroy the Americans at Fort Anne. At the time, the skirmish seemed like a minor engagement, but it was a missed opportunity for Burgoyne.

Burgoyne's prospects, however, continued to look very good. From the time he began his approach to Fort Ticonderoga on June 30 until he consolidated his army at Skenesborough ten days later, he had accomplished a great deal. He had seized the "Gibraltar of North America," captured or destroyed tons of ordnance, gunpowder, food, clothing, and other provisions and stores, taken

hundreds of prisoners and destroyed or captured the remnants of the American Lake Champlain fleet. He had conducted an aggressive pursuit of St. Clair and his Ticonderoga garrison, forcing it far to the east and away from Schuyler and the rest of the Northern Army, causing widespread panic throughout the region. Fraser had suffered a bloody nose at Hubbardton, and Burgoyne had failed to complete the destruction of the Americans at Skenesborough, but all signs pointed to success. With most of the army gathered at Skenesborough, Burgoyne was now only about 35 miles north of Fort Edward and the Hudson River. Albany, the great prize, was now less than 75 miles away.

On Thursday, July 10, Burgoyne informed Germain of his victories at Ticonderoga, Hubbardton, and Skenesborough. He commended his officers and men and was particularly effusive in his praise for Fraser, who "by his judicious orders and spirited execution of them obtained a share for himself and his Troops in the glory of the Action." Burgoyne was thrilled over the quick succession of victories on July 6–8 and told his troops that they had done a "material service to the King" and had given a "signal honor to the profession of Arms."[61]

Burgoyne was right: the campaign had gotten off to a solid start. While he could expect the Americans to put up a defense, getting to Albany should be a simple proposition. However, Burgoyne was now faced with two tough decisions: how to reorganize and consolidate the army for future operations, and which route south to take that would best facilitate his movement to Albany. In London five months earlier, decisions like these looked straightforward. Now in the oppressive heat and humidity of an upstate New York summer, deep in the heart of enemy territory, seemingly straightforward choices were anything but clear-cut.

Burgoyne wrote another note, marked "private," to the secretary that same day, identifying some concerns. First, the Indian allies had turned out to be more trouble than they were worth. Unless they were strictly controlled, "enormities too horrid to think of would ensue; guilty and innocent, women and infants would be common prey." Although Burgoyne had originally planned to send the Native forces farther east to cut off American supplies and threaten New England, the enemy had gathered at Fort Edward. Hence, he decided instead to "employ their terrors that way" and perhaps later use them to move toward Connecticut. Despite the challenges, "I am confident of fulfilling the object of my orders." In fact, wrote Burgoyne, the quality of his army was so good that "my merit will be

small." Burgoyne was so confident in his ability to complete his part of the campaign that he concluded this letter to Germain with a request for leave upon arriving at Albany, saying that his constitution was "not fitted for an American winter." This was a bold request for a general in the middle of a campaign, though not necessarily one for an officer who was "in the fullest confidence."[62]

Thursday, July 11, was a busy day for Burgoyne at his Skenesborough headquarters. He met with his generals for the first time since the Americans had abandoned Ticonderoga. He also dashed off a letter to Howe with news of his victories, which only served to assure the commander-in-chief that he did not have to worry about Burgoyne's army.[63] He also wrote to Carleton, asking him to supply "from Canada a garrison for Ticonderoga." Because his lines of communication would be so long and "the drain upon the army for posts will be so considerable," Burgoyne argued, he would need all his troop strength. Anticipating Carleton's objections, Burgoyne maintained that since Ticonderoga lay on Lake Champlain, it could reasonably be considered "as the *frontier* of the province of Quebec" and thus was within Carleton's area of responsibility. Burgoyne urged him to use his initiative and send some of the three thousand soldiers held back for the defense of Canada to garrison Ticonderoga. Should Carleton garrison the fort, it would free up more than one thousand troops for Burgoyne to use on his campaign.[64] The fact that the two generals had not settled the garrisoning of Ticonderoga ahead of time was yet another planning failure.

Not surprisingly, Carleton refused Burgoyne's request, explaining that because of Germain's strict orders, it was not "left in my power to send any more troops out of the province." For one thing, Ticonderoga was clearly outside the boundaries of Canada. If Carleton's loathing of Germain was not obvious to Burgoyne before, there could be doubt now. "Whatever I may think of his lordship as an officer, and as a statesman, I must respect his office, and . . . he must be obeyed." His inability to properly support Burgoyne, Carleton assured him, was due solely to Germain's "private enmity and resentment."[65] In reality, there was little risk of an American invasion of Canada in the summer of 1777, and if there had been, it would be a relatively simple matter to recall soldiers sent to Burgoyne. Carleton would ultimately relent and provide troops to help man Burgoyne's outposts, but not enough to relieve the northern army from the responsibility to secure its lines of communications.

The exchange between Burgoyne and Carleton illustrated a major flaw with the 1777 British strategy: Who exactly did Burgoyne

General Sir Guy Carleton, by unknown artist (unknown date, probably late 18th century). Carleton's skillful defense saved Canada for Britain in 1776, but his personal and professional relationship with Lord Germain fell apart soon after. He would be the last British commander-in-chief during the American Revolution. Library and Archives Canada/Mabel Messer Collection.

Lord George Germain, by James McArdell (1777) after Sir Joshua Reynolds. As Secretary of State for the Colonies, Germain was responsible for devising and overseeing military strategy and operations in North America during the American Revolution. Yale Center for British Art, Yale University.

A View of Quebec from the Sout Heast, by Joseph F. W. Des Barres, engraver (1777). Library of Congress, LC-USZ62-447.

A north view of Crown Point c. 1759, by Thomas Davies (ca. 1759). Located only 10 miles north of Fort Ticonderoga, Crown Point was an important position for both sides during the 1776 and 1777 campaigns. Library of Congress, LC-USZ62-23831.

Frederick North, 2nd Earl of Guilford, by Nathaniel Dance (ca. 1773–1774). As King George III's prime minister, Lord North urged conciliation with the Americans in late 1777 and 1778. The king declined his offers to resign in the months after Burgoyne's surrender at Saratoga. © National Portrait Gallery, London.

King George III, by Benjamin West (1779). The king eagerly embraced Burgoyne's proposed military strategy for 1777, but he contributed to the confusion over how the competing plans unfolded in North America. Royal Collection Trust/© Her Majesty Queen Elizabeth II 2017.

Lieutenant General John Burgoyne, by Sir Joshua Reynolds (ca. 1766). Burgoyne's experience and expertise made him a logical choice to devise and execute a major portion of the British military strategy in 1777. An ambitious and confident career cavalry officer, he was well-liked by his soldiers. © The Frick Collection.

General Sir William Howe, Knight of the Bath, & Commander in Chief of his Majesty's forces in America, by Richard Purcell. Howe's strategy for 1777 was to seize Philadelphia and lure Washington into a decisive battle. He knew that defeating the rebel army was the only sure way to end the American Revolution. Courtesy Anne S. K. Brown Military Collection. Brown Digital Repository. John Hay Library, Brown University Library.

Major General William Phillips as a lieutenant colonel, by Francis Cotes (ca. 1764). A veteran artilleryman, Phillips acted as Burgoyne's second-in-command during the Saratoga campaign. Courtesy of the Council of the National Army Museum, London.

Major General Friedrich Adolph Riedesel, by Max von Eelking (1856), engraved by M. Lammel. Burgoyne had great respect for Riedesel, who commanded the left wing of his army. He had less regard for Riedesel's German soldiers. Courtesy of the Fort Ticonderoga Museum.

Brigadier General Simon Fraser, engraved by James Watson, after James Scouler (1778). A highly capable and experienced Scottish officer, Fraser commanded the Advanced Corps of Burgoyne's army. Courtesy Anne S. K. Brown Military Collection. Brown Digital Repository. John Jay Library, Brown University Library.

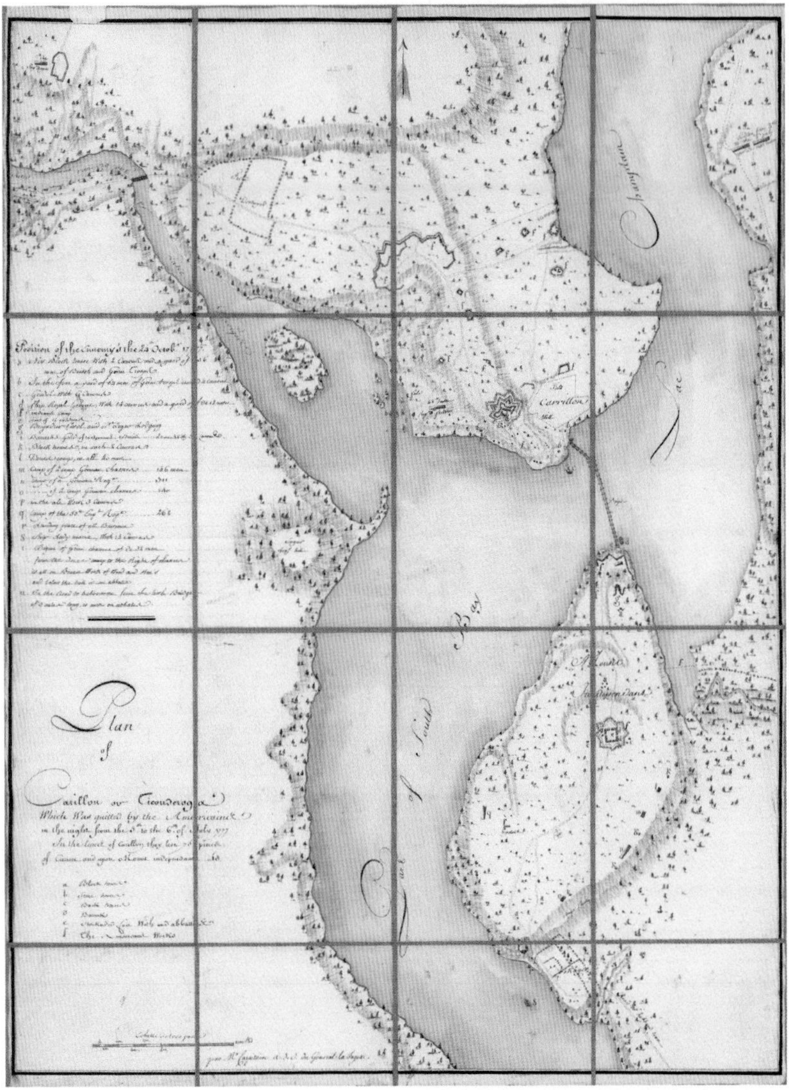

Plan of Carillon ou [sic] Ticonderoga: which was quitted by the Americaines in the night from the 5th to the 6th of July, by Capitaine Du Chesnoy, Michel, and Marie-Joseph Paul Yves Roch Gilbert du Motier Lafayette (1777). Library of Congress, Geography and Map Division.

Fort Ticonderoga from above Mount Defiance, Carl Heilman II, © Fort Ticonderoga.

A view of the Hudson River near Fort Edward, by William Guy Wall, engraved by John Hill (ca. 1821–1825). Burgoyne's soldiers were relieved to finally reach the Hudson River when they arrived at Fort Edward in late July 1777. Many remarked on the natural beauty of the countryside. Library of Congress, LC-DIG-pga-03811.

Frederike Charlotte Luise Riedesel (unknown artist and date) and her three children joined her husband midway through the campaign. Her letters and journal provide an important eyewitness account of Burgoyne's expedition. Library of Congress LC-DIG-pga-05513.

Joseph Brant or Thayendanegea (1742–1807), by Charles Willson Peale, from life (1797). Brant, through his familial ties to British officials in the Mohawk River Valley, was comfortable moving in both European and Native American circles, which gave him an edge as a military and political leader against the Patriots. Courtesy of Independence National Historical Park.

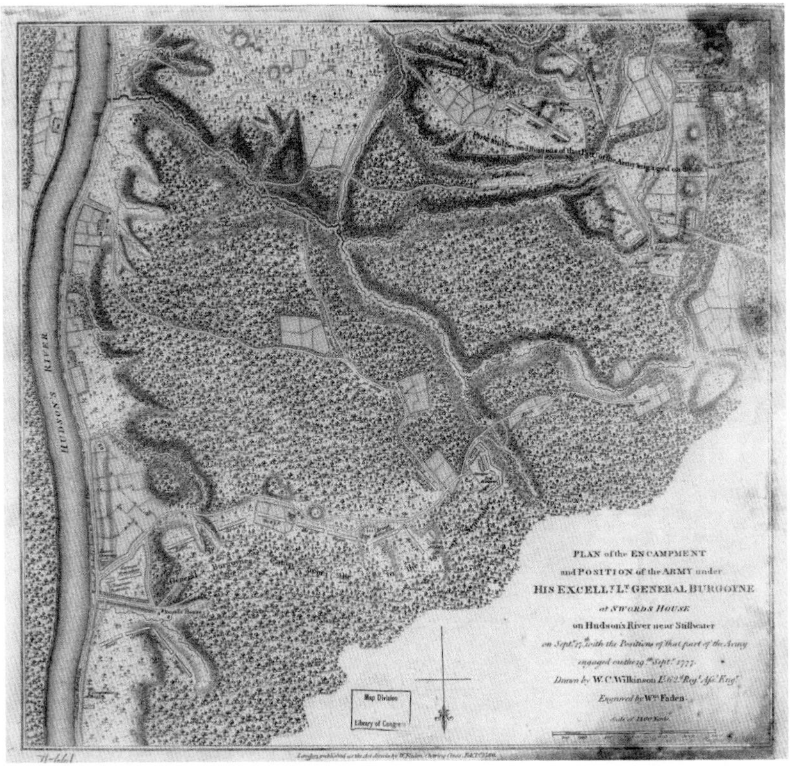

Plan of the encampment and position of the army under His Excelly. Lt. General Burgoyne at Swords House on Hudson's River near Stillwater on Septr. 17th with the positions of that part of the army engaged on the 19th Septr. 1777, by William Cumberland Wilkinson (1780). Library of Congress, Geography and Maps Department.

Lieutenant General Sir Henry Clinton in General Officers' Undress Uniform, by John Smart (ca. 1777). Clinton disagreed with General Howe's military strategy and attempted to assist Burgoyne with an offensive up the Hudson River in October 1777. He would replace Howe as commander-in-chief in 1778. Courtesy of the Council of the National Army Museum, London.

View near Fort Montgomery, by William Guy Wall, engraved by John Hill (ca. 1821–1825). This view gives some idea of the formidable terrain encountered by British soldiers when they attacked Forts Clinton and Montgomery in October 1777. Library of Congress, LC-DIG-pga-03822.

The Burial of General Simon Fraser after the Battle of Saratoga, 1777, by unknown artist, after the original by John Graham (ca. 1794). Courtesy of the Council of the National Army Museum, London.

Lieutenant General John Burgoyne (1722–1792), a study for a detail of *The Funeral of General Simon Fraser, who was shot after the action at Saratoga, October 7, 1777,* by John Graham (c. 1794). Courtesy of the Council of the National Army Museum, London.

A Picturesque View of the State of the Nation for February 1778, from the March 1, 1778, edition of *Westminster Magazine*. This cartoon satirizes the state of the British war effort after Saratoga and Howe's failure to destroy Washington's army. It shows the British cow being dehorned by an American with a Frenchman and Spaniard eagerly awaiting the spoils of fresh milk. The British lion is asleep while a dog urinates on him, and a distressed Englishman is observing it all. In the background is the city of Philadelphia with Lord Howe's flagship aground and the two Howe brothers at a table getting drunk. Library of Congress, LC-USZC4-5293.

Jeffrey Amherst, 1st Baron Amherst by Thomas Gainsborough (ca. 1785). In early 1778, Sir Jeffrey Amherst was the king's first choice to replace Howe as commander-in-chief because of his extensive experience in North America during the French and Indian War. Amherst was instrumental in devising the British post-Saratoga military strategy. © National Portrait Gallery, London.

work for, and according to what timeline? Howe was to take charge of Burgoyne's army once it reached New York, but the command structure of the two British theaters of operation in North America made this very difficult if not impossible. Howe and Carleton were temporarily promoted to full general in 1775 as independent theater commanders. Burgoyne and Sir Henry Clinton were likewise upgraded to lieutenant general, as seconds-in-command to Carleton and Howe, respectively. Per Germain's March 1777 orders, once Burgoyne left Canada, he came under Howe's command, except that Howe was on his way to Philadelphia and in no way capable—even had it been his inclination—to direct the northern army's operations. Howe's second-in-command, Clinton, left behind in New York City, and enjoying the same seniority and position as Burgoyne, did not have the authority, or the knowledge, to issue orders to the army from Canada.[66] That left Carleton and Burgoyne two options: either Carleton had to maintain command and control longer than he would normally have, or Burgoyne was on his own. This hopelessly jumbled command and control arrangement could only lead to confusion and frustration. Howe's April letter to Carleton had tried but failed to make this point.

On July 14, after days in the dark about the whereabouts of the Ticonderoga garrison, Schuyler could report to Washington that St. Clair had finally shown up just south of Fort Edward on the Hudson River. As noted, after the Skenesborough fiasco, St. Clair had been forced to take a circuitous route farther east to Rutland, then south and back west until he arrived at the Hudson River. With St. Clair's arrival, Schuyler now had about four thousand men at or near Fort Edward.[67] Yet even after the reunion, "the Greatest Confusion imaginable prevails here," Schuyler noted. He nonetheless promised to do his best with what he had. He advised Washington that he had sent a regiment into Vermont to drive away livestock and remove any ground transport that might prove useful to Burgoyne. In addition, General Nixon's newly arrived brigade was dispatched to reinforce other units felling trees across the road from Fort Anne to Fort Edward. Finally, Schuyler told Washington that he planned to evacuate Fort George and all its supplies. "Desertion prevails and Disease gains Ground . . . for we have neither Tents, Houses, Barns, Boards or any Shelter." It rained almost every day, and Schuyler wondered whether he would be able to mount an effective defense with his demoralized and poorly equipped troops.[68]

Washington questioned Schuyler's plan to evacuate Fort George to consolidate the Northern Department's forces farther south along

Burgoyne's probable route of march. He also assured Schuyler that the decision was his alone. But if he could hold Fort George, he would keep Burgoyne from crossing Lake George and "oblige him to take a much more circuitous & difficult Rout."[69] Washington's advice was prescient as Burgoyne's next major decision turned on Lake George's accessibility.

Two days after the Ticonderoga garrison arrived at Fort Edward, St. Clair offered to Congress—addressing John Hancock—his first official account of the evacuation. He made a vigorous and lengthy defense of his conduct and decisions. The "weakness of the garrison" and the fact that the "whole of the encampment, on the Ticonderoga side" was exposed to the fire of enemy batteries, had left him no alternative. " The Skenesborough action had forced him to change his retreat route and only after "a fatiguing march of seven days, in which the army suffered much from bad weather and want of provision," he made it to Fort Edward. Although Ticonderoga's loss might seem like a setback, St. Clair assured Hancock that "I may yet have the satisfaction to experience, that, altho' I have lost a post, I have eventually saved a state."[70]

Saving anything seemed a long way off. By July 11, Burgoyne had essentially consolidated the army at Skenesborough, an unforeseen outcome which was the result of the fall of Ticonderoga. Although Fraser's and Riedesel's units could have returned to Ticonderoga after the Battle of Hubbardton, Burgoyne had instead ordered them to march to Skenesborough, where the water chase had also concluded. The pursuit brought much of the rest of the army to Skenesborough. As Burgoyne settled into Phillip Skene's comfortable manor house, he confronted a decision that he had anticipated back in February, when he had argued that "the immediate possession of Lake George would be of great consequence as the most expeditious and most commodious route to Albany." However, should the enemy try to hold the lake, "the route by South Bay and Skeensborough may be attempted, but considerable difficulties may be expected."[71]

Now he was faced with the same choice, but for different reasons. Circumstances had put his army at Skenesborough, out of position for a move up Lake George. Burgoyne could use his abundant water transport to move the entire army back to Ticonderoga and then re-embark them on bateaux and transport them south on Lake George to continue the campaign. Or he could also resume the campaign from Skenesborough by marching overland up Wood Creek to Fort Anne, continuing on to Fort Edward and Albany beyond. This course

of action placed a premium on ground transportation, of which Burgoyne was critically short. He needed those horses and carts.

Both choices offered pluses and minuses. The Lake George option would require considerable labor to load up the army, sail back north to Ticonderoga, haul the boats overland to Lake George, then embark the troops and sail them up the lake to Fort George. However, the road network from Fort George all the way to Albany was fairly good. The overland route from Skenesborough had the advantage of being shorter and more direct, and the army would not have to retrace their steps to Ticonderoga before turning south. In addition to the transport shortage, and as Lieutenant Colonel Hill and his 9th Regiment discovered when they pursued the Americans retreating from Skenesborough to Fort Anne, the route along Wood Creek might be short, but it was anything but easy. Burgoyne decided to split the difference. He chose to move his artillery train and some bulky supplies over water from Ticonderoga to Fort George and the rest of the army overland from Skenesborough to Fort Anne to Fort Edward and then on to Albany.[72] He would now have to wait for the horses and wagons from Canada before he could proceed.

As he later explained, loading up and moving the army back to Ticonderoga would hurt morale and embolden the enemy. Plus, by going overland, he would cut off and isolate Fort George. The first belied his many reports describing the army's excellent morale. The second part of Burgoyne's justification, however, makes more sense. A move south from Skenesborough to Fort Anne and Fort Edward would soon put the army in Fort George's rear, rendering that post untenable. This saved him from having to besiege Fort George. Had he moved the entire army by water on Lake George, the Americans would have retained Fort George, leading to a costly siege and thus delaying his advance on Albany. By taking the "short cut" from Fort Anne to Fort Edward, however difficult, he could effectively dislodge the enemy from Fort George "without a blow." In addition, Burgoyne maintained, he wouldn't need the "great number of boats" that would have been necessary to transport troops and could instead be used to transport supplies and ammunition.[73] Thus, Burgoyne's decision reduced temporarily the requirement for land transport—at least until the army was ready to move.[74]

CHAPTER 8

Aftershocks

LIEUTENANT THOMAS BLAKE AND the rest of the First New Hampshire Regiment arrived at Fort Edward on July 12 after fleeing from their British and German pursuers for almost seven full days, during which, as Blake wrote in his journal, "we were almost without provisions, entirely without shelter, and the weather chief of the time was rainy."[1] Another New Hampshire officer thought, "Such a Retreat was never heard of since the Creation of the world."[2]

The New Hampshire soldiers were not the only ones traumatized by the loss of Fort Ticonderoga. The loss "lays open all New England to the incursions of the Enemy," declared Colonel Jonathan Trumbull, the Northern Department's paymaster. Schuyler was now desperately trying to prepare a stand against Burgoyne, but "if Running Comes into Vogue," he reported gloomily, "I know not where they may Stop." The only thing that could impede Burgoyne now was a massive militia turnout.[3]

Once Surgeon Thacher caught his breath after escaping the British pursuit, he reflected that letting go of Ticonderoga and Mount Independence "has given our cause a dark and gloomy aspect." As the remnants of the troops recovered at Fort Edward, the recriminations started, and some began to accuse St. Clair of treachery. Even General Schuyler, Thacher explained, "is not altogether free from public reprehension," even to the point of being accused along with St. Clair of being "traitors to their country" who were "paid for their treason by the enemy in *silver balls*, shot

from Burgoyne's guns into our camp." Thacher's silver bullet story demonstrates that conspiracy theories are not limited to modern times. The American troops were grasping for an explanation for what was to them inexplicable.[4]

Patriot newspapers reacted to the news with predictable outrage. The Boston *Independent Chronicle* saw the loss of Fort Ticonderoga as a wake-up for the cause: "A campaign is now opening, which may probably determine our fate." Ticonderoga was lost due to unaccountable neglect, or worse, "villainy and treason in its strongest colours."[5] Most everyone agreed that Burgoyne should never have been able to capture the fortress.

Philadelphia's *The Pennsylvania Packet* simply reported the news of the loss of Ticonderoga on July 15, though a week later, the paper published St. Clair's July 14 letter to Hancock, which led to sharp responses from the paper's readers. One letter writer dismissed St. Clair's litany of excuses and declared that if the general's actions "are not deserving of censure . . . I don't know what [are]." He asked the question many Americans had on their minds: would an English officer have acted as St. Clair did? Harkening back to the losses of the Manhattan forts a year before, the writer demanded, "Are we ever like to have our fortifications properly defended if such precedents pass, and such reasoning admitted in excuses?"[6]

The *Providence Gazette and Country Journal* was more optimistic. While the people were rightly "extremely uneasy" at the news about Ticonderoga, wrote the anonymous author: "The States have sufficient resources left and the success of the enemy there may finally turn out to their disadvantage." However, even if American arms overcame the loss of the fort, there simply could be "no good reason" that it should have been abandoned without a fight.[7] Since the French and Indian War, Americans had taken it at face value that Ticonderoga was impregnable and so the loss of the fort was simply inexcusable.

Congress felt the same way, starting with Hancock. The president of Congress was, further, baffled at the lack of information coming out of the Northern Department on the fate of St. Clair, "which is of such a Nature as to increase our apprehensions without removing our Suspense."[8] New Hampshire delegate Nathaniel Folsom spoke for many in Congress when he wrote that "the Loss of Ticonderoga considerably alarmed Congress as they were informed but a Little Time before by General St. Clair that it was in a good state of defence."[9] "No Event since the Commencement of the War has excited such Indignation and Astonishment," a Boston friend of John

Adams wrote, "as the Evacuation of Tyconderoga in so disgraceful a Manner!" He lamented, "How unhappy that the able experience'd Gates left the Command!"[10]

Samuel Adams agreed and used the unfortunate event to renew his objections to Schuyler's reinstatement to the command of the Northern Department. The fort's loss was bad enough, but Congress was also forced to "*guess* what is become of the *Garrison*." The remedy to their troubles was close at hand: "Gates is the Man of my Choice."[11] Additional "rueful" reports from Schuyler did little to assuage Adams. Like many other members of Congress, he had noted with dismay the demoralized tone of Schuyler's letters and hoped that the dreadful loss of Ticonderoga might just clear the way for Gates to return to his old post.[12]

Congress feared that the loss of Ticonderoga and, perhaps more importantly, how it was lost, would be an overwhelming diplomatic blow. The Americans had long pursued negotiations with European powers, especially the French, during which they sought military support and recognition of their independence. In these tense and prolonged diplomatic maneuverings, American negotiators realized that success on the battlefield was critical. The key to gaining French support and recognition was to demonstrate that America could win. One leader observed that "What vexes me most is the disgrace which the evacuation of such a strong-post will fix upon our arms, in Europe."[13] It was, therefore, with the greatest reluctance the Congress's Committee on Foreign Affairs informed the American commissioners at Paris "that we have lost Ticonderoga; whether by neglect or necessity, cowardice or good conduct."[14]

The American commissioners at Paris had a challenging task. Not only did they have to conduct sensitive negotiations, but they also had to handle day-to-day diplomatic tasks, such as caring for American citizens abroad, obtaining loans, coordinating shipping and material support for the war, and lodging protests with Britain about the treatment of American prisoners and sailors. The diplomatic delegation was led by seventy-year-old Benjamin Franklin, whose reputation was built on his scientific exploits as well as his political acumen. Franklin and his sometimes fractious colleagues, Silas Deane and Arthur Lee, worked tirelessly to handle all their responsibilities. Still, it was Franklin who was the key to the American commissioners at Paris. Arriving in Paris in December 1776, he worked for months to convince the French to recognize the fledgling country, but he was put off time and time again, as the French waited for just the right moment.[15]

Franklin dazzled the French court and Paris society. Women were drawn to him. They had never seen anyone quite like Franklin—diplomat, politician, philosopher, scientist, raconteur, and polymath—he was a sensation wherever he went. Befitting a representative from republican America, he always appeared in simple dress, even to the most formal events. His image adorned countless items of dress and everyday use "even (it was said) on an envious King Louis XVI's chamber pot."[16] In 1777, Franklin was probably the most famous man in the world, and this worked to his own and America's advantage. The Congress could not have sent a better representative. He was so effective that he drove his British counterparts in Paris to distraction, and their spies constantly reported on his activities.

Charles Gravier, the Comte de Vergennes, Louis XVI's Minister of Foreign Affairs and a capable career diplomat, was Franklin's main focus. For quite some time, Vergennes had supported covert aid to the rebelling colonies to weaken Great Britain. He wanted to restore France to its rightful place as the strongest European power, a position it had lost mainly due to British gains during the Seven Years War, and he saw the American rebellion as the best chance to do just that.[17] But the Americans wanted and needed more than only covert aid. Franklin was pushing for a formal treaty between the two nations, and, hopefully, Spain as well. Burgoyne's easy capture of Ticonderoga was a blow to those efforts, or so the Americans thought. When news reached Paris in late August, however, Vergennes's response was surprisingly restrained, and he urged caution and patience. In a letter to the Marquis de Noailles, French ambassador to Great Britain, the minister observed that the "capture of Ticonderoga is an event which must have caused the most agreeable sensation in England." However, "In order to give a sound opinion on the present position of the insurgents," he added, "we must await the sequel of General Burgoyne's operation." The swift capture of Ticonderoga will mean little to Burgoyne, Vergennes argued, if the British did not capitalize on their victory.[18] He concluded that unless Burgoyne moved swiftly, Ticonderoga's loss might not be as dire as the Americans imagined, nor as decisive as the British hoped.

The British saw Burgoyne's victory as essential to ensuring that France remained neutral in the American conflict. The British government was well aware that the Americans were actively lobbying the French to recognize the new nation openly; it simply could not afford an expansion of the war. Consequently, David Murray, Viscount Stormont, the British ambassador to France, had been the first to

tell Vergennes of Burgoyne's victory. On August 26, Stormont confirmed the "capture of Ticonderoga," for Vergennes and wrote that he was "persuaded of the interest you will be good enough to take in our success."[19] If the British expected a significant reaction, however, they were disappointed. Vergennes replied that the victory would "raise the very drooping hopes of the ministers." If General Howe was not moving north to cooperate with Burgoyne, the victory might be "of little importance" after all. Therefore, Vergennes concluded, they would have to see what Burgoyne did next.[20] This was not the answer the British government wanted to hear.

Not surprisingly, the reaction in England was much different. On Saturday, August 23, Germain received Burgoyne's July 11 letter announcing the capture of Fort Ticonderoga. The ecstatic secretary immediately informed the king of the glorious news.[21] This was the note that prompted the king's impromptu celebration in Queen Charlotte's chambers reported by Horace Walpole. Of course, the king and his loyal minister Germain could not know that in the six weeks that it took for Burgoyne's report to reach them, the situation in America had changed dramatically.

Many saw Burgoyne's capture of Fort Ticonderoga as confirmation that the 1777 military strategy was a war-winner. "Appearances cannot be more favorable than those of the success at Ticonderoga, which will I trust enable Burgoyne to get soon to Albany," declared the happy monarch, "and must put Washington into a most unpleasant situation." The king predicted the Americans would soon give up the fight.[22] General James Murray, a senior British Army officer, congratulated Germain after hearing Burgoyne's news and predicted the army's arrival at Albany with Howe in support "must open the eyes of the deluded, unshackle the constrained, and accomplish your most sanguine wishes without much bloodshed."[23] Just as Burgoyne believed when he wrote his July 11 letter, the decision makers in Britain also thought that the 1777 strategy was unfolding as planned.

Germain wasted no time publishing the entirety of Burgoyne's letter in a special edition of the *London Gazette*.[24] Walpole could not resist poking fun at the victorious general. In a letter to a friend written the day before the *Gazette* appeared, he announced that Burgoyne's message was the "counterpart to the *Iliad* in a nutshell!"[25] Walpole believed that Ticonderoga's capture had "given a new complexion to the aspect of affairs, which was very wan indeed." Despite the victory, Walpole was not at all confident in Britain's ultimate success: "In one thing alone all that come from America agree, that

the alienation from this country is incredible and universal." Even if Britain achieved a military victory, "the conquest would only entail boundless expense to preserve it."[26] Like the king and his ministers, however, the general population, weary of the two-year-long war against what many viewed as deluded fellow British citizens, were not as jaded as Walpole and thrilled at the news. To many, it meant that the end was in sight.

Germain delayed his reply to Burgoyne's July 11 letter for three weeks, hoping to receive more news. The secretary was not known for dispensing fulsome praise, but in his September 15 letter, Germain commended Burgoyne's "spirit and activity," which only confirmed "His Majesty's wisdom in appointing you to the command." Germain assured him of "the high opinion that His Majesty entertains of the services which you have rendered him." Also lauding Generals Riedesel, Phillips, and Fraser, Germain reminded Burgoyne that he must not "for a single moment lose sight of the grand point in view," and his progress must not be "either slackened or retarded."[27]

Despite the reaction from members of Congress to the loss of Ticonderoga, not all Americans were completely discouraged by the news. At army headquarters on July 13, Alexander Hamilton expressed the thoughts of many of his fellow Patriots, and probably also reflected the mood at headquarters, when he wrote, "We must not be discouraged by misfortune; we must rather exert ourselves the more vigorously to remedy the ill-consequences of it." Indeed, if St. Clair's lost garrison was recovered safely, it all might actually turn out to be a blessing in disguise. "I am in hope that Burgoignes success will precipitate him into measures that will prove his ruin. The enterprising spirit, he has credit for, I suspect, may easily be fanned by his vanity into rashness."[28]

After an initial burst of anger and frustration, John Adams accepted the news with surprising calmness and, like Hamilton, saw a potential opportunity in the disaster. While everyone was decrying the "Disgrace and Disaster," Adams reported to his wife, Abigail, from Philadelphia, that he for one, will "suspend my Judgment, until I know the Facts." Further, he hoped the people in Massachusetts would take heart, given that the British were being led by a "wild Man," who would "rush into some inconsiderate Measures" that would be to their advantage.[29] Nonetheless, Adams was still aghast that the Americans had lost yet another important fortified position, just like they had the Manhattan forts. "I think We shall never defend a Post, untill We shoot a General. After that We shall defend Posts."[30]

As noted, the loss of Fort Ticonderoga and the subsequent reverses suffered by the Northern Department shocked Washington. He was heartened to learn that St. Clair and most of the Ticonderoga garrison had successfully eluded their pursuers, but told Schuyler that the loss of the critically important post was beyond "the Compass of my reasoning." How a garrison of almost five thousand men could have abandoned the fort was simply baffling.[31] He was perhaps most worried about the effect on Schuyler and, indeed, the entire Continental Army. In an obvious attempt to help his general revive his fighting spirit, Washington noted that despite recent events, which "have a dark and gloomy Aspect," he hoped that a combination of Schuyler's defense and Burgoyne's overconfidence would play in their favor. They had no choice but to move on. "We should never despair." He reminded Schuyler that American military affairs had been in dire straits before, and circumstances had always "changed for the better." Schuyler and his officers and men had to do whatever it took to succeed, urged Washington, "If new Difficulties arise, we must only put forth new Exertions and proportion our Efforts to the Exigency of the Times."[32] The commander-in-chief focused his considerable talents on trying to reverse Schuyler's gloom and low morale, but Washington rightly worried that his subordinate's defeatism was infecting his army.

CHAPTER 9

Burgoyne Moves South

SOLDIERS IN ALL ARMIES in all ages are known for grumbling, and even a string of victories did not insulate Burgoyne from criticism. Some in the army questioned his decision to move the main army overland from Skenesborough to Fort Anne and then on to Fort Edward and the Hudson River. Lieutenant Digby had even questioned the army's movement to Skenesborough in the first place, for they had gained nothing from Fort Anne or Hubbardton "except proving the goodness of our troops at the expense of some brave men." Instead of waiting for the horses and carts from Canada, Digby explained, they should have pushed immediately on Fort George from Ticonderoga. Had they done so, they could have captured everything they needed from the disorganized and dispirited Americans. Instead of keeping the pressure on the rebels, the delay at Skenesborough was allowing the Americans to regroup. Still, the young lieutenant reasoned, Burgoyne must have "had his proper reasons for so acting though contrary to the opinion of many."[1]

It wasn't yet clear to the soldiers what Burgoyne's reasons were. The route from Skenesborough to Fort Anne to Fort Edward was about 22 miles, but it was also little more than a primitive track through the wilderness, and not nearly as substantial as the road between Fort George to Fort Edward. The route crossed numerous marshes and creeks, made virtually impassable due to recent heavy rain, and ran through dense forest filled with thick undergrowth. A man on foot would find it difficult to negotiate, let alone an army encumbered

with hundreds of carts filled with heavy cargo and the animals needed to pull them. In addition, hundreds of camp followers accompanied the army, including more than three hundred women and children, among them Lady Harriet Acland, wife of Major John Acland, and, joining the army later, Frederike Charlotte Riedesel and her three children.[2] Inevitably, they slowed the army down. Burgoyne sent the artillery and the heaviest stores up Lake George, but the rest of the army still had to haul the tons of provisions and baggage along the overland route, forcing them to build bridges "not only over creeks, but over ravines and gullies."[3] Plus, they had to contend with the obstacles Schuyler's men had constructed along Wood Creek north and south of Fort Anne.

Thus, Burgoyne's invading army had to transform a country track into a major road.[4] These challenges, combined with the usual biting insects that plagued the region in July and August, meant that the march south was a thoroughly miserable experience. Insects were not the only menacing fauna. The "country round Skeensborough swarms with rattle snakes," wrote one officer, "the bite of which, I believe, is mortal."[5] Heat, rain, rugged terrain, baggage, civilians, bugs, reptiles, and enemy activity all combined to slow Burgoyne's army. The movement south from Skenesborough was turning out to be one of the most challenging features of the campaign for Burgoyne and his men.

Lieutenant Digby and his friends were not the only British officers to question the commanding general's decisions. Lieutenant Hadden, who had been involved in the water pursuit of the Americans to Skenesborough, criticized the decision to abandon Fort Anne after chasing the Americans from that small fort; consequently the rebels "were the real gainers by this affair." The fort itself was inconsequential, but when the British troops retreated back to Skenesborough, they had allowed the Americans to return to the area and emplace obstacles, "The clearing of which cost the Army much labour and time." Had they held on to Fort Anne, they could have prevented this American mischief. Moreover, while the Americans may have been dispirited after their defeats, they seemed to be everywhere along the route—"always keeping near enough to prevent our sending out small detachments."[6] The two young British officers and their colleagues had assessed the situation very well even before the army started moving south from Skenesborough. Had Burgoyne ordered the occupation of Fort Anne immediately after the action on July 8, they might have reduced their overall effort by almost 50 percent. As it was, the British would not occupy Fort Anne until July 25, more

than two weeks after they had left it. Burgoyne's decision to move the army's main body overland, while understandable, had significant implications.

While Burgoyne was preparing his army for their dual movements south toward Albany, Schuyler was desperately appealing to neighboring states for militia assistance to delay them. One of the first states to respond to the loss of Ticonderoga was New Hampshire. Though it already had many troops assigned to the fort's garrison, it immediately pledged additional resources. To lead the effort to protect the state's frontiers, the New Hampshire Court appointed John Stark brigadier general of the New Hampshire militia. Stark, a New Hampshire native, was already a seasoned campaigner. He had fought with the legendary Roger's Rangers during the French and Indian War, and as commander of a New Hampshire regiment at the battles of Bunker Hill, Trenton, and Princeton. He had quit the service after Princeton over a promotion dispute. With Burgoyne's army threatening New York and New England, Stark's leadership and experience was vital. He accepted his new appointment, though only with the understanding that he be independent of the Continental Army and any of its officers.[7] Stark's insistence on an independent command freed him to use his own judgment to raise, organize, and fight his militia units. This proved an effective recruiting tool. Only six days after Stark's appointment, fifteen hundred men had joined the ranks, due largely to the reputation of their leader.[8] However, an independent Stark could also hinder the ability of Schuyler, and even Washington, to convince him to cooperate with other operations.

In the two weeks between July 11 and July 24, when the army was ready to move on, Burgoyne mustered the majority of his units at both Skenesborough and Castleton, 14 miles to the east, while gathering supplies for the upcoming offensive and feigning a movement into Connecticut. In addition, he garrisoned Ticonderoga to protect his line of communication back to Canada, and directed the arduous movement of the artillery across Lake George. Keeping the pressure on Schuyler was vital, and thus the two-week delay—however important the reasons—critical. Some historians argue that the luxury-loving general was simply too comfortable in his headquarters at Phillip Skene's roomy mansion, an oasis in the American wilderness.[9]

More likely, Burgoyne, having maneuvered deep into enemy country while commanding his first independent operation, simply wanted to make sure every detail was addressed before advancing. He also underestimated the enemy and the difficulties involved in

campaigning in this part of North America. While at Skenesborough, Fraser suggested that his commanding general was frustrated by the myriad challenges he faced. "Our Genl is really a fine agreeable manly fellow, but hates lines of resistance when they interrupt his projects, and they will occur here frequently."[10] The trials that went hand in hand with commanding the second largest British Army in North America, an army that was out of supporting distance from any other friendly force, had suddenly become very real.

After Burgoyne ordered an army-wide cannon and musket salute celebrating their victories, accompanied by a "threefold hurrah," British forces started work on the road from Skenesborough to Fort Anne. On the 14th, the portage of the transport vessels from Lake Champlain to Lake George began. Other groups scoured the area for every horse, ox, and wagon they could find. They found very little of use, though were heartened by the arrival of the first batch of 124 horses contracted from Canada.[11] It was still far short of army requirements, but it was a start.

Riedesel's Germans guarded the army's left flank near Castleton. This was mainly to protect them from Colonel Seth Warner's Vermonters, who, after recovering from the mauling at Hubbardton, probed Burgoyne's positions from the east to gather intelligence. After Hubbardton, the largest portion of Warner's regiment had retreated to Manchester, while the rest ultimately moved to Fort Edward. Warner assumed command of the Vermont militia stationed at Manchester and reported to Schuyler that he was ready to conduct operations again. Schuyler told Warner that the British would almost certainly come by way of Fort George rather than Skenesboro. To complicate life for Burgoyne, Warner was directed to find and secure all the carriages and cattle that he could. He was also to round up Tories and send them to "the interior of the country." "Be vigilant," cautioned the general, "A surprise is inexcusable." Schuyler knew that he could not allow Burgoyne to live off the land, so Warner had to focus on countering enemy foraging efforts. "If we act vigorously, we save the country," Schuyler assured Warner, "Why should we despond?"[12]

At Schuyler's urging, Warner appealed to New Hampshire for additional militia, arguing that with three thousand Germans at Castleton, they needed as many troops as possible to "defend this post against any force which the enemy may bring against it."[13] Over the subsequent two weeks, Warner and his men gave Riedesel's Germans fits by harassing Loyalists and conducting raids against small German units. Soon a frustrated Riedesel had had enough and

proposed to Burgoyne that he conduct a major raid into Vermont to punish the rebels and collect supplies. Given that the army was getting ready to move, the commander-in-chief refused. Riedesel would have to be content with sending small detachments "to maintain the enemy's respect in some shape or manner."[14]

Even Warner's best efforts could not prevent all of the enemy foraging activities. On July 21, for example, a small detachment of Braunschweig troops accompanied by "20 friendly Provincials" advanced to within one mile of the rebel camp and seized sixty oxen from under Warner's nose.[15] Such audacious operations were few and far between, however. Although Riedesel's request to mount a major raid into Vermont to seize livestock, horses, oxen, and wagons was put aside for the moment, Burgoyne filed it away for future reference.[16]

Underpinning Burgoyne's and Germain's planning assumptions for the 1777 campaign was the assumption that the region's Loyalists would flock to the British Army and provide any assistance it might require. To help facilitate this support, on July 10, Burgoyne issued a proclamation to the population surrounding Castleton, ordering them to "send deputies, consisting of 10 persons or more from each township" to Riedesel's camp to take an oath of allegiance. When Schuyler learned of this order, he issued a counter-proclamation, forbidding any town to send delegates to the gathering.[17] When four hundred Castleton residents showed up on July 16 near the German base, it looked as if Burgoyne had won the propaganda war. As Phillip Skene, acting as the Crown's senior civilian representative, prepared to administer the oath to these valuable new allies, he found to his disgust that "very few" agreed to it and that most "wished to observe complete neutrality." One witness concluded that instead of a countryside teeming with Loyalists, "3/4 of all the inhabitants of New Hampshire are Rebels."[18] This may have been an exaggeration, but Burgoyne and Germain had nonetheless grossly overestimated the number of Tories in the region, and many Loyalists who did live there were unwilling to offer assistance.[19]

Lack of Loyalist support was not the only disappointment for Burgoyne. His Indian allies were a continual source of frustration. While they provided some intelligence and had terrorized American soldiers, along with the local population, they had not prevented Schuyler's men from obstructing the road from Skenesborough to Fort Edward. They also had not stopped the periodic American raids on Burgoyne's troops working to clear and improve the road. And they had not kept Colonel Warner's men at bay. Carleton's warning

about counting on Indians to play an integral part of the campaign seemed prescient. Despite all of Burgoyne's efforts to control them, the warriors had started to commit atrocities. He began to receive reports of the murder and scalping of civilians and captives, which the commanding general had strictly forbidden at the Bouquet River assembly. Shortly after the fall of Ticonderoga, one incident took place when an American deserter attempted to give himself up to the British and German forces working near the fort. Before he could surrender, he was seized by Indians who "bound the young man hand and foot and wanted to scalp him." Fortunately for the captive, British and German soldiers rescued him. When the incident was reported to Burgoyne, he "again reiterated his orders against scalping [captives], which he had given more than a few times before."[20] Now that the army was stationary for more than two weeks, the Indians had few opportunities for action or looting, and were restive. The number of atrocities soared.

As Burgoyne's warriors became increasingly erratic, Indian arrived at Skenesborough on July 17, saluting the "camp with their shots, and soon afterwards, we heard their horrible cries."[21] It was a sizeable contingent, although accounts vary widely—between four hundred to eighteen hundred warriors.[22] Warriors from several tribes comprised the detachment, all nominally under the control of Chevalier St. Luc de la Corne and Charles Michel de Langlade. Saint Luc, at age sixty-six, was a highly successful and experienced fur trader and merchant. He had developed a good relationship with Native American tribes from the Saint Lawrence River to beyond Lake Superior. He had also served in the French and Indian War against the Americans and British, but now he worked for his former enemy against the rebels.[23] Langlade's military experience was similar to that of Saint Luc's in that he had led warriors during the late war and, like his elder colleague, had switched his loyalty.[24] Saint Luc and Langlade, but especially the elder Frenchman, were perhaps two of the most hated men in New York and New England, and what happened next would solidify their reputations.

Burgoyne welcomed the new arrivals with open arms, because, unlike the warriors already with his army, this new group "are more warlike and less rapacious" and were led by the able Saint Luc.[25] The tribes represented in the new group included Fox, Seneca, Chippewa, and Tuscarora, but it was the Mohawks and Ottawas who really impressed Burgoyne's troops. A Braunschweig surgeon observed that the Mohawks "are very warlike and also the most dangerous of all the Savage nations." The Indians who had joined the

army in Canada "stepped aside in fear while looking at them with frightened eyes."[26]

Burgoyne reprised his Bouquet River assembly and spoke to the new arrivals on July 19, officially welcoming them "into the service of the King." Under a decorative arbor, the eldest chief addressed Burgoyne, urging the general to "Speak, and we will obey." Replying in French, Burgoyne explained that the Americans were "disloyal and unfaithful" to the king and had "engulfed several provinces in war where peace and quiet used to reign." This was why, said the general, "the brave Mohawks and other nations have been called to act in concert and to lead these monsters back to obedience." Burgoyne reminded them that the king wished to punish them but also be merciful. Therefore, the Indians were free to "scalp those whom you have killed in battle and treat them as you are wont," but Burgoyne forbade them to "practice this on any prisoner or wounded," promising a bounty for live prisoners. No harm must come to the elderly or women and children. The Indians "showed their approval by emitting a sound with all their strength," described as a loud groan by Lieutenant Digby.[27]

Even with this Indian reinforcement, Burgoyne was still short of the number he wanted, but it was as many as he was going to get. One of the last pieces of the puzzle was now in place. As soon as the work on the road to Fort Anne was completed and sufficient supplies stockpiled and transport secured, he could finally give the army the order to march.

Idle troops inevitably lead to discipline problems. With the chronic transport shortage, Burgoyne ordered officers to reduce their personal baggage, and he forbade them to appropriate scarce carts for personal use. He had to reissue the order more than once since many officers ignored it.[28] Enterprising local inhabitants took the opportunity to make some extra money by selling alcohol to the soldiers. The officers, who enjoyed their own private stock of spirits, moved quickly to stamp out this illegal trade. Fraser issued a general order on July 17 in which he reprimanded his men for their "licentiousness" after they had acquitted themselves so well at Hubbardton. He reminded the men that "no Exertion of Courage or Labour" could trump discipline and "order, which constitutes the real honour of the Soldier." The no-nonsense brigadier then charged the officers to enforce discipline and to expel from camp any "Woman, who promotes Intemperance among the Men." Access to alcohol and the relatively easy duties during the long delay at Skenesborough led to numerous fights between German and British

troops. This came to a head the day before the great Indian assembly when Burgoyne scolded the soldiers for these incidents, which had been "occasioned by Liquor." Any repeat of these clashes "between the two Nations," warned Burgoyne, "will be punished as a Crime."[29] The army's fine edge was being dulled by inactivity as they lingered at Skenesborough.

On Wednesday, July 23, Burgoyne was finally ready to resume the campaign and move the army toward Fort Anne and, ultimately, to Albany. Another ninety-eight horses arrived from Canada on July 19 and 20. The army was still short, but the general could wait no longer.[30] As usual, Fraser's troops led the way, with parties of Indians serving as the corps' vanguard. As the army's eyes and ears, the advanced corps was charged with protecting the main body from surprise in the event of enemy contact. Fraser had to quickly assess any situation he encountered and react accordingly. It was a challenging task, but one that was perfectly suited to the experienced professional.

Despite the extensive preparations over the previous two weeks, the movement from Skenesborough to Fort Anne was tough going both on the road and Wood Creek. The Americans constructed obstacles faster than the British and Germans could clear them. Because of the trees the Americans had felled over Wood Creek, complained Digby, the army was "obliged to cut a road through the wood, which was attended with great fatigue and labour, for our wagons and artillery."[31] The rainy weather turned the road into a muddy morass. The boots of hundreds of marching troops and the wheels of the heavy carts and the hooves of horses and oxen sank deep into the mud, and with the passage of every animal, soldier, and wagon, the road deteriorated. Although Fort Anne was less than 15 miles from Skenesborough, it took the army more than two days to cover the distance. Parties of Indians attacked and scattered a group of American soldiers, killing and wounding nineteen. At Fort Anne, the sweat-soaked, exhausted soldiers of Fraser's corps discovered the unburied bodies of several British soldiers who had been killed during the action on July 8 and left behind in the wake of the 9th Regiment's hasty withdrawal. The decomposing corpses, "which caused a violent stench," was a reminder of the dangers they all faced.[32] After their two-week respite at Skenesborough, the condition in which they found their comrades once again drove home the harsh realities of war.

While Burgoyne made the final preparations to reach Albany, Washington was seeking a clear picture of what was happening in

the Northern Department. As he marched the main army toward the Hudson River, he told Hancock that he had "no doubt but the Militia from the Western parts of New England will turn out to Genl Schuyler's Assistance."[33] Although happy to learn that St. Clair and most of the Ticonderoga garrison had made their way to Fort Edward, he was incensed by the conduct of the officers and soldiers in the Northern Department and their unrelenting tales of woe. Washington did all he could to assist Schuyler, but as commander-in-chief, he also had to counter the movements of Howe's main force, which is why he had moved the army to the east. From there, he could support Putnam's force at Peekskill, should Howe attempt to support Burgoyne, or to the south and west, should Howe move on Philadelphia.[34] A wrong move could cost him the war.

As Schuyler frantically tried to obstruct Burgoyne's path, St. Clair found time to write a long apologia to the commander-in-chief, in which he repeated all the old excuses for not holding Ticonderoga: he had been outnumbered, outmaneuvered, and his council of war was unanimous for evacuation. He blamed Congress for suggesting that "no serious Attempt in that Quarter was intended" by the British Army. He reminded the commander-in-chief that he had never asked him for help, "as your Operations might thereby be rendered less vigorous; and I know too that you could very ill spare them."[35] St. Clair would not receive the absolution from Washington that he so fervently craved. The commander-in-chief never answered his letter.[36]

Anticipating Burgoyne's movement, on July 17, Schuyler began preparing entrenchments on favorable ground 4 miles south of Fort Edward at a place called Moses Creek. Riders left Schuyler's headquarters daily with frantic demands for Washington. The commander-in-chief expressed astonishment at one request for horses since there were so many in the Northern Department already. Schuyler agreed with Washington's assessment, while also complaining that the horses he did have could not pull carriages in pairs. Despite Schuyler's best efforts, few Vermonters had joined the army. Given that so much Toryism prevailed in the area, Burgoyne could "march as far as Bennington, in order to procure Cattle & Carriages."[37] One month later, Schuyler's prediction would prove to be remarkably accurate.

Schuyler was making some sensible decisions as he slowly moved the army south in the face of Burgoyne's advance, though that was not the signal received by Washington and Congress. He had evacuated and destroyed Fort George and strewn obstacles in Wood Creek. He

also ordered Colonel Kosciuszko to take charge of two brigades to construct obstructions on all the roads the enemy might use, delaying Burgoyne's advance.[38] Indeed, if it was not for his inability to project confidence and competence to his superiors, Schuyler had demonstrated a surprising degree of grip in the weeks after the loss of Ticonderoga.

Washington still hoped that once Schuyler and his army had recovered a bit, they would counter Burgoyne "in a Country which, I am informed, is very strong by nature."[39] To that end, he sent as many reinforcements as he could spare, but the problem was that he could detect little indication that Schuyler was up to the challenge. Washington remained concerned with Schuyler's state of mind. Schuyler always "represents matters in a distressing point of view," Washington admitted to Hancock while hoping things were "not so alarming as they are painted by him." He told the president of the Congress that he was rushing additional powder and shot to Albany to replace some of that lost at Ticonderoga and that Arnold was on his way. Once Arnold arrived, "I flatter myself, his presence and assistance in that Quarter, will be attended with happy consequences."[40] Unspoken was Washington's belief that Arnold would instill some sorely needed backbone in Schuyler as well as in the army.

Washington warned Schuyler that Arnold believed that he should be senior to St. Clair, but he was willing to set aside his claims should they have to act in unison against Burgoyne. Further, Washington reminded Schuyler that "the well known Activity Conduct & Bravery of General Arnold," will endear him to "The Eastern Troops in particular."[41] Washington could tell that Schuyler needed help with the New England militia.[42] Soon yet another Schuyler report came in. He agreed with Washington's earlier admonition that they needed to do whatever they could against the challenges facing them but also warned him about the "true State" of things. He claimed that he had "neither dispaired or desponded" in his previous letters to Washington.[43]

Schuyler never seemed to grasp the extent of outrage over Ticonderoga's loss, and how his post-evacuation letters were being received at army headquarters and in Philadelphia. He commanded not a regiment but an entire department and an army, one that was directed by both Congress and Washington. Schuyler commanded one of the two major armies of the United States. In addition to his army, Schuyler had many more constituencies—Congress, Washington, the army, local and state governments, militia units, and the surrounding population. As a senior leader, he had to

project assurance that he was able to handle any contingency. He had a duty to keep his superiors informed about his requirements and situation, of course. Nonetheless, his letters to Washington and Congress instead suggested an officer who was in over his head and who at times seemed on the verge of panic. Had Schuyler displayed more self-assurance under pressure, he might have kept his job. But by the time Burgoyne started to move south from Skenesborough, Congress and Washington were already losing confidence in their northern commander.

On July 20, as the letters between Schuyler and Washington passed each other on their way back and forth between their respective headquarters, the Northern Department's generals met in a council of war. Schuyler knew that Burgoyne's army would finish their preparations and "visit us soon." He was still short New Hampshire militia, he maintained, and those he did have were "extremely uneasy at being detained here in the very Time of Harvest." He had a force of 4,661, plus an additional 1,600 militia, to face Burgoyne.[44] To retain at least some of the militia with the main army, Schuyler and his generals decided to allow half of them to return home for the fall harvest. Despite this generous—overly generous considering the military situation—decision to release more than eight hundred militia, Schuyler glumly predicted that he wouldn't retain a quarter of those remaining.[45] American militia required careful handling and an appreciation of their abilities and limitations. Indeed, working with the militia was not unlike fighting with a coalition partner: differences in equipment, leadership, training, tactics, and objectives could easily lead to friction. In general, militia could only be called out for local or regional emergencies and for relatively short periods of time. Otherwise, they might not respond to future crises. As Schuyler was painfully aware, counting on militia during harvest season was problematic, even in emergency conditions.

While Schuyler and his generals dealt with their militia, Burgoyne continued his advance south. On July 25, Fraser's advanced corps occupied Fort Anne and began moving toward Fort Edward. Lieutenant Digby and his fellow soldiers were getting heartily sick of the New York wilderness and the American ability to slow the army's advance. On the first days' march, they only managed 6 miles, "the road being broke up by the enemy." The next day's march was not much better. As the British approached, Schuyler pulled the army back away from Fort Edward and toward Fort Miller, but "it was not thought they intended to make a stand," Digby wrote.[46] By July 28,

Schuyler had established his headquarters at Saratoga, on the west bank of the Hudson, as his weary army prepared to make a stand somewhere along the road to Albany.[47]

Finally, on July 30, twenty-four days after marching unopposed into Fort Ticonderoga, the army from Canada emerged from the deep woods onto the banks of the Hudson River, one mile above Fort Edward. The men rejoiced as they made camp "on a beautiful situation from whence you saw the most romantic prospect of the Hudson's river."[48] In their trek to the fort, they began to encounter more small settlements and scattered farms and saw that "the corn in most fields is all ready for the harvest." Fort Edward itself was not a great prize. Once a handsome post, the fort, like many on the New York frontier, had fallen into disrepair and the British found that the "outworks are in a ruinous condition as well as the body of the fort."[49] They had been delayed by the annoying Americans to be sure, but in the end, the enemy's efforts to stop them would be about as effective as the swarms of insects they had endured. Now that they were on the Hudson, Albany was less than 50 miles away. Success seemed assured.

Nine days earlier, around the time Fraser's corps was preparing to depart Skenesborough for Fort Anne, Arnold had reported to Schuyler at Fort Edward. When the army pulled back, he left a message for Burgoyne nailed to a tree, which warned, "Thus far thou go and no farther." The British viewed the letter as nothing more than bluster from a beaten enemy. Despite the increasing logistical challenges facing the army as it penetrated farther into Patriot territory, morale was high.[50] By Wednesday, July 30, almost the entire British Army had reached Fort Edward, when General Phillips arrived with the heavy artillery that had been moved by water on Lake George and then on the good roads from Fort George to Fort Edward.[51]

While some horses had, as we've seen, arrived from Canada, Burgoyne's army still suffered from severe shortages of ground transport, both in oxen and horses and in carts, wagons, and carriages, so the logistical situation remained precarious. If they could move quickly to Albany without encountering significant resistance, all would probably be well. If not, they might be in trouble. As he had at Skenesborugh, Burgoyne now called for another lengthy halt at Fort Edward, to amass enough provisions to maintain the army as it continued south. Given Schuyler's steady retreat in the face of Burgoyne's advance—and all indications pointed to an American retreat all the way to Albany—this seemed like a prudent move.[52]

Once Burgoyne had stockpiled the provisions at Fort Edward and Fort Miller, he could recall the men securing his supply line from Skensborough and Ticonderoga and push on.

Upon arrival at Fort Edward, Burgoyne dispatched another report to Germain, his first since July 11. The enemy had steadily retreated, avoiding battle, but there had been constant skirmishing with rebel detachments "without any loss to the regulars." The Americans, on the other hand, had lost "almost three hundred men." The march to Fort Edward was not easy, Burgoyne wrote, as the Americans had dropped large trees on both sides of the road "so as to fall across and lengthways with the branches interwoven."[53] In an accompanying private letter to Germain, Burgoyne dismissed the American efforts to delay his advance as "an act of desperation and folly." While the rebel activities "retard me for a time," he wrote, they "cannot finally impede me." Burgoyne had heard nothing whatever from General Howe, despite sending ten messages. "I am in total ignorance of the situation or intentions of that general," making no mention of Howe's April 5 letter. He learned that the Americans had sent a large corps up the Mohawk River to oppose St. Leger. Still, he was confident he would make it to Albany in good time to assist his supporting force and catch the Americans between two friendly armies.[54]

To support St. Leger—instead of the other way around, as called for in the original plan—Burgoyne had to move quickly to Albany. Nothing in either letter to Germain indicated that he was worried in the least he couldn't do this unaided. He did not discuss his logistical challenges and mentioned Howe only in passing. This was not the communication of a commander entertaining worry or doubts but of a general certain of his ability to accomplish his mission.

CHAPTER 10

The Ordeal of Philip Schuyler

AS CONFIDENT AS BURGOYNE was of success, his opponent was anything but. During Burgoyne's advance south, Schuyler and Washington kept up their correspondence, with the commander-in-chief trying to prop up his dispirited subordinate. On July 22, Washington had approved Schuyler's previous efforts as "certainly right and judicious." He urged Schuyler to keep faith. "I trust General Burgoyne's Army will meet, sooner or later an effectual Check."[1] On the same day, Schuyler told Washington that instead of the sixteen hundred militia he had previously reported, he had fewer than one thousand, and many of those were leaving. If he were not heavily reinforced, "I leave your Excellency to reflect on what will be the Consequences." Burgoyne had a "superior Body of Troops; well disciplined, flushed with Victory: daily augmenting with Tories, with plenty of Military Stores." The Americans, on the other hand, were "few naked, dispirited, ill provided Troops." Without a significant increase in numbers, there was nothing to stop Burgoyne, and if the enemy continued to Albany, they would be met there by St. Leger's detachment, along "with the whole of the Indians in the six Nations."[2] The next day, Schuyler reported more militia defections. He had only about three hundred remaining and was "morally sure most of these will run off." He also complained that he could not move his cannon, that Indians were harassing his units, and the Berkshire militia had dwindled from twelve hundred to only three hundred men.[3] There was one bright spot: Arnold had arrived.

Schuyler had decided to split his army into two divisions, with St. Clair commanding one and Arnold the other. Still, if he entertained any hopes that the two men would work well together, they were dashed almost immediately. Just days after Arnold joined the army, the two division commanders exchanged heated words over Arnold's sharp criticism of St. Clair's generalship at Ticonderoga. When St. Clair confronted Arnold, Arnold replied that he was "only repeating the Sentiments of the Army & Country." St. Clair complained to Washington that "he had been deceived into thinking he could get a fair hearing at a court of inquiry, given that Arnold's opinion was apparently shared by so many."[4] Washington never answered this letter; he had bigger things to worry about, having just learned that Howe had embarked the main British Army onto ships and was probably heading for the mouth of the Delaware River.[5] After weeks of uncertainty, Washington was now reasonably certain what his opponent was up to.

As he often did, Washington forwarded Schuyler's July 22 letter to Hancock, who had it read to Congress on July 26, setting off a spirited and acrimonious debate. A couple of days later, Schuyler received disturbing news from William Duer. Many of Schuyler's enemies in Congress, particularly the New England delegates, "are leaving no means unessayed to blast your character," blaming him for the loss of Ticonderoga. Schuyler must find a way to "establish your Character on such a basis that even suspicion itself shall be silent." Duer warned Schuyler that he might have to "give an account of the loss of Ticonderoga." The reading of Schuyler's July 22 letter on the floor of Congress did great damage to his reputation. Many understood that Schuyler's "strong coloring used in it was done with a design to induce [General Washington] to reinforce you with Continental troops." Others interpreted it much differently. "Congress," Duer explained, "like an hysterical woman want cordials." Therefore, counseled his friend, "[w]rite truths, without making any reflections of your own."[6] This was sound advice, though it arrived much too late to do Schuyler much good.

Schuyler's continuing issues with the militia alarmed the commander-in-chief so much that he decided to send yet another key leader to Schuyler's department. On July 24, he ordered Major General Benjamin Lincoln to join the Northern Army. Lincoln was to join Schuyler and take over command of the New England Militia, "over whom . . . you have influence and who place confidence in you." He was reluctant to send Lincoln, who had been suffering from

bad health, but Schuyler's recent pessimistic reports had convinced him that it was "absolutely necessary to send a determined Officer."[7]

Lincoln had made his name and reputation in the early years of the war as a recruiter and leader of Massachusetts militia, having served in that capacity from the beginning of the war. Although he had little actual combat experience, Lincoln's organizational and administrative abilities had impressed Washington.[8] His steady, quiet, competent leadership style complemented Arnold's and gave Schuyler another quality subordinate. To Washington, the most significant shortage in the Northern Department was in senior level leadership. He hoped that the addition of Generals Arnold, Nixon, Glover, and Lincoln would rebuild morale and provide the enlightened leadership required by both Continentals and militia soldiers. These leaders should provide Schuyler the building blocks necessary to oppose Burgoyne effectively.

The same day Washington ordered Lincoln north, he wrote to Schuyler, questioning his decision to dismiss some of the militia because of the harvest, "even of those that have come to your Assistance, notwithstanding their presence is at this Time so urgently wanting." Still, Washington was optimistic that the New England states would soon help "check the progress of the Enemy." In the meantime, Schuyler could supplement his trained gunners with ordinary soldiers to fill shortages. He also informed Schuyler that Lincoln was on his way north to take over command of the militia, as he thought their new leader would have a "powerful Tendency to make them turn out with more cheerfulness." Finally, he recommended that Schuyler send Arnold, "or some other sensible spirited Officer," to command at Fort Stanwix (Schuyler) to lift the spirits of the local population and to "improve the favorable Disposition of the Indians."[9] Washington's counsel was getting more explicit.

On July 26, Schuyler thanked the commander-in-chief for sending Glover's brigade as they offset declining numbers. Meanwhile, the militia went "home in crowds," and he worried they would not be replaced. Partly this was because some New Englanders were "industriously propagating that the General Officers who were at Tyconderoga, and myself [were] all a Pack of Traitors." This malicious rumor had spread throughout the army and undermined faith in its officers.[10] This was disturbing news, indeed.

If Schuyler was bewildered by the militia's actions, Connecticut governor Jonathan Trumbull had absolutely no doubts. The approaching harvest season was partly to blame for the paltry response by Connecticut and the rest of the New England states,

but it was not the main issue. The big problem was "the Distress of being Commanded by Officers whose Conduct in evacuating the Posts at Tyconderoga was so much censur'd," otherwise they would turn out "with the Freedom & Spirit." Given the loss of Fort Ticonderoga, explained the governor to Washington, it was unsurprising that "some Cry Treachery, others Cowardice, & all blame." In the Northern Department, the governor explained, "the *Distrust of the Officers* is so *great*, that it will be impracticable to procure Men to go."[11] The implication of Trumbull's letter was clear: Schuyler and St. Clair had to go. Only then would the militia turn out in numbers that would make a difference.

Benedict Arnold provided Washington with his initial impressions of the Northern Department's situation on July 27. From the west side of the Hudson River south of Fort Edward, Arnold wrote, the "Woods being so full of Indians, Canadians, and Regulars that it is almost impossible for small Partys to escape them." This made it very difficult to gather intelligence on Burgoyne's movements. Given the significant advantage Burgoyne enjoyed with his Indians, Arnold asked Washington to send Colonel Daniel Morgan and his Provisional Rifle Corps to join Schuyler. Arnold was intimately familiar with Morgan, with whom he had served on several occasions. The unit's soldiers were comfortable in the woods and highly capable in unconventional warfare. Filled with expert marksmen with a unique set of skills, the unit was a high-demand but low-density asset—everyone wanted Morgan's regiment, but there was only one of them to go around. If Washington could spare Morgan, Arnold confidently predicted that "we should then be in a Condition to see Genl Burgoyne with all his Infernals on any Ground they might choose." This was despite the fact that they were short of salt meat, and the militia was poorly equipped. Arnold also assured Washington that Schuyler had "done every thing man could do in his Situation," and that the "spiteful rumors" about him were unfounded.[12]

Washington must have been buoyed by Arnold's letter, though its positive tone presented the opposite of Schuyler's previous messages. The difference was that one general was a good administrator and manager who had found himself overwhelmed. The other was a dynamic leader who was always looked for opportunities, and who not only functioned but thrived in the most challenging circumstances. As Arnold described, Schuyler's actions had been sound, even if he had not communicated that impression to Washington and Congress and indeed had given the opposite sense of what was happening in the north.

Two days before Burgoyne entered Fort Edward, Schuyler continued to warn that catastrophe was right around the corner. The militia troops were leaving so fast that in ten days, Schuyler predicted, "we shall not have five hundred left." Provisions were low, disease rampant, and although he had begged the surrounding states to send more militia, "I doubt much if any will come up," especially from the New England states "where the Spirit of Malevolence knows no Bounds, and I am considered a traitor." Schuyler was pleased to hear that Washington had sent Lincoln who "may possibly be able to do something with the New England Militia."[13]

Congress continued its debates over Schuyler's and St. Clair's fate. "Schuyler's Friends are endeavoring to clear him from all Blame [for Ticonderoga], because, they say, he was not there," explained Samuel Adams in a July 31 letter to James Warren. While this was true, wrote Adams, Schuyler should have been there: "It is well known he has never been used to keep his own Person near his Army." Adams, and other delegates from New England, thought Schuyler should never have been reinstated to the command of the Northern Department and argued that their militia did not want to serve under him. Despite Adams's belief that Schuyler was wholly unsuited to command the Northern Department, he thought the New Yorker was "excellently well qualified for a Commissary or Quartermaster."[14] Adams expressed what many were thinking: "The Letters we receive from G. Schuyler, are enough to frighten any Body who does not know him."[15]

The debates in Congress over the command of the Northern Department took on a familiar pattern: The New England delegates demanded Schuyler's dismissal, and the New Yorkers argued that he should be retained. They also grew rancorous, with some delegates accusing other members of being influenced by "resentment or partial, private motives." The New York delegates argued that the fault lay with the New England states' failure to supply adequate militia and that the eastern states were ganging up on the others. The New Englanders countered that the generals themselves were responsible for the multiple disasters. Elbridge Gerry from Massachusetts demanded that Schuyler be relieved because "everything [was] in disorder" and the situation "can only be put right by change." Gerry also contended that "Gates has shewn what he can do." Pennsylvanian James Wilson believed relieving Schuyler and St. Clair was "unjust," and while he acknowledged that there was fault somewhere, the generals were "not to blame."[16] Finally, on Tuesday, July 29, Congress ordered an investigation into the loss of Fort Ticonderoga and the next day voted to recall St. Clair. Two days later, they relieved Schuyler.[17]

On Sunday, August 3, after reading more of Schuyler's letters to the delegates, including his alarming July 27 note, Congress directed Washington to "order the general who he shall judge proper to relieve General Schuyler in his command." Congress also ordered that the states ready their militia to march "at a moment's warning" to the Northern Department and serve until the middle of November unless they were relieved sooner.[18]

It was perhaps inevitable that Schuyler would lose his command after the loss of Fort Ticonderoga. It may not have really mattered what he did or wrote or said in the weeks following the disaster because his enemies in Congress were alert for any missteps. As Arnold had observed, Schuyler had instituted measures that significantly contributed to the delay of Burgoyne's advance from Skenesborough, and he had skillfully maneuvered the army south, always keeping it between Burgoyne and Albany. Still, Schuyler had done himself no favors by giving the impression that he was a demoralized, depressed, and pessimistic strategic leader. In letter after letter, his reports of the situation in his command constituted a constant drumbeat of defeatism. By the end of July, Congress believed they had no choice but to relieve Schuyler.

As James Duane explained to his friend, while the loss of Ticonderoga was troubling, there were two primary reasons for Schuyler's relief: The New England militia was suspicious of his "military character" and would not turn out in defense of New York, and because his reports were so "gloomy" that "the Southern members were alarmed."[19]

The New England delegates immediately started lobbying Washington to appoint Gates as Schuyler's replacement. On August 2, seven members from Massachusetts, New Hampshire, Rhode Island, and Connecticut wrote Washington to make their case: "In our Opinion, no Man will be more likely to restore Harmony, order & Discipline, & retrieve our affairs in that Quarter, than Majr. Genl. Gates." The delegates argued that shortages of militia would not be a problem with Gates in command of the Northern Department, because he had "acquired the Confidence, & stands high in the Esteem of the eastern States & Troops."[20] But Washington wanted nothing to do with the lobbying efforts once again concerning the command of the Northern Department. Under normal circumstances, he would have been more than happy to pick a new commanding general for the Northern Department in his role as commander-in-chief. But, since Congress had been responsible for appointing commanders of the Northern Department from the birth of that organization, and

because the position was so politically sensitive, he begged off the disagreeable task.

Upon learning of the congressional directive, Washington wrote to Hancock that "I should wish to be excused from making the appointment." He gave two major reasons for his reluctance: first, the Northern Department and the appointment of its senior officers had always been Congress's prerogative, and second, Washington argued that since the situation was so "delicate and critical," the "Choice of an Officer to that command may involve very interesting and important Consequences."[21]

The first reason for his refusal to appoint the new commander made sense; the second reflected his concern over the political fallout from whoever was appointed. Anyone Washington might select would incur the wrath of either one or another powerful faction in Congress. Also, given the deterioration of the relationship between him and Gates, who was the most obvious successor to Schuyler, Washington wanted no part of that process. It is likely that he simply did not want to appoint someone he did not like. He was only human. However, despite his admirable concern for civil-military relations, Washington should have appointed Schuyler's replacement. After all, he was the commander-in-chief, and he had been directed by his civilian superiors to make the appointment. This should have eased his concern that he was somehow usurping congressional authority.

On August 4, Congress voted to direct Washington to dispatch Gates "with all possible expedition, to the northern department, to relieve Major General Schuyler."[22] Later that same day, Washington dutifully informed Gates that Congress had appointed him. He wished him success, and "that you may speedily be able to restore the face of affairs in that quarter."[23] Despite his misgivings about Gates, Washington knew that he was probably their best bet to solve the militia problem. A few days after he ordered Gates to assume his new post, he reassured New York Governor George Clinton that the issue of the New England states withholding reinforcements from the Northern Department would "be obviated by the presence of Major General Gates."[24] Washington may not have liked him but had to grudgingly admit that Gates was probably the right man for the job.

Schuyler learned of his relief on August 13.[25] The news devastated the New Yorker, who had done so much to maintain the core of the army and to retard the progress of Burgoyne's force. Writing two days after getting the news from just south of Stillwater, New York, where he had moved the army, Schuyler told Washington that it was

"extremely chagrining to me to be deprived of the Command, at a Time when we shall probably, or not at all, soon be enabled to face the Enemy; when we are on the point of taking such Ground, where they must attack to a Disadvantage." His new-found belligerency was too late for Schuyler. He informed Washington that he would stay with the army until his replacement arrived and that he would then remain in Albany to provide whatever assistance he could to the army before setting off for Philadelphia.[26]

Washington's young aide Alexander Hamilton provided one of the best contemporary assessments of why Schuyler's leadership problems in the Northern Department were responsible for his downfall. Possibly reflecting Washington's thoughts as well as his own, Hamilton wrote Robert Livingston, the newly appointed chancellor of New York, that while "I am afraid Gates is hardly the Man. . . . his appointment to this Command could not be avoided." He observed that he had always tried to give Schuyler the benefit of the doubt, but that his alarming assessments of the Northern Department's situation were disturbing. They simply did not ring true to Hamilton. Indeed, even in the Revolution's darkest hours, "I never saw anything like a general panic among the Troops. They appeared at the worst of times as resolute & spirited as in the best." Panic in any army, Hamilton concluded, "is generally a Reflection upon the Leader."[27]

CHAPTER 11

The Murder of Jane McCrea

IN SCHUYLER'S JULY 27 letter to Washington, he reported an incident in which a group of Burgoyne's Indians had attacked a small body of American soldiers near Fort Edward, killing, scalping, and capturing several of them.[1] This had become a common occurrence during the campaign, but the attacks had increased in frequency and severity since the mid-July arrival of the Indian reinforcement at Skenesborough. The ferocity of these attacks and the brutality with which the Indians treated their victims had stunned the American troops of Schuyler's army. Many of the victims of these attacks were stripped and mutilated. After capturing one unfortunate soldier, the Indians scalped him, "stabbed him in several places; they then . . . sharpened a stick and erected him on his feet, by bracing the sharp part of the stick under his chin, and left him a standing monument to their barbarity."[2]

Troubling as these incidents were, Schuyler had bigger things to worry about. He also noted in his letter to Washington that in addition to the soldiers lost, the Indians had "also scalped a Woman and carried off another."[3] This was the first official notice of one of the most notorious and controversial episodes of the entire campaign, and perhaps the war: the murder of Jane McCrea.

That Sunday, one of Burgoyne's Indian warriors, a Wyandot Indian brave named Panther, proudly brought into camp near Fort Edward the scalp of a blond young woman. The unfortunate Jane McCrea was the fiancée of a Loyalist officer serving with the British Army and the sister of an American militia officer. She had been

staying at a farm owned by a Mrs. McNeil outside Fort Edward and, at the urging of her brother, was preparing to move out of the path of Burgoyne's advancing army. On the morning of July 27, the two women, along with a female African American servant and McNeil's two young children, were approached by a group of Indians who were scouting to the front of the advanced corps. A young male African American servant spotted the Indians and shouted a warning before fleeing to the American lines. The female servant and children hid in the kitchen cellar, so the braves seized only the two women and started back toward the main body of the army. The Indians had a hard time hurrying the heavy-set Mrs. McNeil along the trail, and the captors of Jane McCrea quickly moved ahead, and soon the two parties separated. Meanwhile, the servant boy reached the American lines with news of the abduction, and a body of militia immediately set out to rescue the women. They caught up with the Indians dragging McNeil, but despite firing on the abductors, they failed to secure her release, and she was successfully borne unharmed to the British camp.[4]

When McNeil arrived in camp, she berated General Fraser for the rough treatment she had received at the hands of Burgoyne's "scoundrel Indians." Soon the second group of Indians arrived, but without Jane McCrea. Instead, Panther displayed the scalp of a young woman with distinctive long, blond hair.[5] Panther was confronted over the scalp's source but denied killing the young woman and instead blamed the pursuing American militia for her death. The Americans had caught up to the Indian party carrying McCrea to the British camp, Panther said, and an errant shot had hit the unlucky woman, killing her instantly. Panther claimed that he had merely taken advantage of her death to acquire the desirable scalp. Few, including Burgoyne, believed Panther's story.[6]

The report of McCrea's death quickly spread throughout the army and varied little from account to account. British and German officers and men were appalled by this atrocity, but few were surprised. Lieutenant Digby wrote that the atrocities committed by the Indians "were too shocking to relate, particularly the melancholy catastrophe of the unfortunate Miss McCrea, which affected the general and the whole army with the sincerest regret and concern for her untimely fate."[7] Another British officer recorded that "One of the Ottawan Savages thro' Jealousy and Spite most inhumanely scalped a Young Woman about 17 Years of Age." He added that she was to have been married to a young man "in the King's service."[8] McCrea's death also made a tremendous impression on the German soldiers.

A Braunschweig officer declared that McCrea's "misfortune caused quite an uproar in the army; everyone mourned the fate of this fine young woman. She was not even 18 years old. What cruelty!"[9]

Burgoyne personally held an inquiry and questioned Panther in the presence of the senior Indian chiefs, who threatened to leave if their fellow warrior was harshly treated. After hearing Panther's testimony and the pleas of the Indian chiefs and their French comrades to spare the young warrior's life, Burgoyne reasoned that keeping the Indians happy was too important and decided not to impose the ultimate penalty. As he explained later, the incident involved "no premeditated barbarity." The two Indians who had taken her "disputed who should be her guard, and in a fit of savage passion in the one from whose hands she was snatched, the unhappy woman became the victim."[10] Burgoyne's account of the crime quickly became the standard narrative, although some, including Fraser, believed Panther's story. Given the rudimentary forensic evidence—McCrea's body was found with three bullet wounds and no head trauma other than the postmortem scalping—it seems likely that Jane McCrea was the victim of "friendly fire."[11] The Indians were temporarily appeased, though they were furious with Burgoyne for not taking their word about the circumstances surrounding McCrea's death.[12] After the McCrea incident, it would not take much to convince the Indians to go home.

The McCrea affair haunted Burgoyne for the rest of his life. Many accused him of being directly responsible for the torture and death of McCrea, other civilians, and wounded and captured soldiers. This was an unfair charge; Burgoyne frequently admonished the Indian chiefs and their nominal French civilian leaders for not exerting better control of their charges and for not strictly adhering to his orders regarding the proper treatment of civilians and prisoners. As the British Army approached Fort Edward, Burgoyne had even declared that no Indian party would go out without being accompanied by a British officer. This was bitterly resented by the Indians and by Saint Luc, who threatened once more to leave. An Indian departure would be a massive blow to the army. Since the Indian reinforcement arrived at Skenesborough, they had successfully screened the army from the prying eyes of American scouts and had gathered vital intelligence on the American Army's movements. Despite Saint Luc's ominous warning, Burgoyne replied to the Frenchman that he "had rather lose every Indian, than connive at their enormities."[13] For the time being, at least, they agreed to Burgoyne's rules and stayed with the army, but the general was diminished in their eyes. He was not the warrior they thought he would be.

The American reaction to the Jane McCrea affair was initially fairly subdued. Schuyler was not particularly disturbed. There had been many such Indian outrages after all, and, while regrettable, this was simply another heinous incident of war. For most Americans, the main impact of the Indian attacks was to force the region's population to move to more defensible settlements. Burgoyne's campaign, and especially the Indian attacks, created what was perhaps the worst refugee crisis in American history up to that point. The *Newport Gazette* described the sorry plight of these unfortunates: "Great numbers of the back inhabitants are flocking down with their families, having left most part of their subsistence behind them.—Their case is truly deplorable."[14]

Schuyler and his officers and men did not call much attention to McCrea's murder, but the American press did. The *Pennsylvania Evening Post* published a lurid account of McCrea's death only two weeks after the incident. It concluded that "is not this sufficient to congeal the heart of humanity with horror, and even oblige a Tory of liberal sentiments to curse the cause which approves or winks at such worse than hell-like cruelties?"[15] Two days later, the *Independent (Boston) Chronicle* printed an account and called for a massive turnout of militia to oppose Burgoyne. While things looked grim in the Northern Department, argued the newspaper, this was no time to submit in the face of such barbarism, because even while the enemy "tender us the *olive branch*, we may be assured, a fatal dagger is concealed under its leaves."[16]

Jane McCrea was being transformed into an American martyr. The next step in her figurative canonization took place a month after her death, when Gates assumed command of the army from Schuyler on August 19. As he took stock of the army he had inherited from Schuyler, reviewed the strategic situation, and weighed his options, Gates wrote to Hancock that "The Horrid Murders and Scalpings, paid for and encouraged by Lieut General Burgoyne [whom Gates referred to as "this *polite Macaroni*" elsewhere in the letter] . . . will forever stain the Honour of the British Arms."[17] On September 2, in response to a letter from Burgoyne protesting the American treatment of prisoners, Gates responded with his own complaint, making sure to make the letter public. He declared that he was shocked that Burgoyne would dare use the word "inhumanity" in relation to the conduct of American troops when the British employed barbaric savages. The use of Indians in North American warfare was not new, Gates admitted, but to think that someone as seemingly honorable at Burgoyne "in whom the fine Gentleman is united with the Soldier

and Scholar, should hire the savages of America to scalp Europeans and the decedents of Europeans . . . is more than will be believed in Europe."[18]

Gates invoked the murder of McCrea, "a young woman lovely to the sight . . . engaged to be married to an officer in your Army . . . scalped and mangled in a most shocking manner." In addition to McCrea's appalling murder, there had been other atrocities at the hands of Burgoyne's Indians, including the massacre of a couple and their six children "while quietly reading in their once happy and peaceful dwelling." But it was Jane McCrea's death that so outraged the Americans, maintained Gates, because the crime "was particularly aggravated by her being dressed to receive her promised husband, but met her murderer employed by you." Gates estimated that more than one hundred men, women, and children "have perished by the hands of the ruffians to whom it is asserted you have paid the price of blood."[19] He ensured that his letter was widely disseminated throughout the colonies and published in as many Patriot newspapers as possible, intensifying American outrage against the British and stoking disapproval in Britain of Burgoyne's failure to control his Indians.

Burgoyne vehemently denied paying for scalps and described how he had carefully documented all of his interactions with the Indians, which clearly prohibited the taking of scalps "from the wounded and even the dying, and the persons of aged men, women, children and prisoners were pronounced sacred even in assaults." He insisted that Gates's accusations concerning other Indian outrages were completely false.[20]

No matter the accuracy of Burgoyne's protestations, the damage was done to his reputation and to the British war effort. Just how much outrage over the death of Jane McCrea and other innocent civilians contributed to the great influx of American militia units into the Northern Army in August and September 1777 is uncertain. Likely, other events during the campaign, including the threat of Burgoyne's continued advance south, Gates's assumption of the command, and American battlefield victories were far more important factors in the outpouring of militia. However, the death of McCrea and the British employment of Indians against the Americans certainly helped the cause. As Gates and numerous editors of newspapers nationwide recognized, the propaganda value of the alleged atrocity was priceless.[21]

The British press was no less adamant than their American counterparts in condemning the British policy of using Indians

against the Americans in general, and Burgoyne's failure to control his own Indians in particular. Gates's and Burgoyne's early September letters were as widely published in Britain as they were in America, and Burgoyne simply did not come off well in the exchange. One of the main accusations against him after his return to England concerned his use of Indians.[22] Everyone remembered the infamous June 20 proclamation, in which the general threatened to unleash his Indians on all Americans who did not demonstrate loyalty to the Crown. Although the Jane McCrea affair and the American propaganda windfall over the British Indian policy in America did not win the war—or have a significant impact on the Saratoga campaign—it was yet another diplomatic, political, and strategic challenge that the British had to overcome.

CHAPTER 12

Not to Make a Ticonderoga of It

When Burgoyne wrote to Germain on July 11 with the stupendous news that he had captured Ticonderoga and was already at Skenesborough, he mentioned in passing that he had received no report from Lieutenant Colonel Barry St. Leger and his Mohawk River expedition. Consequently, "I have sent some Indians through the woods in hopes of their reaching Lieut.-Colonel St Leger with the account of my progress." "Now is the critical time for his push upon the Mohawk," wrote Burgoyne.[1] Given that the campaign was moving along so quickly and successfully, St. Leger's offensive down the Mohawk to Albany and the Hudson River would keep the Americans off balance.

Burgoyne had first proposed the idea of sending a force down the Mohawk River shortly after his 1776 arrival in Quebec. He argued that an offensive operation in western New York, acting as a diversion, would facilitate the easy movement of the main force up Lake Champlain to Ticonderoga and beyond. Carleton had been intrigued but decided against Burgoyne's idea due to the lack of available troops. However, when Carleton wrote his October 1776 memorandum to Germain suggesting future operations for 1777, he proposed a Mohawk River operation. It was inevitable that when Burgoyne wrote his "Thoughts for Conducting the War" memo that his proposal for the 1777 campaign would include a Mohawk River component.[2]

Germain and the king agreed with Burgoyne's recommendation and included a diversionary operation in the March 26, 1777,

instructions for the campaign. Germain directed Carleton to prepare and dispatch two expeditions from Canada; the first, under Burgoyne, was to "force his way to Albany, and the other under the command of Lieutenant-Colonel St Leger who is to make a diversion on the Mohawk River."[3] The king, Germain, and Burgoyne considered the Mohawk River expedition to be an integral component of the overall campaign. St. Leger and his troops would tie down precious American regulars and militia, and it would force Schuyler to divide his attention between the two British offensives. To maintain the security of the western part of the state, Schuyler would be forced to send forces to counter St. Leger. The British planners also assumed that St. Leger would be able to advance with relative ease since the Americans would only be able to put up token resistance. The small forts guarding the approaches to Albany, most dating from the French and Indian War, were few, small, and in poor condition.

On paper, Lieutenant Colonel Barry St. Leger was exactly the right officer to command the Mohawk River expedition. Born in County Kildare, Ireland, to an upper-class family of Huguenot descent, he was highly educated, attending both Eton and Cambridge. Because of his attendance at these schools, he entered the army in 1756 at the relatively advanced age of twenty-three. (Unfortunately, no images of St. Leger are known to exist.)[4] As a young officer, he served in the French and Indian War. He quickly earned a reputation as an expert in frontier warfare, able to work effectively with both Canadians and Indians. While in North America, St. Leger served with James Wolfe at Quebec and Jeffrey Amherst at Louisbourg. By the time he participated in the relief of Quebec in 1776, he was a lieutenant colonel in the 34th Regiment of Foot and came to the attention of Burgoyne, who months later would ask for him by name to command the Mohawk River expedition. To ensure that there would be no disputes over rank with the other officers assigned to the expedition, St. Leger was given the temporary rank of brigadier general.[5]

Like Burgoyne, St. Leger had problems with the Canadian militia forces assigned to their armies. They tended to be unreliable, prone to high rates of desertion and were often poorly led. This was not a major issue for Burgoyne, as these troops made up a small percentage of his army. For St. Leger's small detachment, however, the unreliable Canadians were problematic. St. Leger's nominal second-in-command was Colonel Sir John Johnson, an American who commanded the King's Royal Regiment of New York, a unit composed primarily of New York Loyalists from the Mohawk Valley also known as the "Johnson Greens." Johnson was the illegitimate son of

Sir William Johnson, a prominent resident of the Mohawk Valley, well known for his close ties with the region's Mohawk Indians. Sir William was fluent in the Mohawk language, led units of Indians and provincials during the French and Indian War, and took a common-law Mohawk wife—the sister of the Mohawk military and diplomatic leader Thayendanegea, also known as Joseph Brant—in his later years. Before his death in 1774, and as tensions escalated between the Americans and British, Sir William worked to maintain Mohawk loyalty to the Crown. His son carried on his legacy with St. Leger's expedition. John Johnson hated the Patriots and their cause, fleeing to Canada, where he offered his services to Great Britain.[6]

The Canadians were not the only challenges St. Leger would face as he prepared his part of Burgoyne's campaign. The largest contingent in his little army was Indian warriors under Joseph Brant.[7] Brant, age 34, may have been the most famous Native American in the world in 1777. He was able to move easily between Indian, American, and European circles. Brant was born near the Cuyahoga River in present-day Ohio. After his father's death, his family moved to a village along the Mohawk River in western New York. His mother was a friend of Sir William Johnson, who lived nearby. Brant's sister Mary, or Molly, fell in love with Johnson, and the young Joseph soon went to live with the couple in Johnson's mansion near the Mohawk Valley. Sir William oversaw Brant's upbringing, which included his education and helping him establish connections with important officials. As a teenager, Brant participated in the French and Indian War with other Mohawks supporting British operations. He also fought with the British in Pontiac's War and in campaigns against competing tribes. Brant was one of the few Indians of his generation who was able to maintain a life in both cultures and even converted to the Anglican Church. When Sir William Johnson died in 1774, his nephew Guy Johnson took over as the British superintendent of Indian affairs and took the young Mohawk chief under his wing. Brant accompanied Johnson on a visit to London in 1775 to secure Native lands and guarantee Indian loyalty to Great Britain. Brant was presented to prominent figures and government officials. Although he had worn European-style clothing for years, he appeared only in traditional Native American dress during his London trip. Brant's visit was a sensation, and he was even presented to King George III at court. Supposedly, when Brant was asked to bow to the king, he said to the monarch that "I will bow to no man, for I am considered a prince among my own people; but I will gladly shake your hand."[8] By all accounts, the king was captivated with this confident and well-spoken young man.[9]

When Brant returned to America, outright rebellion had broken out, and the young Mohawk leader fought with Howe on some of his early campaigns, including the battles on Long Island. Howe asked Brant to carry his personal request to the Iroquois Confederacy to ally themselves officially with the British. Upon his arrival at Fort Niagara, in western New York, Brant found to his dismay that the Six Nations had already promised the Americans that they would remain neutral in the war. Using his considerable persuasive skills, Brant was able to raise a large body of warriors, who, like him, sided with the British to retain their lands and even eject the Europeans from the Mohawk Valley.[10]

Almost from the beginning of the war, the American senior leaders recognized the importance of convincing the Six Nations to maintain their neutrality. As early as April 19, 1776, Washington had written Schuyler that "I have urged to Congress the Necessity of Engaging them on our Side, to prevent their taking an Active Part against Us."[11] Schuyler and Gates had worked to that end, and, although conscientious, were often ham-handed and usually unsuccessful. Schuyler had already set back American-Indian relations when he prohibited trading with Indians in western New York. This new policy was intended to protect merchants, but it only further alienated the tribes.[12]

Both Schuyler and Gates recognized how dangerous Joseph Brant was to American interests in general, and to western New York in particular. Gates had met with representatives of the Six Nations in late May 1777 in Albany, where the chiefs expressed alarm over Brant's recruiting of Mohawks to fight the Americans. They asked Gates to negotiate with Brant to convince him to stop "removing Mohawks from the Country [Mohawk River Valley]."[13] Washington even met with Seneca chiefs at his headquarters on June 19, 1777, at Schuyler's request, hoping to demonstrate the military power the Americans had marshaled in their fight against the British. After the meeting, he confidently wrote Schuyler that they "seemed to be extremely pleased . . . declaring they had seen what was entirely satisfactory."[14] The chiefs might have been impressed with the American Army, but Washington was wrong about the meeting's success. Less than six weeks later, the Senecas would openly join the British.

As Brant pulled other Indians into his small band, Schuyler became increasingly alarmed that the entire Mohawk Valley, and western New York, would be destabilized and thus vulnerable to British offensive operations. In mid-June 1777, he sent Brigadier General Nicolas Herkimer and more than three hundred Tryon

County (New York) militia to meet with Brant and convince him to disband. Brant only had about 150 warriors with him, so Herkimer greatly outnumbered the Indians. Through bluster and subterfuge, Brant convinced Herkimer that the Indian force was much larger than the militia. Tensions ran high, and a fight seemed imminent, but Indian boldness convinced Herkimer not to seize Brant and his men. Despite having all the power, Herkimer gave in to Brant and lost an opportunity to end, or at least greatly reduce, the Indian threat in the Mohawk Valley.[15]

In dealing with the Six Nations—consisting of the Mohawk, Oneida, Onondaga, Cayuga, Seneca, and Tuscarora nations—the American generals had a tough diplomatic mission. Because of deep-seated animosities throughout the region, and because Germain had vowed to support Mohawks against American settlers in the valley after the war, the Patriots operated at a distinct disadvantage. Despite Washington's, Schuyler's, and Gates's best efforts, most of the tribes of the Six Nations were tottering between neutrality and outward support of Great Britain.[16]

In late July 1777, British Indian agent John Butler and Brant convened an assembly of the Six Nations at Three Rivers south of Oswego (not be confused with Trois-Rivières, located midway between Quebec and Montreal) to convince the Six Nations to renounce their neutrality. The news of the fall of Fort Ticonderoga arrived just before the council, and that proof of British power, along with the persuasive abilities of Brant and Butler, succeeded in convincing all but the Oneidas and Tuscaroras to renounce their neutrality and join the British in fighting the Americans. The Oneidas, due largely to their embrace of Christianity, decided to ally themselves with the Americans, as did the Tuscaroras.[17] Brant, along with his recruits, both Indian and Loyalist, joined St. Leger's expedition. Based on the available intelligence of a weak Fort Stanwix and few enemy troops in the Mohawk Valley, St. Leger, Johnson, and Brant promised the Indians an easy campaign with little fighting and lots of plunder.[18]

The feverish preparations for the expedition lasted about four weeks, during which St. Leger, with Carleton's help, gathered the provisions, ammunition, and transport necessary to complete his mission. Along with Canadians, AmericanLoyalists, and Indians, St. Leger's force included his own 34th Regiment of Foot, the 8th Regiment of Foot, and a Hesse-Hanau Jäger (light infantrymen armed with rifles) Company, numbering around sixteen hundred soldiers. Finally, on June 26, 1777, about a week after the departure

of Burgoyne's army from Fort Saint-Jean, St. Leger departed the village of Lachine, 5 miles southwest of Montreal, to sail up the Saint Lawrence River. Once on Lake Ontario, St. Leger's detachment would sail south to Fort Oswego, near present-day Oswego, New York. From there, the party would sail south up the Onondaga River, cross Oneida Lake, then up Wood Creek (present-day Fish Creek and not to be confused with the Wood Creek that ran south from Skenesborough, New York) as far as he could go. At the head of Wood Creek, 60 miles from Oswego, he would encounter a 6-mile portage from Wood Creek to the Mohawk River, known as the Oneida Carrying Place. Once St. Leger and his force reached the Mohawk River, which led directly to the Hudson River and Albany about 110 miles away, he anticipated an easy move down the river and a successful link-up with Burgoyne's army.[19]

The only obstacle standing in the way of St. Leger accomplishing his mission was a small fortification named Fort Stanwix, known to the Americans as Fort Schuyler.[20] Stanwix guarded the Oneida Carrying Place site and between Wood Creek and the Mohawk River, and thus controlled the route from Lake Ontario all the way to Albany. Like most of New York's frontier fortifications, the fort had been built during the French and Indian War. St. Leger assumed Stanwix and its American garrison, if the rebels even bothered to defend it, would be easily swept aside.

Two weeks after St. Leger's expedition began its journey up the St. Lawrence River toward Lake Ontario, the detachment stopped at Buck Island, near the entrance to Lake Ontario. There he made final preparations for the expedition's movements and waited for a report from a reconnaissance party he had sent forward to determine the rebel activity in and around Fort Stanwix. However, he was unconcerned about Stanwix because Carleton had assured him that the Americans had decided to abandon the fort back in the spring.[21] When the scouts returned, their report, which included prisoner testimony, was disturbing. The Americans were, in fact, working diligently to man and strengthen Stanwix. If true, St. Leger realized that he did not have enough heavy artillery to besiege the fort. He dismissed the intelligence as unreliable and instead chose to believe Carleton's much more optimistic assessment of the American defenses.[22]

On July 17, St. Leger learned that Fort Ticonderoga and with it "a large Quantity of provision & artillery & stores . . . were abandoned by the rebels to the grand army the 6th instant" and that the army was "in hot pursuit."[23] This was certainly excellent news, though it also posed

a problem for St. Leger. He thought that it would take some time, perhaps weeks, to reduce and capture Fort Ticonderoga. Now it looked like Burgoyne would be approaching Albany much sooner than anyone had anticipated. St. Leger realized he needed to move quickly if his expedition was to benefit Burgoyne and the main army. The good news from Ticonderoga not only obliged St. Leger to hurry his men and to complete his final preparations for the advance quickly, it also reinforced his preconceived beliefs that the American soldiers and their leaders were poor. There was no reason to believe that those who opposed him in the Mohawk Valley would be any different.[24] Even if he encountered any sizable rebel forces on his journey to Albany, St. Leger believed there was no way they could stand up against his mixed force of British and Hesse-Hanau regulars, provincial militia, and Indians. Two days after the news of Fort Ticonderoga's capture, St. Leger departed Buck Island for Fort Oswego.

Carleton's intelligence about the state of Fort Stanwix and its garrison could not have been more wrong. While the bulk of Schuyler's and Gates's attention had been focused on Ticonderoga, they had not neglected Stanwix. The fort was much smaller than Ticonderoga, but it was vitally important for the defense of the region. The star-shaped fortification boasted four bastions constructed primarily of logs and dirt, with each of the four walls measuring slightly under a football field in length. The thickness of the 9-foot-tall walls ranged from 18 to 20 feet. The projecting bastions themselves were 120 feet deep, with two sides, each about 38 feet long and two 90 feet. The walls and bastions were surrounded by a wide, 18-foot-deep ditch bristling with thick sharpened stakes, or pickets, to guard against infantry assault. Casemates, where the garrison's soldiers could seek shelter from enemy bombardment, were located within the fort's walls, and the primary magazine was situated deep under one of the bastions. Also located within the fort's central courtyard were barracks buildings and other structures designated for officer housing, kitchens, and administrative and storage purposes. Like most other fortifications on the American frontier, Fort Stanwix was built primarily of wood and soil, requiring almost constant maintenance, especially after the harsh New York winters.[25]

In June 1776, Schuyler had been ordered by Congress to repair and man the fort, which he did under the direction of Colonel Elias Dayton of the 3rd New Jersey Regiment of Continentals, who renamed the fort in honor of Schuyler. Dayton and his men completely rebuilt the fort by the end of August, when he reported to Schuyler that he was confident it could withstand anything the

British might throw at it.[26] By the time Dayton's men were replaced in October 1776 by Colonel Samuel Elmore and his Connecticut regiment of Continentals, the only major item left unfinished was a barracks building suitable to house the garrison. Schuyler directed Elmore to improve the fort and sent Captain Bernard De Lamarquise, a French engineer, to take charge of the construction efforts.[27] The work had not progressed far when in the spring of 1777, Colonel Peter Gansevoort Jr., and his 3rd New York Continental Regiment were ordered to Stanwix to replace Elmore and his troops.[28]

Born in Albany, Gansevoort's father was a prosperous brewer. His mother was directly related to the Van Rensselaer family—about as close to royalty as one could get in eighteenth-century New York. Although the family had been in America for at least three generations, they often spoke Dutch at home, and the native-born Gansevoort was always a little self-conscious about his accented speech. Gansevoort continued in his father's brewing business in Albany and joined the local militia as a lieutenant. Only twenty-seven years old at the time of his appointment to command Fort Stanwix, the 6-foot-tall Gansevoort had already distinguished himself in the war. Although only a major, he commanded the 2nd New York Continental Regiment during the invasion of Quebec, the capture of Fort Saint-Jean, and the fighting withdrawal from Canada. In recognition for his service, he was promoted to full colonel and given command of the 3rd New York Regiment and Fort George. Gansevoort was commanding at Fort George when he received the order to move his regiment to Fort Stanwix and to take command of that important post.[29]

Gansevoort arrived at Fort Stanwix on May 3 with about half of his regiment and immediately put them to work on the fort. Lieutenant Colonel Marinus Willett, Gansevoort's second-in-command, and the rest of the regiment arrived at Stanwix on May 29. Like his boss, Willett was a native New Yorker, but from Long Island and not the Albany or Mohawk River Valley area, so he had to work hard to earn the respect of the local men. Ten years older than his regimental commander, Willett served in the French and Indian War when he participated in the failed attack on Fort Ticonderoga.[30] Exhibiting patriotic fervor in the years before the start of the Revolution, he was commissioned as a captain in the Continental Army at the start of the war and served with the 1st New York Regiment in the invasion of Canada. In November 1776, he was promoted to lieutenant colonel in the 3rd New York Regiment when he first met Gansevoort.[31] Together they made a good team.

After surveying his new command, Gansevoort reported to Gates that very little effective work had been done during the preceding months and that it was virtually "untenable." The ditches were filled with earth and trash, and many parts of the wooden walls were rotting and on the verge of collapse, a common problem with earthen fortifications.[32] He was dismayed to learn that the fort's meager treasury contained very little to procure local supplies, and he requested that Gates send out "a Quantity, of Rum . . . as our fatigue & work men have already been 7 days without it." This was vital for morale and for trading with the Indians. Gansevoort assured Gates that except for necessary guard duty, all of his men were working on the fort in accordance with Lamarquise's plan, but because the captain's scheme called for "the whole of the Fort & Barracks is to be new Moddelled" he did not have enough men to do everything, even after the arrival of Willett and the rest of his regiment. In other words, instead of simply repairing the fort, Schuyler's French engineer officer wanted to completely redesign the fort and its supporting structures, a task that required many more soldiers.[33] By the time Gansevoort's letter reached Albany, Congress had reinstated Schuyler to the command of the Northern Department, and Gates was out.

Lamarquise's elaborate plan frustrated Gansevoort and Willett. As Willett recalled, "Instead of repairing the works after the manner of their original construction, which could easily have been done," the Frenchman ordered new construction in locations they thought unsuitable. Consequently, much unnecessary work was being done and time wasted. Finally, after watching his exhausted soldiers wasting their precious time, Willett appealed to Gansevoort to fire Lamarquise. The colonel refused at first because the engineer was on Schuyler's orders, but Willett ultimately prevailed, and soon the Frenchman was on his way to Albany.[34]

Lamarquise was replaced by Major Nathaniel Hubbell, and from then on, Gansevoort, Willett, and Hubbell carefully prioritized the work so that only the most important tasks were undertaken in preparation for an enemy attack.[35] Gansevoort and Willett redoubled their efforts to prepare the fort for St. Leger's attack, with both officers and men working around the clock. Some repairs had to be made after the enemy arrived, which meant that the men "were unavoidably exposed," as Willett recalled, leading to several casualties.[36] In addition to making repairs where necessary and improvements where possible, issues like clearing fields of fire, securing defensible water sources, sanitation, storing and protecting food, powder, and other important supplies—all the necessities for withstanding a

siege—now occupied all of the leaders' time and attention. Wasted effort was not a luxury they could afford.

As June faded, Gansevoort began to receive numerous reports of enemy activity and rumors of an upcoming offensive. On June 30, Schuyler correctly warned Gansevoort that "Sir John Johnson intends to attack your post," and that "you will therefore put yourself in the best position of Defence you possibly can." Schuyler further counseled the young colonel to "Keep out Scouts continually towards Oswego and every other Quarter from which the Enemy may approach—Be very watchful and alert that you may not experience the disgrace of a Surprize." Schuyler also urged Gansevoort to coordinate with Brigadier General Herkimer, in command of the Tryon County militia, because he had been directed "to support you with the Militia in Case you are attacked."[37] However, as Gansevoort well knew, counting on Herkimer and the Tryon County militia was problematic.

The military situation in the summer of 1777 in the Mohawk Valley was extremely complicated, reflecting the diverse population. Populated largely by Palatine Germans, who were lured to the region's wilderness by promises of land grants, the citizens of Tryon County were insular and close-knit. Many second- and third-generation descendants of the original German pioneers maintained their language and religion. Herkimer, for example, spoke German almost exclusively, and it was difficult for him to communicate in English, especially in writing.[38] Making his fortune through fur trading, flax, and shipping, Herkimer was one of the most prominent and wealthy of the county's citizens, perhaps second only to Sir William Johnson, with whom he got along well. In addition, Herkimer and Joseph Brant, neighbors, regarded each other with mutual respect and admiration. The Herkimer, Johnson, and Brant relationship was just one part of the complex web of associations found in Tryon County that summer. Many families were committed Tories, many more were Patriots, and some were split in their loyalties. The clashing allegiances in the valley often led to bitter conflicts that, at times, broke into violence. Suspected Tories were harassed and persecuted.[39] In the Mohawk River Valley, the American Revolution was a bitter, fraternal conflict. Given his prominent position in the community, Herkimer became the region's senior militia commander at the outbreak of the war. After the Loyalists in the county's militia fled to Canada, Herkimer was promoted to brigadier general.[40] Herkimer's and Gansevoort's legacies would be inextricably tied together.

As June gave way to July, Gansevoort continued to improve the fort and tried to convince the Six Nations to maintain their neutrality.[41]

He requested additional ammunition, especially for his meager artillery battery of thirteen cannon, but assured Schuyler that "nothing in my power shall be wanting to Maintain this important post."[42] Gansevoort ordered that Wood Creek be blocked with obstructions to prevent the British vessels from approaching too close to the fort.[43] This required a large work party, and on July 3, an officer and soldier wandered away from the rest of the group and were ambushed by Indians and Loyalists from the scouting party that had been sent ahead by St. Leger. The soldier was killed, and the officer seriously wounded. The next day another work party cutting turf for the fort's walls was attacked, with six men, five privates, and an officer, taken prisoner, and five men killed. One man's body was "inhumanly mangled," a warning for the Stanwix garrison. Gansevoort dutifully reported this attack to Schuyler on July 4, accurately predicting, "This success will no doubt encourage them to send out greater numbers and the intelligence they may possibly require will probably hasten the main body determined to act against us in these parts."[44]

At Schuyler's urging, Herkimer had been trying to raise troops to face St. Leger's expedition, but few responded because they had heard many false alarms in the past. After getting little reaction to his multiple pleas and after more prodding from Schuyler, Herkimer issued a proclamation on July 17 to the citizens of the valley, explaining the threat and appealing to the population's patriotism: "I think it proper and most necessary for the defense of our country," that his fellow citizens "march to oppose the enemy with vigor . . . for the just defense of their country." If the people came out in force, Herkimer concluded, he did not doubt that "victory cannot fail on our side."[45] Herkimer's proclamation worked; when he really needed them, the Tryon County militia started to come out.

A few days after the attack on the work party, Gansevoort received the alarming news that Ticonderoga had fallen.[46] Two days later, a letter arrived from his younger brother, who predicted that Stanwix would soon be attacked. If so, he urged Peter not to evacuate like St. Clair had, and he trusted that he "will not be a disgrace to New York arms." Further, he assured him that their father "flatters himself that you will Conquer or die."[47] (No family pressure there.) Gansevoort assured his frightened fiancée, Catherine Van Schaick that they were working day and night to prepare for the British and "doubt not but [we] shall give them a warm Reception if they should pay us a Visit."[48]

Schuyler had ordered Herkimer to send two hundred Tryon County militia to reinforce the fort, but by the end of July, none

had appeared. Gansevoort reported this fact to his commander on July 26, along with the intelligence that a large body of Loyalists and Indians were at Oswego and were thus only a few days' sail and march from the fort. Knowing that time was running out, he redoubled his efforts to impede the enemy's advance by sending a quarter of his entire force out to obstruct Wood Creek.[49] The attacks in early July and the numerous sightings of Indians patrolling near the fort were indicators that something was up. It would be only a matter of days before the enemy was upon them.

The next day an incident occurred outside the fort that was even more shocking than the Jane McCrea murder. While it received very little nationwide notice, it profoundly affected Gansevoort, Willett, the Stanwix garrison, and the entire region. Three young girls from local farms were picking berries in the woods near the fort when Indians attacked them. Two of the girls were killed and scalped, and the other, though critically wounded, managed to make it to the safety of the fort. Gansevoort was furious because the Indians lying in ambush had ignored a group of soldiers passing by before attacking the girls, "but the mercenaries of Britain came not to fight, but to lie in wait to murder; and it is equally the same to them, if they can get a scalp, whether it is from a soldier or an innocent babe."[50] Unlike the McCrea incident, which took place the day before the atrocity at Fort Stanwix and therefore not yet known to Gansevoort and his men, the murder of the two girls galvanized the Mohawk Valley and contributed to the enthusiastic militia turnout.[51] Gansevoort knew that he had but a short time to make his final preparations for St. Leger, and in the light of the increased Indian attacks, he gathered all the women, children, and sick in and near the fort and sent them down the valley to relative safety.[52]

As St. Leger approached, Herkimer asked Schuyler to send more Continentals to help defend the region, which drove the harassed general, who was dealing with his own problems facing Burgoyne, to exasperation: "I am very, very sorry," wrote Schuyler, "that you should be calling upon me for assistance of Continental troops." Schuyler then offered Herkimer the kind of message he was getting from Washington. "For God's sake do not forget that you are an over-match for any force the enemy can bring against you, if you act with spirit."[53]

At this point, Gansevoort had only 550 soldiers to man the fort and protect the critical piece of land that controlled access to the Mohawk River, Albany, and the Hudson, so Schuyler reluctantly dispatched a small reinforcement of two hundred Continental

troops from the 9th Massachusetts Regiment to Stanwix.[54] This was a critical decision and demonstrated that Schuyler had a firm grasp of the situation throughout his department and not just along the Hudson.

One of Gansevoort's primary sources of intelligence was Thomas Spencer, an Oneida mixed-race blacksmith and stalwart Patriot. Spencer moved freely throughout the region and provided excellent information. On July 29, he reported that "there is but four Days remaining of the Time set for the Kings Troops to come to Fort Schuyler." He further warned the colonel that any militia coming to assist the fort should "take Care on their March" and that the friendly Oneida chiefs "desire the Commanding Officers at Fort Schuyler to exert themselves in their Defense [and] not to make a Ticonderoga of it but they hope you will be courageous."[55] St. Leger's approach posed a direct threat to the Oneida Indians, who had thrown in their lot with the Americans against the British. Stanwix controlled the entire Mohawk Valley, and if the British and their Loyalist and Indian allies were able to seize it, Oneida settlements in the valley would be vulnerable.

On August 1, Gansevoort issued a general order to the entire garrison, which established the standards the American troops would follow for the entire siege. He set out the rules for the guards and procedures for calling out the whole garrison in an emergency. Gansevoort also reminded his men that they needed to guard against one of the biggest threats facing anyone during a prolonged siege, disease. "It is recommended that the Officers be Careful to inculcate the Necessity of cleanliness to their Men," urged Gansevoort, "as much as the preservation of their Health depends upon it." Finally, he emphasized the importance of responding immediately to any alerts: "And it is not doubted but the men at this Important Crisis will be Very alert in turning out in Time of an Alarm."[56]

Spencer's estimate—August 2nd—was accurate. On Friday, August 1, upon learning that an American resupply convoy was coming up the Mohawk to the fort, St. Leger issued the order for the final advance of his army to Fort Stanwix. A raiding party of Indians and soldiers under Lieutenant Henry Bird was sent ahead of the main body to intercept the small flotilla that included the two hundred Massachusetts troops Schuyler had dispatched, along with six weeks' extra provisions. The garrison was still dangerously short of artillery ammunition. Indian ill-discipline and the obstructions on Wood Creek delayed Bird and his detachment, and they barely missed the American convoy, which succeeded in landing its precious cargo.

Bird's men were able to seize the lower landing south of the fort, however, effectively cutting Stanwix off from the river.[57] The effort made by Gansevoort, Willett, and their soldiers to obstruct the creek was starting to pay off. With the arrival of the two hundred Continental troops from the 9th Massachusetts and extra supplies, Gansevoort and the Stanwix garrison were as ready as they would ever be.

Having failed to cut off the American relief party, St. Leger pushed the main body forward. After an arduous and fatiguing march, they began to encircle the fort on August 3. Lieutenant Bird improved his position south of the fort and set up a blocking position along the road leading to Albany. Now the fort was cut off from both routes

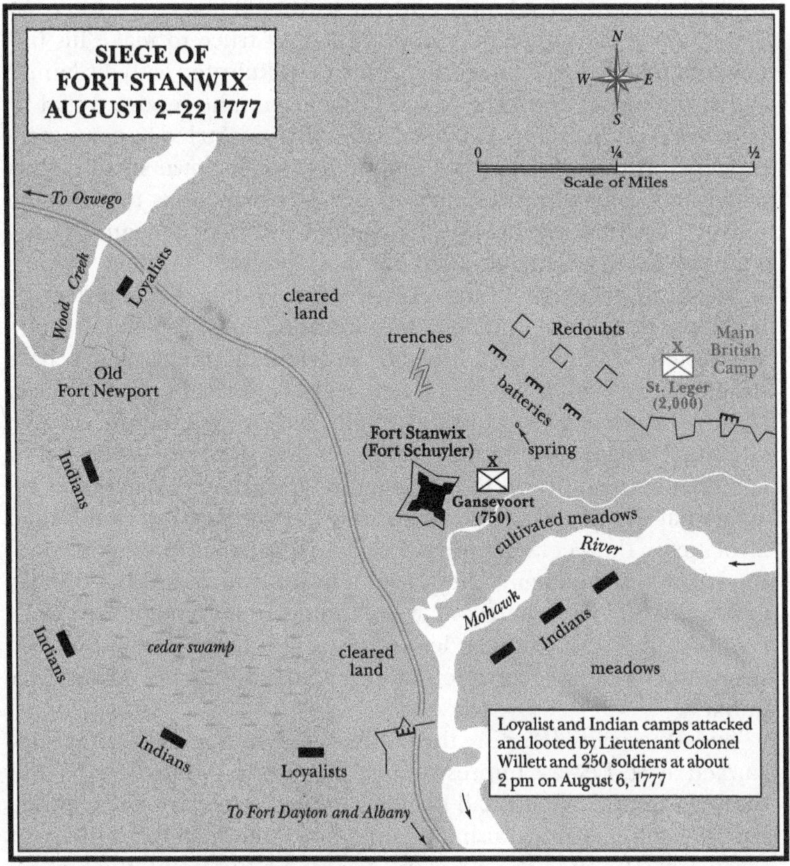

Map 7 Siege of Fort Stanwix, August 2–22, 1777

down the valley. Getting the artillery and supplies to Stanwix was extremely difficult, and St. Leger's plans were delayed for several days as they labored to open Wood Creek and build a temporary road for supplies and the artillery.[58] This was not a task St. Leger had anticipated, and what he found at the fort was even more distressing than the toil involved in approaching it. "Instead of the unsuitable and unfinished work we were taught to expect," wrote St. Leger to Carleton, "I found it was a respectable Fortress strongly garrisoned with seven hundred men and demanding a train of artillery we were not master of for its speedy subjection."[59]

Despite the disappointment, St. Leger moved his troops into positions in front of the fort late in the afternoon of the 3rd. In their full regalia, almost a thousand Indians encircled the fort and mocked its defenders in a frightening manner. After the show of force, St. Leger sent a Loyalist officer under a flag of truce to make his first demand for the fort's surrender, "which was Rejected with disdain."[60] When the officer returned to the British camp, he reported that he had observed an efficient and professional garrison led by competent officers.[61] Although short of ammunition for his own small battery of artillery, Gansevoort had plenty of other provisions to withstand a siege of at least six weeks. The colonel and his 750-man garrison were confident they could hold out until relieved.

Meant to intimidate and terrify the fort and its commander, the incoming troops, the Indian demonstration, and surrender demand was wasted on Gansevoort. Indeed, the ostentatious display may have backfired. As Willett recalled a few weeks later, St. Leger's emissary "told us of their great power, strength and determination, in such a manner as gave us reason to suppose they were not possessed or [of?] strength sufficient to take the fort."[62] The Americans knew exactly what was at stake. They had, after all, witnessed several Indian atrocities in the weeks before St. Leger's arrival; they understood well the nature of the enemy they faced. On this sunny and hot Sunday in August, St. Leger faced one more thing he had not counted on: a resolute American commander and a spirited garrison. A protracted siege now seemed probable, and a rapid advance to Albany was unlikely.

The Americans manning the parapets of Fort Stanwix that Sunday gawked at St. Leger's impressive display outside the fort's walls. But Gansevoort and Willett had decided to boost the garrison's morale and determination by raising a brand-new American flag with great ceremony. Although there is some dispute on this point, the first appearance of the stars and stripes in combat may have taken place at

Fort Stanwix on the first full day of the British siege. The men from the 9th Massachusetts Regiment who arrived the day before had brought news of a new congressional resolution directing "[t]hat the flag of the United States be thirteen stripes, alternate red and white: that the union be thirteen stars, white in a blue field, representing a new constellation."[63] Gansevoort ordered that a makeshift flag be created with the materials on hand at the fort. The flag was quickly sewn together and hoisted up the flagpole on the southwest bastion, in full view of St. Leger and his men.[64] Like the rebuffed surrender demand, the new flag billowing in the soft breeze was a potent symbol of American defiance and resolve. Gansevoort was determined that the colors would fly until St. Leger gave up his siege, or he and his garrison died in its defense.

After Gansevoort rebuffed St. Leger's surrender demand, the British Army settled down to begin a siege. St. Leger set up the main British camp about 1,000 yards northeast of the fort and began to construct three batteries 600 yards to the northeast of the fort and positioned between the fort and the camp. The northernmost battery consisted of three guns, the middle battery three mortars, and the southern battery, an additional three guns. Each battery was to be protected by a separate redoubt. Constructing the batteries and redoubts would take some time, plus St. Leger had to assign over more than one hundred troops to clear Wood Creek, a task that took nine days.[65] The British artillery could do some damage to Stanwix and its garrison, but the shells were not heavy enough to breach the fort's earthen walls. A detachment of the 8th Regiment, supported by a 3-pounder cannon, established a position guarding access to the Albany road and the Mohawk River landing south of the fort. St. Leger's Loyalists and Indians established multiple camps in the woods to the west of the fort and southeast on the river's east bank.[66]

As St. Leger and his men began the investment of Fort Stanwix and embarked on the grueling labor to clear Wood Creek, the two sides exchanged small arms fire that resulted in the siege's first casualties outside of the Indian raids that occurred before the main body's arrival. St. Leger's Jäger company from Hesse-Hanau was particularly effective. Their riflemen acted as snipers against American soldiers exposed on the fort's parapets, inflicting eight American casualties on July 4. Gansevoort and Willett adjusted the positions of the men manning the walls to protect them better, so that the next day "all the damage sustained by us this day was one man killed by a rifle ball." That evening the garrison was kept awake by demonstrations coming from the Indian camps, as "they made most horrid yellings

great part of the evening in the woods hardly a mile from the fort," as Willett noted.[67] The jumpy Americans grabbed their muskets and prepared to repulse an attack, but none came. After a while, they assumed that the terrifying noise was simply another attempt to intimidate the garrison. In fact, the warriors were preparing for battle based on intelligence that had fallen into St. Leger's hands. The American militia was marching toward Stanwix.

CHAPTER 13

Oriskany and Relief

WORD OF ST. LEGER'S approach to Fort Stanwix reached Herkimer, who immediately raised the alarm.[1] His earlier proclamation and the gruesome deaths of the two young girls at Fort Stanwix helped. After a few days, he was able to raise almost one thousand men, who were ordered to assemble at Fort Dayton, on the north side of the Mohawk River near the present-day town of Herkimer, across the river from German Flatts about 32 miles southeast of Fort Stanwix. In part, at least, the enthusiastic response was because many of the citizen soldiers relished the opportunity to settle scores with St. Leger's Loyalists—many from the Mohawk Valley. In addition to the troops and using his business connections as well as invoking his position as commander of the region's militia, Herkimer also gathered dozens of carts and wagons to haul supplies and baggage. This ground transport, probably numbering between 250 and 400 individual vehicles, was hauled by horses and oxen, and some were even dragged along by the men themselves.

Once he gathered his detachment, Herkimer divided the men into regiments of about 175 men per unit, each commanded by a senior militia officer. Recognizing the importance that each militiaman placed on serving alongside his neighbors, Herkimer made sure each regiment was organized around the valley's major localities. On August 4, the day after St. Leger's army demonstrated on the plain north of Fort Stanwix, Herkimer's four regiments—Palatine, Canjoharie, Mohawk, and German Flatts—departed Fort Dayton with almost eight hundred men. Observing all of Herkimer's

preparations, which included the largest assembly of militia anyone in the region had ever seen, was Molly Brant, who immediately wrote a letter describing what she had seen to her brother, who had just arrived at Fort Stanwix with St. Leger's besieging force.[2]

Rain had turned the narrow road to Utica, about 15 miles northwest of Fort Dayton, slick with mud. It was tough going for Herkimer and his men. They cursed the weather, the road, the wilderness, the carts that often slipped off the road into the woods or ditches, and the British for dragging them away from their homes and farms as harvest season approached. Still, Herkimer was able to instill a sense of urgency in the militia officers and men, and the detachment made excellent time, arriving in Utica late on August 4. Early the next morning, the 3-mile column departed Utica on their way to the Oneida settlement of Oriska. Once again, despite the poor road and the hardships involved in dragging along dozens of wagons, the militia kept up a good pace, arriving at Oriska in the early evening. In two days, they traveled 28 miles, a respectable rate of march for untrained and inexperienced soldiers.[3]

That evening, as they rested and prepared for what they were sure would be a triumphant arrival at Fort Stanwix, a small detachment of thirty to sixty Oneida warriors joined Herkimer's force.[4] The addition of the Oneidas to Herkimer's force should have significantly improved their chances of success. Herkimer planned to employ these friendly Indians as scouts for the next day's final approach to the fort, now only a few miles away. Herkimer assumed that St. Leger would try to prevent the relief column from reaching the fort, and he decided to ask Gansevoort to send out some troops from the fort to meet the column. This way, the combined force would keep St. Leger off guard and, if necessary, fight their way to the fort. Early that evening, Herkimer sent three men, a lieutenant and two privates, on a mission to inform Gansevoort of the relief column's approach and to request his cooperation.[5]

The morning of Wednesday, August 6, was unusually quiet at the fort. Willett noticed an enemy detachment marching south along the road to Albany. This was undoubtedly the first detachment of Loyalists and Indians sent out to confront Herkimer. Late in the morning, Herkimer's three men made their way through enemy lines and into the fort, but avoiding St. Leger's army around the fort had taken them much longer than the general had anticipated. Herkimer had sent them on their perilous journey in mid-afternoon of August 5, thinking it would only take them a few hours to cover the 8 miles. Instead, they did not arrive until around 11:00 a.m. the next day. The men

were forced to wade through swampy ground south and west of the fort that St. Leger had foolishly left unguarded because he thought it impassible.[6] As Willett recalled, the men delivered to Gansevoort "a letter from General Harkeman [Herkimer] of the Tryon County militia; advising us that he was at Ercsks [Oriska] (8 mile off) with party of his militia, and proposed to force his way to the fort for our relief."[7] The message also asked Gansevoort to fire three cannon shots as a signal if the three messengers arrived safely to the fort, and he further requested that the colonel meet the militia on their way in.[8]

If Herkimer could successfully bring his men into the fort, it would almost double the garrison's size at a stroke. With a total troop strength of more than fourteen hundred men, Gansevoort and Herkimer would be only at a slight disadvantage in manpower, making the odds of resisting the siege very good indeed. Following Herkimer's direction, Gansevoort and Willett prepared to send out a detachment to meet the militia and guide them to the fort, fighting their way through enemy lines if necessary. "In order to render him what service we could in his march," Willett recalled, "it was agreed that I shou'd make a sally from the fort with 250 men consisting of one half Gansevoorts [3rd New York Regiment], one half Massachusetts [9th Massachusetts Regiment] ditto and one field piece (an iron three pounder)."[9] Things were looking up for the besieged Patriots at Fort Stanwix. What the officers inside the fort could not know was that by the time Herkimer's letter arrived, the general and the Tryon County militia were already in a desperate fight for their lives.

Late on the 5th, the same day Herkimer halted at Oriska, Joseph Brant received Molly's letter. Brant immediately showed the letter to St. Leger. Molly had provided a precise account of the composition and organization of Herkimer's militia relief column. As St. Leger related to Carleton three weeks later, this intelligence revealed "that a reinforcement of eight hundred militia conducted by General Herkimer were on their march to relieve the garrison." Because many of his men were at work clearing Wood Creek, St. Leger had few available regulars, "and therefore could not send above eighty white men, rangers and troops included, with the whole corps of Indians."[10] He placed Sir John Johnson in command of this mixed detachment, which left the camp early in the morning to intercept Herkimer. The detachment included Johnson's Royal Regiment of New York, Butler's Rangers, both Loyalist units, and almost all of St. Leger's Indians, mainly Mohawks and Senecas, nominally led by Joseph Brant.

This was undoubtedly the force Willett observed heading south along the Albany road, and it also explained the loud Indian demonstrations the garrison heard. Although the force included few regulars, the detachment's leaders—Johnson and Brant—had superb knowledge of the local terrain and conditions. Molly's message provided an accurate estimate of Herkimer's numbers and informed St. Leger that the relief column planned to halt at Oriska. Seldom do commanders get such accurate and timely knowledge of both enemy capabilities and intentions. This was an intelligence coup of the first order. If he could turn back or destroy Herkimer's column, St. Leger would buy the time necessary to capture Stanwix and push on to Albany. Everything depended on his Loyalists and the Indians.

As St. Leger's mixed force prepared to march toward Oriska, the Tryon County militia was not faring well. Like most American militia units, Herkimer's force was a collection of farmers, merchants, traders, and craftsmen, most of whom had little or no training or experience, and who tended to be unfamiliar and uncomfortable with military discipline. Men and officers alike felt that they could freely and frankly voice disagreements with their leaders and offer suggestions and demands for different courses of action. Not all militia units were the same, but as they were all composed of Americans who resented being ordered around, they required a special kind of leader. Early in the march, Herkimer's officers began to grumble about some of the commander's decisions. Tensions began to rise shortly after the men assembled. Herkimer wanted to delay their departure to wait for additional militia units to arrive from Albany. Some of his officers would have none of it and demanded they depart immediately to relieve the fort. Despite his protestations, the general agreed to depart early the next morning.[11]

While the initial disagreement was resolved, it was only the first conflict between the general and his men. They also argued about which route to the fort to take. The officers maintained that they should march on the north side of the Mohawk River, which was higher ground where they would avoid many low, swampy areas on the south side of the river. Herkimer wanted to advance on the south side of the Mohawk River, to avoid a potentially dangerous river crossing closer to the enemy forces. The general prevailed this time, but the breaches in discipline were worrisome.[12] By the time the column arrived at Oriska, the discontent was palpable.

As the sun rose on the militia camp early on Wednesday, August 6, the men listened intently for the three cannon shots that would indicate that Gansevoort had received Herkimer's message, but nothing

was heard. This was troubling: if the enemy had not intercepted the advanced party, they should have arrived at the fort by now. Several officers approached Herkimer, demanding that they march immediately despite the lack of response from Fort Stanwix. The general refused, arguing that they must be patient and wait for Gansevoort's cannon signal. The tensions that had already been smoldering due to past grievances and earlier arguments between Herkimer and his officers exploded. The senior officers broke into two camps: those who supported Herkimer's more cautious approach and a much larger group led by Colonel Ebenezer Cox, who demanded that they advance immediately to catch the enemy off balance. Cox and others also objected to Herkimer's use of the friendly Oneida warriors. They were deeply mistrusted by many of the men—another legacy of generations of conflict between Indians and Europeans in the Mohawk Valley. Herkimer explained that he would not lead them into a premature and rash attack, but the disaffected officers complained that the column was so close to the fort that their best course of action was to advance at once. Some officers even suggested that Herkimer was a coward, or worse, a closet Loyalist. This was too much: the proud Herkimer raged at the men but ultimately gave in. Herkimer called for his horse and shouted, "March on!"[13] Yet another source claims that the general bellowed, "You want war? . . . I give you war! You'll see the enemy. . . . And you'll be the first to run!"[14] Against his better judgment, the general had been provoked into a decision for an action he believed was wrong.[15]

Not only had Herkimer permitted his officers to override his better judgment, thereby undermining him in the eyes of the soldiers and diminishing his authority, but his understandable anger at the episode affected his decision-making. As the militiamen gathered their gear and assembled on the road for their march to the fort that morning, Herkimer, still trembling in anger over the incident with his officers, failed to assign men to guard the column's flanks as they marched. The Oneida warriors attached to Herkimer's detachment, instead of serving as the column's eyes and ears as they marched through the dense woods, took up position in the middle of the column ahead of the 4th Regiment from German Flatts, with whom they were friendly.[16] The 1st Regiment took up the lead for the column, followed by the 2nd Regiment, then the Oneidas along with Herkimer and his staff, followed by the 4th Regiment, with the 3rd Regiment split in two to protect the detachment's wagons bringing up the rear. As they marched west toward Fort Stanwix, the column was strung out along the narrow military road that cut through dense

woods, deep and narrow ravines, and through low swampy ground that was crossed by crude bridges.

The evening before Herkimer yielded to the demands of his rebellious officers, St. Leger was involved in his own drama in the British camp outside Fort Stanwix. Molly Brant's intelligence that an American relief column was marching to the fort's aid was not completely unexpected. Still, it did touch off a bitter disagreement between Joseph Brant and Sir John Johnson over how to confront the enemy force. Brant demanded that they immediately set up an ambush with the goal of destroying the approaching Americans. Sir John instead argued that they negotiate with the militia. Johnson believed that because he had deep and long-standing relationships with many of the Americans that he could convince them to disperse and return home. Johnson thought they should at least try his approach; plus, he understood that a bloody brother-against-brother battle could potentially poison the valley for generations. But Herkimer's approaching column was clearly a major threat to the expedition's success, so St. Leger decided to attack the American relief column with Johnson in overall command and with Brant in charge of planning the attack.[17]

Brant used his considerable local knowledge to plan the ambush. He knew that Herkimer and his men were marching along the military road from Stanwix to Albany, which ran along the Mohawk River. Just a few miles west of Oriska, the road crossed some heavily wooded high ground cut by three ravines. The column would first negotiate a ravine about 50 feet deep and about 300 yards wide on a part of the road that crossed a piece of swampy ground and a small stream. The road at this point was corduroy—hundreds of logs laid down on the marshy ground to enable men and wagons to move across the watery obstacle without getting bogged down. After crossing the swampy area, the road skirted a deep ravine to the north that ran to the Mohawk River, and then a few hundred yards farther on, a third ravine crossed the route of march. Brant decided to place most of his Mohawks along the southern side of the road between the two large ravines. More Indians were to attack the enemy along the corduroy road, where the column had to slow down. A fifty-man detachment from Johnson's King's Royal Regiment of New York and elements of German Jäger and John Butler's Rangers would block the road at the western ravine. Their job was to stop the Americans' forward progress, which would allow the Indians to inflict maximum damage on the rest of the column halted in the dense woods. Although accurate numbers are impossible to determine, Johnson and Brant's Indian and Loyalist force probably totaled around seven hundred men.[18]

Once the head of the column reached the western ravine, Brant reasoned that the tail of the enemy force would be climbing out of the eastern ravine or crossing the marshy ground along the corduroy road. If they timed it right, the head and tail of the column would be in low ground and extremely vulnerable, while the middle of the column would probably bunch up as they were forced to halt. This would leave them at the mercy of the Indians along the road on the high ground, and the American relief force would be quickly surrounded and destroyed. On Wednesday morning, August 6, Brant and Johnson placed their men in their positions, ensuring that they were well concealed as they settled down to wait for the American column.[19]

Allowing the insubordinate and headstrong Colonel Cox to lead the column proved a mistake. The more dependable 4th Regiment of German Flatts men under Colonel Peter Bellinger would have been a better choice. They were more loyal to their commander, and, more importantly, they were on good terms with the Oneidas, who could have been used effectively as scouts and flank guards. The Oneidas would have almost certainly detected the presence of Johnson's and Butler's Loyalists and Brant warriors. Herkimer's anger and embarrassment over the morning's incident had clouded his judgment.

As Cox's 1st Regiment of Canjoharie militia approached the western ravine, Johnson's and Butler's men waited with tense anticipation for the signal to open fire. The colonel had sent ahead a detachment of about twenty men as a small advanced guard. As they started down the ravine, the hot, sweaty men noticed a small creek at the bottom of the gully. Abandoning what little discipline they had, they immediately forgot their screening mission for the entire column and made a beeline to the water where they began to drink their fill. It was 10:00 a.m. The Americans were not the only ones on the field that day who lacked discipline. The virtually defenseless detachment of hated Patriots within easy range of their muskets overcame any restraint placed on the jumpy and impatient Loyalists by their officers. One Tory could not contain himself and fired, followed immediately by his comrades. The Senecas quickly joined the premature attack, and in a few minutes, the 1st Regiment's scouting detachment was all but wiped out. Among those killed in the first moments was Thomas Spencer, last seen alive in hand-to-hand combat. Only one man is known to have survived. The Battle of Oriskany had begun.[20]

Seconds after the first volleys, the rest of Johnson's force attacked, including Brant's Mohawks. Although the ambush did not go as planned, the impact and ferocity of the attack were devastating. Even

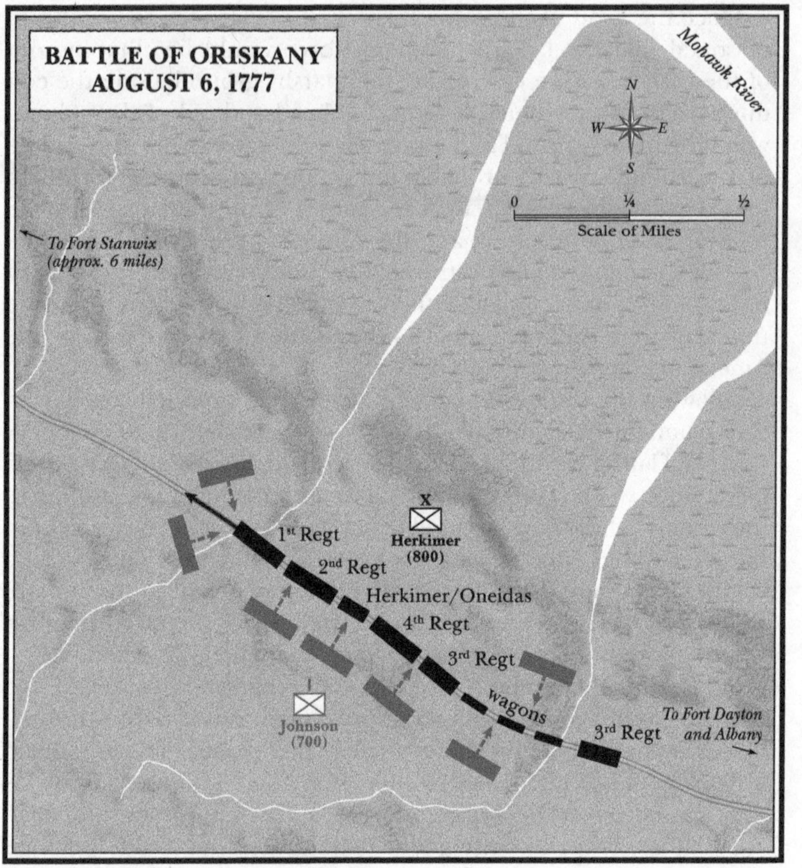

Map 8 Battle of Oriskany, August 6, 1777

well-trained troops can be temporarily incapacitated with shock at the surprise of a well-executed ambush. For the untrained militia, the viciousness of the attack was overwhelming, and the American response was slow. Many of the Indian were armed only with spears, knives, and tomahawks, and these warriors rushed in shrieking to grapple with the startled Americans while they fumbled with their muskets, which were unloaded for the march. Colonel Cox, who was mounted and riding with his regiment at the front of the column, tried to regain control of his men and impose some order, but was shot from his horse and killed.[21] Herkimer was riding toward the head of the column when a musket ball shattered his left leg. In

unspeakable pain, the general slid from his saddle as his mortally wounded horse fell on top of him. With Herkimer pinned under his dying horse, it looked like the militia was about to lose its commander in the first minutes of the fight. Fortunately, several men who had escaped the initial enemy fusillades and taken cover in the woods on the north side of the road saw Herkimer's plight and rushed forward under fire to pull their chief out from under the writhing animal. Dragging him into the woods and at least some semblance of cover, they hastily dressed Herkimer's wounds.[22]

As Brant's Mohawks waited for the signal to attack the vulnerable rear of the column as it reached the first ravine, they were shocked to hear gunfire to the west. Surprise lost, they immediately attacked the 3rd Regiment and the wagons. Many of Colonel Frederick Visscher's men broke and fled east down the road, believing that the way forward meant certain death. To these terrified men, it seemed that their only salvation was back the way they came. Discipline was lost as dozens of panic-stricken troops sprinted down the road and away from the chaos. Brant's Mohawks quickly and methodically chased them down, killing and scalping along the way until the road east of the ravine and the surrounding woods were littered with mutilated corpses. Brant captured almost all the wagons, and the teamsters were killed or dispersed. Despite the carnage he was inflicting in the east ravine, Brant failed to block the road completely, and some militiamen managed to escape.[23]

All along the road, from the east to the west ravine, the militiamen fought for their lives against Johnson's and Brant's Loyalists and Indians. The dense woods, combined with the choking black powder smoke from hundreds of muskets made it hard to pick out targets. The Mohawks and Senecas rushed forward, some firing their muskets at close range and the rest charging the militiamen while they loaded their weapons, a laborious procedure that took at least twenty seconds, and more when the soldier was under extreme stress. Many were cut down during the first minutes of the attack. Some tried to surrender but were hacked to death; the militiamen quickly realized that they had no choice except fight or die.[24] Countless hand-to-hand fights to the death took place on and near the road in the first few minutes of the battle. Soon the road and the surrounding woods were filled with dead and wounded men. The road itself was covered in blood and viscera. American soldiers watched helplessly as many of their comrades—close relatives, life-long friends, and neighbors—suffered brutal and gruesome deaths. The friendly Oneida warriors fought bravely and with reckless abandon

side by side with their Patriot allies. One Oneida brave killed nine Mohawks before being cut down himself.[25]

The battle was truly brother against brother: Oneida warriors fought their Iroquois cousins the Mohawk and Seneca; Loyalists fought their Patriot neighbors and former friends and business partners. The deep familiarity with the foe made the fighting even crueler than normal, if close-quarters combat can ever be called normal. Surviving militia officers screamed commands in German and English as they tried to restore order and organize the traumatized survivors into some kind of defense.

Fortunately for the American cause, Herkimer remained conscious despite his horrible wound. Propped up against a tree in the woods north of the road and near the east ravine's western crest, Herkimer slowly rallied his men. In the aftermath of the brutal ambush, Herkimer rose to the occasion, though grievously wounded and surrounded by his dead, wounded, and demoralized men. He realized that if he did not immediately galvanize his men, they would be wiped out in minutes. Calmly and deliberately, Herkimer issued orders delivered by intrepid messengers and slowly assembled the dazed survivors, managing to organize a defense on the high ground just west of the large, deep east ravine and north of the road.[26] Refusing his men's pleas to move him to a more covered and concealed position, Herkimer instead declared, "No, I will face my enemy!"[27] He quickly organized a defensive perimeter manned by between two hundred to three hundred surviving militia. John Butler would later write that the Americans "recovered themselves, fell back to more advantageous ground, maintaining a running fight."[28] It took a herculean effort to restore the fighting ability of the ragged remnants of the column. By this point—a half-hour after the initial attack—well over 50 percent of the American force was either dead, wounded, had fled, or worse, had been captured by the Indians. While they endured the worst of Johnson's and Brant's onslaught, the situation was still grim for the Americans. One or two determined attacks would probably have been enough to seal the fate of the exhausted remnants of the column that had proudly marched out of Fort Dayton only two days earlier.

As the Americans began to recover their senses and offer some resistance, Johnson ordered a bayonet attack by his regiment. After more hand-to-hand combat, the Loyalists were thrown back. Despite holding higher ground, the Americans were still in deep trouble. Many had still not recovered from the shock of the initial attack and the horrific fighting they had witnessed and endured. Nonetheless,

once the militiamen had regrouped, many fought well, causing significant casualties to Johnson's and Brant's forces.

Particularly critical were the casualties suffered by the Indians. The traditional Native American way of war was characterized by hit-and-run tactics, capturing enemy warriors and women and children, seizing booty, and avoiding pitched battles at all costs. The small Indian populations could simply not afford to take heavy casualties, and by noon on August 6, they had already lost many warriors. After the ambush's initial success, Herkimer's leadership had succeeded in staving off disaster, and the battle settled down into a more conventional affair. It did not take long before the Indian leaders began to complain to Johnson and Brant that they must either destroy the Americans or withdraw back to Fort Stanwix. The friendly Oneida warriors, who had fought so well and suffered grievous losses during the early phase of the attack, began to melt back into the woods and soon disappeared from the militia perimeter.

Johnson was concerned that he would lose control of his Indians and that the American survivors would escape, so he rushed back to the British camp outside Fort Stanwix to gather reinforcements. While he was at the camp, a severe thunderstorm rumbled through the area, halting the fighting for an hour. Soldiers and Indians on both sides struggled to keep their powder and weapons dry as heavy rain fell in sheets through the leaves and branches of the woods, sheltering the combatants. St. Leger approved Johnson's request for reinforcements, and Sir John hurried back to the battlefield with about seventy-five men. Johnson was determined to finish off the militia once and for all, but he needed to move quickly, or he would lose all of his Indians, who were growing increasingly disgruntled and restless.[29]

While Herkimer and the Tryon County militia were fighting for their lives, Gansevoort, in accordance with Herkimer's request, had organized a detachment of 250 men and one piece of field artillery under Willett to sally out of the fort to meet the relief column. Gansevoort fired his three cannon shots at around 1:00 p.m., about the same time the thunderstorm hit. The torrential rain also delayed Willett's departure from the fort. Finally, at around 2:00 p.m., Willett and his detachment poured out of the fort and headed south. They immediately encountered the Loyalist and Indian camps located south of the fort and flanking the road leading southeast toward the battlefield and ultimately all the way to Albany. The only occupants of the camps were women and children and a few warriors. Using his initiative, Willett seized on this unexpected opportunity and ordered

his men to destroy the camps. As they went about this task, they killed several Indians, captured four Loyalists, and seized or destroyed great quantities of papers, possessions, stores, and supplies. As Willett noted with considerable understatement, "Nothing could be more fortunate than this enterprise." Willett proudly recalled that they also captured five sets of enemy colors and that he had prevented the men from scalping the Indians and that they "were much better employed, and kept in excellent order." It took quite some time for Willett's men to destroy the Indian camps and transport their prizes back to the fort, which included Sir John's personal baggage and papers. The Americans also discovered, to their horror, the scalps of the two murdered girls, the grisly trophies "being neatly dressed and the hair plaited." They narrowly avoided Herkimer's fate by dispersing an enemy ambush with their lone artillery piece, which "did considerable execution," enabling Willett and his men to make it safely back to the fort with their prisoners and captured supplies. Although Willett changed the mission from meeting Herkimer to looting and destroying the Loyalist and Indian camps, his instincts were sound, and he did not know that the relief column was in the fight for its life. Not a single American soldier was lost in this action.[30]

After interrogating the enemy prisoners, Gansevoort discovered that Herkimer and his column had been intercepted on their way to the fort.[31] He and Willett reluctantly decided not to send out a rescue force, as they would most likely face a much larger combined Indian and British force and might even share Herkimer's fate. Sending Willett on his brief sally outside the fort had been a huge gamble. While they were not able to march to Herkimer's aid, the impact of Willett's brief but violent expedition outside the gates of Fort Stanwix was enormous. Although Gansevoort would not know it for some time, by destroying the Indian camps, he had come to Herkimer's rescue. In fact, Willett's raid had more of a positive effect on the battle than had he marched directly to the battlefield itself, 6 miles away.

As the thunderstorm dissipated, the battered remains of the relief column braced themselves for a renewed onslaught by the Loyalists and Indians that surrounded them. As one of Brant's Mohawks recalled later, "Soon after the rain stopped, the Indians and Troops began to creep forward through the drenched undergrowth."[32] Wounded from both sides caught in the blood- and rain-soaked no-man's-land between the two forces were slaughtered where they lay. As the killing continued, the Indians began to hear reports that the Americans had looted their camps. The rumors quickly spread and

were soon confirmed. First one by one, then in small groups, the Mohawks and Senecas began to leave, dissolving into the woods to make their way back to Fort Stanwix. Just as they could not afford heavy casualties, the Indians also had very few possessions, and what they had was highly prized. The battle and Willett's raid proved a double blow.

At about 3:00 p.m., a desperate Johnson realized that he had to end the battle immediately or all his Indians would soon be gone. He ordered his men to turn their green uniform coats inside out to reveal the white lining. He hoped that Herkimer's men would think the Loyalists were, in fact, American Continentals, some of whom wore white. This deception almost worked. As the Loyalists marched forward, many militiamen bolted toward their supposed saviors. Others suspected a trick, and an alert officer shouted out, "They're Tories, shoot, shoot."[33] Despite the warning, the men who had moved forward continued and were shot down or seized and killed with knife and bayonet. The militia recovered their senses and immediately opened fire at close range, killing and wounding many Loyalists. The battle once again degenerated into close-quarters combat. Johnson's ruse had failed, and the militiamen held their positions.[34]

The battle ended for the most part after this final attack. The Tories fell back, and the few remaining Indians rushed to their camps outside Fort Stanwix to assess the damage caused by Willett's raid. The rest of Johnson's force followed and returned to the British camp a few hours later. At a little after three in the afternoon of Wednesday, August 6, the contest was over after more than five hours of no-quarter combat.

The American militia hastily fashioned crude stretchers to recover their wounded, including Herkimer, and set out back down the road toward Fort Dayton, leaving their dead behind. As they marched, they found the bodies of their comrades who had tried to escape the ambush by fleeing east. Herkimer's family and friends hoped he would survive his terrible wound, but a botched amputation led to gangrene, and he died in agony ten days after the battle. Tragic as this was, his reputation was secure. Everyone remembered his cool leadership under fire, not the reasons he led his men into the ambush. The Battle of Oriskany, fought at a spot the Iroquois would forever call the "Place for Sorrows," was by far and away the bloodiest battle of the American Revolution by the percentage of men engaged. The Americans lost about five hundred men killed, wounded, or captured. Somewhere around 160 men were killed or died of their wounds, a loss rate of more than 62 percent. Johnson's

Loyalists and Indians lost about seventy killed, wounded, and missing. Around forty died in action, or about 15 percent of the men engaged.[35] Compared with the horrific American losses, the numbers seem small, but Johnson's Indians had not reckoned on losing so many warriors, and this affected them deeply.

By the evening of August 6, Johnson's entire force had made their way back to their camps surrounding Fort Stanwix. The Indians were furious and disheartened. Not only had they lost many fellow warriors, but most of their possessions and provisions. A day that had started with the promise of a great victory ended in mortification. Adding to their gloom, a disturbing sight greeted the returning Indians and Loyalists. As the fort came into view while they approached their camps along the Albany road, they saw that Gansevoort had attached the five captured enemy colors to the fort's flagpole under the American flag. Their humiliation was waving above the fort's southwest bastion for all to see.[36]

The Battle of Oriskany was technically an American victory: Herkimer and his survivors held the terrain after Johnson and Brant withdrew back to the British camp outside Fort Stanwix. But it certainly did not seem like it to the exhausted militiamen as they made their way back to German Flatts and Fort Dayton. They had suffered appalling casualties, and they had not accomplished their mission to relieve the fort. On the other hand, the British had turned back the relief column and were able to continue the siege unmolested. In his report to Carleton, St. Leger certainly thought it was a great success. Indeed, he wrote, despite the fact they were not able to destroy the American militia column, "the two hundred who escaped only served to spread the panic wider."[37]

Despite its immediate impact, in the longer term, the battle was devastating for all concerned. The combination of Johnson's inability to destroy Herkimer's force and Willett's destruction of the Loyalist and Indian camps had an enormous strategic impact. Gansevoort and Willett were able to seize the initiative, resulting in the demoralization of St. Leger's Indian allies, which led in turn to their premature departure from his ranks. The battle led to more animosity and hatred between families along the Mohawk. The heavy casualties suffered by the Indians on both sides led directly to a bloody civil war within the Iroquois Confederacy that lasted for years. For all sides—Patriots, Tories, and the various Indian tribes—it would take generations for the hatred and animosities to dissipate.

St. Leger was only concerned with the here and now, and he and most of his men thought they had just won a great victory. They had

almost completely annihilated Herkimer's relief column and forced the survivors to retreat back down the valley. If nothing else, the Battle of Oriskany had bought the British commander time to complete his siege and capture the fort. Once that was accomplished, he could get back on his timetable and march to Albany and then link up with Burgoyne. Even if things had not gone according to plan, St. Leger had every reason to think that he would still accomplish his part of the campaign.

Colonel Gansevoort was under no illusions. He knew that the relief column had been attacked and probably turned back and that the fort and its garrison were still in great danger from St. Leger and his force, which outnumbered the Americans by more than two to one. Still, he took some satisfaction in what he had been able to do. "At 11 o'Clock this Evening the Enemy came near the Fort [and] called to our Centinels," wrote one American officer, "telling them to come out again with Fixed Bayonets and they would give us Satisfaction for Yesterday's work. . . . We laughed at them heartily."[38]

Two days after the battle, however, Gansevoort learned the fate of Herkimer's militiamen when St. Leger sent his adjutant and Butler to the fort under a flag of truce with a letter from two of Herkimer's militia officers who had been captured at Oriskany. The letter informed the colonel that the column had been destroyed and that all communication between the fort and the rest of the Mohawk Valley was severed. Gansevoort was also told that no other relief force was coming because Burgoyne was already in Albany. St. Leger's representatives demanded that the colonel and his garrison surrender immediately. Gansevoort refused, replying, "I will answer no verbal summons but at the mouth of a cannon, unless delivered by Colonel St. Leger himself."[39]

Early the next day, St. Leger sent Gansevoort a written surrender demand. He informed Gansevoort that the Indians under his command were so enraged over their loss of men at the Battle of Oriskany and the American raid on their camps that they "were determined, unless they got possession of the fort to go down the Mohawk river, and fall upon its inhabitants." Even women and children would not be spared. In addition, it was only with great difficulty that St. Leger was able to convince them not to kill the entire garrison if they surrendered. If the Americans resisted, "the consequences to the garrison, should it afterwards fall into their hands, must be terrible."[40]

St. Leger obviously thought he could overawe the young colonel and his garrison with threats, but Gansevoort would have none of it and sent Willett out with his written reply. When Willett met

St. Leger's representatives outside the fort, he scolded the enemy officers for the outrageous threats contained in the surrender demand: "By your uniform you are British officers. Therefore let me tell you that the message you have brought is a degrading one for a British officer to send and by no means reputable for a British officer to carry."[41] Gansevoort's written response to St. Leger's message was eloquent in its simplicity and directness, and spoke volumes about the colonel's resolve: "Your Letter of this days Date I have Receiv'd, in Answer to which I say, that it is my Determined resolution with the Forces under my Command to defend this Fort [to] the last Extremity in behalf of the United American States who have placed me here to Defend it against all Enemies."[42] Gansevoort would not make a "Ticonderoga of it."

After receiving Gansevoort's reply, St. Leger began to bombard the fort. The cannonade continued throughout the day, stopped for the few hours, and then picked up again late in the evening and continued until the next morning. The artillery fire did no damage to the walls but did cause casualties, and Gansevoort worried that if the buildings inside the walls caught fire, he could lose a significant amount of stores and ammunition. After the flurry of artillery fire ended early on August 10, St. Leger tried to trick Gansevoort into thinking he had abandoned the siege by setting fire to valuable haystacks. The colonel did not fall for the ruse. "Fearing they meant to lull us to sleep and Storm us in the Night," recalled one officer, "the Colonel ordered the Guard & Piquet doubled and the Troops to lay on their Arms."[43] St. Leger continued a desultory cannonade of the fort day and night for the rest of the siege.

Despite the success of Willett's destruction of the Loyalist and Indian camps south of the fort, the situation was still grim for the garrison. They could not hold out indefinitely. Reluctantly, Gansevoort decided that he had to send for help. This was a difficult decision. Enemy forces surrounded the fort, and whoever he picked to make their way to Schuyler would have to slip through St. Leger's lines, and specifically, through the Indians south and east of the fort. These were the same angry and disgruntled Indians who had fought at Oriskany and seen their camps looted by the hated Americans. If the men Gansevoort sent were captured, they could expect a certain and gruesome death. For this perilous mission, Gansevoort selected the redoubtable Willett. Before he left the fort, Willett wrote a farewell letter to the men of the 3rd New York Regiment. Assuring them that he would soon be "Congratulating you on a Glorious Deliverance from your Present Enemies," Willett urged them not to be afraid of

their enemies, who were "truly a Contemptable pack," lacking the power to put their "Diabolical purposes into execution."[44] Willett's letter suggests that St. Leger's threats to unleash the Indians were not working.

Willett's mission to summon help for the fort was every bit as daring and spectacular as any special operation in American history. At 10:00 p.m. on August 10, he and Lieutenant Levi Stockwell, "a good woodman," slipped out of the fort and into the surrounding woods and swamps, carefully skirting the Indian camps using roughly the same route that Herkimer's men had used several days before.[45] Under cover of darkness, they crept through the marsh south and west of the fort, bypassing enemy sentinels who, at times, were only feet away. Crossing the Mohawk River on a log, they made their way through woods teeming with angry Indians. To hide their tracks, they walked on rocks as much as possible and waded through the river. Often having to crawl through thickets, they were forced to halt until daylight revealed a track through the undergrowth and they could continue their perilous mission. To maintain absolute silence, they traveled unarmed and without provisions, so they subsisted on wild berries found along the way.[46] As the men made their way through the woods, they stumbled upon the horrific Oriskany battlefield where the unburied bodies of friends and enemies alike lay strewn about the road and nearby woods. They finally arrived at German Flatts in the afternoon of August 12, having traveled almost 50 miles in less than 48 hours. At Fort Dayton, they learned that Schuyler had already dispatched a relief expedition to Stanwix. The two officers, though exhausted, commandeered horses and rode toward Albany to meet the troops.[47]

Unknown to Gansevoort, Schuyler had already received news of the Oriskany disaster and, against the advice of his fellow general officers, dispatched Brigadier General Ebenezer Learned and a small detachment of troops from the main army to relieve Gansevoort.[48] Schuyler wrote Gansevoort on August 10 that the force was on its way to Fort Stanwix, and "Every Body here believes you will defend it to the last, and I strictly enjoin you to do so." As more New England militia units joined the main army, Schuyler finally began to express some optimism. He assured Gansevoort that despite the fact that Burgoyne's army was at Fort Edward and the Americans continued their steady withdrawal, "Great Reinforcements [are] coming from the Eastward, and we trust all will be well and that the Enemy will be repulsed."[49]

Unaware that another American relief force was en route from Albany, St. Leger continued the siege. The day after Willett's and

Stockman's departure, St. Leger's men attacked the fort's main water supply by diverting the stream that ran just east of the fort. St. Leger's action "wou'd have done us much Damage," wrote one officer, had Gansevoort not already ordered his men to dig "two Wells in the Garrison, which with on We had already proved a Sufficient Supply."[50] Gansevoort had anticipated St. Leger's move.

On August 11, sensing that he might not be able to capture the fort with the resources on hand, St. Leger wrote to Burgoyne with a plea for assistance. Not knowing exactly where the main army was, he sent one of his trusted Indians to deliver the message. St. Leger explained that despite the Battle of Oriskany, the Americans manning the fort were still stubbornly resisting, "A diversion therefore from your army" would "greatly expedite" his movement down the river to Albany.[51] Instead of St. Leger leading a diversionary attack designed in part to ease Burgoyne's passage to Albany, the shoe was on the other foot. The intrepid but anonymous Indian finally found Burgoyne, but he could offer no assistance. In his response to St. Leger, Burgoyne blamed the heavy rains "that prevented me getting forward." Burgoyne suggested that St. Leger simply attack and seize the fort or bypass it and head for Lake George. Burgoyne explained that it would be at least two weeks before he could dispatch any assistance.[52] St. Leger was on his own.

St. Leger now had to deal not only with the tenacious Gansevoort and the determined American garrison but with his own discontented Indians allies. The losses from Oriskany and Willett's raid were proving too much, and the desertions began. As St. Leger dryly reported, the "same zeal no longer animated the Indians: they complained of the thinness of troops and their former losses."[53] For the Indians, the campaign had simply become too costly.

With Gansevoort resisting St. Leger's attempts at intimidation and with inadequate artillery to penetrate the fort's stout ramparts, the British commander decided to send Butler with a small detachment of soldiers and Indians down the Mohawk to threaten the civilian population with slaughter unless they supported the invading enemy army. Butler's mission ended in failure when American soldiers captured him and his men near Fort Dayton. St. Leger was running out of options.[54]

Although the fort's garrison had enough food and water to last for weeks, the rigors of the siege began to tell. The crowded conditions, the round-the-clock British shelling, and constant vigilance against enemy surprise attack were exhausting the men. After St. Leger's second surrender demand, Gansevoort ordered the entire garrison

to "turn out to their Alarm Posts at 2 oClock every morning."[55] This action required every soldier to report to his assigned post in and around the fort fully dressed and under arms. They had to stay at their posts until sunrise, after which the normal duty day began. As the weary garrison went about their duties under the sporadic artillery bombardment, St. Leger's men began to build zigzag approach trenches north of the fort that slowly began to work their way toward Stanwix's walls.[56] To Gansevoort and his men, it was a clear sign that St. Leger had begun an extended, conventional siege, and it was not at all clear that the garrison could hold out before the trenches reached the walls of the fort.

On August 13, Schuyler decided to place the relief force under the command of the newly arrived Arnold, as Washington had suggested three weeks earlier. This was a mission tailor-made for Arnold, who immediately left the main army's camp to join Learned's men already marching up the Mohawk. At Albany, he met with Willett, who gave him valuable intelligence on the conditions in the fort, the strength and dispositions of St. Leger's force, and the route. By August 17, Arnold and his small force arrived at Fort Dayton to prepare for a final push to Stanwix. Aware of the disaster suffered by the Tryon County militia relief force at Oriskany, the ordinarily aggressive Arnold was reluctant to simply march up the Stanwix-Albany road as had the unfortunate Herkimer. He tried and failed to encourage the local population to join his detachment. The bloody Battle of Oriskany had dampened any residual patriotic fervor that might have still existed in the Mohawk Valley. Still, Arnold could not linger too long at Fort Dayton; Stanwix had to be relieved. While he considered his next moves, he received a letter from Gates, who had just arrived at Albany to relieve Schuyler and take command of the Northern Department. "As soon as you have put a happy finishing to our affairs to the Westward," urged Gates, "I desire you to immediately return to the Main Army with all the force you carried with you."[57] Arnold replied on August 21, expressing his pleasure at the news of Gates's arrival. He reported that he was departing Fort Dayton "for Fort Schuyler, which is still besieged by a number equal to ours, nothing shall be omitted that can be done to raise the siege." He assured Gates that "you will hear of my being victorious or no more, and as soon as the Safety of this part of the Country will Permit I will fly to your assistance."[58]

Arnold did not tell Gates that he had decided to employ a deception operation focused directly at St. Leger and his remaining Indian allies. One of the men captured with Butler on his ill-fated

attempt to mobilize the local Mohawk Valley populace to the British cause was a local distant relative to Schuyler, Hans Yost Schuyler. Schuyler was probably mildly mentally disabled and was regarded by the Indians with great respect. As a Loyalist who had taken up arms against his Patriot neighbors, he was tried by a military court and sentenced to receive one hundred lashes. Arnold threatened Hans Yost with the wholesale arrest and execution of his family if he did not agree to travel to the British camp outside Stanwix and report to St. Leger that a large force of three thousand Americans was on the way to relieve Gansevoort and the garrison. As one American officer recalled, Arnold further ordered Schuyler to tell St. Leger that "if he did not, without delay, raze the siege, they might expect he would march his army and cut them off, or make prisoners of the whole."[59] Schuyler agreed to Arnold's demands and left immediately for Stanwix, arriving on August 22.[60]

While Arnold was finalizing his plans for relieving Stanwix, St. Leger redoubled his siege efforts by increasing the workforce assigned to dig the approach trenches. Gansevoort recognized that if the trenches were allowed to get close to the fort, even St. Leger's small-caliber cannons might be able to breach the fort's walls when employed at point-blank range. The threat to the fort was very real. The American commander, therefore, ordered his men to keep up a harassing fire on the trenches. Even if he could not stop St. Leger's progress on the trenches, he might at least slow it down. One American officer reported that their fire forced the British to work at night and that they were under constant "fire of our Cannon and small Arms."[61] St. Leger also directed his men to increase their own harassing fire against the garrison resulting in several American casualties. The approach trenches and increased sniper fire indicated an imminent British assault on the fort, resulting in several American desertions.[62] Still, the garrison's overall morale was good, and Gansevoort reported that the Americans at Stanwix "are still in high Spirits and Determined to Defend it to the Last."[63]

But no British attack was forthcoming. Instead, before his approach trenches could get close to the fort, St. Leger received two devastating pieces of intelligence: Burgoyne's army had experienced a serious setback at Bennington, and Hans Yost Schuyler arrived with the news that Arnold was on his way with an overwhelming relief force. At first, St. Leger wanted to personally lead an attack on the advancing Americans along the Stanwix-Albany road, aiming for a repeat of the Oriskany ambush. After announcing to the Indians his plans, St. Leger sensed they were reluctant to resume offensive

operations. "It was at that moment I began to suspect cowardice in some and treason in others," St. Leger reported, "but I returned to camp not without hopes . . . of inducing them [the Indians] to meet the enemy." It was not to be. At a council with the Indian leaders, St. Leger learned that some two hundred warriors had already decamped and that he must retreat, or the rest would abandon him. He simply could not continue without Indian assistance.[64] In a matter of hours, St. Leger's army abandoned their camp, the trenches, and a large store of supplies, and began the long trek back the way they came over twenty days before. The siege was over.

On the afternoon of August 22, seven British deserters came into the fort and told an astonished Gansevoort that St. Leger with his army was "retreating with the utmost precipitation." The colonel promptly sent out a reconnaissance party that confirmed the startling news.[65] Arnold received Gansevoort's news the next day while on the march to the fort and immediately informed Gates that the enemy had lifted the siege. While Arnold thought the enemy army was probably heading back to Canada, he argued that St. Leger might have "retire[d] with a view of engaging us on the road." He told Gates that he would dispatch nine hundred men on a forced march to the fort, hoping to catch up with them.[66]

True to his word, Arnold covered more than 30 miles in less than a day and arrived at Fort Stanwix at mid-afternoon on August 24. On the way, the Stanwix-Albany road passed through the Oriskany battlefield, and Arnold's men had to march past the unburied corpses of hundreds of men. One officer described the horrific scene: "the weather [was] warm, and they were much swollen and of a purple colour, which represented the frailty of man in a very figurative sense."[67]

The tired but grateful Stanwix garrison greeted their saviors with a cannon salute, "Attended with the Cheers from the Troops."[68] Arnold found that Gansevoort had the situation well in hand. "Colonel Gansevoort had anticipated my design," he reported to Gates, "by sending out a small party, who brought in . . . a considerable quantity of baggage, with a number of prisoners and deserters." Arnold praised Gansevoort and his men, telling Gates that the colonel and the fort's garrison "deserve great applause for their Spirited Conduct and vigorous defence."[69]

Arnold rested his men that day and set out in pursuit of St. Leger's force early the next morning as they moved toward Oneida Lake. The Americans "arrived just in time to see the last Boats of the Enemy going off," he reported. Arnold and his detachment

stayed at Stanwix another two days to make sure St. Leger had indeed retreated to Oswego, and then he started the long march back down the Mohawk Valley toward Albany to rejoin the main army. Before he left, he ensured that the Stanwix garrison was resupplied with enough food and ammunition to last five months, and he did the same to all the key forts throughout the Mohawk Valley. On August 28, he was already near Fort Dayton, where he wrote to Gates to tell him that he would soon rejoin the army with twelve hundred men and a few friendly Indians. Arnold assured the commander of the Northern Department that there was "nothing to fear from the Enemy in this quarter at Present."[70]

Gansevoort and his garrison had successfully defended Fort Stanwix in the face of heavy odds. Their losses had been slight: seven soldiers killed in action; eighteen wounded in action; and nine deserted, for a total of fifty men, or about 5 percent.[71] Given the importance of the post, the price the Americans paid to keep it was very small. By comparison, St. Leger later reported that he lost thirty-seven men since the siege began, thirteen fewer than the Americans, but these numbers were probably much higher since he did not record Indian casualties.[72]

When St. Leger arrived at Oswego, he found a letter from Burgoyne waiting for him, urging him to move quickly to join the main army either down the Mohawk Valley, or, if that route were no longer possible, to sail back up the St. Lawrence to Canada and then south up Lake Champlain to Fort Ticonderoga and Fort Edward. St. Leger wrote to Carleton, blaming his lack of success at taking Stanwix on his Indian allies, despite the advantages in numbers he enjoyed and his victory at Oriskany. Every misstep could be laid at the feet of treasonous Indians failing to fight or being "misled by the information of a cowardly Indian," and so on.[73] Others blamed the failure on a lack of heavy artillery.[74] To his credit, St. Leger moved quickly in an attempt to reinforce Burgoyne, but the distances were simply too great, and the transportation challenges too complex, and in the end, he never made it to the main army.

While St. Leger embarked on vessels to begin his move back to Canada, news of his retreat spread throughout the region and beyond. Arnold was just the first key official to commend Gansevoort. Gates passed on his appreciation, as did the commander-in-chief himself. When Washington received official news of the raising of the siege, he wrote Gates to say that the victory "will free us from any further Apprehensions of an Invasion in that Quarter this campaign." Washington was also prescient when he opined that St. Leger would

no longer be a factor in the northern theater due to the enemy's "Loss of Provisions and baggage, and the distance they have to go."[75] Alexander Hamilton wrote that "The relieving [of] Fort Schuyler is a very happy and important event" that will surely help "to reverse the state of affairs and turn the scale against Mr. Burgoigne."[76]

Congress, too, gave its thanks to Gansevoort and Willett.[77] John Hancock wrote them both to forward the official "Thanks of Congress" for their "Defence of Fort Schuyler." Gansevoort was given the honorary title of "Colonel Commandant of the Fort," while Willett was presented with "an elegant sword" in recognition of his "Successful Sally . . . made on the Enemy while they invested Fort Schuyler."[78] John Adams, who had been frustrated by the seeming inactivity and lack of drive of so many American commanders, happily wrote to his wife that "Gansevoort has proved, that it is possible to hold a Post."[79]

Like every good leader, Gansevoort credited his men with the victory. In a speech to his regiment after he returned from a short leave of absence after St. Leger's retreat, he told his soldiers that they had done "essential Service to your Country and acquir'd the immortal Honour to yourselves." Gansevoort closed his address by saying that the success of the 1777 campaign "will effectually establish the Independence of the United States and thereby Secure to ourselves the Spirits and Liberties for which we have nobly stood forth."[80] Gansevoort had exhibited a high degree of grip.

Holding Fort Stanwix was significant in many ways. The failure of St. Leger to penetrate down the Mohawk Valley disrupted Burgoyne's plans; he had counted on St. Leger to divert critical American military resources to the western part of New York and away from the main effort, and as a supporting effort that would link up with the main army at or near Albany.[81] As Burgoyne's situation grew increasingly grim in late August 1777, he needed St. Leger to succeed. The latter's failure was a blow to Burgoyne, especially in the wake of other setbacks. With Fort Stanwix remaining firmly in American hands, the western part of the Northern Department was safe from British and Indian threats for at least another year. Moreover, the Americans proved that the British did not have a monopoly on capable and professionally competent leaders.[82]

St. Leger was ultimately forced to move his army back to Canada and up Lake Champlain to reinforce Burgoyne, but he never made it farther than Ticonderoga. The Americans exploited interior lines, and the British were forced to go the long way around. When Schuyler dispatched the relief force while facing Burgoyne's army, he (and

later Gates) weighed the pros and cons. Then, he calculated that the detachment under Arnold could reach Stanwix, lift the siege, secure the region, and return to the main American Army before Burgoyne could strike. It was a gutsy move made while Burgoyne and his army were moving south.

The American victory at Stanwix provided a major morale boost to both the Northern Army and the American population. Until Stanwix, they had endured disaster after disaster, including the loss of Ticonderoga and other key posts, the Battle of Hubbardton, the headlong retreat of the American Army, and the Battle of Oriskany. Stanwix and, as we will see, the Battle of Bennington provided a much-needed corrective to the litany of calamities. The social, political, and military balance of power had started to swing to the Patriot side.

Many of the families who lost loved ones at Oriskany wreaked vengeance on Loyalists and Mohawk settlements in the valley, driving many families out of the region. Ultimately, the British would employ more Loyalist Rangers and Indians for the defense of Canada and raids into the frontiers of Pennsylvania and New York, which led to the infamous Wyoming Massacre and the start of a terrible frontier war that lasted on and off from the summer of 1778 until 1781. But in the short term, at least, the enemy Indian and Tory threat was eliminated from the Mohawk Valley.[83]

The leadership demonstrated by Gansevoort and Willett stood in stark contrast to that exhibited by American senior leaders at Fort Ticonderoga. Gansevoort sought opportunities to gain an advantage over the enemy despite being heavily outnumbered. He consistently anticipated St. Leger's actions. He always kept his men informed by regularly addressing the garrison and sought out ways to lift their morale. Together, he and Willett provided what the American cause most needed at this critical juncture: grit.

CHAPTER 14

Cat and Mouse

WHEN LIEUTENANT GENERAL CLINTON arrived in New York City on July 5 from England, he was appalled at what he found. After witnessing firsthand the strategic planning done in London over the winter and into early spring, he was convinced that Howe would be preparing to move the army up the Hudson River to link up with Burgoyne's army from Canada. Instead, he found that Howe was getting ready to move the army by sea to Philadelphia. Unlike Howe, Clinton had discussed the 1777 campaign with Germain, so he was familiar with the secretary's intent. Clinton knew that the king and Germain saw the linkup of Burgoyne's and Sir William's army as a necessary condition for winning the war. Howe, on the other hand, was focused on Philadelphia, part of a campaign that had been approved by both the king and Germain. During the three weeks between his return to America and the embarking of Howe's army onto Lord Howe's ships at the end of July, Clinton tried in vain to convince Howe to abandon Philadelphia and cooperate with Burgoyne.[1]

Never shy about voicing his opinion, Clinton confronted the commander-in-chief and expressed his concern over what he thought was a disastrous strategic decision, but "my proposal was very coldly received at first." As the days passed, Howe gave no indication that he would change his mind, but "by degrees I was heard," recalled Clinton, and "at least I was encouraged to speak my mind very freely." In a series of meetings between the two generals during that month of July in New York, Clinton attempted to clarify "all

the disadvantages of the move proposed, and all the good which might be expected from mine." Still, no amount of cajoling could move Howe.[2] The Philadelphia expedition was moving forward, and nothing Clinton could say would divert Howe from attacking the home of the hated Continental Congress.

On July 7, the same day that General Fraser was fighting for his life against the stubborn American rear guard at Hubbardton, Howe wrote Germain that he would be unable to join with Burgoyne. Such a linkup "I do not suppose can happen this campaign as I apprehend General Burgoyne will find full employment for his army against that of the rebels opposed to him." In other words, Burgoyne had to fight his own fight in upstate New York. Howe would focus on Philadelphia. He also told the secretary that Clinton would stay in New York because of the city's importance. Clinton's primary mission was to act on the "defensive, with power to act otherwise . . . without losing sight of the principal object in the security of this place," suggesting that Clinton might be able to do something in support of Burgoyne. Howe closed by noting that he had received nothing of consequence from Carleton and Burgoyne, suggesting that the operation to Albany would have no impact, positive or negative, on his Philadelphia campaign.[3]

By this time, the relationship between Howe and Clinton had hit rock bottom. Whatever facts, logic, and persuasive rationale may have been behind Clinton's arguments, Howe was unlikely to take his subordinate's advice. He had invested months of planning and thought into the Philadelphia campaign, which had been approved by his superiors, and he was the commander-in-chief, after all. Unlike Carleton and Germain, whose relationship had degenerated into mutual hatred, Clinton and Howe respected each other, but simply could not work together. For the good of the British war effort, Germain and the king probably should have taken Howe's advice when he suggested that Clinton take command of the Canada army with Burgoyne assigned as his, Howe's, second-in-command. Burgoyne and Howe were much closer in temperament and probably would have worked quite well together. Clinton, the senior of the two, had already conducted independent operations and was better suited for the Albany mission. As things stood, dysfunction at the highest level of the British chain of command was hindering operations.

Like Howe, Washington had to divide his attention, but he was better at it. Although most Americans expected another British attempt to repeat the 1776 campaign, Washington had to be prepared

to counter several enemy options. He consolidated the main army in the hills around Boundbrook, New Jersey, 20 miles west of New York and only a few miles northwest of Howe's army at Brunswick, New Jersey. From there, Washington could keep a close watch on Howe and move north to reinforce the American units in the Hudson Highlands or even the Northern Department. He could also fall back to cover Philadelphia, if necessary.

For his part, while Howe was preparing for his expedition by sea to Philadelphia, he also tried to lure Washington into battle. If he could do that, he might end the war in one stroke. To force Washington to move out of his virtually unassailable positions at Boundbrook, Howe planned to march his army from Brunswick toward Philadelphia. If Washington took the bait, Howe might get his long-sought decisive battle.[4]

On June 13, Howe started moving the army but quickly ran into scattered American forces. After marching a few miles, his troops were forced to halt when they encountered a destroyed bridge across the Millstone River. After repairing the bridge, Howe waited for Washington to react. Washington quickly and correctly determined what Howe was doing and reported to Congress that Sir William "designs Philadelphia to be the Object of his pursuits—or the defeat of this Army &c, for one or both of these purposes."[5] Washington immediately ordered several units from the Hudson Highlands to reinforce the main army. In addition, he directed the newly promoted Arnold to defend Philadelphia.[6]

Alexander Hamilton was a firm believer in the commander-in-chief's overall strategy, even in the event Howe succeeded in seizing Philadelphia. It was critical to "avoid a general action," though they might in the process give "up objects of first importance," like the city, as he wrote in a letter to Hugh Knox. As long as the army remained intact, they could "take advantage of favorable opportunities and waste and defeat the enemy by piece-meal."[7] This was the essence of Washington's military strategy.

Although not convinced he fully understood Howe's intentions, Washington started to get a pretty good idea. As he explained to Arnold, the "views of the Enemy must be to give a severe blow to this Army and to get possession of Philada." He was, again, right on both counts, but in this letter, Washington also incisively noted that "Both are objects of importance; but the former of far the greatest." So long as the Continental Army existed, "every acquisition of territory they make will be precarious and perhaps burthensome." An attack on Howe would be ruinous.[8] On June 18, five days after he

marched out of Brunswick, Howe returned the army to their camps, and shortly after that, marched his troops all the way back to Amboy, New Jersey, and from there to Staten Island, abandoning his effort to force Washington to give battle by maneuvering his army overland.[9]

By early summer, Howe had turned his attention back to the Philadelphia campaign. His New Jersey adventure, however, had pushed back the start of that operation. Once the British Army arrived on Staten Island, they started to load the waiting transport ships. The delay, coupled with the absence of a favorable wind, meant that it would be almost impossible for Sir William to provide any material assistance to Burgoyne, even had he wanted to sail north rather than south. Little things were starting to add up and taken together they would determine the fate of the army from Canada.

Washington soon figured out that Howe was going by sea, but guessed they would go up the Hudson rather than south to the Delaware River.[10] Using the Royal Navy's superior mobility, Howe could move in multiple directions, which placed Washington at a distinct disadvantage, forcing him to be reactive. Howe could move the army to Rhode Island. He could also go up the mouth of the Delaware to Philadelphia, or, now, most likely in Washington's view, he could sail up the Hudson to cooperate with Burgoyne. Two days later, Washington warned General Putnam, still commanding troops in the Hudson Highlands, that "If Genl Howe should make a push up the River, the importance of the Highland passes will demand the utmost attention & every exertion for their Security."[11] A week later, Washington became even more convinced Howe was aiming to go up the Hudson and ordered Brigadier John Nixon's brigade of Continental troops to join Schuyler's army.[12] It was the first of many resources Washington would provide to the Northern Army over the next several weeks.

By July 5, Washington knew that Burgoyne had started his campaign and was convinced that Howe was moving north to join with him.[13] Although that was Howe's most likely course of action, Washington could not confirm it through his various intelligence sources, which meant he still had to stay flexible. He had to be ready to move north to reinforce the American troops guarding the Hudson Highlands, move even further north in support of Schuyler, or protect Philadelphia. Only two days after concluding that Howe was going up the river, Washington received intelligence from a Staten Island resident who had observed the British Army making preparations that seemed more elaborate than those for a simple trip up the Hudson. Not only were the troops embarking on the waiting

ships, but "small Craft are constantly lying between N. York and the Fleet laden with Officer's Baggage and Stores put up in packages." It also appeared as if stalls for horses were being fitted on the vessels. These things indicated that "[t]his looks as if a longer Voyage was intended than up the North River," as Washington wrote to Hancock on July 7. Consequently, he warned the New England states to "be on their guard."[14]

The loss of Fort Ticonderoga again altered Washington's assessment of the strategic situation. "Whatever might have been General Howe's intentions a few days ago," Washington observed to one of his officers, "there remains little doubt of what they will be when he gets intelligence from Northward."[15] Surely Howe would now sail up the Hudson to exploit Burgoyne's success. Washington responded by marching the army to the northeast, closer to the Hudson, where he could better react to Howe.

But the commander-in-chief was wrong. When Howe received confirmation of Burgoyne's victory at Ticonderoga and learned that the fort would be garrisoned in part from Canada, he became more resolved than ever to move on Philadelphia. After all, if Burgoyne could seize the greatest fortress in North America so effortlessly, he did not need Howe's help to complete his mission. Besides, Washington was sure to follow Howe to Philadelphia and leave Burgoyne alone.[16] If Howe had ever had any nagging doubts about going to Philadelphia instead of up the Hudson, they were gone.

By the time Howe received the news about Ticonderoga, his army had been packed aboard the anchored transports for more than a week, waiting for a favorable wind to carry them out of their anchorage and south to either the mouth of the Delaware or the Chesapeake Bay. Conditions on these ships were never comfortable, and as the idle men and horses languished in the great wallowing vessels, the hot weather started taking its toll. Frustration grew, including among Howe's staff. One of his aides complained in his diary that "no one seems to be able to figure out why we are waiting so long, considering the fact that everyone, except Howe and few officers, are aboard ship."[17]

As Washington maneuvered the army closer to the Hudson River and Peekskill to guard against a British thrust up the Hudson, Howe, comfortably ashore and therefore not sharing in his troops' discomfort on the transports, took a break from his preparations to assure Germain that all was well and that nothing could derail the Philadelphia expedition. In the unlikely event that Washington moved north up the Hudson River or showed signs of attacking

New York, Howe would leave Clinton behind with additional troops. He had no worries about Burgoyne. "I apprehend General Burgoyne will meet with little interruption otherwise than the difficulties he must encounter in transporting stores and provisions for the supply of his army." In the unlikely event that Washington marched north to attack Burgoyne, "the strength of General Burgoyne's army is such as to leave me no room to dread the event." Washington would quickly find himself trapped by Northern Army and Clinton's New York force at the same moment, a situation from which "I flatter myself he would find it difficult to escape."[18] In all these rosy scenarios that Howe laid out for the secretary, he never once even mentioned Schuyler's army.

Not all British generals were as sure of success as Howe and Burgoyne. As Howe readied his amphibious expedition, Clinton seethed. Howe was going to Philadelphia despite his best efforts to convince him otherwise. Clinton's frustration over his chief's inability to see reason boiled over in a blunt letter to Howe. "I confess I more and more see the necessity of making a diversion in his [Burgoyne's] favor," argued Clinton. Howe should have moved north weeks sooner, and now it was probably too late. However, Howe could still help the northern army with an operation along the Connecticut River instead of Philadelphia. At any rate, supporting Burgoyne was critical because "such things may be at this instant done there as will decide the war." Clinton hoped that he was not too frank with the commander-in-chief. "If I am not so lucky to have you agree with me, I sincerely hope that your success (go where you will) be such as may make it appear that your opinion has been the best." However, Clinton had second thoughts and wrote on the letter, "not sent, I repent I did not."[19] It is doubtful that Clinton's letter, had he sent it, would have made any difference to Howe.[20] Howe persisted in believing that only a threat to Philadelphia could lure Washington into a decisive, war-winning battle.

As Howe made final preparations for his joint amphibious operation with his brother, Lord Howe, he also prepared his instructions for Clinton, who would remain behind in New York with a force of about seven thousand men.[21] His subordinate's mission was twofold: first, and most importantly, he had to defend New York, Long Island, and the eastern part of New Jersey bordering on the New York harbor. Second, "if you can make any diversion in favor of Genl Burgoyne's approaching Albany . . . I need not point out the utility of such a measure."[22] Accomplishing both missions with seven thousand men would be very difficult indeed.

Finally, on July 23, after seemingly interminable delays, Howe and his army of sixteen thousand soldiers set sail, escorted by Royal Navy warships.[23] Howe knew exactly where he wanted to go, though he was unsure of his route to get there. There were two options available for the fleet to sail to Philadelphia: the Delaware River or the Chesapeake Bay. The Delaware route had the advantage of being the most direct, while the Chesapeake Bay approach would take longer but might contain an element of surprise.[24]

Putting aside his unsent letter to Howe, Clinton vented instead to a friend about the intolerable position in which he found himself. He would do his best to be cheerful about the campaign, but "declared, "I cannot serve another" with the current commander-in-chief. He simply could not get along with Howe, and he did not believe in or support his boss's action, which "I fear . . . bears heavy on Burgoyne." The overall strategic picture did little to brighten Clinton's outlook. "Operations since Trenton have not pleased me. On that day Britain lost the opportunity of an honorable peace never, I fear, to return again."[25]

While all of the intelligence indicators now seemed to point to Philadelphia or another destination that could be reached by sea as Howe's destination, Washington still could not be sure. His spy network worked overtime to discover the enemy's destination. Now that they had weighed anchor and gone to sea, the commander-in-chief's frustration mounted. Howe's unmatched superiority in sea power gave him almost unlimited flexibility and negated in no small degree Washington's advantage of interior lines. As an exasperated Washington explained to Hancock from his headquarters near Ramapo, New York, "the amazing advantage the Enemy derive from their ships and the command of the Water, keeps us in a State of constant perplexity and the most anxious conjecture." Thus, he and his officers could not be sure where Howe was going.[26]

Washington had faced many tough situations during the war, but never in his role as commander-in-chief did he confront a more daunting challenge than in July of 1777. He was not only the commanding general of the main American Army, but he also had to direct, coordinate, and provide resources to the Northern Army and the army guarding the Hudson Highlands, all while trying to determine what Howe and Burgoyne were doing and taking steps to counter them. As in an enormous chess game, he had to move his pieces in response to his opponents' maneuvers, without opening himself up to an unexpected assault, and he had to do it on land. In contrast, his opponent enjoyed an indisputable advantage—sea power.

The preponderance of the evidence led Washington to move the army once again, this time in stages over 70 miles to Coryell's Ferry, New Jersey, about halfway between New York and Philadelphia. Near present-day Lambertville, New Jersey, the ferry was a major crossing point over the Delaware River. He also left major units closer to the Highlands to support Putnam if necessary. This allowed Washington to be near Philadelphia while still being able to march northeast should the enemy move in that direction, a slim possibility but one that still haunted him. "Genl Howe's, in a manner, abandoning Genl Burgoyne, is so unaccountable a matter," he explained to Gates, "that till I am fully assured it is so, I cannot help casting my Eyes continually behind me."[27] Washington, if not always right in his assessment of what Howe would do, was always mindful of what he could do.

At 10:00 a.m. on July 31, Washington learned that Howe and his fleet had been sighted off the Delaware Capes, which seemed to finally confirm that Philadelphia was the objective. He directed Putnam to forward the news to Schuyler and the governors of the New England states, telling the general, "I hope as they now have nothing to fear from Genl Howe that they will now turn out their force both Continl & Militia to oppose Burgoyne."[28] The next day, however, just as Washington was developing his plan to confront Howe's imminent amphibious landing, he learned that instead of sailing up the mouth of the Delaware River and on to Philadelphia, the British fleet had turned abruptly and sailed east, out into the Atlantic. Howe was once again up to his old tricks. In a flurry of letters, Washington moved brigades back to the Highlands and directed General George Clinton to occupy and reinforce Fort Montgomery.[29] Exasperated, he wrote that the "conduct of the Enemy is distressing, and difficult to be understood."[30] For weeks, the American Army had been "marching & countermarching" in the midsummer heat and humidity.[31] Washington finally decided to maintain the bulk of the army in the vicinity of Coryell's Ferry. "Till we can get some trace of the Course of the Enemy," he explained to John Taylor on August 5, "it will be a folly to move."[32]

Washington and his generals spent the next five days anxiously waiting for news of Howe's whereabouts. Washington knew that it was entirely possible that Howe could suddenly appear at the Hudson. If the wind was right, he could quickly overwhelm the Patriot Forts Clinton and Montgomery guarding the Hudson Highlands and be on his way up the river before the main American Army could react. Finally, on August 10, Washington received word that the fleet was sighted off Sinepuxent Bay (about 25 miles south of the Delaware

River) and headed south toward the Virginia Capes at the mouth of the Chesapeake Bay.[33] There could be only two possible objectives for Howe given the fleet's course: Charleston or Philadelphia.

On August 16, while still at sea, Howe received Germain's May 18 letter. He must have felt both relieved and vindicated that day, because not only did Germain approve of his plan to conduct his operation to Philadelphia by sea, the secretary also informed him that "His Majesty entirely approves of your [April 5] letter to Sir Guy Carleton," the one in which Howe frankly stated that he would not be coming north up the Hudson River to cooperate with Burgoyne. The only thing that gave Howe pause was Germain's statement that although the Philadelphia expedition by sea was approved, the king and the secretary expected "it will be executed in time for you to cooperate with the army ordered to proceed from Canada and put itself under your command."[34] This was virtually impossible. After all, Howe had no idea when he might even land at the head of the Chesapeake Bay. It was already mid-August, and it could be days or even weeks before they started the overland portion of the campaign. The chances of concluding the Philadelphia campaign in time to reposition the army and cooperate with Burgoyne were nonexistent. Everything was dependent on the wind and the Americans. Howe's conscience was clear. Burgoyne's last message had announced the Ticonderoga triumph and suggested an army in no need of assistance. Plus, he left a very competent, albeit annoying, subordinate behind in New York with instructions to assist the army from Canada if necessary. Germain's letter, combined with Burgoyne's last message, swept away any lingering concern Howe may have had about not supporting the army from Canada.

As Howe's fleet continued south off the coast of Maryland and Virginia, Washington weighed his options. After analysis of all his available intelligence, he concluded that Howe was probably heading for Charleston. If so, there was no way the American Army could follow. For one thing, with Howe's superior mobility, the Americans would never get there in time. Also, an operation in the Deep South in the middle of the summer made little sense strategically or for the army's health. Washington could stay near Philadelphia or march back to the Hudson and on to Albany to combine with the Northern Army and counter Burgoyne or attack the British base at New York. He was leaning toward the former when his decision was made for him.[35] On August 21, Washington received word that Howe's fleet had sailed up into the Chesapeake Bay. Finally, Howe's intentions were confirmed: he was going to attack Philadelphia from

the south. Four days later, Howe started landing his army at Head of Elk (present-day Elkton, Maryland), about 50 miles southwest of Philadelphia.[36] The final phase of the Philadelphia campaign had begun. Though technically a separate operation, it was inextricably linked to the campaign on the Hudson River north of Albany.

Howe finally answered Germain's letter on August 30 from Head of Elk. Pleased that the king had approved his plan to go to Philadelphia by sea, he was concerned about His Majesty's expectation that he could quickly wrap up the campaign in time to assist Burgoyne. Despite their successful, although monotonous and fatiguing, forty-day voyage, all was not well. By this time, Howe had heard rumors that Burgoyne had suffered some setbacks. Not only that, but in the five days he was on the ground in Maryland, Howe discovered to his dismay, just as Burgoyne had done before him, that he was mistaken in his assumption that he would be supported by legions of Loyalists. The Philadelphia campaign was not going to be as easy as he had thought. In fact, he concluded, he needed large reinforcements "for bringing the war to a conclusion with this campaign, which I have not the smallest hope of effecting with my present force."[37] This was not the message Germain expected.

In early September, well before he had received Howe's August 30 letter, Germain learned that the British fleet had been sighted in late July off Cape Henlopen in Delaware. His reaction to this information demonstrates the secretary's misunderstanding of the strategic realities involved in conducting a North American campaign. "Having had the pleasure of hearing that the troops were all safely embarked," Germain wrote to Howe, "I flatter myself that I shall soon have the satisfaction of receiving advice of consequence from Philadelphia." Since the last news Germain received from Burgoyne reported the capture of Ticonderoga, he enthused, "In the meantime you will give me leave to partake of the joy you will have derived from the account of General Burgoyne's rapid progress." So far, so good, but he closed by saying that because things were going so well, he was certain that there was a "fair prospect which you now have of an earlier junction than you lately supposed likely to be effected."[38]

If Germain truly believed this and was not simply ensuring that his concerns were on the record, he was oblivious to the operational challenges involved. The campaign could take weeks or even longer. Assuming Howe was successful in defeating Washington—which was not certain—he had to garrison the city and then either march almost 300 miles north to cooperate with Burgoyne, which could take weeks, or re-embark on Lord Howe's ships to transport the army up the

Hudson, hoping for favorable winds. The odds of any of these scenarios playing out prior to the onset of the New York winter, or before Burgoyne's part of the campaign was completed, were slim to none. Germain did not seem to understand these fundamental facts, which was troubling for the man responsible for developing and directing British military strategy in North America. This disconnect was driven home to Germain in late September when Howe's August 30 letter arrived in the Whitehall offices of the Colonial Department. A frustrated Germain wrote to Under Secretary of State for the Colonies William Knox, "I am sorry the Canada army will be disappointed in the junction they expect with Sir William Howe, but the more honour for Burgoyne if he does the business without any assistance from New York."[39]

The contrast between the two commanders-in-chief could not have been more pronounced during 1777. From the very start, Howe had focused solely on his own operations and only paid lip service to Burgoyne's expedition. In part, this was understandable. He was in charge of British forces in North America, and it was his job to develop plans and direct campaigns to achieve British strategic goals. Nonetheless, he was being directed from 3,000 miles away to subordinate his plans to those generated by an officer junior to him. Washington, on the other hand, though reporting to Congress, was his own man. He let his subordinate commanders command their organizations, but he directed them when needed and provided them with the resources they required to accomplish the mission. And perhaps most importantly, he was able to do something Howe could not or would not: coordinate the actions of all of his armies.

CHAPTER 15

Burgoyne's Dilemma

PHILIP SCHUYLER WAS OFFICIALLY relieved of his command on August 3, though he did not get the news for quite some time. In the meantime, he had a lot on his mind. In late July, the American general had moved the Northern Army out of Fort Edward farther south to Fort Miller. Like many outposts in the region, Fort Miller was little more than a wooden stockade. It was hardly a defensible position, and so Schuyler moved the army again to the west side of the Hudson River near Saratoga.

As the Americans withdrew south, General Fraser's advanced corps and his attached Indians continually probed and harassed them. Since the British Army arrived at Skenesborough on July 6, its movements had been deliberate in the extreme. Burgoyne had waited more than two full weeks at Skenesborough before moving to Fort Anne, and once he had arrived at Fort Edward, he delayed yet again by another two full weeks and then some. Indeed, by the time his army finally departed Fort Edward on August 13, Burgoyne's expedition had covered 31 miles in thirty-nine days. Few campaigns have been won by armies moving at that speed.

The potential impact of the slow rate of march was not lost on the men. One young German officer, reflecting a year later on the army's leisurely pace in July and August, thoughtfully observed that "if it was absolutely essential to occupy Albany, why was there such a great delay at Fort Edward and did the English not advance at a rapid pace as they had first done?" If they had, "One may almost take it for granted that they would have succeeded since the rebels still

had not been strengthened by the troops Washington would later dispatch upriver."[1] Although writing with the benefit of hindsight, the officer was right. After capturing Fort Ticonderoga and seizing the initiative, Burgoyne ought to have retained and exploited his advantage.

As we have seen, in the face of constant pressure from Fraser's advanced corps, Schuyler had continued his steady retreat south to Saratoga, on the west bank of the Hudson, and finally to Stillwater, 24 miles south of Fort Edward, on August 4. A few days before, General John Glover's brigade of twelve hundred troops, as well as a detachment of militia troops, arrived to reinforce Schuyler's army. On his arrival at Stillwater, Schuyler's army probably outnumbered Burgoyne's.[2] General Lincoln, who had been dispatched to Manchester in Vermont to gather militia, reported to Washington that on August 2, he "found here about five or six hundred Militia—A number have since come in; I expect in three or four days, probably, they will increase to two thousand."[3] Things were starting to look up for the Americans, though one would not know this based on Schuyler's report. Only with a large reinforcement did he have a chance to stop Burgoyne, but neither Massachusetts nor Connecticut had answered Schuyler's multiple requests for militia. Worse was that their "Continental Force is daily decreasing," and as his army grew smaller, "that of the Enemy augments by a constant Acquisition of Tories." While some Loyalist recruits had augmented Burgoyne's army since their arrival in New York, they were too few to make a difference.[4] Nine days after writing the last of his fatalistic letters to Washington on August 4—and as he continued to withdraw the army from Stillwater to Van Schaick Island 10 miles north of Albany—Schuyler received the news of his relief and orders directing him to report to Washington's headquarters. Six days after that, on August 19, Gates arrived at Schuyler's headquarters to take command of the army and the Northern Department.

Days after complaining to Germain that he had not heard from Howe, Burgoyne received a letter from the commander-in-chief dated July 17. As Burgoyne's army penetrated deeper and deeper into American territory, it had become increasingly difficult to get messages through the lines, so Howe resorted to smuggling the letter through hostile country in a hollow lead ball. Howe first congratulated Burgoyne for successfully taking Ticonderoga: "a great event, carried without loss." The news that Burgoyne had taken the great fort was undoubtedly a great relief for Howe, who reminded Burgoyne that "My intention is for Pennsylvania, where I expect to

meet Washington." Indeed, Howe's army was already embarked on transports and waited for only a favorable wind before sailing to Philadelphia. However, he pledged to Burgoyne that if Washington "goes to the northward . . . be assured I shall soon be after him to relieve you." Once Burgoyne got to Albany, Howe counseled, "the movements of the enemy will guide yours; but my wishes are, that the enemy be driven out of this province before any operation takes place in Connecticut. Sir Henry Clinton remains in the command here, and will act as occurrences may direct."[5]

For the first time in the execution of the 1777 British military strategy, Burgoyne had received direction from the commander-in-chief, but it was nebulous at best. Still, it answered vaguely the question that should have been addressed when the campaign of 1777 was devised: what was the goal? Howe wanted him to clear the state of New York of enemy troops and suggested that he or perhaps Clinton would at some point come up the river to meet him. This was an impossible task for Burgoyne's small army, even if it was augmented. That sentence suggests that Howe had no idea of the challenges Burgoyne faced or how difficult it was to wage war in the New York wilderness. The task of clearing the state of American military forces would have required tens of thousands of troops that Britain simply did not have. Even had Howe's main army combined with Burgoyne, an objective such as the one Howe stated in this letter would have been unrealistic at best.

Eagerly responding to his new boss, Burgoyne described the army's torturous march south from Skenesborough to Fort Edward, which "was very laborious through a country naturally difficult, the roads and bridges all broke up, and in the face of the enemy, who retired nevertheless from post to post with considerable loss in killed and prisoners." Despite the difficulties they encountered, Burgoyne wrote that "I have had the fullest satisfaction in the alacrity of the army," which justified his choice of the route of march. Unfortunately, taking all the artillery and provisions had cost him time. He also had had to leave behind a good number of troops to maintain lines of communication. Given that it had taken him so long to reach Fort Edward, Burgoyne explained to Howe that it would not be possible to take Albany, even supposing the enemy didn't oppose him before August 22.[6]

Burgoyne's reply to Howe reveals no concerns about getting to Albany. Indeed, the tone of the letter was almost as optimistic as those that had preceded it. Burgoyne would later claim that Howe's letter reinforced Germain's original orders that Albany had to be

reached no matter what, and that he had interpreted Howe's mention of Henry Clinton being "left in New York to act as occurrences might direct," to mean that he could expect assistance from his old friend. All these ex post facto rationalizations by Burgoyne were disingenuous. Howe's letter was clear: he was not coming to Albany, and Burgoyne was on his own. Burgoyne suggested that Howe's July 17 letter gave him his first inkling that the commander-in-chief was not coming to Albany and going to Philadelphia instead.[7] This was simply not true. But even if it was, as Burgoyne sat in his tent at Fort Edward on August 6, composing his reply to Sir William, he was clearly unconcerned over his ability to get safely to Albany. If he had truly believed what he later testified, Burgoyne gave no indication in his August 6 response to Howe.

News of Howe's letter quickly made its way around the British and German camps.[8] The fact that Burgoyne did not reveal the contents of Howe's message may not be as sinister as some have made it out to be. One argument has been that Burgoyne was so shocked and disappointed to learn that Howe was not coming to Albany that to maintain morale, he deliberately concealed that fact to his officers and men. But Burgoyne had known for months that Howe did not intend to come up the Hudson. However, he did suggest to his men that Clinton might soon send some forces up the river.[9] And in general, he seemed unconcerned to be on his own. He was determined to get to Albany and from there to follow Howe's instructions to the best of his ability.

But the prospect of getting to Albany was growing dimmer. For one thing, the army's health was declining.[10] The miserably hot and humid weather conditions, the insects, and the rain—"almost every day there is a thunderstorm," wrote one German officer in his journal—led to a rise in the sick rate. A British officer noted that many men in his unit, including his company commander, were sick "of fevers & agues so common to the climate." The heat affected food supplies. "All sorts of meat were tainted in a very short time, and the stench was prejudicial."[11] On August 4, Burgoyne's British regiments reported a sick rate of almost 15 percent. This was a significant drain on the army, especially when added to the 30 percent employed to protect the line of communications.[12] Troops began to desert. July's arduous campaigning and the promise of a prosperous life in America proved tempting. Although the number of deserters was small, it alarmed Burgoyne enough to issue a General Order to the army on August 6. He vowed that upon learning of any new absconders, Indians would be "immediately sent in pursuit, who have orders to scalp all deserters."[13]

Yet another serious issue arose in early August, one that Burgoyne had not anticipated. The Indians decided to leave the army. The Ottawas explained to Burgoyne that they had originally told Carleton that they could only stay until early August, and they were already hundreds of miles from home. It was time for them to leave. Other Native warriors attached to the expedition were growing restless and not just because of the lateness of the season. They had joined Burgoyne in the anticipation that they would raid and collect loot, and they had bristled at the restrictions imposed on them. Now the army had once again halted for an extended period, this time at Fort Edward, as they gathered supplies and repaired roads. The frustrated warriors no longer viewed the expedition as a profitable one. A desperate Burgoyne moved quickly to convince his Indians to stay with the army. He appealed to their honor, promised booty, and liberally plied them with rum. The Indians "asked to be granted the freedom of practicing revenge . . . and to be allowed to treat the enemy more harshly than before."[14] Burgoyne replied that he could not permit them to commit "cruelties against the enemy on behalf of other Savage nations." Burgoyne's arguments—and his rum—convinced the warriors to stay with the army at least until they reached Albany.[15]

In addition to the army's precarious health and disgruntled Indian allies, Burgoyne also had to face the army's increasingly shaky logistical situation. His supply lines stretched back to Fort George and Fort Ticonderoga, over 50 miles of wilderness, watercourses, and poor roads, under constant threat of American attack and disruption. As he wrote Germain, "Exceeding heavy rains augmented the impediments."[16] As the army continued to move south toward Albany, supplying it would get progressively more difficult. To enable it to continue to march, Burgoyne would have to stockpile several weeks of supplies, and this was proving impossible. Only with great effort could his quartermaster gather much more than four days' supply, and typically the army had only one days' supply on hand. The army continued to suffer from a lack of transport. Only 180 of the five hundred carts that Burgoyne had contracted for in Canada had made it to Fort Edward.[17]

Exacerbating the logistical challenge was the immense train of artillery accompanying the army, which required more than four hundred horses to move. Burgoyne argued later that he needed the artillery to destroy American fortifications. True or not, it only served to slow the army and suck up precious supplies that could be used elsewhere. He later claimed that the hundreds of horses required to haul the artillery did not interfere with the transport of provisions,

but the horses had to be fed, which took up resources that could have been better used elsewhere.[18] The logistical situation was not the only reason for the deliberate approach toward Albany, but it was perhaps the most important.

On August 7, Burgoyne ordered that all forms of transport—"ox teams, carts, horses and oxen"—be gathered together "in order to their being immediately employed in the Transport for the Army."[19] Two days later, he dispatched Fraser and his advanced corps to Fort Miller, located about 8 miles south of Fort Edward on the east bank of the Hudson River, with the main army to follow a couple of days later. He was determined to move south, and the logistical situation was now Burgoyne's top priority and precipitated a crucial decision. As Burgoyne explained to Germain two weeks later, he had "either to relinquish the favourable opportunity of advancing upon the enemy or to attempt other resources of supply."[20] Since he was determined to advance, he decided to send a large raid deep into enemy-held territory to seize supplies, forage, animals, and transport.

CHAPTER 16

Battle of Bennington

EVEN BEFORE BURGOYNE HAD made his move, Washington recognized an opportunity. As we have seen, Schuyler had mentioned in mid-July that Burgoyne might try to seize vital supplies at Bennington. Washington observed that given that the British general "Appears to be pursuing that Line of Conduct which of all others is most favorable to us," could they not send some troops and cut them off? If Burgoyne divided his forces in any way, Schuyler had to seize the opportunity and strike. If that happened, the militia would also surely "lose Sight of past Misfortunes" and leap at the chance to help the effort.[1] Two days later, Washington continued to urge Schuyler to attack Burgoyne's supply bases or one of his separated units. However, he agreed with Schuyler's suggestions that a large body of troops should be maintained in Vermont.[2] Washington knew that Burgoyne's army was necessarily shrinking because of the nature of the countryside and his logistical requirements. He knew that the militia would certainly respond to the imminent threat to their homes that Burgoyne's army represented. Schuyler's reports that Burgoyne had detached a major force for gathering supplies meant that he would be vulnerable, if only the Americans would react aggressively. This was clear evidence of Washington's grip.

There were other positive signs for the Americans. Benjamin Lincoln reported to Washington from Manchester, Vermont, that Burgoyne's Indians were "murdering and scalping the inhabitants without discrimination" and that the civilians in the area were "greatly agitated." As a result, more militia troops were coming in

from New Hampshire, and Massachusetts and, hopefully, these new forces would help "reduce his main body."[3] Schuyler did not see things in quite the same way. He told Washington that he had pulled the army back to Stillwater, his militia was getting ready to leave the army, and that Tories were reinforcing Burgoyne.[4] Despite the conflicting reports, Washington was optimistic about the situation in the Northern Department and was confident the northern states would fulfill their militia obligations and, he wrote to Governor Jonathan Trumbull, "put things right again." The widespread panic that followed the loss of Ticonderoga "is nearly subsided."[5]

By the first week in August, in the face of mounting logistical pressure, Burgoyne decided to proceed with a raid similar to that proposed by Riedesel two weeks earlier. Riedesel had envisioned a foray into Vermont to capture supplies and deter attacks by enemy militia. This was not a difficult decision. Despite the Americans' best efforts to slow down the army's advance and harass and interdict his lines of communication back to Forts George and Ticonderoga, British forces had routed them at every opportunity. It was clear to Burgoyne that Schuyler and his troops had no stomach for direct confrontation. Even if the Americans could scrape together a force to oppose the raid, they would be swept aside by the European regulars. Burgoyne was confident that his men could easily handle anything the Americans could throw against him, but the success of his expedition now turned on easing his supply problems. A successful raid would do the trick.

Since Riedesel had first suggested the idea of a raid, in part to seize horses to mount his dragoons, Burgoyne decided to assign Lieutenant Colonel Friedrich Baum to command an operation to Manchester composed mainly of German units. Riedesel yearned for action since his men had done little since the Battle of Hubbardton. A raid, Burgoyne explained, would offer a chance "to give in to their ideas and solicitations because in exerting their zeal to fulfil their favourite purpose they necessarily would effect the greater purpose of my own."[6] This was not the best of reasons for making a crucial operational decision. And the timing was off. The situation had "materially changed," as Riedesel later noted, between July 22 when he suggested it in the first place and when the raid actually took place.[7]

Burgoyne put together a mixed force, composed of several units that had never worked together before. Baum's force, numbering 762 German, British, Loyalists, Canadian, and Indian soldiers and warriors, was accompanied by two 3-pounder artillery pieces. In addition to the Indians, who would scout ahead of the main force as

it moved into enemy territory, Burgoyne added Captain Alexander Fraser's marksmen to the raid, along with some extra British officers to assist with translation issues. To provide local knowledge and to help recruit Loyalists, the former British officer Phillip Skene also accompanied Baum. Baum's task force would consist of units that spoke at least four languages: German, English, French, and several Native American dialects.[8]

Baum was a curious choice to lead such an important mission deep into enemy territory. He spoke no English and would have to rely on Loyalists and a few British officers to help negotiate with Americans encountered along the way. Although Baum had served in the Seven Years War, he had no experience with independent command, and he had seen no combat in America. Burgoyne had a force that was ready-made for such a mission: Fraser's advanced corps. Fraser had proven himself again and again to be a tough, capable, and aggressive leader. He and his unit had led the army throughout the campaign and had actually fought Americans at Hubbardton, so he had a healthy respect for the enemy. Fraser and the advance corps were proven and capable commodities; Baum and his pick-up team were not.

Fraser was thus furious when he learned that the Germans had been assigned this critical mission. He protested to Lieutenant Colonel Kingston, Burgoyne's adjutant general, arguing that the Germans were simply unsuited for this kind of task, having earlier observed that they were "a helpless kind of troops in the woods."[9] Kingston replied that Riedesel "was desirous of having the Germans employed," since the advanced corps had received the lion's share of the credit for Hubbardton. Fraser muttered an oath, prompting Kingston to urge the brigadier "to mention his objections, if he had any, to General Burgoyne." Resigned, Fraser replied, "the Germans are not a very active people; but it may do." This was hardly a ringing endorsement. Kingston, therefore, pressed Fraser again to go to Burgoyne, but he refused.[10]

With the advanced corps in the lead, the army moved from Fort Edward to Fort Miller, and Baum prepared to march his task force into Vermont. As the final preparations for the raid were being made, the men built a bridge of boats across the Hudson in anticipation of the army's further advance toward Albany. Until Burgoyne was ready to continue, the advanced corps crossed the river to keep the American Army off-balance as well as to divert its attention from Baum's expedition.

Burgoyne provided Baum with a very clear and unambiguous mission statement: "to try the affections of the country, to disconcert

the councils of the enemy, to mount the Riedesel's dragoons . . . and to obtain large supplies of cattle, horses, and carriages." While the objectives were straightforward, they were not going to be easy. Burgoyne was asking a lot of Baum's small force. At all times, Baum's expedition "must be proceeded upon with caution," and he must at all times keep track of enemy militias around him. Using his Indians would be key. Burgoyne also directed Baum to find horses, wagons, carriages, and "as many draft oxen as will be necessary to draw them, and all cattle fit for slaughter." Skene was to assist in helping him "distinguish the good subjects from the bad, [and] to procure you the best intelligence of the enemy." He cautioned Baum to always to be on guard against ambush. He added another mission to Baum's already lengthy list of tasks: "to make the country believe that the troops under your command are the advanced corps of the army, and that it is intended to pass the Connecticut [River] on the road to Boston."[11] In other words, not only was he to mount the dragoons, recruit Loyalists, awe the inhabitants, and gather horses, cattle, oxen, and carriages but spread disinformation and conduct a diversion.

Burgoyne was particularly nervous about large bodies of enemy troops, specifically mentioning Colonel Seth Warner's unit, which had given the expedition trouble earlier in the campaign. Should the Americans "contrary to expectation, be able to collect a large force," cautioned Burgoyne, it was up to Baum whether to attack the rebels or not. If Baum ran into Continental troops from Schuyler's army, Burgoyne advised him to send word immediately, assume a good defensive position, and await the arrival of the main army. Burgoyne assumed that Baum's mission would be done in a fortnight, telling Baum that if he, Burgoyne, was in Albany before the raid was completed, he would send word.[12] Burgoyne thought that the army would make it to Albany in two weeks with or without Baum's detachment.

The Manchester raid was originally proposed to gather horses, transport, and supplies for the army's continued advance toward Albany. By the time it was organized, Burgoyne had piled task upon task upon task on an inexperienced commander with a hastily formed force that had never worked together. Meanwhile, as Baum came to grips with Burgoyne's orders, the advanced corps sat on the Hudson's west bank.

While spending more than two weeks in Skene's mansion, Burgoyne and the wealthy landowner had hit it off. He began to lean on Skene for advice and to act as his primary liaison with the local population. Burgoyne, Germain, and the king had assumed that

the expedition's ranks would swell with Loyalist supporters. So far, there was little evidence of it. Still, Burgoyne thought Skene could be useful to Baum's expedition. Burgoyne prepared a separate set of instructions for him, focusing on the disinformation and deception plan and securing Loyalist support.[13]

When Riedesel learned of the expansion of Baum's mission, he complained to Burgoyne. The German general thought that the original plan, calling merely for a raid to Manchester, was still the right course of action. Burgoyne replied that they needed enough provisions to last four weeks and that Baum's raid would pull enemy forces away from both St. Leger and the main army as it moved toward Schuyler's force at Stillwater. Riedesel countered that when he had first proposed a raid to gather supplies in mid-July, he envisioned a straightforward out-and-back operation during a moment when the American militia had not yet been energized. The new plan was much larger, more complex, and hazardous. Burgoyne could not be moved. The raid would go on.[14]

On the morning of August 11, as Baum and his men made ready to march from Fort Miller, they were surprised to see the commanding general himself ride up. Burgoyne directed Baum to change his objective from Manchester to Bennington, Vermont. Intelligence sources indicated that large quantities of cattle, horses, oxen, and carriages were gathered there for the American forces. With Burgoyne's detailed written orders and his verbal instructions changing the objective to Bennington, Baum and his diverse detachment of Braunschweig, Hesse-Hanau, British, Canadian, and American Loyalist soldiers and Indian warriors departed at noon. As they marched south, they waded across the Batten Kill creek, which flows into the Hudson just north of the little town of Saratoga, located on the west bank of the river. Though a small collection of buildings, including General Schuyler's manor house, it was the first settlement of any size they had seen since they departed Canada.[15]

That night as they made camp south of the Batten Kill, another violent thunderstorm struck.[16] For troops on both sides, the summer of 1777 was anything but pleasant, consisting of relentless heat and humidity, punctuated by drenching rains. Early the next morning, they resumed their journey, but traveled only a mile before Baum, spooked by reports of a large American force ahead, turned the column around and returned to their starting point. When this turned out to be false, Baum was determined to make up ground, and the detachment departed again, at 5:00 a.m. on August 13.[17]

In late July and August, the Americans in Vermont, Massachusetts, and New Hampshire were not sitting idle. The states' leaders took steps to pull together a force to defend their homes from the enemy invasion. Colonel Warner and the survivors from the Battle of Hubbardton had retreated to Manchester, Vermont, located about 26 miles north of Bennington, and had engaged in harassing operations against Burgoyne. On July 15, with Burgoyne's army threatening, the Vermont Council of Safety had desperately asked New Hampshire and Massachusetts for assistance: "so as to put it immediately in our power to make a sufficient stand against such strength as they [the enemy] may send."[18] The New Hampshire General Court promised to raise three battalions under the command of Brigadier General John Stark.[19] Although the newly promoted Stark had accepted his new appointment under the condition that he and his command would be independent of the Continental Army, he was keen to defend Vermont and New Hampshire from a British invasion. Almost immediately after Stark was promoted, the New Hampshire militia began to come out. Hundreds of men responded, and in less than a week, more than 10 percent of the state's military-age men came forward.[20] The men who flocked to Stark's side knew that leadership was the key to success. They did not respond well to Schuyler's or St. Clair's many pleas for assistance but felt no hesitation in answering the call when they knew they would be under Stark's command.

John Stark was a remarkable man. A lifelong resident of New Hampshire, Stark was born to Irish and Scottish parents. He served with Robert's Rangers during the French and Indian War, and at the outbreak of the American Revolution, was appointed colonel of the New Hampshire militia. After fighting at Bunker Hill, he accepted an appointment as a colonel in the Continental Army. He participated in the invasion of Canada and the battles of Trenton and Princeton, before resigning his commission over a promotion dispute. Stark was a combat leader who could quickly forge unbreakable bonds with his men, and his wide-ranging experience had given him tactical and operational expertise.[21]

Throughout the rest of July and into early August, Stark gathered his forces at Charleston, New Hampshire, and from there, sent some of his men to Manchester to reinforce Warner's units. When he was ready to move into Vermont, Stark went to Manchester to confer with Warner, with whom he was close, and Lincoln, who was charged with managing militia operations in the region. Lincoln tried to persuade Stark to join Schuyler's army at Stillwater, but he refused to take orders from any Continental officer.[22] Stark was there to defend

Vermont and his own state. However, he did agree to work with Lincoln, to "fall into the rear of Burgoyne who from the best information we can obtain hath left a very naked and uncovered rear."[23] To both protect the Vermont frontiers and "harass Burgoyne's flank," both Warner and Stark ordered their men to meet at the little town of Bennington, located only about 3 miles east of the New York border, and less than 35 miles from Fort Miller and Burgoyne's army. The American leaders, along with rapidly growing militia units, arrived at Bennington three days before Baum first departed Fort Miller on August 11.[24] The stage was now set for an inevitable clash.

After their slow start, Baum's expedition made good progress on August 13, and by late in the afternoon, the column arrived in Cambridge, New York, after a march of more than 20 miles. Several small American detachments fired on Baum's column. They did little damage but helped spread the news of the enemy's approach throughout the region. Baum's force had achieved some success by the time they arrived at Cambridge, confiscating fifteen horses and some cattle and capturing several prisoners. After they made camp that night, they received a report from Burgoyne that St. Leger had won the Battle of Oriskany. This good news was quickly disseminated throughout the camp, though one German officer cynically remarked, "This is only being spread to inspire our men with courage."[25]

At Cambridge, Baum received the first indication from Loyalists and prisoners that a large body of American militia was starting to form. They were consolidating at Bennington, 12 miles away, and the main objective of the expedition. He informed Burgoyne that "the number of the enemy amounted to 1800." This was a much larger force than anyone anticipated, but Baum assured Burgoyne that he would take "precautions to fulfil the orders . . . of your Excellency." Besides, Skene was confident that Loyalists "outnumbered rebels five to one in the area."[26] Baum prepared to continue the march toward Bennington at first light the next morning.

As the detachment resumed its march from Cambridge, they encountered dozens of self-proclaimed Loyalists. Skene vouched for their reliability, and he, therefore, did nothing to restrict their comings and goings. Meanwhile, Stark was aware of Baum's strength and movements through reports from many of these same "Loyalists" and other Patriots. He sent out from Bennington a small detachment of about two hundred New Hampshire militia under Colonel William Gregg to gain intelligence and to "stop their march."[27] Gregg's men met Baum's column at a small settlement only 7 miles

from Bennington called Sancoick, the site of a mill and a bridge over which the column had to pass. The New Hampshire men fired at the approaching enemy, wounding an Indian, destroyed the bridge, and withdrew in the face of Baum's superior numbers. As Baum stopped to repair the bridge and to consider his next move, he dashed off a message to Burgoyne. The enemy "in their usual way, fired from the bushes, and took their road to Bennington," reported Baum. In addition, a few prisoners claimed that "1500 to 1800 men are at Bennington; but are supposed to leave it at our approach."[28] This intelligence confirmed what Baum had learned earlier about the American strength at Bennington and was reasonably accurate. His assessment of their intentions, however, was not.

Meanwhile, Burgoyne planned to move the army across the Hudson River, sever his supply line to Fort George, and continue to Albany. The army would subsist on the supplies captured by Baum's raid. For three straight days, August 14–16, Burgoyne directed that "the Army will hold themselves in readiness" in anticipation of Baum's success.[29] Responding to Baum's Sancoick note late on the 14th, Burgoyne praised the lieutenant colonel's actions as "very satisfactory." Anticipating that he may have to send a large force to assist, Burgoyne asked whether Baum's route was "convenient for a considerable corps with cannon." He warned Baum, again, that if the enemy at Bennington was too strong, "I wish you to take a post where you can maintain yourself till you receive an answer from me; and I will either support you in force or withdraw you." In the meantime, Burgoyne directed Baum to send back to the main army all the horses, oxen, carriages, and supplies he had already secured.[30] By the time Baum received this letter, he had already found what he thought was a defensible spot to wait for help.

Stark recognized that he had a chance to strike a major blow against Burgoyne, just as Washington had predicted. When Stark and Warner decided to consolidate their militias at Bennington, Burgoyne had almost simultaneously detached a large force from the main army. Baum's column was advancing toward Bennington, and with his significant numerical advantage, Stark was not about to squander this opportunity. He met with Warner and his other colonels to prepare their plan of attack.[31]

Baum resumed his pursuit of Gregg's New Hampshire troops late on the morning of the 14th. They had advanced along the Hoosic River toward Bennington, and at Sancoick, the column turned east and followed the Walloomsac River to a little hamlet know today as Hoosic, New York, about 4 miles west of Bennington. There, on

the opposite bank, Baum was shocked to see most of Stark's brigade, which had advanced out of Bennington to support Gregg. These Americans did not run away at the regulars' approach; they stayed put and were ready to fight. This was not what Baum had expected. Not willing to take on Stark's militia with his inferior force, the Braunschweig lieutenant colonel occupied a 300-foot hill west of the river. There he posted his dragoons and most of Fraser's marksmen, whom he ordered to dig in. To cover a bridge crossing the Walloomsac, he ordered his men to build a smaller redoubt at the base of the hill manned by more dragoons with the artillery. Finally, the Loyalists and Canadians occupied positions on both sides of the bridge, the largest on the south side of the river called the Tory Redoubt. Except for the large dragoon redoubt on the high ground north of the river, however, the rest of Baum's defensive dispositions were poorly sited. Most were too far apart, not located on key terrain, and few of Baum's positions were mutually supporting. Hence, they were vulnerable to separate attacks. As Baum's detachment prepared their defensive positions, he sent off his second note of the day to Burgoyne, asking for reinforcements.[32]

Stark did not let Baum prepare his defenses uncontested. One of Baum's Mohawk chiefs was shot when he ventured too far forward across the bridge. Other American forces attacked the separated detachments from the cover of the surrounding woods. "We have seen today how the enemy attacks: either lying on the ground or standing behind trees," complained a German surgeon. "They load their guns and shoot. They run from one tree to another and then forward as circumstances demand." Despite Americans swarming through the woods, Baum failed to take the most basic precautions, such as posting sentries during the night, which led to thirty men killed and wounded, including two Indian chiefs. The Indian losses were felt dearly, and they "were so enraged about their loss that they wanted to depart for Canada tonight." Some of Baum's officers were angry over his handling of the skirmishes and disgusted that he did not allow them to pursue the Americans as they melted back into the woods to their positions on the south side of the river. "Now they will become bold," a captain grumbled. "We leave them too much time, for they will gather by the thousands during the night." Baum, he said, had exhibited "no military expertise at all, cannot take proper measures, particularly here in the wilderness."[33]

When Burgoyne received Baum's request for help at 5:00 a.m. on August 15, he told Riedesel that the raiding column faced a large enemy contingent and that they must dispatch a relief force "either

to make a new attack or to call back the detachment." Burgoyne cautioned Riedesel that there would be grave consequences if the relief operation failed. At all costs, they must give "no cause for discouragement to the Indians" and keep all the animals and wagons they had captured.[34] Burgoyne directed Riedesel to send Lieutenant Colonel Heinrich Breymann to head the relief unit. What had happened to Baum was what the Braunschweig general (and Fraser) had feared all along: a small force deep in enemy territory, out of supporting distance, and facing a numerically superior foe. Although Riedesel thought that the best course of action was to order Baum to withdraw and rejoin the main army at once, he did not lodge a formal protest and instead issued the necessary orders.

At 9:00 a.m., Breymann, and a battalion of grenadiers and a Jäger battalion, totaling almost 650 men of all ranks, and two 6-pounder artillery pieces set out to cover the 24 miles that separated the main army from Baum's detachment.[35] The selection of Breymann and his German units to form the relief detachment made more sense than Baum to command the Bennington expedition. The relief force's mission was straightforward, and there would be no language issue. However, the advanced corps was still available. Just as he had done when he learned that Baum and his Germans had been tapped for the original raid, Fraser objected to the relief force's composition. Once again, he was rebuffed.[36]

It rained heavily all day on August 15, again. Some minor skirmishing took place near the bridge across the Walloomsac, and both sides sent out patrols to probe the enemy positions. Baum's scouts reported that they did "not see anything in particular," which was highly unlikely since the countryside between Baum's positions and Bennington were teeming with American militia.[37] Baum's men could not understand his inaction. Many believed that they should fall back to Sancoick instead of staying in a place where "every 40 paces a man is standing behind a tree," but they were relieved to learn that Breymann was on his way with a large body of men.[38] Despite Baum's poor dispositions, all should be well if Breymann moved swiftly to his colleague's aid.

On that rainy Friday, Baum wrote to Burgoyne, describing his dire situation and the fact that the Americans "expected more [militia] to come in, having sent about a hundred miles round for that purpose." Except for a few places, he assured Burgoyne that the Cambridge to Sancoick to Bennington road was good, and a relief column should have little difficulty reaching him. In the meantime, Baum had "secured my post as advantageously as possible" and "will

wait your excellency's instructions."[39] In general, Baum had complied with Burgoyne's original orders. Since he was clearly outnumbered and further movement toward Bennington would be foolhardy, he had assumed a defensive posture to await either reinforcement or the order to withdraw. What he did not do, however, was make the most basic, mutually supporting, defensive dispositions on the most favorable terrain.

It did not look promising for the Germans. Stark had three big advantages: detailed knowledge of the local area and the terrain; a command that probably exceeded two thousand men; and a good idea of Baum's dispositions. Throughout the 15th, Stark, Warner, and the rest of the key American officers put the finishing touches on their plan. By the time the 16th dawned hot and clear, Stark's force had been reinforced yet again, this time by Warner's Vermonters and some Massachusetts militia. Stark decided to split his force into three columns, which was a dangerous tactic since the Americans faced a force composed primarily of well-trained regulars. With his edge in numbers, however, Stark was willing to gamble on total victory. Lieutenant Colonel Nichols and 250 men were to work their way around to the north then west to fall on Baum's left rear flank at the dragoon redoubt. Three hundred men under Colonel Herrick were directed to make their way west, fording the Walloomsac River to attack Baum's dragoon redoubt from the right and rear flanks. Colonels Hobart and Stickney and two hundred men would attack Baum's center at the bridge and the Tory Redoubt. Finally, Stark and the remaining men would back up the attack on the center.[40] Stark addressed his troops before they moved out: "My men, yonder are the Hessians. They were bought for seven pounds and tenpence a man. Are you worth more? Prove it! Tonight the American flag floats from yonder hill, or Molly Stark sleeps a widow."[41]

The American columns set out at noon and worked their way into position. Baum's scouts and sentries noticed movement in the woods, but the colonel, again reassured by Skene, assumed they were Loyalists. As Baum's men waited behind their makeshift fortifications, they received word that Breymann's relief force was approaching. Now it was just a question of who would get there first, the Americans or the reinforcements. While the Americans moved into their assigned positions, Stark and Warner rode forward to get a good look at the Tory Redoubt. The enemy immediately opened a brisk but inaccurate artillery fire on the two mounted officers. As they prudently "came galloping back," the irrepressible Stark "cried

out to his men: 'Those rascals know I am an officer; don't you see they honor me with a big gun as a salute!' "[42]

At about 3:00 p.m. Herrick's men started the battle by firing a heavy volley against the dragoon redoubt, followed shortly after by the other American columns. The combat veteran Stark characterized the resulting battle as "the hottest engagement I have ever witnessed, resembling a continual clap of thunder."[43] Soon, the dragoons on the high ground were enveloped in a maelstrom of fire. One German participant recalled that as the dragoons "rose to take aim, bullets went through their heads. They fell backwards and no longer moved a finger. Thus, in a short time, our tallest and best dragoons were sent into eternity." The American fire grew heavier. The artillerymen were quickly shot down, and the officer who was covering the left flank and rear was driven back and captured with his men. "We were thus completely encircled."[44] Once they realized they were surrounded, the Indians fled. After the Indians bolted, Baum's positions were under constant attack. But the men fought ferociously because they knew that they only had to hold on until Breymann's arrival, "now momentarily expected."[45]

The Germans on the hilltop redoubt tried several times to break out of their encircled position. Baum personally led one of the charges but fell mortally wounded. Americans soon overran

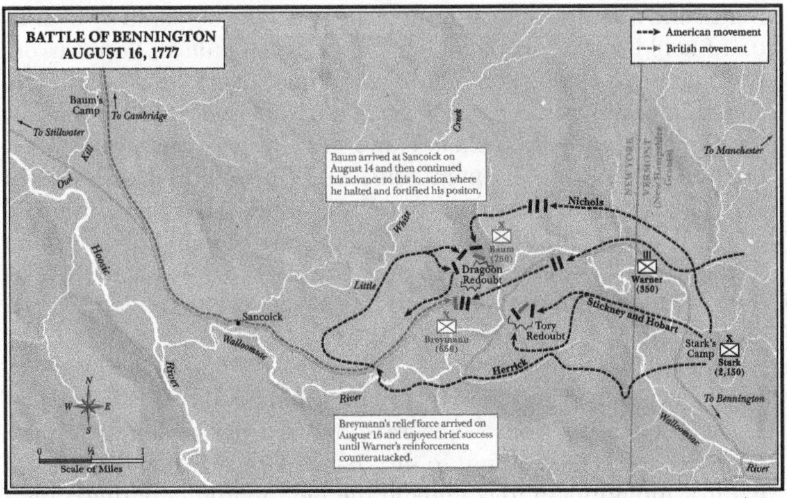

Map 9 Battle of Bennington, August 16, 1777

Baum's positions, and the fighting devolving into hand-to-hand combat: "The bayonet, the butt of the rifle, the sabre, the pike, were in full play, and men fell, as they rarely fall in modern war, under the direct blows of their enemies," wrote one of the few survivors. Under these conditions, discipline and unit cohesion soon crumbled. It did not help that Baum's units were drawn from across the army. "Outnumbered, broken and somewhat disheartened by late events," the officer recalled, "our people wavered and fell back, or fought singly and unconnectedly, till they were either cut down at their posts, obstinately defending themselves, or compelled to surrender."[46] The other positions faced similar onslaughts, and in an intense fight that lasted less than two hours, all of Baum's outposts were quickly overrun, and the men manning them killed, wounded, or captured.

Stark had succeeded beyond his expectations. "Our people behaved with the greatest spirit and bravery imaginable," he reported later. "Had they been Alexanders, or Charleses of Sweden, they could not have behaved better."[47] Stark's report omitted the fact that as the American officers tried to consolidate their gains and process the enemy prisoners and treat the wounded, many of the militia troops began to loot the camps, and soon discipline and unit cohesion dissolved. Just as the American victors were at their most vulnerable, Breymann's relief force arrived.[48]

Although Breymann's detachment started to march to Baum's aid at 9:00 a.m. on August 15, their progress was painfully slow. After fording the Batten Kill, the "great number of hills, the bottomless roads, and a severe and continuous rain, made the march so tedious that I could scarcely make one-half an English mile an hour," wrote Breymann days later. The men labored mightily to pull the artillery and ammunition on the muddy roads.[49] Nonetheless, the rain, hilly terrain, and unwieldy artillery could not alone account for a three-quarters-of-a-mile-per-hour rate of march. It would take Breymann and his column 32 hours to march 24 miles. Had they advanced at about 2 miles an hour—the standard rate of march for German soldiers—they would have arrived at Baum's position late in the evening of the 15th, hours before Stark's men attacked at mid-afternoon on the 16th.[50]

Instead, Breymann dithered, fussing with the wagons and artillery carriages, and making camp that night when he should have pressed on to Baum's position. Many reasons have been offered for the failure of the relief column to save Baum: Breymann was jealous of Baum's appointment to command the Bennington raid; there was a long-standing feud between the two officers; the German forces were

too burdened with unnecessary equipment and accouterments.[51] There is no way to know for sure, and while the poor conditions due to the heavy rains must have contributed, they were certainly not responsible for the entirety of the delay. The Germans had proven during the campaign that they could march quickly when they had to. The most likely explanation is the simplest: Breymann allowed the cannons to slow down the main column and failed to exhibit the kind of urgency required in a crisis.

When Stark learned of Breymann's approach near Sancoick, he immediately dispatched four small detachments to delay the enemy's advance until he could get his forces back under control. At Sancoick, Breymann met Skene, who had barely escaped Baum's camp to meet the relief force. Skene urged Breymann to hurry to Baum's side, only 2 miles away. Breymann agreed, and shortly after the column continued its march, they spotted bands of armed men in the woods. At first, Skene was deceived again, believing the men were Loyalists, but soon discovered his error when they opened fire on the advancing Germans. Breymann deployed his men and his two pieces of artillery on the road, and the small skirmish soon escalated into another tough fight. Colonel Stickney's New Hampshire militia regiment bore the brunt of the fighting against the enemy newcomers because they had occupied Stark's left flank. It was hot work. One private recalled stopping to get a drink from a nearby brook when he was confronted by an angry officer threatening to run him in with his sword as a deserter. "On my complaining of thirst," the soldier recalled, "he handed me his canteen, which was full of rum. I drank and forgot my thirst."[52]

The fighting continued for more than three hours, with Breymann's men gaining the upper hand on the Americans. Soon the German relief detachment began to outflank Stickney's weary men, who had by this time been reinforced by Stark with additional New Hampshire militia. As the American officers urged their spent soldiers to hold their ground, the Patriots were overjoyed to see Warner's regiment approaching on the double down the road. Recalled Stark, "Colonel Warner's regiment came up, which put a stop to their career. We soon rallied, and in a few minutes the action became very warm and desperate, which lasted until night."[53] One of Breymann's grenadiers recalled that they enjoyed initial success and pushed the Americans back, "but because they were as yet 4 or 5 times as strong as us and were better acquainted with this region, they encircled us, and our right wing had to withdraw," forcing them to abandon the guns, which were quickly captured.[54] After hours of

hard fighting, Breymann led a small party of men to recover the artillery, but they failed, and most were wounded, including their commander.[55]

Finally, as the sun set, their ammunition exhausted, Breymann's detachment fell back. The retreat was orderly at first, but then discipline began to collapse. "Soon the Germans ran," recalled one American soldier, "and we followed. Many of them threw down their guns on the ground, or offered them to us, or kneeled, some in puddles of water. One said to me: 'Wir sind ein, bruder!' [We are one, brother!] But I pushed him behind me and rushed on."[56] Breymann's shattered units fell back across the bridge at Sancoick, and, after a short pause during which some order was restored, they started back toward the main British camp. Stark claimed later that if they'd had one more hour of daylight, they would have captured the whole detachment.[57] On their retreat, Breymann's party met Burgoyne at the head of the 20th Regiment of Foot, which had marched out to come to Breymann's and Baum's assistance. One look at the disheveled and bloody survivors, and the commander-in-chief knew it was hopeless. He wordlessly turned back toward Fort Miller, arriving early on the morning of Sunday, August 17. Breymann's relief force was able to cover the 24 miles back to the main camp—minus their artillery—in less than twelve hours. This time there was no question about the urgency.[58]

For several days after the August 16 disaster, stragglers from Baum's and Breymann's commands made their way back to the British lines. Still, Burgoyne's losses of almost one thousand men were staggering, which put the campaign's continued viability into question. To complicate matters, on the 18th, the runoff from the heavy rains washed away the bridge the British had built in anticipation of the army's next major move to the west bank and then south. Burgoyne had to decide whether to resume the offensive south toward Albany or fall back to Fort George or Fort Ticonderoga and secure lines of communication back to Canada. For the time being, at least, there would be no lightning move across the river and on to Albany.

Sunday's general orders revealed to the army a hint of the Bennington disaster and of Burgoyne's immediate intentions: Baum's raid "failed of success through the chances of War." It was now necessary that they spend "some days" gathering the sick and wounded and those straggling back.[59] Bennington was no minor setback, however. Of Baum's 762 men, only fourteen soldiers escaped death or capture, with many of the prisoners being wounded. Breymann's relief force fared little better, with twenty men killed, seventy-one wounded,

and 142 missing, most of them captured. Of the combined total of about fourteen hundred Loyalists, German, British, and Canadian troops, and Indian warriors in Baum's and Breymann's commands, a stunning 70 percent became casualties. In one day, Burgoyne had lost almost 15 percent of his total force, which now numbered fewer than five thousand men fit for duty. In contrast, Stark's casualties amounted to thirty killed and forty wounded.[60]

In exchange for the heavy losses, Burgoyne gained little of value. Baum had sent back some cattle and provisions before he was cut off by Stark's militia, but not nearly enough to sustain Burgoyne's army for any length of time. Few Loyalists had come to the expedition's aid, and no one was deceived into believing that Baum was heading for Boston. In short, Burgoyne had incurred crippling losses for almost nothing, and now the army had to remain in place while they stockpiled provisions for future operations. "Some days" turned into a week, then two, and finally four and a half weeks passed before they were ready to move again.[61]

Recriminations began well before the last stragglers stumbled into camp. In a letter to Riedesel written a few days after he received Breymann's after-action report, Burgoyne pointed out, not unreasonably, that although there was no question of bravery, "the march of Mr. Breymann was very slow." Burgoyne was baffled that Breymann allowed the cumbersome artillery to slow him down: "It would have been better if he had left his artillery behind to follow after him under an escort, than to have delayed reenforcing the troops."[62] Had Breymann moved smartly, "success would probably have ensued; misfortune would certainly have been avoided."[63] Burgoyne was right, but it is unlikely that the combined force of Breymann and Baum could have beaten Stark.

There is plenty of blame to go around for Bennington. Baum failed to fulfill the most fundamental military obligations to his units, and Breymann's conduct on the march to Sancoick was deplorable. Burgoyne had picked the expedition's leader, specified the units, prepared the detailed instructions, and personally designated the relief force, against the advice of both Riedesel and Fraser, albeit for different reasons. Baum's and Breymann's soldiers paid the price for the multiple failures of their leaders.

The full implications of the Battle of Bennington were not apparent to Burgoyne in the days immediately following the disaster. Still, for the first time since the campaign began, he realized that the army was in real jeopardy. Three days after Breymann's detachment stumbled into camp, Burgoyne wrote Germain about the catastrophe.

Two letters went out on August 20, one of them suitable for public consumption, the other for the secretary's eyes only. In the public, official account, Burgoyne praised the military ability and bravery of the German troops and the two Braunschweig commanders. He also described the action at Bennington by lowballing his casualties by more than 50 percent and claiming that American "loss in killed and wounded being more than double to ours," which was grossly inaccurate. Despite the setback, they had replaced the bridge knocked out by the flooding Hudson River, and once they were ready to move, Burgoyne assured Germain that he would be ready for whatever came next, particularly if his "endeavours may be in some degree assisted by the cooperation of the army under Sir William Howe."[64] For the first time since he had departed Canada, Burgoyne acknowledged needing Howe's help in accomplishing his immediate objective of getting to Albany. Indeed, he had given every indication of being sure to reach Albany unaided, even expressing a desire to reach his objective quickly so he could help St. Leger, and not the other way around. Burgoyne's public letter was still full of optimism and purpose.

The private letter, however, was blunt. Bennington was an utter debacle. Breymann's conduct was appalling, as "if ever there was a situation to justify enterprise and exertion," it was the affair at Bennington. Had the raid succeeded, Burgoyne declared, "I should have effected a junction with St. Leger and have been before now at Albany." He had sent German troops on the raid and the relief column because they were the most expendable. Although the morale was still high, prospects for overall success, Burgoyne admitted, were "far less prosperous than when I wrote last." Admitting that his assumptions concerning Loyalist support in the region had been wrong, he noted, "Wherever the King's forces point, militia to the amount of three or four thousand assemble in twenty-four hours." Due to the "active and rebellious" population, Burgoyne acknowledged that he could no longer secure his lines of communication.[65]

Gates now commanded the American Northern Department, reported Burgoyne, and he and his army were "now strongly posted near the mouth of the Mohawk with an army superior to mine in troops of the Congress and as many militia as he pleases." This was an exaggeration at the time of writing but would be proved accurate in less than a month. If only he could use his own initiative, Burgoyne maintained, he would either stay where he was or fall back to Fort Edward, where his communications "would be perfectly secure." However, since Germain's orders required him to "force a

junction with Sir Wm Howe," he had to push forward.[66] Of course, this was wrong: both Germain and Howe had counseled Burgoyne always to use his initiative.

Everything had shifted. Only two weeks earlier, Burgoyne believed he would reach Albany by the end of August. Now he had to remain near Fort Miller until he could accumulate "25 days provisions." Only then would he cross the river to the west bank, sever his lines of communication, and march on to Albany. His predicament, in other words, was all Carleton's and Howe's fault. When he wrote his earlier upbeat reports, he had not known he would be on his own and solely responsible for garrisoning Ticonderoga.[67] This was pure sophistry. Burgoyne did not expect, nor did he believe he required, any assistance, and had predicted in a letter to Howe on August 6 that the army would reach Albany by the 22nd or 23rd, even if the Americans opposed him.

Burgoyne also complained about Howe. The only message he had received from the commander-in-chief was the July 17 letter confirming, once again, that he was heading to Philadelphia. Burgoyne protested that nothing "has yet been done in my favour."[68] This was highly disingenuous. He already knew that help from New York was unlikely anytime soon. Clinton had already written Burgoyne after Howe sailed to the Chesapeake to say that he had been left with very few troops with which to "make any effectual diversion in your favor," but that he might be able to do something "towards the close of the year." Clinton felt no pressure or urgency to make a move because he had seen a copy of Burgoyne's August 6 letter to Howe saying all was well and that he would be in Albany by August 22. Since his return to New York in early July, Clinton worried about the fate of the army from Canada, but, after reading Burgoyne's letter, he had little reason to fear for his friend's welfare. All accounts agreed that Burgoyne was "in a most flourishing way."[69]

It appears that the main purpose of the private letter to Germain was to prepare the groundwork for his defense should the Albany mission fail.[70] He held his German troops responsible for the Bennington defeat and Carleton and Howe for his overall predicament. In truth, Burgoyne had only himself to blame. He ordered the raid on Bennington because he had dallied, and his logistical problems had become acute. After Bennington, he should have admitted that preserving the army took precedence over getting to Albany.

In addition to his combat losses, Burgoyne lost most of his Indians after Bennington. They were already demoralized by the restrictions

placed on them by the Europeans, but the Battle of Bennington was the last straw. On August 19, the Indians held a council, and most decided to leave. Many of the British and German rank and file and junior officers were not sorry to see them go: "No great effort was made to persuade them," a German officer recalled, "and still less to beg them to stay longer." Five days later, the same German observer recorded that most "of the Savages have returned via Fort George to Canada." The Indians assigned to Fraser's advanced corps, the majority of Burgoyne's warriors, were reduced to fewer than fifty, and many of these would soon depart as well. On August 28, Joseph Brant and three fellow warriors came into Burgoyne's camp, offering their assistance and carrying the news of St. Leger's withdrawal back to Canada, but this was not enough to make up for the mass exodus. By the beginning of September, almost all of his Indians were gone. Fraser tried to make up for their departure by using Loyalists to patrol and scout, but they were not suitable substitutes. "Our Provincials were neither careful nor agile enough . . . to give the camp the same security that the Savages had been able to do."[71]

While the Indians had been troublesome and caused frequent headaches for Burgoyne and his officers, they had been invaluable for screening the army from American patrols and raids and intelligence-gathering. Burgoyne's ability to get an accurate intelligence assessment of the Americans was now severely degraded.

Nonetheless, despite the dire logistics situation, Indian desertion, combat losses, and the double setback of Bennington and St. Leger's withdrawal, Burgoyne still believed that all was not lost. He still had a large, highly disciplined, and dangerous army. The Americans were still amateurs with limited military resources led by a motley collection of lawyers, shopkeepers, farmers, and merchants. Surely he could complete the final part of the campaign. Albany was less than 40 miles away.

Yet after Bennington, Burgoyne faced an American Army that started to increase in numbers, and not just because of Washington's reinforcements. Schuyler's appeals to nearby states for reinforcements had been largely ineffective. Still, with Washington's own personal pleas, coupled with his assignment of militia-friendly Generals Arnold and Lincoln to the Northern Department, Gates's command appointment, the direct enemy threat to Vermont and New Hampshire, and Gansevoort's determined resistance, the militia began to respond in greater and greater numbers. The greatest motivating event for militia turnout was Stark's stunning victory. As one American soldier reported, the Battle of Bennington produced

"the happiest effects on the spirits of our militia, by increasing their confidence in their own prowess."[72] Stark himself thought revenge was the impetus for the militia's positive response. As he wrote to the Council of New Hampshire, "I think in this action we have returned the enemy a proper compliment for their Hubbardston engagement."[73]

During the four and a half weeks the army camped at Fort Miller, Burgoyne was forced to extend the left wing under Riedesel all the way back to Fort Edward to secure the lines of communication to Fort George and Skenesborough. Fraser's advanced corps returned to the east bank on bateaux after the bridge was destroyed by the flooding Hudson and camped near the mouth of the Batten Kill until the bridge was rebuilt. Once again, the army sat immobile, with the troops knowing full well that each day they sat at Fort Miller, the more vulnerable they became. A frustrated Lieutenant Digby wrote, it "is scarce to be conceived the many difficulties we had to encounter in carrying on a war in such a country."[74] Foraging parties roamed the countryside searching for fodder, cattle, grain, and other foodstuffs, but their efforts were only partly successful. The desertion rate started to climb after Bennington as well. If captured, the miscreant could expect little leniency, and at dawn, the ringing sound of musketry from firing squads was often heard during the army's extended interlude at Fort Miller. Rumors spread throughout the camps that told of overwhelming American forces, St. Leger's retreat, and Howe's movement to Philadelphia and not Albany. "Various were the reports then circulating thro our camp," wrote one concerned officer, "not of the most pleasing kind, which might easily be perceived on the faces of some of our great men, who I believe began to think our affairs had not taken so fortunate a turn as might have been expected."[75] Still, the army waited.

While Burgoyne was launching the Bennington raid, Schuyler resumed his steady retreat and withdrew the Northern Army from Stillwater to Van Schaick Island, located 10 miles north of Albany near the mouth of the Mohawk River. Here he waited for his replacement, and hopefully, militia reinforcements. Schuyler informed Congress of the Bennington victory on August 18: "I have the honor to congratulate Congress on a signal victory obtained by General Stark." In addition, he hoped that "Congress will very soon have the satisfaction to hear that Gen. Arnold has raised the siege of Fort Schuyler."[76] The lame duck Northern Department commander at least had the satisfaction of knowing that he had helped set the conditions for Gates's success.

Schuyler's dispatch announcing the great triumph arrived at the Congress on August 21. John Adams wrote Abigail that "Gen. Starks has acquired great Glory, and so has his Militia."[77] Thomas Jefferson received the news from fellow Virginian Richard Henry Lee: "This was an important victory, well timed, and will probably occasion Mr. Burgoyne to retire very quickly."[78] On August 28, the Patriot *Pennsylvania Evening Post* announced news of the victory and concluded that the British Army was trapped: "[W]e may infer, that the instant Burgoyne got into the country, he was at a loss how to go *on*, and perhaps by this time he is at as great a loss how to get *out*." The *Post* believed that if a substantial number of militia worked in conjunction with the Northern Army, the British would be routed.[79] Americans were starting to realize that Burgoyne was in deep trouble, and they sensed that there was an opportunity for a great victory—if only the British Army would stay put just a little longer.

In Britain, the reaction to Bennington was understandably more subdued when word arrived in October. Most were simply unaware of the magnitude of the defeat. Horace Walpole noted that "General Burgoyne has had but bad sport in the woods."[80] Burgoyne's August 20 public report had, of course, downplayed his losses and their impact on the strategic situation. Even the private letter to Germain did not reveal the true extent of his dilemma. However, it was clear to the secretary that the Bennington disaster, coupled with Howe's focus on Philadelphia, meant that Burgoyne's campaign was now "totally ruined." From 3,000 miles away, the secretary knew that Burgoyne would be hard-pressed to accomplish his mission. He assumed that after Bennington, Burgoyne would certainly withdraw back north to Ticonderoga. Surely, believed Germain, Burgoyne knew that saving the army was more important than blindly pursuing a plan that no longer made any sense. "What alarms me most," Germain complained to William Knox, is that Burgoyne seemed to think that "his orders to go to Albany to force a junction with Sir William Howe are so positive that he must attempt at all events the obeying them."[81] Burgoyne's original orders clearly—to Germain, at least—directed that at all times the general was to use his initiative and to "act as exigencies may require."[82] It appeared now that Burgoyne was not controlling events. Instead, events were controlling him.

Germain may not have fully understood the tactical and operational realities of conducting complex military operations in North America, but at this point in the campaign, he had a better strategic grasp than Burgoyne. He was rightly shocked that Burgoyne's letter indicated that he was blindly following orders written five months

before and 3,000 miles away that could not possibly have anticipated every contingency he might face.

As the British commander-in-chief disembarked his army at Head of Elk, Maryland, to start his offensive toward Philadelphia, Howe saw rebel newspapers with sketchy accounts of an American victory north of Albany. In his August 30 letter to Germain, Sir William reported that he could not confirm the intelligence, but even if true, he sincerely hoped Burgoyne would be able to capitalize on the great success he had already achieved.[83] The next day he updated Sir Henry Clinton on the possible Burgoyne defeat, concluding that "it is much exaggerated as the generality of the accounts are."[84] The report quickly spread throughout the army. The men knew the news was bad. Precisely how bad was anybody's guess.

CHAPTER 17

Gates Takes Command

HORATIO GATES ARRIVED AT Albany on Monday, August 18, after an unhurried two-week journey.[1] He found the town transformed since he departed the Northern Command in a fit of pique almost three months earlier. The small settlement (consisting of roughly three hundred buildings) did not appear as grim. Bennington had changed the mood from panic to cautious optimism. Nonetheless, the improving situation did not mean that the task facing Gates would be easy. There was still a large army of British and German regulars within striking distance, and it showed no sign of withdrawing. Reaching army headquarters at Van Schaick Island late afternoon the next day, Gates had been instructed by Congress to shake things up, including suspending officers for misconduct to prevent disciplinary problems that were "apt to prevail in a retreating army."[2] The delegates did not want a repeat of Ticonderoga.

The reunion with Schuyler at headquarters was anything but cordial. Gates brusquely rebuffed Schuyler's suggestions and advice and declined the New Yorker's attempt to renew their previous relationship and settle their differences.[3] At one time or another, both men felt that they had been mistreated by Congress: Gates by his unceremonious removal from the department three months earlier, and Schuyler's dismissal in the wake of Ticonderoga. Both were proud men who felt abused and maligned by the other's allies in Philadelphia. Now Gates had been vindicated while Schuyler had to seek exoneration through a court of inquiry. Despite Gates's snub, Schuyler, on his own initiative, returned to Albany, where he

continued to push supplies forward to the army for the rest of the campaign, essentially resuming the role he had played during the 1776 campaign.[4]

After the tense meeting with Schuyler, Gates immersed himself in his new duties. Most of the army was delighted with the change of commanders. After learning of Gates's arrival, the surgeon Thacher declared that his appointment "will be very satisfactory to our army, as General Gates has the respect and confidence of the New England troops."[5] Brigadier General John Nixon's brigade of Massachusetts Continentals congratulated Gates and assured him that when his appointment was announced, "Gladness appear'd in every Countenance, Joy circulated thro the Camp." Any implied censure of the army's previous conduct was due solely to Gates's predecessor. They assured Gates that he could count on them to "acquit themselves like Men."[6] Major Henry Dearborn of the 3rd New Hampshire Regiment wrote in his diary that the new commander would "Put a New face upon our affairs."[7]

Over the next few days, Gates sent a flurry of letters from Van Schaick's Island to all parts of the Northern Department and the surrounding states. One of his first notes went to John Stark. "The whole Country resounds with the Fame of your Victory," Gates wrote, and "in a few days, perhaps hours, I think I may be able to transmit you the News of the like happy termination of Our Affairs at Fort Stanwix." Once that happened, he told Stark, he looked forward to the moment when he, with Stark's and Arnold's assistance, would go after Burgoyne's main army. Gates was aware of Stark's previous refusal to place himself and his men under federal control and clearly wanted to convince him to do just that, or at least to effectively cooperate with it. He assured Stark that he and Warner and their men would certainly "meet with all the Honour & Reward Congress can bestow."[8] Gates understood all too well that militia commanders had to be carefully cultivated and could not simply be ordered about by Continental officers.

Stark, maintaining his steadfast refusal to place his men under the command of a Continental officer, replied from Bennington and suggested instead that he and his men cooperate with Lincoln and harass Burgoyne's left flank from the Hudson's east bank. Lincoln had agreed with Stark's suggestion, so Gates concurred, although he would have much preferred to have Stark's battle-hardened New Hampshire and Vermont men with the main army.[9]

Lincoln also provided a piece of valuable intelligence that he had received from three escaped American militiamen who had been

captured at Bennington. After spending a few days in Burgoyne's camp, they learned that the enemy was stockpiling supplies brought down from Forts George and Ticonderoga, where they had also dispatched regiments to secure those posts. In addition, the "Indians are leaving them—the Canadians disaffected" and fear to "even go for water after dark." Nonetheless, said the militiamen, the British hoped to make Albany their winter quarters.[10]

The day after his arrival, Gates informed Hancock that "I shall not wait to be attacked, but endeavor to turn the tables upon my antagonist."[11] To do that, he would need the militias. To Governor Trumbull of Connecticut, he was even more optimistic, urging him to send along his militia as soon as possible, but also suggesting that they might very well be released to return home sooner than expected because "I think there is the fairest prospect of a Happy finishing of the Northern Campaign."[12] While things were looking up, Gates still had to deal with several challenges, not the least of which involved staff officers who were still loyal to Schuyler. Prominent among these men were Lieutenant Colonels Richard Varick and Henry B. Livingston, who temporarily joined Arnold's staff as supernumerary aides-de-camp. Both men kept up an active correspondence with Schuyler and did everything they could to undermine the new Northern Department commander.[13]

Gates inherited an army that was gaining in strength and ability. Stark's action had galvanized the army's rank and file and encouraged the surrounding states to call out their militia units. Another reason was that Washington lavished considerable attention on the Northern Department, sending substantial reinforcements and experienced combat leaders, including Nixon, Glover, Lincoln, and, of course, Arnold. On August 16—while he anxiously awaited information on Howe's whereabouts—Washington ordered Colonel Daniel Morgan and his corps of riflemen to march as quickly as possible to Peekskill and from there take ships north to Albany, putting in place the final piece of the puzzle.

The situation in the Northern Department and the "approach of the Enemy in that Quarter, has made a further reinforcement necessary, and I know of no Corps so likely to check their progress in proportion to its Number as that under your command," Washington wrote Morgan.[14] This was a key decision and not one that Washington took lightly. Only recently formed, Morgan's riflemen were nonetheless the most elite unit in the Continental Army.

Since Morgan's men were "well acquainted with the use of Rifles and with that mode of Fighting which is necessary to make them a

good Counterpoise to the Indians," Washington assured New York Governor George Clinton, that "I expect the most eminent Services from them." To enhance their fearsome reputation, Washington urged Clinton to "circulate these Ideas with proper Embellishments" and to "take pains to communicate them to the Enemy." Clinton wasted no time forwarding Washington's advice to Gates.[15] By the time the corps of riflemen joined the Northern Army, Burgoyne's Indian threat had all but vanished, but Morgan's small but potent force soon proved to be a combat multiplier.

As Morgan and his men set out on their journey, Washington considered his overall command situation. If Howe headed toward the Carolinas, Washington might have to march the main army north to join Gates, so he asked Hancock to reaffirm his status as the commander of the main army and commander-in-chief of all the American armies and departments. Given the prospect of fighting side by side with Gates, this was an extremely shrewd maneuver. Congress responded two days later with a measure that unambiguously defined Washington's position: "Congress never intended by any commission hitherto granted by them, or by the establishment of any department whatever, to supersede or circumscribe the power of General Washington as the commander in chief of all the continental land forces within the United States."[16] Washington clearly thought that because Gates had been appointed directly by Congress and not by the commander-in-chief, he might cause trouble. By the time he received a copy of the resolution, Washington had confirmed that Howe's objective was Philadelphia and not the Carolinas. Still, it was a critical endorsement of his status and authority over Gates.

Three days after he assumed command and two days after sending an update to Hancock, Gates wrote to Washington. Although very busy, Gates should have owed his superior timelier assessments of the situation, yet he continued to ignore Washington throughout the campaign. He treated Hancock and Congress as his real superiors and Washington merely as someone who could help him out from time to time. "Upon my leaving Philadelphia the Prospect this Way appeared most gloomy," reported Gates, but Bennington and Stanwix had "given a more pleasing View of public Affairs." Arnold would soon return with the brigade sent to relieve Fort Stanwix, Lincoln was operating with Stark near Bennington, and General Enoch Poor's brigade was camped on the south bank of the Mohawk River near headquarters. "I cannot sufficiently thank Your Excellency for sending Col. Morgan's Corps to this Army," Gates wrote. Prior to his arrival, "the Army were quite Panic Struck by the Indians, and

their Tory, and Canadians Assassins in Indian Dress."[17] Things were looking up for the Northern Department, and Washington could now focus most of his energy on Howe.

The Northern Department's situation was much improved by the end of August, but Gates was still not ready to confront Burgoyne. In a meeting with Lincoln and George Clinton, he assessed their current situation and laid out the way ahead. Lincoln was to return to Bennington and gather incoming militia and use them to strike Burgoyne's flanks and British outposts at Fort George, Skenesborough, and Ticonderoga. Other plans would have to form in due course. Arnold and his troops had not yet returned from relieving Fort Stanwix. Morgan and his riflemen were still on the Hudson River south of Albany, delayed by contrary winds. And although Gates had been promised great bodies of militia, few had as yet arrived. However, once these units joined the army, he planned to march north to meet Burgoyne.[18]

On August 29, Morgan and his men reached Albany, and Gates personally welcomed the Virginian to the army. To enhance the combat effectiveness of the riflemen, Gates selected men from every regiment in the army to form an ad hoc Corps of Light Infantry under the command of Major Henry Dearborn to augment Morgan.[19] Gates intended to make good use of Morgan's unique capabilities. Two days later, Arnold arrived from his successful expedition to Fort Stanwix with Learned's brigade following a couple days' march behind. Soon Gates's Continental troops would be at full strength with the happy prospect of joining the army over the next few days and weeks.

The arrival of Morgan's riflemen delivered a considerable boost to the army's spirits and, more importantly, to its combat effectiveness. The impact of this small unit composed primarily of frontiersmen was out of all proportion to its size, and not merely because its soldiers were equipped with rifles. Morgan's leadership was perhaps the rifle corps's most potent weapon. Born in New Jersey, Morgan had left home at an early age to make his own way as a teamster on the Virginia frontier. During the French and Indian War, his occupation was in high demand as British Major General Edward Braddock prepared to conduct offensive operations against the French. During his service, the impetuous 6-foot-tall Morgan struck a British officer during a quarrel and was sentenced to receive five hundred lashes, a punishment that often ended in death. Miraculously he survived, but he harbored a lifelong and profound hatred for the British Army and refused to use corporal punishment himself.[20] He settled down

after the war, married, and joined the local militia, quickly rising to the rank of captain. At the outbreak of the Revolution, he raised a company of light infantry and joined Washington's army at Boston. His company was assigned to Benedict Arnold's Kennebec River expedition, where his backwoods skills and abilities as a natural leader became clear. During the December 1775 attack on Quebec, Morgan displayed courage by leading his riflemen on several failed assaults against prepared enemy positions. Captured by the British, he was released in August 1776 and promoted to colonel shortly after.[21]

Because of Morgan's extensive experience leading light infantry units in combat, in June 1777, Washington assigned him to command the army's newly formed rifle corps. Almost immediately, the unit established a unique identity. Their uniform consisted of distinctive off-white, fringed hunting shirts. Morgan's frontiersmen were not only excellent marksmen; they were adept at moving easily through the woods and using terrain to their advantage. They used what was called the Pennsylvania rifle, which could hit targets out to 300 yards, and was highly accurate to 200 yards, a four-fold improvement over the standard-issue smoothbore musket. The rifle enabled Morgan's men to pick off high-value targets, including officers, noncommissioned officers, artillery crews, and enemy patrols and scouts. While it afforded Morgan's corps a great range advantage, the rifle's rate of fire was very slow owing to the unique characteristics of a muzzle-loading rifle.[22] This made the riflemen vulnerable as they laboriously reloaded. This limitation led to Gates's order to form the corps of light infantrymen under Dearborn. The young New Hampshire native had already established himself in Quebec and Fort Ticonderoga and was a perfect fit for the command. The combination of Morgan's riflemen and Dearborn's light infantry created a synergistic effect that was very effective.

On Monday, September 8, the American Army began to march north. By the next morning, it reached Stillwater. As they marched, Gates continued to work on the stubborn Stark. Gates desperately wanted Stark's combat-hardened militia at his side when he did battle with Burgoyne's regulars. After failing to convince Stark to join the army, he asked him to take up positions forward of the army on the west bank of the Hudson. Stark refused. Gates next suggested that Stark and his men move to the east side of the river, directly opposite the army, appealing to the brigadier's sense of pride; he wrote, "I entreat you will not Tarnish the Glory you have gained but march instantly to the post assigned you." Stark refused again. He would stay on the east side of the river, but he would maneuver his men as he

saw fit.[23] Despite Stark's persistent resistance, Gates was nonetheless confident that he would ultimately convince him to do his duty and wrote Hancock that Stark would soon "occupy a strong Height upon the right of this Camp." He further predicted that days or even hours would "determine whether General Burgoyne will risque a Battle, or return to Ticonderoga, for I cannot think he will stay long Inactive in his present position."[24]

When the army arrived at Stillwater, Colonel Morgan Lewis, Gates's deputy quartermaster general, was charged with setting up the camp and assigning units to their positions. Thaddeus Kosciuszko, for one, was appalled at the site selection. With his keen eye for terrain, the Polish officer observed that the location was dominated by high ground, telling Lewis the enemy could either cannonade the Americans or "take aim at your shoe-buttons."[25] After a hasty conversation with James Wilkinson and Gates, the engineer, Lewis, Arnold, and another staff officer were sent forward to scout for more favorable terrain on which the army could prepare for Burgoyne's advance. Although Gates was moving toward Burgoyne, he wanted to fight a defensive battle on favorable ground. Kosciuszko and his team had to find terrain that would allow Gates to "Defend the main Chance; to Attack only by Detail; and when a precious advantage Offers."[26] Because the assumption was that Burgoyne would advance and attack, according to one of the participants, Kosciuszko insisted on an exhaustive examination of the terrain, and thus, the party went "up hill and down dale," as they journeyed north.[27]

About 2 miles north of Stillwater, Kosciuszko found exactly what he was looking for in a place called Bemis Heights, named after the owner of a nearby tavern. The Heights overlook the Hudson River at a point where it makes a sharp bend to the west. When Kosciuszko saw that the high ground towered 100 feet over both the Albany road and the Hudson River, he cried out to his companions, "This is the spot!"[28] After the men reported the results of their reconnaissance to Gates, he ordered the army to occupy the Heights and take up defensive positions designated by Kosciuszko, which they did on September 12. The Pole made sure each unit was given a spot on the perimeter that maximized its defensive capability. He developed an overall plan consisting of several field fortifications that were incorporated into the natural terrain, giving the Americans a very formidable position. As Burgoyne's army prepared to cross the Hudson River, it faced an American force of roughly equal numbers, but one that enjoyed a distinct tactical advantage on favorable terrain behind defensive fortifications.

The Americans were determined and confident as they advanced toward what most anticipated would be the campaign's climax. Henry Livingston also assured Schuyler that "Mr. Burgoyne has got himself stuck in a situation that he can neither advance or retire without fighting. And at all events, I think a very capital battle might soon be fought." Still, Livingston was "chagrined to the soul" that Gates was about to "reap the fruits of your [Schuyler's] labor."[29] Both Livingston and Varick were fiercely loyal to Schuyler and Arnold, and both detested Gates.

Bemis Heights was the perfect location for Gates to fight his kind of battle. Not only did it tower over the main Albany road and the river, the route Burgoyne had to control if he was to accomplish his mission, it was also topped by scattered meadows and open, cultivated fields. The fields were intersected by deep, steep gullies and ravines, cut through the soft soil by Mill Creek and other small watercourses, which hampered cross-country mobility. The Heights were further bordered on the west by dense woods that would hinder the movement and maneuver of large forces. To get past the Heights with his extensive artillery and logistics trains, Burgoyne would ultimately have to control the riverside Albany road. It was, in almost every way, "a very advantageous Post," as described by Major Dearborn.[30] Once the Americans secured their positions on the high ground overlooking the Hudson River, placed their artillery, and prepared their field fortifications, Burgoyne's challenge was very simple but very difficult: if he wanted to force his way to Albany, he had to defeat or somehow bypass the Americans on Bemis Heights.

As the army prepared their defensive positions on Bemis Heights, Gates sent a series of letters to Governors Trumbull and Clinton and various committees of safety, telling them that since Burgoyne seemed bent on continuing his advance to the south, all Patriots must "exert themselves in reinforcing this army without one moment's delay."[31] He also informed Hancock that all his intelligence indicated that Burgoyne had crossed the Hudson with his entire army plus his artillery, which clearly indicated that he "designs at all Hazzards to Force his way down the Country." Gates assured Hancock that "nothing is left unattempted to Defeat this rash project."[32]

In Albany, Schuyler continued to assist his former command. Hoping to smooth over tensions exacerbated by the fighting in the Mohawk River valley, Schuyler called for a council of the Six Nations. Only warriors from the Oneida and Tuscarora tribes attended. Gates asked Schuyler to convince these friendly tribes to send men to join the army. Schuyler was skeptical, but putting aside any lingering

hostility toward Gates, he urged the Native Americans to fight Burgoyne: "Our Cause is the same . . . and We have nothing to hope for but Tyranny & oppression should we be defeated." Schuyler's speech did the trick. By September 20, 150 Oneidas and a few Tuscaroras joined Gates's army.[33] When Schuyler willingly took on a supporting role, he relieved Gates of extra responsibilities. The new commander of the Northern Army could concentrate his efforts on purely operational and tactical matters.

On the same day Gates put his men into motion, Burgoyne and his army were still trying to accumulate enough provisions to continue their march to Albany. They had languished near Fort Miller for four weeks and were beginning to see ominous signs that they had stayed in one place for too long. Fresh provisions and forage for the animals "began then to turn very scarce," complained one officer, and their food stores were steadily declining. The hot and humid weather they had experienced almost from the day they left Canada began to turn cold, which added to their discomfort. Their winter clothing had been sent from Skenesborough to Ticonderoga in July to reduce the transport required for the army.[34] The change in weather that was an annoyance in early September would soon become a major issue. As the army made final preparations to move, an American deserter was brought in with the news that Gates had almost fifteen thousand men and was almost certainly going to move forward to meet the army from Canada. In addition, as Riedesel noted, the "inhabitants of Albany had already received orders to drive their cattle into the back country, that the army of the enemy might be deprived of the means of subsistence should it reach that point."[35] Even this worrisome intelligence failed to persuade Burgoyne to change his mind about continuing to Albany.

On September 10, the army moved south across the Batten Kill, waiting to cross the Hudson the next day. Also on the 10th, Burgoyne learned from a scout that the American Army was on the move and had advanced all the way to Stillwater. The scout informed them that "in consequence of that unfortunate affair at Bennington," the Americans were joined by large numbers of Militia, "who in all probability would have remained neuter had we proved successful."[36] The intelligence was wrong about the numbers, but militiamen by the score were undoubtedly on the move.

Burgoyne was delayed yet again on the 11th when heavy rains once more spoiled his plans. Still, after weeks of unremitting toil, the army had stockpiled five weeks of provisions that had, as one officer remarked in amazement, "been forwarded from Quebec

upwards of four hundred Miles by Land or water."[37] They also had hauled several bateaux from Lake George to Fort Miller to transport the supplies across and down the Hudson. It required a herculean effort on the part of Burgoyne's officers and men, but it had just taken too long. As the army waited for the rain to subside, they spent the 12th making final preparations to cross the river on the newly completed floating bridge. Given the army's fragile logistical situation, Burgoyne issued an order calling for "the preservation and distribution of Provisions."[38] Burgoyne hoped he could get to Albany in one or two weeks, but if not, his supplies had to last as long as necessary to complete his mission.

Finally, on September 13, a beautiful and clear Saturday, the British expedition from Canada crossed the Hudson and established their camp at Saratoga on the Schuyler estate grounds. Burgoyne set up his headquarters in his former counterpart's mansion. With the breaking up of the temporary bridge over the Batten Kill, Burgoyne cut his line of communications to the north and was now committed to march on Albany.[39] For the first time in six weeks, the two armies were now on the same side of the Hudson and only 10 miles apart.

The delightful weather seemed to offer the promise of future success. Frederike Charlotte Riedesel—who, along with their three children, had joined her husband on August 15 after an arduous journey—recalled that "when we passed the Hudson river, and General Burgoyne said, 'The English never lose ground,' our spirits were greatly exhilarated."[40] Not only did Burgoyne's army enjoy the beautiful weather, but it also appreciated the prosperous farms and settlements they began to encounter in the midst of harvest season, which "greatly pleased our eyes." One field was already filled with "sheaves of wheat and rye [that] provided camp straw for almost the entire army, [a situation] which we had so far not encountered in all of America."[41]

The Americans did not allow their enemy to enjoy their new surroundings for very long. No sooner had they halted to set up camp near the Schuyler mansion than American detachments began probing the British and German perimeters. After the departure of most of Burgoyne's Indians, this became common and made the most routine tasks very dangerous. One officer wrote that the presence of the American scouting parties meant that the "duty here turned very severe, such numbers being constantly on either guards or picquets."[42]

Crossing the Hudson River was arguably the most consequential choice Burgoyne had made to date. After learning of St. Leger's

withdrawal to Canada in late August, he had everything he needed to make an informed decision: St. Leger's retreat, no support from Howe, the logistical situation, the Bennington defeat, the Indian exodus, and widespread American militia mobilization. Even with all of this information, Burgoyne fell back on Germain's March 26 orders to justify his decision to proceed.

Once the army crossed the Hudson, conserving supplies and ammunition became a deadly serious matter. Burgoyne's general order for September 14 rebuked the army for the "enormous mismanagement" of the army's carts and wagons during the last move. In the future, field-grade officers (majors and above) had to personally inspect each cart to ensure that it was loaded with nothing but "Camp Equipage."[43] General Phillips, the career artilleryman, gathered all of his fellow gunners together and "exhorted them to be cautious of expending their Ammunition in case of an Action, reminding them of the impossibility of a fresh supply." They still had a long way to go before they reached Albany and should "avoid firing on a retreating Enemy unless almost certain of great success."[44] The army's overall health was not much better than it had been in early August, with an overall sick rate of almost 14 percent.[45] This was another drag on the army. Nevertheless, on Monday, September 15, the army resumed its march toward Albany and Gates.

The army marched in three columns with the British troops, the right wing, in the lead, the artillery train following, and Riedesel's left wing bringing up the rear. The bridge over the Hudson was dismantled and floated down the river for future use, as were some of the heaviest equipment and supplies, on bateaux manned by Royal Navy officers and sailors. The army was slowed when they encountered numerous bridges destroyed by the Americans as they retreated through the area weeks before. After only 3 miles, Burgoyne halted the army at Dovegat (present-day Coveville, New York), 6 miles from Bemis Heights. Burgoyne knew Gates and the American Army were somewhere ahead of him, probably astride the Albany road, but its exact location, size, and disposition was a mystery. All of his attempts to gather intelligence were thwarted by American pickets and patrols employed to screen the army. As the British inched closer to the Americans' positions on Bemis Heights, Burgoyne's intelligence picture was increasingly vague. The army keenly felt the exodus of their Indian allies after Bennington.[46]

The leaves on many of the trees and bushes had begun to change, and the daylight hours waned as the army continued to trudge south. "It was then pretty certain and generally believed, and indeed wished

for, that we should shortly have a decisive engagement," Lieutenant Digby recalled, "I say wished for, as they [the Americans] never would allow us to go into winter quarters, till we had gained some great advantage over them." Once they defeated the Americans, Digby hoped, "many of the country people would join us, but not till then—they choosing to be on the strongest side."[47] Digby was not the only British soldier itching to get at the Americans at long last. Captain John Money, Burgoyne's deputy quartermaster general, thought that the army "did think it was their indispensable duty to proceed forward and fight the rebels," and Captain John Harrington, the Earl of Harrington, recalled that it was "impossible for any army to have been in higher spirits than they were at that time, or more desirous of coming to an engagement with the enemy."[48]

The ubiquitous and aggressive American patrols made it difficult to repair the bridges that Schuyler had ordered destroyed weeks earlier. So many Americans lurked in the woods that Burgoyne had to ban foraging, except by large bodies of men supervised by an officer. As the increasingly cool evenings heralded the coming of autumn, they also led to the formation of thick ground fog that clung to the low-lying areas and along watercourses that persisted until burned off by the sun in the mid- to late morning. This, along with the destroyed bridges and skulking Americans, contributed to slow the British advance. To help smooth the next jump toward Albany, on September 16, Burgoyne led a two-thousand-man detachment to scout the route forward, push away any American troops in the vicinity, and protect the work parties repairing the bridges. This was successful, and the next day the army marched on a roundabout route through the woods, avoiding the worst of the damaged Albany road, but they were still only able to advance 3 miles. They made camp that night at Swords's house, three and a half miles from Bemis Heights.[49]

A combination of hunger and lack of discipline led to the death and capture of more than a dozen British soldiers on the 18th when they were ambushed after venturing outside the camp without permission in search of potatoes. A furious Burgoyne issued yet another order banning foraging, which promised that anyone disobeying "will be instantly hanged." He simply could not afford to lose anyone at this critical juncture in the campaign, especially for "the pitiful consideration of potatoes." Burgoyne had to remind his men that "The life of a Soldier is the property of the King."[50]

In the meantime, Braunschweig soldiers from the left wing had been repairing the Albany road and its many bridges. After

rebuilding one bridge that morning and starting work on a second, an American force of four hundred men appeared in the distance giving "the impression of intending to prevent" the repairs. Major von Ehrenkrook, of the Regiment von Specht, arrived at the first bridge with one hundred men and two cannons to reinforce and defend the security detachment and work party. Soon they realized that the "enemy reinforced his own troops to an appreciable degree," recalled the German officer, and "several of his regiments were discovered with their flags in view."[51] The Germans had encountered Arnold and fifteen hundred men, who had been sent out to ambush an element of Burgoyne's army.[52] Things escalated as the Germans dispatched an entire regiment to support the men at the bridge. After a tense standoff, the Americans finally backed away. That night Burgoyne's entire army slept with their weapons at their sides.

As Burgoyne's army edged closer to Gates's position on Bemis Heights, Benjamin Lincoln successfully gathered almost two thousand militia troops at Pawlet, Vermont (located about 35 miles west of Fort George), and, following the guidance Washington, Schuyler, and Gates had given him, dispatched three American militia detachments of about five hundred men each to attack enemy outposts. Colonel Benjamin Woodbridge seized Fort Anne and Skenesborough on September 14 and 15. Colonel John Brown captured the critical British supply base at Fort George on September 15 and then marched north. Three days later, he overran the portage between Ticonderoga and Lake George. Brown captured hundreds of British soldiers, including four companies of the 53rd Regiment of Foot, tons of provisions, and two hundred bateaux. He also succeeded in freeing one hundred American prisoners. Colonel Samuel Johnson, commanding the third detachment, marched to Fort Ticonderoga and, on September 18, demanded the surrender of the British garrison. Brigadier General Henry Watson Powell, detached by Burgoyne from the main army along with almost one thousand men to garrison the fort, refused, and the Americans were forced to retreat down the west shore of Lake George. Colonel Brown then tried but failed to seize the British supply base on tiny Diamond Island at the southern end of the lake.[53]

Despite their failure to retake Fort Ticonderoga, the militia detachments inflicted considerable damage. Gates was understandably pleased with these actions, but with Burgoyne only a few miles away, he ordered Lincoln and his militia to join the main army. Now Burgoyne was completely cut off. He had to press on with his advance

southward or face the prospect of having to fight all the way back to the safety of Ticonderoga.[54]

The morale of the American forces had undergone an almost miraculous transformation. The twin victories at Bennington and Stanwix, coupled with the militia-friendly Gates's assumption of command, combined with the constant and steady arrival of militia and reinforcements from Washington's army—as Gates's army got bigger, Burgoyne's steadily declined—had caused American optimism to soar. An army that was disorganized and disillusioned in mid- to late July was itching for a fight a few weeks later. There was now a widespread belief that the invading enemy army was in deep trouble. One officer assured Schuyler that a battle was now virtually certain and predicted that soon "I shall have the pleasure of seeing the Enemy's spirits crushed."[55] Gates urged the army to avenge the innocent civilians murdered by Burgoyne's Indians, and told his troops that "the time is now come, when they are called on by their country, by their general, and by every thing divine and human, to vanquish the foe."[56]

As the armies edged closer toward one another, Schuyler's former officers, now on Arnold's staff, ridiculed the new army commander. Livingston wrote Schuyler that Gates now estimated Burgoyne's army to total around eight thousand men, when just a short time before the commander believed the number was closer to about five thousand. "The Riddle is Plain," wrote Livingston, "It was *his* interest then, to diminish, now to magnify the number of the enemy."[57] Richard Varick could not resist a jab at Gates's nearsightedness when he wrote the next day that although everyone seemed optimistic about the upcoming battle, "I wish to God we had a commander who could see for a little distance before him without spectacles and we would probably make as Brilliant a stroke as that of Bennington."[58] Varick and Livingston soon discovered that Gates's eyesight was up to the task.

CHAPTER 18

The Battle of Freeman's Farm

BY THURSDAY, SEPTEMBER 18, only 3 miles separated the two armies. About halfway between Swords's house and Bemis Heights was a deep gully cut by a stream framed by steep banks that later became known as the Great Ravine. Any Burgoyne advance would have to negotiate not only the Great Ravine, described by one of his aides as "one of the deepest I ever saw," but many smaller valleys that crisscrossed the landscape, formed by creeks as they made their way to the Hudson River.[1] He also had to contend with more downed and destroyed bridges along the Albany road and the densely wooded areas, traversed by narrow paths and crude roads and pockmarked by scattered, cultivated fields and small farms.

Burgoyne wanted to keep moving. He knew the Americans were on favorable terrain that guarded the road to Albany, but he lacked the detailed intelligence that would allow him to plan and conduct a thorough, deliberate attack. Hence he decided to conduct a forward movement to find and engage Gates and to develop the situation to his advantage.[2] Burgoyne most likely wanted to fix Gates in position and then outflank him from the west, hoping to force the Americans to abandon their strong position on Bemis Heights and retreat south.[3]

Delayed by thick ground fog, Burgoyne's forces prepared themselves to battle the Americans. Ammunition, a hundred rounds for each man, and rations were distributed, baggage packed onto carts, bateaux loaded and readied to be floated down the river parallel to the army's advance, and the men formed into ranks. Burgoyne began

his advance at 9:00 a.m. on the 19th, using three columns, with his remaining Indians, Loyalists, and Canadians in the lead acting as scouts. The columns would advance together along different routes while remaining within supporting distance of each other. The right column consisted of the advanced corps (2,400) and Breymann's Corps (530) along with two 6-pounder guns. Fraser's mission was to skirt the Great Ravine and seize and hold the high ground to the west of Bemis Heights. The center column, referred to as the "British Line" and accompanied by Burgoyne himself, consisted of the 9th, 20th, 21st, and 62nd Regiments of Foot and an artillery detachment of four 6-pounders (1,700). Brigadier General James Hamilton commanded the center column, which acted as the army's main effort. The left column, commanded by Riedesel and accompanied by Phillips, consisted of Riedesel's Corps of the three Braunschweig musketeer regiments, the surviving Braunschweig dragoons, and the Hesse-Hanau artillery (1,600). This column was followed by the hospital, the army's baggage and artillery train, and the followers. The Hesse-Hanau infantry regiment (590) acted as the army's rear guard at Swords's house. Riedesel was charged with opening the Albany road and fixing Gates in position. A signal gun fired from the center column would announce the launch of a synchronized attack on the American positions on Bemis Heights.[4]

Burgoyne and Hamilton's center column made good time, crossing the Great Ravine quickly and without opposition, the Americans having failed to destroy a bridge across the stream, reaching the vicinity of Freeman's Farm by noon. The Americans passed up an opportunity to inflict serious damage on the center column by failing to defend the south bank of the Great Ravine. Burgoyne's men quickly crossed the unattended obstacle. The other two columns took much longer to get into their assigned positions, hindered by the dense woods, poor roads, fallen trees, morning fog, and three bridges along the river road that had been destroyed by the Americans. Fraser and the right column also had to negotiate a longer, more circuitous route to march. The movement was particularly frustrating for Riedesel and his troops, who seemed to encounter a downed bridge every quarter mile. Although Burgoyne had established a system of cannon signals to coordinate the three columns' movements, managing an army divided into three parts across miles of rough terrain and thick woodlands was a difficult task. By noon the columns had all reached their designated positions, and a signal of three cannon shots announced the order for the columns to continue their advance. Hamilton dispatched

Major Gordon Forbes and one hundred men to scout ahead of the main column and to brush away some American pickets who had harassed the British advance.[5]

As Burgoyne and his army approached the Americans' positions, Gates enjoyed some major advantages over the enemy. He only had to defend, not attack. This was Gates's preferred mode of fighting, and using the militia fit it perfectly. Militia forces were most effective when used on the defensive and behind fortifications. Gates could, therefore, afford to wait for Burgoyne's advance. Gates also had a secure line of communications to Stillwater and then on to Albany.

Still, all was not rosy in the American camp. Gates and his temporary second in command Arnold (Lincoln was senior to Arnold but was still in Vermont) disagreed on the best way to counter Burgoyne's advance. Arnold wanted to seize the initiative and attack; he believed they could catch Burgoyne on the move and inflict maximum damage. Gates settled on a compromise course of action, one that failed to appease his fiery subordinate and led to a bitter disagreement between the two men in the coming days.[6]

The American positions on and around Bemis Heights were formidable indeed, but mainly due to the terrain since the fortifications were still incomplete. Because the river and the road to Albany were critical to Burgoyne's movement southward, the Americans put most of their efforts into denying the enemy access to both. They built trench lines across the floodplain from the base of Bemis Heights to the road and the river, along with batteries covering the earthworks and the river itself. Three artillery batteries—the North Redan, the Bemis Heights Redoubt, and the South Redan—were also posted on the eastern summit of Bemis Heights, where they commanded the low ground, the road, and the river. From the batteries covering the road and river, the entrenchments extended almost a mile west along the northern slope of the heights and all the way to the Neilson Farm, which was located on high ground that anchored the defenses.[7]

This long line of field fortifications faced another deep ravine (not the Great Ravine) just to the north, making a frontal attack difficult. The army's right wing, commanded personally by Gates, manned the positions along the river and to the front, while Arnold's left wing occupied the western entrenchments. At the Neilson Farm, the line angled back south for about a half-mile until it reached an east-west road that ran all the way to the river near the Bemis Tavern. This part of the line guarded against an enemy flank attack from the west. Gates's headquarters was located at the Woodworth Farm, about

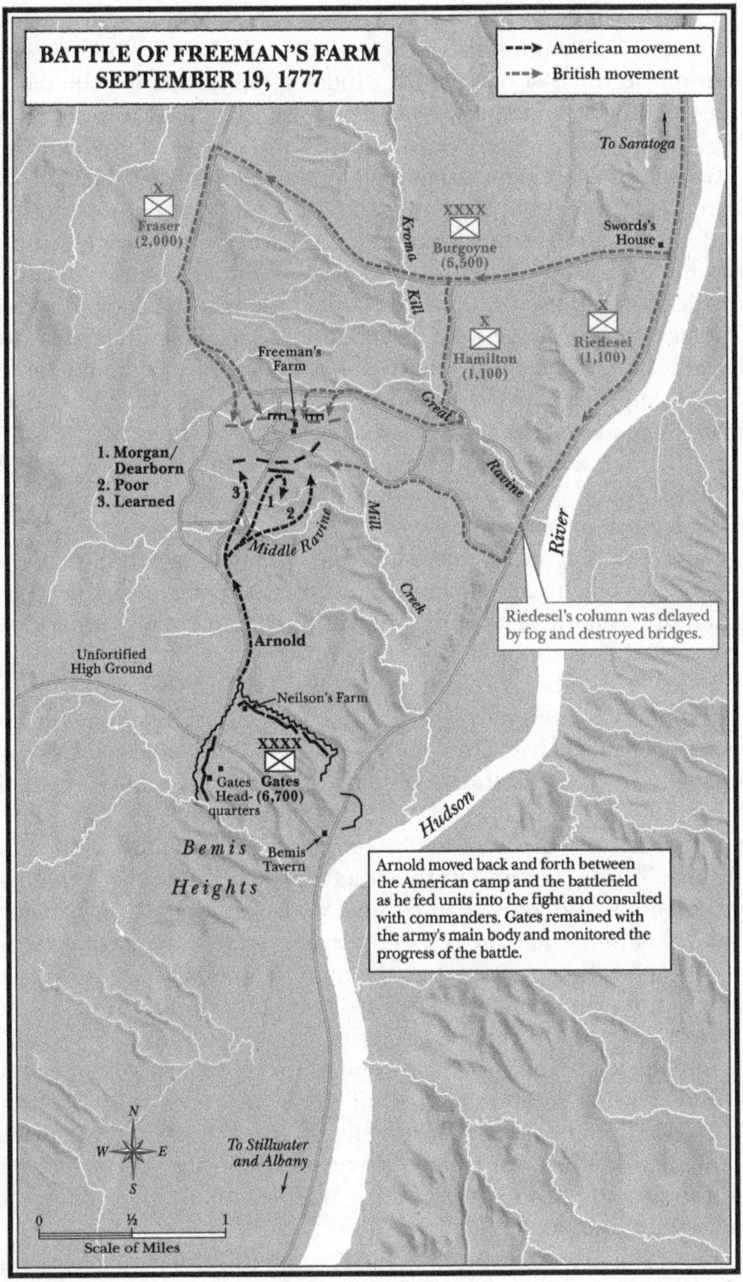

Map 10 Battle of Freeman's Farm, September 19, 1777

a third of a mile south of the Neilson Farm. The Americans had constructed a floating bridge near the Bemis Tavern, linking their positions to the east bank of the Hudson and facilitating the movement of troops and supplies, and especially militia from the New England states. Kosciuszko had done his work very well, indeed.[8]

In addition to being incomplete, the American defenses on Bemis Heights, though strong and well sited, were not impregnable. If Burgoyne could place a sizeable force on the high ground to the west of Neilson Farm, they could potentially outflank Gates's fortifications. However, given that the American positions formed a horseshoe-like shape with the open end facing south, Gates had the advantage of tactical interior lines and thus could shift forces to face any threat, whether they came along the Albany road or through the woods against his weaker left flank. Burgoyne, on the other hand, had to operate on exterior lines, forcing him to march farther through dense woods along unmapped paths and in and out of a labyrinth of ravines.

Gates was well aware that Burgoyne's army was getting ready to move. Though he anticipated that they would head in the direction of the American positions, he was unable to get his scouts close enough to have an exact sense of the British preparations. He, therefore, on September 18, sent some New Hampshire troops under Lieutenant Colonel Andrew Colburn to the east side of the Hudson directly across the river from Swords's house. When Burgoyne's army broke camp, and the three columns moved out, Colburn immediately sent word to Gates and Arnold. Taking Arnold's advice, Gates sent Morgan and his men "to observe their direction, & harrass their advance."[9] Morgan and Dearborn left the security of the American fortifications and moved into the woods and toward the enemy middle column, while the rest of the army manned the fortifications.

They made their way through the uneven, wooded terrain, crossed walls and fences, meadows, streams, and gullies until they reached the outskirts of an L-shaped clearing known locally as Freeman's Farm. One leg of the clearing extended south, toward the American positions, with the other angled off to the east toward the Hudson River. The latter, which was longer, consisted of 66 acres and was planted with wheat and rye. The north-south leg was mostly uncultivated and, although cleared, contained many trees scattered throughout the field.[10]

About a quarter-mile south of the Freeman's Farm clearing was another deep east-west gully called the Middle Ravine. A small dwelling and several outbuildings were located on high ground near the

junction of the two legs. To the west of the clearing and extending into the woods was more high ground, consisting of several small hills. Fences and deep woods surrounded the entire perimeter of the clearing.[11] Any American forces approaching from the south would have to climb the gently sloping ground from the Middle Ravine to the Freeman's Farm buildings. Dealing with the difficult and unfamiliar terrain while facing uncertain enemy dispositions was precisely the kind of mission for which the corps of riflemen was created.

Just as Morgan's men arrived at the edge of the woods on the south edge of the Freeman's Farm clearing, a mile and a quarter north of the American positions, the lead elements of Hamilton's column under Major Forbes appeared out of the woods. At 12:45 p.m., they encountered and scattered the American sentries posted in the Freeman's Farm buildings. The American riflemen immediately opened a deadly fire on Forbes's men from the cover of the woods and the fence line. Soon Forbes and his men were forced to give way and retreat into the safety of the woods with significant losses. Hearing the heavy firing to their front, the rest of Hamilton's men mistook the soldiers stumbling toward them through the undergrowth for Americans and opened fire on their own troops, killing and wounding a number of Forbes's men. The leaders were particularly hard hit, lamented one British lieutenant, "every officer being killed or wounded except one." Forbes was among the casualties.[12]

Burgoyne had planned the advance so that the three columns would be mutually supporting. If one group encountered trouble, the other columns could quickly march to its aid or, conversely, if one column achieved success, the others could pile on. Morgan soon learned how effective this tactic could be when he tried to follow up on his initial success by ordering his men to rush across the open fields in pursuit of Forbes's troops. The riflemen spread out and lost unit integrity as they single-mindedly rushed after the vulnerable stragglers. Fraser, commanding the British right column, also heard the firing, and on his own initiative, sent two companies of the 24th Regiment to support the middle column. Just as Morgan's men were about to catch the retreating enemy, they were struck from their left by Fraser's troops. This timely British response to the overly aggressive and undisciplined American attack threw the riflemen into further disarray. Morgan ordered a hasty retreat into the woods about a mile and a half to the southeast of Freeman's Farm, where he eventually succeeded in regaining control of his men.[13]

Morgan had exceeded his orders to "observe & harass," but his zeal and that of his troops was understandable. He had been able

to inflict significant damage on the enemy with little loss. Dearborn and his light infantry detachment had been following Morgan and supporting the riflemen, but they, too, were forced to withdraw to the high ground a few hundred yards southwest of Freeman's Farm. James Wilkinson, who always seemed to be in the thick of every action, claimed that he encountered a distraught Morgan who exclaimed, "I am ruined, by God!"[14] Given Morgan's reputation for courage under fire and exceptional leadership, this account seems highly exaggerated, and perhaps designed to make Wilkinson look better by comparison, as with many of his accounts. More likely, the emotional Morgan, who was undoubtedly frustrated, was shrieking curses as he struggled to regain control of his men. What is certain is that the American riflemen and light infantry were forced to regroup after overextending themselves. The opening round of the Battle of Freeman's Farm was over in only 30 minutes but was costly to both sides and a harbinger of things to come.[15]

With the Americans temporarily out of action and consolidating their new positions southeast and southwest of Freeman's Farm, the British center column moved forward. Captain Thomas Jones ordered his artillerymen to fire a round into the farmhouse to make sure no American troops had taken refuge there. No enemy emerged, but young Lieutenant James Hadden proudly declared that "by that accident I fired the first Shot from the main body of this Army."[16] The four British regiments that made up the middle column, the 9th, 21st, 62nd, and 20th, were ordered forward and they took up positions to the east of the farm buildings, forming a line of battle facing south. The 9th Regiment was directed by Burgoyne to move to the right (west) and hold a position near two outbuildings to anchor the middle column's right and facilitate the linkup with the advanced corps approaching from the west. Burgoyne ordered the 9th to "defend them to the last extremity." The British artillery consisting of light 6-pounders under the command of Captain Thomas Jones were placed with the 62nd, between the 9th and 21st regiments.[17] Burgoyne sensed that the biggest threat he faced came from the high ground to his right front, where Dearborn's men were located and to where American reinforcements were marching. This was also where the vulnerable junction between the middle column and Fraser's advanced corps was located. If the enemy succeeded in splitting the two forces, they could conceivably defeat each in detail.

From 2:00 and 3:00 p.m., there was a lull in the fighting as the units prepared to resume the battle. While the British were getting their units into position, Arnold ordered Colonel Joseph Cilley's

1st New Hampshire Regiment of Poor's brigade, one of the units humiliated at Ticonderoga, to reinforce Morgan and Dearborn. They arrived just as the British 21st and 62nd Regiments were advancing toward Dearborn's light infantry. Heavily outnumbered, the 1st New Hampshire bore the brunt of the British attack. They held out for 20 minutes, suffering heavy losses despite attempts by Dearborn to assist, before Cilley was forced to order his men back toward Bemis Heights. Now it was just Morgan and Dearborn left to face almost two-thirds of Burgoyne's army, but they were not alone for long. While Cilley and his men staggered back toward camp, they ran into Colonel Alexander Scammell's 3rd New Hampshire Regiment, also of Poor's brigade, followed by the 1st Regiment of Connecticut Militia, commanded by Colonel Thaddeus Cook, hurrying toward the firing. Arnold had dispatched them as additional reinforcements. Not wanting to be shown up by their New Hampshire comrades, Cilley and his men turned and rushed back to the fight. Soon the Americans filled the woods on the high ground in and around Dearborn's light infantry and in the fields to the south of Freeman's Farm and immediately "began a very vigorous attack" on the British regulars. Using the cover afforded by the ravines to the south and left of the British line, Morgan's riflemen began a constant harassing fire, specifically targeting enemy officers and noncommissioned officers.[18]

Uncharacteristically for Arnold—he was almost always at the scene of the action—he shuttled back and forth between his headquarters inside the American fortifications and the edge of the clearing south of Freeman's Farm, while he received reports from the battlefield, consulted with officers, and gauged the intensity of the fighting. Arnold managed the battle but did not personally lead the engaged units in the fighting.[19] He soon sensed that even more reinforcements were necessary to check Burgoyne's advance, so he sent in Poor along with the rest of his brigade, consisting of the 2nd New Hampshire Regiment (Lieutenant Colonel Winborn Adams), the 2nd New York Regiment (Colonel Philip van Cortlandt), the 4th New York Regiment (Colonel Henry Livingston), and the 2nd Regiment Connecticut Militia (Colonel Jonathan Lattimore). By 3:00 p.m., the American line consisted of Dearborn's light infantry, anchoring the left flank with their position on the high ground in the woods; next came the 3rd New Hampshire to the southwest of Freeman's Farm; extending to the right was the 2nd New Hampshire, the last unit to arrive at Freeman's Farm, followed by the 1st New Hampshire, angling its line to the northeast. Cook's Connecticut militia regiment

secured the American right flank along with Morgan's riflemen. The 2nd and 4th New York Regiments and Latimer's Connecticut militia regiment took up positions to the west of Dearborn, facing Fraser's advanced corps. The positions of the two New York regiments essentially refused the American left flank—a maneuver by which a part of a unit moves to a position at right angles to the main line—making it very difficult for Fraser's troops to outflank the rebels.[20]

The fight resumed at about 3:00 p.m. with heavy firing up and down the line. In a short time, the 20th and 62nd Regiments on the British left became hard-pressed by the New Hampshire and Connecticut troops, but counterattacks with bayonet and artillery fire soon thwarted the American flanking attempts. Generals Hamilton, Fraser, and Phillips, and Burgoyne himself were conspicuous throughout the action, exposing themselves to enemy fire, encouraging the troops, and even personally leading counterattacks. Hadden's artillery detachment supporting the 62nd Regiment experienced some of the heaviest fire of the entire campaign. Because his gunners were vulnerable to American fire, Hadden asked General Hamilton for infantry support for his gun crews, and "while speaking to him my cap was shot thro."[21] Additional heavy guns located at Swords's house had been called up at the start of the action, and they finally arrived on the field, led by Phillips, who had heard the firing and hurried to the sound of the guns on his own initiative. These guns were placed with the center column on the northern side of the field where they could fire at the distant tree lines from a position of relative safety.

The fighting at Freeman's Farm was vicious, often at close quarters, chaotic and confused, with much of it taking place in or near broken terrain and woods. Digby, with the advanced corps, noted that they experienced "an explosion of fire I never had an idea before, and the heavy artillery joining in concert like great peals of thunder, assisted by the echoes of the woods, almost deafened us with noise." It kept up until darkness had fallen.[22]

The 62nd, reinforced with Breymann's German light infantry, attacked the Americans again and again. Although they were thrown back with heavy losses, the pressure on the militia and New Hampshire troops was severe, and the Connecticut troops began to give way. In response to the bitter fighting on the American right, Arnold threw together an ad hoc force, comprised of men on guard duty and commanded by Major William Hull of the 8th Massachusetts, and directed them to reinforce the right. Hull's men immediately came under fire from Hadden's guns, but they arrived in time to

help repulse one of the 62nd's attacks. As the battle on the east side of the field ebbed and flowed, Americans captured Hadden's guns at least twice but were unable to remove them without horses. Each time British counterattacks recaptured the guns, with one of these efforts led personally by General Phillips. Thirty-six of the forty-eight British gunners on the field were killed or wounded, including Captain Jones, but the artillerymen fought bravely and probably saved the day by preventing the Americans from turning the British left flank.[23]

The late afternoon fighting on September 19 was some of the most intense of the entire war. "A bullet carried off my cap, another grazed my side," recalled a British soldier, and "a third broke the lock of my fusil."[24] Throughout the middle and late afternoon, the area around Freeman's Farm was shrouded in thick gray smoke from the discharge of thousands of black powder weapons, making it difficult to see targets and for officers and noncommissioned officers to keep order. Adding to the confusion and terror was the noise: thundering volleys of musketry, the ringing single shots from Morgan's riflemen as they targeted individual officers, conspicuous and active noncommissioned officers, artillerymen, and their horses, the ear-splitting crack of the cannon, and the distinctive sound of shot whistling overhead. Officers shouted orders, and noncommissioned officers exhorted their men to maintain their lines, so they could deliver effective fire. Perhaps worst of all was the screaming of wounded and dying men.

As Jones, Hadden, and their gunners repelled the repeated American assaults, one mile to the west, Fraser's advanced corps moved south and occupied Marshall Farm, anchoring the right flank of the British line. The battle soon progressed there as it had on the British left—Americans from the 2nd and 4th New York Regiments and Latimer's Connecticut militia turned back the British advance. They then briefly pursued the retreating Redcoats, only to be repulsed in return. But Fraser's advancing units soon heavily outnumbered the New York Continentals and Connecticut militia, and so were able to hold their position. The American light infantry, still in the woods between the two British columns, primarily faced Fraser's 24th Regiment, which "Brought their whole force against us, together with 8 pieces of Artilery," recalled Dearborn. Nonetheless, the stubborn light infantry held firm. Dearborn proudly explained that they were able to "keep our ground till Night," because the Americans "had Something more at Stake than fighting for six Pence pr Day."[25]

To support Dearborn and the left flank, Arnold ordered Learned's brigade forward, reinforcing the American forces south of Marshall's Farm. The reinforcements included the 2nd Massachusetts Regiment (Colonel John Bailey), the 8th Massachusetts Regiment (Lieutenant Colonel John Brooks), 9th Massachusetts Regiment (Colonel James Wesson), and the only right wing unit to fight that day, the 10th Massachusetts Regiment, under Colonel Thomas Marshall. They would be the last influx of fresh American troops. They arrived just as the fighting ended, at about 6:30 p.m., and briefly engaged Fraser's regiments. Including Learned's brigade, more than thirty-five hundred Americans were committed to the fight by Arnold and Gates.[26]

Throughout the bitter early fighting taking place at and near Freeman's Farm, Burgoyne's left column under Riedesel had inched forward along the river road as they repaired or replaced the bridges already destroyed by the Americans. It soon became clear to them that the fortifications on Bemis Heights and the troops covering the road rendered the American positions virtually impregnable, certainly beyond Riedesel's modest offensive capability. The Germans assumed a defensive posture as they waited for orders from Burgoyne. Few expected the left column to play a major role that day. On the contrary, Riedesel was responsible for controlling the key river road, protecting the army's logistical train, and reacting according to the situation as things developed. General Phillips, who had accompanied Riedesel's column, had already left to determine the middle column's situation once he heard firing coming from the west at around 2:00 p.m. When the firing picked up again at around 3:00 p.m. and did not let up, the anxious Riedesel sent several patrols to scout the route between the German column and the middle column and another with one of his aides to find Burgoyne and request orders. After an arduous journey through miles of unfamiliar terrain, the patrol returned at about 5:00 p.m. with orders directing Riedesel to "assist General Burgoyne with as many troops as he could spare and try to attack the enemy's right flank."[27] As a seasoned soldier, Riedesel had already prepared a force that was ready to march at a moment's notice. By the time Burgoyne's orders arrived, his men were heading west within minutes, with their general in the lead.

Leaving Brigadier General Johann Specht in charge of the remaining troops covering the river road and protecting the hospital and supplies, Riedesel moved out with his own regiment, two companies of the Rhetz Regiment, and two 6-pounder cannons under the command of Captain Georg Pausch. They followed the

route already scouted by his patrols and headed toward the sound of continuous musketry, which signified that the rest of the army was engaged in a furious fight with the Americans. The sun was starting to set as they reached the high ground near the eastern edge of the Freeman's Farm clearing. Riedesel could clearly see that the Americans were advancing in strength against the struggling British left flank. He witnessed the final assault by Hull's detachment and the New Hampshire Continentals on the 20th and 62nd Regiments, which were barely hanging on. He immediately ordered his troops to attack the exposed rebel flank, which they did "with great vigor," supported by Captain Pausch, who with his two artillery pieces, "directed a murderous grapeshot fire against the enemy."[28] The Brunswickers' timing was flawless. The "Englishmen were about to yield, but when they saw us coming, they regained their courage. They bellowed one hurrah after another, and. . . . The air fairly resounded with noise." The Americans retreated.[29]

The 20th and 62nd Regiments, heartened by the reinforcements, charged one last time, the 20th with Phillips in front. Although the British units had fought continuously for more than three hours and were exhausted and their ranks depleted, with the artilleryman leading the way, they "moved on to the charge with spirit."[30] The Americans on the east side of the battlefield recoiled from the unexpected German onslaught and the newly energized British regiments and soon limped back to their entrenchments; the advanced corps resumed its attack in the west at 6:30 p.m. just as Learned's brigade arrived on the battlefield. The battle's final action was short and sharp as the Americans slowly pulled back in the fading light, their withdrawal covered by the 8th Massachusetts. Soon night descended on the battlefield, ending the carnage and the hope of a British pursuit, though not the suffering of the wounded.[31]

During the night, the temperature fell to almost freezing, but the British and German troops remained in their positions with their weapons close at hand, expecting the fighting to break out again at any moment.[32] Their rest was often interrupted by the cries of the wounded. "Sleep was a stranger to us," recalled one officer.[33] Another noted that the "battlefield was covered in corpses."[34] A German officer recalled the plight of the men lying in the field: "Our wounded were taken to our hospital that, was following us. But as there were only a few wretched houses and 3 barns in this region, most of these unfortunate men had to remain in the open air during the night."[35] The bodies of enlisted men were hastily interred in mass graves, which were "scarcely covered with the clay," while "the only tribute

of respect to fallen officers was, to bury them by themselves, without throwing them in the common grave."[36]

The casualties were heavy on both sides, the Americans losing almost 100 killed, 325 wounded, and 40 missing (most of them prisoners), and Burgoyne's army 160 killed, 364 wounded, and 42 missing.[37] Both sides lost a number of leaders, but the British losses were mostly confined to the lower officer ranks. As Corporal Roger Lamb of the 9th Regiment recalled, "In this battle an unusual number of officers fell, as our army abounded with young men of respectability at this time. . . . Three subalterns of the 20th regiment on this occasion, the oldest of whom did not exceed the age of seventeen years, were buried together."[38] This was in stark contrast to the Americans, who lost an alarming number of captains and field officers because they tended to lead from the front.

Despite casualties that amounted to well over 10 percent of his total combat force, Burgoyne's army retained control of the field, which allowed him to claim victory. It was a pyrrhic triumph at best and did nothing to enhance the British strategic situation. Indeed, the heavy losses and the necessity to care for the significant number of wounded—something for which the army was unprepared—only exacerbated Burgoyne's already precarious logistical situation.[39] As he bitterly recalled four weeks later, "It was soon found that no fruits, honours excepted, were attained with the preceding victory."[40]

Nonetheless, Burgoyne's army was pleased with their success, and morale was still high. Digby recalled that "we were all in good spirits and ready to obey with cheerfulness any orders the general might issue."[41] But they had also been surprised by and profoundly impressed with the quality of the American troops they had faced. Up until this point, Burgoyne and many of his men had dismissed the fighting ability of the American troops. This was reinforced by their initial engagements with rebel troops at Fort Ticonderoga and Skenesborough. Many, including Burgoyne, viewed the Bennington disaster as an aberration caused by the failures of the German commanders. Freeman's Farm was something else entirely. They had witnessed American Continental and militia troops who fought as well as or better than any European army. One German officer involved in some of the fiercest fighting on September 19 declared with amazement that "I question whether any war has ever witnessed regular troops withstand hostile fire so courageously and stubbornly as these farmers and burghers."[42] Balcarras, the British light infantry commander, recalled that the "enemy behaved with great obstinacy and courage."[43] Another officer, Lord Harrington, seconded this

when he described the Americans as fighting "very obstinately."[44] Years later, Burgoyne testified that anyone who doubted after the battles that "the Americans possess the quality and faculty of fighting (call it by whatever term they please) they are of a prejudice that it would be very absurd longer to contend with."[45] If there were to be another battle, it would not be an easy one.

On September 21, Burgoyne issued a general order in which his praise for his own troops was measured. The commanding general was pleased to "give his publick testimony to the exemplary spirit of the Officers in general, and in many instances of the private men." Generals Phillips, Riedesel, Hamilton, and Fraser and the artillery under Captain Jones were singled out for special recognition, but "the impetuosity and uncertain aim of the British Troops in giving their fire, and the mistake they are still under, in preferring it to the Bayonette, is to be much lamented."[46] For relatively inexperienced soldiers—regulars though they were—Burgoyne's men fought bravely and well, yet the general was clearly disappointed that his men had not crushed the rebels.[47]

This was more than empty rhetoric. Throughout the fighting, the British generals led from the front. Burgoyne, Hamilton, Phillips, and Fraser were almost always in full view of their men, exposed to heavy enemy fire, including that of Morgan's riflemen, who were aiming to pick off "Gentleman Johnny" or one of his fellow general officers. One eyewitness noted that "General Burgoyne during this conflict behaved with great personal bravery, he shunned no danger; his presence and conduct animated the troops."[48] With the terrain making it difficult for the British to bring all of the combat power from Fraser's and Hamilton's columns to bear on any of the American weak points, the leadership of the British generals had been vital. Nonetheless, it also meant that Burgoyne was unable to step back and consider the battle as a whole. He had concentrated his efforts on the tactical actions of the center column. Had he focused on coordinating the movements of all three columns, the outcome might have been very different.

Although the timely arrival of Riedesel and his troops forced them to retreat, the Americans were generally pleased with their performance against Burgoyne's army. But the effort was costly, especially in leaders. They had lost two lieutenant colonels and several other officers. The day after the battle, Arnold criticized his regimental commanders and other field grade officers for allowing their "Zeal and Spirit" to propel them to "the front of their Companies," exposing themselves to enemy fire when their correct place was in

the rear. Arnold reminded them that in future, they must "observe their proper stations."[49]

Arnold may have found a reason to complain about how his men, or at least their leaders, had conducted themselves during the battle, but others were more positive. Dearborn enthusiastically explained that "on this Day has Been fought one of the Greatest Battles that Ever was fought in Amarrca, & I Trust we have Convincd the British Butchers that the Cowardly Yankees Can & when there is a Call for it, will, fight."[50] Gates agreed with his light infantry commander and wrote Hancock three days after the battle that "[t]he general good behavior of the troops, on this important occasion, cannot be surpassed by the most veteran army," and that "to discriminate in praise of the officers, would be injustice, as they all deserve the honour and applause of Congress."[51]

Although Generals Poor and Learned did make an appearance on the field toward the end of the battle, virtually all the fighting at Freeman's Farm was directed and fought by field officers—majors, lieutenant colonels, and colonels—on the American side. It was the regimental and battalion commanders like Morgan, Dearborn, Cilley, Scammell, Adams, Colburn, and Cook and detachment commanders like Hull, who led their units in taking on some of the best trained and led regulars that Europe had to offer. Arnold's role convincing Gates to check Burgoyne's advance, monitoring the progress of the battle, and the timely employment of additional troops was critical to stopping the enemy. Yet the engagement at Freeman's Farm was a battle of field grade officers for the Americans. These leaders coordinated with each other, mutually supported each other, and fought Burgoyne's army to a standstill.

Some have been critical of Gates's conduct during the Battle of Freeman's Farm, castigating him for being too passive and not yielding to Arnold's demands for a major attack.[52] He was the army commander, however, not Arnold. It is easy for a subordinate to urge aggression when he does not have the commander's responsibility. Gates wanted to fight a predominately defensive battle to protect the road to Albany. Arnold was also right to argue that Burgoyne's advance had to be checked because while the American right was almost impregnable, the positions on the left were not yet complete, and the army was vulnerable there. As the army's de facto second-in-command, he provided advice and was Gates's tactical point man in the field. As the army commander, Gates made the key decisions and oversaw the battle while staying with the army's main body. With the advantage of hindsight, had the Americans attacked Burgoyne

in mid-afternoon with the entire army at Freeman's Farm, they might have succeeded in defeating all three enemy columns in detail. That would have meant abandoning fortified key terrain and leaving the vital river road uncovered when the size, exact locations, and movements of Burgoyne's army were unclear. In the end, both Arnold and Gates did their jobs well that day.

The day after the battle, a British deserter alerted Gates that Burgoyne was planning a follow-on attack on the American left. So the exhausted troops, who, like their counterparts, endured the haunting cries of the wounded during the frigid dark night, manned their positions in the cold autumn morning. No attack materialized. Burgoyne had indeed planned to attack early on the 20th, but canceled it, deciding to rest his men. He considered yet another assault for the next day. That, too, was called off. Instead, Burgoyne's army went to work consolidating their lines and preparing extensive field fortifications anchored on Freeman's Farm and extending east to the heights overlooking the river, the Albany road, and northwest to McBride's Farm. Burgoyne hoped to protect his hospitals, now overflowing with battle casualties, and the army's vital supplies at Swords's house. After the false alarm, the Americans continued to improve their positions, concentrating their efforts on the left flank.[53]

While all this was happening, the minor ill will that had developed between Gates and Arnold now exploded into outright hostility. As the Americans tried to determine what Burgoyne was up to, Arnold's supernumerary aide-de-camp, Richard Varick, penned Schuyler that a "very *Capital* battle was fought with Great gallantry and Heroic spirit on both sides," with Arnold at the center of the action. Although reluctant to provide details, Varick had been offended by something Gates said at dinner. This only aggravated his hatred for the commanding general. "I will sooner see him drawn and quartered," Varick wrote, "than do anything for him out of my line."[54] Clearly, in Varick's mind, at least, Gates had disparaged Arnold in some way, and the word got back to the general.

Gates exacerbated the dispute between the two men with a September 22 general order. He instructed that Morgan was henceforth to report not to Arnold but to headquarters, "from whence alone he is to receive orders."[55] This formally removed Morgan and Dearborn from Arnold's command, stripping away much of the credit Arnold earned for his units' performance during the battle.

On the same day, he issued the general order, Gates sent off his official account of the battle to Congress, heaping praise on the conduct

of the troops and mentioning by name only two of the officers who had been killed in the action. The report was relatively inoffensive. However, the fact that it did not specifically single out Arnold and his units for winning the battle infuriated the left wing commander, who stormed into Gates's headquarters demanding an explanation for the report and the newly issued general orders about Morgan. Arnold arrived "in great warmth [and] asserted his pretensions to the command of the elite [Morgan's riflemen]."[56] Gates replied to Arnold by saying that he was not actually a major general and that because Benjamin Lincoln was on his way to join the army, he, Arnold, did not have a command either. Gates meant that since General Washington had sent Lincoln, who was senior to Arnold, to the Northern Department, he was technically second-in-command. Arnold only temporarily fulfilled that role until Lincoln arrived at Bemis Heights, which was expected any day. As the Northern Department was only authorized two major generals, once Lincoln arrived, Arnold technically did not have a command. Gates's crack about Arnold not being a major general was because Arnold had recently submitted his resignation. These were all minor technicalities, but Gates clearly wanted to get under Arnold's skin by invoking them, and he succeeded. Arnold's reply was equally heated, and the discussion quickly degenerated into an exchange of profanities.[57]

Varick confided to Schuyler that "matters between Genl. Gates and Arnold are got to such a Pitch, that I have the fullest Assurance Arnold will quit the Department in a Day or two." He blamed this sorry state of affairs solely on Gates, who he said had been "insufferably rude" to Arnold. Arnold was upset mainly because Gates had detached Morgan and Dearborn and that he had been given no credit for the September 19 fight. If not for Arnold's insistence, claimed Varick, Gates would have never even fought Burgoyne: "If I do him injustice, it arises from an Opinion founded on mistaken notions of his Character."[58]

In a second letter written that same night, Varick informed Schuyler that Arnold "had the full Confidence of the Troops and they would fight Gallantly under him." He also made a thinly veiled accusation of cowardice at worst, or of indifference at best, against Gates, claiming that while the battle raged on and as Arnold was ordering out troops, the commanding general was in Dr. Jonathan Potts's (medical director for the Northern Department) "tent backbiting his neighbors."[59] Had Gates been hiding in a tent while his men were fighting and dying, it would have most certainly been remarked upon by more objective observers.

After the verbal altercation, relations between Gates and Arnold deteriorated so badly that the two men were reduced to exchanging letters instead of speaking face to face, even though their two headquarters were only a half-mile apart. Arnold fired the first salvo that night—in a battle of written messages that would continue off and on for the next eight days—with a letter to his chief. He laid out his case that Morgan's riflemen were assigned to his division from the start, and thus, he deserved to command them. Gates himself acknowledged this, maintained Arnold because he, Arnold, had been ordered to send them out by Gates, and he had obeyed the order. Gates's written reports might contradict these facts, but Morgan and Dearborn "have been in and done duty with my division for some time past." Arnold reminded Gates that he had brought up all of these arguments to him in person earlier that day and that the commanding general had cavalierly dismissed him. As a major general, Arnold commanded upward of four thousand men. They had performed with "spirit and firmness in action," and are "justly entitled to the applause due to a proper division." "I mentioned these matters," Arnold wrote, "as I wish justice done to the division as well as particular regiments or persons."[60]

Arnold finished his letter with a lengthy paragraph in which he complained about the personal abuse and disrespect he had received both from Gates himself and his headquarters staff. Few of his recommendations had been accepted, and "I have been received with the greatest coolness at head quarters." Since Gates remarked that as soon as Lincoln arrived, he would take command of the left wing and that "you thought me of little consequence to the army," Arnold asked to be sent back to Philadelphia to join Washington.[61] This angry letter suggests that Wilkinson's description of the generals' conversation as being full of "high words and gross language" was an understatement.[62]

Gates waited a day to respond, but the delay did little to heal bruised feelings or cool hot tempers. In a brief two-sentence reply, Gates formally told Arnold that his request to leave the army was approved.[63] Arnold was not assuaged in any way by this and immediately dashed off another note to Gates, demanding that he respond to the many points he had made in his September 22 message. He expected that the commanding general "would at least have condescended to acquaint me with the reasons which have induced you to treat me with affront and indignity." Arnold was baffled by Gates's ill-treatment of him unless he had "been traduced by some designing *villain*."[64] Just who this villain might be, Arnold did not say, but he was probably

referring to someone on Gates's staff. The dueling letters continued when Gates responded that same day, arguing that he had already answered all of Arnold's objections in their face-to-face meeting the night before, and he "gave you such answers to all your objections as I think were satisfactory." He added that "I know not what you mean by insult or indignity."[65]

All of this added needless stress to what was already a hazardous operational situation. Burgoyne's army was still dangerous and sat only a mile from the American lines, yet the two senior Patriot generals were engaged in a juvenile quarrel. Part of the problem was that the two men could not have been more different. However, they had worked together before and had gotten along fairly well. One or both should have put their disagreements, resentments, or hurt feelings aside for the good of the army and the cause. But as the days went by, neither man seemed willing to take that crucial first step toward reconciliation.

Varick's friend and fellow aide Henry Livingston continued the campaign to disparage Gates and praise Arnold. He wrote to Schuyler, lamenting Arnold's decision to leave the Northern Department. "His presence was never more necessary. He is the Life and Soul of the troops," and to a man, his soldiers and officers would "follow him to Conquest or Death." On the other hand, Gates was not half the man Arnold was, yet treated him with "great coldness, and in many instances even disrespect."[66] The similarities between the wording and construction of Livingston's letter to Schuyler and that of Arnold's letters to Gates is striking and suggests that Livingston and probably Varick were spurring on Arnold by appealing to his vanity, prolonging and even escalating his conflict with Gates.

While Gates and Arnold fought their war of words, news arrived from Lincoln of the American attack on Fort Ticonderoga and other British outposts. Gates ordered a thirteen-gun salute—one for each of the states—fired in celebration.[67] The commanding general urged Lincoln to send all the militia soldiers he could muster to Bemis Heights, because "you may be satisfied that New York and not Tyconderoga is General Burgoyne's object."[68] The troops were further buoyed by the fact that additional militia units had started to arrive, answering Gates's and Washington's calls and responding to the victories at Bennington and Freeman's Farm, reported an officer from Albany.[69] On September 22, Lincoln and two thousand militiamen arrived on Bemis Heights, while at the same time, deserters from the British side appeared daily.[70] Gates's army was growing as Burgoyne's was diminishing.

As he oversaw the arrival of militia units and the continued improvement to the army's fortifications, Gates found time to write his wife to complain about Washington being "out Generaled in that Department upon the Whole," by Howe. He believed that the finale with Burgoyne was close at hand: "One week more will determine the great business of this campaign," he wrote, "in that time, the Enemy will either retire, or by one violent push, endeavor to recover the almost ruined State of their Affairs."[71] His estimate was off by about a week, but otherwise, it was a pretty good assessment of Burgoyne's situation.

Five days after Freeman's Farm, Gates and Arnold were still not on speaking terms. Arnold's threat to leave the army "is made public," reported Livingston, "and has caused great uneasiness among the Soldiery." Some of the army's senior officers expressed their dismay, including Enoch Poor, who proposed a petition to convince Arnold to stay. His plan was quashed by a number of general officers and colonels who might have agreed with it but were afraid of offending Gates. Livingston was furious that the petition failed but reported to Schuyler that Lincoln was asked to intervene and "is anxious for Arnold to stay and will pursue the matter."[72] When Lincoln arrived in the army's camp, he automatically became Gates's second-in-command by seniority and assumed the leadership of the army's right wing, which had previously been personally directed by the army commander. Despite his quarrel with Gates, Arnold retained command of the left wing.[73]

Varick and Livingston continued their extensive correspondence with Schuyler the next day, and, as usual, their letters were filled with news of the Gates-Arnold dispute. Livingston bridled at the army's inaction and blamed Gates's overcautious nature. "And in the last battle, had a certain Great Person, had the direction, not a man would have been sent out to support the riflemen and the infantry."[74] Varick wrote to Schuyler on the 25th reporting that Gates maintained "that Arnold's mind was poisoned by some of those about him," probably referring to the two aides.[75] Livingston also complained that "it has been several times insinuated by the Commander in Chief to Genl Arnold that his mind has been *poisoned* and *prejudiced* by some of his Family. And I have been pointed out as the person who had this *undue influence* over him." This accusation further enraged Arnold, who exploded at a militia officer sent as a Gates emissary to work out their disagreements that the commanding general had a "Face of Clay."[76]

On September 26, Arnold was presented with a petition signed by almost all the army's colonels and generals except Lincoln, requesting that he remain in camp. "He has consented," Livingston reported to

his old chief, "tho' no accommodation has taken place."[77] Arnold had chosen to remain at his post for two reasons. First, the gratifying support from his fellow general officers and senior field officers must have fed his healthy ego, which certainly influenced his decision. Second, and perhaps most importantly, had he left the army in a fit of pique while Burgoyne lay nearby, it would not help his prospects for regaining the seniority he felt was owed to him by Congress.

While most accounts of the two battles of Saratoga would lead one to believe that Gates was without supporters in the army, that was not the case. Wilkinson certainly supported Gates, at least at the time of the battles, but certainly not after, as did almost all of the officers and soldiers from New England. These officers certainly recognized Arnold's value to the army, and many supported the petition urging him to stay with the army, but they also had great faith in Gates's abilities, which were instrumental in the enlargement of the army with the flood of militia units.

Arnold's decision to remain with the army and the left wing still did not end the back-and-forth between the two generals. On September 27 and 28, Arnold and Gates again exchanged letters over another petty dispute, this time concerning a fifty-dollar reward Arnold promised to a soldier for killing an infamous Native ally of the British, of which Gates had disapproved. This was tantamount to Gates accusing him of "deceit," Arnold fumed.[78] A clearly frustrated Gates replied that "I am surprised you should be offended at my answer to your certificate in favour of the continental soldier." Even though the sum was small, Gates explained, "that is no reason for my breaking my instructions," on issuing such payments. "I have never called in question, nor suspected you of deceit in that particular," explained Gates, "so cannot see the shadow of a reason for the last part of your note."[79]

Gates's attempt at reconciliation was unsuccessful, and he still had a discontented general on his hands. The tone of his letters indicates that Gates had cooled down by the end of September and hoped that Arnold would do the same in due time. Unlike Arnold, he had avoided personal insults, in writing at least, and seemed willing to give his passionate subordinate some time and space. Plus, Gates had to know that if the army had to fight another battle, Arnold was one of his biggest assets. What is not clear is what Lincoln's role was as Gates's new second-in-command. He had not signed the petition urging Arnold to stay, an action that would have been altogether improper, but it is not clear whether he tried to mediate the conflict.[80]

Arnold fired the last salvo on October 1, in a letter in which he once again repeated all the slights he had endured in an epic one-sentence paragraph:

> Notwithstanding the ill treatment I have met with, and continued daily to receive, treated only as a cypher in the army, never consulted or acquainted with any occurrence in the army, which I know only by accident, while I have every reason to think your treatment proceeds from a spirit of jealousy, and that I have every thing to fear from the malice of my enemies, conscious of my own innocency and integrity, I am determined to sacrifice my feelings, present peace and quiet, to the public good, and continue in the army at this critical juncture, when my country needs every support.

After his grand announcement of his intention to stay with the army, Arnold then proceeded to give Gates the benefit of his advice, a duty for "which nothing shall deter me from doing." The army, cautioned Arnold, "are clamoring for action. The militia who compose a great part of the army are already threatening to go home." In two weeks' time, should Gates make no attempt to attack Burgoyne, the army will be reduced by "sickness and defection [by] at least four thousand men," which would allow the enemy to pull their forces back. Arnold then criticized Gates for failing to follow up their September 19 success at Freeman's Farm with an attack on the 20th, but "that is past, let me intreat you to improve the present time." "I hope you will not impute this hint to a wish to command the army, or to outshine you, when I assure you it proceeds from my zeal for the cause of my country in which I expect to rise or fall."[81]

Gates did not rise to Arnold's bait and never answered the letter. Gates knew that he needed the dynamic combat leadership that he lacked, and Arnold provided. Indeed, he had made the argument to Hancock in 1776 that someone with Arnold's talents was indispensable, despite his flaws. The written exchanges between the two men ended with Arnold's October 1 letter. They resolved their differences at least to the point of civility and perhaps even further and were able to work—and fight—together once again by October 7. Somehow between October 1 and October 7 the rift was healed. Perhaps one or the other walked the half-mile between each other's headquarters to make amends. Or someone invited the other for dinner. Or perhaps Lincoln acted as a go-between and convinced the two to talk it out. Or they both simply let the matter drop. One or more of those events must have happened; it is, after all, what human beings tend to do in such situations, and it is what senior leaders must do.

CHAPTER 19

Sir Henry Clinton to the Rescue

AS THE BITTER DISPUTE raged between Arnold and Gates and militia from New York and the New England states flocked to Bemis Heights, Burgoyne found himself faced with yet another critical decision: to press on to Albany and there wait out the fast-approaching winter, or retreat across the Hudson River and then north to Ticonderoga and perhaps all the way to Canada. By this point in the campaign, neither choice was a particularly good one. If he succeeded in defeating or getting past Gates's army and making it to Albany, he faced a bitter winter deep in enemy territory, in a small town ill-equipped to provide shelter and provisions for more than five thousand men. If he attempted a retreat to Ticonderoga or Canada, he would be vulnerable to enemy attack along the route, especially from militia on his flanks, while perilously short of supplies and in increasingly deteriorating weather conditions. He should have known by this time that whoever commanded the American Army would be happy to see the British Army merely depart back into Canada, so a vigorous pursuit was unlikely. But time was not on his side; Burgoyne's choices narrowed with each passing day.

While Burgoyne weighed his options, he received a message from Henry Clinton two days after the Battle of Freeman's Farm. Throughout the campaign, Burgoyne and Clinton—who had, of course, been left behind by Howe to secure New York City—exchanged several letters. The last was received in early August when Burgoyne still believed that his prospects were very good. Howe had not given Clinton much advice concerning Burgoyne, though at the

end of July, he had told him that "if you can make any diversion in favor of Genl Burgoyne's approaching Albany . . . I need not point out the utility of such a measure."[1] Clinton had been worried about Burgoyne's expedition from the start and thus vehemently opposed Howe's Philadelphia operation, instead advocating cooperation with the northern army. Although Burgoyne had told him that he expected to reach Albany by the end of August, Clinton knew from reports and rumors that he was still far short of that goal. Once word of Bennington arrived at his headquarters in early September, Clinton decided he would conduct a "little diversion" against the Americans. Clinton hoped that such an expedition would draw off the enemy units blocking Burgoyne's route south. Given his small force, he did not anticipate going much beyond the American Hudson Highland forts, even if successful.[2]

On September 21, a British officer arrived at army headquarters near Freeman's Farm with a ciphered letter from Clinton that must have seemed to Burgoyne like a godsend. The messenger had made his way through countryside teeming with American militia as they were being mobilized and sent to reinforce Gates. He was one of a lucky few who was not caught and hanged. Clinton wrote that although Howe had left him with just a small force with which to defend New York, he was willing to make a demonstration on Burgoyne's behalf: "If you think 2,000 men can assist you effectually, I will make a push on [Fort] Montgomery in about ten days." If he did mount an expedition up the river, he cautioned, his flanks would be vulnerable to American attacks, and if the enemy were to make "a move on force to either of them I must return to save this important post." Howe had made it crystal clear to Clinton that his priority was to defend New York, but if he could spare the resources, he was authorized to make some demonstration on Burgoyne's behalf. Clinton hinted to Burgoyne that he would not be able to make a move until reinforcements, expected any day, arrived from England. "Let me know what you would wish."[3]

Burgoyne immediately sent two replies—on September 21 and 23, hoping one would get through the American lines—urging Clinton to make the move up the Hudson. "An attack or even the menace of an attack upon Fort Montgomery will be of use," Burgoyne advised, "it will move them from hence and I will follow them close. Do it, my friend, directly."[4] He could not express the actual desperate state of his army for fear that the message, like so many others, would be intercepted, but it was clear he wanted and needed Clinton to move quickly. Burgoyne believed Clinton and his small army were in the

process of attacking Fort Montgomery on the very day he wrote his reply. However, Clinton was waiting for two things to happen before committing to his expedition against Fort Montgomery and Fort Clinton: reinforcements and Burgoyne's answer, and neither had yet come.

Clinton's reference to the attack starting in ten days in his September 11 letter to Burgoyne was an estimate only; the increasingly desperate Burgoyne took it as a firm commitment, and, as he later recalled, would have opened the way to Albany.[5] Hence he decided to continue to dig in and wait for Clinton's expedition to work its magic, forcing Gates to move south to face the new threat or at least weaken his army. The decision reflected a misunderstanding of geography and the strategic situation, both his own and Clinton's. By hoping that he would find deliverance from a source almost 200 miles away, he squandered the slight advantage he had gained on September 19.

Clinton was frustrated with Howe. He had received no messages from the commander-in-chief for more than a month, and he was unsure of Burgoyne's situation. He knew he had to defend New York, but with the arrival of almost two thousand reinforcements from home—they came on September 24—he had a little more flexibility than before. Finally receiving the news of Howe's September 11 victory over Washington at the Battle of Brandywine, Clinton congratulated his chief for the success, but "Being totally unacquainted with your present situation . . . I wait with some impatience to receive your commands." Even without orders, Clinton was determined to act, and he informed Howe that if he did not hear from him in a week, "I shall probably make an attempt upon Fort Montgomery," to support Burgoyne. Forts Montgomery and Clinton were key to the American defenses along the Hudson, yet the risk was worth it because even if they were to fail, they would not lose much and might gain a lot. Plus, continued Clinton, "I shall have the satisfaction to think that I have at least attempted something in favour of Genl Burgoyne's army." Such a small operation against the Hudson Highland forts might look "a little desperate," he admitted, "but the times may possibly require such an exertion."[6] Clinton's message to Howe was clear: *someone* had to help Burgoyne, and if Howe would not, he would.

On September 26, five days after the reinforcements arrived in New York, so did Burgoyne's messenger with his response to Clinton's proposed lifeline. Clinton immediately set to work preparing his expedition. Soon he and his small force of about three thousand men and several warships and transports were ready to proceed up the Hudson River toward the American forts on October 3.

Major General Israel Putnam commanded the small army of about twelve hundred American soldiers charged with defending the Highlands. His force was inadequate to the task, but given the limited resources, Washington was willing to accept risk in the Highlands and had ordered Putnam to send many of his units to reinforce the main army and the Northern Army. The commander-in-chief judged that the rugged terrain and the forts would increase the effectiveness of whatever troops were tasked with defending them.

Beautiful but forbidding, the Hudson Highlands, 40 miles north of New York, stretch all the way to Newburgh Bay about 12 miles upriver. Heading north, the Hudson makes a sharp jog to the east just after Verplank's Point to Peekskill, and then back west before continuing upriver toward West Point. Fort Clinton and Fort Montgomery were perched about 100 feet above the river and separated by a deep gully through which ran the Popelopen Creek. Although between them the two forts boasted 67 artillery pieces of various sizes, ranging from 3-pounders to 32-pounders, the fortifications themselves were relatively small, only partly finished, and inadequately manned. About fifty American soldiers were stationed at Fort Independence, a small fortification located on the Hudson's east bank where the river turns back to the west. Somewhere around three hundred men occupied Fort Clinton, the southernmost of the two main forts, and another five hundred garrisoned Fort Montgomery. To impede river traffic, the Americans had constructed a chain obstacle across the river from Fort Montgomery on the west bank to the foot of a 900-foot mountain called Anthony's Nose on the eastern side, and they supplemented their river defenses with two 24-gun frigates. Towering more than 1,000 feet over the river and located just to the south of Fort Clinton was Dunderberg Mountain (also known as Thunder Mountain). Just behind Fort Clinton was a large oblong-shaped pond, and to the west of that lay Bear Mountain, with an elevation of 1,300 feet. Both mountains and the rugged countryside surrounding the forts made an overland attack very difficult. The narrow channel and fast river currents meant that a waterborne assault faced its own challenges.

At first glance, it might seem odd that the Americans would have built two forts on the same side of the river and only a half-mile apart. The reason was geography. The chain-boom river obstacle was placed at the narrowest part of the river in the area. However, an obstacle is useless unless covered by observation and fire, as Arthur St. Clair and the Fort Ticonderoga garrison learned to their dismay. Fort Montgomery was built to cover the water obstacle. Given that

directly across the steep gorge carrying Popelopen Creek to the Hudson lay higher ground, it was necessary to build Fort Clinton to protect Fort Montgomery.[7]

Seizing both Highland forts was going to be a challenge, and Clinton decided early on that he would take the forts simultaneously using a *coup de main.* But first, he had to get there, and to do that, he needed close cooperation between the army and the Royal Navy. Fortunately for Clinton, he enjoyed good relations with Commodore William Hotham. Hotham agreed to provide the vessels to transport and land the troops, and escorting warships to protect the transports and counter any American attempts to move troops across the river or interfere with their frigates.

On October 3, the expedition began their journey upriver. Two days later, a small flotilla under the command of Captain Sir James Wallace sailed past Verplank's Point to Peekskill to cut the American escape route across the river.[8] Following closely behind Wallace's warships, Clinton landed a small force at Verplank's Point and chased away a detachment of American militia. To General Putnam, head of that militia, it looked like Clinton's objective was Peekskill, not the river forts, but it was a feint. Keeping a small residual force on the east bank, Clinton landed the rest of his army, consisting of about twenty-one hundred troops, early on the morning of October 6 at Stoney Point, located directly across the river from Verplank's Point.[9]

By the end of September, Burgoyne's situation was grim. Gates's army was increasing in size daily, and Burgoyne would soon be heavily outnumbered. He suspected this but couldn't be sure of the numbers. However, since most of his Indians were gone, he knew that his flanks and rear were threatened by groups of enemy militia. The rations so painstakingly collected before the crossing of the Hudson on September 13 were rapidly disappearing. Under these circumstances, on September 28, Burgoyne sent another appeal to Clinton using two couriers, Captain Alexander Campbell and Captain Thomas Scott. The messengers used different routes and, amazingly, both made it through enemy lines and found Clinton soon after he began his operation up the Hudson. The written notes themselves were innocuous, but the real message was conveyed verbally to Sir Henry by the two officers.[10]

What the captains told him bore no relation to Burgoyne's relatively positive notes of September 21 and 23. According to Clinton's secretary, Captain Scott said that the army was outnumbered at least two to one and that Burgoyne "can remain in his present position"

until October 16, if lines of communications were opened between his army and Clinton's. If not, "it will be necessary he should make good his retreat to Canada before the ice sets in." Scott told Clinton that Burgoyne needed to know whether to push on to Albany or retreat to Canada. For his part, Burgoyne still believed he "could force his way to Albany," but that unless "communication between that place and New York could be kept open, he could not subsist his army during the winter."[11]

This was stunning intelligence to Clinton. Until Campbell and Scott showed up, every message he had received from Burgoyne seemed so positive.[12] Now the two captains described an army that was in dire straits. He also complained that he was rapidly running out of provisions to last a couple of weeks without resupply and that he "would not have given up his communications with Ticonderoga had he not expected a cooperating army at Albany."[13]

This last point was utter nonsense. Howe had given Burgoyne only the vague suggestion that Clinton might be able to offer some assistance. The timing and substance of that assistance were always unclear. Now Burgoyne was asking more than Clinton could possibly accomplish with his available resources. An attack on Fort Montgomery and Fort Clinton was no longer enough. Clinton needed to establish a fully functioning line of communication between New York and Albany. Even if Clinton was somehow able to make it to Albany, it would take many more troops and ships than he had to maintain control of 150 miles of river. As Clinton recalled years later, this suggestion "surprised me not a little."[14]

Burgoyne was in a desperate situation, and the British command and control structure in America did not help. Both Clinton and Burgoyne were seconds-in-command in their respective theaters: Canada under Carleton and the rest of North America under Howe. Once Burgoyne crossed into Howe's command (around the time he reached Fort Ticonderoga), only Howe could give him direction. Even though he was Howe's second-in-command, Clinton could give advice but not issue orders to Burgoyne in Howe's absence. Clinton not only did not have the information required to issue orders to Burgoyne, but he also lacked the authority.[15] Although captains Scott and Campbell had now given him a better sense of Burgoyne's predicament, Clinton knew very little about the enemy between him and the northern army. At any rate, any orders he issued might not arrive in time to be of any use. Burgoyne was equally aware of all these facts. Still, his request to Clinton for instructions was either an indication that he was desperate and totally out of

his depth, or another attempt to redirect responsibility and blame, or both.

While Clinton oversaw the diversion on October 5, Burgoyne's couriers had arrived with his message describing the army's woeful state. After digesting Burgoyne's communication and its implications, and as he made final preparations to attack Forts Montgomery and Clinton, Clinton dispatched Campbell back to Burgoyne with a message. In formal, third-person prose, a clearly annoyed Clinton wrote, "Sir Henry Clinton cannot presume to give orders to General Burgoyne. Genl Burgoyne could not suppose that Sir Henry Clinton had an idea of penetrating to Albany with the small force he mentioned in his last letter. What he offered in that letter [the attack on the American Hudson Highland forts] he has now undertaken." Clinton added that he could not be sure of success but hoped that even the "menace of an attack" might be useful.[16] Both knew that Burgoyne was asking the impossible of Clinton's tiny force and that the taking of the forts might not make a material difference. The fate of the northern army would be resolved in a very few days, one way or the other, and while there was very little Clinton could do about it, he was determined to try.

American Brigadier General George Clinton was responsible for the defense of the two forts. With the news of the enemy's landing on the west bank of the Hudson, he hurried to Fort Montgomery and dispatched patrols to gather intelligence on their movements. He also appealed to Putnam for reinforcements, but Captain Wallace's warships effectively shut down American communications between the two riverbanks. He would, therefore, have to face the British attack with only about eight hundred men.

Sir Henry Clinton had envisioned an ambitious simultaneous attack from the rear on the two forts. The British landing force at Stoney Point included the advanced guard commanded by Lieutenant Colonel Mungo Campbell and consisting of the 52nd and 57th Regiments, the Loyal American Regiment, New York Volunteers, and a company of Emmerich's Chasseurs, for a total of about 950 troops. The main force was commanded by Major General John Vaughan and included the 26th and 63rd Regiments, separate companies from the 7th Regiment and 17th Light Dragoons, and the grenadier company of the 1st Anspach-Bayreuth Regiment, totaling about twelve hundred men. A seven-hundred-man rearguard composed primarily of Loyalist and Hessian soldiers and commanded by Major General William Tryon, the Royal Governor of New York, rounded

General George Washington (1732–1799), by James Peale, after Charles Willson Peale (ca. 1787–1790). After losing multiple battles in 1776, Washington began to adopt a modified Fabian military strategy. To Washington, maintaining the Continental Army was the key to success in the war. After Saratoga, Washington successfully outmaneuvered the officers associated with the so-called Conway Cabal, further strengthening his position as commander-in-chief of the American forces. Courtesy of Independence National Historical Park.

Major General Philip John Schuyler (1733–1804), by Jacob Hart Lazarus, after John Trumbull (ca. 1886). Schuyler was an excellent manager and a logistics expert, but his New York upbringing and patrician background made him unpopular with New England militia and delegates to Congress. Courtesy of Independence National Historical Park.

Major General Benedict Arnold (1741–1801), from an engraving by Benoît-Louis Prévost of a drawing by Pierre Eugene du Simitiere (ca. 1777). Arnold was perhaps the most dynamic and aggressive combat commander in the American Army. He was also ambitious, vain, and took offense easily, but Gates thought his positive attributes far outweighed his liabilities. Gates dismissed Arnold's critics by observing that "men of little merit, are ever jealous of those who have a great deal." Digital Collections, New York Public Library.

Major General Horatio Gates, by James Peale after Charles Willson Peale (ca. 1782). A former British Army officer, Gates joined the American cause early in the war and served with both the main army under Washington and in the Northern Department under Schuyler. He assumed command of the department upon Schuyler's relief in August 1777. National Portrait Gallery, Smithsonian Institution; gift of Mr. Lawrence A. Fleischman and Gallery Purchase.

Carrying the bateaux at Skowhegan Falls, by Sydney Adamson and engraved by C. W. Chadwick, from the January 1903 edition of *The Century Illustrated Monthly Magazine.* This print depicts Benedict Arnold's troops on their 1775 expedition to Canada and shows the appearance and construction of a typical bateau. Bateaux were used extensively by both sides and varied in size. Library of Congress, LC-USZ62-108231.

Lieutenant Colonel Thaddeus Kosciusko (1746–1817), by Julian Rys, after an unidentified source (1897). The young Polish military engineer was valued by Gates for his keen eye for terrain and the placement and construction of field fortifications. Courtesy of Independence National Historical Park.

Major General Arthur St. Clair, attributed to Jean Pierre Henri Elouis. A former British Army officer turned Patriot, St. Clair assumed command of Fort Ticonderoga three weeks before the arrival of Burgoyne's army from Canada. National Portrait Gallery, Smithsonian Institution; gift of Mr. and Mrs. Arthur St. Clair Johnson. Conserved with funds from the Smithsonian Women's Committee.

Mount Defiance from Mount Independence. Author Photo.

Major General Benjamin Lincoln (1733–1810), by Charles Willson Peale, from life (ca. 1781–1783). Lincoln's excellent rapport with militia troops contributed significantly to American success during the Saratoga campaign. Courtesy of Independence National Historical Park.

Fort Stanwix reconstruction. Courtesy of the National Park Service.

Colonel Peter Gansevoort, as a brigadier general, by Gilbert Stuart (1794). Gansevoort's leadership before and during the siege of Fort Stanwix was one of the few bright spots for the Americans in the summer of 1777. © Munson-Williams-Proctor Arts Institute/Art Resource, NY.

Battle of Oriskany, by James Reuben Chapin, Charles F. Damoreau, engraver (1857). The wounded General Herkimer is depicted on the left directing his soldiers during the height of the battle. Library of Congress, LC-USZC4-12376.

Lieutenant Colonel Marinus Willett, by Ralph Earl (ca. 1791). As Gansevoort's second-in-command at Fort Stanwix, Willett proved himself on numerous occasions. The two men made an effective command team. © The Metropolitan Museum of Art/Art Resource/NY.

Brigadier General John Stark, as a major general, by Washington Irving. Stark's refusal to put himself and his militia soldiers under Continental Army control in the summer and fall of 1777 was outweighed by their outstanding performance at Bennington. Digital Collections, New York Public Library.

Colonel Daniel Morgan (1736–1802), by Charles Willson Peale, from life (ca. 1794). The impact of Morgan's riflemen on the outcome of the campaign was out of all proportion to the size of the unit. Courtesy of Independence National Historical Park.

Major Henry Dearborn (1751–1829), by Charles Willson Peale, from life (1796–1797). Dearborn commanded a unit of select light infantry that worked closely with Morgan's riflemen at the battles of Freeman's Farm and Bemis Heights. Courtesy of Independence National Historical Park.

Bemis Heights, overlooking the Hudson River and the road to Albany. Author photo.

Colonel James Wilkinson (1757–1825), by Charles Willson Peale, from life (1796–1797). Wilkinson was a valuable staff officer for both Schuyler and Gates, but his memoirs sometimes misrepresent his central role in the campaign. Courtesy of Independence National Historical Park.

Arnold Boot Monument, Saratoga National Historical Park. This monument memorializes Benedict Arnold's performance during the Saratoga campaign and the serious leg wound he suffered on October 7, 1777. Due to his later treason, the monument does not include his name. Courtesy of the National Park Service.

Country Home of Philip Schuyler at Saratoga (present-day Schuylerville, NY). Burgoyne's army burned Schuyler's country estate at Saratoga during their October 1777 retreat. Schuyler rebuilt the home shortly after the surrender. Courtesy of the National Park Service.

Surrender of John Burgoyne, by John Trumbull (1821). In one of the monumental paintings displayed in the capitol rotunda, Trumbull depicted the moment when Gates graciously declined Burgoyne's sword at Saratoga. Next to Burgoyne on the left is Major General Phillips. Fifth from right, in a brown coat, is Major General Schuyler. Colonel Daniel Morgan, conspicuous in the white shirt of the elite riflemen, is center right. Courtesy of the Office of the Architect of the Capitol.

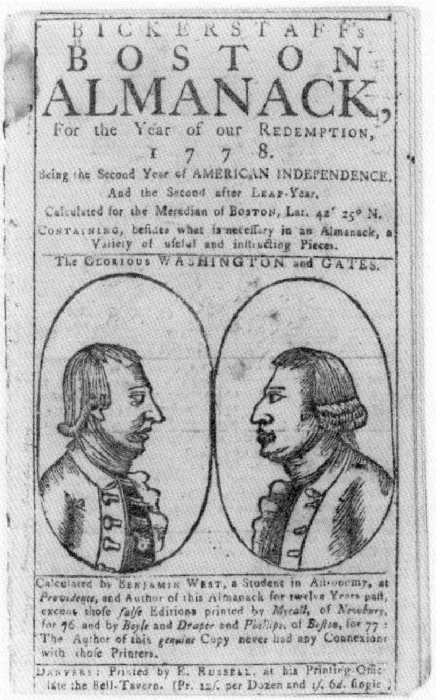

BICKERSTAFF's
BOSTON
ALMANACK,
For the Year of our REDEMPTION,
1778.
Being the Second Year of AMERICAN INDEPENDENCE.
And the Second after LEAP-Year,
Calculated for the Meredian of BOSTON, Lat. 42' 25° N.
CONTAINING, besides what is necessary in an Almanack, a Variety of useful and instructing Pieces.
The GLORIOUS WASHINGTON and GATES.

Calculated by BENJAMIN WEST, a Student in Astronomy, at *Providence*, and Author of this Almanack for twelve Years past, except those *false* Editions printed by *Mycall*, of *Newbury*, for 76 and by *Boyle* and *Draper* and *Phillips*, of *Boston*, for 77: The Author of this *genuine* Copy never had any Connexions with those Printers.

DANVERS: Printed by E. RUSSELL, at his Printing-Office late the Bell-Tavern. (Pr. 12/. per Dozen and 1/. 6d. single.)

The glorious Washington and Gates from the title page of *Bickerstaff's Boston Almanack* (Boston, 1778). For many Americans, Gates was at least the equal to Washington after Saratoga. Library of Congress, LC-USZ62-45321.

Benjamin Franklin (1706–1790), by an unidentified French artist, after Joseph Siffred Duplessis (possibly late eighteenth or early nineteenth century). Along with the other commissioners at Paris, Franklin's brilliant diplomacy was instrumental in exploiting the American success at Saratoga and securing an alliance with France. Courtesy of Independence National Historical Park.

Saratoga Battle Monument, Schuylerville, NY, c. 1901, by Detroit Publishing Company. The monument is located at the site of Burgoyne's final camp at Saratoga (present-day Schuylerville). Library of Congress, LC-DIG-det-4a09232.

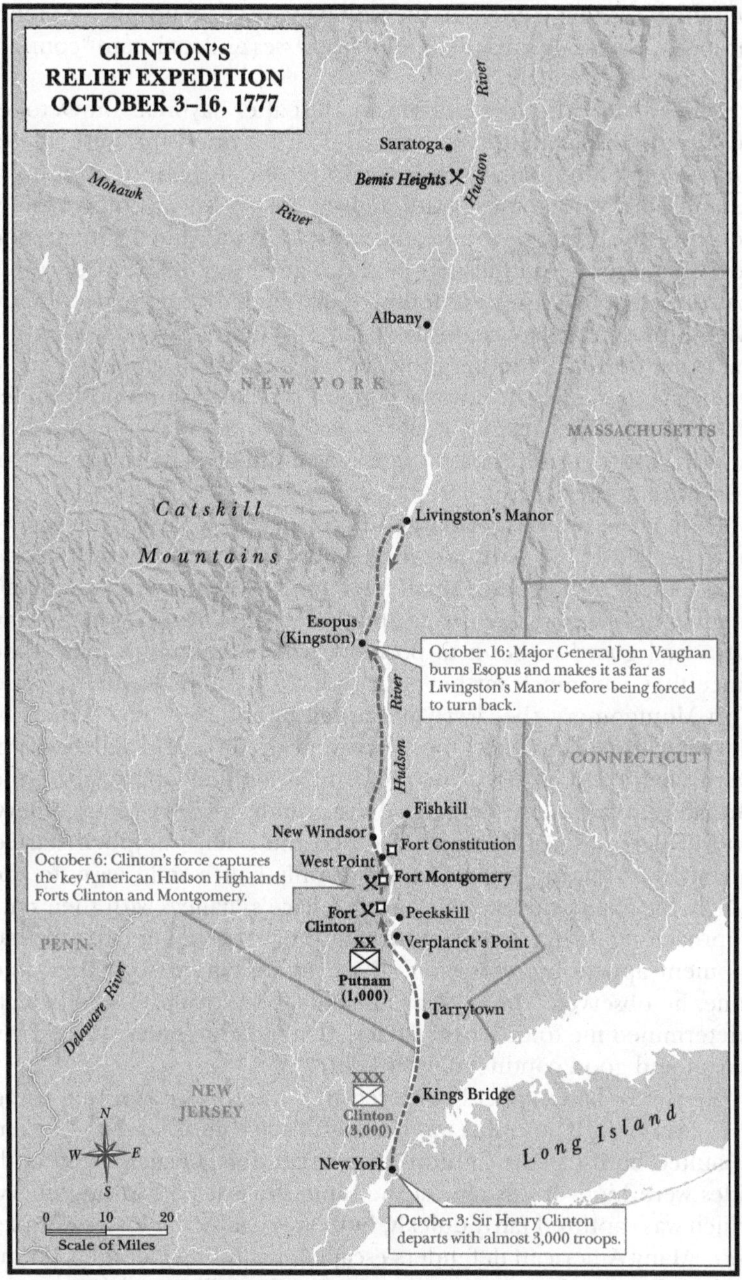

Map 11 Clinton's Relief Expedition, October 3–16, 1777

out the force that landed on the west bank of the Hudson. Sir Henry ordered Tryon to guard the mountain passes and maintain "communication with the fleet."[17]

Immediately after the landing and just after daybreak on October 6, Clinton dispatched his advanced guard around the west side of Dunderberg Mountain to clear the route and to get into position to assault Fort Montgomery. Although Stoney Point was only 2 miles south of the forts, the route the men took was much longer, and their march was complicated by the rugged terrain and the rough paths. Campbell's force was followed by Vaughan and the main body, whose mission was to assault Fort Clinton. Once they arrived in the valley between Dunderberg and Bear Mountains, Vaughan's main body halted to give the advanced guard time to get into position for their assault. The advanced guard split off to the west to make their way around Bear Mountain to take a position to the northwest of Fort Montgomery.[18]

Late in the morning, George Clinton received word from one of his patrols that two British columns were headed for each fort and immediately dispatched a small force to slow them down. Vaughan's main body brushed them aside and then settled down to wait for the advanced guard to get into position, which took quite some time since they had much farther to march. As Campbell's men neared Fort Montgomery, they were ambushed by another small American delaying force, but they, too, were quickly forced to fall back toward the fort. At around 5:00 p.m. and as nightfall approached, the British sent a party to demand the surrender of Fort Montgomery, and while George Clinton considered the offer, Campbell started his attack. Hearing the heavy firing only half a mile away to the north, Sir Henry noticed Sir James Wallace's "galleys with their oars approaching, firing and even striking the forts, the men-of-war that moment appearing, crowding all sail to support us." At the same time, he observed "the extreme ardour of the troops," all of which "determined me to order the attack. General Vaughan's spirited behavior and good conduct did the rest."[19]

Sir Henry had explicitly ordered that the fort be stormed using the bayonet only, and this was successfully accomplished as his men assaulted both of Fort Clinton's main redoubts. Casualties on both sides were high. It was almost the same story at Fort Montgomery, which was captured fairly quickly, but, once again, the losses were severe. Many American defenders escaped, including George Clinton and his brother James, who commanded Fort Clinton, but 70 were killed, 40 wounded, and 240 captured. Although Sir Henry Clinton

claimed afterward that "our loss was not very considerable,"[20] British casualties were 40 killed and 150 wounded, but they also lost several officers, including Campbell, who was cut down in the initial assault on Fort Montgomery.[21] In their headlong flight from the forts, the Americans burned their vessels and retreated north. Fort Constitution, a small fortification located directly across the river from West Point, was quickly abandoned in the face of the British threat. By the morning of October 8, when the chain and boom obstacle was broken, the Hudson Highlands lay open at Sir Henry Clinton's feet.

Flush with victory, on October 8, Clinton sent another courier, Private Daniel Taylor, to Burgoyne with a note that contained a much more positive message than the one he had dispatched two days earlier. Datelined "Fort Montgomery," he wrote his friend that there was now "nothing . . . between us but *Gates.*" He hoped that "this *little* success of ours may facilitate your operations." He added that in response to Burgoyne's earlier letter about seeking instructions, he still could not "presume to order or even advise for reasons obvious. I heartily wish you success."[22] The very next day, he dispatched the intrepid Scott with a similar message.[23] He assured Burgoyne "that if on hearing of our success, he had determined to push for Albany, we would do everything in our power to communicate with him."[24]

Unfortunately for Burgoyne, none of the messengers—including Captains Scott and Campbell—made it through the American lines. Taylor was quickly captured and was seen to swallow something by his captors. He was immediately taken to George Clinton, who threatened Taylor with immediate disemboweling if he did not agree to take a "severe tartar emetic" that would evacuate his stomach and bowels. The emetic worked, and Clinton was soon in possession of a hollow silver ball that contained his namesake's letter to Burgoyne, which was read to the troops and published in the *New York Packet* newspaper of Fishkill, New York, on October 16. For his efforts, Taylor was hanged as a spy a week later.[25]

Sir Henry Clinton was unaware of the fate of his messengers and the northern army because he had received no updates since Burgoyne's anxious September 27 and 28 notes. However, the Highlands forts had fallen quickly, and he felt like he could push on farther up the river. Hurrying back to New York on October 11, because of the illness of two of his general officers left behind to defend the city, Clinton prepared another expedition to sail up the river to Albany. On October 13, he ordered Vaughan, with seventeen hundred men, to continue up the river from the Highlands toward

Albany. The diversion against the American forts "has succeeded beyond my utmost hope," he wrote to family members, and "the communication with Albany is now open but I fear Burgoyne is not there to avail himself of it," and may have retreated. Despite his success, Clinton was worried that the entire 1777 British strategy was turning into a fiasco: "Good God, what a fair prospect blasted if Burgoyne is retreated as he seemed under no apprehension of difficulties in his retreat."[26]

The Americans were powerless to stop Vaughan's British flotilla. On October 16, they landed at Esopus (present-day Kingston, New York), which they promptly burned to the outrage of Americans throughout the country.[27] The *New York Packet* reflected the disgust with Vanghan's action: "Britain, how art thou fallen!" The pro-British *Pennsylvania Ledger* saw it differently and asserted that the town was burned only after "the rebels having fled to the houses of Kingston . . . fired upon the royal army from the windows." The newspaper further reported that Vaughan "proceeded on to join General Burgoyne, and in a few days we hope to hear of the two generals having formed a junction at Albany."[28]

Vaughan did advance up the Hudson, and after another 20 miles, his ships reached Livingston's Manor. The local pilots refused to go any farther. The relief force was still 45 miles south of Albany and 70 miles from Burgoyne and his army. Although Vaughan had faced spotty opposition at best, he learned that the countryside was swarming with American militia. He could not hazard his small force by an overland march to Albany. At Livingston's Manor, Vaughan's detachment was joined by Captains Scott and Campbell, who, after days of trying to slip through the American lines to reach their embattled comrades with Clinton's news of the capture of the Highland forts, finally admitted defeat.[29] Burgoyne would receive no assistance from Clinton or anyone else.

While Vaughan was pressing up the Hudson past Esopus, Clinton finally received a message from Howe. The commander-in-chief had been busy since the army landed at Head of Elk on August 25. After the soldiers and animals recovered from their six-week sea journey from New York, they started toward Philadelphia, hoping to engage Washington and the main American Army in a decisive battle.

Washington supplied that opportunity when he tried to block Howe's route to Philadelphia by positioning his army along the north bank of the Brandywine Creek. In a departure from his usual strategy, Washington decided to try to defend the city. After a close-fought battle that lasted almost all day, Howe was able to outflank

the American right, forcing Washington to fall back. It was a very close call. Although the Americans suffered more than twice the number of Howe's casualties, Washington was once again able to slip away and live to fight another day. The price of the American defeat at Brandywine, however, was Philadelphia. After some indecisive actions outside the city, Congress evacuated to Lancaster, and ultimately, York, Pennsylvania, and Howe's men marched into Philadelphia on September 26.[30]

Washington informed Gates that the "Army has not been able to oppose General Howe's with the success that was wished." Therefore, the main American Army needed reinforcement, and Washington asked that if "circumstances will admit, that you will Order Colo. Morgan to Join me again with his Corps." Despite his pressing need for Morgan and his riflemen to oppose Howe, the commander-in-chief assured Gates that his letter was a request, not an order, and he would "leave you to determine upon it, according to your situation."[31] Gates replied to Washington on October 5—the first letter to his chief since August 28—to say that he could not possibly release Morgan.[32] Washington would have to face Howe without his most elite unit.

Howe kept about a third of his force, three thousand troops, in Philadelphia on garrison duty and stationed the rest at Germantown, a small community located a few miles to the north. Howe's decision to divide his forces while still seeking a decisive victory over Washington was questionable. If his primary goal was to destroy Washington and use Philadelphia as bait for the main object, destroying the American Army, as he claimed to the House of Commons two years later, dividing his force made little sense. As Alexander Hamilton observed months before, "any object short of our army is a bad one."[33]

Splitting his force also made him vulnerable to attack. After Trenton and Princeton, Howe should have known that Washington was capable of doing the unexpected—attacking—and on October 4 he did just that. Advancing in multiple columns in dense fog—a situation in which Morgan's men would have been most useful—the Americans surprised the British, and for a while, it looked like they might achieve a victory. However, the attack was uncoordinated, and Howe's outnumbered soldiers reacted well after the initial shock with Sir William personally in the thick of the fighting. The battle, during which American units fired on each other by mistake, ended in Washington's withdrawal. Howe pursued the retreating army for a while, but Washington managed to remain just outside of Howe's

reach. The British commander-in-chief soon shifted his focus to clearing the Delaware River of American defenses, a process that took weeks.[34]

Howe's letter to Clinton—his first to his second-in-command in weeks—written shortly after his victory at Germantown, acknowledged that while Clinton might still be moving on the Hudson Highlands, he should send four thousand men as reinforcements to Howe—"unless you may be on the eve of accomplishing some very material and effectual stroke, in which case you will be pleased to proceed upon it, provided you judge it may be accomplished in a few days after you receive this."[35] Howe did not want a repeat of his near-disaster at Germantown, and four thousand extra troops would strengthen the hold on Philadelphia and allow him to pursue his elusive final battle with Washington. After receiving letters from Howe on October 18 demanding that he send a large portion of his available troops south to Philadelphia, messages that Sir Henry could not ignore, and with Vaughan stymied 70 miles from Burgoyne, Clinton had no choice but to cancel any further movement toward Albany.[36] He recalled Vaughan, ordered the destruction of the newly captured forts, and withdrew all his forces back to New York.[37] Clinton now feared that Burgoyne and his army might well be doomed. The best he could hope for was that they succeeded in retreating to Ticonderoga, or better yet, Canada.

From the time he learned of the overall 1777 strategy in the spring, Clinton had argued in vain that the commander-in-chief should have moved the main army up the Hudson to cooperate with Burgoyne.[38] He was furious with Howe for frustrating what appeared to be an excellent opportunity to assist Burgoyne. "What a prospect we must quit," he wrote glumly to a fellow general officer the day he had received Howe's orders. Even Howe's victories over Washington could not make up for the strategic debacle because neither battle, Clinton wrote, had been "in the least decisive."[39] Yes, Howe had taken Philadelphia, but as Clinton feared would happen all along, the campaign looked like it would end up in a strategic cul-de-sac.

CHAPTER 20

The Battle of Bemis Heights

NEWS OF SIR HENRY Clinton's September 11 message and the prospect of a relief expedition quickly spread throughout Burgoyne's army, temporarily boosting morale. The men redoubled their efforts to build field fortifications strong enough to withstand an American assault while they awaited deliverance from the south. More than one thousand soldiers were put to work cutting timber for the emplacements "to strengthen our camp and wait some favourable accounts from General Clinton," as Lieutenant Digby wrote in his journal.[1] The lack of forage for the animals on the west side of the river forced Burgoyne to order the building of a bridge across the Hudson, along with fortifications to secure it, to facilitate the search for provisions. Heavy rain fell off and on throughout the week after the battle, making these jobs even harder. It was almost impossible to get dry and warm by this time in the campaign, because many of the tents had started to rot, adding to the troops' misery.[2] To make matters even worse, the heavy rains led to unexpected and unwelcome consequences: the stench of decaying bodies exposed by the waters.[3]

The British field fortifications were constructed out of logs and soil along almost the entire front line with artillery positions located at key points.[4] In general, the lines were manned by units in relation to where they ended up after the Battle of Freeman's Farm. The Great Redoubt was an enclosed fortification located on the highest hill facing the Great Ravine. It also overlooked the Hudson River and was designed to protect the hospital and the artillery

park, both located on the flood plain directly below the redoubt's fortifications, as well as the precious logistical train. The flood plain and the river road was the only real retreat route available to the army. The fortifications in and around the Great Redoubt were manned primarily by the Hessen-Hanau Regiment Erbprinz. The rest of the fortified line consisting of shallow trenches and abates—tree branches and sharpened sticks placed in trenches facing the enemy—was located south of the Great Ravine and continued west until it reached Freeman's Farm, the site of the heaviest fighting on September 19. It then angled northwest to prevent an attack from turning the British right flank. Anchoring the British right were two major fortifications, the British Light Infantry Redoubt and Breymann's Fortified Camp (known today, incorrectly, as Balcarres Redoubt and Breymann's Redoubt).[5]

Major Alexander Lindsay, Lord Balcarres, and his light infantry battalion, along with a battery of eight artillery pieces, manned the British Light Infantry Redoubt. This fortification incorporated the Freeman's Farm buildings and formed a long narrow rectangle that extended some 1,200 feet south from the farm's high ground. The redoubt faced west instead of south or southwest as one might expect, given the location of the American camp, with half the artillery located at the southern end of the fortification. Because of the poor digging conditions, like the other major fortifications, the redoubt's walls were constructed out of cut-down trees and earth. Two smaller field fortifications covered the right and left, or north and south, flanks of the British Light Infantry Redoubt, one positioned on high ground just to the west of the southern end of the main works and the other to the northwest. Also located to the northwest were two small cabins, later called the "Canadian Cabins," that were turned into strongpoints and manned by companies of Burgoyne's Canadian provincial troops.[6]

About 500 yards northwest of Freeman's Farm and the British Light Infantry Redoubt and just north of the Canadian cabins was Breymann's Fortified Camp, manned by German grenadiers, light infantry, and Jägers, commanded by Lieutenant Colonel Heinrich Breymann. Archeological studies have revealed the exact layout of this small system of fortifications that, in combination with the British Light Infantry Redoubt, guarded the army's right flank. The camp consisted of three major elements, like the others, constructed of logs and dirt. The first was a zigzag wall of 100 yards in length that faced to the northwest. Another similar 85-yard-long wall was located on high ground at right angles to the first a little less than 100 yards

to the north facing to the north. The final element of the position was a smaller square-shaped fortress about midway between the two walls and 70 yards west, also situated on high ground.[7]

The location of Breymann's Fortified Camp, like its counterpart to the south, was peculiar at best: there was a major blind spot between the square-shaped fort and the main zigzag wall.[8] While this blind spot was partly covered by two light artillery pieces positioned in the middle of the main works, it was vulnerable to an attack from the west. Because the three major components of Breymann's Fortified Camp were not mutually supporting, an enemy force could conceivably get between the camp's three parts and defeat each one in detail, without worrying about accurate fire from the other works.

Another drawback was the fact that the two major right flank defenses, and thus the most important part of Burgoyne's defensive lines, were located more than 500 yards apart, with only the Canadian Cabins to cover the yawning gap, representing a significant weak spot in Burgoyne's defensive scheme.[9]

As the work on Burgoyne's defensive fortifications progressed, the weather and the proximity of the enemy took a toll on the men. There was constant skirmishing between the two sides, which made sleep almost impossible to get in restorative doses. The "picquets and advanced parties were almost continually firing and skirmishing," a British soldier recalled, "so much so that the officers and men refreshed and slept exposed to the enemy's fire."[10] The relentless alarms and firefights continued day and night. "Sometimes it was so intense that we had to stand to arms at midnight, something which occurred anyway two hours before dawn on a regular basis throughout camp."[11] Rations and feed for the animals started to run low, and heavily guarded foraging parties had to range far and wide on the east bank of the Hudson and north and west of camp. Sometimes they succeeded, as on September 28, when a "large detachment was ordered out to forage for the army, which was greatly wanting, as all our grass was ate up and many horses dying for want. We brought in some hay."[12] Other forays were less fruitful. A German officer complained, "Our daily nourishment was thus one and a half loaves of bread and twenty ounces of salt pork. It is disgusting even to touch the meat, not to mention the bad smell. Vegetables or rice could not be had for hard cash."[13]

All of the hardships, combined with the army's precarious tactical and operational situation, resulted in increased desertions.[14] On October 2, another German officer noted with alarm that desertion "was now beginning to gain ground in both corps." The

constant fatigue duties, skirmishes, poor food, oncoming winter, and American propaganda were taking their toll. The officer maintained that neither Burgoyne nor Riedesel were doing anything about it.[15] If the soldiers had been uncertain about their situation before, they were made painfully aware of how perilous it was when on October 3 Burgoyne decided to reduce rations.[16] A German officer wrote in his journal that the diminished rations, which were now "barely enough for three weeks," led to even more desertions, and so the officers were forced to double the guards and use only "reliable persons."[17]

In the same General Order that cut the food allowance, Burgoyne also announced that help was on its way: "There is reason to be assured," he declared, "that other powerful Armies are actually in co-operation with these Troops."[18] Although he did not mention him by name, he was clearly referring to Clinton's expedition against the Hudson Highland forts. Of course, Burgoyne and his men could not know that as the October 3 General Order was published, one that promised imminent deliverance, Clinton was only beginning to move out of New York and up the Hudson. He was still almost 200 miles away—with the enemy in between.

In the days leading up to Burgoyne's October 3 General Order, the troops speculated about the army's next move. Digby of the advanced corps observed that some thought "we should be ordered to retreat," while others believed that would be impossible with all of the sick and wounded. Some "were certain our general would try another action before a retreat was thought on." At the same time, others thought that they would wait for reinforcements either from Ticonderoga or New York, particularly the latter. While many of the troops were hopeful that Clinton's movements would force the Americans to reduce their numbers, most believed that unlikely. It was widely known that reinforcements were arriving daily at the enemy camp.[19] Probably the majority of the men, however, reflecting their chief's hopes, were "expecting General Clinton would come up the north River and we would have them between two fires."[20]

For days Burgoyne ordered that rockets and guns be fired at intervals to mark their location, making it easier for Clinton to navigate the final miles to reach the army and salvage the campaign. Some speculated that this was done simply to raise morale.[21] But whether the troops thought they would soon fight, retreat, or be delivered by Clinton's timely arrival, Digby observed that "most people's opinions and suppositions were rather founded on what they wished, than on the certain knowledge of what would happen."[22] Only time would tell how things would work out, and time was not on Burgoyne's side.

While Burgoyne waited for Clinton—continuing to work on their defensive positions and foraging for food and fodder—Gates and the American Army were far from idle. His clash with Arnold continued to preoccupy him. Still, Gates had other matters to attend to, such as exchanging information with Burgoyne about prisoners, especially the wounded men captured on September 19.[23] Perhaps the biggest task he faced was incorporating the inflow of militia units from New York and the surrounding states. These units had been arriving steadily starting a few days after the September 19 battle. They would ultimately swell the army's numbers to over eleven thousand men by October 7, and seventeen thousand a week later. They had to be given their assignments, camp locations, and to be supported with rations, ammunition, and other supplies. This was no small job, and the lamps burned at his headquarters on Bemis Heights late into the night, every night. Small bands of friendly Oneida and Tuscarora Indians also arrived in camp to join the army.[24] Gates dispatched raiding parties and patrols to gather intelligence, probe Burgoyne's defenses, disrupt their ability to forage throughout the surrounding countryside, and generally keep the enemy off guard.

In early October, Burgoyne had little information about anything that lay much beyond the perimeter of the army's camp. However, from British and German deserters, prisoners, and captured messengers, Gates was able to put together an accurate intelligence picture of Burgoyne's situation and, therefore, his available courses of action. For example, Brigadier General John Nixon reported that deserting Germans complained that they had not eaten "one mouthful of fresh provisions since they left Canada."[25] Gates knew that Burgoyne's situation was becoming increasingly grim. His confidence soared, confiding to an officer that "I think this Campaign will have a happy Issue for the Cause of Freedom & America."[26]

Gates was not the only American who was optimistic about the prospects in the Northern Department. New York congressional delegate James Duane rejoiced over Bennington and "the late gallant Behaviour of the left wing of our Army" at Freeman's Farm.[27] The next day Congress promoted John Stark to brigadier general in the Continental Army and presented the Thanks of Congress to him, Gansevoort, and Willett for their actions at Bennington and Stanwix. Congress also wrote Gates to "highly approve of the prowess and behavior of the troops under his command, in their late gallant repulse of the enemy under General Burgoyne."[28] The Committee on Foreign Affairs dispatched a detailed account of the favorable situation in the Northern Department to the American commissioners

at Paris, declaring that since Burgoyne had "little prospect of safe retreat" and since Gates was growing stronger every day, "we hope e'er long to be able to give you information of definitive success over the British army in that quarter."[29] After the loss of Philadelphia and Congress's hasty evacuation to York, hopes and expectations for Gates and his army ran high.

From British deserters, Gates gathered that Burgoyne expected that Sir Henry Clinton would help him with his approach to Albany by opening a passage through the Highlands. He also learned that the enemy had only three weeks' provisions. Gates's intelligence was very good, indeed. "Perhaps his Despair may dictate to him to risque all upon one throw," surmised Gates of Burgoyne: "He is an old gamester, and in his time, has seen all chances. I will endeavor to be ready to prevent his good fortune, and, if possible, secure my own."[30] Despite his outward optimism, Gates was worried about Clinton's relief expedition and reminded Hancock that everything must be done to protect against that.[31] Despite Gates's knowledge of Burgoyne's vulnerabilities, he was not about to make the first move and attack the British Army. He would not deviate from the plan. He assured Hancock that "every means that can be devised" was being taken to withstand the British attacks and cut their line of retreat. If Burgoyne's "destressed situation" forced him to retreat toward Ticonderoga, Gates would adopt "the most active measures to attack him to advantage."[32] This was the very wait-and-see attitude that infuriated Arnold. Gates, however, was not going to tinker with success.

And Gates was not about to give up Morgan and his riflemen to Washington. At least not yet. On the 5th, he replied to Washington's request with a long letter to the commander-in-chief. Because "the Enemy have kept the Ground they Occupied the Morning of that Day; And fortified their Camp," Washington would surely "not wish me to part with the Corps the Army of General Burgoyne are most Afraid of." He assured Washington that all would soon be resolved, because Burgoyne would have no choice except to "risque, at infinite Disadvantage, to Force my Camp, or Retreat to his Den." Whether the enemy attacked or retreated, Gates was sure of success, and once that happened, he confidently predicted that he would soon be able to do more than send Washington just one regiment.[33]

As the first week of October drew to a close, Burgoyne was growing more and more apprehensive. The jubilation over the victory at Freeman's Farm had long since worn off, and it had been more than two weeks since Sir Henry Clinton's last message made

it through enemy lines; there was still no evidence of a relief expedition. Provisions were quickly running out, desertions had risen to an alarming rate, and the enemy army was growing by the hour. To help boost morale, Burgoyne ordered that twelve barrels of rum be distributed to the men, an action described by a grateful German officer as "a special favor which the army can boast of having had twice during this campaign."[34]

The continued silence from Clinton and the rapidly diminishing supplies, especially forage, forced Burgoyne's hand. He had to make a move, or his animals would starve. The many foraging parties sent out by the army enjoyed some limited success, but it was never enough to sustain the army for very long.[35] He decided to probe the American left flank to see whether there was a route by which they might either slip by or force Gates to fall back. But most importantly, Burgoyne had to find more food and forage. The army was in the "greatest distress" and "a supply could only be obtained by a movement of the army."[36]

Conferring with his senior officers, Burgoyne considered several options. He rejected a wide turning movement to the right to get into Gates's rear, because it would take too long. Without his Indians, his patrols could not venture far without running into American soldiers, so he did not know the roads and Gates's exact positions. Riedesel argued that unless they could attack and defeat Gates in the next few days, the army should fall back to the Hudson's east bank, and there wait for Clinton. But because Burgoyne "hated to retrogress," he decided instead to order a large-scale reconnaissance on October 7 with two objectives: to forage and to examine the nature of the American left flank positions to determine if an attack was even possible. If feasible, he would attack Gates's army with his entire force the next day, the 8th. If not, the army would retreat north to the Batten Kill not later than the 11th.[37] The stage was set for the closing act of the drama that began the year before, with General Carleton's abortive attempt to invade the rebellious colonies from Canada and Lake Champlain.

To make sure he was able to put as many trustworthy sets of eyes on the terrain, the roads, and the enemy positions as possible, Burgoyne decided to lead the detachment himself, accompanied by Generals Riedesel, Phillips, and Fraser. The seventeen-hundred-man reconnaissance force was drawn from units across the army but was primarily drawn from the advanced corps and Breymann's Reserve Corps, which manned the defenses on Burgoyne's right flank. Although the right was the most vulnerable part of Burgoyne's line, he most

likely pulled men from these positions instead of the left because the Americans had been aggressively probing the defenses that protected the army's artillery park, hospital, supplies, and the potential retreat route. Plus, when they returned from the reconnaissance, the troops could simply fall back into their prepared positions.[38]

Except for a few complete units, such as Captain Alexander Fraser's Rangers—reconstituted after Bennington—most of the reconnaissance force was thrown together in a more or less ad-hoc fashion, mixing German and British and Canadian troops, which complicated command and control. The artillery attached to the force consisted of ten guns: two 12-pounders, six 6-pounders, and two 5½-inch howitzers. These guns and their crews came from no fewer than three artillery companies, both British and German. Likewise, Riedesel's German line detachments were pulled from four different regiments.[39] Burgoyne was not particularly worried about the mission or the improvised nature of the detachment. This was to be a relatively low-risk, out-and-back operation. The critical decisions and maneuvers would be made after the reconnaissance force had done its work.

Early on the morning of the 7th, Burgoyne's reconnaissance in force assembled behind the British Light Infantry Redoubt. The generals met in Simon Fraser's tent to discuss the plan for the day and afterward addressed the army's few remaining Indians. The latter, along with Captain Fraser's Rangers, would scout ahead of the main body and protect its right flank. At 10:00 a.m., they moved southwest toward the American lines. Since almost all the army's senior leaders accompanied Burgoyne on the reconnaissance, the main defensive positions left behind were under the direction of Brigadier Generals Hamilton, Specht, and von Gall. As the detachment proceeded in three separate columns, they found the rude pathways and roads made for slow going, and they had to continually hack through the woods and undergrowth, repairing bridges over small creeks to clear the way for the artillery. Major Griffith Williams, commanding the British artillery, had objected to the use of the heavy guns, arguing that an unwieldy 12-pounder employed in the deep American woods was as good as lost.[40]

After about 30 minutes, the columns halted, having marched about three-quarters of a mile. Burgoyne ordered the men to stop at two abandoned farms surrounded by large clearings that were separated by woods. The reconnaissance detachment found itself in the middle of two unharvested wheat fields. The fields included high ground that provided good places to site artillery. The light

infantry took up a position on the right and defended from the base of a wooded hill across the west field, which measured about 350 by 250 yards, and was known to the Germans as the Weisser Farm. Captain Fraser's Rangers and the army's remaining Indians maneuvered around to the right to take possession of a hill, located a mere quarter of a mile west of the American defenses. The 24th Regiment of Foot defended the east edge of the west field and the woods between the two clearings. The various detachments from the German units defended the eastern field, known as Barber's Farm, the larger of the two clearings measuring about 250 by 550 yards. The British grenadiers under Major Acland extended the line to the left, defending the rest of the eastern field and stretching to the northeast into the woods, thereby protecting the detachment's left flank. Finally, the rest of the British detachments positioned themselves at right angles to the grenadiers. They extended their line east toward, though not all the way to the British Light Infantry Redoubt. The artillery was placed in two-gun sections all along the line.[41]

The British-German line was long, stretching over three-quarters of a mile, much of it through rough, wooded terrain, and it was very thin. They were close to the American defenses, yet despite several officers attempting to gain better vantage points by climbing onto the roofs of the farm buildings, the heavy woods south of the fields blocked their view. American sentries were stationed at the farms located in both fields, where they were watching for enemy movements. These men were quickly chased away. Burgoyne's sally out of his fortifications, however, was no longer a secret.[42]

Burgoyne immediately directed his men to start cutting and gathering the ripe crop. Soldiers and transport from the main camp were hurried forward to help. As the men began their work, Burgoyne considered his next step.[43] They planned to stay in place only long enough to gather the wheat and would not be vulnerable for long. After they harvested the fields, they could move on. All they needed was a little time.

Morgan's riflemen and Dearborn's light infantry were tired, wet, and hungry on the morning of October 7. A day earlier, they had been sent out to gather intelligence on the enemy's right and rear. After capturing several prisoners but failing to prompt an enemy response, they started back toward friendly lines. The mission took longer than expected, the sun set, and a steady rain began to fall. Soon the detachment got lost and spent the night in the dark thickets, not making it back to the American camp until well after daybreak. "By the Time we had Refresh'd our Selves," Dearborn wrote in his journal, "which

was about 12 O Clock we found a Body of the Enimy were Advancing towards out Lines."[44] Gates's far greater numbers allowed him to make sure the no man's land between the two armies was filled with American sentries and patrols. This served the dual purpose of keeping eyes on the enemy and screening the American fortifications from British information-gathering efforts. The Americans could never have placed so many sentries and scouts in the area, nor could they have conducted so many patrols and probed Burgoyne's lines virtually unopposed, had Burgoyne's full complement of Indians remained with the army. This was just one of the reasons that Burgoyne ordered the large-scale reconnaissance mission in the first place, and because of it, American scouts stationed at the Wiesser and Barber farms spotted Burgoyne's columns.

Word of the enemy's movements quickly reached Gates, who according to Wilkinson, dispatched the colonel to confirm the reports of enemy movements. The young staff officer rode forward and saw "several columns of the enemy . . . entering a wheat field which had not been cut." Wilkinson also saw several officers standing on the top of a cabin, trying to reconnoiter the American left, concealed from their view by woods.[45] After fifteen minutes observing the enemy, Wilkinson hurried back to Gates and reported what he had seen. Years later, Wilkinson recalled that he had told the general what the enemy was up to and added, "I think Sir, they offer you battle." The colonel thought, not unreasonably, that Burgoyne's force was too large to be a mere foraging party. Gates asked about the nature of the terrain and enemy dispositions. "Their front is open, and their flanks rest on woods," Wilkinson answered, "under cover of which they may be attacked; their right is skirted by a lofty height. I would indulge them." "Well, then," Gates replied, "order on Morgan to begin the game." According to Wilkinson, he went to Morgan and gave the order, while Arnold, who was without a command, acted "rash and intemperate" and, contrary to orders, rushed onto the field.[46]

The only problem with this account is that Arnold gave the orders to Morgan, not Wilkinson. Wilkinson, in his memoirs, essentially took on Arnold's initial actions on October 7 for himself. However, several disinterested witnesses contradict Wilkinson. Dearborn, ironically providing an account of the battle to Wilkinson in 1815, wrote that upon learning that the enemy was on the march "[a]s usual, the light troops advanced and soon received orders from Gen'l Arnold [not Wilkinson] to file to the left . . . and advance in a direction to meet any part of the enemy."[47] Years later, Benjamin Lincoln, Gates's

second-in-command, wrote that when Burgoyne's October 7 movement was discovered, Gates had ordered Arnold to advance with the left.[48] In addition, Oliver Wolcott, a Connecticut militia brigadier general and signer of the Declaration of Independence, wrote three days after the battle that when the enemy approached the army's left flank, Arnold's division had been "sent out to oppose the enemy."[49] Wolcott and Lincoln were on the battlefield that day, and both men were most likely at army headquarters when the battle began. Lincoln certainly was, and if anyone had firsthand knowledge of how the battle unfolded on October 7 and who made what decisions, it would be he. Both generals clearly acknowledged that Arnold was in command of the army's left division or wing, and neither mention any insubordination or heated exchanges between the two generals that day, something they would surely have mentioned.

Even more remarkable is the narrative of an American regimental commander, Lieutenant Colonel John Brooks of the 8th Massachusetts Regiment. Brooks dined with several senior officers at midday on October 7, including Arnold and Gates. The fact that Gates and Arnold were taking a meal together in itself contradicts the prevailing narrative of two officers who were not on speaking terms at the time of the second battle. "While at table," Brooks recalled, "we heard a firing from the advanced picket." Arnold asked Gates whether he should "go out, and see what is the matter." Gates didn't answer immediately, and Arnold repeated his request. "I am afraid to trust you, Arnold," replied Gates, obviously with their recent quarrel front and center in his mind. But Arnold reassured his chief: "Pray, let me go: I will be careful; and, if our advance does not need support, I will promise not to commit you." Gates told Arnold to go ahead, and Morgan and Dearborn soon moved toward the enemy.[50]

Many accounts of the Saratoga campaign have relied heavily on James Wilkinson's 1816 memoirs throughout the years, but this source must be used with great caution. Key participants Dearborn and Brooks and their two independent and disinterested narratives demonstrate Wilkinson's unreliability. In addition, Wilkinson soon proved himself to be highly self-serving, and he had a bitter falling out with Gates not long after the battle. Wilkinson's memoirs, along with other sources including the anti-Gates letters from Varick and Livingston, have painted a thoroughly negative portrait of the American commanding general. Many describe a passive Gates who stayed at his headquarters and played a very small role in the October 7 battle while the gallant, rebellious, out-of-control, and even disobedient Arnold, who had been relieved of his command by

the querulous commanding general, violated orders and saved the day. This story suggests that the dispute between Gates and Arnold that erupted after the Battle of Freeman's Farm continued through the second battle on October 7.[51] However, the evidence indicates that the feud between Arnold and Gates ended sometime between October 1 (the date of Arnold's last letter to Gates related to the dispute) and October 7, the date of the second battle. Just when and how it ended is unknown, but before the Battle of Bemis Heights, Arnold and Gates were once again on speaking terms, and Arnold was still in active command of the army's left wing.[52]

Morgan's riflemen and Dearborn's light infantry—which by now had been working together as a unit for more than a month—were directed to skirt around Burgoyne's right, seize control of the hill on the western edge of the west clearing, and attack the enemy flank. Whether it was Morgan's idea to conduct a flank attack or Gates's or Arnold's is unknown. In any case, the riflemen and light infantry set off at about 2:00 p.m. Just as they had on September 19, these elite units would play a major role. Gates then directed Arnold to dispatch the three New Hampshire regiments of General Enoch Poor's brigade to move through the woods and attack Burgoyne's left flank. The 1st and 2nd Regiments went out first, with Colonel Alexander Scammell's 3rd Regiment bringing up the rear. Gates decided to send out relatively small forces one-by-one in a piecemeal fashion to develop the situation and avoid stripping his fortified positions of combat power. Poor's brigade had fought very well at the Battle of Freeman's Farm, and here was yet another opportunity. It took some time for the American troops to get into position. By 2:30 p.m., the German units defending the east field (Barber's wheat field) began to see significant enemy activity in the woods to their front and left. These were Poor's New Hampshire men, maneuvering through the trees and using the natural terrain to mask their movements, thereby gaining a decided tactical advantage. Morgan's men had much farther to go; hence Poor started his attack before Morgan was in place.[53]

Upon seeing the Americans forming in the woods, Major Williams immediately opened fire with his two 12-pounders, and Captain Georg Pausch of the Hesse-Hanau artillery quickly followed with his 6-pounders, but the trees obscured their aim, and the artillery fire did little to disrupt Poor's attack. Indeed, recalled British Captain Thomas Blomefield, despite the vigorous artillery fire, "they drew up along the skirts of the wood behind trees."[54] Soon, the Americans were surging forward. The second battle of Saratoga had begun.

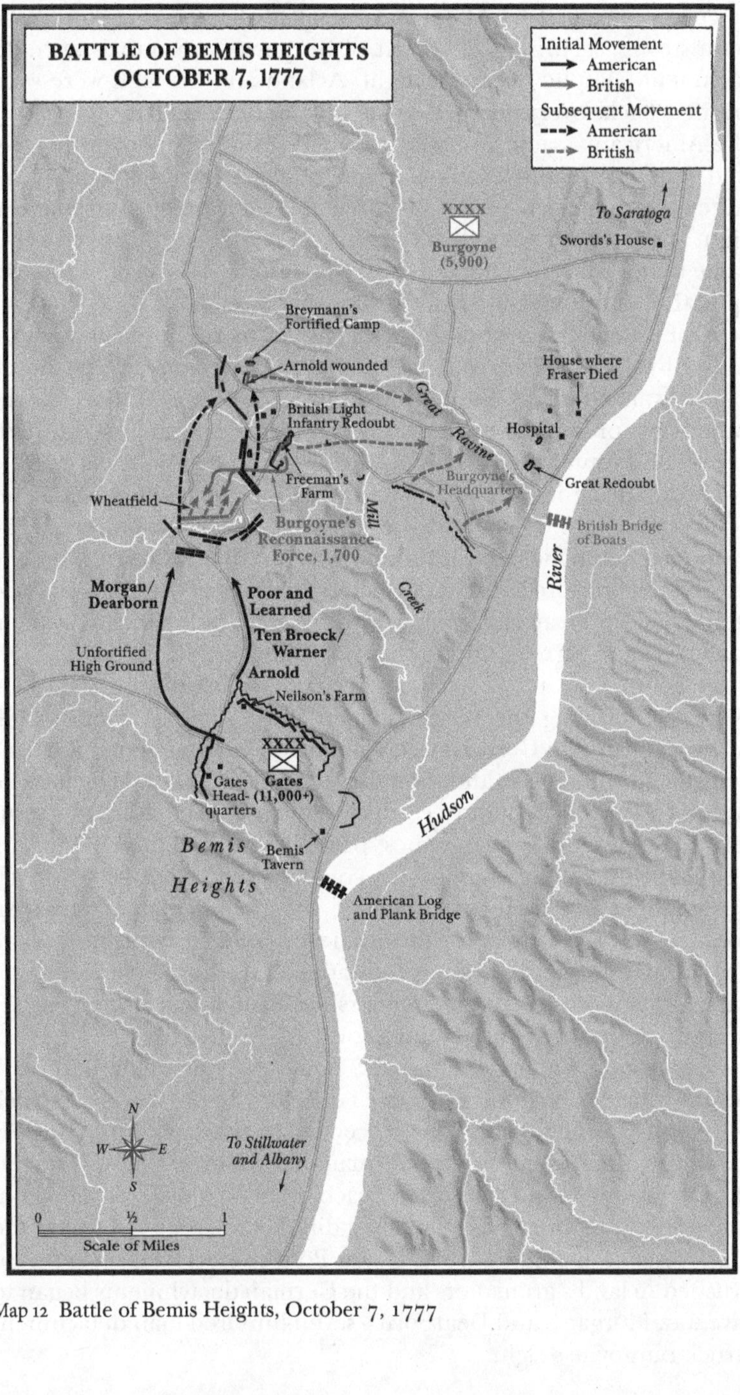

Map 12 Battle of Bemis Heights, October 7, 1777

Poor's men first hit Major Acland's British grenadiers, only 266 men strong, securing the far left of Burgoyne's reconnaissance detachment. Despite a spirited fight, Acland and his men were soon pushed back, overwhelmed by sheer numbers and the ferocity of the American assault.[55] Acland received serious wounds to his legs and was soon captured. A German officer remembered that the Americans attacked "with such force and such violent fire that our right and left flanks as well as our front were all being attacked at the same time." They defended themselves as well as they could, but despite their advantage in artillery, "it was no use."[56]

Poor threw more units into the fight "to reinforce those who were already engaged with us," Captain Pausch wrote that night, "and advanced madly and blindly in the face of furious fire." As the Americans pressed forward, the two British 12-pounders and their crews soon found themselves on their own. Major Williams tried to continue the fight, but soon all his horses had been killed, and many of his crew were down, and the rest were quickly captured.[57] The guns changed hands again. Colonel Joseph Cilley, commanding the 1st New Hampshire Regiment, vaulted onto one of the guns, claimed it for "the American cause," and "then with his own hands assisted in loading it and turned it upon the retreating enemy."[58]

At about 3:00 p.m., Acland's grenadiers finally gave way completely, unhinging the reconnaissance force's far left flank. This, in turn, made the German detachments defending across Barber's wheat field vulnerable, and soon they too fell back. What began as an orderly retreat turned into a confused collapse. "At this junction, our left wing retreated in the greatest possible disorder, thereby causing a similar rout among our German command," wrote Pausch, "which was stationed behind the fence in line of battle." Pausch and his men soon shared the fate of the British 12-pounder crews as they were abandoned by their retreating comrades and left on their own. In an amazing feat of courage and leadership, Pausch was able to extract his guns under heavy fire and deploy them farther back.[59]

This respite was only temporary, however. Poor's men had inadvertently made an almost perfect en echelon attack. They first struck the enemy's far left flank, then proceeded to attack all along the line, extending their assault to the German detachments. This prevented the enemy units from reinforcing each other by moving troops from one hot spot to another and made it difficult to judge just where the main threat was coming from. Just as Poor's New Hampshire troops crushed Acland's grenadiers and the German detachments began to give way, Morgan's and Dearborn's seven-hundred-man detachment struck Burgoyne's right.

Morgan had swung all the way around Burgoyne's right flank and hit the advanced corps units from the right rear. Dearborn, hugging Morgan's right, attacked directly into their flank. The combination was devastating. Morgan's attack placed Burgoyne in an impossible position. He knew his left was crumbling, but before he could provide support to those beleaguered units, the American riflemen and light infantry were assaulting his right. British troops were pushed off the high ground and began to fall back in disarray. It soon became apparent that about all Burgoyne could do was get the entire detachment back into their prepared positions in the main defensive lines, so he ordered, as he later wrote Germain, "the light infantry and part of the 24th regiment . . . to form a second line and to secure the return of the troops to camp."[60]

Balcarres tried to establish another line behind a fence, but he was forced to fall back once more. Morgan pushed forward and moved into Barber's wheat field, pursuing the advanced corps units and putting still more pressure on the German detachments. With both flanks collapsing, showers of American bullets buzzing by—musket balls pierced Burgoyne's clothing in several places and his horse was hit, but the general himself was miraculously unscathed—and units falling back in disarray, Burgoyne dispatched his aide, Sir Francis Clarke, to Generals Phillips and Riedesel with orders to withdraw back to the army's fortifications. But Clarke was mortally wounded before he got very far, and the general officers never got the word.[61] From the woods, Arnold had observed it all and saw an opportunity.

Lieutenant Nathaniel Bacheller's unit was ordered to join Arnold's division early in the afternoon of October 7, which they did, just as Morgan, Dearborn, and Poor's New Hampshire regiments moved forward to counter Burgoyne. Shortly afterward, Bacheller observed Arnold ride out of the camp and into the woods to the north, apparently to observe the British forces, which were then engaged with Morgan's riflemen.[62] Not long after Arnold had galloped off and as the battle raged less than a mile away, Gates rode up and asked for Arnold. He was told that he was "out of the lines to View the Enemy." After waiting a few minutes, Gates dispatched an officer on horseback to find Arnold and tell him to make sure that Morgan's and Dearborn's men did not fire on the regiments of Poor's brigade. Gates was specifically concerned about the 3rd New Hampshire Regiment, commanded by Colonel Scammell, the last of Poor's units to be sent into the fight.[63] Few things will sap an army's morale quicker than a friendly fire incident. Gates wanted to make sure that Morgan's men did not direct their fire into the woods south

of the British-German positions where parts of Poor's brigade were maneuvering and fighting.

Before long, Arnold raced back into the lines to consult with Gates. According to eyewitness Bacheller, Arnold informed Gates "that the Enemy Design was To Take Possession of a hill about a Quarter of a mile To the west of our lines." He was undoubtedly referring to the high ground that Captain Fraser's Rangers and Indians had occupied. As the sounds of the battle intensified, Arnold, having witnessed the successful flank attacks of Poor's New Hampshire troops, Morgan's riflemen, and Dearborn's light infantry, turned to Gates and said: "it is Late in the Day but Let me have men & we will have some Fun with them Before Sun Set!" Gates agreed and ordered out Brigadier General Ebenezer Learned's brigade of Massachusetts regiments along with the rest of Poor's brigade, including two New York Continental regiments and the Connecticut militia, and most likely Brigadier General Ten Broeck's Albany County, New York, militia brigade (also known as "Schuyler's Brigade) and Brigadier General Jonathan Warner's Massachusetts militia brigade as well. Conspicuous on his huge bay horse, Arnold led his men into the fight.[64]

Wolcott recalled that "Genl Arnold came up with a reinforcement about four, upon which the fire of musketry became violent and incessant," which clearly supports Bacheller's eyewitness account.[65] Bacheller had no axe to grind, nor did Lincoln, Dearborn, Brooks, and Wolcott, unlike Wilkinson, Varick, and Livingston. The picture these men paint of the situation on Bemis Heights on that Tuesday afternoon is much different from almost all accounts of the battle. This was not a passive, almost disinterested, or cowardly Gates, sulking at his headquarters and leaving the fight to others. Gates was actively managing the battle and taking his subordinate's advice to reinforce the success enjoyed by Poor's brigade, Morgan's riflemen, and Dearborn's light infantry. On the other hand, Arnold was clearly still in command of the left wing, contradicting Wilkinson and others. He may have been excited in the heat of combat, but he was also poised and in complete control as he urged Gates to strike as the enemy faltered.

At this point, the Americans engaged in the fighting outnumbered Burgoyne's detachment almost two to one. The addition of Learned's thirteen-hundred-man brigade, the rest of Poor's brigade, and Ten Broeck's and Warner's brigades, all being led forward by Arnold, dashed any hopes Burgoyne might have had for an orderly retreat back to his fortified lines. Learned's brigade and the remainder of

Poor's brigade hit the detachment's center. It was just too much combat power. Pausch and his gun crews tried to stem the American advance and furiously loaded and fired their two 6-pounders, "which became so heated that it was impossible for any man to lay his hands on them." The German artillerymen fell back once again, "hoping to meet a body of our Infantry and with them make a stand," Pausch later wrote in his journal, but it was not to be: "Some of the men ran in one direction, and others in another." Pausch could see that "all was irretrievably lost, and that it was impossible to save anything," so he ordered a retreat.[66] Burgoyne later wrote that the "troops retreated hard pressed but in good order," and some units did.[67] Pausch's account confirms that many did not.

With the fresh American troops led by Arnold hitting the center of Burgoyne's detachment, the British-German lines, inevitably, gave way. Some detachments that were already without their normal commanders broke and ran. Others held out for a while and attempted an orderly withdrawal. These soon found themselves in danger of being overwhelmed. Quickly sizing up the desperate situation, Simon Fraser established a line formed by the 24th Regiment and the light infantry on the southern edge of the Marshall Farm field. This rear guard action enabled a number of units to escape being overrun, but the cost was very high. As Fraser directed the rear guard on horseback, leading by example, he was hit in the stomach and slipped from his horse, mortally wounded.[68] Burgoyne had now lost his most respected and gifted combat commander. When his commander was shot, it "helped to turn the fate of the day," Digby recalled, and only then did General Burgoyne sense "in the highest degree our disagreeable situation."[69]

Balcarres assumed command from the stricken Fraser and slowly pulled the rear guard back until they reached his redoubt. Arnold and the American brigade commanders conducted a vigorous pursuit and followed close on the heels of the withdrawing rear guard. As the 24th Regiment, the light infantry, and other British and German units reached their fortifications, Poor immediately attacked and seized the outer works that protected the Light Infantry Redoubt. Arnold and Poor then focused on the main redoubt itself. Many of the survivors of the afternoon's fighting, British and German, had taken refuge in the Light Infantry Redoubt, and thus, Balcarres had plenty of firepower with which to defend the works. With Arnold and Poor leading their men forward, they advanced right up to the redoubt's walls but were repulsed with heavy losses. Digby was amazed at the rebels' bravery and remarked that they "still advanced

upon our works under a severe fire of grape shot, which in some measure stopped them, by the great execution we made among their columns."[70] Poor's men fell back to the outer works and from there directed a constant harassing fire on the redoubt.[71]

After failing to seize the British Light Infantry Redoubt with a direct assault, Arnold turned his attention to Breymann's Fortified Camp; he could do this without interference because of the faulty placement of the fortifications. Not only was Breymann's Fortified Camp poorly sited, but by late afternoon on October 7 it was also sparsely manned. Many of Breymann's soldiers who had participated in the reconnaissance had taken refuge in the British Light Infantry Redoubt after the retreat, so fewer than two hundred men occupied the position. While Poor's brigade focused on the British Light Infantry Redoubt, Morgan, Dearborn, and Learned's units moved north to confront Breymann's Fortified Camp, with Ten Broeck's brigade linking with Poor's brigade to the south. Since the British Light Infantry Redoubt was out of supporting distance and Poor's and Ten Broeck's brigades were keeping the garrison pinned down, Breymann could not count on any assistance from the southeast. Learned's brigade, now led by Arnold once again, directly assaulted and quickly overwhelmed the fortified Canadian Cabins, which protected the redoubt's southern flank. Breymann and his tiny force were now almost completely isolated, the fortified camp's defenders outnumbered by the Americans facing them by almost ten to one. Arnold sensed that the enemy was faltering.[72]

After taking the Canadian Cabins, and as daylight began to wane, Arnold wasted no time and immediately attacked Breymann's Fortified Camp from the south. Lieutenant Colonel Richard Butler, Morgan's second-in-command, recalled the action as they stormed the redoubt: "Genl Arnold was the first who Entered, one Major [Joseph] Morris with about 12 of the Rifle men followed him on the Rear of their . . . flank while I led up the Rest of the Riflemen in front." The rest of Learned's brigade and Morgan's and Dearborn's men conducted a frontal attack on the western face of the fortification; the soldiers rapidly made their way in, some through the gap between the log walls and others through the embrasures, openings in the wall for the artillery. Still others made their way in "by climbing over the breast work, which was formed by small timbers, seven or eight feet high."[73]

As Arnold spurred his horse into the camp, he was shot in the left leg (the leg that had already sustained a serious wound during the Quebec expedition). His horse was also shot several times, and as it fell, Arnold's wounded leg was crushed under the weight of the

dying animal. Dearborn raced to the scene and assisted in pulling the horse off the left wing commander. "I asked him if he was badly wounded," Dearborn recalled. Arnold gasped that he "wished the ball had passed his heart." Despite the excruciating pain of his wound, Arnold continued to give orders and cheer on Learned's and Morgan's men.[74]

After a brief, sharp fight, the American assault swamped the defenders, and Breymann was killed in the crossfire. The survivors promptly fled to the northeast away from the threat, and soon they "were all gone Except here and there a Scatering one behind a Tree," remembered Samuel Armstrong, a lieutenant with the 8th Massachusetts Regiment and serving temporarily with Dearborn's light infantry.[75] A small force of Braunschweig troops tried to recapture Breymann's fortified camp, but darkness and the great number of American troops in the vicinity quickly put a stop to the attempt, and the commanding officers of the detachment were captured. As the sun set, Arnold had accomplished what he promised Gates with such bravado: he had some fun with them.

Armstrong later wrote that although they tried to chase the fleeing enemy, the American troops soon had to "give over pursuing, it being very dark in the woods." The young officer proudly reported that they had captured several guns and "Horses and all compleat." They also seized the "Camp-Equipage with all their Baggage, where their Kettles were boiling on the fires!"[76] All of the artillery pieces that had gone out with the reconnaissance force were captured, along with quantities of ammunition and baggage, and the all-important forage was lost.

Impressive as the spoils was, the critical fact was that the Americans had severely damaged Burgoyne's army. British and German losses were dreadful. Burgoyne's casualties totaled 894 men, well over 15 percent of his total force. Captain John Money, the army's quartermaster, and Majors Acland and Williams had been captured, Breymann killed, and General Fraser and Captain Clarke mortally wounded, along with many other brave officers and men. The Americans suffered about two hundred casualties.[77]

Once Breymann's Fortified Camp fell, Burgoyne's right flank was unhinged, and the entire line was threatened. Almost half of the American Army now sat on his fully exposed flank. As an experienced professional soldier, Burgoyne recognized the futility of his tactical situation: "Under the disadvantages thus apparent in our situation, the army was ordered to quit the present position during the night and take post" at the Great Redoubt.[78]

Nightfall ended any chance for a larger American success, but by any measure, the Battle of Bemis Heights—the second battle of Saratoga—was a ringing American victory. This time the Americans not only held the field, but they also turned Burgoyne's right flank, forcing him to abandon much of his fortified lines and to move the entire army to the east and the vicinity of the Great Redoubt and the river road. It was also a triumph of leadership. Gates's management of the battle was critical: gradually committing units as the situation developed just as he had at Freeman's Farm acting on Arnold's advice and enabling the decisive stroke by sending into the fight the entire left wing, always keeping in mind that he had to cover the Albany river road. Gates's insistence that Burgoyne make the first move paid off. And Arnold's intuitive feel for how the battle was progressing and his aggressive nature spurred him to keep pressing the enemy when they began to falter. His dynamic and inspiring "lead from the front" example was decisive in the battle's outcome. Benjamin Lincoln's calm presence as Gates's second-in-command and his adept handling of the militia in August and September was critical to the successful outcome. American units—in particular Morgan's, Dearborn's, and Poor's New Hampshire regiments—used the natural terrain to their advantage during their approach, deployment, and initial and follow-on attacks. Once again, the well-led American units, both Continentals and militia, fought aggressively and with competence and determination.

And, once again, Burgoyne had gotten himself into trouble by his single-minded insistence on continuing toward Albany despite the dramatically different operational situation after the twin disasters at Bennington and Fort Stanwix, and the inconclusive Battle of Freeman's Farm. He had grossly underestimated American military capabilities and leadership, and their ability to respond effectively and quickly to his movements. He failed to exert effective command and control during both battles. He had thrown together a mixed force of units and parts of units, and he further mixed them as they advanced and halted in the clearings. This disrupted the units' normal command structures, contributing to the defeat. Another key factor in the disaster was the poor placement of the two fortifications that were charged with protecting Burgoyne's vulnerable right flank.

At the Battle of Bemis Heights, Americans—especially Gates and Arnold, along with their subordinate leaders—capitalized on the situation and made the right moves at the right time, despite the chaos. On that Tuesday, October 7, 1777, they demonstrated initiative, flexibility and, most importantly, grip.

As Burgoyne's army abandoned their right-wing fortifications and moved toward the Great Redoubt, the Americans were temporarily disorganized because of the darkness and loss of Arnold. Gates sent Lincoln and Brigadier General John Glover to feel out Burgoyne's right to try to determine his intentions. After examining the British lines as thoroughly as possible in the darkness, Lincoln reported back to Gates early in the morning of October 8 that "the enemy appeared to be a state of inquietude lying upon their arms and that appearances indicated a retreat if not a flight."[79] Lincoln's intelligence was not entirely accurate, but his report seemed to offer Gates the opportunity to deliver the knockout blow. Instead, he ordered his second-in-command to move the right wing forward "to feel the enemy, and, if possible, to obtain a more perfect knowledge of their designs."[80]

As Lincoln led the brigades north through the thick woods, ravines, and undergrowth, Burgoyne's men braced for the worst. Digby wrote that at about "8 in the morning we perceived the enemy marching from their camp in great numbers, blackening the fields with their dark clothing."[81] As Lincoln led his men through the dense woods, the Massachusetts general stumbled upon a German unit in the thickets. At first, he thought they were friendly troops, but before he recognized his mistake, dozens of Braunschweig muskets fired in his direction. Lincoln wheeled his horse around but was hit in the right leg. He barely avoided capture, but his wound sidelined him for months.[82] In the space of a few hours, both of Gates's senior generals were gravely wounded in action and out of the fight.

The movement of the American right wing amounted to little except for some small clashes along the newly constituted British-German lines and some ineffective artillery contests. The American guns targeted the enemy bridge across the Hudson and the hospital—likely mistaking the tent complex for a headquarters—located below the Great Redoubt. Effective or not, the artillery forced Burgoyne to relocate the hospital, necessitating the movement of many critically wounded soldiers, "which was a most shocking scene," wrote Digby, "some poor wretches dying in the attempt, being so severely wounded."[83]

Late in the day, the American gunners turned their attention to a group gathered on the parapet of one of the fortifications that made up the Great Redoubt. Although they could not know it, they were firing at mourners gathered for the funeral of Brigadier General Simon Fraser. After he was shot trying to protect the withdrawal of the reconnaissance detachment on October 7, Fraser was carried to

the small cabin occupied by Frederike Riedesel and her children. Fraser asked the surgeon attending him if he might recover. On hearing the negative prognosis, he sent the surgeon away to care for other wounded men. During the night, Fraser suffered unspeakable pain, and the Baroness heard him cry out again and again: "Oh, fatal ambition! Poor General Burgoyne! Poor Mrs. Fraser!" He died the next morning.[84]

Before he died, Fraser asked to be buried in the Great Redoubt, a request Burgoyne fulfilled at 6:00 p.m. that evening, in a funeral ceremony attended by all the generals and most of the army's senior officers. Digby, who had served under Fraser for the entire campaign and greatly admired and respected the general, wrote that the service "was performed I think in the most solemn manner I ever before saw; perhaps the scene around, big with the fate of many, caused it to appear more so."[85] The Baroness also described the scene: "At precisely at six o'clock the body was actually carried away, and we saw all the generals and their staffs take part in the funeral services on the hilltop. . . . Cannon balls constantly flew around and over the heads of the mourners."[86] Fraser's death was a shattering blow to the army and to Burgoyne personally.

Two hours after Fraser's funeral, the British Army slipped out of camp under cover of darkness and heavy rain, abandoning the hospital along with its three hundred wounded and sick men along with a note from Burgoyne asking Gates to care for the stricken soldiers left behind. Riedesel commanded the lead elements with Phillips commanding the rear guard. Burgoyne, fearing that Gates would turn his right and cut off any possible retreat route, had no choice but to fall back toward Saratoga. He was still not convinced that the game was up.

CHAPTER 21

Retreat, Pursuit, and Surrender

BURGOYNE'S SOLDIERS NEVER FORGOT that miserable night march. Heavy rain turned the roads into ankle-deep rivers of mud. The constant threat of American attack only added to the distress of a defeated army exhausted and on reduced rations. As they slowly moved north, the advanced corps brought up the rear, destroying bridges behind them. Digby remarked with irony that "this was the second time of their being destroyed that season—the first by the enemy to prevent our pursueing them. What a great alteration in affairs!"[1] The long column stopped after only a few miles, at 5:00 a.m. on October 9, in the vicinity of Dovegat. To lighten their load, "we set fire to a portion of the baggage and carts," recalled a German officer, and all "the houses and bridges that we encountered along our route experienced the same fate."[2] The men expected to be back on the road in short order, but the hours dragged on and on with no orders to resume the march.

Burgoyne's decision to halt for such an extended period while "it rained in torrents," baffled many in the army, and the delay allowed the Americans to react.[3] Many in the British Army knew, even if their commanding general seemed not to, that they had to execute "an uninterrupted retreat in order to thwart the enemy's intentions and to return at least one corps of soldiers to the King even if we had to abandon all our baggage."[4] Burgoyne argued later that the halt had been necessary to refresh the troops and give the bateaux time to catch up as they struggled against the river current.[5] Some delay may well have been necessary, but not ten hours. Early in the afternoon,

the men were issued six days of rations that they had to carry themselves due to the loss of transport.[6] Lady Acland was given a pass by Burgoyne that allowed her to safely negotiate the enemy lines so she could join her wounded husband already in American hands. She promptly embarked on a small boat down the river, accompanied by a chaplain. When she reached American lines, she was met by Dearborn, who found her shelter for the night and secured her safe passage to her husband.[7] The delay dragged on.

Gates's instinctive caution, which was aggravated by the loss of Arnold and Lincoln, prevented him from making an energetic pursuit. Nonetheless, he still directed units to try to block the enemy on the west bank and dispatched militia units to the east bank of the Hudson to guard against a river crossing. These units harassed the worn-out enemy army, firing on bateaux moving the rest of Burgoyne's meager supplies upriver. A Massachusetts militia brigade commanded by Brigadier General John Fellows had been sent to cut off Burgoyne's retreat, but they were discovered sound asleep by a reconnoitering British battalion, blissfully unaware of the danger. The British unit was too small to attack the vulnerable Americans by itself, but Burgoyne passed up a chance for an easy victory by not supplying reinforcements in time. Fellows, finally altered to the danger, escaped and crossed to the river's east bank.

Finally, late in the afternoon, Burgoyne ordered the march to resume, and they set off. Though it "rained horribly and was likewise extremely cold," remembered one German officer, the men slogged on. The army's lead elements reached Saratoga late that evening. However, the troops' suffering was not over as many of the men had to sleep on the bare ground in little more than their sodden uniforms because they had burned their tents in retreat.[8]

It took a while for the rest of Burgoyne's army to arrive at Saratoga. The troops found it particularly difficult to drag the artillery over the muddy roads and across numerous small creeks swollen twice and three times their normal width and depth with the runoff from the heavy rain. They left behind baggage, broken wagons, dead animals, and other debris abandoned by men who wanted nothing more than to get away from the rebels and find refuge somewhere in the seemingly endless American wilderness.[9]

Burgoyne intended to continue the march after a brief pause at Saratoga, cross the river to the east side, and then continue to Fort Edward. This hope was quickly dashed when he discovered American militia in large numbers on the east side of the river. On October 10, Gates ordered the entire army in pursuit of Burgoyne, and by

late that afternoon was facing the enemy army, which had started to dig in across the Fishkill Creek just north of Saratoga. This was familiar ground for Burgoyne and his army as they had made camp at Saratoga four weeks earlier. Their primary defensive position for the British units was located on high ground north of the Fishkill Creek and just west of Philip Schuyler's estate. The German troops were located on rocky ground in their own camp about a half-mile to the north.[10] Burgoyne ordered the burning of Schuyler's mansion and the extensive array of outbuildings to clear fields of fire for his artillery. "The enemy have burned all the Houses before them as they retreated," reported an outraged Gates to Hancock, "The extensive Buildings and Kills &c belonging to Major General Schuyler are also laid in Ashes." This "shameful behavior" shocked the Americans and only redoubled their desire to finish the work they had started at Freeman's Farm.[11]

Americans on both banks could now fire on the British bateaux in the river. They destroyed several along with their precious cargo, forcing Burgoyne to order the rest of the supplies hauled ashore and into the main fortifications. This action "was effected under fire and with great difficulty," as Burgoyne later wrote Germain.[12] On the morning of October 11, Gates almost made a major mistake. Burgoyne had arranged his artillery to rake a flat plain just east of the main British camp. That morning a dense fog covered the low ground and hid Burgoyne's main position. Gates sent a large force across the creek near its outlet into the Hudson, thinking that Burgoyne was heading for the river crossing about a mile and a half to the north. Glover's, Nixon's, and Learned's brigades were almost caught in the open by the enemy guns. Fortunately for the Americans, Gates recognized his error and recalled the attack before any harm was done.[13]

By midday on October 11, Burgoyne and his army were surrounded, and the noose was beginning to tighten. Stark and his New Hampshire militia controlled the river crossing north of Saratoga and the road to Fort Edward; General Fellows and his brigade commanded a ford across the river east of the British camp; the American Army's right wing was south of the Fishkill Creek, facing Burgoyne's main camp; and General Poor's brigade was just to the northwest of the enemy camp, with Morgan and Dearborn to the north.[14] Digby believed that many of the dispirited troops felt that the long halt at Dovegat "was the cause of our being surrounded."[15]

Conditions inside the main British camp were appalling. "We were obliged to bring our oxen and horses into our lines, where they had

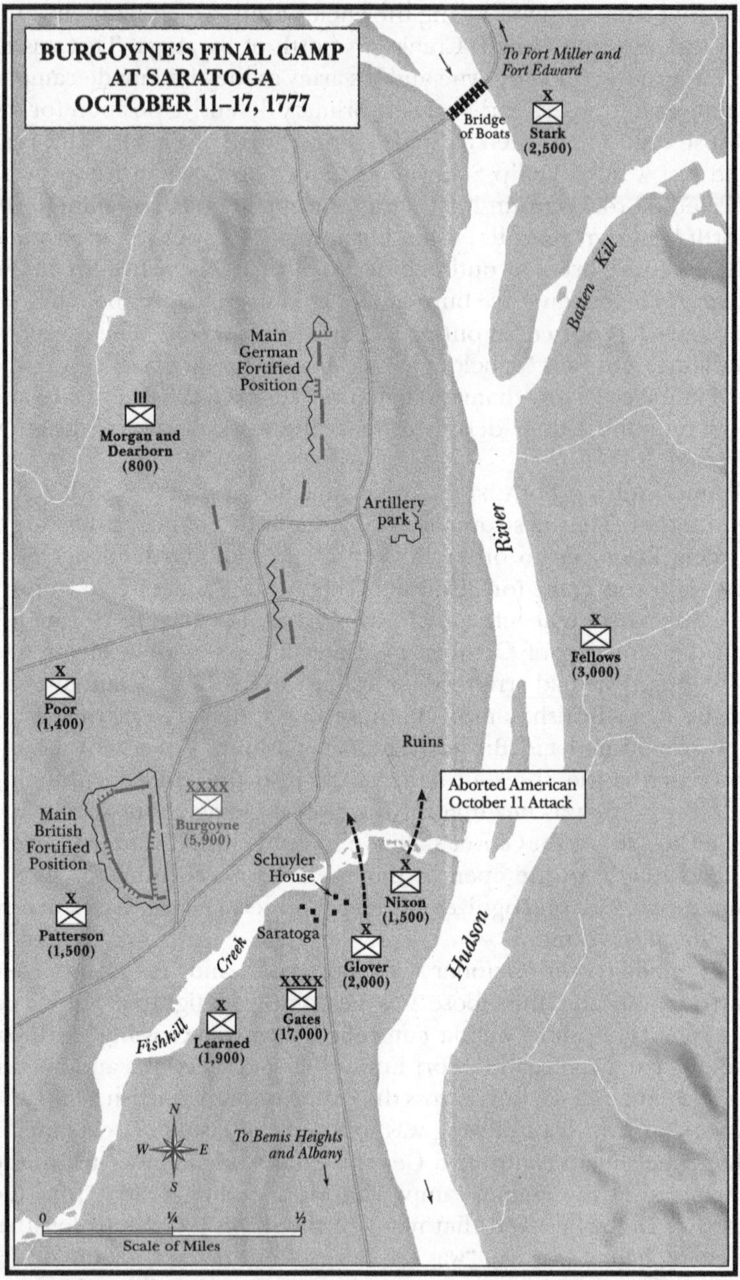

Map 13 Burgoyne's Final Camp at Saratoga, October 11–17, 1777

the wretched prospect of living but a few days," moaned Digby, "as our grass was all gone, and nothing but the leaves of trees for them." True to the lieutenant's predictions, the animals quickly began to die, "and the stench was very prejudicial in so small a space."[16] Still, although "very great indeed were the distresses which the army had to encounter at this period," wrote Corporal Lamb, "they were borne with fortitude."[17] Perhaps that was the case for most of the troops, but for many others, it was just too much. Desertions soared. Each day dozens of Burgoyne's soldiers slipped away to give themselves up to the Americans. Gates informed Hancock that "I am happy to acquaint your Excellency that Desertion has taken a deep Root in the Royal Army particularly among the Germans who come to us in Shoals."[18] From their lines, the British and German troops could clearly observe the growing numbers of militia now joining the Americans as they swarmed "around the little adverse army like birds of prey."[19]

Until they surrounded Burgoyne at Saratoga, the Americans had displayed no great proficiency with their artillery. Now, however, they were so close they could hardly miss. They began a relentless bombardment of the British lines, one of the rounds nearly striking Burgoyne. "Roaring of cannon and whistling of bullets from their rifle pieces, were constantly heard day and night," wrote Lamb.[20] Even with all his advantages, Gates showed no signs of attacking. As he had during the preceding four weeks, he was content to let Burgoyne make the first move. He finally did.

After enduring two days of constant sniping and artillery fire, Burgoyne could detect no signs that the Americans would attack their hastily constructed field fortifications. He had also received no word from Sir Henry Clinton on his expedition through the Hudson River Highlands, so on the afternoon of Sunday, October 12, Burgoyne called a council of war to consider his options. He met with Generals Riedesel, Phillips, and Hamilton and reviewed their situation. He estimated that Gates's army approached fourteen thousand Continentals and militia with more on the east bank of the Hudson. They had lost all their bateaux through enemy action, and thus, "no means appear of making a bridge over the Hudson's River." Burgoyne explained that their only options for retreat were to cross the river at a ford near Fort Edward or stay on the west bank of the river all the way to Fort George. If they took their artillery with them, "some bridges must be repaired under fire of the enemy," which would cause a very long delay. Burgoyne reminded his fellow generals that they had only about one week of provisions remaining.

With these unpleasant facts in mind, the generals considered five courses of action: attack the Americans; wait for Gates to attack; retreat with the artillery; retreat without the artillery; and try again for Albany. Obviously, waiting was unacceptable, and they simply did not have the combat power to attack and defeat the Americans. To retreat with all their artillery and baggage was also unthinkable: The slow-moving columns would be easy pickings for the swarming enemy forces.[21]

Although there was some initial disagreement, in the end, all the senior officers agreed that the army should abandon their guns and baggage and retreat north that very night. But as preparations were being made for the night movement, patrols sent out by Burgoyne reported back that the Americans were everywhere, including to the north, and that they would spot any major movements almost immediately.[22] The breakout was cancelled, and Burgoyne waited "in the anxious hope of succor from our friends [Sir Henry Clinton's expedition] or the next desirable expectation, an attack from our enemy."[23]

As the two armies settled into what looked like an extended siege, Gates announced to the world the great victory of October 7. From his headquarters at "Camp Saratoga," Gates wrote, "From 3 o'clock in the afternoon till almost night the Conflict was very warm and bloody, when the Enemy, by a precipitate Retreat, determined the fate of the day." American losses were comparatively light, wrote Gates, but among the casualties was "the gallant Major General Arnold, whose Leg was fractured by a Musket Ball as he was forcing the Enemy's Breast-work." Gates's prominent mention of Arnold provides yet more evidence that their feud was over, and refutes the story that his dynamic general had disobeyed orders, as so many accounts later claimed. Gates was also fulsome in his commendation of Morgan and his men and those under Major Dearborn.[24] He closed by describing Lincoln's wounding, Burgoyne's retreat, and the burning of General Schuyler's estate. Significantly, Gates wrote this letter to Hancock, president of Congress, and not to Washington, his commander-in-chief.[25]

The next day the British continued to endure an unabated American cannonade, with no signs of an attack and no news from Sir Henry Clinton. "The enemy had now completely encircled us," wrote a German officer, "and taken his position in such a way that we could not attack him without obvious disadvantage for us. The moment for the retreat had definitely passed."[26] Gates's army was now so big that he could afford to send two thousand militia under General

Jacob Bayley to seize Fort Edward, shutting off yet another retreat route.[27] The Americans thus controlled all the Hudson River fords in the area and the entire eastern bank, from opposite Stillwater to Fort Edward.

The situation within the British and German fortified camps grew worse with each passing hour: "Our poor sick and wounded crept around in the camp to look in part for safe spaces of refuge," as the harried and weary surgeons did their best to alleviate their suffering, but it was almost impossible.[28] Aggravating their hunger and illness was exhaustion. Digby wrote that after October 7, "the men lay constantly upon their arms,—Harassed and fatigued beyond measure, from their great want of rest."[29]

Burgoyne called yet another council of war, and this time he included all commanding officers down to the rank of captain. The American artillery fire was relentless, making it difficult to find a sheltered place for the gathering. Burgoyne again addressed the assembled officers, men who in the space of just three months had experienced the highest of highs with the capture of Fort Ticonderoga and the lowest of lows with their defeat six days earlier. The minutes of that meeting reveal that while he told them that he was more than willing to place himself at the head of the army and attempt a breakout, he knew that "a capitulation had been in the contemplation of some, perhaps of all, who knew the real situation of things." He had expanded the council's attendance to include junior officers to ensure he had "a full representation of the army." He would not ask Gates for terms unless all the commanders agreed. The commanding general then asked his fellow officers to consider two questions: First, "whether an army of 3500 fighting men and well-provided with artillery were justifiable upon the principles of national dignity and military honour in capitulating in any possible situation." The vote was a unanimous yes. Second, he asked, "Is the present situation of that nature?" Once again, the officers all answered yes, and that the "situation justifies a capitulation upon honourable terms."[30] General Phillips, disgusted that the campaign had come to this sad end, asked to take a few men and try to break out and make his way to Ticonderoga. Burgoyne refused.[31]

Lieutenant Colonel Kingston was immediately dispatched under a flag of truce to Gates's headquarters with the following message: "Lieutenant-general Burgoyne is desirous of sending a field officer to Major-general Gates, upon a matter of high moment to both armies."[32] Gates agreed to meet with Burgoyne's representative at 10:00 a.m. the next day, the 14th. At the appointed time, Colonel

Wilkinson met Kingston between the two armies at the ruins of the destroyed bridge over the Fishkill, blindfolded the protesting British envoy, and escorted him to headquarters, where the negotiations for the surrender of the army from Canada began.[33]

Kingston carried with him Burgoyne's opening statement. Whatever his shortcomings as a general may have been, Burgoyne was a good negotiator. Because any further fighting would surely result in "a scene of carnage on both sides," Burgoyne was "impelled by humanity" to "to spare the lives of brave men upon honourable terms." He proposed a temporary truce to allow ample time to "communicate the preliminary terms."[34] Gates agreed to a ceasefire until sunset and surprised Kingston by handing him a list he had already prepared of six proposed articles that basically demanded an immediate and unconditional surrender. Kingston was shocked and initially refused to deliver the message to his chief. Gates convinced him to do so, arguing that since the lieutenant colonel "had brought the message, he ought to take back the answer."[35]

Once again, a British council of war was formed, and once again, the verdict was unanimous, this time rejecting Gates's proposals. Burgoyne was furious with the American terms and immediately drafted a response, which Kingston duly delivered late in the afternoon. Gates had demanded that the enemy army "ground their arms" in their camps, which insulted Burgoyne and his officers and was "inadmissible in any extremity." If Gates did not eliminate the demand, the ceasefire would end "at once."[36] Along with his emphatic rejection of Gates's terms, Burgoyne countered that the army should be afforded the full honors of war, that they be allowed to return to Great Britain "upon condition of not serving in North America during the present contest," that the army not be broken up, that Burgoyne be allowed to send messengers with letters to Sir William Howe, Sir Guy Carleton, and Lord Germain, and a few other smaller points.[37] Few among the British forces thought Gates would agree to such liberal terms, especially given the army's obviously poor condition. The men grimly prepared for the resumption of hostilities.

Riedesel noted in his journal on October 15 that "It seemed now as if negotiations were at an end." However, at 10 in the morning, Wilkinson "very unexpectedly arrived at our outposts bearing the propositions of General Burgoyne with the signature of Gates."[38] Gates had agreed to virtually everything Burgoyne had asked for with just a few minor alternations, and that "this capitulation was to take place at two o'clock on the afternoon of the same day."[39] Burgoyne was suspicious. Gates had agreed too readily to terms that

were extremely favorable to the defeated army, and he seemed to be rushing things. He was especially surprised that Gates had agreed without argument to allow the army to return to Great Britain. Was it possible that Sir Henry Clinton and his relief expedition were finally approaching and that Gates, therefore, needed to quickly conclude the negotiations so he could turn and face the threat from the south?

Burgoyne's suspicions were correct. Gates had indeed received reports from Generals Putnam and George Clinton, Governor Trumbull, and others on Sir Henry Clinton's and later General Vaughan's progress, though the intelligence picture was far from clear. He thought it unlikely that a British force was nearing Albany, but he could not be sure.[40] Gates needed to wrap up negotiations, dispose of Burgoyne's army, and then turn south. Having guessed this, Burgoyne stalled for time, asking that representatives from both sides meet to iron out all the details before he would sign any formal agreement. This frustrated Gates because he had already jumped the gun, announcing to Putnam and George Clinton that Burgoyne had surrendered. He reluctantly agreed.[41] He could do little else. For once, time was on Burgoyne's side.

Staff officers from both sides met throughout the day on October 15 in a tent pitched near Philip Schuyler's ruined mansion. Negotiations concluded, or so the officers thought, at 8:00 p.m. At 10:30 p.m., Wilkinson received a message from one of Burgoyne's aides, Captain James Craig, with one final demand: Although he reported that the commanding general had approved all the articles, in their "zeal to complete it expeditiously," they had allowed a mistake to pass by unnoticed in the document. "We have, Sir, unguardedly called the treaty a *capitulation*, which the army means only as a treaty of convention."[42] Craig promised that if Gates approved the title change, Burgoyne would be ready to sign the next morning. This was a face-saving measure as well as a delaying tactic, but Gates immediately approved the change. He wanted to end it there and then, and squabbling over the name of the treaty was counterproductive.

Burgoyne had one more trick up his sleeve. During the night, a Loyalist came through the lines with third-hand news that Sir Henry Clinton's expedition had captured the Hudson Highlands forts and was pushing on to Esopus and Albany. The man did not know exactly where they were, but they could already be at Albany or even closer. This intelligence seemed to confirm Gates's haste to conclude the treaty. Burgoyne was elated; the news offered him one more chance at redemption. He called yet another council of war and put two key

questions to the officers. First, "Whether a treaty, which was about to be completed by his deputies, and which he himself had promised to sign, could be broken?" The officers decided fourteen to eight that it could not. Second, "Whether the report of a man, whom nobody knew, was sufficient in our present situation to justify refusal of so advantageous a treaty?" Again, the vote was fourteen to eight against.[43] Even were Clinton trying to come to their aid, he was probably still some distance off, and there was no telling how long it might be until he arrived. In any case, most of the senior officers felt that they simply could not in good conscious renege on the pending treaty.

The next morning, in one final attempt to gain a little more time, Burgoyne sent another note to Gates, accusing him of detaching major elements of the American Army. This action was "subversive of the principles on which the treaty originated, viz. a great superiority in numbers in General Gates's army." Burgoyne then asked that Gates allow him to send two officers to inspect the rebel force to confirm that Gates had not weakened the army.[44] Gates was furious at Burgoyne's demand and obvious delaying tactic and immediately dispatched Wilkinson with a very pointed reply: Gates assured Burgoyne that "no violation of the treaty has taken place," he would not allow British officers to inspect his army, and that "it now remains with your excellency to ratify or dissolve the treaty; Major-general Gates expects your immediate and decisive reply."[45] Gates had called Burgoyne's bluff. Burgoyne dejectedly consulted his officers one last time, though the officers "had as little to say in answer to this reply of Gates, as Burgoyne himself."[46] As Phillips explained to Sir Henry Clinton a week after the surrender, "Your movement was too late and we had no alternative but to capitulate or starve. Attack we could not, and attack they would not."[47]

Burgoyne signed the treaty, which contained thirteen articles in all, and returned it to Gates. The army's remaining Loyalists, fearing reprisals, were allowed to slip out of camp and make their way home. Riedesel returned to the German camp and ordered the burning of the regimental colors to keep them from falling into enemy hands. However, some were hidden from the Americans by being sewn into a pillow and smuggled back home.[48] The formal treaty signing was scheduled for the next day, October 17, at 9:00 a.m., followed by the surrender of Burgoyne's army.

Crestfallen as he may have been over the campaign's final act, Burgoyne had negotiated an agreement that could not have been more advantageous to Britain. "There is not, perhaps, a single instance in history," Riedesel reflected, "or certainly very few, where

troops could be reconciled to a capitulation with so much honour."[49] Burgoyne himself was heard to remark that the Convention's terms were "easier than we could have expected from our situation."[50] Under the circumstances, Gates could have stuck with his initial demand for immediate and unconditional surrender. The British Army was in no condition to do much of anything, offensively nor defensively. Burgoyne's remaining officers and men were willing to fight on; their morale was as good as could be expected given all they had endured. American forces, however, would likely have made short work of them. But, as Burgoyne had suspected, with Sir Henry Clinton's whereabouts unknown, Gates was unwilling to prolong the negotiations.

Britain had only two major field armies in North America, and with the decisive defeat at Saratoga, they had lost one of them. Nonetheless, despite all his disadvantages, Burgoyne had out-negotiated Gates. He had convinced his counterpart to call the treaty a "Convention," which helped him and his soldiers retain their self-esteem. But the biggest concession was Article II of the Convention: "A free passage to be granted to the army under Lieutenant-general Burgoyne to Great Britain, on condition of not serving again in North America during the present contest."[51] This provision allowed the entire vanquished army, almost six thousand strong, to return to England. Soldiers are fungible. Assuming both sides abided by the treaty, the British could simply replace Burgoyne's troops one-for-one with soldiers stationed elsewhere. Burgoyne was right when he explained later in a speech to Parliament that "by the treaty of Saratoga the army was saved to the state," at least on paper.[52]

Gates can be faulted for many things, but given the overall operational and strategic situation, he can hardly be blamed for accepting the bulk of Burgoyne's terms, including the provision to exchange the British Army. Despite the tremendous American victory, the terms of the Convention of Saratoga would be a continued sore point for both sides.

Early on Friday, October 17, 1777, a day Digby called, "famous in the annals of America," Burgoyne left his tent wearing his dazzling scarlet dress uniform.[53] Observing the cold, fog-shrouded landscape, he met with his officers one last time before the formal surrender. He told them how proud he was of their conduct and what an honor it had been to command such an army. Having to pause several times to collect himself, he explained that his orders had given him little leeway in conducting the campaign, which why he had to "push to Albany *at all Events*, and that his Obedience to those Orders was the

cause of his present Situation," as one of those present recorded in his journal.[54] According to Digby, he assured them that if only they had enough supplies, "he never would have accepted any terms."[55] But Burgoyne's rationalizing rang hollow. A bitter Digby wrote in his diary that "thus ended all our hopes of victory, honour, glory," and whoever was responsible for the disaster—Germain, Howe, Burgoyne, or even the army's officers and men—"let them suffer to the utmost extent, and by an unlimited punishment, in part blot out and erase, if possible, the crime charged to their account."[56]

Colonel Wilkinson guided Burgoyne and his senior commanders to the flood plain near the Hudson where the army was to stack their weapons. The young officer gestured to the numerous militia soldiers in clear view across the river and asked Burgoyne if he saw them. "Yes," he said ruefully, according to what Wilkinson wrote in his memoirs, "I have seen them too long."[57] Wilkinson then escorted Burgoyne, Phillips, Riedesel, and the other British and German general officers and their staffs to meet Gates at his headquarters. The two army commanders knew each other slightly from their previous service in the same regiment more than thirty years earlier. The contrast between the two was striking. Burgoyne was tall and impeccably attired, as befitted a lieutenant general in His Majesty's service. Gates, on the other hand, was short, stooped, bespectacled, as a German eyewitness observed "with the thin hair of an old man hanging about his head," and wore the rather plain blue coat of a Continental major general.[58] He was hardly the image of a triumphant general. Burgoyne dismounted. The two men exchanged greetings under a makeshift American flag stirring gently in the breeze, and the defeated general offered his sword to the victor, who graciously returned it. Gates then welcomed the enemy generals and other officers into his tent for a meal.[59]

Joining them were all the American general officers and colonels, plus one more familiar face. Philip Schuyler had come up from Albany to see the surrender for himself. It was perhaps a minor breach of protocol, but after all, much of the success enjoyed by the Northern Department was due to his efforts, and Gates did not object, at least publicly. The Baroness soon arrived with her children; she was personally greeted by Schuyler, who led her to Gates's tent, where she found Generals Burgoyne and Phillips "upon an extremely friendly footing" with the American officers. Schuyler, who was perhaps feeling a little out of place celebrating with his former colleagues, could see that she was also uncomfortable and said, as the Baroness later recounted, "Come now with your children into

my tent, where I will give you, it is true, a frugal meal, but one that will be accompanied by the best of wishes."[60] She gratefully accepted the meal and an offer to stay at the general's house in Albany until other arrangements could be made. For the rest of her life, the Baroness spoke fondly of Schuyler and his kindness on and after that melancholy day.

The British and German soldiers marched out of their camps with "the drums beating & the honours of war," to ground their arms in the field north of the Fishkill, near the site of a ruined French and Indian War fort. Digby recalled that although the band played the stirring "Grenadiers march . . . it seemed by its last feeble effort, as if almost ashamed to be heard on such an occasion." The young lieutenant who had experienced so much over the past several months tried but failed to hide his tears.[61] Almost all the eyewitnesses to the surrender recalled that it was marked by silence and solemnity, restraint that "can only be demanded from the best disciplined troops."[62] There was no reveling, nor any boisterous outbursts from the American soldiers. Even the militiamen were on their best behavior. The Americans treated their vanquished foes with dignity and respect, much to the surprise of the British and German soldiers. Gates's general orders for that day were explicit: the entire army was to act with decorum.[63]

As Lord Napier's unit marched through two lines of American soldiers, he noted with astonishment that they "behaved with the greatest decency and propriety, not even a Smile appearing on their Countenances." He was sure that the British reaction would have been quite different, "had the case been reversed."[64] After meeting Gates, Captain von Geismar recalled a couple of days later that "I cannot say enough about how extremely polite this man has been."[65] These were not backward provincials. Instead, the men who received the British surrender at Saratoga were tough, hardened, and in many cases professional soldiers who earned the respect of their vanquished foes.

The American soldiers may have behaved well enough during the formalities of the surrender, but that did not mean they were not elated at the campaign's outcome. Surgeon Thacher, who had participated in the headlong flight from Ticonderoga, exulted at their great victory: "Thus we witness the incalculable reverse of fortune, and the extraordinary vicissitudes of military events, as ordained by Divine Providence." The unparalleled triumph would most certainly, predicted Thacher, strike at the British government like a "thunderbolt, and demonstrate to them the invincibility of a

people united in the noble cause of liberty and the rights of man."[66] Henry Dearborn exulted in his journal that this was "the Greatest Conquest Ever known."[67] Brigadier General John Nixon called the surrender the last act of "the compleat victory."[68]

The spoils reaped from the American victory were staggering: in addition to the almost six thousand troops, the Americans captured more than forty-five hundred muskets (many of them damaged by disgruntled German and British soldiers); thirty artillery pieces along with their carriages, ammunition, and tools; uniforms and other clothing; tents; and tons of other useful military stores.[69] On top of that, for now, at least, the American northern flank was secure.

For many of Burgoyne's men, the surrender ceremonies offered them the first chance to see the Americans up close. An observant German officer noticed that the American Continental officers "were wearing any old uniforms," but "light blue coats with red or straw-colored facings were seen quite frequently." The American generals and their staff officers typically "wore blue coats with white turn ups," but militia officers, "on the other hand, wore their usual dress with all kinds of wigs." While all the American soldiers seemed to be reasonably well equipped with muskets and bayonets, even the Continental regiments did not have matching uniforms. One German officer was struck most by the American regimental colors, which were quite striking and "covered with all sorts of emblems aiming at freedom."[70]

After the formal rituals were observed, Gates directed that Burgoyne's army, now American prisoners of war, begin their long march toward Boston and, in accordance with the Convention, their repatriation to Britain. That night they reached as far as the Freeman's Farm battlefield, and two days later, they crossed the Hudson and began their trek east, escorted by General Glover's brigade.

This was just the beginning of a six-year odyssey for what would henceforth be referred to as the "Convention Army." Burgoyne's men were marched first to Boston, where they languished for more than a year while each side accused the other of violating the treaty in one way or another. The army was later marched to Charlottesville, Virginia, and ultimately to Frederick, MD. (Today, driving through the mid-Atlantic countryside, motorists may be mystified to see roadside markers noting the various locations of the "Convention Army." These mark the places where the nomadic prisoners of Saratoga were marched by their captors to prevent their rescue by British forces.) The British and German officers who were not exchanged or paroled typically received decent treatment. The

enlisted men were often subjected to horrible living conditions and inadequate diet, and many soldiers died of disease. Thousands escaped or deserted, many ultimately becoming American citizens. The few remaining were not repatriated until the war's end in 1783, thus concluding an unfortunate epilogue to an otherwise splendid American victory.[71]

Gates had very little time to savor his triumph. After the ceremonies concluded, he immediately ordered the army to march to Albany. Were Clinton still coming up the Hudson, he had to be ready to face him. Before he set out for Albany, Gates informed Congress of the triumph: "I have the satisfaction to present your Excellency with the convention of Saratoga by which His Excellency Lt Gen. Burgoyne has surrendered himself & his whole Army into my hands & they are now on their march to Boston, this signal and important event is the more glorious as it was effected with so little loss to the Army of the United States."[72]

Gates accorded Wilkinson the singular honor of delivering the message by hand to Hancock. Although Wilkinson would turn out to be less than loyal, his actions and counsel had proved invaluable to Gates throughout the campaign. The victorious general asked Congress to promote his young prodigy. "[B]elieve me," he assured them, that from the very beginning of the war, "I have not met with a more promising Military Genius than Colonel Wilkinson."[73]

As the colonel set off on his journey to York, where Congress had established itself after the loss of Philadelphia, the commanding general departed for Albany, arriving late on October 18. Now that Burgoyne's army was no longer a threat, Gates shifted his gaze from the north to the south, focusing on "pushing the Army forward to stop the cruel cancer of General Vaughan up the Hudsons River."[74] After ensuring his army was properly positioned south of the city and prepared to meet Clinton or Vaughan should they appear, he dispatched reinforcements to Putnam and George Clinton, who had been clamoring for them. By October 25, Gates received word from Enoch Poor that General Vaughan had moved back down the river and that the immediate threat to Albany was over.[75] After the crisis subsided, Gates finally found time to write to Elizabeth: "The Voice of Fame ere this reaches you, will Tell how greatly Fortunate we have been in This Department: Burgoyne and his whole Army have laid down their Arms, & Surrendered themselves to me and my Yankees." Gates had harsh words for his native land: "If Old England is not by this lesson Taught Humility, then She is an Obstinate Old Slut, bent upon her Ruin."[76]

The same day Gates wrote to his wife, Burgoyne was also in Albany, though he had not arrived as he originally imagined he would. Comfortably lodged in Philip Schuyler's Albany home, along with the Riedesels, he wrote two letters to Germain, describing the events that occurred over the preceding five weeks. After "hard toil, incessant effort, stubborn action," the "total defection of the Indians, the desertion or the timidity of the Canadians and Provincials," with critically short provisions, after being abandoned by other British armies, and surrounded by an enemy army of sixteen thousand men, "I called into council all the generals, field officers, and captains commanding corps, and by their unanimous concurrence and advice I was induced to open a treaty with Major-General Gates." Arguing that his orders gave him no latitude, he explained that he was forced to cross to the west bank of the Hudson and make for Albany.[77]

He described the Battle of Freeman's Farm and the false hope of Sir Henry's Clinton's Hudson Highlands expedition. Explaining part of his rationale for not retreating after the first battle, he argued that a withdrawal would free up "such an army as General Gates's to act against Sir William Howe." Indeed, he claimed that he had to hold out for as long as possible because the "expedition I commanded was evidently meant at first to be *hazarded.* Circumstances might require it to be *devoted* [sacrificed]. A critical junction of Mr. Gates's force with Mr. Washington might possibly decide the fate of the war." This was a new twist. Now Burgoyne was arguing after the fact that his actions following the Battle of Freeman's Farm were meant to protect Howe's main army when he was actually focused on getting to Albany and hoping for assistance from Clinton. His last resort was a retreat back to Canada. The wellbeing of Howe's army most likely never entered Burgoyne's mind from early September onward, and he instead desperately hoped that Gates would send units south to face Sir Henry Clinton. It was yet another rationalization after the fact. Burgoyne hoped that Germain would view the Convention as "unavoidable and which I trust in that situation will be esteemed honourable."[78]

In his second letter written on October 20 to Germain, Burgoyne was not only very frank, he added to the defense he had already begun. He reminded Germain that forcing his way to Albany to link up with General Howe "was the principle, the letter, and the spirit of my orders." He suggested that he would not have pressed across the Hudson after the Battle of Bennington "had my orders instead of being preemptory been discretionary." He complained that the "promises of professing loyalists" had not come to fruition," and nor

had coordination with Howe or Clinton. Since he had no choice other than to advance, Burgoyne argued, the actions that took place in late September and October on the west bank of the Hudson must be viewed as "honourable misfortunes." He praised Riedesel but argued that if only his "force been *all* British," they might have held out longer. Still, he reassured Germain that all was not lost because the treaty with Gates preserved the army to defend the home country. In short, Burgoyne was very, very proud of the Convention.[79]

He admitted that his poor opinion of American troops after Ticonderoga had been dead wrong, and it was now his "duty to the state to confess it." Indeed, he said, the rebel soldiers "I have seen are disciplined. I do not hazard the term but apply it to the great fundamental points of military institution, sobriety, subordination, regularity and courage." Although the militia troops were not as disciplined, they were effective in fighting in the woods. The poor performance and outright panic they witnessed at Ticonderoga and afterward was "confined and of short duration," and American "enthusiasm is extensive and permanent."[80]

However right he was on some of these points, Burgoyne's defense doesn't stand up, and his gratuitous demeaning of the German troops was wholly unjustified. Months later, while in American captivity in Boston, Riedesel learned of the contents of Burgoyne's letter to Germain. In a public rebuttal, a furious Riedesel criticized his former chief for failing to retreat when he had the opportunity and for not taking the advice of his generals. He defended his troops, declaring that he would "rather be deprived of all praise than see his troops robbed of the same glory in a public and unjust manner."[81] Burgoyne's oft-repeated claim that he had no choice other than to push on to Albany was simply not true. His orders explicitly authorized him to use his discretion. As a senior independent commander, he was to apply his professional judgment and initiative to every situation, especially when his orders were written six months before and 3,000 miles away.

In another rambling letter to Colonel Richard Burton Phillipson, aide-de-camp to the king, also on October 20, Burgoyne offered a spirited defense of his conduct during the campaign. He wanted to ensure his story got out "in case the Ministry should mangle or curtail any part of it." He insisted that his orders were to blame for the disaster, not his own actions: "I expect ministerial ingratitude will be displayed, as in all countries and all times has been usual, to remove the blame from the order to the execution." Burgoyne complained that his army "has been totally unsupported by Sir William Howe."

This point contradicted Burgoyne's own claim that he was supposed to sacrifice the army for Howe. In a letter that he obviously wanted Phillipson to show the king, Burgoyne insisted that when all the details surrounding the campaign were finally revealed, "I am clear I shall receive honour and not disgrace from the public."[82]

While at Albany, Burgoyne apologized to Schuyler for destroying his Saratoga estate, calling it a regrettable "calamity." Schuyler shrugged it off as an unpleasant but unavoidable act of war.[83] A few days later, while still enjoying his erstwhile enemy's hospitality, Burgoyne wrote Sir Henry Clinton, offering yet more excuses. Burgoyne blamed Howe, his German allies, the massive American force, and finally Germain, for his downfall. "I seek no pardon; I only want justification," he wrote. If only Howe "enabled you to make the same movement you lately made one month sooner, or perhaps half that time, I believe our junction would have been effected." He then ripped into his German allies. The engagement on October 7 would have turned out much differently, he claimed, had only "the Germans fought like the British." He also laid out his preliminary case against Germain, arguing that he was sure the secretary would attack him for his conduct, continuing his grossly faulty line of reasoning that he and his army "have been a sacrifice of the minister to assist great purposes" of keeping Gates from linking up with Washington, which might have "decided the fate of the war." If Germain dared to blame him, "Such ingratitude would not surprize me—I think it will not sink me."[84] This letter, along with the others written both before and after he rejoined his army en route to Boston, defined how Burgoyne planned to defend himself from the attacks that would almost certainly come his way. He would assume no personal responsibility. He would instead blame Germain, Howe, the Germans, and just about everyone else.

As Gates prepared to take on Sir Henry Clinton or Vaughan, Washington was growing increasingly frustrated. He had been beaten twice by Howe at the battles of Brandywine and Germantown. The British had marched into Philadelphia, the Congress had moved to York, and he had received almost no news from or about the Northern Department. What intelligence he did have came from sources other than Gates. He had heard nothing from Gates since his brief October 5 letter refusing to return Morgan and his riflemen to the main army. Finally, on October 18, he received news from Israel Putnam that Burgoyne had surrendered to Gates. This was the result of Gates's premature announcement of the surrender to Putnam on October 15. An ecstatic Washington issued a general order to the

army announcing the glorious news, which he hoped would boost morale and spur the main army toward its own victories: "Let every face brighten, and every heart expand with grateful Joy and praise to the supreme disposer of all events, who has granted us this signal success." He also directed that the army fire a salute in recognition of the Northern Army's feat of arms.[85]

Washington immediately forwarded Putnam's news to Hancock, though he assumed that Congress had already received the report directly from Gates.[86] He was wrong. Washington and Congress soon learned that Putnam's news might have been premature. All they knew for certain was that Gates and his army were in a favorable position north of Albany, but could not dismiss the possibility of yet another setback. "We have been in a state of tormenting Uncertainty concerning our Affairs at the Northward," wrote John Adams. "On Sunday, We had News, from the Committee of Albany, through Governor Clinton and G. Washington, of a Capitulation of Burgoine and his whole Army. To this Moment We have no Express from Gates, nor any Authentic Confirmation."[87]

James Wilkinson was taking his sweet time getting to York with Gates's official report. A trip that should have taken just a few days took Wilkinson almost two weeks. At one stop in Reading, Pennsylvania, less than 60 miles from York, Wilkinson met with two delegates from Congress, Major General Thomas Mifflin, former quartermaster general of the Army, and Brigadier General Thomas Conway, an Irishman who had joined the American cause and commanded a brigade at Germantown. Over dinner, the five men praised Gates and criticized Washington's handling of the army. Wilkinson took the opportunity to regale his companions with Gates's unflattering commentary about the commander-in-chief. Also present was an aide to Major General Lord Stirling (William Alexander), who saw a letter from Conway to Gates disparaging Washington. The aide passed on the contents to Lord Stirling, who forwarded it several days later to his good friend, George Washington.[88] While the young colonel—the "promising military genius," as Gates had described him—dawdled and mocked Washington, an anxious Congress waited.

After enduring three days of heavy rain in York, John Adams wrote to Abigail that they were still waiting for authentic news from the Northern Department. Adding to the "Gloom is the Uncertainty in which We remain to this Moment," grumbled Adams, "concerning the Fate of Gates and Burgoigne. We are out of Patience. It is impossible to bear this suspence, with any Temper."[89] In a letter to Patrick Henry, Richard Henry Lee echoed Adams's sentiments: "For nine

days past, we have hourly expected the arrival of a Messenger."[90] Finally, on Friday, October 31, thirteen days after he departed the American camp at Saratoga, Wilkinson arrived in York and presented Gates's report to Congress.[91] The same day Congress dispatched a message to the American commissioners in Paris who were trying to negotiate a treaty with France. The commissioners were to use "this intelligence to depress our enemies and produce essential aid to our cause in Europe."[92] Congress instantly recognized the strategic implications of Gates's victory. Burgoyne's surrender was just what they were hoping for: a victory of such significant dimensions that the European powers—especially France—would not only recognize American independence but provide overt support.

Congress, now under the direction of its new president, South Carolinian Henry Laurens, reconvened late in the afternoon on Monday, November 3, and Wilkinson was called before the delighted delegates. He formally delivered a copy of the Convention, Gates's report, which listed returns of the troops, ordnance, and other provisions captured, and copies of all the messages exchanged between Burgoyne and Gates during the treaty negotiations. These were read to the delegates. Obviously anticipating that some members of Congress would view the Convention's terms as overly generous, Wilkinson argued that because attacking Burgoyne at Saratoga would have cost significant casualties, and rumors of Sir Henry Clinton's approach seemed reliable, "I am ordered to say that this delicate situation, abridged our conquest and procured Lieut: Genl. Burgoyne, the terms he enjoys."[93] The delegates promptly voted the Thanks of Congress to Gates, Arnold, Lincoln, "and the rest of the officers and troops under his command, for their brave and successful efforts in support of the independence of their country." In addition, they voted that a special gold medal be struck and presented to Gates. They also agreed to promote Wilkinson to brevet brigadier general for his services during the campaign.[94] Laurens joyfully assured Gates that "Your Name Sir will be written in the breasts of the grateful Americans of the present Age & sent down to Posterity in Characters which will remain indelible when the Gold shall have changed its appearance."[95]

The tributes had only just begun. While news of the victory may have taken a long time to make its way to York, the entire city of Boston erupted in spontaneous celebrations when they received word on October 20. The *Boston Gazette* reported that numerous toasts were drunk, and cannons and fireworks shot off and in "consequence [of the news] of which the colleges were beautifully illuminated in high

taste and elegance." A large bonfire was made on the Common and salutes fired in honor of Gates and his army. In most of the American colonies, as in Boston, when the news of Saratoga arrived, "Joy was in every face without a cloud."[96]

Throughout late October and November, Gates received many accolades and congratulations. "I most sincerely Congratulate you on the glorious Success with which the Almighty has Crowned your most faithful Indeavours in the cause of your Country," wrote Connecticut delegate Eliphalet Dyer to Gates.[97] Massachusetts delegate James Lovell also rejoiced in the "happy events which have taken place since you returned to the northern Department which had gone almost to ruin in your absence from it." Even those in Congress who favored Schuyler grudgingly approved of Gates's conduct, wrote Lovell: "If you are not Sincerely regarded here in general, yet there is at least a modesty as to any appearance of the old Opposition."[98] Those members of Congress who had voted for Gates to replace Schuyler back in the dark days of late July certainly felt vindicated now.

Some began to make the obvious comparison between successes in the Northern Department and operations around Philadelphia. In a letter to Adams, Benjamin Rush wrote that "General Gates's unparalleled success gave me great pleasure, but it has not obliterated the remembrance of the disorders I have seen in the army of this department." Some of Gates's senior officers of his acquaintance, Rush claimed, "compared Genl. Washington's imitation of an Army to an unformed mob," while Gates's army was a "well regulated family." Whereas Gates had planned his operations with "wisdom and executed with vigor and bravery," Washington was "outgeneraled and twice beaten . . . and forced to give up the capital of a state."[99] Rush was not the only prominent figure in and out of Congress and the army who began to think that Gates, rather than Washington, was the man who could secure independence for the new nation.

As Congress and the rest of America rejoiced over the news of Saratoga, the last remnants of the great British expedition from Canada abandoned the site of their first triumph and returned north. Brigadier General Powell, who had been assigned by Burgoyne to command the British-German garrison at Ticonderoga and its surrounding fortifications, received confirmation of Burgoyne's surrender on October 20. After deliberating with his officers, Powell decided to return to Canada and there rejoin Carleton in the defense of the province. Now that the army was in American hands, and no other British forces were coming up the Hudson River, there was

no reason to hold on to Ticonderoga and Mount Independence. In early November, Powell led the garrison out of Ticonderoga, but not before "the barracks and blockhouses [were] burnt and razed to the ground, and not the least vestige of what it was left." By November 11, Powell and his one-thousand-man detachment (including the small parties stationed on Lake George) reached Saint-Jean on the Richelieu River, the exact spot from which Burgoyne's army had confidently departed five and a half months earlier to begin the campaign that would end the American rebellion. With Powell's arrival at Saint-Jean, the Saratoga campaign was over.[100]

CHAPTER 22

British Strategic Reassessment

THE NEWS OF BURGOYNE'S surrender reached London late in the evening on December 2, 1777, and had an immediate and profound impact on British civilian and military leadership.[1] The loss of an army was only the most obvious result. Direct foreign intervention in the war by Britain's historic enemies France and Spain was now a very real possibility. Homeland defense took on new urgency. Saratoga meant that the war would drag on into the foreseeable future and be the catalyst for a major transformation of British naval and land strategic concepts and significant changes in key military leadership.[2]

Writing to Sir Henry Clinton from London, Lieutenant General Sir Hugh Percy noted that the news of the Saratoga defeat "you will readily conceive, has occasioned the greatest consternation." He added that he would not be surprised if "a change of both men and measures" resulted.[3] There would indeed be a change of both men and measures, though any strategic choices Great Britain made at this point in the war were sure to be unpalatable and expensive.

Less than two weeks before hearing the stunning news, while opening Parliament on November 20, the king expressed confidence that he would continue to receive full support "for the suppression of the revolt" in America.[4] To members of Parliament, the king spoke ominously of "the necessity of preparing for such future operations, as the contingencies of war, and the obstinacy of the rebels, may render expedient." Yet he also "shall be ever watchful of an opportunity of putting a stop to the effusion of the blood of my

subjects." Further, he gave conflicting reports of the threat Britain faced from its traditional enemies: "I receive repeated assurances from foreign powers, of their pacific dispositions. My own cannot be doubted: but . . . I have thought it advisable to make a considerable augmentation to my naval force." The speech did not go over well with the Whig opposition in Parliament.[5]

William Pitt, the 1st Earl of Chatham, the country's leader during the Seven Years War and now a vocal critic of the American conflict, criticized the king and especially his ministers by saying that despite George III's optimism, the country's condition was "perilous." He argued that they should not be fighting the Americans but preparing to defend themselves against France and Spain.[6]

By the Tuesday, December 2, meeting of Parliament, the rumors of a major military setback in America were running rampant. The opposition stepped up its pressure on the government to unprecedented levels.[7] Diplomat William Eden received a report from one of his agents in France whose humor was surely not appreciated: "Burgoyne has been forced to capitulate. . . . This news won't help you digest your supper."[8] Later that evening, the king finally received confirmation he expected, but desperately hoped was wrong, and "fell into agonies on hearing this account."[9] The next day, Germain was forced to admit to the Commons that Burgoyne, his army having "been surrounded by a force greatly superior," had surrendered.[10]

The normally raucous House of Commons erupted with outrage. Edmund Burke, so overcome with emotion that he had to pause before speaking, blamed the defeat on Germain and the cabinet.[11] Prominent anti-war Whig Charles James Fox accused the cabinet of criminal negligence.[12] North rose to express "sorrow at the unhappy news" and defend himself and the cabinet for their conduct of the war. He offered faint praise for Germain who "had acted on the soundest principles of candour and deliberation."[13] The government's experience in the House of Lords was no different from that in the Commons. Chatham praised the military and its leaders while condemning North, Germain, and the rest of the king's cabinet for Burgoyne's "melancholy disaster," declaring that "the glory of British arms . . . had been sacrificed to the ignorance, temerity, and incapacity of ministers."[14]

Burgoyne's defeat forced British leaders to reassess their overall situation and devise a new military strategy for the American war. The 1778 strategy formulation process was quite different from the one a year earlier. The 1777 strategy had been created and executed

almost exclusively by Germain, Howe, and Burgoyne, with input from the king. The rest of the cabinet had approved the 1777 military strategy, making few meaningful contributions. In contrast, a number of players were involved in Britain's strategic reassessment after Saratoga. North, Germain, and the king were intimately involved, of course, but input from other advisors was sought. John Montagu, the Earl of Sandwich and First Lord of Admiralty, played a significant role as did several key diplomats.[15]

While the diversity of opinion consulted during the reassessment was impressive, neither Germain nor North talked to their commanders in America. The British leadership requested no input from the Howe brothers or their replacements. Thus those with the most extensive knowledge of the overall situation—the enemy, the terrain, and the people—had virtually no role in the post-Saratoga strategic reassessment. Howe's and Burgoyne's advice had not borne fruit in 1777, and the government, especially Germain, did not enjoy good relations with any of the senior officers in America. Nonetheless, this was a noteworthy omission.

Even before the news of Saratoga reached London, Howe asked to be relieved. "From the little attention My Lord [has] given to my recommendations since the commencement of my command," he wrote in October, "I am led to hope I may be relieved from this very painful service."[16] Howe's request was granted, and he was replaced by his subordinate, Sir Henry Clinton, on February 4, 1778.[17] Sir Guy Carleton, still bristling over the fact that Germain had relieved him of his military command in Canada, also demanded once again to be replaced.[18] Future prime minister William Petty, the Earl of Shelburne, observed that it was not surprising that the military setback at Saratoga had occurred when one considered the fact that Clinton was "jealous of general Burgoyne," that Howe had little "confidence in Mr. Clinton," and that the governor of Quebec, Sir Guy Carleton, "had shewn the utmost indifference for all these gentlemen." Only when senior officers work hand-in-hand can a war be won, he said, but the "opposite to this had been the case in America."[19]

Not only did these men not get along, but they had also lost confidence in their political leadership, and their political leadership had lost confidence in them. By the start of the strategic reassessment in late 1777, relationships between British Army leaders in America, and between Germain and the senior British military, were simply dysfunctional. By the early summer of 1778, all the major commanders of British land and naval forces in America had been replaced.[20]

A few weeks after he had asked to be relieved, Howe offered a few strategic options for Germain to consider. Howe cautioned him that unless the British forces in America were heavily reinforced, "I do not apprehend a successful termination to the war from any advantages His Majesty's troops can gain while the enemy is able to avoid, or is unwilling to hazard, a decisive action." This was a concise description of Washington's military strategy. He went on to offer other options. The British could give up one of its major bases (New York, Philadelphia, or Rhode Island) and then use troops thus freed up to conduct offensive operations. Britain could also continue to act on the defensive, which could hamper American logistical efforts, but "it might on the other hand, by protracting the war produce events, which may not be prudent to risk."[21] Howe had contributed to the failure of the campaign of 1777, but he was right that only a military strategy that ended in the destruction of Washington's army could achieve victory. His advice was sound, and the government should have listened to their most strategically able general.

The king started the strategic reassessment on December 4 with a letter to Lord North. He urged the cabinet to view Saratoga in its "true light, as very serious, but not without remedy." He suggested that the remaining forces in American go on the defensive and urged that "those who have served in those parts" be consulted, as they "will be able to point out what is best." The king had in mind Lord Jeffrey Amherst rather than Clinton or Howe.[22] Amherst had been commander-in-chief of the British Army in America during the French and Indian War and presided over the capture of Canada.[23] Most importantly, he was the king's confidant and therefore played a crucial role in developing the new military strategy for 1778. The king suggested they retain several bases in North America but omitted Philadelphia. Howe had expended considerable army and navy resources, effort, and time to capture Philadelphia, yet he had not lured Washington into a decisive battle.[24] Holding on to the city now was looking increasingly counterproductive.

Sandwich was the first to submit his ideas for going forward, arguing that although the Royal Navy had "been employed in convoying, embarking and disembarking the troops, and attending the operations of the army," it should return to its traditional roles of blockading and hunting down American privateers, merchant ships, and naval vessels. He proposed that the army seize additional naval bases so the king's ships "can be maintained so as to answer the purposes expected."[25] He reminded his cabinet colleagues that with the Saratoga defeat, the French would likely enter the conflict.

Not only were they vulnerable at home, but they were also at risk in the Leeward Islands, Jamaica, and in North America, and more ships were needed to secure these possessions. France and Spain were "only waiting for the favourable moment to strike a blow."[26] Before Saratoga, homeland defense and protecting overseas possessions were low priorities. Not anymore.

During the parliamentary recess, which took place from December 1777 to January 1778, North worked on his plans for a conciliation scheme with the Americans. The prime minister had long advocated a major diplomatic effort that offered generous terms to the rebels, but now he wanted to combine it with the new military strategy. Anticipating the cabinet's plans, George Spencer, the Third Duke of Marlborough, hoped that North was not thinking "of sending more troops, for I suppose, they may as well think of subduing the ocean by force of arms."[27] When in early January the duke heard about the conciliatory scheme that North proposed, he wrote William Eden that "I really truly do not know . . . of any better plan of operations than the one you mention." However, he also thought there was little chance the Americans would accept it.[28]

Throughout all of the discussions on what steps to take in North America, the king was crystal clear in reaffirming Britain's overall strategic objective when he told North that while they may have to temporarily scale back military operations in North America due to the loss of Burgoyne's army, "to treat with Independence can never be possible."[29]

George III's major contribution to the strategic reassessment was insisting that Lord Amherst play a key role. In the absence of Howe's and Clinton's input, Amherst's professional military advice was critical. The king directed the cabinet to consult him on the subject of "conducting the American war." Amherst thought that an army of forty thousand men would be required to conduct "an offensive land war." Since that was impossible, he agreed with Sandwich that a sea war was the "only wise plan." At this point in the war, destroying American commerce would have a greater chance of success than land-based operations.[30] Amherst and Sandwich recommended a naval blockade of America, the occupation of a few key bases, and targeted and limited offensive operations because "under our present circumstances the future Operation must be principally Naval, to distress their Trade and prevent their Supplies from Europe."[31] Saratoga had significantly changed the art of the possible in military strategic terms. After Saratoga the choices available to the British planners were very limited. If France entered the war—and

almost everybody in Great Britain believed it would—there would be even fewer.

As discussions of a predominately naval war progressed, Germain saw an opening to pursue a concept that he had favored for a long time: subduing the southern colonies. Howe had considered this option the year before but dropped it when it became clear that taking Philadelphia would be challenging enough. Germain thought a move into the American South made great sense. For some time, the southern Royal governors had pushed for a major operation into the region, which would not require extensive extra resources—an important consideration if the French intervened. It was generally believed that Loyalist sentiment prevailed in the South, and this would help facilitate military operations. Germain successfully inserted a southern component into the strategy.[32]

As the new military strategy took shape, the king urged North to push forward his conciliation plan. Once the naval war was implemented, the United States would be "more ready to treat that at the present hour."[33] Before Saratoga, George III flatly refused to negotiate with the rebels, but with the threat of French intervention, he was willing to try almost anything. On February 11, North announced the conciliatory proposal to Parliament, igniting a boisterous debate in both houses. North maintained that his proposal was offered not out of weakness after Saratoga, but because the war's uncertainty persuaded him that the Conciliatory Acts be issued with terms that were "substantially the same as he should propose in the height of victory."[34] Parliament was stunned: "A dull melancholy silence for some time succeeded to this speech," recorded an observer, "Astonishment, dejection, and fear, overclouded the whole assembly."[35] Fox told North that his proposals were too little too late and demanded to know if the prime minister was aware of a treaty between France and America. Were this true, Fox declared, North's proposals were worthless. North admitted that the rumor might well be correct. The stories were true: although London did not get an official notification for weeks, France and the United States had signed a Treaty of Amity and Commerce and a Treaty of Alliance on February 6, 1778.[36]

The legislation finally passed in March and led to the formation of the so-called Carlisle Peace Commission, led by the king's friend, Frederick Howard, 5th Earl of Carlisle, and composed of diplomats and senior military officers. The commission, it was hoped, in combination with Parliament's repeal of many of the acts that Americans found so repugnant, would coax the errant colonies back into the

British fold. In short, as one historian has observed, the commissioners were authorized to give the Americans "any terms short of independence."[37] These were major concessions to the Americans, but, as Fox had warned, they were too little and too late.

The specter of a formal Franco-American alliance worried British decision makers more than anything, compelling the king to warn that should the French expand the war, it would mean that any operations against the rebels and against Great Britain's rivals "must be feeble in all parts and consequently unsuccessful."[38] George III's assessment of the situation in the likely event of direct French involvement was on the mark. He was right to warn against strategic overreach.

A sense of urgency animated the ministers in late February and early March. North urged his cabinet colleagues to "go forward with our military preparations with great diligence."[39] Finally, after months of deliberations, on March 8, 1778, Germain dispatched the final military strategy to Sir Henry Clinton. The new plan promised ten to twelve thousand reinforcements and directed Clinton to seek opportunities to defeat Washington's army. His primary mission, however, was to support the Royal Navy's effort to strangle American trade. Once this was accomplished, he could begin operations into the South, where he could "raise and employ the well affected inhabitants in all the provinces where any posts are maintained, or operations carried on." Operations against Savannah and Charleston, in particular, claimed Germain, would convince American planters of "the necessity of abandoning, or being abandoned by, their slaves, or submitting to the King's authority."[40] The new commander-in-chief was also authorized to evacuate Philadelphia, informed of the Carlisle Peace Commission, and, probably as a reaction to Burgoyne's justifications for his recent decisions, was explicitly directed to use his own best judgment.

Three days after the new strategy was dispatched to Clinton, the French ambassador to Great Britain informed the king of the treaties between the United States and France. Although the intelligence was expected, it still caught the government flat-footed. The new strategy just sent to Clinton only indirectly addressed the very real probability of direct French military intervention. The treaties, which were "certainly equivalent to a declaration" of war, "must entirely overturn every plan proposed for strengthening the army under the command of Lieut.-Gen. Clinton with an intent to carry on an active war in North America," wrote an outraged George III. With France now in the war, retaining Pennsylvania was "a joke."[41] The troops

garrisoning Philadelphia were now needed to invade the French West Indies and increase the troop levels in Ireland.[42] Amherst agreed with the king's assessment and told him that orders should immediately be sent to America to take troops from Philadelphia and send them to New York.[43] The beginning of a French war "will be the end of an offensive American one."[44] On March 17, 1778, Great Britain declared war on France.

In late March, North told the king that the country was not ready for a war with America, France, and Spain. He believed that Britain would lose such a war, not because of military defeats, but because the enormous expense would ruin the country. "Great Britain," North argued, "will undo herself while she thinks of punishing France." If the expanded war led to disaster, it would be attributed to the government's "obstinate perseverance in the American War."[45]

With France's entry into the war, Britain faced an almost unprecedented strategic challenge. Even with considerable effort, only ten to twelve thousand troops had been scraped together to reinforce Clinton before France came into the war. Now, most of these troops would have to be used elsewhere, including defending British possessions in the West Indies and Canada, not to mention the home islands. A British fleet that was already too small would be pulled in many directions. Great Britain was now in a global war without allies or enough resources to conduct the operations it needed to achieve its objectives. Despite almost universal recognition that America was now a secondary theater, British decision makers—particularly George III—were unwilling to let the colonies go. Without taking that bold step, they would have to find a way to conduct the American war on the cheap, while refocusing their efforts on France.

As the opposition attacks intensified, North put on a brave face in the House of Commons, but with the king he was brutally frank. North begged the king to release him from his post, arguing that "the present Ministry cannot continue a fortnight as it is."[46] The king flatly refused: "I would rather lose the Crown I now wear than bear the ignominy of possessing it under their [the opposition's] shackles."[47] North argued that the king needed "*new* men and *able* men" to provide fresh perspectives. North ultimately agreed to stay on but warned the king that his loyalty to his prime minister "may prove ruinous to the Public."[48]

Amherst recognized that the war in America was now "a secondary consideration," and thus, "our principal object must be distressing France and defending and securing our own possessions against their hostile Attempts."[49] The cabinet agreed and decided to attack French possessions in the West Indies—a region critical to Britain's

economic security.[50] Still, the king and his ministers were not ready to give up America.

In new orders to Clinton dated March 21, the king directed five thousand troops to seize the French island of St. Lucia and reinforce British possessions in the West Indies. Clinton was ordered to evacuate Philadelphia and move the army to New York. Once in New York, he was directed to "wait the issue of the treaty which we have authorized our commissioners to pursue."[51] Clinton was also told that he could no longer expect the reinforcements he had previously been promised, though it was still hoped that he would "keep up an alarm on the seacoasts of the rebellious provinces and perhaps disable them from materially annoying their trade."[52] For now at least, operations against the Southern colonies were on hold. Maintaining the economic security of Great Britain and striking a blow against French interests trumped almost all other considerations.[53] This meant that the new and hastily conceived strategy could not possibly achieve the newly modified British objectives—defeat the French and prevent American independence—at least for the foreseeable future.[54] Six days after Clinton's new instructions were sent to North America, George III was so determined to "avenge the faithless and insolent conduct of France" that he seemed to indicate an openness to reconsidering independence for America.[55] Sadly this was not pursued.

Once France intervened in the war, British leaders needed to address the central question: in a war with France, America, and potentially other European powers, did they have what it would take to achieve their goals, meaning defeat the French and subdue the Americans? It is not that this question was never asked—North, Amherst, and even the king considered it—but they simply could not and would not act on it. They would have done well to consider something Carl von Clausewitz observed early in the next century: "Once the expenditure of effort exceeds the value of the political object, the object must be renounced and peace must follow."[56]

Clinton evacuated Philadelphia on June 18, 1778, and began a long march back to New York with Washington following close behind. In an attempt to inflict some damage on the British Army, Washington attacked on June 28 near Monmouth Courthouse (present-day Freehold Borough, New Jersey). Although the battle ended in a standoff, it increased American confidence and proved that they could stand toe-to-toe with British regulars. Monmouth was probably the last chance the British had of forcing a decisive battle with Washington, but as ever, the American commander-in-chief made sure he did not get himself into an impossible situation.

The Carlisle Peace Commissioners failed. Congress flatly rejected any peace overtures that did not include unconditional independence. On June 17, 1778, the same day that Congress rejected the Carlisle Commission's proposals, Henry Laurens observed in a letter to Gates, "If all the fine things now offered had been tended some time ago . . . there can be no doubt but that the people of America would joyfully have embraced the proposition." Instead, the British "seem to mistake our understanding as once they did our resolve."[57] Later that summer, upon hearing that their negotiations with the Americans had gone nowhere, an exasperated George III wrote, "Farther concession is a joke; all that can now be done is steadily to pursue the plan very wisely adopted in the spring."[58] The commissioners returned to England empty-handed in November 1778. A joint British Army-Navy operation seized St. Lucia in December 1778, and the "Southern Strategy" was finally begun late in 1778.

The post-Saratoga strategic reassessment was not conducted in a vacuum. British strategy makers confronted many challenges. George III, Lord North, Germain, and the other ministers had not only to deal with the loss at Saratoga, and greatly improved American morale and confidence, they also had to face the possibility of a general war with France and Spain; they had to provide for the defense of the homeland and protection of British trade at home and abroad; they faced a vocal and increasingly effective political opposition; and they had to work through personality conflicts among senior military commanders.[59]

Saratoga prompted a wide-ranging, thorough, and sober review and reworking of British military strategy. The king and his advisers considered numerous points of view and were willing to change the strategic concepts they had previously adopted. The process was iterative: the leaders were willing to revisit concepts and issues again and again until satisfied that they had made the best choices available. All of this was accomplished while under intense political pressure. Some of their assumptions—that Loyalist sentiment in the Southern colonies was widespread, for example—turned out to be wrong. An assumption that should have been made, but was not, was that French intervention after Saratoga was inevitable. Although the king made some slight adjustments to the war's objectives in the face of political pressure and military reality, once the Franco-American treaties were made public, decision makers should have conducted an honest reconsideration of Britain's war aims as part of creating their new strategy, but because they did not, the war continued for another five years.

CHAPTER 23

The Fruits of Victory

FOR TWO WEEKS AFTER it happened, as we've seen, Washington had received only second-hand reports of Gates's victory at Saratoga. Commiserating with Benjamin Lincoln about his leg wound, the commander-in-chief hoped that the "glorious termination of the Campaign against Genl Burgoine" might "in its consequences, free us from all our oppressors."[1] Washington knew that it would have profound effects far beyond the confines of North America. Finally, on October 26, he received a letter from General Putnam confirming Burgoyne's surrender and a copy of the Convention. He had, of course, not heard the news directly from Gates, and therefore, he grumbled, did "not know what steps he is taking with the Army under his command."[2] Two days later, Washington wrote to Richard Henry Lee that while Burgoyne's surrender was a "great, and glorious event," he could not "help complaining, most bitterly, of Genl Gates's neglect in not giving me the earliest authentic advice of it."[3] Since late August, all of Gates's official correspondence had been with Congress and John Hancock. Washington was acutely aware that he had lost two battles and that many blamed him for losing Philadelphia as well, while Gates was suddenly the toast of the country. It was only natural that he would view his subordinate's actions with suspicion. Gates's cavalier attitude toward his commander worsened their already shaky relationship.

On October 30, the commander-in-chief had still not heard from Gates, so he wrote the Northern Department commander. Washington began with hearty congratulations for "the signal

success of the Army under your command." Formalities observed, Washington got right to the point: "At the same time, I cannot but regret, that a matter of such magnitude and so interesting to our General Operations, should have reached me by report only."[4]

To drive home his displeasure, Washington dispatched Alexander Hamilton to hand-deliver the letter and ensure that Gates quickly transferred units from the Northern Department to the main army. Washington directed Hamilton to explain to Gates "in the Clearest and fullest manner . . . the absolute necessity that there is for his detaching a very considerable part of the Army at present under his Command to the reinforcement of this." If Washington received these reinforcements in a timely manner, he could "in all probability reduce Genl Howe to the same situation in which Genl Burgoine now is, should he attempt to remain in Philadelphia." Washington specifically asked for three New Hampshire and twenty Massachusetts Continental regiments, Morgan's riflemen (if they were not already on their way south), as well as Glover's and Nixon's brigades.[5] This was a delicate mission for a twenty-one-year-old officer, but Hamilton left immediately, met Morgan's men on their way to join Washington, and continued north, arriving at Putnam's headquarters in Fishkill, New York, on November 2 and Gates's headquarters in Albany on Wednesday, November 5.

That same day Hamilton arrived in Fishkill, Gates wrote Washington his first letter in a month, informing him that Morgan and his riflemen were on their way to join the main army. In defense of his failure to keep Washington personally informed, Gates maintained that "Congress having been requested, immediately to transmit Copies of all my Dispatches to them, I am Confident Your Excellency has long ago received all the Good News from this Quarter."[6] Gates was correct to keep Congress informed, given the unusual relationship between that body and the Northern Department. However, that did not relieve him of the responsibility of communicating and coordinating with Washington.[7] Well aware of Howe's twin victories over Washington outside Philadelphia, Gates wrote that it was his "Ardent Wish" that "Conquest, and Triumphs, may be the final Results of Your Excellencys Campaign."[8]

Gates took the arrival of the brash and supremely self-confident Hamilton as Washington probably anticipated: badly. The two officers clashed almost immediately. In accordance with his instructions from Washington, Hamilton proposed that two of Gates's three remaining brigades be sent to join the main army. Gates made a case for one brigade, his smallest, which Hamilton rejected, arguing that he did

not consider the offer "compatible with the good of the service or my instructions from His Excellency George Washington." He insisted that another brigade be added to it.[9] Gates refused, reasoning that he had no good intelligence on Sir Henry Clinton's movements, and such a move would open New England up for invasion. Hamilton wrote Washington to say that he had failed in his mission. He had done everything he could to get Gates to give up two brigades but found him "inflexible" on the subject. "The force of these reasons did by no means strike me," wrote Hamilton, "and I did everything in my power to show they were unsubstantial." When Gates continued to insist on parting only with the one small brigade, Hamilton didn't know what to do. He felt he could not afford to push much harder. Given Gates's increased stature, if anything went wrong, "there would be too fair a pretext for censure [of Washington], and many people are too-well-disposed to lay hold of."[10]

Hamilton was walking a tightrope, trying to wrest as many troops as possible out of Gates while avoiding anything that might damage Washington's status. Hamilton gave Gates a day to cool down. "Having given General Gates a little time to recollect himself," Hamilton explained to Washington, "I renewed my remonstrances on the necessity and propriety of sending you more than one Brigade."[11]

Gates was furious that Washington had sent the young upstart officer to his headquarters. On November 7, he complained that Hamilton had "verbally Demanded" almost two-thirds of his remaining troops. Gates warned Washington that "every good Effect of the ruin of Genl Burgoyne's Army" would be lost if the enemy should strike at Albany with his army in its weakened state. Gates conveniently omitted the fact that there was no imminent threat of enemy action in the region. Despite his misgivings and "Upon mature consideration of all Circumstances," Gates ordered General Glover's brigade to join the rest of the troops he was sending to Washington, but his anger persisted. The loss of troops was bad enough, but it was Washington's dispatch of Hamilton, along with the colonel's prickly nature, that really upset Gates. In a draft of the November 7 letter, Gates wrote, but subsequently omitted, a passage that revealed just how angry he was: "Although it is Customary & even Absolutely necessary to direct Implicit Obedience to be paid to the Verbal Orders of Aids de Camp in Action, as while upon the Service & with this Army upon this Spot—yet I believe it is never practiced to Delegate that Dictatorial power to One Aid de Camp sent to an Army 300 Miles distant."[12]

Washington nevertheless had conveyed two very clear signals to Gates by sending Hamilton on his mission to Albany. First, he

reminded Gates that he was in charge, and it did not matter how many victories Gates won. Second, sending very pointed orders to be delivered by a very young aide was a message in and of itself. Gates's defiance forced his hand.

Washington's dreams of surrounding Howe in Philadelphia with his heavily reinforced army and forcing his surrender, just as Gates had done to Burgoyne at Saratoga, were soon dashed. Sir William Howe, with support from Royal Navy warships, succeeded at great cost in opening the Delaware River to shipping, despite defensive operations by elements of the Continental Army. By November 16, the British established a reliable line of communications to Philadelphia by sea, ensuring they could maintain control of the city almost indefinitely. Washington first moved the army on to Whitemarsh, 14 miles north of the city. Finally, in mid-December, Washington led the army 20 miles to the west of Philadelphia to a place called Valley Forge.[13]

Washington carefully read the Saratoga Convention and immediately recognized that the terms were highly favorable to Great Britain, especially the article that allowed Burgoyne's army to be sent home and replaced one-for-one with other troops. After the Convention Army arrived in Boston, there arose several disputes over whether or not Burgoyne had lived up to the agreement. As these disputes surfaced, Washington instructed Major General William Heath, who was responsible for supervising Burgoyne and his army in Boston, not to give in on any point, explaining that it was not in "our interest to expedite the passage of the prisoners to England," given that they could easily be replaced. Heath was not to approve any request from Burgoyne or Sir William Howe that did not strictly adhere to the letter of the Convention. Any "indulgence will be attended with most obvious & capital disadvantages to us."[14]

In early November, Washington began to fear that certain American senior leaders were aiming to remove him from his post. While it is unlikely that there was an organized plot to replace Washington with Gates, dissatisfaction with the commander-in-chief ran high, and Washington knew it. Washington had his critics—James Lovell, John Adams, Benjamin Rush, John Dickinson Sergeant, Brigadier General Anthony Wayne, and Major General Thomas Mifflin among them.[15]

On November 4, as he was supervising the setup of the army's camp at Whitemarsh, Washington received Lord Stirling's note forwarding Brigadier General Conway's disparaging comments. Stirling sent the offending passage without comment: "In a Letter from Genl Conway to Genl Gates he says—'Heaven has been determind to save

your Country; or a weak General and bad Councellors would have ruind it.' "[16] This was the first hint of what historians have dubbed the "Conway Cabal." Washington had little respect for Conway and had in mid-October adamantly opposed his promotion to brigadier general, explaining to Richard Henry Lee that he was a man whose principle merit "as an officer, and his importance in this Army, exists more in his own imagination than in reality."[17] Instead of directly attacking Conway or Gates, or defending his honor with an elaborate response, Washington merely forwarded the offending quote to its author, writing, "a Letter which I received last Night, containd the following, paragraph."[18]

Conway protested in reply that while he may have voiced some criticism in the past on how the army was being managed, he had never written the words quoted in Washington's letter. Indeed, Conway insisted, he only had the greatest respect for Washington, "a Brave man, an honest Man, a Patriot, and a Man of great sense." He should have left it there. Instead, Conway charged the commander-in-chief with allowing himself to be "influenc'd by men who Were not equal to you in point of experience, Knowledge or judgment." He denied ever calling Washington a "Weak General," and blamed unnamed staff officers for spreading lies. Conway concluded with a subtle warning: "I mean to Write an impartial account of the operations Which I saw During this campaign. this account Will be such that i am sure you Will acknowledge to be true. and I pledge my Word of a Gentleman and of an officer that I Will Write nothing in that account but What i Will impart to you" in person.[19]

Conway immediately sent word to Mifflin that Washington had obtained a copy of the letter to Gates, and Mifflin, in turn, warned Gates that Conway's letter to him had been sent to headquarters. "The extract was a collection of just sentiments; yet, such as should not have been entrusted to any of your family." Mifflin meant Wilkinson. Mifflin assured Gates that Conway did not apologize, "on the contrary, although some reflections were made on some people, yet the practice was pleaded boldly, and no satisfaction given." He cautioned Gates to be careful with what he shared with his officers because his words and letters "cannot injure yourself, but may injure some of your best friends."[20]

While there may not have been an established conspiracy between Mifflin, Conway, Gates, and others, the exchange of correspondence between the three men show that they were undermining the commander-in-chief.[21] Once Gates learned that Washington had possession of his embarrassing, and perhaps worse, correspondence

with Conway, he went on the offensive. Acting as if he were the injured party, Gates told the commander-in-chief that he was mortified to discover that "confidential Letters" had been "exposed to public Inspection." Gates, like Conway, tried to deflect the blame elsewhere when confronted with the damning evidence. He asked Washington to help him find the "Author of the Infedelity" who must have "stealingly copied" the communication. Since no one on his staff could possibly have done such a thing, Gates argued, Washington must help him "by detecting a Wretch, who may betray me, and capitally injure the very Operations under your immediate Direction."[22] Gates was accusing Hamilton of surreptitiously copying Gates's private correspondence when he had visited Albany.

Hoping to head off any potential blowback from Congress, Gates uncharacteristically went on the offensive and sent Laurens a copy of his letter to Washington, adding that the "same Anxiety dictates this Letter, that the whole being communicated to Congress, the Criminal may be the sooner detected." He assured Laurens that "the traiterous Thief" would soon be identified.[23] By deflecting and then going directly to Congress about the incident, he played into Washington's hands. Washington waited a full month before answering Gates, letting him hang in the wind.

As if Washington did not have enough to worry about, Congress appointed both Mifflin and Gates to the Board of War, a body established in 1776 at Washington's urging to relieve some of the commander-in-chief's heavy administrative burdens. It was originally composed of delegates to Congress, but in early November 1777, Mifflin was added to the board along with several other officers. He, in turn, convinced Congress to appoint Gates as the board's president. To add insult to injury, the reorganized board was given powers that allowed it to supervise the army and its commander. James Lovell urged his friend to accept the appointment, arguing that it was the next best thing to replacing Washington.[24] Gates accepted, seeing the high-profile post as another way to boost his prestige. In December, over Washington's protest, Congress promoted Conway to major general and appointed him as the new inspector general. Now all three of the major players intriguing against Washington had been elevated to important positions.[25]

Washington handled these slights, some trivial, others more significant, with aplomb. When he finally responded to Gates December 8 letter, Washington expressed surprise that Gates had sent a copy of his letter to Congress, which meant he had "the disagreeable necessity of returning my answer through the same channel, lest any member

of that honble body, should harbour an unfavourable suspicion of my having practiced some indirect means, to come at the contents of the confidential Letters between you & General Conway." It was his own Colonel Wilkinson, not Hamilton, nor anyone else connected to Washington, who had leaked the offending letter. He had sent a copy to Conway "without having any thing more in view than merely to shew that Gentn that I was not unapprized of his intrieguing disposition." Washington informed Gates that he never imagined that there was any malicious leak of the original letter. Instead, he believed that Gates, through Wilkinson, had given it "with a friendly view to forewarn, and consequently forearm me, against a secret enemy," or, in other words, Conway. Washington sadly concluded, however, that "in this, as in other matters of late, I have found myself mistaken."[26] Washington adroitly redirected Gates's attacks back against him, taking the high road, while Gates sputtered and dissembled.

Gates, now at York as president of the Board of War, responded three weeks later that he was "relieved" that Washington thought he had only been warning him about Conway. Nonetheless, he also claimed that Conway's insulting letter "conveyed to Your Excellency, as a genuine Part of it, was in Words, as well as in Substance, a wicked Forgery." Even while he argued that the passage was wholly made up, he maintained that frank assessments of senior officers were by no means unusual and that Conway had written "to me as a candid Observer, as other Officers in every Service freely write to each other." He then suggested that the forger might well be Colonel Wilkinson, or Hamilton, or some other staff member. Gates regretted that Washington had attacked Conway in his last letter because he had always found "that Gentleman a firm, and constant Friend to America." Besides, he claimed, he hardly knew Conway and had, in fact, just recently met him in person.[27] The lecturing tone was typical of Gates, especially after Saratoga.

From the army's camp at Valley Forge, Washington replied to Gates on February 9 and proceeded to dissect his arguments. First, Washington found "no small difficulty in reconciling the spirit and import of your different Letters, and sometimes of the different parts of the same Letter with each other." He dismissed out of hand Gates's claim that the critical passage was faked as it "must appear somewhat strange that the forgery remained so long undetected; and that your first Letter to me from Albany of the 8th of Decemr should tacitly recognize the genuineness of the paragraph in question." He also questioned why Gates was outraged over the violation of his confidential correspondence when both he and Conway had

shown it to members of Congress and others. Washington closed by refusing to back down from his assessment of Conway in his last letter to Gates: "I cannot perswade my self to retract the prediction concerning him; which you so emphatically wish had not been inserted in my Last." Washington was an able judge of Conway's character since he had a "better acquaintance with him, than I have reason to think you have had, from what you say."[28] Washington had essentially accused Gates of obfuscation and even duplicity, and the case he made was unassailable.

When the commander-in-chief's letter finally made its way to York, Gates realized that he had no more cards to play. He had tried outrage, he had gone on the offensive, he had blamed others, he had defended Conway, and he even claimed to be a victim of a forgery. On February 19, he pleaded with Washington that they devote no more time "upon the Subject of General Conways Letter, whether that Gentleman does, or does not deserve the Suspicions you Express, would be intirely indifferent to me." Gates then swallowed his pride and apologized: "I Solemnly declare that I am of no Faction; & if any of my Letters taken aggregately, or by paragraphs, convey any meaning, which under any construction, is Offensive to Your Excellency; that was by no means the intention of the Writer."[29] Washington's reply was short and direct and is worth quoting in full to reveal the completeness of his victory over Gates:

> I am as averse to controversy, as any Man, and had I not been forced into it, you never would have had occasion to impute to me, even the shadow of a disposition towards it. Your repeatedly & solemnly disclaiming any offensive views in those matters, which have been the subject of our past correspondence, makes me willing to close with the desire, you express, of burying them hereafter in silence, and, as far as future events will permit, oblivion.
>
> My temper leads me to peace and harmony with all Men; and it is particularly my wish, to avoid any personal feuds or dissentions with those, who are embarked in the same great national interest with my self; as every difference of this kind must in its consequences be injurious.[30]

Washington still suspected that Gates and others wanted him out, and he was probably right. Still, the immediate crisis passed, and, if anything, he emerged from the incident more secure in his authority as commander-in-chief.[31]

Whether or not there was an organized conspiracy to oust Washington is unclear, but he certainly thought there was, and his understandable suspicions drove his actions. Shortly after he accepted Gate's apology, he explained his position on the conspiracy

to Patrick Henry: "I cannot precisely mark the extent of their views, but it appeared in general, that General Gates was to be exalted, on the ruin of my reputation and influence. . . . Genl Mifflin it is commonly supposed, bore the second part in the Cabal; and General Conway, I know, was a very active, and malignant partizan but I have good reasons to believe" that the tables have been turned back on them.[32]

With Gates's apology, the so-called conspiracy disappeared, and although criticism of Washington's conduct continued, his position was safe. The three primary members of the cabal also faded from the scene in surprisingly short order. Thomas Mifflin was accused of malfeasance as the quartermaster general and forced to resign. Conway succeeded in antagonizing much of Congress and the army and resigned from the service in March 1778. Gates soon left the Board of War and, in 1780, assumed command of the Southern Department, where he was defeated at the Battle of Camden on August 17. The conspiracy ended in appropriately sordid fashion. On Independence Day 1778, Conway fought a duel with Brigadier General John Cadwallader, a close friend of Washington's, over his insults concerning the commander-in-chief. Cadwallader shot Conway in the mouth, almost killing him. Cadwallader strode up to his prostrate, bleeding victim, and exclaimed, "I have stopped that damned rascal's lying anyway."[33]

In the end, Washington emerged from the conspiracy with his power and prestige, if not strengthened, at least preserved.[34] The American victory at Saratoga had many far-reaching impacts, and one of them was the direct challenge to Washington's authority by key members of the army and Congress. They were emboldened by Gates's success, as well as by Howe's victories at Brandywine and Germantown and his occupation of Philadelphia. The direction of America's military strategy was almost completely in Washington's hands. If he been forced from his position or his influence significantly weakened, final independence might well have remained elusive.

While Washington was trying to establish the extent of the internal threat against him, news of the Saratoga victory was slowly making its way across the Atlantic. The American commissioners—Benjamin Franklin, Silas Deane, and Arthur Lee—had been working for months in Paris to convince the French to recognize American independence and to come out in open support of the new nation. France had been providing covert aid with military supplies and professional expertise since 1775. Still, if the Americans could negotiate

overt French assistance and the formal recognition of their independence, it would change the character of the war and greatly enhance the chances for ultimate success.

The commissioners had received only scraps of news for months, and they feared for the safety of Philadelphia and the Northern Department. On Thursday, December 4, 1777, the news of Burgoyne's surrender finally reached Paris. Having heard rumors that a messenger was on his way from the coast with important intelligence, they assembled in great anticipation at Benjamin Franklin's home in Passy, Paris, on the Seine's Right Bank. They did not have long to wait as shortly thereafter, a rider appeared, and before he even had a chance to dismount, Franklin called out, "Sir, is Philadelphia taken?" "Yes, sir," the messenger responded. With a look of anguish, Franklin, who had made Philadelphia his home, turned and began to walk away. Before he had taken two steps, the rider exclaimed, "But, sir, I have greater news than that. General Burgoyne and his whole army are prisoners of war!" As one eyewitness noted, "the effect was electrical"—an appropriate remark given that the subject of his observation was Benjamin Franklin. The commissioners immediately drafted a letter for public release announcing the victory and distributed copies throughout the city, specifically targeting key ministers and public figures. The letter contained several errors, but the essence was true enough: one of only two British field armies in North America had surrendered to an American Army and an American general. Paris erupted in celebration. "Joy filled the court," wrote one American diplomat, while another claimed that "the people greeted the victory as it had been their own."[35]

One copy of the announcement was signed by all three commissioners and sent to Vergennes, Louis XVI's Minister of Foreign Affairs, and, for their purposes, the most important man in France. Vergennes had the king's ear, and any request for French support and negotiations leading to a formal alliance had to go through him. For many months Vergennes had supported covert aid to the Americans and suggested to Franklin that an official alliance would be forthcoming. Indeed, the Americans had proposed the terms of such a treaty a year before, but Vergennes had always put them off, sensing that the right moment had not yet arrived. After the twin American victories at Trenton and Princeton, there were no military successes that the American diplomats could use as leverage. Ticonderoga, Brandywine, and Germantown did not inspire confidence in America's potential European allies. Saratoga changed everything.

While Franklin and his colleagues were disseminating the news of Saratoga across Paris, Lord Stormont, the British ambassador to France, tried to counter their efforts by telling anyone who would listen that Howe had captured Philadelphia. The dueling diplomats' reports were not equal, as Vergennes well knew. On December 6, he wrote to his ambassador in London that Lord Stormont "has hastened to let me share his modest satisfaction" about the seizure of the American capital. "I have duly thanked him for his attention," Vergennes wrote, "to which I might have replied by sending him General Burgoyne's capitulation, but I prefer to let him learn it from others."[36]

Also on the 6th, Conrad-Alexandre Gérard, Vergennes's chief secretary, met the Americans at Passy, congratulating them on Saratoga and assuring "them of the great pleasure it gave at Versailles." Most importantly, since the United States had proven the "ability and resolution" to maintain its independence by forcing Burgoyne's surrender, Vergennes and the king were open to discussing a formal alliance, and that such negotiations "could not be done too soon." This was the moment toward which the commissioners had been fighting for so many months. Franklin immediately began to draft a memorial that called for reopening negotiations on a draft treaty proposal that the commissioners had already submitted almost a year before.[37]

Vergennes had anticipated the American request and had already convinced the king to receive them. He assured the American diplomats of the interest that "His Majesty has always shown in their cause; but that circumstances now appearing more favourable to the establishment of a close understanding between his Crown and the United States of North America, His Majesty will not be averse to listen to such proposals as the Deputies may have to make to him."[38] This was a major diplomatic breakthrough for the Americans.

Two days later, the memorial was complete and personally delivered to Vergennes by William Temple Franklin, Franklin's illegitimate eighteen-year-old grandson, and secretary. He was surprised when the great man received him in person. In the memorial, Franklin "most urgently" urged Vergennes to "resume the consideration" of a proposed treaty between the two countries. Given the "present circumstances," Franklin argued that the "completing of such a treaty at this time must have the most happy effect." The present circumstance was, of course, the news of Saratoga. Such a treaty would strengthen American morale, improve its credit abroad, and suppress internal resistance to independence. American's success would

increase the "wealth and strength" of France. The commissioners asked Vergennes to appoint a "speedy day" to receive them. After "establishing their own liberty," the United States promised a "firm and everlasting union" with France. Vergennes told young William that he would meet with the commissioners in a few days.[39]

Pierre Beaumarchais, who supervised the distribution of covert French aid to the Americans, advised Vergennes on December 11 that it was in France's national interest to support the rebels, and "the real moral meaning of the crisis" was that "of the two nations, England and France, the first who recognizes American independence will alone gather from it all the fruits, whilst that independence will be certainly fatal to the one who allows her rival to take the lead." With Burgoyne's surrender, "ce moment accomplit tout."[40]

Vergennes needed no reminding that timing was important. To the French ambassador to Spain, he noted that while Burgoyne's surrender though "very fortunate in that it humiliates English pride, may, however, produce consequences which might upset our forecasts." Now that the Americans had achieved a great military victory, the British might "renounce the pompous plan of wishing to conquer the continent of North America," and instead offer the Americans terms for reconciliation. If the French were to be drawn into a war, "is it not more expedient to venture on it with the Americans for friends, rather than have them our enemies?"[41]

The meeting between Vergennes and the commissioners took place on Friday, December 12—a date that should be memorialized in American history. The meeting went surprisingly well, considering the large stakes for both parties. As Arthur Lee recorded, Vergennes admitted that the initial news of the fall of Ticonderoga and Burgoyne's "rapid advance" had "brought upon him a total overthrow." But Saratoga, and especially the militia's performance, had changed everything. He asked Franklin what he thought of the war now. Franklin replied that the British would "soon be tired of it," and America would win. The minister emphasized that France had no desire to take advantage of the Americans and that any treaty between the two countries must be based on "mutual interest." Vergennes announced that treaty negotiations would go forward, though he cautioned "that entering into a treaty with us would be declaring our independency, and necessarily draw on a war."[42] Franklin reported only that "some Difficulties were mention'd and remov'd, some Explications ask'd and given, to Satisfaction."[43]

For his part, Arthur Lee was confident of success. In a letter to Samuel Adams, he wrote that Burgoyne's defeat had "given

a sensation that is likely to produce the most speedy and decisive effects." He assured Adams that "the United States will not make another campaign without allies." Still, Americans must not "think the danger over" just because of the Saratoga victory and the impending treaty with France because the British were still "formidable."[44]

Signifying yet another delay, Vergennes said that before they could finalize the agreement, Spain had to consent, a process that could take weeks. Franklin told Vergennes that he had been approached by Paul Wentworth, one of Lord North's agents, who informed him that the British were willing to offer America something "a little short of independence." Franklin had told Wentworth that America would fight for fifty years "before she would give up [Independency]," but he did not tell Vergennes that.[45] Instead, Franklin told the minister that as a result of the Saratoga disaster, Britain "would be making some propositions for accommodation," and that indeed the commissioners had received serious feelers offering negotiations.[46]

Both the Americans and the French were well aware of the acrimonious debates in Britain's Parliament that had erupted after the news of Saratoga, during which opposition members were calling for an end to the American war. This was the last thing Vergennes wanted, and Franklin knew it. If Saratoga compelled the British to reopen negotiations, they might offer terms that would lure the Americans back into their fold, dashing Vergennes's dreams of fatally weakening France's historic foe. Vergennes could not afford to let this opportunity pass.

With a renewed sense of urgency prompted by British attempts to reopen negotiations with the rebels, Vergennes convinced the king to go ahead without first hearing from Spain, and on December 17, the minister sent his secretary to inform the commissioners "by order of the King, that after long and full Consideration of our Affairs and Propositions in Council, it was decided and his Majesty was determined to acknowledge our Independence and make a Treaty with us of Amity and Commerce." The king agreed to the treaty and was determined "not only to acknowledge but to support our Independence, by every means in his Power." Louis XVI recognized that France would probably "be soon engag'd in War, with all the Expences, Risque and Damage usually attending it," but he did "not expect any Compensation from us on that Account." The king and Vergennes also made it very clear that the decision to go ahead with the treaty was because "it was manifestly the Interest of France that the Power of England should be diminish'd by our Separation from

it." To the French, American independence was purely a means to an end, and that end was to shrink British power and influence.[47]

All the months of careful, patient, and often frustrating diplomacy, crowned by the victory at Saratoga, had paid off. As Franklin, Deane, and Lee reported to Congress, the only real condition that the French imposed on the Americans was that they would not "give up our Independency, and return to the Obedience of that [Britain's] Government."[48] The last was an important point for Vergennes, who even a few days later expressed his deep concern that Britain might find a way to lure back the Americans.[49] He need not have worried, for on Saturday, November 22, the Congress had already declared that "all proposals for a treaty between the King of Great Britain . . . and the United States of America, inconsistent with the independence of said states . . . will be rejected by Congress."[50] A delighted Arthur Lee wrote a friend that the "last ray of British splendor is passing away, and the American sun is emerging in full glory."[51] There was no going back.

While the diplomats conferred over the details of the treaty with France, Franklin was in his element. As always, he was in great demand in Paris social circles. One British agent reported that "Doctor Franklin is all life and full of spirits." It was hardly a secret that an alliance was close at hand. Franklin was seen dining with a doctor from *Les invalides* who toasted "success to American arms" and "perpetual and everlasting understanding between the House of Bourbon and the American Congress." The agent further related that "the general opinion of the people is that an alliance is absolutely concluded between the court and the Americans."[52]

When an acquaintance expressed his concern over the loss of Philadelphia, Franklin confidently replied with his characteristic humor and wisdom that "you mistake the matter, instead of *Howe* taking *Philada.—Philada.* has taken *Howe.*"[53] He was right: there was simply no comparison between Saratoga and Philadelphia. The capture of Philadelphia was a strategic dead end that failed to force Washington into a decisive engagement. Instead, the one remaining large British Army in North America was shut up in the city with no prospect of gaining any further advantage.

Throughout January 1778, Franklin, Deane, Lee, and Gérard worked out the fine print. Both sides argued over certain points, such as when France would actually supply troops and ships to support American operations, Spain's entry into the war, and French claims on Canada. At one point, Franklin argued that since a treaty would certainly draw France into the war, why not simply declare

war against Great Britain concurrent with the signing of the agreement. Gérard categorically refused.[54] In the end, the Americans, "almost panting after an alliance"—as one historian has put it—dropped their demands and agreed to the final French proposals.[55] On January 27, they settled on the final terms. Less than two months after the news of Burgoyne's capitulation had reached Paris, the French and Americans formally agreed to an alliance.[56]

Despite American eagerness to conclude the treaties and the fact that France held most of the cards, the agreements were mutually beneficial to both parties, though perhaps especially to the United States. Just as France insisted that the United States not negotiate any peace that did not include independence, Vergennes agreed to the same clause. They also agreed to keep fighting with the Americans until a formal treaty granting independence from Great Britain was concluded. This meant that even if they had second thoughts, or the war dragged on, France was committed by treaty to the final American victory. Everyone involved knew that once the treaties were announced, France would soon be in the war, one way or another.[57]

The agreements were translated into English and French. On February 6, the representatives of France and the United States put their signatures to a Treaty of Amity and Commerce and a Treaty of Alliance.[58] On March 20, Louis XVI received the Americans at Versailles, and as usual, Franklin stole the show as he arrived at the glittering reception attired in his provincial clothes. The king asked Franklin to "assure Congress of my friendship," and that he hoped that the agreement "will be for the good of the two countries." Franklin replied, "Your Majesty may count on the gratitude of Congress and its faithful observance of the pledges it now makes."[59] The war, and the world, were forever changed.

While recognition of United States independence through the Treaty of Amity and Commerce was important for reasons both material and psychological, the Treaty of Alliance provided a vital addition to American military strategy. In the event Britain declared war against France or tried to affect commerce, it stated, the parties "should then make common Cause of it, and join our Forces and Councils, &c. &c."[60]

The French ambassador officially announced the existence of the treaties in London on March 13. Four days later, Great Britain declared war on France. Now, theoretically at least, Washington would have access to or at least could expect cooperation with, French naval power and land forces.

On May 4, the Congress ratified both agreements.[61] After Saratoga, Congress had no desire to entertain British offers of reconciliation. The arrival of the signed treaties ensured that compromise on anything short of full independence from Great Britain was unthinkable, as the members of the Carlisle Peace Commission found out to their dismay later that summer.

Prominent Americans celebrated the news of the treaties. Samuel Chase wrote to Maryland Governor Thomas John that "America has now taken her rank among the Nations & has it in her power to secure her Liberty & Independance."[62] Pennsylvania delegate Jonathan Bayard Smith observed that "It now only remains with ourselves to act in spirit."[63] North Carolinian Thomas Burke wrote that because of the treaty, the "Prospect of a free, happy, gallant, flourishing People obtrudes every moment on my Imagination and I enjoy by anticipation the future felicity of my Country."[64] To Thomas Jefferson, fellow Virginian Richard Henry Lee predicted that Great Britain had now "two Cards to play." She could either "acknowledge the Independency of America and make a Treaty of Commerce with her and thus be at peace with us and with all the World," or she could double down and try to end the American war by concentrating all of her troops "for a last effort."[65] Lee was sure of one thing: "England alone will pay for her wickedness and folly by the loss of North America."[66] General Oliver Wolcott, who served with Gates during the Saratoga campaign, wrote his wife that "Our Peace I consider as now dawning upon us. And whenever it shall be established, may these Independent States thankfully Acknowledge that Great Goodness of God who by his kind Providence so evidently affords us his Protection."[67]

Washington, while rejoicing at the prospect of the French joining the war, nevertheless remained sober in his assessment: "Notwithstanding the immense advantages which we shall derive from the acknowledgement of our Independency by, and our late alliance with the Court of France," he wrote to one of his generals, "yet much remains to be done to extricate ourselves intirely from our oppressors."[68] Washington knew that unless suddenly Britain gave up and agreed to American independence, an unlikely event, the war would continue for an extended period. It was now all the more important that he preserve the army and carry on with his plans.

And devise new ones. With the entry of France into the war, Washington could now adjust the modified Fabian strategy to take advantage of the greater flexibility and mobility that France's sea

power could give him. With more combat power at his disposal, the commander-in-chief could afford to accept additional operational risk by conducting selective offensive operations. Nonetheless, as Washington also knew, the high expectations of immediate French military assistance were largely illusionary, at least in the short term.

The first attempt at a combined operation between American and French forces took place in late August 1778 with an attempt to capture British-held Newport, Rhode Island. Bad weather, miscommunications, and disagreements between commanders, and a stout British defense, foiled the Franco-American efforts. In the meantime, the Fabian strategy would continue in the main theater of operations until reaching a virtual stalemate in late 1778, when the British shifted their strategic focus south. Washington and his southern theater commander, who, as of October 1780, was Major General Nathanael Greene, never wavered in their single-minded determination to maintain the armies in the field. They continued to avoid decisive battles when they did not have the upper hand, no matter how tempting such opportunities might be.[69]

Finally, in October 1781, Washington's patient strategy paid off at the siege of Yorktown in September and October 1781, where French land and naval forces played a decisive role. A combined American and French army under Washington and his allied counterpart, the Comte de Rochambeau, captured a British Army under Lieutenant General Lord Charles Cornwallis. The Battle of Yorktown led directly to the negotiations that eventually ended the conflict.

The final American victory at Yorktown would never have been possible without Saratoga. The British not only lost the troops, artillery pieces, and equipment for the duration of the war, but perhaps most importantly, their war effort was deprived of hundreds of key leaders from general officers down to experienced noncommissioned officers. Burgoyne's defeat, coupled with the strategically barren Philadelphia campaign, forced Great Britain to reevaluate its military strategy and embark on one that reflected the new realities. In Britain, the political opposition was emboldened to redouble their efforts to end the war. Experienced and capable senior leaders, such as the Howe brothers and Sir Guy Carleton, stepped down from key positions after the 1777 campaigns.

Saratoga gave the Americans a vital morale boost just when they needed it. Howe's capture of Philadelphia had been a blow, but Saratoga countered it. In the wake of Gates's understandable surge in popularity, Washington withstood a challenge to his authority and skillfully defeated the so-called Conway Cabal, emerging from

the post-Saratoga crisis with a strengthened grasp on his position as commander-in-chief. This enabled him to continue to pursue his war-winning military strategy. The victory was the catalyst that propelled the French to formally recognize American independence and conclude treaties that ensured she would enter the war, bringing her considerable naval and land forces into the fight, opening new strategic and operational possibilities for Washington.

In the summer and early autumn of 1777, America's prospects had looked grim indeed. After October 17, the very character of the war changed. Although the fighting would go on for several more years, the fate of the new nation was assured. No other campaign of the American Revolution had as many far-reaching consequences. Saratoga was simply the most decisive campaign of the war, and its effects are with us still.

CONCLUSION

Men and Measures

The execution merits equal censure perhaps more than the design.

—Hugh Elliot

FOR THE BRITISH, SARATOGA was not merely a battlefield defeat; it was a strategic, operational, and tactical catastrophe. The loss of a priceless field army, along with its now battle-hardened soldiers and officers, was simply impossible to replace. American morale soared. France exploited the rebel victory, sensing a strategic opening that was too tempting to ignore. The British now had to deal with a widened war, which would lead to the loss of the American colonies in 1783. The roots of this calamity can be traced directly to the British plans developed in early 1777.

Another factor was the quality of leadership on both sides. Even the best strategy cannot succeed unless it is executed by capable leaders. In 1777, the Americans exhibited better leadership than the British at all levels of war, and the Patriot leaders showed again and again that they had grip. In large part, the Americans not only skillfully handled soldiers on the battlefield, but they also understood the bigger picture and how they fit into the overall scheme. The senior leaders envisioned how the campaign would unfold, and, after the initial shock of losing Fort Ticonderoga wore off, were

able to anticipate and counter Burgoyne's maneuvers. These resilient leaders used their initiative when required and made sound decisions throughout the campaign.

While eighteenth-century British military and civilian leaders did not use the term "strategy" as we do today—the calculated application of ways and means to achieve a political objective—they certainly understood the concept. They fell victim to some of the same traps as strategists before and since while creating the 1777 campaign, including the use of schemes laden with unexamined assumptions. When Burgoyne presented his "Thoughts for Conducting the War from the Side of Canada," on February 28, 1777, he gave Germain and the king exactly what they wanted. They were so obsessed with invading New York via Lake Champlain that they failed to question their own underlying assumptions about executing a complex operation in such a forbidding environment. The focus on reprising the failed 1776 Lake Champlain-Ticonderoga-Hudson River strategy also kept them from fully exploring all of their strategic options. They also focused on the junction of Howe's and Burgoyne's army, not on what it was supposed to produce.

British leaders never gave their two senior commanders—Howe and Burgoyne—a clearly defined and decisive objective, except to effect a junction of two armies at Albany. Any discussion of an overall objective—the "what" of strategy—was either an afterthought or an assumption. They took it as an article of faith that the mere linking of Burgoyne's army from Canada and Howe's main army would somehow generate victory. After Howe's and Burgoyne's armies combined at Albany, good things would happen. What those good things were was not well-conceived.

Howe had the best grasp of the realities of conducting a war in North America. Not long after the Battles of Trenton and Princeton in late 1776 and early 1777, he recognized that only the decisive defeat of Washington and his army could possibly win the war. Almost all of his efforts in 1777 were directed toward that goal. Howe instinctively understood that there had to be a distinct, clearly defined, and decisive objective guiding their efforts. For Howe, that could be only one thing: Washington's army. Defeat Washington and you end the rebellion. Yet Germain viewed Howe's Philadelphia campaign and his quest to lure Washington into a decisive battle merely as something to wrap up quickly so the commander-in-chief could shift his focus to the true British main effort: moving up to Hudson to Albany and Burgoyne. Howe was, in any case, unable to get his decisive battle. But his strategy for 1777 held out a much greater prospect for overall success than did Burgoyne's and Germain's.

Alexander Hamilton agreed. Responding in April 1777 to the concerns of the New York Committee of Correspondence that the British might try to repeat their 1776 attempt to invade from Canada and to seize control of the Hudson River, Hamilton assured them that they had little to fear. The committee worried that should the Americans lose control of the Hudson River valley, communications between the New England states and the rest of the country would be cut. This concern was misplaced, according to Hamilton: "Unless the Geography of the Country is far different from anything I can conceive, to effect this would require a chain of posts and such a number of men at each as would never be practicable or maintainable but to an immense army."[1] Writing a few weeks later on the same subject, Hamilton assured fellow New Yorker Gouverneur Morris that "Any object short of our army is a bad one."[2] Hamilton had identified the major flaw in British military strategy.

The alternate option was one that Burgoyne proposed in his "Thoughts" memorandum. Instead of linking up with Howe's army at Albany, the army from Canada could embark on Royal Navy ships at Quebec and "effect a junction" with Howe by sea.[3] Exactly where that junction was to happen, Burgoyne did not say, but Howe would have certainly wanted Burgoyne's army to join him at New York City. But because of their focus on an invasion from Canada, neither Burgoyne nor the intended audience for his memorandum—the king and Germain—believed meeting in New York was a viable or desirable option. But, given the Royal Navy's complete control of the sea, it was a low-risk and low-cost alternative to a land campaign, and one with the potential for a big payoff. Had Howe's main army had been reinforced with an additional nine thousand soldiers from Canada, he might very well have had enough combat power to seek out and destroy Washington somewhere in New Jersey or Pennsylvania in the summer or fall of 1777. After Saratoga, the British would never again have that opportunity.

In addition to being fundamentally unsound, the 1777 plans were unsynchronized and badly implemented. The tyranny of space and time that the British had to constantly battle was an issue the Americans did not face. Developing a strategy and then trying to oversee it from thousands of miles and many weeks away from the scene of the action proved impossible. But the British could have avoided that trap by providing an overall objective to the commanders on the ground—such as "destroy Washington's army"—supplying them with adequate resources and then relying on their judgment and ability to achieve the objective. By dictating from London almost every aspect of the strategy, and without the ability to confer face-to-face with Howe and

Carleton, Germain and George III guaranteed that the plans would be uncoordinated. Instead of massing combat power at a decisive point (Washington's army), it was frittered away.

When British leaders allowed Howe to go to Philadelphia while also giving the green light to Burgoyne's march to Albany, they demonstrated a fundamental misunderstanding of the realities of campaigning in North America. By hoping that Howe could conclude his campaign quickly and still link up with Burgoyne, they were inviting failure. They had ended up with a plan that had to go perfectly in almost every respect to achieve the desired result. Only an extremely gifted commander of the army from Canada might have been able to salvage something out of the campaign when events did not unfold as anticipated. Burgoyne was not that officer.

So what are the strategic lessons Saratoga offers? First, leaders must clearly define an objective for their military commanders. They must make clear what exactly they want the military operation to accomplish. The objective must also lead to accomplishing a larger, usually political, goal. How much blood and treasure have been wasted by those who simply send troops into harm's way to "do something," with no defined goal other than hoping that the action, in and of itself, would somehow lead to a happy result?

Examining planning assumptions is key, and leaders must prepare for the very real possibility that their initial assumptions are wrong. British strategists should have considered the possibility that Loyalists would not come out by the hundreds and thousands to support the army, or that only a few hundred Native Americans could be convinced to fight with the army, or that the army from Canada might not be able to reach Albany unaided. A strategy must be fully coordinated with all parties understanding their roles, as well as the overall goal.

Assumptions are not the only things that strategists must consider. Senior leaders cannot envision, create, and implement a strategy without understanding that geography, enemy actions, and intangibles such as chance, weather, and human frailties will all play a part once a campaign begins. Thus, they must conduct constant reassessments of their strategy. The British did not do this. As the 1777 campaign unfolded, starting from the moment Burgoyne landed in Canada, all the senior leaders—Germain, Carleton, Howe, and Burgoyne—should have been watchful for unforeseen circumstances, or faulty assumptions, or any of a hundred different things that might prevent success. When these issues surfaced—a shortage of forage, insufficient vehicles, unexpected American

resilience, and so on—the commanders had to determine whether the plan was still viable, regardless of their initial orders. None of the British leaders performed this basic task, not in London, New York, Quebec, or north of Albany. Burgoyne and Howe stuck to their basic designs; Carleton followed the exact letter of his instructions as he denounced Germain, and the secretary hoped for the best.

Even on today's widely dispersed battlefields, where commanders enjoy instantaneous communications, a strategy must have a clear objective, operations must be fully coordinated and synchronized to achieve unity of effort, and combat power must still be concentrated at the decisive point. Commanders and civilian leaders must constantly assess and reassess their strategy. The failure of British leaders to follow these fundamental tenets led inevitably to their defeat at Saratoga.

On the other hand, the Americans, facing a more straightforward strategic challenge, showed greater flexibility, largely due to Washington's leadership. Washington skillfully exploited the American advantage of interior lines on both the strategic and operational levels of war. This advantage enabled Washington to coordinate military strategy between the Northern Department and the main army in New Jersey and Pennsylvania.

Aside from highlighting strategic failure, the Saratoga campaign offers instructive illustrations of senior-level leadership. Both sides possessed exceptional leadership at the tactical level of battalion commander and below. Officers led their men effectively, and most were good role models. There were very few, if any, instances of officers abandoning their men or hanging back.

This was also the case at the regimental and brigade level. Brigadier Generals Stark and Herkimer and Colonels Morgan, Warner, and Gansevoort on the American side are but a few examples of outstanding leadership during the campaign. Brigadier General Simon Fraser, Lord Balcarres, Major Acland, Major Grant, and many other British and German officers also distinguished themselves. Tactically, there was little distinction between the British and American forces. It was at the operational and strategic levels where the difference becomes clear.

Here again, a major factor was grip. I have expanded Montgomery's notion of grip to include not only a commander who has a firm grasp of a battle through close supervision and personal involvement but one who also understands the strategic or operational problem in its full complexity. A leader with grip is also one who can envision how a campaign or battle might unfold and anticipates what is on

and over the horizon and how to handle it. This quality of intuition is present in the best senior leaders, and it is developed and enhanced through exercise, experience, and study.[4] Senior military leaders are routinely forced to operate in extremely challenging and complex strategic and operational environments, and the very best thrive. These officers have grip. There are abundant examples of exceptional, adequate, mediocre, and dreadful leadership in the Saratoga campaign. We have much to learn from Germain, Howe, Carleton, Burgoyne, Washington, Schuyler, Gates, St. Clair, Arnold, Stark, Morgan, and Gansevoort.

The British war effort in 1777 was hampered by dysfunctional relationships between senior military commanders in America and their civilian leader in London. Lord George Germain had lost all confidence in Sir Guy Carleton; and Carleton despised Germain. Carleton's personal animosity may well have led to his failure to do the utmost to support Burgoyne's expedition. Sir Henry Clinton lost all respect for his superior, Howe, and Howe ignored Clinton's advice. And Howe, the commander-in-chief, also became disgusted with Germain, who tended to ignore his advice and achievements. The lesson is very clear. Senior-level leadership is, in many ways, a process of negotiation, and commanders must cultivate healthy interpersonal relations with subordinates and peers to accomplish the mission.[5] In senior level leadership, trust is the coin of the realm.

The Americans had challenges on this same front as well. The difference was that they were able to overcome them and continue to work toward a shared mission. The bitter quarrel between Gates and Arnold is a perfect example. The two generals ultimately resolved their differences to the point where they could function at a high level. Human relationships are often fragile, and it is not unusual for them to fray, but senior military leaders cannot allow them to deteriorate to the point where military operations are negatively affected. To their credit, Gates and Arnold put aside their differences for the good of the army and their cause, at least for the duration of the second battle. In too many cases, the British found this much more difficult.

After the war, Sir Henry Clinton wrote a devastating assessment of Howe, concluding that he had brought "infamy to himself and indelible dishonor to his Country."[6] This sentiment was typical of Clinton, who could find fault with almost everyone and everything. Even with his flaws, however, Howe's performance in 1777 had many strengths. He had the best grasp of the overall situation and what it would take to win the war. The government had been disappointed in Howe's

failure to defeat Washington in 1776 and in the losses at the battles of Trenton and Princeton. Still, they should have allowed Howe maximum latitude to conduct operations as he saw fit. Instead, they viewed his Philadelphia campaign as a secondary effort compared with Burgoyne's expedition.

Howe can, however, be faulted for not acting as a true commander-in-chief when it came to Burgoyne's army. When Howe got wind of the expedition from Canada, he immediately sent that April letter to General Carleton, informing him unequivocally that the main army was going to Philadelphia and not up the Hudson. After that, he effectively put Burgoyne out of his mind. Once Burgoyne passed Lake Champlain, he became the direct subordinate to Howe, who did not take on this responsibility. Instead, he left Clinton behind in New York City with vague instructions about Burgoyne and few resources to do much of anything in support of the army from Canada. This muddled situation between Howe and Burgoyne only exacerbated an already flawed plan. Howe's performance in 1777 was not brilliant, but neither was it worthy of the condemnation he has received from contemporaries and historians alike. Howe was a good soldier who knew what the objective for 1777 should have been. The Americans were fortunate that his British colleagues did not listen to him.

On reading Burgoyne's account of the last battles in the campaign and his surrender, British diplomat Hugh Elliot wrote a friend that the conduct of the campaign "merits equal censure perhaps more than the design."[7] Leaving aside Burgoyne's central role in formulating British strategy, Elliot was right. That raises one of the most interesting questions to come out of the campaign: Why did Burgoyne make so many poor decisions from May through October 1777? We can begin with hubris. From the start, Burgoyne allowed himself to get drawn into the American wilderness despite grossly inadequate logistical support simply because he believed in his superior ability to overcome any challenge. Although Burgoyne campaigned in the region with Carleton's 1776 expedition, he progressed no farther than Crown Point, and so never fully appreciated the difficulties of conducting military operations in that part of North America.

Burgoyne underestimated the enemy, especially after encountering St. Clair's defense and evacuation of Ticonderoga, which contributed to his overconfidence. He did not push his men, and only when he started to encounter real difficulties did he exhibit anything like a sense of urgency. Burgoyne failed to use his initiative, despite instructions to rely on his best judgment. Personally

fearless—a byproduct of his hubris, perhaps—Burgoyne allowed both major battles to get away from him, in part because he was in the thick of the fighting and did not step back to assess the overall situation and adjust accordingly. Despite his considerable experience as a professional army officer, Burgoyne demonstrated overconfidence and pride, but very little grip.

Burgoyne's and his army's fate can be traced through a series of decisions, any one of which, had it been different, may have altered the course of the campaign. If Burgoyne had pushed on aggressively after his unexpected victory at Ticonderoga, instead of delaying at Skenesborough, he might well have successfully exploited American disarray and panic. It is tempting but unfair to study history backward and evaluate decisions based on perfect information that leaders never enjoyed. We must assess these figures based on what they knew at the time. After the Battle of Bennington, Burgoyne had all the information he needed to make a sound decision. He knew his logistics situation was bleak, his casualties severe, that the Americans had rebounded from the initial shock of losing Ticonderoga, that the Patriot militia would fight, and that Howe was not coming to his aid. At this point, saving the army should have been Burgoyne's first and only mission, despite his orders. Perhaps it was because of his inexperience with independent command or the shock of the Bennington disaster, but for whatever reason, the decision to continue the campaign was a fundamental miscalculation.

Had he withdrawn back north after Bennington or even after Freeman's Farm, he might have saved the army. Indeed, an intact British army at Fort Ticonderoga would have created a significant strategic headache for Washington. But instead, he pressed on, falling victim to both status quo bias—the tendency to stick with a plan, even after it no longer makes sense—and confirmation bias—the inclination to see what you want to see. He remained fixated on getting to Albany and interpreted every message from General Clinton in the most positive light, even in the face of contradictory evidence.

None of Burgoyne's individual shortcomings was enough by itself to doom the expedition. Taken together, however, they led to the loss of an army. Burgoyne's soldiers loved him because he cared about them, but he also failed them. General Fraser observed at the start of the campaign that his chief "hates lines of resistance when they interrupt his projects."[8] Burgoyne was a good man and a decent soldier who was simply out of his depth trying to execute what was one of the most challenging operations of the American Revolution, and when he ran into "lines of resistance," he was ill-equipped to

deal with them. There is plenty of blame to go around for the failure of the 1777 campaign, but responsibility for the loss of the army from Canada rests solely on Burgoyne's shoulders.

The British lost at Saratoga. The Americans also won it. Throughout the campaign, especially in the later stages, British tactical merit was simply overwhelmed by American operational and strategic excellence. This is not to say that every American senior leader performed well. They had their own issues to overcome. Arthur St. Clair's leadership was sorely lacking at Ticonderoga. He failed to take fundamental measures to defend the fortress and to prepare for evacuation, and he failed to cover the water obstacle or destroy the bridge across the lake, which led to the battle at Hubbardton and the loss of critical supplies and troops at Skenesborough. He also did little to delay Burgoyne's advance. St. Clair and his generals were handed a tough mission, and the challenges were daunting, but the American troops at Fort Ticonderoga deserved more. Some have argued that St. Clair's decisions at Ticonderoga led to American victory because he saved the army from certain capture. But the Americans won despite St. Clair's conduct, not because of it.

The self-serving antics of Philip Schuyler and Horatio Gates over who was to command in the spring of 1777 jeopardized the security of the Northern Department and the entire American northern flank. Congress's and Washington's neglect of the Northern Department in the winter and spring of 1777 unnecessarily impaired its readiness to repel an enemy invasion from Canada. Indeed, no American senior leader performed particularly well prior to the loss of Fort Ticonderoga. The sharp quarrel between Gates and Benedict Arnold after the Battle of Freeman's Farm threatened to undermine the combat capability of the army at a critical time. But they did not let it fester.

The two commanders of the Northern Department—Philip Schuyler and Horatio Gates—both contributed enormously to the American victory. Schuyler did a much better job after the loss of Ticonderoga than his messages to Washington and Congress suggested. He appealed for militia from the surrounding states, and he applied his deep knowledge of the countryside and of logistics to delay Burgoyne's move south and, at the same time, reconstitute the Northern Army.

Schuyler's major failing after Ticonderoga was his inability to communicate effectively with his superiors. His many competent decisions belied the tone of despair and even panic that infected almost every message he sent to Congress and Washington. The commander-in-chief was rightly concerned that Schuyler's gloom

and defeatism were infecting the army. This was a recipe for disaster. If Schuyler's reports to his superiors had been more encouraging, he would have retained command and fought Burgoyne somewhere along the route to Albany. Schuyler did not have grip—he was too often in alarm mode, at least outwardly, and he failed to understand his responsibilities to those above him on the chain of command—but he did set the conditions for success in the Northern Department. Schuyler was a selfless servant and a Patriot, but circumstances of war and his own leadership flaws led to his tragic downfall during the Saratoga campaign.

Gates, Schuyler's successor, enjoyed the benefit of assuming command of the Northern Department after it had endured its most difficult period. It had nowhere to go but up. A number of observers, including Schuyler's staff officers (and not a few historians), believed that Gates deserved none of the Saratoga tributes he received and that the accolades rightfully belonged to Schuyler or Arnold or both. Major General Nathanael Greene wrote of Gates after the campaign that "This Gentleman is a mere child of fortune. The foundation of all the Northern successes was laid long before his arrival there."[9] While there is a kernel of truth in Greene's statement, it does not give the full story. Gates was steady, a good manager, understood terrain and was able to handle—eventually—the brilliant but mercurial Arnold. He successfully directed both major battles. The defensive and reactive battle management that he oversaw at Freeman's Farm and Bemis Heights was exactly what was called for under the circumstances, despite Arnold's complaints. He skillfully managed both battles while maintaining the defensive position on Bemis Heights, and he refused to allow himself to be bullied by Arnold into making out-of-character decisions.

Had the campaign required something other than a primarily defensive effort, Gates would not likely have been up to the challenge, as he proved three years later at the Battle of Camden, where he failed after trying a more aggressive and offensive-minded approach. But the unique circumstances that Gates encountered in September and October 1777—the slow approach of a weakened Burgoyne, giving the Americans time to find and prepare superb defensive positions, and the time for militia to gather—played into his strengths and overcame his weaknesses. Gates was not a team player—as was evident in his disregard and even disrespect toward the commander-in-chief. And his arrogance after a great victory led him astray. However, his performance during the Saratoga campaign showed that he could be a capable commander with grip, given the

right conditions. He deserves to be remembered as the victor of Saratoga.

Last, but more important, there was Washington. Fully embracing his responsibilities as commander-in-chief, Washington, through spotty reports and panicked messages, was quickly able to assess the situation after the loss of Ticonderoga. He could sense what Burgoyne was doing and what the Northern Department needed to face the threat and to act accordingly. He could see that Schuyler needed help and responded with sound advice, wise counsel, veteran troops, experienced leaders, and other resources.

Washington was able to do all of this while also commanding his own army, defending the American capital, campaigning against Howe's superior force, simultaneously answering to Congress, and coordinating with state governors and assemblies. Notwithstanding these many competing priorities, he was able to exercise exceptional judgment throughout the summer and fall of 1777. He also knew that every decision he made would be closely scrutinized by Congress, his subordinates, and the enemy. His communications—both written and verbal—had to exude confidence and optimism, even in the face of defeat. Despite reverses, some severe, he was able to dodge Howe's attempts to corner and destroy the army, and with it the promise of American liberty. That was where the entire war hinged. The main army lived on, Burgoyne surrendered, and the American Revolution entered a new phase. Of all the senior leaders involved in the Saratoga campaign, it was Washington who had the strongest grip.

Though he stands apart, Washington did not stand alone. Schuyler, Gates, Gansevoort, Stark, Willet, Morgan, Dearborn, and many more all contributed to the ultimate American victory at Saratoga. When faced with a seemingly overwhelming and irresistible enemy invasion, they did not flinch. When knocked down, they and their soldiers rebounded. When they finally enjoyed an advantage, they exploited it. In short, most of the American leaders from Washington at the top, to Schuyler and Gates at the operational level, to the men at the tip of the spear, demonstrated better grip than did their foes.

After the surrender ceremony at Saratoga, a disillusioned Lieutenant Digby blamed the British loss on Germain's "blundering," Howe's "stupid inaction," and Burgoyne's insistence on "penetrating so far, as to be unable to return."[10] Digby was right, but only in part. In the end, the American victory at Saratoga—a victory that Surgeon Thacher predicted "will make one of the most brilliant pages of American history"—stemmed from faulty British

strategy and superior American leadership.[11] The decisions taken by leaders on both sides, from offices in Whitehall to headquarters in Canada, New Jersey, Pennsylvania, and New York City, to tents along the Hudson River, determined the outcome of a campaign that ultimately guaranteed American independence.

APPENDIX A

What Became of Them?

BRITISH AND GERMAN PARTICIPANTS

Lieutenant General John Burgoyne: Burgoyne returned to England in mid-May 1778 and spent the next several years justifying his actions during the Saratoga campaign. The bitter general joined the opposition party and continued to write plays, several of which were critically acclaimed. Burgoyne died in August 1792 at age seventy and is buried at Westminster Abbey.[1]

Brigadier General Barry St. Leger: St. Leger conducted several unsuccessful operations after his failure at Fort Stanwix and was involved in negotiations with some of Vermont's leaders hoping to convince the republic to return to Crown control. Nothing came of the effort. He continued to serve in Canada after the war and died in 1789 at age fifty-two in Quebec.[2]

Major General Friedrich Adolf Riedesel: Riedesel and his wife stayed with the Convention Army as it marched to Boston and then to Charlottesville, Virginia, until paroled. He continued to serve in North America until 1783 when he returned home. He retired after an admirable career and was recalled from retirement and made commandant of the city of Braunschweig, where he died at age sixty-one in January 1800.[3]

General Sir William Howe: Howe returned to England in May 1778 and reverted to his permanent rank of major general. Despite his failure to crush the American rebellion, he was ultimately promoted to lieutenant general in 1782 and full general in 1793. In 1799 he became the 5th Viscount Howe. He was the last survivor of those senior British leaders who had a major role in the Saratoga campaign when he died after a long illness in 1814 at the age of eighty-five.[4]

General Sir Henry Clinton: Clinton's term as Howe's successor as commander-in-chief was not a happy one. Although he enjoyed some successes with the taking of Charleston and other victories in the southern states, a series of British blunders coupled with a winning military strategy orchestrated by American Major General Nathaniel Greene and George Washington led to the British disaster at Yorktown in October 1781. Clinton was recalled soon afterward and replaced by Sir Guy Carleton. He served on and off in Parliament and, in 1793, was promoted to full general. He was then appointed to the post of governor of Gibraltar but died at age sixty-five in December 1795 before he could assume the position.[5]

General Sir Guy Carleton: Carleton's oft-repeated request to resign was finally accepted, and he was replaced as the governor of Canada by General Frederick Haldimand. Carleton returned to England and remained there until he was appointed American commander-in-chief, replacing Sir Henry Clinton, who had been relieved after Yorktown. He presided over the successful evacuation of British troops in November 1783 and returned to England as the last British commander-in-chief in the American Revolutionary War. He returned to Canada as governor for the second time and was elevated to a peerage as 1st Baron Dorchester. He lived a quiet retirement until his death at age eighty-four in November 1808.[6]

Lord George Germain: After Saratoga, Germain reestablished himself as the primary architect of military operations in North America, but only two months after the news of Yorktown arrived in London, the king pressured Germain to resign in February 1782. The North ministry fell a few weeks later. Germain was raised to a peerage as Viscount Sackville and took his seat in the House of Lords despite protests; the specters of Minden, Saratoga, and Yorktown would haunt him for the rest of his life. Declining health forced his retirement to his country home in Sussex where he died at age sixty-nine in August 1785, justifying his conduct to the end.[7]

AMERICAN PARTICIPANTS

Major General Horatio Gates: After the so-called Conway Cabal, Gates resigned from the Board of War, and Congress appointed him commander of the Southern Department in July 1780. On August 16, 1780, at the Battle of Camden, Gates's army and his reputation suffered a shattering defeat.[8] Gates rejoined the army at Washington's headquarters at Newburgh, New York, where he and the commander-in-chief worked well together in the short time before the war ended. In his retirement, Gates dabbled in politics and generously gave away a large percentage of his fortune to disadvantaged veterans and served as vice president of the Society of the Cincinnati. He died quietly at his New York estate at age seventy-eight in April 1806.[9]

Major General Philip Schuyler: After his removal from command of the Northern Department, Schuyler was court-martialed and acquitted of all charges in the loss of Fort Ticonderoga. He resigned his commission in April 1779 and continued his successful political career. One of his daughters married Alexander Hamilton, and Schuyler fought for the ratification of the Constitution. Schuyler's final years were marred by ill health and personal tragedy with his wife's death by illness and his son-in-law through his duel with their mutual political rival, Aaron Burr. Schuyler died shortly after enduring these personal blows at his Albany mansion at age seventy in November 1804.[10]

General George Washington: After the bitter winter of 1778 and the Monmouth campaign, Washington continued to exercise his duties as commander-in-chief but was not involved in direct military operations himself as the focus of the war moved south. After abortive and frustrating attempts to coordinate combined operations with his new French allies, he orchestrated the successful and decisive Yorktown campaign in 1781. He also brilliantly resolved the Newburgh Conspiracy in 1783 and resigned his commission in December 1783, establishing the uniquely American concept of civil-military relations. He retired to his beloved Mount Vernon, but, inevitably, he was recalled to public service to act as the presiding officer of the Constitutional Convention, where his prestige and mere presence gave legitimacy to the proceedings. He was the unanimous choice to be the first president of the United States under the new Constitution. Washington's long-delayed and much-coveted final retirement took place in March 1797 after a second presidential term, when he returned again to Mount Vernon. He enjoyed robust health until he contracted his final brief illness, dying after great suffering at age sixty-seven on December 14, 1799. Washington was arguably the most important figure in American history, and inarguably of the American Revolution.[11]

Major General Arthur St. Clair: More than a year after he ordered the evacuation of Fort Ticonderoga, St. Clair was acquitted of all charges at a court martial. He returned to the army and served on Washington's staff for the rest of the war. After the war, he was elected as a delegate from Pennsylvania to the Confederation Congress and was elected its president in early 1787. Under his presidency, Congress passed the Northwest Ordinance in 1787, perhaps the most important piece of legislation to come out of the Confederation period of United States history. He was soon appointed governor of the newly created Northwest Territory. In 1791, St. Clair was named commander of the United States Army at his old rank of major general. He personally led a one thousand-man expedition (plus about two hundred camp followers) into what is now western Ohio. In the battle that would become to be known as "St. Clair's Defeat,"

the United States Army suffered one of its worst losses by percentage of men engaged in its history. A congressional inquiry absolved him of blame, but St. Clair resigned from the army and returned to his position as governor of the Northwest Territory. President Thomas Jefferson removed him from office in 1802 over a policy dispute, and he returned to Pennsylvania to live with his daughter. He died destitute at age eighty-one in August 1818.[12]

Major General Benedict Arnold: As Arnold recovered from his severe leg wound, Congress finally corrected his date of rank as a major general, thereby restoring his seniority. But Arnold still harbored bitter feelings toward Congress, and his pride was severely hurt by real and imagined slights, so he burned with resentment.

Washington assigned him to command the important Hudson Highland post at West Point, where his duties would not be overly onerous. Through various machinations, the disgruntled Arnold offered to hand over his new post to Sir Henry Clinton for the sum of £10,000. To wrap up the negotiations and take possession of West Point, Clinton sent Major John André to meet with Arnold. After the meeting, André was captured, and Arnold's treason exposed. The unfortunate André was ultimately hanged as a spy, and Arnold barely escaped arrest to join the British cause.

Even though they never received West Point, the British honored their agreement and, financially at least, Arnold was fixed for life. He was subsequently commissioned in the British Army as a regular army cavalry colonel and a provisional brigadier general. Arnold led several raids against his former countrymen in Virginia and Connecticut. After Cornwallis's surrender at Yorktown, Arnold took his family to London, where he was distrusted, and he was unable to secure any other military assignments. His health declined over many years, and he died in London, largely forgotten by friend and foe, at age sixty in June 1801.[13]

Major General Benjamin Lincoln: Lincoln's leg wound never fully healed, but he was appointed to command the Southern Department in the fall of 1778. Lincoln surrendered Charleston and his command to a large British expedition May 12, 1780. The likable general's reputation emerged unscathed, and after he was exchanged, Lincoln rejoined the army and led the American contingent that helped besiege and defeat Cornwallis at Yorktown. Shortly after the last great battle of the war, Lincoln was named the first secretary of war by Congress, a post he held until October 1783. Lincoln came out of retirement to help put down Shay's Rebellion in 1787, and he was a member of the Massachusetts convention that ratified the new United States Constitution. He served one term as lieutenant governor of Massachusetts, and Washington appointed him Collector of the Port of Boston. He died in Hingham, Massachusetts, in his childhood home at age seventy-seven in May 1810.[14]

Brigadier General John Stark: The victor of the Battle of Bennington stayed in the army for the rest of the war and commanded the Northern Department three times from 1778 through 1781. Unlike many, if not most of his contemporaries, Stark retired completely from public life after the war. He returned to his farm in Derryfield, New Hampshire, where he lived out the rest of his life until his death at age ninety-three in May 1822, but not before coining the wonderful phrase that would become New Hampshire's state motto: "Live free, or die!" Stark was the last survivor of the Saratoga campaign's senior American military participants.[15]

Colonel Daniel Morgan: Morgan and his riflemen returned to the main army after Saratoga and were involved in the subsequent operations through the Monmouth campaign in June 1778. He was promoted to brigadier general and sent to the Southern Department, where he routed a British-Loyalist force in a tactical tour de force at the Battle of Cowpens on January 17, 1781. Poor health forced his retirement from the army soon after. In retirement, Morgan led Virginia militia during the Whiskey Rebellion and, as an ardent Federalist, resisted Thomas Jefferson's policies. He was elected to Congress in 1797 on his second try and served one term. His many physical infirmities, aggravated by years of arduous campaigning, finally caught up with him when he died in Winchester, Virginia, at the age of sixty-six in July 1802.[16]

Colonel Peter Gansevoort: After receiving the Thanks of Congress for his performance as commander of Fort Stanwix during the Saratoga campaign, Gansevoort unaccountably received no further promotions or assignments of any consequence in the Continental Army. After the war, he presided over a number of prosperous businesses but was unsuccessful in politics. In 1809, he was appointed a brigadier general in the United States Army and commanded the Northern Department. Gansevoort died at his home in Albany at age sixty-two in July 1812.[17]

APPENDIX B

Chronology of the Saratoga Campaign, 1776–1778 (Including Key Dates from General Howe's Philadelphia Campaign)

1776

October 11	Battle of Valcour Island
October 14	Americans abandon Crown Point
November 4	General Sir Guy Carleton abandons Crown Point and returns his army to Canada
December 10	Lieutenant General John Burgoyne meets with Lord George Germain in London to discuss the 1776 campaign and the military strategy for 1777
December 13	Burgoyne meets with King George III to discuss the 1776 campaign and ideas for 1777
December 25–26	Battle of Trenton

1777

January 3–4	Battle of Princeton
January 20	General Sir William Howe submits his plan for the 1777 military strategy with Philadelphia as the bait to lure Washington into a decisive battle
February 28	Burgoyne submits his "Thoughts for Conducting the War from the Side of Canada," outlining his ideas for the 1777 military strategy, to Germain
March 25	Major General Horatio Gates ordered by Congress to take command at Fort Ticonderoga
March 26	Major General Philip Schuyler departs his headquarters at Albany, New York, and travels to Philadelphia
March 26	Germain issues orders to Carleton for the 1777 military strategy, and he sends a copy to Howe
April 5	Howe informs Carleton that he will be going to Philadelphia and not up the Hudson River. Burgoyne is on his own and must use his initiative

May 3	Colonel Peter Gansevoort arrives at Fort Stanwix
May 6	Burgoyne arrives in Quebec
May 10	Lieutenant Colonel Marinas Willett arrives at Fort Stanwix
May 18	Germain tells Howe that his plan to travel by sea to Philadelphia is approved; but he trusts Howe will assist Burgoyne once the Philadelphia campaign is complete
May 22	Congress reappoints Schuyler as commander of the Northern Department
June 12	Major General Arthur St. Clair takes command at Fort Ticonderoga
June 12–26	Howe tries and fails to maneuver Washington into a decisive battle
June 13	Burgoyne's army departs Saint-Jean and begins its journey south up Lake Champlain toward Fort Ticonderoga
June 18	Gates addresses Congress in Philadelphia protesting Schuyler's reappointment to command of the Northern Department
June 20	Burgoyne issues a proclamation to be distributed to American civilians urging cooperation with the invading army
June 20	Schuyler convenes a council of war at Fort Ticonderoga
June 21	At the army's camp at the Bouquet River, Burgoyne addresses an assembly of his Indian allies and urges them to follow the rules of civilized warfare against the American rebels
June 23	Brigadier General Barry St. Leger and his force departs Canada for Oswego to begin his campaign down the Mohawk River valley to Albany as the supporting effort for Burgoyne's army
June 25	Lead elements of Burgoyne's army arrives at Crown Point
July 1	Burgoyne's army moves from Crown Point toward Fort Ticonderoga
July 2–4	Burgoyne's army begins to surround the American fortresses at Fort Ticonderoga and Mount Independence, by seizing Mount Hope and landing German forces on the east shore of Lake Champlain
July 4–5	British soldiers succeed in hauling two artillery pieces to the summit of Mount Defiance
July 5	St. Clair convenes a council of war; the generals agree to evacuate Fort Ticonderoga and Mount Independence
July 6	Americans abandon Fort Ticonderoga and Mount Independence and retreat toward Castleton, Vermont
July 6	Brigadier General Simon Fraser occupies Fort Ticonderoga and Mount Independence and begins pursuit of St. Clair's army
July 6	Action at Skenesborough
July 7	Battle of Hubbardton
July 8	Howe's main British Army embarks on ships for the Philadelphia campaign
July 8	Action at Fort Anne
July 9–27	Burgoyne is at Skenesborough while the route is cleared to Fort Anne
July 14	St. Clair and the Fort Ticonderoga garrison rejoins Schuyler's main army near Fort Edward

July 17	Brigadier General Nicholas Herkimer issues a proclamation calling for the Tryon County militia to muster for the purpose of defending Fort Stanwix
July 19	Burgoyne addresses another Indian assembly upon the arrival of Indian reinforcements
July 19	General George Washington orders Major General Benedict Arnold to report to the Northern Department
July 22	Howe's main British Army departs by ship from Sandy Hook to Philadelphia
July 23	Burgoyne's army begins movement from Skenesborough to Fort Anne
July 24	Washington orders Major General Benjamin Lincoln to report to the Northern Department
July 25	St. Leger arrives at Oswego
July 25	Burgoyne's army occupies Fort Anne
July 26	Jane McCrea killed
July 27	Murder of two children outside Fort Stanwix
July 28	Schuyler establishes his headquarters at Saratoga
July 29	Final American forces abandon Fort Edward
July 30	British fleet sighted off the Capes of Delaware
July 30	Burgoyne's army occupies Fort Edward
August 2	Fort Stanwix garrison reinforced by 200 Continental troops and supplies; St. Leger's Advanced Party just misses intercepting reinforcements
August 3	St. Leger's main force arrives at and invests Fort Stanwix
August 3	Congress relieves Schuyler of command of the Northern Department
August 4	Congress orders Washington to send Gates to command the Northern Department
August 4	Herkimer and his detachment depart Fort Dayton to relieve Fort Stanwix
August 6	Battle of Oriskany
August 6	Willett raids Indian camps outside Fort Stanwix
August 8	Willett clandestinely departs Fort Stanwix to seek help
August 10	Schuyler dispatches Arnold to relieve Fort Stanwix
August 11	Lieutenant Colonel Friederich von Baum and his detachment depart for Bennington, Vermont, to gather provisions
August 14	Main body of Burgoyne's army arrives at Fort Miller
August 16	Battle of Bennington
August 16	Washington orders Colonel Daniel Morgan and his riflemen to join the Northern Department
August 19	Gates formally relieves Schuyler of command of the Northern Department
August 20	Most of Burgoyne's Indian allies depart for home

August 22	St. Leger departs Fort Stanwix for Canada
August 23	Congress reaffirms Washington's position as the commander-in-chief of all land forces within the United States
August 24	Arnold and relief force arrive at Fort Stanwix
August 25	Howe lands his army at Head of Elk, Maryland
August 26	Arnold and relief force departs Fort Stanwix to rejoin main army
August 28	Burgoyne receives news that St. Leger has abandoned the siege of Fort Stanwix and returned to Canada
August 29	Morgan and his riflemen arrive at Albany
August 29	Gates organizes a corps of light infantry under Major Henry Dearborn to work with Morgan's riflemen
September 11	Battle of Brandywine
September 11	Congress evacuates Philadelphia
September 12	Gates's army begins to dig in on Bemis Heights
September 13	Burgoyne and his army cross to the west bank of the Hudson River after more than four weeks in the vicinity of Fort Miller
September 15	Burgoyne's army at Dovegat (Coveville), New York
September 15–18	American raids on Fort Ticonderoga, Skenesborough, Fort George, and Diamond Island
September 19	Battle of Freeman's Farm
September 21	Burgoyne receives message from Lieutenant General Sir Henry Clinton offering to attack the American forts in the Hudson Highlands
September 22	Benjamin Lincoln arrives at the American camp at Bemis Heights
September 26	British Army marches into Philadelphia
October 3	Burgoyne cuts the army's rations
October 3	Clinton begins campaign up the Hudson River
October 4	Battle of Germantown
October 4	Congress votes that the "Thanks of Congress" be presented to Brigadier General John Stark and Colonel Gansevoort and that an "elegant sword" be presented to Lieutenant Colonel Willett
October 6	Clinton captures Forts Clinton and Montgomery in the Hudson Highlands
October 7	Battle of Bemis Heights
October 8	General Fraser dies
October 8–11	Burgoyne's army retreats north to Saratoga
October 13	Burgoyne requests that negotiations be opened between the commanders of the two opposing armies
October 14–16	Negotiations between Gates and Burgoyne
October 16	Burgoyne receives word that Clinton has captured the Hudson Highland forts
October 16	Saratoga Convention signed by Gates and Burgoyne
October 16	Major General John Vaughan burns Esopus (Kingston), New York

October 17	Burgoyne and his army surrenders to Gates
November 4	Congress votes that the "Thanks of Congress" be presented to Generals Gates, Lincoln, and Arnold
November 4	Washington receives first evidence of the existence of the so-called "Conway Cabal"
November 5	Lieutenant Colonel Alexander Hamilton arrives at Gates's headquarters in Albany carrying Washington's orders
November 6	Burgoyne's army arrives in Boston under guard
November 8	British garrison abandons Fort Ticonderoga and retreats to Canada
December 2	News of Saratoga reaches London
December 4	News of Saratoga reaches Paris
December 7	First post-Saratoga meeting of the British cabinet to discuss a new military strategy
December 12	Charles Gravier, the Comte de Vergennes, the French Foreign Minister, meets with the American commissioners at Paris: Benjamin Franklin, Silas Deane, and Arthur Lee
December 17	Washington leads the American main army into winter encampment at Valley Forge, Pennsylvania

1778

January 17	British cabinet meeting to discuss Lord Jeffrey Amherst's recommendations for a new military strategy for 1778
January 27	After weeks of negotiations, French and American diplomats agree to the terms of treaties between the two countries
February 6	France and the United States sign a Treaty of Amity and Commerce and a Treaty of Alliance
March 7	Germain orders Clinton to replace Howe as British commander-in-chief
March 13	French ambassador to Great Britain delivers news of the two treaties between France and the United States
March 16	Parliament authorizes the Carlisle Peace Commission to reopen negotiations with the Americans
March 17	Great Britain declares war on France
March 20	Louis XVI receives the American commissioners at Paris at Versailles
March 21	Germain dispatches a new military strategy to Clinton
April 5	Burgoyne departs Boston for England ostensibly for health reasons
May 4	Congress ratifies the Treaty of Amity and Commerce and the Treaty of Alliance with France
June 15	British Army evacuates Philadelphia—begins march to New York
June 28	Battle of Monmouth

APPENDIX C

Key British Letters/Orders/ Meetings, 1776–1777

	Letter/Orders Date Sent	Sender	Recipient	Date Received	Subject/Remarks
1	Mid-October 1776	General Sir Guy Carleton	Lord George Germain	December 9, 1776	Carleton's ideas for 1777, delivered to Lord George Germain and King George III by Lieutenant General Burgoyne
2	October 10, 1776	Germain	General Sir William Howe	December 1776	News that the king has knighted Howe
3	October 18, 1776	Germain	William Howe	December 1776	Germain hopes Howe will "pay a visit to Philadelphia" in a future campaign
4	November 30, 1776	William Howe	Germain	December 30, 1776	Howe's first plan: offensives to Rhode Island, Albany, threats to Philadelphia, preparation to conduct operations in the southern colonies
5	December 10, 1776*	Lieutenant General John Burgoyne	Lord George Germain	N/A	Meeting to discuss 1776 campaign and Burgoyne's ideas for 1777
6	December 10, 1776	Germain	King George III	December 10, 1776	Results of meeting with Burgoyne—Carleton's failure in Oct. 1776
7	December 13, 1776*	Burgoyne	George III	N/A	Meeting to discuss 1776 campaign and Burgoyne's ideas for 1777

(*continued*)

	Letter/Orders Date Sent	Sender	Recipient	Date Received	Subject/Remarks
8	December 13, 1776	George III	Lord North	December 13, 1776	Results of meeting with Burgoyne—Burgoyne should command in Canada in 1777
9	December 20, 1776	William Howe	Germain	February 23, 1777	Howe alters first proposal and now calls for the main effort to capture Philadelphia; Howe does not believe northern army could possibly reach Albany until mid-Sept. 1777
10	December 31, 1776	William Howe	Germain	February 1777	Informs Germain about Trenton; requests Clinton be given the Canada expedition and Burgoyne be named Howe's second-in-command
11	January 1, 1776	Burgoyne	Germain	January 1, 1777	Tells Germain he's met with the king; asks for Germain's assistance in securing a major command
12	January 14, 1777	Germain	William Howe	March 9, 1777	Germain criticizes Carleton's actions in Oct. 1776 and declines to comment on Howe's first plan dated Nov. 30, 1776
13	January 20, 1777	William Howe	Germain	Sometime just before March 3, 1777	Trenton and Princeton changes everything: Howe thinks Philadelphia is the key. Discusses movement by sea
14	February 24, 1777	George III	Lord North	February 24, 1777	King declined to fire Carleton
15	February 28, 1777	Burgoyne	George III and Germain	February 28, 1777	"Thoughts for Conducting the War from the Side of Canada"—Burgoyne's detailed proposed plan for 1777 Lake Champlain—Hudson River campaign

	Letter/Orders Date Sent	Sender	Recipient	Date Received	Subject/Remarks
16	March 3, 1777	Germain	William Howe	May 8, 1777	Response to Howe's January 20, 1777, letter. Howe's modified plans to take Philadelphia are approved
17	March 26, 1777	Germain	Carleton and Burgoyne; Copy to William Howe	May 6, 1777; Howe received a copy on June 5, 1777	Detailed plan for the 1777 Campaign; Relieved Carleton of his military command. It contained no direct orders for Howe, but implied he had to cooperate with Burgoyne's army from Canada; no similar orders were dispatched to Howe
18	March 26, 1777	Germain	Carleton	May 6, 1777	Orders Carleton to recruit Indians for Burgoyne's and other campaigns
19	April 2, 1777	William Howe	Germain	May 18, 1777	Informs Germain that he will transport his entire army by sea for the Philadelphia campaign; encloses a copy of his April 5, 1777, letter to Carleton; see below
20	April 5, 1777	William Howe	Carleton; Howe also sent a copy to Germain enclosed with the April 2, 1777, letter above	Before May 6, 1777; Carleton sent a copy to Burgoyne after his arrival in Quebec on May 6, 1777	Howe will not be able to come up the Hudson River because he will be in Pennsylvania; Burgoyne must use his initiative and not expect any direct assistance from Howe
21	May 15, 1777	Burgoyne	Germain	Mid- to late June 1777	Burgoyne provides Germain with the status of his preparation for the campaign; he does not mention Howe's April 5, 1777, letter; he expresses confidence in the upcoming campaign

(*continued*)

	Letter/Orders Date Sent	Sender	Recipient	Date Received	Subject/Remarks
22	May 18, 1777	Germain	William Howe	August 16, 1777; at sea; in the Chesapeake Bay	Reply to Howe's April 2, 1777, letter; Germain and the king approve Howe's alterations to his plan including going to Philadelphia by sea; trusts that Howe will complete his campaign in Pennsylvania in time to "cooperate with the army ordered to proceed from Canada." The letter closes with the king's approval of Howe's April 5 letter to Carleton
23	ca. May 22, 1777	Carleton	Lord North	ca. July 2, 1777	Carleton asks for permission to resign his position as governor of Canada
24	June 3, 1777	William Howe	Germain	Late July 1777	Howe acknowledges receipt (he actually received it on May 8) of Germain's March 3 letter in which Germain and the king had approved Howe's plan to take Philadelphia; Howe tells Germain that he cannot conduct a diversion to Massachusetts that had been recommended by the secretary "without interfering with the more important operations of the campaign [Philadelphia] that have received the Royal Approbation"

	Letter/Orders Date Sent	Sender	Recipient	Date Received	Subject/Remarks
25	June 5, 1777	William Howe	Germain	Late July 1777	Howe asks for reinforcements, especially artillery; "I trust your Lordship may expect a successful campaign to the southward; yet I fear little can be done to the northward other than to give security to this province." Note: Howe had not yet received Germain's May 18 letter in which the secretary urged Howe to complete his Philadelphia campaign in time to cooperate with Burgoyne
26	June 5, 1777	Germain	George III	June 5, 1777	Germain expresses frustration that he has not received adequate updates on the commander-in-chief's activities; he had received rumors that Howe had sent two expeditions up the North (Hudson) River and so the secretary assumed they "must be intended to assist each other. It is surprising that the General should be so fond of Concealing his operations"
27	July 2, 1777	Lord North	George III	July 2, 1777	North transmits Carleton's May 22 letter (#23) to the king asking to resign, as well as the governor's May 20 and 22 letters to Germain (not in this table) discussing Burgoyne's preparations and responding to Germain's insults

(*continued*)

	Letter/Orders Date Sent	Sender	Recipient	Date Received	Subject/Remarks
28	July 2, 1777	George III	Lord North	July 2, 1777	King replies to North's July 2 letter earlier that day (#27) and says he fully understands why Carleton wants to resign

*Meeting, not a letter or set of orders.

APPENDIX D

Orders of Battle

BRITISH ARMY FROM CANADA—LIEUTENANT GENERAL JOHN BURGOYNE[1]

Headquarters Staff
Major General William Phillips and Staff
Headquarters Units
Prinz Ludwig Dragoons (Lieutenant Colonel Friederich von Baum)
Indians (typically operated with the Advanced Corps)

Royal Artillery—Major Griffith Williams
Brigade of the Park of Artillery—Captain John Carter
8th Company, 1st Battalion, Royal Regiment of Artillery (Major Griffith Williams)
5th Company, 1st Battalion, Royal Regiment of Artillery (Captain John Carter)
Additional Company, 33rd Regiment of Foot (Lieutenant George Anson Nutt)
Right Division (two medium 12-pounders, two light 6-pounders) (Lieutenant Samuel Rimington)
Center Division (two light 24-pounders, two 8-inch howitzers, two 5½-inch howitzers) (Captain Thomas Blomefield)
Left Division (two medium 12-pounders, two light 6-pounders) (Captain Thomas Hosmer)

Advanced Corps—Brigadier General Simon Fraser
Company of British Marksmen (also called Fraser's Rangers) (Captain Alexander Fraser)
British Light Infantry Battalion (Major Alexander Lindsay, 6th Earl of Balcarres)
British Grenadier Battalion (Major John Acland)
24th Regiment of Foot (Major Robert Grant)
7th Company, 3rd Battalion, Royal Regiment of Artillery (four 6-pounders, four 3-pounders, two 5½-inch howitzers) (Captain Ellis Walker)

Right Wing—Brigadier James Hamilton and Major General William Phillips
Artillery (four 6-pounders) (Captain Thomas Jones)

First Brigade—Brigadier General Henry Watson Powell
9th Regiment of Foot (Lieutenant Colonel John Hill)
47th Regiment of Foot (Lieutenant Colonel Nicolas Sutherland)
53rd Regiment of Foot (Major Paul Irving)

Second Brigade—Brigadier General James Hamilton
20th Regiment of Foot (Lieutenant Colonel John Lind)
21st Regiment of Foot (Major George Forster)
62nd Regiment of Foot (Lieutenant Colonel John Anstruther)

Left Wing—Major General Friedrich Riedesel
Hesse-Hanau Artillery Corps (four 6-pounders) (Captain Georg Pausch)

Advance Corps—"Breymann's Corps"—Lieutenant Colonel Heinrich Breymann
Hesse-Hanau Artillery Corps (two light 6-pounders, two light 3-pounders) (Lieutenant von Spangenburg)
Grenadier Battalion (Major Otto von Mengen)
Light Battalion (Major Ferdinand von Barner)
Jäger Company (Captain Carl von Geyso)

First Brigade—Brigadier General Johann von Specht
Regiment von Rhetz (Major Balthasar von Lucke)
Regiment von Riedesel (Lieutenant Colonel Ernst von Speth)
Regiment von Specht (Major Carl von Ehrenkrook)

Second Brigade—Brigadier General Wilhelm von Gall
Regiment Prinz Friedrich (Lieutenant Colonel Christian Praetorius)
Regiment Erbprinz (Hesse-Hanau) (Lieutenant Colonel Otto von Lentz)

Loyalist Corps (these units typically served with the Advanced Corps)
The King's Loyal Americans (Jessup's Rangers) (Lieutenant Colonel Ebenezer Jessup)
The Queen's Loyal Rangers (Peters' Corps) (Lieutenant Colonel John Peters)
The Loyal Volunteers (Captain Samuel MacKay)
Captain Adams's Company of Rangers (Captain Samuel Adams)
Wilcox's Pioneer Company (Captain Hazard Wilcox)
Van Alstine's Bateaux Company (Captain Peter Van Alstine)
King's Royal Regiment of New York Detachment (Ensign William Phillips)

Other Units and Groups
47th Regiment of Foot (Lieutenant Colonel Nicholas Sutherland)
Royal Navy detachment (1st Lieutenant William Brown)
Corps of Engineers (Lieutenant and Sub-Engineer William Twiss)
His Majesty's General Hospital (Acting Physician Vincent Wood)
Quartermaster Department (Deputy Quartermaster-General Captain John Money)
Commissary Departments (Commissary-General Jonathan Clarke)
Artificers (Captain George Lowes)
Bateaux-men, teamsters
Followers: Women, children, and servants

British and German Troops Assigned to Garrison Duties
53rd Regiment of Foot—Fort Ticonderoga Garrison
Braunschweig Regiment Prinz Friedrich—Fort Ticonderoga Garrison
Two-thirds of Captain William Borthwick's Company, 3rd Battalion, Royal Artillery—Fort Ticonderoga Garrison
Two Companies of the 47th Regiment of Foot—Diamond Island Garrison, Lake George

Totals:
July 1, 1777—**9,500** (ca. **4,000** British soldiers in the Right Wing and Advanced Corps and ca. **3,600** German soldiers in the Left Wing)[2]
September 15, 1777—**6,530** fit for duty
October 7, 1777—ca. **5,900** fit for duty

Notes: It is impossible to know how many Indians accompanied Burgoyne's expedition, but at its peak, the contingent probably exceeded 500 warriors. However, fewer than 80 remained with the army by mid-September. Although Phillips was technically Burgoyne's

second-in-command and commander of all the artillery, as an artillery officer, he was prohibited by regulation from commanding infantry units. However, he received special authorization to command infantry units as necessary during the campaign, which he did. After the capture of Fort Ticonderoga, General Hamilton, along with 1,000 soldiers, was assigned to secure the fort and surrounding area. General Powell replaced him in August, and Hamilton returned to the army for the rest of the campaign. The total number of camp followers is unknown, but they probably amounted to about 300 women and 100 children. Additionally, an unknown number of refugees, civilian contractors (such as teamsters), and sutlers accompanied the army.

AMERICAN ARMY AT FORT TICONDEROGA—MAJOR GENERAL ARTHUR ST. CLAIR[3]

Headquarters and Staff
Brigadier General Enoch Poor
1st New Hampshire Regiment (Colonel Joseph Cilley)
2nd New Hampshire Regiment (Colonel Nathan Hale)
3rd New Hampshire Regiment (Colonel Alexander Scammel)

Brigadier General John Paterson
10th Massachusetts Regiment (Colonel Thomas Marshall)
11th Massachusetts Regiment (Colonel Ebenezer Francis)
12th Massachusetts Regiment (Colonel Samuel Brewer)
14th Massachusetts Regiment (Colonel Gamaliel Bradford)

Brigadier General Roche de Fermoy
Additional Continental Regiment (Colonel Seth Warner)
8th Massachusetts Regiment (Colonel Michael Jackson)
New Hampshire Militia (Colonel Pierce Long)
Massachusetts Militia (Colonel Leonard)
Massachusetts Militia (Colonel Wells)
Total: ca. 4,553 fit for duty

BATTLE OF HUBBARDTON—JULY 7, 1777[4]

Americans—Colonel Ebenezer Francis
11th Massachusetts Regiment (Colonel Francis)
Additional Continental Regiment (Colonel Seth Warner)
2nd New Hampshire Regiment (Colonel Hale)
Total: 1,300

British-German Pursuit Force
British—Brigadier General Simon Fraser
Corps of Marksmen (Captain Fraser)
Loyalists and Indians (Lieutenant Colonel Peters)
24th Regiment of Foot (Major Grant)
Grenadier Battalion (Major Acland)
Light Battalion (Major Lindsey)
Total: 850

German—Major General Friedrich Riedesel
Men from the Grenadier and Light Infantry Battalions (Captain Schottelius)
Jägers (Captain von Geyso)
Total: 180

SIEGE OF FORT STANWIX—AUGUST 2–22, 1777

British-German Mohawk River Expedition—Brigadier General Barry St. Leger:[5]
Royal Artillery (two 6-pounders, two 3-pounders, four mortars) (Lieutenant Glennie)
8th Foot (Captain Lernoult)
34th Foot (Brigadier General St. Leger)
Jäger Company (Hesse-Hanau) (Lieutenant Hildebrandt)
King's Royal Regiment of New York (Colonel Sir John Johnson)
Rangers (Colonel John Butler)
Canadian Militia
Bateaux Men
Iroquois (Chief Thayendanegea—Joseph Brandt)
Total: ca. 2,000

American Fort Stanwix (Schuyler) Garrison—Colonel Peter Gansevoort[6]
3rd New York Regiment (Colonel Peter Gansevoort)
9th Massachusetts Regiment (Lieutenant Colonel James Mellen)
Total: 750

BATTLE OF ORISKANY—AUGUST 6, 1777

American Fort Stanwix Relief Force—Brigadier General Nicholas Herkimer
1st Regiment (Canjoharie) (Colonel Ebenezer Cox)
2nd Regiment (Palatine) (Colonel Jacob Klock)
3rd Regiment (Mohawk) (Colonel Frederick Visscher)
4th Regiment (German Flatts) (Colonel Peter Bellinger)
Oneida Warriors
Teamsters
Total: ca. 800

British-Indian Ambush Detachment—Colonel Sir John Johnson and Joseph Brant
King's Royal Regiment of New York (Colonel Sir John Johnson)
Rangers (Colonel John Butler)
Iroquois Warriors (Chief Thayendanegea—Joseph Brant)
Total: ca. 700

BATTLE OF BENNINGTON—AUGUST 16, 1777[7]

German-British Detachment—Lieutenant Colonel Baum
Prince Ludwig Dragoons (Major Maiborn)
Grenadier Battalion (Lieutenant Burghoff)
Light Battalion (Captain Thomas)
Line Infantry Detachment (Ensign Andrea)
Hesse-Hanau Artillery (two 3-pounders) (Lieutenant Bach)
Queen's Loyal Rangers (Lieutenant Colonel Peters)
Corps of Marksmen (Captain Fraser)
Loyalists (Lieutenant Colonel Pfister/Captain Covel)
Canadians
Indians (Captain de Lanaudiére/Captain Campbell)
Total: 762

American—Brigadier General John Stark[8]
New Hampshire Militia (Colonel William Gregg)
New Hampshire Militia (Lieutenant Colonel Moses Nichol)
New Hampshire Militia (Colonel Thomas Stickney)
New Hampshire Militia (Colonel David Hobart)

Reserve New Hampshire Militia
Vermont Rangers/Militia (Colonel Samuel Herrick)
Massachusetts Regiment of Militia (Colonel Benjamin Simonds)
Warner's Vermont Regiment (Colonel Seth Warner)
Additional Continental Regiment (Lieutenant Colonel Safford)
Total: ca. 2,150

German Relief Force—Lieutenant Colonel Heinrich Breymann[9]
Grenadier Battalion
Jäger Battalion
Hesse-Hanau Artillery (two 6-pounders)
Total: 644

AMERICAN NORTHERN ARMY—MAJOR GENERAL HORATIO GATES[10]

Headquarters Staff
Artillery
Independent Continental Artillery Battalion (one 9-pounder, four 6-pounders, fifteen 4-pounders, two 3-pounders) (Major Ebenezer Stevens)

Cavalry
2nd Connecticut Light Dragoons (Captain Jean Louis de Vernejoux)
2nd Connecticut Light Horse (Major Elijah Hyde)

Left Wing—Major General Benedict Arnold
Morgan's Corps—Colonel Daniel Morgan
Corps of Riflemen (Colonel Daniel Morgan)
Corps of Light Infantry (Major Henry Dearborn)

Brigadier General Enoch Poor's Brigade
1st New Hampshire Regiment (Colonel Joseph Cilley)
2nd New Hampshire Regiment (Colonel Hale was captured on July 7 and Lieutenant Colonel Winborn Adams was killed in action on September 19, 1777; command devolved to Captain John Drew)
3rd New Hampshire Regiment (Colonel Alexander Scammell)
2nd New York Regiment (Colonel Philip van Cortlandt)
4th New York Regiment (Colonel Henry Livingston) 1st Regiment Connecticut Militia (Colonel Thaddeus Cook)
2nd Regiment Connecticut Militia (Colonel Jonathan Latimer)

Brigadier General Ebenezer Learned's Brigade
2nd Massachusetts Regiment (Colonel John Bailey)
8th Massachusetts Regiment (Lieutenant Colonel John Brooks)
9th Massachusetts Regiment (Colonel James Wesson)
1st Canadian Regiment (Colonel James Livingston)
Battalion of New Hampshire Militia (Colonel Stephen Evans) (arrived on October 7)
Battalion of New Hampshire Militia (Colonel Abraham Drake) (arrived on October 7)

Right Wing—Major General Horatio Gates and Major General Benjamin Lincoln
Brigadier John Glover's Brigade
1st Massachusetts Regiment (Colonel Joseph Vose)
4th Massachusetts Regiment (Colonel William Shepard)

13th Massachusetts Regiment (Major John Porter)
15th Massachusetts Regiment (Colonel Timothy Bigelow)
Battalion of Albany County, New York Militia (1st Regiment) (Colonel Abraham Wemple)
Battalion of Albany County, New York Militia (2nd Regiment) (Colonel William Whiting)
Battalion of Dutchess and Ulster Counties, New York Militia (Colonel Morris Graham)

Brigadier General John Nixon's Brigade
3rd Massachusetts Regiment (Colonel John Greaton)
5th Massachusetts Regiment (Colonel Rufus Putnam)
6th Massachusetts Regiment (Colonel Thomas Nixon)
7th Massachusetts Regiment (Colonel Ichabod Alden)
One Regiment of Massachusetts Militia (Colonel Ezra May) (arrived on October 5 and departed on October 14)

Brigadier General John Paterson's Brigade
10th Massachusetts Regiment (Colonel Thomas Marshall)
11th Massachusetts Regiment (Lieutenant Colonel Benjamin Tupper)
12th Massachusetts Regiment (Colonel Samuel Brewer)
14th Massachusetts Regiment (Colonel Gamaliel Bradford)
1st Berkshire County Battalion, Massachusetts Militia (Colonel John Ashley) (arrived on October 3)
3rd York County Battalion, Massachusetts Militia (Lieutenant Colonel Joseph Storer) (arrived on October 3) [d]

Brigadier General Jonathan Warner's Command
Five Battalions of Massachusetts Militia (arrived on September 24)

Brigadier General Abraham Ten Broeck's Brigade (also known as "Schuyler's Brigade")
Elements of Ten Albany County Regiments, New York Militia (arrived on October 4)

Brigadier General John Fellows's Brigade
Unknown number of Massachusetts militia regiments (arrived after October 7)

Independent Commands
Brigadier General John Stark
Unknown number of New Hampshire militia regiments (arrived after October 7)

Brigadier General William Whipple
Unknown number of New Hampshire militia regiments (arrived after October 7)

Brigadier General Jacob Bayley
Unknown number of Vermont militia regiments (arrived after October 7)

Brigadier General James Brickett
Unknown number of Massachusetts militia regiments (arrived after October 7)

Brigadier General Oliver Wolcott
Wolcott's brigade consisted of his own battalion of Connecticut militia (arrived on October 4)

Totals:
September 19, 1777—6,693 fit for duty
October 7, 1777—ca. 11,000
October 16, 1777—16,930 fit for duty

Notes: Although Arnold requested that he be relieved of his command during the quarrel with Gates, this never happened. He retained command of the left wing through the Battle of Bemis Heights. Gates commanded the army and the right wing until Lincoln's arrival. Once Lincoln joined the army on September 22, he assumed command of the right wing and replaced Arnold as Gates's second-in-command. The total strength of the American units is impossible to know for sure, given the inaccuracy of personnel returns and conflicting sources, especially regarding the militia. It is clear that Gates slightly outnumbered Burgoyne in everything but artillery on September 19. Due to the massive influx of militia reinforcements, the American army grew to over 11,000 troops by October 7. After the Battle of Bemis Heights, militia troops continued to flow into the area, and Gates's army numbered almost 17,000 men when Burgoyne surrendered.

BRITISH-GERMAN OCTOBER 7, 1777, RECONNAISSANCE FORCE[11]
Canadian Volunteers
Royalists
British Grenadiers
British Light Infantry
24th Regiment of Foot
Breymann's Reserve Corps
British Line Detachments
German Line Detachments
Artillery
Total: ca. 1,700

NOTES ON MAPS

The maps for this book were created by Glen Pawelski from Mapping Specialists Limited of Fitchburg, Wisconsin. Glen patiently endured my many change requests. We used many existing period and modern maps as baseline sources for identifying key features such as locations of buildings, roads, and units, and the movements of soldiers throughout the theater and on the battlefield. Key among these existing maps were National Park Service maps, American Battlefield Trust maps, and several created by cartographers of the History Department at the US Army Military Academy, especially the maps depicting Fort Ticonderoga and Burgoyne's final camp. In addition, we consulted period maps such as the François Louis Tesseidre de Fleury map of the siege of Fort Stanwix and the William Cumberland Wilkinson maps of Saratoga, all easily accessible online. In addition, all the maps include input and modifications based on research, walks through the grounds, and extensive discussions with park rangers and other staff at the Saratoga National Historical Park, the Fort Stanwix National Monument, the Oriskany Battlefield State Historic Site in New York, and the Hubbardton Battlefield State Historic Site in Vermont.

NOTES

ABBREVIATIONS

AHP Harold C. Syrett, ed., *The Papers of Alexander Hamilton, Volume 1* (New York: Columbia University Press, 1961)
DAR K. G. Davies, ed., *Documents of the American Revolution: Colonial Office Series* (Dublin: Irish University Press, 1976)
DLAR David Library of the American Revolution
GGP Lord George Germain Papers, Clements Library, University of Michigan
GWP *The Papers of George Washington, Revolutionary War Series*
HCP Sir Henry Clinton Papers, Clements Library, University of Michigan
HGP Horatio Gates Papers, Microfilm Edition, Army Heritage and Education Center
JCC *Journals of the Continental Congress* (Washington, DC: Government Printing Office, 1905)
LDC *Letters of Delegates to Congress* (Washington, DC: Library of Congress, 1976–2000)
STOE John Burgoyne, *A State of the Expedition from Canada as Laid before the House of Commons by Lieutenant-General Burgoyne*, 2nd Ed. (London: J. Almon, 1780)

INTRODUCTION

1. Journal entry for August 22, 1777, in Horace Walpole, *Journal of the Reign of King George the Third from the Year 1771 to 1783*, Vol. 2, ed. John Doran (London: Bentley, 1859), 131. For an excellent biography of the king, see Jeremy Black, *George III: America's Last King* (New Haven, CT: Yale University Press, 2009). See also Stanley Weintraub, *Iron Tears: America's Battle for Freedom, Britain's Quagmire: 1775–1783* (New York: Free Press, 2005), 110.
2. George III to Earl of Sandwich, September 3, 1777, in *John Montagu, The Private Papers of John, Earl of Sandwich, First Lord of the Admiralty, 1771–1782*, Vol. 1, ed. G. R. Barnes and J. H. Owens (London: Navy Records Society, 1932), 293.
3. For an excellent discussion of the shock and near-panic that gripped Britain after Saratoga, see Brendan Simms, *Three Victories and a Defeat: The Rise and Fall of the First British Empire* (New York: Basic, 2007), 610.
4. Congress designated the Northern Department of the Continental Army, which extended from the Canadian border to south of Albany. The army assigned to this department was commonly called the Northern Army. Burgoyne's invading army from Canada was generally referred to as the Northern Army as well. To avoid confusion, in this book the American Northern Army will be capitalized, and the British northern army will be in lowercase. Robert K. Wright Jr., *The Continental Army* (Washington, DC: Center of Military History, 2006), 41.
5. For a good explanation of Montgomery's concept of grip, see Edward J. Erickson, *Gallipoli: Command Under Fire* (New York: Osprey, 2015), 19; and Stephen Ashley Hart, *Colossal Cracks: Montgomery's 21st Army Group in Northwest Europe, 1944–45* (Mechanicsburg, PA: Stackpole Books, 2007), 116.
6. Carl von Clausewitz, *On War*, ed. and trans. Michael Howard and Peter Paret (Princeton, NJ: Princeton University Press, 1976), 100–112.
7. The three levels of war are tactical, operational, and strategic. Tactics are the techniques used to fight battles and engagements; operations link tactical actions on the battlefield—battles, engagements, and other operations—to strategic goals, through the conduct of

campaigns; and strategy is the calculated application of ways and means to achieve a political objective. All three levels can overlap. Joint Staff, *Joint Publication (JP) 3.0, Joint Operations* (Washington, DC: Joint Staff, August 11, 2011): I-12–I-14.

CHAPTER 1

1. Andrew Jackson O'Shaughnessy, *The Men Who Lost America: British Leadership, the American Revolution, and the Fate of the Empire* (New Haven, CT: Yale University Press, 2013), 87.
2. Richard M. Ketchum, *Decisive Day: The Battle of Bunker Hill* (New York: Holt McDougal, 1999), 183.
3. William Howe to unnamed fellow officer, June 22 and 24, 1776, in Henry Steele Commager and Richard B. Morris, eds., *The Spirit of 'Seventy-Six: The Story of the American Revolution as Told by Participants* (New York: Bonanza Books, 1983), 132.
4. For an excellent discussion of the increasingly dysfunctional relationship between Clinton and Howe, see William B. Willcox, *Portrait of a General: Sir Henry Clinton and the War of Independence* (New York: Knopf, 1964), 66. See also Ira Gruber, *The Howe Brothers and the American Revolution* (New York: Athenaeum, 1972), 230.
5. As General William Howe's second-in-command, Clinton enjoyed the temporary rank of lieutenant general because of his position. When Burgoyne became General Sir Guy Carleton's second-in-command in Canada, he was also temporarily promoted. The ranks can cause confusion as both officers are often referred to by their permanent ranks of major general.
6. Horace Walpole to Horace Mann, September 20, 1776, in Paget Toynbee, ed., *The Letters of Horace Walpole, Fourth Earl of Orford*, Vol. 9: 1774–1776 (Oxford: Clarendon Press, 1903), 415.
7. Myron Magnet, "When George Washington Became Great: Those Were the Times that Tried Men's Souls," *City Journal* (Winter 2012). http://www.city-journal.org/html/when-george-washington-became-great-13458.html
8. Richard W. Stewart, ed., *American Military History, Vol. 1: The United States Army and the Forging of a Nation, 1775–1917* (Washington, DC: Center of American History, 2005), 67–68.
9. Chernow has described the battle as a "searing loss; it was a defeat without redeeming features." Ron Chernow, *Washington: A Life* (New York: Penguin Press, 2010), 262.
10. Stewart, *American Military History*, 68–69.
11. Lee to Gates, December 13, 1776, in Allan Kulikoff, ed., *American Archives: Documents of the American Revolutionary Period, 1774–1776* (DeKalb: Northern Illinois University Libraries). http://amarch.lib.niu.edu/islandora/object/niu-amarch%3A104112
12. Washington to Hancock, November 16, 1776, in Edward G. Lengel, ed., *This Glorious Struggle: George Washington's Revolutionary War Letters* (New York: Harper Collins, 2007), 77.
13. For a good account of both William and Richard Howe's attitude toward the Americans and their cause, see Gruber, *The Howe Brothers and the American Revolution.* See also Chernow, *Washington*, 263.
14. Washington to Charles Lee, November 30, 1776, in Commager and Morris, *The Spirit of 'Seventy-Six*, 499.
15. Donald Stoker and Michael W. Jones, "Colonial Military Strategy," in *Strategy in the American War of Independence: A Global Approach*, ed. Donald Stoker, Kenneth J. Hagan, and Michael T. McMaster (London: Routledge, 2010), 8–13.
16. Washington to Hancock, September 25, 1776, in Lengel, *This Glorious Struggle*, 69–73. In this letter, Washington called, again, for long-term enlistments for the Continental Army, because "To place any dependence upon the Militia, is, assuredly, resting upon a broken staff."
17. Alexander Hamilton to Robert R. Livingston, June 28, 1777, in *The Papers of Alexander Hamilton, Volume 1*, ed. Harold C. Syrett (New York: Columbia University Press, 1961), 274–77 (hereafter AHP).

18. Washington to Hancock, December 8, 1776, in Lengel, *This Glorious Struggle*, 78.
19. Washington to Lund Washington, December 17, 1776, in Commager and Morris, *Spirit of 'Seventy-Six*, 504.
20. Thomas Paine, *The American Crisis*, ibid., 505.
21. Washington to Hancock, December 20, 1776, in Lengel, *This Glorious Struggle*, 81.
22. Chernow, *Washington*, 272.
23. The best account of the key American victory at Trenton is David Hackett Fischer, *Washington's Crossing* (New York: Oxford University Press, 2004). See also Chernow, *Washington*, 269–77.
24. Washington to Hancock, December 27, 1776, in Lengel, *This Glorious Struggle*, 87–89.
25. William Tryon to George Germain, December 31, 1776, *American Archives: Documents of the American Revolutionary Period, 1774–1776*. http://amarch.lib.niu.edu/islandora/object/niu-amarch%3A101040
26. Howe to Germain, January 20, 1777, in K. G. Davies, ed., *Documents of the American Revolution: Colonial Office Series*, Vol. 14 (Dublin: Irish University Press, 1976), 33 (hereafter DAR).
27. Sources vary widely on the casualty count for this battle. Fischer, *Washington's Crossing*, 324–40. See also Chernow, *Washington*, 277–84, and Stewart, *American Military History*, 71–72.
28. Washington to Hancock, January 5, 1777, in Lengel, *This Glorious Struggle*, 97.
29. Horace Walpole to William Mason, February 27, 1777, in Toynbee, *The Letters of Horace Walpole*, Vol. X, 22.
30. Worthington Chauncey Ford, ed., *Journals of the Continental Congress, Vol. II, 1775* (Washington, DC: Government Printing Office, 1905), 109–10 (hereafter JCC).
31. The French and Indian War was the name for the North American theater of operations during the larger Seven Years War. Ibid., 109.
32. Paul David Nelson, *General Sir Guy Carleton, Lord Dorchester: Soldier-Statesman of Early British Canada* (Cranbury, NJ: Fairleigh Dickinson University Press, 2000); Paul H. Smith, "Sir Guy Carleton: Soldier-Statesman," in *George Washington's Generals and Opponents: Their Exploits and Leadership*, Vol. 2, ed. George Athan Billias (New York: De Capo Press, 1994); and René Chartrand, *American War of Independence Commanders* (Oxford: Osprey, 2003), 27–30.
33. Quoted in Smith, "Sir Guy Carleton," 105.
34. Ibid., 103–41; and see also Nelson, *General Sir Guy Carleton*.
35. John H. G. Pell, "Philip Schuyler: The General as Aristocrat," in Billias, *George Washington's Generals and Opponents, Vol. 1*, 55.
36. Ibid., 55–58, and Don R. Gerlach, *Proud Patriot: Philip Schuyler and the War of Independence, 1775–1783* (Syracuse, NY: Syracuse University Press, 1987), 1–25. Although there was no United States on June 19, 1775, when Congress appointed Schuyler as a major general, the birthdate of the United States Army is June 14, 1775, with the creation of the Continental Army.
37. Gerlach, *Proud Patriot*, 39.
38. Willard M. Wallace, "Benedict Arnold: Traitorous Patriot," in Billias, *George Washington's Generals and Opponents, Vol. 1*, 163–64; and James Kirby Martin, *Benedict Arnold, Revolutionary Hero* (New York: New York University Press, 1997), 11–64.
39. Wallace, "Benedict Arnold," 166–70, and Martin, *Benedict Arnold*, 106–16.
40. Washington to Benedict Arnold, September 14, 1775, in Lengel, *This Glorious Struggle*, 21–22.
41. Washington's "Address to the People of Canada," September 14, 1775, ibid., 22–24.
42. Gerlach, *Proud Patriot*, 59–66. See also John Ferling, *Almost a Miracle: The American Victory in the War of Independence* (New York: Oxford University Press, 2007), 83–87; Robert Middlekauff, *The Glorious Cause: The American Revolution, 1763–1789* (New York: Oxford University Press, 2005), 309–10; Stewart, *American Military History*, 53–54; Martin, *Benedict Arnold*, 104–23; and Clare Brandt, *The Man in the Mirror: A Life of Benedict Arnold* (New York: Random House, 1994), 42–44.

43. Philip Schuyler to Washington, July 31–August 2, 1775, in *The Papers of George Washington*, Revolutionary War Series, Vol. 1, June 16, 1775–September 15, 1775, ed. Philander D. Chase (Charlottesville: University Press of Virginia, 1985), 202–3 (hereafter GWP).
44. Washington to Schuyler, August 14, 1775, ibid., 305–7.
45. Benedict Arnold to (probably) Philip Schuyler, November 27, 1775, in Commager and Morris, *Spirit of 'Seventy-Six*, 201.
46. Martin, *Benedict Arnold*, 104–28; and Colin G. Calloway, *The American Revolution in Indian Country: Crisis and Diversity in Native American Communities* (New York: Cambridge University Press, 1995), 72.
47. "Letter of an Officer of the New York Troops in Canada," November 3, 1775, in Commager and Morris, *Spirit of 'Seventy-Six*, 189–90.
48. Stewart, *American Military History*, 53–54; and Ferling, *Almost a Miracle*, 87–88. See also the excellent biography of Guy Carleton, Nelson, *General Sir Guy Carleton.*
49. Ferling, *Almost a Miracle*, 88. See also Benjamin Trumbull, journal entry, November 14, 1775, in Commager and Morris, *Spirit of 'Seventy-Six*, 191; and Nelson, *General Sir Guy Carleton*, 66–83.
50. Richard Montgomery to Schuyler, December 5, 1775, in Commager and Morris, *Spirit of 'Seventy-Six*, 202–3.
51. Benedict Arnold to Hannah Arnold, January 6, 1776, in ibid., 210.
52. Ferling, *Almost a Miracle*, 97–99; Stewart, *American Military History*, 54–55; Martin, *Benedict Arnold*, 151–74; and Mike Laramie, "The Last Invasion of Canada," *Military History Matters* (August 2019), 40–46. Included among the American prisoners was a relatively unknown but highly capable officer, Daniel Morgan, who twenty-one months later would play a pivotal role in the Saratoga campaign. Carleton released his prisoners in August 1776.
53. Nelson, *General Sir Guy Carleton*, 84. As soon as Lord George Germain, the newly appointed Secretary of State for America, heard that the Americans had taken Montreal and Carleton had retreated to Quebec, he put into motion plans to reinforce Canada and expel the Americans. Journal entries, November 9 and 30, 1775, in Walpole, *Journal of the Reign of King George*, Vol. 1, 530–31.
54. Ferling, *Almost a Miracle*, 108–11 and Martin, *Benedict Arnold*, 180–209. Like Sir Henry Clinton, Burgoyne enjoyed the rank of temporary lieutenant general by virtue of his position as second-in-command to a full general commanding a major department.
55. Journal entry, June 3, 1776, Walpole, *Journal of the Reign of King George*, Vol. 2, 56.

CHAPTER 2

1. Nelson, *General Sir Guy Carleton*, 87–88; and DAR, Vol. 12: 7–8.
2. Martin, *Benedict Arnold*, 218–20.
3. Ibid., 221.
4. Nelson, *General Sir Guy Carleton*, 90.
5. Journal entry, July 2, 1776, in Walpole, *Journal of the Reign of King George*, Vol. 2, 60. See also Alan Valentine, *Lord George Germain* (Oxford: Oxford University Press, 1962), 151.
6. Nelson, *General Sir Guy Carleton*, 90–91, and Smith, "Sir Guy Carleton," 123–24.
7. Walpole believed that the source of the animosity between the two men was because Carleton had testified against Germain at his court martial, but this never happened. More likely, Germain was predisposed to dislike Carleton because of his friendship with the Duke of Richmond, one of the secretary's enemies. Valentine, *Lord George Germain*, 151n.
8. Germain to Carleton, June 21, 1776, in DAR, Vol. 12: 154.
9. Guy Carleton to George Germain, September 28, 1776, in DAR, Vol. 12: 232–33.
10. Nelson, *General Sir Guy Carleton*, 94–95. For a good discussion of the personal and professional conflict between Carleton and Germain, see ibid., 88–99; DAR, Vol. 12: 9–10; and Valentine, *Lord George Germain*, 149–55.
11. Valentine, *Lord George Germain*, 40.
12. Quoted in ibid., 40.
13. Germain to Henry Conway, July 8, 1758, in Toynebee, *The Letters of Horace Walpole*, 156.

14. Surprisingly, there is only one full-length biography of Germain that covers his entire life: Valentine, *Lord George Germain.* However, Piers Mackesy has written an excellent book that concentrates on the Minden controversy: Piers Mackesy, *The Coward of Minden: The Affair of Lord Sackville* (New York: St. Martin's Press, 1979). See also the excellent essay on Germain in O'Shaughnessy, *The Men Who Lost America,* 165–203.
15. Valentine, *Lord George Germain,* 49.
16. Ibid., 58. See also Gerald S. Brown, "The Court Martial of Lord George Sackville, Whipping Boy of the Revolutionary War," *William and Mary Quarterly* 9, no.3 (July 1952): 328–34.
17. Valentine, *Lord George Germain,* 68; and Mackesy, *The Coward of Minden,* 224.
18. Walpole to George Montagu, April 19, 1760, in Toynbee, *Letters of Horace Walpole,* Vol. 4, 370. Many were surprised at Sackville's sentence because only three years before, Admiral John Byng had been found guilty by a court martial and executed for failing "to do his utmost" while fighting the French in the Mediterranean.
19. Valentine, *Lord George Germain,* 68–69.
20. The *Parliamentary History of England* and Walpole's journals during this period are replete with examples of Germain being attacked and ridiculed in the House of Commons. Walpole, *Journal of the Reign of King George,* Vol. 2, 34.
21. Late in 1769, Lady Betty Germain left her large estate in Northhamptonshire to Sackville with the provision that he assume the Germain name. This he did, and in 1770 he became known as Lord George Germain; see Mackesy, *The Coward of Minden,* 249–50; and Valentine, *Lord George Germain,* 98. As Valentine notes, it seems strange that Sackville would choose to abandon his illustrious family name, but as the third son, he could certainly use the fortune bequeathed by Lady Germain, and a new name could distance him from the Minden affair. Germain's title of Secretary of State for the Colonies was also commonly referred to as the Secretary of State for the American Department.
22. Journal entry, foNovember 9, 1775, in Walpole, *Journal of the Reign of King George,* Vol. 1, 519.
23. Both O'Shaughnessy and Mackesy discuss the impact of his homosexuality on his political career; see O'Shaughnessy, *The Men Who Lost America,* 171–73; and Mackesy, *The Coward of Minden,* 253–58.
24. Mackesy, *The Coward of Minden,* 36.
25. For an excellent summary of senior level leadership theory that emphasizes the importance of building and maintaining strong interpersonal relationships between leaders, see Stephen J. Gerras, *Strategic Leadership Primer,* 3rd edition (Carlisle Barracks, PA: Department of Command, Leadership and Management, US Army War College, 2010), 32–33.
26. Germain to Carleton, August 22, 1776, in DAR, Vol. 12: 187–88.
27. Nelson, *General Sir Guy Carleton,* 96–97. Historians have argued that Carleton was essentially relieved of the military part of his responsibilities in Canada because he failed to take Fort Ticonderoga in October 1776 after the British naval victories of October 11 and 13, 1776, on Lake Champlain. But the August 26 letter clearly shows that Germain wanted to relieve Carleton well before 1777. Thus, it was the secretary's loss of confidence in the general in the summer of 1776, as well as their deteriorating relationship, that led to Carleton's relief.
28. Quoted in ibid., 8.
29. Carleton to Germain, September 28, 1776, in DAR, Vol. 12: 232–34.
30. Nelson, *General Sir Guy Carleton,* 99.
31. For a description of the British fleet, see Gregory M. Tomlin, "Valcour Island: Setting the Conditions for Victory at Saratoga," in *Key to the Northern Country: The Hudson River in the American Revolution,* ed. James M. Johnson, Christopher Pryslopski, and Andrew Villani (Albany: State University of New York Press, 2013), 272.
32. Bateaux is the plural of bateau. For an excellent description of the origins, uses, dimensions, capability, and construction of bateaux, see Nathan A. Gallagher, "The Lake George Bateaux: British Colonial Utility Craft in the French and Indian War," Unpublished Master's Thesis, Texas A&M University, May 2015, 7–16.

33. Tomlin, "Valcour Island," 272; Richard M. Ketchum, *Saratoga: Turning Point of America's Revolutionary War* (New York: Henry Holt, 1997), 41; and Bowler, R. Arthur, *Logistics and the Failure of the British Army in America, 1775–1783* (Princeton, NJ: Princeton University Press, 1975), 223.
34. Resolves of Congress, June 17, 1776, in JCC, Vol. 5: 448. Major General John Thomas, who had replaced General David Wooster, who had in turn replaced Arnold outside Quebec, died of the disease during the retreat from Canada. Paul David Nelson, *General Horatio Gates: A Biography* (Baton Rouge: Louisiana State University, 1976), 56.
35. Washington to Gates, June 24, 1776, in GWP, Vol. 5: 84–86.
36. Gates to John Adams, June 24, 1776, *National Archives, Founders Online.* http://founders.archives.gov/documents/Adams/06-04-02-0137.
37. Philip Schuyler to George Washington, July 1, 1776, in GWP, Vol. 5: 172–78. For discussions of the roots of the Northern Department's command issues, see Gerlach, *Proud Patriot*, 160–65; and Nelson, *Horatio Gates*, 58–61.
38. Resolves of Congress, July 8, 1776, in JCC, Vol. 5: 526.
39. John Adams autobiography, part 1, "John Adams," through 1776, sheet 36 of 53 [electronic edition]. *Adams Family Papers: An Electronic Archive.* Massachusetts Historical Society. http://www.masshist.org/digitaladams/
40. Douglas R. Cubbison, *The American Northern Army in 1776: The Ruin and Reconstruction of the Continental Force* (Jefferson, NC: McFarland, 2010), 129–30.
41. For discussion of the July 7, 1776, council of war and its key decision to abandon Crown Point, see ibid., 135–37; Gerlach, *Proud Patriot*, 166–72; Martin, *Benedict Arnold*, 234–35; Brandt, *Man in the Mirror*, 93–94; and Nelson, *Horatio Gates*, 61–68.
42. George Washington to Horatio Gates, July 19, 1776, in GWP, Vol. 5: 380–81. A number of New England officers went so far as to protest in writing the decision to abandon Crown Point, which was forwarded to Schuyler; see Gerlach, *Proud Patriot*, 169.
43. Horatio Gates to George Washington, July 29, 1776, in GWP, Vol. 5: 498–501.
44. Ibid.
45. Ibid.
46. Horatio Gates to John Hancock, July 29, 1776, Horatio Gates Papers, Microfilm Reel 3, Army Heritage and Education Center (hereafter HGP).
47. Benedict Arnold to George Washington, June 25, 1776, in GWP, Vol. 5: 96–97. See also Martin, *Benedict Arnold*, 227.
48. George Washington to Horatio Gates, August 14, 1776, in GWP, Vol. 6: 20–22.
49. George Athan Billias, "Horatio Gates: Professional Soldier," in *George Washington's Generals and Opponents: Their Exploits and Leadership*, Vol. 1, 79–86; and John R. Elting, *The Battles of Saratoga* (Monmouth Beach, NJ: Philip Freneau Press, 1977), 17–18.
50. Billias, "Horatio Gates: Professional Soldier," 79–86; and Elting, *The Battles of Saratoga*, 17–18.
51. Will Monk, "The Myth of 'Granny Gates,'" *Journal of the American Revolution* (October 2, 2014). http://allthingsliberty.com/2014/10/the-myth-of-granny-gates/
52. Quoted in Nelson, *General Horatio Gates*, 6, and Thomas Fleming, *Washington's Secret War: The Hidden History of Valley Forge* (New York: HarperCollins, 2005), 109–10.
53. For Washington's initially favorable impression of Gates, see Chernow, *Washington*, 101–2, 190.
54. Washington to John Jay, April 14, 1779, quoted in Chernow, *Washington*, 190. See also Nelson, *General Horatio Gates*; Billias, "Horatio Gates: Professional Soldier," 79–108; Max M. Mintz, *The Generals of Saratoga: John Burgoyne and Horatio Gates* (New Haven, CT: Yale University Press, 1990); and Alan Cate, "Horatio Gates," in Cate, *Founding Fighters*, 50–67.
55. Horatio Gates to John Hancock, July 29,1776, in HGP, Reel 3.
56. Skenesborough was the location of the extensive estates of the Loyalist Phillip Skene, a prominent local prewar citizen, that included a manor house and a shipyard with mills and specialized shops. Arnold spent much of the summer splitting his time between Skenesborough and Ticonderoga. Cubbison, *The American Northern Theater Army*, 200–201; and n.a., "Philip Skene of Skenesborough," *Bulletin of the Fort Ticonderoga Museum* 6 (January 1943): 159–60.

57. Benedict Arnold to Washington, June 25, 1776, in GWP, Vol. 5: 96–97.
58. John Trumbull to Jonathan Trumbull, July 12, 1776, in Commager and Morris, *Spirit of 'Seventy-Six*, 222.
59. Journal entry, August 5, 1776, in Thomas Williams Baldwin, ed., *The Revolutionary Journal of Col. Jeduthan Baldwin, 1775–1778* (Bangor, ME: Printed for the DeBurians, 1906), 65. Baldwin also reported that as the ships were completed at Skenesborough, they were sailed down the lake to Ticonderoga where they were fitted out; see journal entry for August 31, 1776, ibid., 73.
60. For the construction and manning of the American fleet, see Tomlin, "Valcour Island," 274, and Cubbison, *The American Northern Theater Army*, 181–82. See also Nelson, *General Horatio Gates*, 69n.
61. Tomlin, "Valcour Island," 274; and Cubbison, *The American Northern Theater Army*, 181–82. See also Nelson, *General Horatio Gates*, 69n.
62. Quoted in Barry K. Wilson, *Benedict Arnold: A Traitor in Our Midst* (Montreal: McGill-Queens University Press, 2001), 133. See also Martin, *Benedict Arnold*, 248.
63. Cubbison, *The American Northern Theater Army*, 227.
64. Gates to Arnold, August 7, 1776, in HGP, Reel 3.
65. Horatio Gates to John Adams, May 4, 1776, in Robert J. Taylor, ed., *The Adams Papers: Papers of John Adams*, Vol. 4, February–August 1776 (Boston: Belknap Press, 1983), 164–65. Controversy often followed Arnold. During those very busy and pressure-filled summer months in 1776, Arnold was accused of impropriety over the British capture of American provisions during the retreat from Canada. Gates convened a court of inquiry in late July 1776. The court recommended that Gates arrest Arnold, but he refused and dissolved the court. In a letter to Hancock, Gates said that both sides were probably at fault to some degree, but in spite of his second-in-command's prickly personality, "the United States must not be deprived of that excellent officer's service at this important moment." Gates pleaded with Hancock to "represent this affair in the most favourable light to Congress." See Gates to John Hancock, September 2, 1776, HGP, Reel 3. See also Martin, *Benedict Arnold*, 237–43; Wilson, *A Traitor in Our Midst*, 132; and Brandt, *Man in the Mirror*, 114–15.
66. Quoted in Cubbison, *The American Northern Theater Army*, 141.
67. John Trumbull to Jonathan Sr., July 12, 1776, in Commager and Morris, *Spirit of 'Seventy-Six*, 221.
68. For a good contemporary description of the fort, see James Thacher, *A Military Journal During the American Revolutionary War from 1775–1783* (Boston: Richardson and Lord, 1823), 73–74. For an excellent study of Mount Independence, see Michael Barbieri, "Mount Independence: The Most Intact Revolutionary War Site in America," *Journal of the American Revolution* (May 5, 2016). https://allthingsliberty.com/2016/05/mount-independence-the-most-intact-revolutionary-war-site-in-america/
69. Gates to Thomas Hartley, July 20, 1776, in HGP, Reel 3.
70. General Order, July 30, 1776, "Colonel Anthony Wayne Orderly Book," in *Engineers of Independence: A Documentary History of the American Engineers in the American Revolution, 1775–1783*, ed. Paul K. Walker (Washington, DC: Historical Division, U.S. Army Corps of Engineers, 1977), 93.
71. Baldwin, *The Revolutionary Journal of Col. Jeduthan Baldwin, 1775–1778*, xv–xxxii.
72. Journal entry, July 28, 1776, ibid., 63.
73. Autobiography of John Trumbull, in Walker, *Engineers of Independence*, 86–87. See also Cubbison, *The American Northern Theater Army*, 198. For the elevations of the various key points at Fort Ticonderoga, a topographic map was consulted. http://www.cnyhiking.com/MountDefiance.htm
74. Nelson, *General Sir Guy Carleton*, 99.
75. Carleton to William and Richard Howe, October 4, 1776, quoted in ibid., 99.
76. In September an officer commanding one of Arnold's patrols was captured. This officer told his captors that the American force at Fort Ticonderoga numbered almost twenty thousand and that Arnold commanded the Patriot naval force. Digby, journal entry,

September 25, 1776, William Digby, *The British Invasion from the North, The Campaigns of Generals Carleton and Burgoyne from Canada, 1776–1777*, introductory chapter and notes from James Phinny Baxter (Albany, NY: Joel Musell's Sons, 1887), 145–47; Martin, *Benedict Arnold*, 252 and 256; and Tomlin, "Battle of Valcour Island," 275.
77. Arnold to Gates, September 15, 1776, quoted in Martin, *Benedict Arnold*, 260–70.
78. Wilson, *A Traitor in Our Midst*, 133.
79. Arnold to Philip Schuyler, October 12, 1776, in Commager and Morris, *Spirit of 'Seventy-Six*, 222. See also Tomlin, "Valcour Island," 275–78; Wilson, *Traitor in Our Midst*, 133–35; Nelson, *Sir Guy Carleton*, 100–102; Martin, *Benedict Arnold*, 259–84; and Brandt, *The Man in the Mirror*, 101–9.
80. Benedict Arnold to Philip Schuyler, October 12, 1776, in Commager and Morris, *Spirit of 'Seventy-Six*, 222. See also Tomlin, "Valcour Island," 275–78; Wilson, *Traitor in Our Midst*, 133–35; Nelson, *Sir Guy Carleton*, 100–102; Martin, *Benedict Arnold*, 259–84; and Brandt, *The Man in the Mirror*, 101–9.
81. Benedict Arnold to Philip Schuyler, October 12, 1776, in Commager and Morris, *Spirit of 'Seventy-Six*, 222. See also Tomlin, "Valcour Island," 275–78; Wilson, *Traitor in Our Midst*, 133–35; Nelson, *Sir Guy Carleton*, 100–102; Martin, *Benedict Arnold*, 259–84; and Brandt, *The Man in the Mirror*, 101–9.
82. Benedict Arnold to Philip Schuyler, October 12, 1776, in Commager and Morris, *Spirit of 'Seventy-Six*, 222. See also Tomlin, "Valcour Island," 275–78; Wilson, *Traitor in Our Midst*, 133–35; Nelson, *General Sir Guy Carleton*, 100–102; Martin, *Benedict Arnold*, 259–84; and Brandt, *The Man in the Mirror*, 101–9.
83. James M. Hadden, *Hadden's Journal and Orderly Books: A Journal Kept in Canada and upon Burgoyne's Campaign in 1776 and 1777*, ed. Horatio Rogers (Albany, NY: Joel Munsell's Sons, 1884), 24–25.
84. Arnold to Schuyler, October 12, 1776, in Commager and Morris, *Spirit of 'Seventy-Six*, 223.
85. Quoted in Tomlin, "Valcour Island," 277.
86. Tomlin, "Valcour Island," 276–78; and Martin, *Benedict Arnold*, 281–84.
87. There are many excellent accounts of the two naval battles on Lake Champlain: Tomlin, "Valcour Island," 275–78; Wilson, *Traitor in Our Midst*, 133–35; Nelson, *General Sir Guy Carleton*, 100–102; Martin, *Benedict Arnold*, 259–84; and Brandt, *The Man in the Mirror*, 101–9.
88. William Maxwell to William Livingston, October 20, 1776, quoted in Martin, *Benedict Arnold*, 288.
89. Carleton to Germain, October 14, 1776, in DAR, Vol. 12: 237.
90. Burgoyne's General Order of October 17, 1776, in Digby, *British Invasion from the North*, 177.
91. Gates to Schuyler, October 24, 1776, in Digby, *British Invasion from the North*, 172n.
92. Carleton to Germain, October 14, 1776, in DAR, Vol. 12: 237.
93. Burgoyne to Henry Clinton, November 7, 1776, Sir Henry Clinton Papers, Clements Library, University of Michigan (hereafter HCP). For excellent discussions of the conflict between Burgoyne and Carleton over continuing the offensive in October 1776, see Nelson, *General Sir Guy Carleton*, 104; and Richard J. Hargrove Jr., *General John Burgoyne* (Newark: University of Delaware Press, 1983), 95–96.
94. Gabriel Christie to Germain, October 26, 1776, Lord George Germain Papers, Clements Library, University of Michigan (hereafter GGP).
95. Alfred Thayer Mahan, "Major Operations of the Royal Navy, 1762–1783," in *The Royal Navy: A History from the Earliest Times to the Present*, Vol. 3, ed. William Laird Clowes (London: Sampson Low, Marston and Company, 1898), 368.
96. Carleton to Germain, October 14, 1776, in DAR, Vol. 12: 237 and "Memorandum of General Carleton relative to the Next Campaign, Communicated to LtGen'l Burgoyne to be Laid before Government," n.d. but probably late October 1776, GGP.
97. Charles Douglas to Philip Stephens, October 21, 1776, in DAR, Vol. 12: 238.
98. Riedesel to the Duke Ferdinand of Brunswick, November 10, 1776, *Memoirs, and Letters and Journals, of Major General Riedesel*, Vol. 1, ed. William L. Stone (Albany, NY: J. Munsell, 1868), 83.

CHAPTER 3

1. Burgoyne to Henry Clinton, November 7, 1776, in HCP.
2. Journal entry, December 9, 1776, in Walpole, *Journal of the Reign of King George the Third*, Vol. 2, 88.
3. For a wonderful description of eighteenth-century London, see M. Dorothy George, *London Life in the Eighteenth Century* (New York: Penguin, 1966), 15–33, 73–86.
4. "Memorandum of General Carleton relative to the Next Campaign, Communicated to LtGen'l Burgoyne to be Laid before the Government," Carleton to Germain, n.d., but probably mid-October 1776, in Germain, Lord George Sackville Papers, Clements Library, University of Michigan. See also Hargrove, *General John Burgoyne*, 102–3; and Nelson, *Sir Guy Carleton*, 106–7. Burgoyne had originally suggested a diversion down the Mohawk River early in the 1776 campaign, so it is safe to assume that Carleton borrowed that idea from his second-in-command for his own concept that Burgoyne carried to Germain.
5. Keeping track of the letters and orders during this period can be very confusing. Appendix B should help the reader make sense of the messages.
6. For the lure of the Hudson River–Lake Champlain strategic concept, see Ketchum, *Saratoga*, 79–80; and Eliot Cohen, *Conquered into Liberty: Two Centuries of Battles along the Great Warpath that Made the American Way of War* (New York, NY: Free Press, 2011), 1–15, 197–202.
7. Hargrove, *General John Burgoyne*, 102–3; and Nelson, *Sir Guy Carleton*, 106.
8. Germain to King, December 10, 1777, in *The Correspondence of King George the Third from 1760 to December 1783*, Vol. 3, ed. John Fortescue (London: Macmillan, 1928), 405–6.
9. King to Lord North, December 13, 1776, in ibid., 406–7.
10. Ibid. See also, Hargrove, *General John Burgoyne*, 102; Nelson, *Sir Guy Carleton*, 106–8; and Valentine, *Lord George Germain*, 135–36.
11. O'Shaughnessy, *The Men Who Lost America*, 19–28; and Boatner, *Encyclopedia of the American Revolution*, 416–19.
12. Burgoyne to Germain, January 1, 1777, in GGP. Also, in John Burgoyne, *A State of the Expedition from Canada as Laid Before the House of Commons by Lieutenant-General Burgoyne*, 2nd ed. (London: J. Almon, 1780), Appendix i (hereafter STOE).
13. O'Shaughnessy, *The Men Who Lost America*, 124.
14. Hargrove, *General John Burgoyne*, 17–34; O'Shaughnessy, *The Men Who Lost America*, 124–27; and George Athan Billias, "John Burgoyne: Ambitious General," in Billias, *George Washington's Generals and Opponents*, Vol. 2, 142–46.
15. Billias, "John Burgoyne," 147.
16. O'Shaughnessy, *The Men Who Lost America*, 127. See also Billias, "John Burgoyne," 148–50; and Hargrove, *General John Burgoyne*, 29–41, 45–46.
17. Journal entry, October 9, 1776, in Digby, *British Invasion from the North*, 157.
18. Quoted in Billias, "John Burgoyne," 153.
19. Horace Walpole to William Mason, October 5, 1777, *The Letters of Horace Walpole, Earl of Orford*, Vol. 6, ed. Peter Cunningham (London: R. Bentley, 1857), 494.
20. O'Shaughnessy, *The Men Who Lost America*, 129–32; Hargrove, *General John Burgoyne*, 49–70; and Billias, "John Burgoyne," 150–54.
21. Germain to William Howe, October 10, 1776, in GGP. On the same date, Germain sent similar congratulations to Vice Admiral Lord Richard Howe, William's brother and the naval commander in North America.
22. Germain to William Howe, October 18, 1776, ibid. Germain's emphasis on Philadelphia must have stuck in Howe's mind as he prepared his plans for 1777.
23. William and his elder brother, Vice Admiral Lord Richard Howe, commanded the army and naval forces in North America (minus Canada) and thus enjoyed outstanding army-navy cooperation, which in part enabled the success of the British amphibious operations on 1776. Maldwyn A. Jones, "Sir William Howe, Conventional Strategist," in *George Washington's Generals and Opponents: Their Exploits and Leadership*, Vol. 2, 1994), 43–47; O'Shaughnessy, *The Men Who Lost America*, 88–91; and Boatner, *Encyclopedia of the American Revolution*, 522–26.

24. William Howe to Germain, November 30, 1776, in GGP. Germain received this letter on December 30, 1776, only days after his and the king's meetings with Burgoyne.
25. William Howe to Germain, December 20, 1776, ibid. Germain received Howe's second plan on February 23, 1777.
26. William Howe to Germain, December 31, 1776, in GGP. In this letter, Howe also told Germain that Henry Clinton was on his way home, and that Clinton "being senior to Gen'l Burgoyne . . . should go to Canada" to take command of that army. If that happens, wrote Howe, he hopes that "Gen'l Burgoyne will join this army." Howe was clearly trying to get rid of Clinton.
27. *Morning Press* for January 6, 1777, in Troy Bickham, *Making Headlines: The American Revolution as Seen through the British Press* (DeKalb: Northern Illinois Press, 2009), 103.
28. *Lloyd's Evening Post* for January 13, 1777, in ibid., 104.
29. William Howe to Germain, January 20, 1777, in ibid.
30. Howe also testified that "I think a stronger, or more solid diversion [in support of the Northern British army from Canada] could not have been made, than that of drawing General Washington, and the whole continental army, near three hundred miles off." Howe never argued until much later that the Philadelphia campaign would assist Burgoyne, even though there was certainly some truth to it, as even Washington maintained. See William Howe, *The Narrative of Lieutenant General Sir William Howe: In a Committee of the House of Commons, on the 29th of April 1779, relative to His Conduct, During His Late Command of the King's Troops in North America: To Which are Added, Some Observations Upon a Pamphlet, entitled, Letters to a Nobleman* (London: H. Baldwin, 1780), 19, 25, and 61.
31. King George III to Lord North, February 24, 1777, in *The Correspondence of King George the Third with Lord North, 1768 to 1783*, Vol. 2, ed. W. Bodham Donne (New York: De Capo Press, 1971), 55–56.
32. Minutes of the February 25, 1777, Cabinet Meeting, *The Private Papers of John, Earl of Sandwich, First Lord of the Admiralty, 1771–1782, Vol. 1, August 1770–March 1778*, ed. G. R. Barnes and J. H. Owen (London: Navy Records Society, 1932), 285.
33. Journal entry, February 13, 1777, in Walpole, *Journal of the Reign of King George the Third*, Vol. 2, 97–98.
34. John Burgoyne, "Thoughts for Conducting the War from the Side of Canada," February 28, 1777, in DAR, Vol. 14: 41–46.
35. Ibid., 45. The official instructions for the campaign issued by Lord Germain on March 26 did not include any direction for follow-on operations, Germain to Carleton, March 26, 1777, in DAR, Vol. 14: 53–56.
36. John Burgoyne, "Thoughts for Conducting the War from the Side of Canada," February 28, 1777, in DAR, Vol. 14: 41–46.
37. Ibid.
38. Ibid.
39. Ibid.
40. Ibid. In the House of Commons two years later, Burgoyne accused Germain of ignoring the last two courses of action "while the ["Thoughts"] paper was in his lordship's hands." This was after he surrendered his army and was trying to defend his actions and actively seeking to pass the blame onto others. But this was quite a reach as he clearly did not intend the last two options to be taken seriously. They were buried in the last paragraph of a multi-page memorandum that advocated one military strategy and one military strategy only. See Burgoyne, "prefatory speech," Burgoyne, STOE, 4.
41. For a discussion of the importance of carefully identifying and confirming assumptions during strategy development, see Ben Lombardi, "Assumptions and Grand Strategy," *Parameters* (Spring 2011): 29–40. See also Joint Staff, *Joint Publication 5.0: Joint Operational Planning* (Washington, DC: Department of Defense, August 11, 2011), GL-5.
42. "Remarks on the Conduct of the War—from Canada," n.a., March 5, 1777, in George III, *Correspondence of King George the Third*, Vol. 3, 443–44.

43. Germain to Howe, March 3, 1777, GGP. Howe received this letter in New York on May 8, 1777, but did not reply until June 3. Howe to Germain, June 3, 1777, in ibid. Two days later, Howe wrote again to Germain asking for reinforcements, especially artillery, and, although he had not received any orders to support any operations of the Canada army, he preemptively informed the secretary that "I trust your Lordship may expect a successful campaign to the southward; yet I fear little can be done to the northward other than give security to this province." Howe to Germain, June 5, 1777, in ibid.
44. Germain to Carleton, March 26, 1777, in GGP.
45. Ibid.
46. Germain to Carleton, March 26, 1777, in ibid.
47. Ibid.
48. John F. Luzader, *Saratoga: A Military History of the Decisive Campaign of the American Revolution* (New York: Savas Beatie, 2008), 25; Richard M. Ketchum, *Saratoga: Turning Point of America's Revolutionary War* (New York: Henry Holt, 1997), 86; John F. Luzader, "The Coming Revolutionary War Battles at Saratoga," in *The Saratoga Campaign: Uncovering an Embattled Landscape*, ed. William A. Griswold and Donald W. Linebaugh (Hanover, NH: University Press of New England, 2016), 11; Valentine, *Lord George Germain*, 175–76 and 284; and Hoffman Nickerson, *The Turning Point of the Revolution, or Burgoyne in America* (Boston: Houghton Mifflin, 1928), 97–98. Even if Knox's story is true, Germain was not overly concerned about Burgoyne's fate. Nickerson and others also claim that the British lost the war because of Germain's failure to send explicit instructions to Howe ordering a linkup of both armies at Albany. This was simply not the case for the strategic reasons laid out in this book.
49. Howe, *Narrative*, 15. Howe has been roundly criticized by historians for not moving his entire army north to assist Burgoyne, but he had already received approval for the Philadelphia expedition, and he would receive confirmation of that approval in a follow-on letter Germain sent on May 18.
50. Germain to Carleton, March 26, 1777, in GGP.
51. Burgoyne, STOE, 3–5.
52. William Howe to Germain, April 2, 1777, in GGP.
53. Ibid.
54. Ibid.
55. Germain to William Howe, January 14, 1777, in ibid.
56. William Howe to Carleton, April 5, 1777, in ibid.
57. Ibid. A copy of this letter was forwarded to Germain along with the April 2 letter from Howe to Germain and received by him on May 18, 1777.
58. Hargrove, *General John Burgoyne*, 117; and Burgoyne, STOE, 31.
59. Burgoyne, STOE, 22. This short passage and another on page 188 is Burgoyne's only mention of Howe's April 5 letter in his privately published testimony; he could not ignore it, but he was clearly trying to downplay its significance.
60. Ibid., 189.
61. Ibid., 9.
62. The full content of the two letters Burgoyne sent to Howe in May 1777 upon his arrival in Quebec are a mystery, as they seem to be missing, except for the very short excerpt Burgoyne's quoted in his *State of the Expedition.* In his correspondence with Germain, Howe mentions these letters only in passing, and seems to have regarded them as being of very little significance. It is likely that they were simply updates on Burgoyne's and the army's preparations; see Howe to Germain, July 10, 1777, in DAR, Vol. 14: 131. In a July 17 message to Burgoyne, Howe mentions the letters, but he simply acknowledged receipt. Once again, it is reasonable to assume that Burgoyne did not challenge Howe's April 5 warning that he was not coming up the Hudson; see William Howe to Burgoyne, July 17, 1777, Gold Star Collection, Clements Library, University of Michigan. Few historians have worked through this exchange of letters, and none have quoted either of Burgoyne's two May letters to Howe except to cite the brief excerpt in *State of*

the Expedition. There is no doubt he sent them, as Howe acknowledged on July 17, but from the context of the commander-in-chief's reply, and Burgoyne's failure to publish them, he did not challenge Howe or request confirmation of his April 5 letter. In his biography of Burgoyne, Hargrove mentions the May letters, and Burgoyne's small quote from one of letters in the *State of the Expedition,* but downplays their significance; see Hargrove, *General John Burgoyne,* 113–14 and 117. Nickerson also mentions the letters in passing and cites a brief quote from Burgoyne's narrative in the *State of the Expedition* but does not quote either of the letters; see Nickerson, *Turning Point of the Revolution,* 103–4. Valentine's biography of Germain mentions Burgoyne's missing May letters to Howe but does not quote them. He does, however, cite Edward De Fonblanque's 1876 book on Burgoyne. Yet, an examination of that book reveals that De Fonblanque simply quoted Burgoyne's tiny excerpt from *State of the Expedition.* See Valentine, *Lord George Germain,* 197; and Edward Barrington De Fonblanque, *Political and Military Episodes in the Latter Half of the Eighteenth Century Derived from the Life and Correspondence of the Right Hon. John Burgoyne, General, Statesman, Dramatist* (London: Macmillan, 1876), 233. No other major work on Saratoga, Sir William Howe, or John Burgoyne mentions these letters. See Ketchum, *Saratoga*; Luzader, *Saratoga*; Elting, *Battles of Saratoga*; Stephen R. Taaffe, *The Philadelphia Campaign, 1777–1778* (Lawrence: University Press of Kansas, 2003); Ira Gruber, *The Howe Brothers and the American Revolution* (New York: Atheneum, 1972); Francis J. Huddleson, *Gentleman Johnny Burgoyne: Misadventures of an English General in the Revolution* (New York: Sun Dial Press, 1939); *Burgoyne and the Saratoga Campaign: His Papers,* ed. Douglas R. Cubbison (Norman, OK: Arthur H. Clark Company, 2012); and William B. Willcox, "Too Many Cooks: British Planning Before Saratoga," *Journal of British Studies* 2.1 (November 1962): 56–90.

63. Burgoyne, STOE, 31. General Howe, on the other hand, testifying in his own Commons inquiry, was quite clear on the purpose of the April 5 letter, although he makes no mention of the two letters Burgoyne sent to him in May 1777. Howe, *Narrative,* 15.
64. Burgoyne to Germain, May 15, 1777, in DAR, Vol. 14: 78–79. Even long after the campaign, Burgoyne continued to praise his old chief for his help preparing the army for the campaign. Burgoyne, STOE, 9–10.
65. Germain to Howe, May 18, 1777, in DAR, Vol. 14: 84–85. See Appendix B to keep track of the numerous letters and meetings between British leaders in late 1776 and 1777.
66. The best analysis of the impact of Trenton and Princeton on the Revolutionary War is Fischer, *Washington's Crossing,* 363–67.
67. Germain to William Howe, May 18, 1777, in DAR, Vol. 14: 84–85. The May 18, 1777, letter from Germain gave Howe a free hand, despite the secretary's clear desire for the army in New York to cooperate with Burgoyne.
68. Howe, *Narrative,* 24.
69. Henry Clinton met with Germain and Burgoyne while on leave in London and hoped, as the senior general, to get command of the northern army for the upcoming campaign, but he was bitterly disappointed. William B. Willcox, *Portrait of a General: Sir Henry Clinton in the War of Independence* (New York: Knopf, 1964), 140–41; Willcox, "Too Many Cooks," 66–68; and Henry Clinton, *The American Rebellion: Sir Henry Clinton's Narrative of His Campaigns, 1775–1782, with an Appendix of Original Documents* Edited by William B. Willcox (New Haven, CT: Yale University Press, 1958), 60–61. Willcox's work on British strategy in the American Revolutionary War is quite good, but he is, in my opinion, unfairly biased against Sir William Howe.

CHAPTER 4

1. William Howe to Germain, January 20, 1777, in GGP. For the actions and operations conducted by the American Army after Trenton and Princeton, see Fischer, *Washington's Crossing,* 346–60.
2. Thomas Fleming, *Washington's Secret War: The Hidden History of Valley Forge* (New York: Harper Collins, 2005), 13.

3. *Joint Publication (JP) 3.0*, I-13-I14.
4. See J. Boone Bartholomees, "A Survey of the Theory of Strategy," in *US Army War College Guide to National Security Issues: Volume I: Theory of War and Strategy*, ed. J. Boone Bartholomees (Carlisle, PA: Strategic Studies Institute, 2012), 30.
5. Stoker and Jones, "Colonial Military Strategy," 8–13.
6. For an excellent discussion of the lack of unity of command during the British campaigns of 1777, see Jeremy Black, "British Military Strategy," in Stoker et al., eds., *Strategy in the American War of Independence*, 63–67.
7. During the Saratoga campaign, it was officially the State of Vermont, as the residents had essentially declared themselves a republic. It also ratified its own constitution, but many during the campaign continued to call it the New Hampshire Grants, the Hampshire Grants, or just, the Grants. Pell, "Philip Schuyler," 62. For an excellent and detailed explanation of Schuyler's pre-Saratoga career and the attacks leveled at him, see Gerlach, *Proud Patriot*, 132–200.
8. Schuyler to Washington, September 16, 1776, in GWP, Vol. 1: 318–19. See also Gerlach, *Proud Patriot*, 194–210, and Pell, "Philip Schuyler," 64.
9. Schuyler to Washington, January 30, 1777, in GWP, Vol. 8: 192–94. See also Gerlach, *Proud Patriot*, 212.
10. Schuyler's biographer places almost all the blame on Washington and Congress for Schuyler's ultimate failure in his command of the Northern Department. See Gerlach, *Proud Patriot*, 216. This is unfair to Washington as Schuyler was the commander and thus bore the primary responsibility for everything his command did or failed to do.
11. Washington to Schuyler, February 9, 1777, in GWP, Vol. 8: 292–94. These exchanges of letters between Schuyler in Albany and Washington in Morristown took on average less than ten days from sending to receipt of an answer. This was much faster than the British were able to achieve, by a factor of six to ten.
12. Washington to Schuyler, February 19, 1777, ibid., 373–74.
13. Washington to Schuyler, March 12, 1777, ibid, 560–63.
14. Schuyler to Washington, March 25, 1777, ibid., 632–33.
15. Schuyler to Goose Van Schaick, March 25, 1777, Philip Schuyler, *Proceedings of a General Court Martial Held at Major General Lincoln's Quarters near Quaker-Hill, in the State of New York, by Order of Excellency George Washington, Commander in Chief of the Army of the United States of America, for the Trial of Major General Schuyler, October 1, 1778. Major General Lincoln, President*, vol. 2, Publication Fund Series (Albany, NY: New York Historical Society Collections, 1879), 27. In this letter, Schuyler placed Colonel Van Schaick in charge of the Northern Department in his absence. He departed Albany for Philadelphia the next day.
16. Nathanael Greene to John Adams, April 5, 1777, in *The Papers of John Adams, Vol. 5: August 1776–March 1778*, ed. Robert J. Taylor (Boston: Belknap Press, 1983), 141–42. Schuyler's biographer argues that the New Yorker's decision to "absent himself from command of the Northern Army was no sign of failure in responsibility." Gerlach, *Proud Patriot*, 219. However, with the campaigning season rapidly approaching, Schuyler's place was at the Northern Department and not arguing over petty grievances in Congress.
17. Gates's biographer, Paul David Nelson, carefully examined three possible reasons for his departure to Baltimore: first, to secure an independent command by personally lobbying Congress; second, that he was a coward; and third, that he was ill. He concludes that Gates was ill and that was the reason he did not participate in the Trenton raid. While I agree that Gates was no coward, the illness excuse is not convincing. I believe he went to Baltimore to lobby Congress; after all, he was well enough to travel. See Nelson, *Horatio Gates*, 75–77.
18. Samuel Adams to John Adams, January 9, 1777, Paul H. Smith, ed., *Letters of Delegates to Congress, Vol. 6: January 1, 1777–April 30, 1777* (Washington, DC: Library of Congress, 1976–2000), 65 (hereafter LDC).
19. Gates to John Hancock, February 28, 1777, in HGP, Reel 4. See also Jonathan Gregory Rossie, *The Politics of Command in the American Revolution* (Syracuse, NY: Syracuse University Press, 1975), 143.

20. Gates to Washington, March 3 and March 7, 1777, in GWP, Vol. 8: 497–98 and 533–34.
21. Washington to Gates, March 10, 1777, in GWP, Vol. 8: 548.
22. Max M. Mintz, *The Generals of Saratoga* (New Haven, CT: Yale University Press, 1990), 123–24.
23. Hancock to Gates, March 25, 1777, in HGP, Reel 4. See also Rossie, The Politics of Command, 144–45; and Gates to Hancock, March 26, 1777, in HGP, Reel 4.
24. Hancock to Washington, April 4, 1777, in GWP, Vol. 9: 59; and Washington to Hancock, April 9, 1777, ibid., 97–98.
25. March 25, 1777, Resolves of Congress, in JCC, Vol. 7: 202. See also Nelson, *Horatio Gates*, 81; and Gerlach, *Proud Patriot*, 222–23. Before Schuyler left Albany for Philadelphia, he was unaware that Gates had been dispatched by Congress to command at Ticonderoga.
26. Schuyler to Richard Varick, April 26, 1777, in LDC, Vol. 6: 661. See also Gerlach, *Proud Patriot*, 223.
27. James Lovell to Gates, May 1, 1777, in LDC, Vol. 7: 5.
28. Here are just a few examples. The Committee of Cachanawago to Gates, May 2, 1777; Committee for the Town of Bennington [John Fay] to Gates, May 4, 1777; Richard Livingston to Gates, May 5, 1777; and John Paterson to Gates, May 4, 1777, all in HGP, Reel 4.
29. Gates to John Jay, May 9, 1777, in HGP, Reel 4.
30. Gates to Washington, April 19, 1777, in GWP, Vol. 9: 208–9.
31. Washington to Gates, April 28, 1777, ibid., 292.
32. Gates to John Hancock, April 29, 1777, in HGP, Reel 4.
33. Gates to Lovell, April 29, 1777, ibid. See also Gates to Washington, April 29, 1777, ibid.
34. Resolves of Congress, April 29, 1777, in JCC, Vol. 7: 306–7.
35. Washington to William Heath, May 2, 1777, in GWP, Vol. 9: 327–28; and Washington to Hancock, May 3, 1777, ibid., 333.
36. Nathanael Greene to John Adams, May 7, 1777, in Taylor, *The Papers of John Adams*, Vol. 5, 181.
37. Gates to Washington, May 13, 1777, in GWP, Vol. 9: 410–11.
38. Washington to Gates, May 19, 1777, ibid., 471–72.
39. Gates to James Lovell, May 25, 1777, in HGP, Reel 4.
40. Gerlach, *Proud Patriot*, 223–25.
41. Nathanael Greene to John Adams, May 28, 1777, Taylor, *The Papers of John Adams*, Vol. 5, 207.
42. Schuyler to Washington, April 30, 1777, in GWP, Vol. 9: 311–12.
43. Washington to Schuyler, May 3, 1777, ibid., 339.
44. Gates to Hancock, May 9, 1777, in HGP, Reel 4.
45. Resolves of Congress, May 22, 1777, in JCC, Vol. 7: 375.
46. Board of War Report, May 15, 1777, ibid., 364. See also Gerlach, *Proud Patriot*, 225–28; Rossie, *The Politics of Command*, 148–49; Hargrove, *Horatio Gates*, 85; and Cate, *Founding Fighters*, 55.
47. Lovell to Gates, May 22, 1777, in HGP, Reel 4.
48. John Trumbull to Gates, May 24, 1777, ibid. Votes for Schuyler: NY, PA, MD, VA, NC, and SC; votes against reinstating Schuyler: NH, MA, CT, NJ, and GA. The remaining states split their delegations.
49. Lovell to Gates, June 8, 1777, LDC, Vol. 7: 178.
50. William Duer to Robert R. Livingston, May 28, 1777, in Edmund C. Burnett, ed., *Letters of Members of the Continental Congress*, Vol. 3, July 5, 1776, to December 31, 1777 (Washington, DC: Carnegie Institute of Washington, 1923), 376.
51. Schuyler to Gates, June 4, 1777, in HGP, Reel 4. See also Gerlach, *Proud Patriot*, 230–31; and Nelson, *General Horatio Gates*, 86.
52. Schuyler to Gates, June 9, 1777, ibid. See also Gerlach, *Proud Patriot*, 230–31; and Nelson, *General Horatio Gates*, 86.
53. Wilkinson to Gates, June 10, 1777, in HGP, Reel 4.

54. James Duane to Schuyler, June 19, 1777, in Philip Schuyler Papers, Letters to Schuyler, Film 659, Reel 9.
55. William Duer to Schuyler, June 19, 1777, ibid.
56. Ibid.
57. Ibid.
58. Ibid.
59. Horatio Gates's Notes for a Speech to Congress, June 18, 1777, in LDC, Vol. 7: 213–16.
60. Duer to Schuyler, June 19, 1777, Schuyler Papers.
61. Ibid. Gates's biographer cautions that the only accounts of Gates's June 18 congressional audience come from two of Schuyler's allies in Congress, James Duane and William Duer. While this is true, their accounts match closely, and it is reasonable to conclude that Gates's performance in Congress did not reflect well on him.
62. Resolutions of Congress, July 8, 1777, Ford, *Journals of Congress*, Vol. 6, 540. See also Rossie, *The Politics of Command*, 151; Fleming, *Washington's Secret War*, 114–15; and Nelson, *General Horatio Gates*, 86–87.

CHAPTER 5

1. Letter from an Unnamed Officer, March 9, 1777, Ray W. Pettengill, trans. and ed., *Letters from America, 1776–1779: Being Letters of Brunswick, Hessian, and Waldeck Officers with the British Armies During the Revolution* (New York: Houghton, Mifflin, 1924), 42–43; and 39, 41–42.
2. Carleton to Germain, May 20, 1777, GGP.
3. Most German soldiers who served on the Burgoyne expedition were from Brunswick, (although some were from Hesse and Hanau) not Hesse, and should therefore be called Braunschweig or Braunschweigers. Thomas M. Barker, ed., "The Battles of Saratoga and the Kinderhook Tea Party: The Campaign Diary of a Junior Officer of Baron Riedesel's Musketeer Regiment in the 1777 British Invasion of New York," *Hessians: Journal of Johannes Schwalm Historical Association* 9 (2007): 28; and Major General Riedesel to Duke Ferdinand of Brunswick, April 10, 1777, *Memoirs, and Letters*, 93.
4. Lord Chatham quoted in Brendon Simms, *Three Victories and a Defeat: The Rise and Fall of the First British Empire* (New York: Basic Books, 2007), 609.
5. Ibid., 596.
6. Georg Pausch, *Journal of Captain Pausch, Chief of the Hanau Artillery During the Burgoyne Campaign*, trans. William L. Stone (Albany, NY: Joel Munsell's Sons, 1886), 107.
7. Ibid., 108.
8. Hadden, *Journal*, lxxxv. See also journal entry, August 16, 1777, in Digby, *British Invasion from the North*, 250–52.
9. Pausch, *Journal*, 116; and Burgoyne, STOE, 128.
10. Quoted in Simms, *Three Victories and a Defeat*, 594–95.
11. Quoted in Colin G. Calloway, *The American Revolution in Indian Country: Crisis and Diversity in Native American Communities* (New York: Cambridge University Press, 1995), 63.
12. Carleton had recruited, or "coerced," as Colin Calloway argues, the Indians from the settlements of St. Regis, Sault St. Louis, Lake of the Two Mountains, and St. Francis. Carleton to Germain, June 26, 1777, in DAR, Vol. 14: 121; Calloway, *American Revolution in Indian Country*, 40, 72; Glenn F. Williams, *Year of the Hangman: George Washington's Campaign against the Iroquois* (Yardley, PA: Westholme Publishing, 2005), 49–50; and Nelson, *General Sir Guy Carleton*, 120. For a good discussion of the background to British relations with Native Americans prior to the American Revolution, see Fintan O'Toole, *White Savage: William Johnson and the Invention of America* (New York: Farrar, Straus & Giroux, 2005).
13. Unnamed officer, n.d. April 1777, in Pettengill, *Letters from America*, 71.
14. Charles Stedman, *The History of the Origin, Progress, and Termination of the American War* (London: Privately Printed, 1794), 319–20.

15. John Burgoyne, *The Substance of General Burgoyne's Speeches: On Mr. Vyner's Motion, on the 26th of May; and Upon Mr. Hartley's Motion, on the 28th of May, 1778. With an Appendix, Containing General Washington's Letter to General Burgoyne. &c* (London: J. Almon, 1778), 3.
16. Journal entry, May 6, 1777, in Digby, *British Invasion from the North*, 188.
17. Helga B. Doblin and Mary C. Lynn, eds., "A Brunswick Grenadier with Burgoyne: The Journal of Johann Bense, 1776–1783," *New York History* 66 (October 1985): 429; and Harrison Bird, *March to Saratoga: General Burgoyne and the American Campaign, 1777* (New York: Oxford University Press, 1963), 18.
18. Nelson, *General Sir Guy Carleton*, 110, 113, and 118–19; and journal entry, May 6, 1777, in Digby, *The British Invasion from Canada*, 187.
19. Digby, *The British Invasion from Canada*, 188n; and diary entry from an unnamed officer, but most probably the adjutant of the Specht Regiment, Lieutenant Anton Adolph Heinrich Du Roi, May 13, 1777, in Helga Doblin, trans., *The Specht Journal: A Military Journal of the Burgoyne Campaign*, ed. Mary C. Lynn (Westport, CT: Greenwood Press, 1995), 42. See also Gavin K. Watt, *Rebellion in the Mohawk Valley: The St. Leger Expedition of 1777* (Toronto: Dundurn, 2002), 46.
20. Stedman, *History of the Origins, Progress, and Termination of the American War*, 318–19.
21. Burgoyne to Harvey, May 19, 1777, quoted in Huddleson, *Gentleman Johnny Burgoyne*, 134.
22. Carleton to Germain, May 20, 1777, in GGP.
23. Ibid. Washington's army was reinforced by soldiers from the Northern Department just days before his raid on Trenton. See also Nelson, *General Sir Guy Carleton*, 110–13.
24. Carleton to Germain, May 22, 1777, in DAR, Vol. 14: 92–93.
25. Nelson, *General Sir Guy Carleton*, 113.
26. Burgoyne to Germain, May 19, 1777, in DAR, Vol. 14: 86. In a letter written the same day to a fellow general officer, Burgoyne essentially repeated the same sentiments that he had with Germain. See Burgoyne to Harvey, May 19, 1777, quoted in Huddleson, *Gentleman Johnny Burgoyne*, 134.
27. R. Arthur Bowler, *Logistics and the Failure of the British Army in America, 1775–1783* (Princeton, NJ: Princeton University Press, 1975), 225.
28. Ibid., 225–26.
29. Ibid., 226.
30. Journal entry, May 2, 1777, Pausch, *Journal*, 109.
31. Carleton to Burgoyne July 28, 1777, quoted in Paul Kopperman, "The Numbers Game: Health Issues in the Army that Burgoyne Led to Saratoga," *New York History* 88 (Summer 2007): 269.
32. Ibid., 273.
33. Ibid., 269–76.
34. Note that "Jäger" is written and pronounced the same for singular and plural usage. See Bruce M. Venter, *The Battle of Hubbardton: The Rear Guard Action That Saved America* (Charleston, SC: History Press, 2015), 127n.
35. Hadden, *Journal*, 15.
36. Robin May, *The British Army in North America, 1775–1783* (Reading, UK: Osprey Publishing Limited, 1974), 8–9 and 13; Elting, *Battles of Saratoga*, 86; Patrick Mercer, "The 9th (East Norfolk) Regiment of Foot, Saratoga, 19 September & 7 October 1777," *Military History Monthly* 77 (February 2017): 55; and Matthew H. Spring, *With Zeal and With Bayonets Only: The British Army on Campaign in North America, 1775–1783* (Norman: University of Oklahoma Press, 2008), 200.
37. Unnamed officer, n.d. circa April 1777, in Pettengill, *Letters from America*, 70–71.
38. May, *The British Army in North America*, 8–9 and 13; Elting, Battles of Saratoga, 86; Mercer, "The 9th (East Norfolk) Regiment of Foot, 55; and Spring, *With Zeal and With Bayonets Only*, 200.
39. Spring, *With Zeal and With Bayonets Only*, 142–43, 202, 205, and 222–32; and Elting, *Battles of Saratoga*, 85–86.
40. Ibid.

41. Spring, *With Zeal and With Bayonets Only*, 57–62, 252–55.
42. Burgoyne to Germain, May 26, 1777, British Colonial Office Records, CO 42/37, David Library of the American Revolution (hereafter DLAR).
43. Burgoyne to Carleton, June 7, 1777, ibid. This letter included Burgoyne's formal request for an additional one thousand horses and five hundred carts.
44. Carleton to Burgoyne, June 10, 1777, ibid.
45. William Howe to Carleton, April 5, 1777, GGP.
46. Journal entry, June 15, 1777, in J. F. Wasmus, *An Eyewitness Account of the American Revolution: The Journal of J.F. Wasmus, German Company Surgeon, 1776–1783*, trans. Helga Doblin, ed. Mary C. Lynn (Westport, CT: Greenwood Press, 1990), 52. See also Bird, *March to Saratoga*, 22–24.
47. Journal entry, June 6, 1777, in Hadden, *Journal*, 51.
48. Journal entry, June 19, 1777, in Wasmus, *An Eyewitness Account of the American Revolution*, 53. See also Major General Riedesel, *Memoirs, and Letters*, 104–5; Journal entry, June 19, 1777, *in Hadden, Journal*, 55–56; Digby, *British Invasion from the North*, 187–88; Anton Adolph Heinrich Du Roi (attrib.), journal entry, June 19, 1777, in Doblin, *Specht Journal*, 47; and Johann Bense, journal entry, June 13, 1777, in Doblin, "A Brunswick Grenadier with Burgoyne," 429.
49. Du Roi (attrib.), journal entry, June 16 and 17, 1777, in Doblin, *Specht Journal*, 47.
50. Journal entry, June 18, 1777, in Hadden, *Journal*, 55–56.
51. Journal entry, June 20, 1777, in Wasmus, *An Eyewitness Account of the American Revolution*, 53.
52. Journal entry, June 20, 1777, in Digby, *The British Invasion from the North*, 200.
53. Undated journal entry, ibid., 188.
54. Burgoyne's June 20, 1777, Proclamation, in Digby, *British Invasion from the North*, 189–92.
55. Journal entry, August 1777, in Walpole, *Journal of the Reign of King George the Third, Vol.* 2, 130.
56. Stedman, *History of the Origin, Progress, and Termination of the American War*, 321–22.
57. Quoted in Troy Bickham, *Making Headlines: The American Revolution as Seen through the British Press* (DeKalb: Northern Illinois University Press, 2009), 220.
58. Ibid.
59. September 28, 1777, edition of the *Independent Chronicle* (Boston), microfilm collection, DLAR.
60. Journal entry, July 1, 1777, James Thacher, *A Military Journal During the American Revolutionary War from 1775–1783* (Boston: Richardson and Lord, 1823), 97.
61. John Hawk to his wife, July 1, 1777, Frank Moore, ed., *Diary of the American Revolution from Newspapers and Original Documents*, Vol. 1 (New York: Charles Scribner, 1860) (Reprint Edition, 1979), 453.
62. Burgoyne, May 26, 1778, speech to the House of Commons, in Burgoyne, *The Substance of General Burgoyne's Speeches*, 6–7.
63. Note that I do not argue that it did not impact any Americans. It certainly made an impression on one senior American leader: see Schuyler to Washington, July 9, 1777, in GWP, Vol. 10: 234–35.
64. Burgoyne to Germain, June 22, 1777, in DAR, Vol. 14: 119–21. The intelligence Fraser was able to gather from this spy, including details on defenses, identities of commanders, and enemy numbers, was remarkably accurate. Simon Fraser, "Examination of a Spy from Ticonderoga, June 16, 1777," *Bulletin of the Fort Ticonderoga Museum* 10.3 (1959): 240–45.
65. "The operational level links the tactical employment of forces to national and strategic objectives. The focus at this level is on the design, planning, and execution of operations using . . . the application of creative imagination by commanders . . . to design strategies, campaigns, and major operations." *Joint Publication (JP) 3.0*, I-13.
66. We see hints that Burgoyne considered independent operations once he got to Albany. See Burgoyne, STOE, 9.
67. Du Roi (attrib.,) journal entry, June 21, 1777, in Doblin, *Specht Journal*, 48–49; Burgoyne, "Substance of the Speech of Lieut. Genl. Burgoyne to the Indians in Congress at the

Camp Upon the River Bouquet, June 21, 1777, And of their Answer," in *Burgoyne and the Saratoga Campaign, His Papers*, ed. Douglas R. Cubbison (Norman: University of Oklahoma Press, 2012), 198–201. See also Burgoyne to Germain, June 22, 1777, DAR, Vol. 14: 119; journal entry, in Digby, *British Invasion from the North*, 200; Roger Lamb, *Memoir of His Own Life* (Dublin: J. Jones, 1811), 168–70; and Nickerson, *The Turning Point of the Revolution*, 123–26.

68. Commager and Morris, *Spirit of 'Seventy-Six*, 544. Burke also argued that using Indians "was no way to treat one's own countrymen," quoted in Bickham, *Making Headlines*, 222–23.
69. Journal entry, June 24, 1777, in Wasmus, *An Eyewitness Account of the American Revolution*, 55.
70. Journal entry, June 21, 1777, in George F. G. Stanley, ed., *For Want of a Horse: Being a Journal of the Campaign Against the Americans in 1776 and 1777 Conducted from Canada, by an Officer Who Served with Lt. Gen. Burgoyne* (Sackville, New Brunswick, Canada: Tribune Press, 1961), 102.

CHAPTER 6

1. Gates to Robert Morris, April 22, 1777, in HGP, Reel 4.
2. Anthony Wayne to Gates, April 25, 1777, ibid.
3. Bird, *March to Saratoga*, 29.
4. René Chartrand, *Ticonderoga, 1758: Montcalm's Victory Against All Odds* (Oxford: Osprey Publishing, 2000), 58. See also "Fort Ticonderoga—A Short History," *Bulletin of the Fort Ticonderoga Museum* 7 (July 1945), 26–29. All the elevations were taken from a 2006 topographic map of the Ticonderoga area. http://www.cnyhiking.com/MountDefiance.htm
5. Baldwin, *Revolutionary Journal*, 94; and Thacher, *Military Journal*, 96.
6. Anthony Wayne to Gates, April 25, 1777, in HGP, Reel 4.
7. John P. Becker, *The Sexagenary: Or, Reminiscences of the American Revolution* (Albany, NY: J. Munsell, 1866), 57.
8. Lieutenant Carl Augustus Sartorious, journal entry, July 4, 1777, Henry J. Retzer, trans., "Journal of the Hessen-Hanau Erbprinz Infantry Regiment," *Hessians: Journal of the Johannes Schwalm Historical Association* 6 (1999): 34.
9. Alex Storozynski, *The Peasant Prince: Thaddeus Kosciuszko and the Age of Revolution* (New York: St. Martin's Press, 2009). See also journal entry, May 12, 1777, in Baldwin, *Revolutionary Journal*, 101.
10. Gates to Paterson, May 8, 1777, in HGP, Reel 4.
11. Storozynski, *Peasant Prince*, 25–26.
12. Kosciuszko to Gates, May 18, 1777, in HGP, Reel 4; and Storozynski, *Peasant Prince*, 27–28.
13. Storozynski, *Peasant Prince*, 27; and Barbieri, "Mount Independence." Baldwin also reported to Gates about his activities at Ticonderoga and emphasized his work on the post's hospital and redoubts near the old French lines, neither of which were critical for the defense of the fort. Baldwin to Gates, May 15, 1777, in HGP, Reel 4.
14. Wilkinson to Gates, May 22, 1777, in HGP, Reel 4.
15. Gates to Paterson, May 23, 1777, in HGP, Reel 4.
16. Wilkinson to Gates, May 26, 1777, ibid.
17. Gates to Enoch Poor, May 27, 1777, and Gates to Baldwin, May 28, 1777, ibid.
18. Wilkinson to Gates, May 31, 1777, ibid.
19. Poor to Gates, June 2, 1777, ibid.; and Baldwin's journal from mid-May through mid-June 1777, in Baldwin, *Revolutionary Journal*, 102–5.
20. JCC, VII: 217; Mark M. Boatner, III, *Encyclopedia of the American Revolution* (Mechanicsburg, PA: Stackpole Books, 1994), 956; journal entry, June 12, 1777, in Baldwin, *Revolutionary Journal*, 105; and Thomas Blake journal entry, June 11, 1777, Frederick Kidder, ed., *History of the New Hampshire Regiment in the War of the Revolution*, reprint of 1868 edition (Hampton, NH: Peter E. Randall, 1973), 26.

21. Gates to Arthur St. Clair, June 12, 1777, in HGP, Reel 4. This episode raises two key questions. First, why did Gates not give a direct order to Generals Wayne and Paterson to seize Mount Defiance? Second, why did St. Clair ignore Gates's suggestion? Things might have turned out very differently during the 1777 campaign had Gates properly exercised his command authority while in the Northern Department.
22. Schuyler to Washington, June 14, 1777, in GWP, Vol. 10: 39.
23. Schuyler to Washington, June 16, 1777, ibid., 55.
24. Washington to Schuyler, June 16, 1777, ibid., 53–54.
25. Washington to Israel Putnam, June 17, 1777, ibid., 63.
26. St. Clair to James Wilson, June 18, 1777, Arthur St. Clair Papers, Film 38, Reel 1, David Library of the American Revolution (hereafter DLAR). A brief account of the Indian raid on June 18 can be found in the journal entry, June 18, 1777, in Baldwin, *Revolutionary Journal*, 106.
27. Richard Varick to Schuyler, June 13, 1777, in Philip Schuyler Papers, Film 659, Reel 9, DLAR.
28. Blake journal entry, June 17, 1777, in Kidder, *History of the First New Hampshire Regiment*, 26. Lieutenant Blake also recorded the arrival at the fort of General Schuyler on June 18, 1777. See also Michael R. Barbieri, "... They Will Not Trouble Us Here this Summer": An Account of Some Incident That Took Place on June 17, 1777 Near Fort Ticonderoga," *Bulletin of the Fort Ticonderoga Museum* 16 (2000): 253–71.
29. James Wilkinson, *Memoirs of My Own Times*, Vol. 1 (Philadelphia: Abraham Small, 1816), 173. Wilkinson's memoirs must be viewed with considerable caution as he is one of the most disreputable and deceitful characters in United States history, and his memoirs are replete with falsehoods and exaggerations, especially when he portrays his own role as central. Still, his recollections of this time period are important, as he was a key player and eyewitness. When he discusses an event in which his own involvement was peripheral, we can be reasonably certain of its accuracy. See also the fascinating biography of Wilkinson, Andro Linklater, *An Artist in Treason: The Extraordinary Double Life of General James Wilkinson* (New York: Walker Publishing, 2009).
30. Ibid., 174–76. See also Arthur St. Clair, *The Life and Public Services of Arthur St. Clair, with His Correspondence and Other Papers*, Vol. 1, ed. Henry Smith (Cincinnati, OH: Robert Clarke, 1882), 404. See also Gerlach, *Proud Patriot*, 240–41. Gerlach calls the decisions of the council of war "perfectly understandable," and agrees with most historians that the generals' judgment and decisions were correct.
31. Washington to Schuyler, June 20, 1777, in GWP, Vol. 10: 90–92.
32. The orders of battle in this book are taken from Morrissey, *Saratoga, 1777*, 24, and match fairly closely the last official return of the troops at the fort recorded on June 28, 1777, which indicated a total of 4,072 officers and men present for duty. See Arthur St. Clair, *Proceedings of a Court Martial Held at White Plains in the State of New York, By the Order of His Excellency General Washington, Commander in Chief of the Army of the United States of America, for the Trial of Major General St. Clair, August 25, 1778* (Philadelphia: Hall and Sellers, 1778), 10–11. See also GWP, Vol. 10: 201n. The two-to-one force ratio assumes a total British fit for duty strength at Ticonderoga of approximately 6,900 officers and men. See journal entry, June 30, 1777, in Digby, *British Invasion from the North*, 201, and Kopperman, "The Numbers Game," 264. These returns contradict the claim by St. Clair, Schuyler, Wilkinson, and others that there were only between two thousand and three thousand soldiers at the fort when the British attacked. By only counting infantrymen, they routinely made the situation look much worse than it was. Based on his own returns and the number of soldiers unfit for duty, on July 5, 1777, the day St. Clair ordered the evacuation of the entire complex, he had well over 3,500 soldiers (and according to Morrissey, probably up to about 4,500) capable of resisting Burgoyne. This meant that the force ratio at Ticonderoga was a little less than two to one in Burgoyne's favor, which in a defensive fight benefited the Americans.

33. Gates in his testimony at St. Clair's court martial in August 1778 testified that if he were commanding at Fort Ticonderoga he would want a "three to two" advantage over Burgoyne. St. Clair had to make do with what he had, and he had enough men to put up an adequate defense. Horatio Gates testimony, in St. Clair, *Court Martial,* 17.
34. During his court-martial Schuyler was asked by St. Clair if he had issued any orders to evacuate the garrison. Schuyler replied: "No. The reason why I did not give you any orders for evacuating these garrisons was, because I had wrote this letter to Congress [a June 8, 1777, letter in which Schuyler assured the delegates that St. Clair could hold the fort] and they did not give me any orders about it; and as the continent conceived them of great importance, and very strong, I did not think myself at liberty to give any orders for an evacuation of them." St. Clair, *Court Martial,* 34. See also Wilkinson to Gates, June 25, 1777, in HGP, Reel 4.
35. St. Clair to Schuyler, June 24, 1777, Philip Schuyler Papers, DLAR.
36. St. Clair to Gates, June 27, 1777, in HGP, Reel 4.
37. Udnay Hay, James Wilkinson, and Arthur St. Clair testimony on the difficulty in gathering intelligence prior to the British attack, mainly due to the Indian activities, St. Clair, *Court Martial,* 19 and 21. See also Barbieri, ". . . They Will Not Trouble Us Here this Summer," 263; and Wilkinson, *Memoirs,* 178–79. St. Clair said much the same in a letter to Schuyler: due to the Indian attacks and British patrols, "We can not venture the teams now without a strong guard"; see St. Clair to Schuyler, June 28, 1777, in Arthur St. Clair, *Life and Public Services of Arthur St. Clair,* 411.
38. St. Clair to Schuyler, June 25, 1777, in St. Clair, *Life and Public Services,* 409.
39. Wilkinson to Gates, June 25, 1777, in HGP, Reel 4. See also Cohen, *Conquered into Liberty,* 208.
40. Schuyler to Hancock, June 25, 1777, in Schuyler, *Court Martial,* 35. The discrepancy between St. Clair's and Schuyler's claims is about 12 percent, which seems like a relatively small discrepancy, but it amounts to over a week's worth of provisions. Schuyler testified at St. Clair's court martial that it would have been very difficult to raise a siege, even if Ticonderoga had held out, but his testimony should be viewed with skepticism since he was facing his own court martial and it was to his advantage to support St. Clair. See the testimony of the Northern Department's Deputy Commissary General and Schuyler in St. Clair, *Court Martial,* 12–13 and 34.
41. John Milsop, *Continental Infantrymen of the American Revolution* (Oxford, UK: Osprey Publishing, 2004), 14–16.
42. Ibid., 20–21 and 23–24.
43. Each bateau held between 25 and 30 men. Hadden, *Journal,* 80.
44. Simon Fraser to John Robinson, July 13, 1777, "General Fraser's Account of Burgoyne's Campaign on Lake Champlain and the Battle of Hubbardton," *Proceedings of the Vermont Historical Society* 4 (1898): 141.
45. Journal entries, June 26 and 29, 1777, in Wasmus, *An Eyewitness Account of the American Revolution,* 56–57. For another similar description of Crown Point, see Anton Adolph Heinrich Du Roi (attrib.), journal entry, June 27, 1777, in Doblin, *Specht Journal,* 50.
46. Journal entry, June 30, 1777, in Hadden, *Journal,* 81.
47. Burgoyne, June 30, 1777, General Order, in *Burgoyne's Orderly Book,* 17.
48. Journal entry, June 30, 1777, in Digby, *British Invasion from the North,* 201.
49. Journal entry, June 30, 1777, in Baldwin, *Revolutionary Journal,* 108.
50. Schuyler to Washington, June 28, 1777, and St. Clair to Schuyler, June 25, 1777, GWP, Vol. 10: 141 and 142n. Schuyler wrote to Washington again on June 30 with essentially the same message; Schuyler to Washington, June 30, 1777, ibid., 159–60.
51. Henry Livingston to Schuyler, June 30, 1777, in Philip Schuyler Papers, Film 659, Reel 9, DLAR.
52. St. Clair to Schuyler, June 30, 1777, in St. Clair, *Life and Public Services,* 414. St. Clair's letter echoes one that Schuyler sent to Congress two weeks before: "[W]e shall be able to hold that pass [Mount Independence] against any effort by the enemy"; see Schuyler

to Hancock, June 14, 1777, in Schuyler, *Court Martial*, 32. See also Cohen, *Conquered into Liberty*, 209.

53. Washington to Schuyler, July 2, 1777, in GWP, Vol. 10: 170–71.
54. Ronald F. Kingsley, Harvey Alexander, and Eric Schnitzer, "German Auxiliaries Project: The Incursion to Mount Independence, the Burgoyne Campaign, July 1777. Part I: An Investigation of the Landing and Encampment," *Hessians: Journal of the Johannes Schwalm Historical Association* 8 (2005): 33 and journal entries, July 1 and 2, 1777, in Hadden, *Journal*, 82–83.
55. Journal entries, July 1 and 2, 1777, in Baldwin, *Revolutionary Journal*, 109–10.
56. Journal entry, July 3, 1777, in Stanley, *For Want of a Horse*, 108. This journal writer recorded that only two men were killed by the American cannonade and "a few Tents knock'd down." See also Cubbison, *The Artillery Never Gained More Honour*, 74–76.
57. Journal entry, July 2, 3, and 4, 1777, in Thacher, *Military Journal*, 98.
58. Fraser to John Robinson, July 13, 1777, "General Fraser's Account of Burgoyne's Campaign," 142.
59. Journal entry, July 3, 1777, in Stanley, *For Want of a Horse*, 108. See also Lord Francis Napier's journal entry for July 2, 1777, in S. Sydney Bradford, ed., "Lord Francis Napier's Journal of the Burgoyne Campaign," *Maryland Historical Magazine* 57 (December 1962): 298.
60. Fraser to John Robinson, July 13, 1777, "General Fraser's Account of Burgoyne's Campaign," 142.
61. Burgoyne to Howe, July 2, 1777, DAR, Vol. 14: 125.
62. St. Clair to Schuyler, July 3, 1777, in St. Clair, *Court Martial*, 24. See also St. Clair to Schuyler, July 1 and 2, 1777, ibid., 23–24.
63. Clausewitz, *On War*, 194–97. The two-to-one ratio is based on the soldiers reported as fit and present for duty: Americans more than four thousand and the British/Germans about seven thousand. See the Orders of Battle appendix.
64. St. Clair had also explicitly stated that he would consolidate his forces on Mount Independence. St. Clair to Schuyler, June 18, 1777, in St. Clair, *Court Martial*, 7.
65. Fraser to John Robinson, July 13, 1777, "General Fraser's Account of Burgoyne's Campaign," 143.
66. Ibid.
67. Cubbison, *The Artillery Never Gained More Honour*, 77–78; Cohen, *Conquered into Liberty*, 211; Barbieri, "Mount Independence"; and St. Clair, *The St. Clair Papers*, 63. For a description of Twiss's and Phillips's work at Mount Defiance, see Burgoyne to Germain, July 11, 1777, in DAR, Vol. 14: 135–36.
68. Journal entry, July 5, 1777, in Bradford, "Lord Francis Napier's Journal," 299; and Burgoyne to Germain, July 11, 1777, in DAR, Vol. 14: 136. For a contrary view of the importance of Mount Defiance, see Ron Morgan, "'Shamefully abandoning the Posts of Ticonderoga and Mount Independence, in His Charge': The Court Martial of Major General Arthur St. Clair and the Verdict of History," Mount Independence Coalition (2013), 34. https://mountindependence.org
69. Journal entry, July 4, 1777, in Digby, *British Invasion from the North*, 205.
70. Journal entry, July 4, 1777, in Baldwin, *Revolutionary Journal*, 109. See also Blake journal entry, July 5, 1777, in Kidder, *History of the First New Hampshire Regiment*, 27–28.
71. Journal entry, July 5, 1777, in Thacher, *Military Journal*, 98–99.
72. Officer journal entry, July 4, 1777, in Stanley, *For Want of a Horse*, 108.
73. Burgoyne to Earl Hervey, July 11, 1777, in de Fonblanque, *Political and Military Episodes*, 247. For another view, see Morgan, "Arthur St. Clair's Decision to Abandon Fort Ticonderoga and Mount Independence," *Journal of the American Revolution* (May 16, 2016). https://allthingsliberty.com/2016/05/arthur-st-clairs-decision-to-abandon-fort-ticonderoga-and-mount-independence/. See also Morgan, "The Court Martial of Major General Arthur St. Clair," 35.

74. St. Clair, Minutes of the Council of War at Fort Ticonderoga, July 5, 1777, in GWP, Vol. 10: 281–82n.
75. Udney Hay's testimony at the St. Clair court-martial, August 29, 1778, in St. Clair, *Court Martial*, 18.
76. All the timings for the July 5 activities come from the St. Clair court-martial testimony of Colonels Hay, Baldwin, and Kosciuszko, ibid., 18, 22, and 30. See also Smith, *The St. Clair Papers*, 65.
77. Hay testimony, St. Clair, *Court Martial*, ibid., 18. See also Ketchum, *Saratoga*, 173–74. Gates had ordered the building of the Ticonderoga-Castleton road the year before to expedite the transport of supplies and troops. See Gates to Jonathan Trumbull, September 30, 1776, *American Archives Online*. http://digital.lib.niu.edu/islandora/object/niu-amarch%3A101895
78. Ibid.
79. Journal entry, July 14, 1777, in Thacher, *Military Journal*, 99.
80. Ketchum, *Saratoga*, 180–81.
81. David M. Ludlum, "The Weather of Independence," *Weatherwise* 29 (October 1976): 237.
82. Blake journal entry, July 6, 1777, in Kidder, *History of the First New Hampshire Regiment*, 28.
83. Smith, *St. Clair Papers*, 65; and Cohen, *Conquered into Liberty*, 212.
84. Journal entry, July 6, 1777, in Digby, *British Invasion from the North*, 208–9.
85. Ketchum's 1997 book on the campaign, which is the standard account, repeats the story of the drunken soldiers, as do Morrissey and many others. However, recent research on the original source, which has been drawn on for more than two hundred years, has convincingly debunked the account. Digby and Fraser, who were both among the first British soldiers to cross the bridge to Mount Independence, made no mention of any Americans contesting the crossing or covering the bridge or obstacle. See Ketchum, *Saratoga*, 183–84; Morrissey, *Saratoga, 1777*, 37; and Ennis Duling, "Thomas Anburey at the Battle of Hubbardton: How a Fraudulent Source Misled Historians." *Vermont History* 78, no.1 (Winter/Spring 2010): 1–14.
86. Kosciuszko's testimony, in St. Clair, *Court Martial*, 22.
87. This critical assessment of St. Clair's leadership failure is not shared by most historians, who have justified St. Clair's actions for a variety of reasons, but mainly because the American Army escaped. One even likened the evacuation to Dunkirk. St. Clair's mission was to hold Ticonderoga for as long as he could, but he made little effort to even try. The fact that everything worked out in the end is no excuse. For contrary views, see Ketchum, *Saratoga*, 172–84; Luzader, *Saratoga*, 55–59; and Morgan, "Arthur St. Clair's Decision to Abandon Fort Ticonderoga" and Morgan, "Shamefully Abandoning the Posts," 65.
88. Gerlach, *Proud Patriot*, 243–44; and Linklater, *An Artist in Treason*, 34–35.

CHAPTER 7

1. Fraser to John Robinson, July 13, 1777, "General Fraser's Account of Burgoyne's Campaign," 144.
2. Burgoyne, "Thoughts for Conducting the War from then Side of Canada," in DAR, Vol. 14: 44.
3. Journal entry, July 6, 1777, in Hadden, *Journal*, 85; and Fraser to John Robinson, July 13, 1777, "General Fraser's Account of Burgoyne's Campaign," 144. Burgoyne reported that it only took 30 minutes to dismantle the boom; see Burgoyne to Germain, July 11, 1777, in DAR, Vol. 14: 136. The light infantry battalion commanded by Major Lindsay, Lord Balcarres, was also often known as the Balcarres light infantry battalion. As a peer, Lindsay was often known by simply by his title, "Balcarres."
4. Anton Adolph Heinrich Du Roi (attrib.) journal entry, July 6, 1777, in Doblin, *Specht Journal*, 53. See also Philipp Theobald, journal entry, July 6, 1777, Henry J. Retzer, ed., and trans., "Journal of the Hessen-Hanau Erbprinz Infantry Regiment—June to August 1777, Kept by Chaplain Philipp Theobald," *Hessians: Journal of the Johannes Schwalm*

Historical Association 7 (2001): 42. An American officer calculated that the total loss at the fort was 127 cannon, 500 barrels of powder, 500 barrels of flour, 1,500 barrels of salt pork, 700 barrels of salt beef, tents for 4,000, and five ships. Blake journal entry, July 7, 1777, in Kidder, *History of the First New Hampshire Infantry Regiment*, 28–29.

5. Unnamed officer journal entry, July 6, 1777, in Barker, "The Battles of Saratoga and the Kinderhook Tea Party," 31. See also J. A. Houlding and G. Kenneth Gates, eds., "Corporal Fox's Memoir of Service, 1776–1783: Quebec, Saratoga, and the Convention Army," *Journal of the Society for Army Historical Research* 68 (Autumn 1990): 18.
6. Journal entry, July 6, 1777, in Digby, *British Invasion from the North*, 205–6.
7. Schuyler to Washington, July 7, 1777, in GWP, Vol. 10: 219.
8. Schuyler to Washington, July 7, 1777, ibid., 220–21.
9. Schuyler to Washington, July 9, 1777, ibid., 234.
10. St. Clair to William Heath, July 7, 1777, in William Heath Papers, Reel 5, DLAR.
11. St. Clair to Schuyler, July 8, 1777, in GWP, Vol. 10: 245–46n.
12. Washington to Hancock, July 10, 1777, ibid., 240.
13. Wallace, "Benedict Arnold," 177–79; and Martin, *Benedict Arnold*, 303–41.
14. Congressional resolution of July 11, 1777, in JCC, Vol. 8: 545.
15. Washington to Schuyler, July 12, 1777, in GWP, Vol. 10: 261–62.
16. Washington to Schuyler, July 13, 1777, ibid., 276. Washington's exasperation was evident in his letters to other officers as well. To General Israel Putnam: "The more Accounts we get—the most astonishing does the evacuation of the posts on the Lakes appear." Washington to Israel Putnam, July 13, 1777, ibid., 274.
17. Schuyler to John Fellows, July 9, 1777, Schuyler, *Court Martial*, 48–49.
18. Schuyler to Ten Broeck, July 10, 1777, ibid., 48.
19. Schuyler to Washington, July 10, 1777, ibid., 244–45.
20. Burgoyne General Order, July 6, 1777, in Major General Riedesel, *Memoirs*, 114.
21. Venter, *Battle of Hubbardton*, 42.
22. For the geography of the area see Duling, "Thomas Anburey at the Battle of Hubbardton," 12; and Venter, *Battle of Hubbardton*, 44–45.
23. Morrissey, *Saratoga*, 34–35; Luzader, *Saratoga*, 60; Venter, *Battle of Hubbardton*, 47; and Dearborn to Wilkinson, December 20, 1815, *Bulletin of the Fort Ticonderoga Museum* 1.5 (January 1929), 4.
24. Fraser to John Robinson, July 13, 1777, "General Fraser's Account of Burgoyne's Campaign," 145.
25. Morrissey, *Saratoga*, 35–36; and Luzader, *Saratoga*, 59–60. See also Burgoyne to Germain, July 11, 1777, in DAR, Vol. 14: 137–38 and Major General Riedesel, *Memoirs*, 115.
26. Morrissey, *Saratoga*, 35–36; and Luzader, *Saratoga*, 60–61. See also Burgoyne to Germain, July 11, 1777, in DAR, Vol. 14: 137–38; Major General Riedesel, *Memoirs*, 115; and Venter, *Battle of Hubbardton*, 50–51. St. Clair would later argue that the Battle of Hubbardton was unnecessary because Warner disobeyed his orders to continue to Castleton close behind the retreating army and there rejoin the main body. However, the many stragglers from the main body would have almost certainly been captured and the rapidly pursing Fraser might well have caught up to St. Clair with disastrous consequences. St. Clair, *Court Martial*, 47; and Venter, *Battle of Hubbardton*, 51–52. For an excellent analysis of Warner's decision making, see John Williams, *The Battle of Hubbardton: The American Rebels Stem the Tide* (Montpelier: Vermont Division for Historical Preservation, 1988), 66–68.
27. Journal entry, July 7, 1777, in Digby, *The British Invasion from the North*, 209–10.
28. Unnamed German officer journal entry, July 7, 1777, Barker, "The Battles of Saratoga and the Kinderhook Tea Party," 31; and Venter, *Battle of Hubbardton*, 53 and 72–73.
29. Burgoyne to Germain, July 11, 1777, in DAR, Vol. 14: 137.
30. Three Hubbardton myths are related directly to the same questionable source as that for the four drunken soldiers at Mount Independence. The first is that Major Acland's grenadiers climbed to the top of Mount Zion. This was highly unlikely. It is an extremely high, rugged, and rocky peak that could be used for observation purposes, but tactically,

Mount Zion was simply unusable. Second, the Americans did not post sentries and were surprised by Fraser while cooking their breakfast. However, Fraser himself wrote a few days later that they encountered American sentries on their approach. Finally, the source claimed that the Americans had faked a surrender and instead had fired at the British at point-blank range as they approached to disarm them, thus violating the civilized laws rules of warfare. These stories, all originating from Anburey's *Travels through the Interior Parts of America*, are easily refuted by referring to Burgoyne's July 11, 1777, letter to Germain, Balcarres's testimony to the House of Commons, Digby's and Hadden's journals, Fraser's letter to a friend, and an examination of the terrain. Still, some or all these myths have persisted in well regarded books on Saratoga including those by Nickerson, Ketchum, Morrissey, and Luzader. Duling, "Thomas Anburey at the Battle of Hubbardton: How a Fraudulent Source Misled Historians," 2–14, and Fraser to John Robinson, July 13, 1777, "General Fraser's Account of Burgoyne's Campaign," 145.

31. Morrissey, *Saratoga*, 35–38; Luzader, *Saratoga*, 61–67; and Venter, *Battle of Hubbardton*, 74–88. See also Burgoyne to Germain, July 11, 1777, in DAR, Vol. 14: 138; Major General Riedesel, *Memoirs*, 115–16; Fraser to John Robinson, July 13, 1777, "General Fraser's Account of Burgoyne's Campaign," 145–46; and Daniel Chipman, ed., *Memoir of Colonel Seth Warner* (Middlebury, VT: L. W. Clark, 1848), 50–52.
32. Venter, *Battle of Hubbardton*, 89–95; and Fraser to John Robinson, July 13, 1777, "General Fraser's Account of Burgoyne's Campaign," 146.
33. Morrissey, *Saratoga*, 35–38; Luzader, *Saratoga*, 62–67; and Venter, *Battle of Hubbardton*, 96–107.
34. Venter, *Battle of Hubbardton*, 89–105; and Unnamed officer journal entry, July 7, 1777, in Barker, "The Battles of Saratoga and the Kinderhook Tea Party," 31.
35. Morrissey, *Saratoga*, 35–38; Luzader, *Saratoga*, 62–67; and Venter, *Battle of Hubbardton*, 96–107. See also Burgoyne to Germain, July 11, 1777, in DAR, Vol. 14: 138; Major General Riedesel, *Memoirs*, 115–16; and Chipman, *Memoir of Colonel Seth Warner*, 50–52.
36. Unnamed officer journal entry, July 7, 1777, in Barker, "The Battles of Saratoga and the Kinderhook Tea Party," 31; and Venter, *Battle of Hubbardton*, 105–7.
37. The British lost 25 percent of their soldiers and the combined allied force lost a total of 17 percent casualties of all engaged. The Americans lost more than 28 percent.
38. Unnamed officer journal entry, July 8, 1777, in Barker, "The Battles of Saratoga and the Kinderhook Tea Party," 31.
39. Fraser to John Robinson, July 13, 1777, "General Fraser's Account of Burgoyne's Campaign," 146.
40. Morrissey, *Saratoga*, 38; Luzader, *Saratoga*, 69–71; journal entries, July 8 and 9, 1777, in Digby, *British Invasion from the North*, 216–23; Fraser to John Robinson, July 13, 1777, "General Fraser's Account of Burgoyne's Campaign," 145–46; and Major General Riedesel, *Memoirs*, 115–18.
41. Venter, *The Battle of Hubbardton*. See also Cohen, *Conquered into Liberty*, 217.
42. Lord Balcarres's testimony, in Burgoyne, STOE, 39.
43. Journal entry, July 7, 1777, in Digby, *British Invasion from the North*, 210.
44. Burgoyne General Order issued at Skenesborough, July 10, 1777, in Digby, *British Invasion from the North*, 223–24; and journal entry, July 12, 1777, in Hadden, *Journal*, 95.
45. Journal entry, July 7, 1777 (obviously Hadden added to this entry after the battle), ibid., 87.
46. Journal entry, July 14, 1777, in Thacher, *Military Journal*, 99.
47. Douglas R. Cubbison, "Catastrophe on Lake Champlain, July 6, 1777," *American Revolution* (July/August 2012): 13.
48. Journal entry, July 14, 1777, in Thacher, *Military Journal*, 99–100.
49. No author, "Phillip Skene of Skenesborough," *Bulletin of the Fort Ticonderoga Museum* 6 (January 1943): 159–60; and Boatner, "Philip Skeen," *Dictionary of the American Revolution*, 1010–12. Skene surrendered with Burgoyne's army and most of his extensive estate was

destroyed during the war. He tried to regain his property after the war, but like many Loyalists was unsuccessful. He lived out the rest of his days in England.
50. Burgoyne to Germain, July 11, 1777, in DAR, Vol. 14: 136–37.
51. Journal entry, July 6, 1777, in Hadden, *Journal*, 89.
52. Journal entry, July 14, 1777, in Thacher, *Military Journal*, 100; and Burgoyne to Germain, July 11, 1777, in DAR, Vol. 14: 137.
53. Cubbison, "Catastrophe on Lake Champlain," 12–18.
54. This list of ships and supplies captured and destroyed at Skenesborough is from unnamed British officer journal entry, July 9, 1777, in Stanley, *For Want of a Horse*, 118.
55. Journal entry, July 14, 1777, in Thacher, *Military Journal*, 100.
56. Journal entry, July 14, 1777, in Thacher, *Military Journal*, 100.
57. Becker, *The Sexagenary*, 56.
58. The reason the British officer had to fake an Indian war cry was because the Indian party accompanying the 9th Regiment had deserted, an ominous portent of things to come for Burgoyne's army. Journal entry, July 14, 1777, in Thacher, *Military Journal*, 101; and Morrissey, *Saratoga*, 38.
59. Burgoyne to Germain, July 11, 1777, in DAR, Vol. 14: 139. See also journal entry, July 9, 1777, in Digby, *British Invasion from the North*, 221.
60. Journal entry, July 9, 1777, in Digby, *British Invasion from the North*, 221.
61. Burgoyne General Order issued from Skenesborough on July 11, 1777, in Hadden, *Journal*, 91–93.
62. Burgoyne to Germain, July 11, 1777, in DAR, Vol. 14: 140–42.
63. Howe received Burgoyne's July 11 letter on or about July 15, only a week before he set sail for Chesapeake Bay on his Philadelphia campaign. Burgoyne's letter suggested that he would need no help getting to Albany. See Morrissey, *Saratoga*, 42.
64. Burgoyne to Carleton, July 11, 1777, in British Colonial Office Records, CO 42/37, DLAR.
65. Carleton to Burgoyne, July 19, 1777, ibid. To Carleton's credit, after another appeal by Burgoyne later in the month, he would send some of his troops to help garrison various posts, but Burgoyne was still forced to devote one thousand soldiers to guard his rear. See Nelson, *General Sir Guy Carleton*, 120–21; and Carleton to Lord Barrington, July 31, 1777, in British War Office Papers, WO1/11, DLAR.
66. Eric Schnitzer email to the author, March 27, 2017.
67. Morrissey, *Saratoga*, 39.
68. Schuyler to Washington, July 14, 1777, in GWP, Vol. 10: 279–81. Participants from both sides remarked often about the unusually rainy summer of 1777.
69. Washington to Schuyler, July 15, 1777, in GWP, Vol. 10: 291.
70. St. Clair to Hancock, July 14, 1777, St. Clair, *Court Martial*, 24.
71. Burgoyne memo "Thoughts for Conducting the War from the Side of Canada," February 28, 1777, in DAR, Vol. 14: 44.
72. Cubbison, *The Artillery Never Gained More Honour*, 90–91; and Bird, *March to Saratoga*, 60–62.
73. Burgoyne's "Narrative" statement, in Burgoyne, STOE, 17–18. Americans abandoned Fort George on June 22, 1777, which was before Burgoyne's main movement south. See William L. Stone, trans., *Letters of Brunswick and Hessian Officers During the American Revolution* (Albany, NY: Joel Munsell's Sons, 1891), 94.
74. Burgoyne to Germain, July 30, 1777, in DAR, Vol. 14: 153.

CHAPTER 8

1. Blake journal entry, July 8, 1777, in Kidder, *History of the First New Hampshire Regiment*, 29.
2. Quoted in Ben Z. Rose, *John Stark: Maverick General* (Waverly, MA: Treeline Press, 2007), 104.
3. Jonathan Trumbull Jr. to Jonathan Trumbull Sr., July 8, 1777, in GWP, Vol. 10: 283n. The different Trumbulls can be confusing. Colonel John Trumbull was the perceptive officer who urged the occupation of Mount Defiance back in 1776. Jonathan Trumbull Jr., the

author of this letter, was John's brother and fellow Patriot officer. Jonathan Trumbull Sr., the father of both men, was the colonial governor of Connecticut.

4. Journal entry, July 14, 1777, in Thacher, *Military Journal*, 102–3. Despite the multiple setbacks, some soldiers thought that "this event, apparently so calamitous, will ultimately prove advantageous by drawing the British army into the heart of the country, and thereby place them more immediately in our power."
5. *(Boston) Independent Chronicle*, July 17 and 24, 1777, Microfilm Newspaper Collection, Film 251, Reel 2, DLAR.
6. *(Philadelphia) Pennsylvania Packet*, July 29, 1777, Microfilm Newspaper Collection, Film 521, Reel 1, DLAR.
7. *Providence (Rhode Island) Gazette and Country Journal*, July 19, 1777, Microfilm Newspaper Collection, Film 251, Reel 2.
8. John Hancock to Schuyler, July 18, 1777, in Burnett, *Letters of Members of the Continental Congress*, Vol. 3, 415.
9. Nathaniel Folsom to the president of New Hampshire, July 26, 1777, in LDC, Vol. 7: 426.
10. Samuel Cooper to John Adams, July 24, 1777, in Adams, *Papers of John Adams*, Vol. 5, 250–51.
11. Samuel Adams to Richard Henry Lee, July 15, 1777, in Burnett, *Letters of Members of the Continental Congress*, Vol. 3, 413.
12. Samuel Adams to Richard Henry Lee, July 22, 1777, in LDC, Vol. 7: 360.
13. Quoted in Simms, *Three Victories and a Defeat*, 606.
14. Benjamin Harrison, et al., to Benjamin Franklin et al., August 3, 1777, in Francis Wharton, ed., *The Revolutionary Diplomatic Correspondence of the United States, Volume 2* (Washington, DC: US Government Printing Office, 1889), 373–74.
15. George Herring, *From Colony to Superpower: U.S. Foreign Relations since 1776* (New York: Oxford University Press, 2008), 19–20. The commissions often distrusted each other. Silas Deane even employed as his secretary a British double agent, Edward Bancroft. Yet they were still ultimately able to succeed in their diplomatic mission.
16. Ibid., 19.
17. For French strategic objectives during this time period, see James Pritchard, "French Strategy and the American Revolution: A Reappraisal," in Stoker et al., *Strategy in the American War of Independence*, 144.
18. Vergennes to Noailles, September 6, 1777, #45, in Benjamin Franklin Stevens, ed. and trans., *B. F. Stevens's Facsimiles of Manuscripts in European Archives Relating to America, 1773–1783*, Vol. 18 (London: Malby and Sons, 1898), heinonline.org
19. Stormont to Vergennes, August 26, 1777, in ibid. .
20. Vergennes to Stormont, September 6, 1777, in ibid.
21. Germain to the King George III, August 23, 1777, in Fortescue, *The Correspondence of King George the Third*, Vol. 3, 471–72.
22. King George III to Earl of Sandwich, September 3, 1777, in Montagu, *The Private Papers of John, Earl of Sandwich*, Vol. 1, 293.
23. James Murray to Germain, September 6, 1777, in GGP.
24. *London Gazette Extraordinary*, August 25, 1777, Newspaper Collection, Microfilm, DLAR.
25. Walpole to the Countess of Upper Ossory, August 24, 1777, in Toynbee, *The Letters of Horace Walpole*, Vol. 10, 100.
26. Horace Walpole to Horace Mann, September 1, 1777, in ibid., 103.
27. Germain to Burgoyne, September 15, 1777, in DAR, Vol. 14: 184–85.
28. Hamilton to Jay, July 13, 1777, in AHP, Vol. 1: 285–86.
29. John Adams to Abigail Adams, July 20, 1777, in LDC, Vol. 7: 355.
30. John Adams to Abigail Adams, August 19, 1777, in LDC, Vol. 7: 506.
31. Washington to Schuyler, July 15, 1777, in GWP, Vol. 10: 289–90.
32. Ibid.

CHAPTER 9

1. Journal entry, July 9, 1777, in Digby, *British Invasion from the North*, 227.
2. Ketchum, *Saratoga*, 140 and 249; and Eric H. Schnitzer, "Organization of the Army from Canada Commanded by Lieutenant General John Burgoyne—September 19 to October 7" (Stillwater, NY: Saratoga National Historical Park, January 2013), 3 and 5n. Some 215 British and 82 German women accompanied the army (at the time of Burgoyne's surrender), about 100 children, and an unknown number of servants, civilian contractors, and suttlers. The Riedesels were baron and baroness, but only he was Baron Riedesel. Frederike was a baroness, but she was not Baroness Riedesel. Her title came down through her maiden line. She also often wrote her name as "von Riedesel," but this was technically incorrect, as the "von" came from her line, not her husband's. He never referred to himself as "von Riedesel." Eric Schnitzer email to the author, March 27, 2017.
3. Stedman, *History of the Origin, Progress, and Termination of the American War*, 326–27.
4. Ibid.
5. Journal entry, July 9, 1777, in Digby, *British Invasion from the North*, 228.
6. Journal entry, July 12, 1777, in Hadden, *Journal*, 94–95.
7. Rose, *John Stark: Maverick General*, 106.
8. Ibid., 108. Stark's character was not the only impetus for New Hampshire's successful raising of their militia. Burgoyne's proclamation also enflamed the passions of the population. See Caleb Stark, *Memoir and Official Correspondence of Gen. John Stark* (Concord, NH: G. Parker Lyon, 1860), 119–21.
9. Hargrove, *General John Burgoyne*, 147; Morrissey, *Saratoga*, 42; and Ketchum, *Saratoga*, 233–39. While this may explain, in part at least, Burgoyne's delay at Skenesborough, few if any of his officers accused their general of neglecting his duties. Despite Carleton's assistance with providing some garrison troops from Canada, Burgoyne was forced to assign about one thousand troops to secure his lines back to Ticonderoga.
10. Fraser to John Robinson, July 13, 1777, "General Fraser's Account of Burgoyne's Campaign," 147. Since Fraser wrote this letter from Skenesborough, it is likely that he witnessed his commander's frustrations with the difficult landscape, logistics, and Schuyler's attempts to obstruct his route of march. This is Fraser's only account written during the campaign, since he was mortally wounded in action on October 7, 1777.
11. Unnamed officer journal entry for July 12, 1777, in Barker, "The Battles of Saratoga and the Kinderhook Tea Party," 32; journal entry, July 13 and 15, 1777, in Hadden, *Journal*, 95–96; and Anton Adolph Heinrich Du Roi (attrib.) journal entry, July 14, 1777, in Doblin, *Specht Journal*, 56.
12. Schuyler to Warner, July 15, 1777, Chipman, *Memoir of Colonel Seth Warner*, 53–54.
13. Warner to the Honorable Council of New Hampshire, July 18, 1777, ibid., 55–56.
14. Anton Adolph Heinrich Du Roi (attrib.) journal entry, for 21, 1777, in Doblin, *Specht Journal*, 57–58.
15. Ibid., 58.
16. Riedesel, *Memoirs*, 120–21.
17. Quoted in Digby, *British Invasion from the North*, 233n; and Schuyler to Washington, July 17, 1777, in GWP, Vol. 10: 312–13.
18. Anton Adolph Heinrich Du Roi (attrib.) journal entry, July 16, 1777, in Doblin, *Specht Journal*, 57.
19. In his testimony at the House of Commons inquiry, Burgoyne mentioned several times that he had been let down by Loyalists. Burgoyne "review of the evidence," Burgoyne, STOE, 151–53.
20. Journal entry, July 16, 1777, in Doblin, *Journal of J. F. Wasmus*, 62–63. Several participants noted that American deserters were reluctant to give themselves up to the British or German troops because they feared they would be intercepted by the Indians and killed, or worse, captured.
21. Ibid., 63.

22. Wasmus reported that 1,800 Indians came into the army's camp at Skenesborough; an anonymous German officer recorded that the number was "almost 1,000"; a member of Fraser's advanced corps said the number was "about 400"; Hadden wrote that the Indian contingent "surpassed all others I had seen before in size and appearance." Journal entry, July 17, in Doblin, *Journal of J. F. Wasmus*, 63; Anton Adolph Heinrich Du Roi (attrib.) journal entry, July 17, 1777, *Specht Journal*, 57 and 120n; unnamed officer journal entry for July 17, 1777, Stanley, *For Want of a Horse*, 119; and Hadden journal entry for July 20, 1777, Hadden, *Hadden's Journal*, 228.
23. Ketchum, *Saratoga*, 111–12; and Boatner, *Encyclopedia of the American Revolution*, 964–65.
24. Ketchum, *Saratoga*, 111–22; and Boatner, *Encyclopedia of the American Revolution*, 597–98. Langlade also led the destruction of the British trading post town of Pickawillany in 1752, which was an accelerant to the start of the French and Indian War.
25. Burgoyne to Germain, July 11, 1777, in DAR, Vol. 14: 140–41.
26. Journal entry, July 17, 1777, in Doblin, *An Eyewitness Account of the American Revolution*, 57, 62–63.
27. Doblin, *An Eyewitness Account of the American Revolution*, 64–65; and journal entry, July 20, 1777, in Digby, *British Invasion from the North*, 229.
28. For just one example of several like orders, see General Order for July 12, 1777, in Burgoyne, *Order Book*, 37–38. Officers also disobeyed Burgoyne's orders not to purchase horses for their personal use. See Bowler, *Logistics*, 229.
29. General Fraser's July 17, 1777, General Order to the advanced corps and General Burgoyne's July 18, 1777, General Order to the Army, in Stanley, *For Want of a Horse*, 119–20.
30. Anton Adolph Heinrich Du Roi (attrib.) journal entry, July 19 and 20, 1777, in Doblin, *Specht Journal*, 57.
31. Journal entry, July 24, 1777, in Digby, *British Invasion from the North*, 233.
32. Ibid., 234.
33. Washington to Hancock, July 15, 1777, in GWP, Vol. 10: 294.
34. Washington marched the army from its main headquarters at Morristown, New Jersey, 18 miles northeast to Pompton Plains, New Jersey, on July 11 in part as a response to the loss of Ticonderoga. A few days later he marched the army again a further 18 miles northeast to Suffern, New York, as he edged toward Peekskill, New York. See Washington to John Sullivan, July 12, 1777, in ibid., 262, and Washington to Colonel Hugh Hughes, July 15, 1777, in ibid., 286–87.
35. St. Clair to Washington, July 17, 1777, in ibid., 308–11.
36. Washington would not write St. Clair again until April 1778, and then only on a purely administrative matter, this after numerous other letters from St. Clair went unanswered. Washington to St. Clair, April 10, 1778, in GWP, Vol. 14: 470–71.
37. Schuyler to Washington, July 17, 1777, in GWP, Vol. 10: 311–13.
38. Schuyler to Kosciuszko, July 16, 1777, quoted in Storozynski, *Peasant Prince*, 29.
39. Washington to John Trumbull Sr., July 17, 1777, in GWP, Vol. 10: 314.
40. Washington to Hancock, July 18, 1777, ibid., 320. See also Rossie, *The Politics of Command*, 160.
41. Washington to Schuyler, July 18, 1777, in GWP, Vol. 10: 323.
42. Washington was aware of Schuyler's poor reputation among New Englanders. As he told General Heath a few days later, "I therefore hope that with Genl Arnold's Assistance, (in whom the Army and Militia in particular place great confidence) matters will be put in a more favourable train" in the Northern Department. Washington to William Heath, July 19, 1777, ibid., 339. Washington also made a separate appeal directly to senior militia officers in Massachusetts and New Hampshire. Washington to "the Brigadier Generals of Militia of Western Massachusetts and New Hampshire," July 18, 1777., ibid., 317–18.
43. Schuyler to Washington, July 18, 1777, ibid., 326.
44. Schuyler's July 21, 1777, return of the Northern Army enclosed in a letter to Washington, in ibid., 351n.

45. Schuyler to Washington, July 21, 1777, in ibid., 348–49.
46. Journal entries, July 28 and 29, 1777, in Digby, *British Invasion from the North*, 239.
47. Schuyler to Washington, July 28, 1777, in GWP, Vol. 10: 450.
48. Journal entry, July 30, 1777, in Digby, *British Invasion from the North*, 240.
49. Anton Adolph Heinrich Du Roi (attrib.) journal entry, August 5, 1777, in Doblin, *Specht Journal*, 62; and journal entry for August 1, 1777, in Bradford, "Napier's Journal," 307.
50. Jjournal entry, July 30, 1777, inDigby, *British Invasion from the North*, 240–42.
51. Unnamed officer journal entry, July 30, 1777, Stanley, *For Want of a Horse*, 124–25; and Hadden journal entry for July 27–30, 1777, in Hadden, *Journal*, 102–9.
52. Anton Adolph Heinrich Du Roi (attrib.) journal entry, July 31, 1777, in Doblin, *Specht Journal*, 60. See also Stedman, *History of the Origin, Progress, and Termination of the American War*, 330.
53. Burgoyne to Germain, July 30, 1777, in DAR, Vol. 14: 153.
54. Burgoyne to Germain, marked "Private," July 30, 1777, in ibid., 154–55.

CHAPTER 10

1. Two letters from Washington to Schuyler, both dated July 22, 1777, in GWP, Vol. 10: 363–65.
2. Schuyler to Washington, July 22, 1777, in ibid., 365–66. The Six Nations of the Iroquois Confederacy consisted of the Mohawk, Oneida, Onondaga, Cayuga, Seneca, and Tuscarora nations.
3. Schuyler to Washington, July 23, 1777, in ibid., 380–81. Three days later Schuyler reported that his army numbered 5,193 of all ranks, with only 3,884 present and fit for duty with almost 1,000 reported sick, 367 assigned to other duties, and 13 on leave. Schuyler's estimate of about 1,000 militia was probably about right. See Morrissey, *Saratoga*, 25.
4. St. Clair to Washington, July 25, 1777, in ibid., 418–19. See also St. Clair to Gates, August 1, 1777, in HGP, Reel 5.
5. Washington to Benjamin Lincoln, July 24, 1777, in GWP, Vol. 10: 385.
6. William Duer to Schuyler, July 29, 1777, in LDC, Vol. 7: 390. For the start of Congress's debates over Schuyler's command of the Northern Department after the fall of Ticonderoga, see journal entry, Saturday, July 26, 1777, in JCC, Vol. 7: 582–83.
7. Washington to Benjamin Lincoln, July 24, 1777, in GWP, Vol. 10: 385. See also David B. Mattern, *Benjamin Lincoln and the American Revolution* (Columbia: University of South Carolina Press, 1995), 41–42.
8. Boatner, *Encyclopedia of the American Revolution*, 635–37.
9. Washington to Schuyler, July 24, 1777, in GWP, Vol. 10: 396–98. At first Schuyler resisted Washington's suggestion to send Arnold to relieve Stanwix, but then later changed his mind. See Schuyler to Washington, July 28, 1777, in ibid., 450.
10. Schuyler to Washington, July 26–27, 1777, in ibid., 430–31. On July 27, Washington wrote to Schuyler saying he was moving the army to Philadelphia to face Howe, who had departed by sea from New York with the main army. Washington assured Schuyler that the British force remaining in New York City was not a threat to the Northern Army. See Washington to Schuyler, July 27, 1777, in ibid., 442. Despite Washington's reassurance, Schuyler believed that Howe would undoubtedly turn back up the Hudson to attack him from the rear. See Schuyler to Washington, August 1, 1777, in ibid., 483. Washington viewed Schuyler's August 1 letter with some alarm. Schuyler seemed woefully unequipped to deal with the situation. On receipt of Schuyler's August 1 letter, the commander-in-chief forwarded it to Hancock remarking that "you will perceive, that Our affairs, at the Northward, have experienced no change for the better. On the contrary, that they are on a more unpromising train." Washington to Hancock, August 7, 1777, ibid., 546.
11. Jonathan Trumbull Sr. to Washington, July 25, 1777, in ibid., 420–23. Washington answered Trumbull's letter saying he was in full agreement with Trumbull's assessment

of the impact of the loss of Ticonderoga, but he was more circumspect in criticizing his officers. See Washington to Jonathan Trumbull Sr., July 31, 1777, in ibid., 471-72.

12. Arnold to Washington, July 25, 1777, in ibid., 433–35. Glover's brigade joined the army on July 27, 1777; see Varick to Schuyler, July 27, 1777, in Philip Schuyler Papers, DLAR, Film 659, Reel 9. Morgan and his riflemen were ordered to join the Northern Army in mid-August. Washington to Morgan, August 16, 1777, in GWP, Vol. 10: 641, and John Fitzgerald to Morgan, August 18, 1777, ibid., 641n.
13. Schuyler to Washington, July 28, 1777, in GWP, Vol. 10: 450. Schuyler wisely took Washington's advice on how to use General Lincoln. Lincoln joined Schuyler on July 30 and on August 1 "set out to take Command on the Grants," where he would not only take charge of the militia there but would also recruit New England militia. Schuyler to Washington, August 1, 1777, in ibid., 483.
14. Samuel Adams to James Warren, July 31, 1777, in LDC, Vol. 7: 397.
15. John Adams to James Warren, August 12, 1777, in Taylor, *Papers of John Adams*, Vol. 5, 273.
16. Charles Thompson's notes on the debate of July 28, 1777, in LDC, Vol. 7: 389.
17. Minutes of Congress's debates, July 29 and 30, 1777, and August 1, 1777, in JCC, Vol. 7: 585, 590, and 595.
18. Ibid., 600. Hancock forwarded the congressional directive to Washington on August 2, 1777. See Hancock to Washington, August 2, 1777, in GWP, Vol. 10: 487.
19. James Duane to Schuyler, August 23, 1777, in Philip Schuyler Papers, DLAR, Film 659, Reel 9.
20. New England delegates to Washington, August 2, 1777, in LDC, Vol. 7: 406. The delegates who signed this letter to Washington included John Adams, Samuel Adams, Elbridge Gerry, Nathaniel Folsom, Eliphalet Dyer, William Williams, and Henry Marchant.
21. Washington to Hancock, August 3, 1777, in GWP, Vol. 10: 492–93.
22. Minutes of the congressional debate for August 4, 1777, in JCC, Vol. 7: 604. See also Hancock to Washington, August 4, 1777, in GWP, Vol. 10: 499.
23. Washington to Gates, August 4, 1777, in ibid., 499.
24. Washington to George Clinton, August 13, 1777, in ibid., 597.
25. Schuyler to Washington, August 13, 1777, in ibid., 606.
26. Schuyler to Washington, August 15, 1777, in ibid., 626.
27. Alexander Hamilton to Robert Livingston, August 7, 1777, in AHP, Vol. 1: 307. Ironically, Hamilton would later marry Schuyler's daughter.

CHAPTER 11

1. Schuyler to Washington, July 26–27, 1777, in GWP, Vol. 10: 430–31.
2. William Scudder, *The Journal of William Scudder, an Officer in the Late New-York Line* (New York: n.p., 1794), 13.
3. Schuyler to Washington, July 26–27, 1777, in GWP, Vol. 10: 430–31.
4. John Koster, "Jane McCrea, Remembered as a Victim of American Indian Brutality, May Have Died under Different Circumstances," *Military History* 17 (June 2000): 12–14.
5. Ibid., 16.
6. Ibid.
7. Journal entry, July 24, 1777, in Digby, *British Invasion from the North*, 236–37.
8. Unnamed British officer journal entry, July 27, 1777, in Stanley, *For Want of a Horse*, 122.
9. Journal entry, August 1, 1777, in Doblin, *Journal of J. F. Wasmus*, 66.
10. Burgoyne to Gates, September 6, 1777, in HGP, Reel 5. For another corroborating account of Burgoyne's questioning of Panther and of the Indian chiefs' pleas for clemency, see unnamed British officer journal entry, July 28, 1777, in Stanley, *For Want of a Horse*, 123.
11. Koster, "Jane McCrea, Remembered," 16. What is unclear is whether or not the Americans knew or suspected that McCrea had been accidently shot by friendly militia.

12. Historian Brendan Morrissey argues that Burgoyne seriously mishandled the McCrea affair and it was this bungling that led to the mass Indian departure a few weeks later. He also maintains that the incident was not the cause of the massive call-out of militia that would ultimately swell the ranks of Gates's army. Morrissey, *Saratoga*, 42n. See also William R. Nester, *The Frontier War for Independence* (Mechanicsburg, PA: Stackpole Books, 2004), 154.
13. Burgoyne, STOE, 66. The quote comes from a Burgoyne question to a witness asking him if the general had uttered these words. The witness replied that he had. See also Grenier, *The First Way of War*, 164.
14. *Newport Gazette* quoted in Jeremy Engels and Greg Goodale, "'Our Battle Cry Will Be: Remember Jenny McCrea!': A Precis on the Rhetoric of Revenge," *American Quarterly* 61 (March 2009): 96.
15. Unsigned letter to the editor dated July 27, 1777, printed in the August 12, 1777, edition of the *Pennsylvania Evening Post*, Moore, *Diary of the American Revolution from Newspapers and Original Documents*, Vol. 1, 475–76.
16. *Independent (Boston) Chronicle* unsigned article, August 14, 1777, American Revolutionary Newspapers, Microfilm Collection, DLAR.
17. Gates to Hancock, August 28, 1777, in HGP, Reel 5. "Macaroni" in late-eighteenth-century British and American slang referred to a man who "exceeded the ordinary bounds of fashion," such as dress, food, leisure pursuits, and so on. *The Macaroni and Theatrical Magazine*, inaugural issue, 1772, quoted in Amelia Rauser, "Hair, Authenticity, and Self-Made Macaroni," *Eighteenth-Century Studies* 38.1 (2004), 101–17. In the British song "Yankee Doodle Dandy" the lyrics "stuck a feather in his hat and called it macaroni" poked fun at Americans, who were so backward as to think that only one feather in a hat would be enough to identify a macaroni. In his letter to Hancock, Gates was returning the favor by ridiculing Burgoyne.
18. Gates to Burgoyne, September 2, 1777, in HGP, Reel 5.
19. Ibid.
20. Burgoyne to Gates, September 6, 1777, and Gates to Burgoyne, September 8, 1777, in ibid.
21. Other events such as the American victory at Bennington and the failure of St. Leger to take Fort Stanwix also played a major role in turning out the American militia. For the impact and propaganda value to the Americans of the Jane McCrea affair, see Engels and Goodale, "Our Battle Cry Will Be: Remember Jenny McCrea!" 93–112; Nester, *The Frontier War for American Independence*, 153–55; Morrissey, *Saratoga*, 42n; and Koster, "Jane McCrea," 12–16.
22. For the reaction of the British press to the McCrea incident and Burgoyne's Indian policy, see Bickham, *Making Headlines*, 220–22. Burgoyne had to defend himself against accusations that his improper handling of the Indians during the campaign led directly to the many atrocities committed on the New York and New Hampshire frontiers. Burgoyne, STOE and Burgoyne, *The Substance of General Burgoyne's Speeches*.

CHAPTER 12

1. Burgoyne to Germain, July 11, 1777, in DAR, Vol. 14: 141.
2. Burgoyne's memo to Germain and George III, "Thoughts for Conducting the War from the Side of Canada," in DAR, Vol. 14: 45.
3. Germain to Carleton, March 26, 1777, in ibid., 53.
4. Watt, *Rebellion in the Mohawk Valley*, 69–70. Almost every book written about Saratoga, the Battle of Oriskany, and the siege of Fort Stanwix includes a portrait alleged to be of St. Leger, but it is actually that of another British officer, John Hayes St. Leger. Eric Schnitzer email to the author, March 27, 2017.
5. Paul A. Boehlert, *The Battle of Oriskany and General Nicholas Herkimer: Revolution in the Mohawk Valley* (Charleston, SC: The History Press, 2013), 61; Watt, *Rebellion in the Mohawk*

Valley, 69; Boatner, *Encyclopedia of the American Revolution*, 960; and Burgoyne, "Thoughts" memo, DAR, Vol. 14: 45.

6. Boatner, *Encyclopedia of the American Revolution*, 561–62; and Boehlert, *The Battle of Oriskany*, 23 and 61.
7. Boehlert, *The Battle of Oriskany*, 61.
8. Ibid., 68.
9. Boatner, *Encyclopedia of the American Revolution*, 110–11; Barbara Graymont, *The Iroquois in the American Revolution* (Syracuse, NY: Syracuse University Press, 1972), 104–5; Calloway, *American Revolution in Indian Country*, 60; and Watt, *Rebellion in the Mohawk Valley*, 47–49.
10. Nester, *The Frontier War for American Independence*, 169; Watt, *Rebellion in the Mohawk Valley*, 82–83 and 95–97.
11. Washington to Schuyler, April 19, 1776, in GWP, Vol. 4: 90.
12. Nester, *The Frontier War for Independence*, 142.
13. Minutes of the Meetings between Gates and the Six Nations, May 25, 1777, and Gates's speech to the Chiefs of the Six Nations, circa May 1777, in HGP, Reel 4.
14. Washington to Schuyler, June 29, 1777, in GWP, Vol. 10: 78.
15. Nester, *Frontier War for Independence*, 142–43; and Graymont, *Iroquois in the American Revolution*, 116–17; see also Watt, *Rebellion in the Mohawk Valley*, 82–84.
16. John Grenier, *The First Way of War: American War Making on the Frontier* (New York: Cambridge University Press, 2005), 162–63; and Graymont, *Iroquois in the American Revolution*, 104–28.
17. Gaymont, *Iroquois in the American Revolution*, 125–28; and Grenier, *The First Way of War*, 162–63. There is some question as to whether or not Brant was at this conference or already on his way to Fort Stanwix. The best study of the Oneida Indians in the American Revolution is Joseph T. Glatthaar and James Kirby Martin, *Forgotten Allies: The Oneida Indians and the American Revolution* (New York: Hill and Wang, 2006).
18. Nester, *Frontier War for Independence*, 143; Watt, *Rebellion in the Mohawk Valley*, 96–97; and Richard Berleth, *Bloody Mohawk: The French and Indian War & American Revolution on New York's Frontier* (Hensonville, NY: Black Dome, 2009), 210–11.
19. Nester, *Frontier War for Independence*, 143; Watt, *Rebellion in the Mohawk Valley*, 96–97; and Berleth, *Bloody Mohawk*, 210–11.
20. Fort Stanwix was renamed Fort Schuyler by the Americans in 1776. To prevent confusion, I will refer to the fort as Stanwix.
21. Watt, *Rebellion in the Mohawk Valley*, 89, 91–93.
22. Ibid., 89. Watt argues that St. Leger discounted the reports that did not agree with Carleton's assessment because Clause interrogated the prisoners and the scouting reports came from Loyalist officers, so he did not trust their intelligence. Plus, even if true, the Americans could not improve the dilapidated fort before the expedition's arrival. See also Nester, *Frontier War for American Independence*, 168–69; Morrissey, *Saratoga*, 43; and Boehlert, *The Battle of Oriskany*, 65.
23. Quoted in Watt, *Rebellion in the Mohawk Valley*, 101.
24. Ibid., 101–2.
25. This description of the fort is based on the author's personal exploration of the Fort Stanwix site and reconstruction and John F. Luzader, *Fort Stanwix: Construction and Military History* (Washington, DC: Office of Park Historic Preservation, National Park Service, 1976), https://www.nps.gov/parkhistory/online_books/fost/history/history-sec4.htm . See also David A. Ranzan and Matthew J. Hollis, eds., *Hero of Fort Schuyler: Selected Revolutionary War Correspondence of Brigadier General Peter Gansevoort, Jr.* (Jefferson, NC: McFarlan and Company, 2014), 37.
26. Ranzan and Hollis, *Hero of Fort Schuyler*, 23.
27. Ibid., 24.
28. Gates to Gansevoort, April 26, 1777, in HGP, Reel 4.
29. Boatner, *Encyclopedia of the American Revolution*, 411; Ranzan and Hollis, *Hero of Fort Schuyler*, 5–6; and Boehlert, *The Battle of Oriskany*, 64.

30. Watt, *Rebellion in the Mohawk Valley*, 62.
31. Boatner, *Encyclopedia of the American Revolution*, 1207–208.
32. Ranzan and Hollis, *Hero of Fort Stanwix*, 40.
33. Gansevoort to Gates, May 23, 1777, in ibid., 44.
34. Luzader, *Fort Stanwix*, Section 3, https://www.nps.gov/parkhistory/online_books/fost/history/history-sec3.htm
35. Gansevoort to Schuyler, June 15, 1777, Ranzan and Hollis, *Hero of Fort Schuyler*, 52. See also Berleth, *Bloody Mohawk*, 206.
36. William M. Willett, ed. *A Narrative of the Military Actions of Colonel Marinus Willett, Taken Chiefly from His Own Manuscript* (New York: G. C. H. Carville, 1831), 49.
37. Schuyler to Gansevoort, July 30, 1777, Ranzan and Hollis, *Hero of Fort Schuyler*, 55. The same day Schuyler wrote Washington that he feared "a considerable Body [of enemy] to Attack on Fort Schuyler. . . . I have requested General Herkemer to keep his Militia in Readiness to march to their Support." Schuyler to Washington, June 30, 1777, in GWP, Vol. 10: 159–60.
38. Berleth, *Bloody Mohawk*, 207.
39. Watt, *Rebellion in the Mohawk Valley*, 43.
40. Boatner, *Encyclopedia of the American Revolution*, 501–2; Boelhert, *The Battle of Oriskany*, 28–29; and Berleth, *Bloody Mohawk*, 207–8.
41. Gansevoort to Brother Schems & Warriors of the Six Nations, July 2, 1777, in Ranzan and Hollis, *Hero of Fort Stanwix*, 56.
42. Gansevoort to Schuyler, July 3, 1777, ibid., 57.
43. This was probably Willett's idea based on his experience in the area during the French and Indian War.
44. Gansevoort to Schuyler, July 4, 1777, ibid., 58. See also Berleth, *Bloody Mohawk*, 217.
45. Watt, *Rebellion in the Mohawk Valley*, 100.
46. John Hanson to Gansevoort, July 7, 1777, in Ranzan and Hollis, *Hero of Fort Stanwix*, 60.
47. Leonard Gansevoort to Peter Gansevoort, July 9, 1777, in ibid., 61.
48. Gansevoort to Catherine Van Schaick, July 12, 1777, in ibid., 62.
49. Gansevoort to Schuyler, July 26, 1777, in ibid., 63.
50. Gansevoort to Goose Van Schaick, July 28, 1777, in William Colbrath, *Days of Siege: A Journal of the Siege of Fort Stanwix in 1777*, Larry Lowenthal, ed. (Fort Washington, PA: Eastern National, 1983), 19; Berleth, *Bloody Mohawk*, 218; and Willett, *A Narrative*, 48.
51. Gansevoort learned of the McCrea incident from a letter from his brother. Leonard Gansevoort to Gansevoort, July 28, 1777, in Ranzan and Hollis, *Hero of Fort Schuyler*, 65.
52. Watt, *Rebellion in the Mohawk Valley*, 114.
53. Berleth, *Bloody Mohawk*, 219.
54. The two-hundred-man detachment of the 9th Massachusetts Regiment arrived at the fort along with several weeks' provisions on August 2, 1777. Boehlert, *The Battle of Oriskany*, 66.
55. Thomas Spencer to Gansevoort, July 29, 1777, in Ranzan and Hollis, *Hero of Fort Schuyler*, 67. As an Oneida, Spencer had been providing accurate intelligence to Gansevoort for weeks, and fought and died with the American militia at the Battle of Oriskany. See also Glatthaar and Martin, *Forgotten Allies*, 89–90; and Graymont, *Iroquois in the American Revolution*, 112.
56. Fort Schuyler General Orders, issued August 1, 1777, in William Colbrath, *Days of Siege: A Journal of the Siege of Fort Stanwix in 1777*, ed. Larry Lowenthal (Fort Washington, PA: Eastern National, 1983), 22.
57. Henry Bird to St. Leger, August 2, 1777, and St. Leger to Henry Bird, August 2, 1777, in Ranzan and Hollis, *Hero of Fort Schuyler*, 70–71; St. Leger to Carleton, August 27, 1777, DAR, Vol. 14: 171; Nester, *The Frontier War for American Independence*, 170; Willett, *A Narrative*, 50; and Watt, *Rebellion in the Mohawk Valley*, 111–24.
58. St. Leger to Carleton, August 27, 1777, in DAR, Vol. 14: 171.
59. Nester, *The Frontier War for American Independence*, 170.

60. Ranzan and Hollis, *Hero of Fort Schuyler,* 72.
61. Watt, *Rebellion in the Mohawk Valley,* 130; and Berleth, *Bloody Mohawk,* 220.
62. Narrative of Lieutenant Colonel Willett, written on August 11 and published in the *Massachusetts Spy* on August 29, 1777, in Ranzan and Hollis, *Hero of Fort Schuyler,* 78.
63. Resolution of Congress, June 14, 1777, in JCC, Vol. 8: 464.
64. Ranzan and Hollis, *Hero of Fort Schuyler,* 72 and 246n; and Willett, *A Narrative,* 50. Luzader and others argue that the flag was not the new stars and stripes but was instead the Continental or Union flag. However, there is no disagreement that Gansevoort ordered that an improvised American flag be made and flown from the fort. Luzader, *Fort Stanwix,* Section 4, https://www.nps.gov/parkhistory/online_books/fost/history/history-sec4.htm
65. St. Leger to Carleton, August 27, 1777, in DAR, Vol. 14: 171; and Ranzan and Hollis, *Hero of Fort Schuyler,* 131.
66. The positions of the various camps and batteries is taken from the map in Morrissey, *Saratoga,* 50, which is a revised version of a contemporary map drawn by Francois Louis Tesseidre de Fleury. https://commons.wikimedia.org/wiki/File:SiegeOfFortStanwix1777FleuryMap.jpg
67. Narrative of Lieutenant Colonel Willett, written sometime on August 11 and published in the *Massachusetts Spy* on August 29, 1777, in Ranzan and Hollis, *Hero of Fort Schuyler,* 78.

CHAPTER 13

1. Boehlert, *The Battle of Oriskany,* 66.
2. Ibid., 69–70; and Watt, *Rebellion in the Mohawk Valley,* 147–48. Molly's presence at Herkmer's home demonstrates the complex web of relationships in the Mohawk Valley. Even though Molly's brother was actively fighting for Britain, she was welcomed into the Herkimer home because of the long-standing connection between the two neighboring families.
3. Boehlert, *The Battle of Oriskany,* 69–70; and Watt, *Rebellion in the Mohawk Valley,* 147–48.
4. The number of Oneida warriors who joined Herkimer's force at Oriska is uncertain. Most sources say that between sixty and one hundred warriors joined the relief column, but this number seems very high. The total number of Indian warriors in each of the Six Nations of the Iroquois Confederacy was very small, typically between 100 and 250. It seems highly unlikely that such a large percentage of the total number of Oneida warriors joined Herkimer's militia on August 5. Discussions with the Oriskany and Stanwix park ranger staff on May 9, 2016.
5. Boehlert, *The Battle of Oriskany,* 70; and Watt, *Rebellion in the Mohawk Valley,* 152.
6. The route the three men traveled to the fort is unclear but based on the topography of the area and the location of the river and the fort, they most likely approached the fort from the south and west, as that route provided the most concealment. These insights based on discussions with the Fort Stanwix National Monument staff on May 9, 2016.
7. Narrative of Lieutenant Colonel Willett, written on August 11 and published in the *Massachusetts Spy* on August 29, 1777, in Ranzan and Hollis, *Hero of Fort Schuyler,* 78.
8. Watt, *Rebellion in the Mohawk Valley,* 152.
9. Narrative of Lieutenant Colonel Willett, written on August and published in the *Massachusetts Spy* on August 29, 1777, in Ranzan and Hollis, *Hero of Fort Schuyler,* 78.
10. St. Leger to Carleton, August 27, 1777, in DAR, Vol. 14: 171. See also Watt, *Rebellion in the Mohawk Valley,* 134–35.
11. Watt, *Rebellion in the Mohawk Valley,* 149.
12. Ibid.
13. Boehlert, *The Battle of Oriskany,* 78–80
14. Berleth, *Bloody Mohawk,* 226.
15. Watt, *Rebellion in the Mohawk Valley,* 53–154; Boehlert, *The Battle of Oriskany,* 78–80; and Berleth, *Bloody Mohawk,* 225–26.
16. Berleth, *Bloody Mohawk,* 226.

17. This account of St. Leger's decision to attack Herkimer is from Berleth, *Bloody Mohawk*, 227.
18. Ibid., 227.
19. Ibid.
20. Ibid., 228; and Glatthaar and Martin, *Forgotten Allies*, 166. The name of the battle is taken from the nearby Oneida settlement of Oriska.
21. Boehlert, *The Battle of Oriskany*, 81.
22. Ibid., 82; Watt, *Rebellion in the Mohawk Valley*, 162–63; and Berleth, *Bloody Mohawk*, 231.
23. Boehlert, *The Battle of Oriskany*, 81–85; Watt, *Rebellion in the Mohawk Valley*, 164; and Berleth, *Bloody Mohawk*, 228–29.
24. Watt, *Rebellion in the Mohawk Valley*, 163.
25. Ibid., 166–67; and Berleth, *Bloody Mohawk*, 232–33.
26. Berleth, *Bloody Mohawk*, 231.
27. Ibid.
28. Watt, *Rebellion in the Mohawk Valley*, 170. The location of Herkimer's stand is a matter of some dispute and confusion. The accounts vary, but the most likely location is the high ground just to the west of the large ravine and north of the road. I am indebted to the Oriskany Battlefield State Historic Site ranger staff for helping clarify some of the confusion over this point.
29. Ibid., 178–79; Berleth, *Bloody Mohawk*, 233–34; and Ludlum, "Weather of Independence," 238.
30. Narrative of Lieutenant Colonel Willett, written on August 11 and published in the *Massachusetts Spy* on August 29, 1777, in Ranzan and Hollis, *Hero of Fort Schuyler*, 78–79; Colbrath journal entry for August 6, 1777, in Commager and Morris, *Spirit of 'Seventy-Six*, 563; Willett, *A Narrative*, 54; and Luzader, *Fort Stanwix*, Section 4, https://www.nps.gov/parkhistory/online_books/fost/history/history-sec4.htm
31. Ibid., 79.
32. Berleth, *Bloody Mohawk*, 235.
33. Ibid., 235.
34. Ibid., 235–36; Watt, *Rebellion in the Mohawk Valley*, 180–85; and Nester, *The Frontier War for American Independence*, 171–72.
35. Casualty figures are from Nester, *The Frontier War for American Independence*, 172.
36. Colbrath journal entry for August 6, 1777, in Commager and Morris, *Spirit of 'Seventy-Six*, 564.
37. St. Leger to Carleton, August 27, 1777, in DAR, Vol. 14: 172.
38. Journal entry, August 7, 1777, in William Colbrath, *Days of Siege: A Journal of the Siege of Fort Stanwix*, ed. Larry Lowenthal (Fort Washington, PA: Eastern National, 1983), 32 and Willett, *A Narrative*, 55.
39. Ranzan and Hollis, *The Hero of Fort Schuyler*, 75.
40. Narrative of Lieutenant Colonel Willett, written on August 11 and published in the *Massachusetts Spy* on August 29, 1777, in ibid, 77.
41. Willett quoted in Nickerson, *The Turning Point of the Revolution*, 271.
42. Gansevoort to St. Leger, August 9, 1777, in Ranzan and Hollis, *The Hero of Fort Schuyler*, 75–76.
43. Journal entry, August 10, 1777, in Colbrath, *Days of Siege*, 38. The garrison lost men killed and wounded with almost every one of St. Leger's bombardments. On August 9 and 10, the garrison lost one man killed and one wounded.
44. Willett to the Men of the Third New York Regiment, August 5, 1777 [the letter was dated August 5, but Willett must have made an error, and was more likely written on August 9], in Ranzan and Hollis, *Hero of Fort Schuyler*, 73.
45. Narrative of Lieutenant Colonel Willett, written on August 11 and published in the *Massachusetts Spy* on August 29, 1777, in ibid, 77.
46. Colbrath, *Days of Siege*, 36; and Willett, *A Narrative*, 59–61.
47. Willett, *A Narrative*, 61.

48. Schuyler to Hancock, August 8, 1777, in GWP, Vol. 10: 557–58n.
49. Schuyler to Gansevoort, August 10, 1777, in Ranzan and Hollis, *Hero of Fort Schuyler*, 77.
50. Journal entry, August 11, 1777, in Colbrath, *Days of Siege*, 39.
51. St. Leger to Burgoyne, August 11, 1777, in British Colonial Office Records, CO 42/37, DLAR.
52. Burgoyne to St. Leger, n.d. but probably immediately after the Battle of Bennington in late August 1777, in ibid.
53. St. Leger to Carleton, August 27, 1777, in DAR, Vol. 14: 173.
54. Ibid.; Nester, *Frontier War for American Independence*, 173; and Watt, *Rebellion in the Mohawk Valley*, 227–29.
55. Gansevoort, "Garrison Orders," for August 15, 1777, in Colbrath, *Days of Siege*, 42.
56. Luzader, *Fort Stanwix*, Section 4.
57. Gates to Arnold, August 19, 1777, in HGP, Reel 4. In this letter, Gates also informed Arnold of the American victory at the Battle of Bennington.
58. Arnold to Gates, August 21, 1777, ibid.
59. Scudder, *The Journal of William Scudder*, 18; Catherine S. Crary, *The Price of Loyalty: Tory Writings from the Revolutionary Era* (New York: McGraw Hill, 1973), 244–45; Willett, *A Narrative*, 62; and Cate, *Founding Fighters*, 111–12.
60. Nester, *The Frontier War for Independence*, 174–75; Berleth, *Bloody Mohawk*, 247–48; and Watt, *Rebellion in the Mohawk Valley*, 243–56.
61. Journal entry, August 20, 1977, in Colbrath, *Days of Siege*, 47.
62. Journal entry, August 21, 1777, in ibid., 48.
63. Gansevoort to John Wesson, August 19, 1777, in GWP, Vol. 11: 52n.
64. St. Leger to Carleton, August 27, 1777, in DAR, Vol. 14: 173.
65. Gansevoort to Arnold, August 22, 1777, in Ranzan and Hollis, *Hero of Fort Schuyler*, 80–81.
66. Arnold to Gates, August 23, 1777, in HGP, Reel 5.
67. Scudder, *The Journal of William Scudder*, 19.
68. Journal entry, August 23, 1777 [but this was incorrect; he meant the 24th], in Colbrath, *Days of Siege*, 52.
69. Arnold to Gates, August 24, 1777, in HGP, Reel 5.
70. Arnold to Gates, August 28, 1777, in ibid. See also Nester, *The Frontier War for American Independence*, 174–75; Berleth, *Bloody Mohawk*, 249–50; and Watt, *Rebellion in the Mohawk Valley*, 259–61. On August 22, Gates dispatched two regiments to reinforce the Stanwix garrison to make sure it stayed secure and in American hands. Gates to Arnold, August 22, 1777, in HGP, Reel 5.
71. Colbrath, *Days of Siege*, 54. These are casualty figures for the dates of the actual siege only.
72. Watt, *Rebellion in Mohawk Valley*, 267.
73. St. Leger to Carleton, August 27, 1777, in DAR, Vol. 14: 171–74. See also Nester, *The Frontier War for American Independence*, 174.
74. Daniel Claus to Guy Johnson, November 12, 1777, in HCP.
75. Washington to Gates, September 1, 1777, in GWP, Vol. 11: 107. See also note by Robert Hanson Harrison added to the letter from Washington to George Baylor, August 25, 1777, ibid., 65.
76. Alexander Hamilton to Gouverneur Morris, September 1, 1777, in AHP, Vol. 1: 320.
77. Congress received news of the successful repulse of St. Leger at Fort Stanwix on September 1, 1777, in JCC, Vol. 8: 699. They had just directed that the commander-in-chief establish courts-martial to investigate the abandoning of Fort Ticonderoga. The contrast between the actions of the commanders of the two posts was not lost on many of the delegates.
78. John Hancock to Gansevoort, October 5, 1777, and Hancock to Willett, October 5, 1777, in LDC, Vol. 8: 53.
79. John Adams to Abigail Adams, September 2, 1777, in ibid., Vol. 7: 589.
80. Gansevoort address to the Third New York Regiment, n.p., n.d., in Ranzan and Hollis, *Hero of Fort Schuyler*, 83.

81. This was another flaw in Burgoyne's plan. St. Leger was conducting both a diversion and a supporting attack, which should not be combined in a single operation.
82. One of the keys to the Americans' success during the Saratoga campaign was their skillful exploitation of interior lines. If an army or a military unit enjoys the advantage of operating on interior lines, it means that the commander can reinforce his separated units faster than the enemy because of central position, superior mobility, or both. Interior lines can be an advantage at all the tactical and operational levels of war. At Fort Stanwix, the Americans exploited interior lines at the operational level of war. *Joint Publication (JP) 3.0*, I-13–I-14.
83. Some of the Indians who served with St. Leger made their way to join Burgoyne's army, but they arrived around the time the Indians already with the army were starting to leave in droves after the Battle of Bennington. Brant and his small band arrived at Burgoyne's headquarters on August 28, carrying with him the definitive news of St. Leger's defeat, but they were too few and too late to make a major impact on the campaign. Journal entry, August 28, 1777, in Digby, *British Invasion from the North*, 256–58; journal entry for unknown British officer, August 28, 1777, in Stanley, *For Want of a Horse*, 139; Grenier, *The First Way of War*, 164–69; Nester, *The Frontier War for American Independence*, 175; Berleth, *Bloody Mohawk*, 250–51; and Watt, *Rebellion in the Mohawk Valley*, 269–78.

CHAPTER 14

1. Willcox, *Portrait of a General*, 154–59.
2. Clinton memorandum, n.p., n.d., but from the contents and context, probably written in early to mid-October 1777, in HCP. See also Gruber, *The Howe Brothers*, 230–33; and Willcox, *Portrait of a General*, 154.
3. Howe to Germain, July 7, 1777, in DAR, Vol. 14: 129–31. Howe was referring to Burgoyne's positive mid-May letters.
4. Stephen R. Taaffe, *The Philadelphia Campaign, 1777–1778* (Lawrence: University Press of Kansas, 2003), 36.
5. Washington to Hancock, June 13, 1777, in GWP, Vol. 10: 26.
6. Transcript of George Washington's Council of War at Middle Brook, NJ, June 12, 1777, ibid., 9–10, and Benedict Arnold to Washington, June 16, 1777, ibid., 48–49. See also Taaffe, *Philadelphia Campaign*, 37–38.
7. Hamilton to Hugh Knox, n.d. July 1777, in AHP, Vol. 1: 301.
8. Washington to Arnold, June 17, 1777, in GWP, Vol. 10: 59.
9. Tench Tilghman to Hancock, June 22, 1777, in ibid., 104–5. See also Taaffe, *Philadelphia Campaign*, 39–41.
10. Washington to Israel Putnam, June 22, 1777, in GWP, Vol. 10: 107.
11. Washington to Putnam, June 25, 1777, in ibid., 125.
12. Washington to George Clinton, July 1, 1777, in ibid., 163 and 164n; and Washington to Israel Putnam, July 1, 1777, in ibid., 165–66.
13. Washington to John Rutledge, July 5, 1777, ibid., 198–99. Washington reacted to Howe's probable move north by marching the main army to Morristown, New Jersey. See Alexander Hamilton to Gouverneur Morris, July 6, 1777, in AHP, Vol. 1: 281–82.
14. Washington to Hancock, July 7, 1777, in GWP, Vol. 10: 215–16.
15. Washington to William Heath, July 13, 1777, in ibid., 271. See also Washington to Heath, July 19, 1777, in ibid., 339, and John Fitzgerald to Daniel Morgan, July 19, 1777, in General Daniel Morgan Papers, Film 568, Reel 2, DLAR.
16. Howe received Burgoyne's letter informing him of his success at Ticonderoga on July 15, 1777, according to his testimony to the House of Commons in April 1779. Howe, *Narrative*, 21.
17. Journal entry, July 13, 1777, in Friederich von Muenchhausen, *At Howe's Side: The Diary of General William Howe's Aide de Camp, Captain Friederich von Muenchhausen*, trans. Ernst Kipping, ed. Samuel Smith (Monmouth Beach, NJ: Philip Freneau Press, 1974), 21.
18. Howe to Germain, July 16, 1777, in DAR, Vol. 14: 145.

19. Henry Clinton to Howe, July 21, 1777 (not sent), in HCP. See also journal entry, July 17, 1777, in Muenchhausen, *At Howe's Side*, 21.
20. On July 24, the king and Germain discussed Howe's attempt to bring Washington to battle, and neither expressed concern that Sir William was not going to cooperate with Burgoyne or that he was starting the Philadelphia campaign late in the season, or that any movement north by large British forces was highly unlikely. North to King, July 24, 1777, and King to North, July 24, 1777, Fortescue, *Correspondence of King George the Third*, Vol. 2, 461. See also Clinton, *The American Rebellion*, 63–64.
21. Howe argued in April 1779 that the Philadelphia expedition had three strategic objectives: drawing off enemy troops away from Burgoyne, seizing the rebel capital, and most importantly, it was "the one object, which would have tempted General Washington to risk a general action." Howe, *Narrative*, 61. Troops' numbers are taken from Howe to Germain, July 7, 1777, in GGP. In this letter, Howe specifies what troops he would leave behind for Clinton: eight regiments of British regulars, eight foreign regiments, and ten provincial regiments, for a total of 7,367 men. See also Morrissey, *Saratoga*, 68.
22. Howe to Clinton, July 30, 1777, in HCP. See also Willcox, *Portrait of a General*, 166–68.
23. Taaffe, *Philadelphia Campaign*, 45.
24. Howe to Henry Clinton, July 23, 1777, in HCP. See also Gruber, *The Howe Brothers*, 235.
25. Henry Clinton to Hugh Percy, July 23, 1777, in HCP. See also Clinton to Henry Pelham, July 27, 1777, in ibid.
26. Washington to Hancock, July 25, 1777, in GWP, Vol. 10: 410.
27. Washington to Gates, July 30, 1777, in ibid., 459. See also Washington to Hancock, July 30, 1777, in ibid., 459–60.
28. Washington to Major General John Sullivan, July 31, 1777, in ibid., 471; Washington to Gates, July 31, 1777, in ibid., 466; and Washington to Israel Putnam, July 31, 1777, in ibid., 468.
29. Hancock to Washington, August 1, 1777, in ibid., 479–80; Washington to George Clinton, August 1, 1777, in ibid., 475; Washington to Elias Dayton, August 1, 1777, in ibid., 475; Washington to Nathanael Greene, August 1, 1777, in ibid., 479; Washington to Alexander McDougal, August 1, 1777, in ibid., 480–81; and Washington to Israel Putnam, August 1, 1777, in ibid., 481–82.
30. Washington to Elias Dayton, August 3, 1777, in ibid., 491–92.
31. Washington to John Langdon, August 3, 1777, in ibid., 500–501.
32. Washington to John Taylor, August 5, 1777, in ibid., 512–13. See also Taaffe, *Philadelphia Campaign*, 48.
33. Hancock to Washington, August 10, 1777, in ibid., 574.
34. Germain to Howe, May 18, 1777, in DAR, Vol. 14: 84–85.
35. Minutes from Council of War including Washington and his key general officers, August 21, 1777, in GWP, Vol. 11: 19–20; Washington to Hancock, August 21, 1777, in GWP, Vol. 11: 21–23; Hancock to Washington, August 21, 1777, in GWP, Vol. 11: 25; Taaffe, *Philadelphia Campaign*, 48; and Justin Clement, *Philadelphia, 1777: Taking the Capital* (Oxford: Osprey Publishing, 2007), 34–35.
36. Washington to John Armstrong, August 25, 1777, in GWP, Vol. 11: 64.
37. Howe to Germain, August 30, 1777, in GGP. Germain received this letter on October 28, 1777.
38. Germain to Howe, September 3, 1777, in GGP.
39. Germain to William Knox, September 29, 1777, Commager and Morris, *Spirit of 'Seventy-Six*, 579.

CHAPTER 15

1. Unknown German officer in Thomas M. Barker, "The British Invasion of New York as Seen by a Braunschweig Subaltern at Fort Ticonderoga: 'Some Frank Thoughts About the Campaign of Lieutenant General John Burgoyne in 1777,'" *Hessians: Journal of Johannes Schwalm Historical Association* 7 (2001): 4.

2. Schuyler to Washington, August 4, 1777, in GWP, Vol. 10: 506 and Nester, *The Frontier War for American Independence*, 155.
3. Benjamin Lincoln to Washington, August 4, 1777, in GWP, Vol. 10: 501. Lincoln was referring to the New Hampshire militia under Brigadier General John Stark and Vermont militia under Colonel Seth Warner.
4. Schuyler to Washington, August 4, 1777, in ibid., 506; and Ketchum, *Saratoga*, 281.
5. Burgoyne to Germain, July 30, 1777, in DAR, Vol. 14: 155, and Howe to Burgoyne, July 17, 1777, in Burgoyne, STOE, xlix. Burgoyne received Howe's letter on August 5. See also Commodore William Hotham to Lord Sandwich, July 26, 1777, in Montagu, *Private Papers of John, Earl of Sandwich*, Vol. 1, 290–91.
6. Burgoyne to Howe, August 6, 1777, in DAR, Vol. 14: 156–57.
7. Burgoyne, STOE, 22. Like he did with other unhelpful evidence, Burgoyne omitted the August 6 letter from his privately printed STOE.
8. Unnamed British officer journal entry, August 4, 1777, in Stanley, *For Want of a Horse*, 126. See also journal entries, August 3–5, 1777, in Doblin, *Journal of J. F. Wasmus*, 67.
9. Anton Adolph Heinrich Du Roi (attrib.) journal entry. August 5, 1777, in Doblin, *Specht Journal*, 62.
10. Anton Adolph Heinrich Du Roi (attrib.) journal entry, August 7, 1777, ibid., 65.
11. Journal entry, August 9, 1777, in Digby, *British Invasion from the North*, 245–46.
12. The best discussion of the state of health of Burgoyne's army is Kopperman, "The Numbers Game," 264.
13. Burgoyne General Order for August 6, 1777, in Burgoyne, *Orderly Book*, 66.
14. Anton Adolph Heinrich Du Roi (attrib.) journal entry, August 5, 1777, in Doblin, *Specht Journal*, 62.
15. Unnamed British officer's journal entry, August 5, 1777, in Stanley, *For Want of a Horse*, 127; and Nester, *The Frontier War for Independence*, 175.
16. Burgoyne to Germain, August 20,1777, in DAR, Vol. 14: 162.
17. Testimony of Captain John Money, the expedition's deputy quartermaster, in Burgoyne, STOE, 53–56. Money testified that with the available transport, the army could only gather "over and above the daily consumption of the army, should suppose all those carriages would not carry more than four days provisions at most." See also Bowler, *Logistics and the Failure of the British Army in America*, 226; and Stedman, *History of the Origin, Progress, and Termination of the American War*, 328.
18. Bowler, *Logistics*, 229. See also Burgoyne, STOE, 13, 47, 78–79.
19. General Orders for August 7, 1777, in Burgoyne, *Orderly Book*, 67.
20. Burgoyne to Germain, August 20, 1777, in DAR, Vol. 14: 163.

CHAPTER 16

1. Schuyler to Washington, July 17, 1777, in GWP, Vol. 10: 312, and Washington to Schuyler, July 22, 1777, in ibid., 363. Washington demonstrated his strategic flexibility when he urged Schuyler to attack Burgoyne's separated units after the fall of Ticonderoga. By 1777, Washington was reluctant to risk his armies on head-to-head encounters with British regulars, but he was willing to depart from his Fabian strategy when an opportunity presented itself. In July, he began to sense that Burgoyne would offer just such an opening.
2. Washington to Schuyler, July 24, 1777, in ibid., 397. This was the kind of mission Washington envisioned for Lincoln when he dispatched him to join Schuyler.
3. Lincoln to Washington, August 4, 1777, in GWP, Vol. 10: 501–2.
4. Schuyler to Washington, August 4, 1777, in ibid., 506.
5. Washington to Jonathan Trumbull Sr., August 4, 1777, in ibid., 506–7.
6. Burgoyne to Germain (Private), August 20, 1777, in DAR, Vol. 14: 165. See also Michael P. Gabriel, *The Battle of Bennington: Soldiers and Civilians* (Charleston, SC: The History Press, 2012), 18; and Burgoyne, STOE, 137.

7. Riedesel to Duke Charles William Ferdinand of Brunswick, September 3, 1777, in Major General Riedesel, *Memoirs,* 260.
8. Gabriel, *Battle of Bennington,* 18. Captain Fraser was Brigadier General Fraser's nephew.
9. Fraser to John Robinson, July 13, 1777, "General Fraser's Account of Burgoyne's Campaign," 142.
10. Robert Kingston testimony, in Burgoyne, STOE, 100. Since Fraser was killed two months later, it is impossible to know what he was thinking, but his only surviving letter from the campaign, written on July 13, suggests some earlier frustration with Burgoyne.
11. Burgoyne's orders to Baum, August 9, 1777, in Burgoyne, STOE, lxiii–lxvii.
12. Ibid., lxvii–lxviii.
13. Burgoyne to Philip Skene, August 10, 1777, GGP.
14. Journal entry, August 11, 1777, in Major General Riedesel, *Memoirs,* Vol. 1, 128. Riedesel made the same argument in a letter written three years later in response to Burgoyne's *State of the Expedition.* Riedesel to Duke Charles William Ferdinand of Brunswick, September 3, 1780, ibid., 259–64; and Report of Riedesel to Duke Charles of Brunswick, ibid., 248–49.
15. Journal entry, August 11, 1777, in Wasmus, *Journal of J.F. Wasmus,* 68–69. See also Riedesel to Duke Charles William Ferdinand of Brunswick, September 3, 1780, Major General Riedesel, *Memoirs,* Vol. 1, 263.
16. Journal entry, August 11, 1777, in Digby, *British Invasion from the North,* 248.
17. Journal entries, August 12 and 13, 1777, in Wasmus, *Journal of J.F. Wasmus,* 69.
18. Ira Allen to the Councils of Safety of Massachusetts and New Hampshire, July 15, 1777, in Caleb Stark, ed., *Memoir and Official Correspondence of Gen. John Stark, With Notices of Several Other Officers of the Revolution* (Concord, NH: G. Parker Lyon, 1860), 122.
19. Meshech Weare to Ira Allen, July 19, 1777, ibid., 123.
20. Rose, *John Stark: Maverick General,* 108; and Gabriel, *Battle of Bennington,* 20.
21. Rose, *John Stark: Maverick General,* 9–100; and Boatner, *Encyclopedia of the American Revolution,* 1052–53.
22. Lincoln informed Schuyler of Stark's position on his independent command, which Schuyler promptly forwarded to Washington and Congress. Schuyler told Hancock that "The untimely Objections of General Stark are a New Source of Distress to us." See Schuyler to Washington, August 8, 1777, in GWP, Vol. 10: 557 and 558n. See also Mattern, *Benjamin Lincoln,* 44–45.
23. Benjamin Lincoln to Washington, August 12, 1777, in GWP, Vol. 10: 592. See also Gabriel, *Battle of Bennington,* 20; Rose, *John Stark: Maverick General,* 109–11; and Mattern, *Benjamin Lincoln,* 45.
24. Gabriel, *Battle of Bennington,* 20.
25. Journal entry, August 13, 1777, in Wasmus, *Journal of J.F. Wasmus,* 69.
26. Baum to Burgoyne, August 13, 1777, in Burgoyne, STOE, lxix–lxx; and Morrissey, *Saratoga,* 52.
27. Stark to the Council of New Hampshire, August 18, 1777, in Stark, *Memoir and Official Correspondence of Gen. John Stark,* 126. See also Morrissey, *Saratoga,* 52.
28. Baum to Burgoyne, August 14, 1777, in Burgoyne, STOE, lxx–lxxi.
29. Burgoyne's General Order for August 14, 1777, in Burgoyne, *Orderly Book,* 72–73. Similar orders were published to the army on August 15 and 16; see ibid., 73–76. Burgoyne had to cross the river because the only good road network to Albany was located on the west bank.
30. Burgoyne to Baum, August 14, 1777, in Burgoyne, STOE, lxxvi.
31. Rose, *John Stark: Maverick General,* 116–17; and Ketchum, *Saratoga,* 297.
32. Gabriel, *Battle of Bennington,* 22; and Thomas M. Baker, "Braunschweigers, Hessians and Tories in the Battle of Bennington (16 August 1777): The American Revolution as a Civil War," *Hessians: Journal of Johannes Schwalm Historical Association* 10 (2007): 28.

33. Journal entry for August 14, 1777, in Wasmus, *Journal of J.F. Wasmus*, 70; and Stark to the Council of New Hampshire, August 18, 1777, in Stark, *Memoir and Official Correspondence of Gen. John Stark*, 127.
34. Burgoyne to Riedesel, August 13, 1777, Major General Riedesel, *Memoirs*, Vol. 1, 272. Note that in the book this letter is dated August 13 at 10:30 a.m. But this is an error, the letter had to be sent early on the morning of August 15. On August 13, Baum was still at Cambridge, New York, and had not yet run into trouble.
35. Riedesel to Duke Charles William Ferdinand of Brunswick, September 3, 1780, in Major General Riedesel, *Memoirs*, , 263; Sir Francis Clark to Breymann, August 15, 1777, in ibid., 259; and Michael R. Gadue, "'Fatal Pique': The Failure of LTC Breymann to Relieve LTC Baum at Bennington, August 16, 1777, A Case of *Braunschweig* Dishonor?" *Hessians: Journal of the Johannes Schwalm Historical Association* 12 (2009): 49. Burgoyne claimed later that it was Riedesel who picked Breymann to lead the relief detachment, but Clark's letter confirms that it was Burgoyne himself who chose Breymann.
36. Journal entry, August 16, 1777, in Hadden, *Journal*, 118–19.
37. Journal entry, August 15, 1777, in Wasmus, *Journal of J.F. Wasmus*, 71.
38. Ibid. For the impact of the rain on operations in and around Bennington, see Ludlum, "Weather of Independence," 238–39.
39. Baum to Burgoyne, August 15, 1777, in Gabriel, *Battle of Bennington*, 32.
40. Stark's plan for the Battle of Bennington is taken from Stark to the Council of New Hampshire, August 18, 1777, in Stark, *Memoirs and Official Correspondence of Gen. John Stark*, 127; and Gabriel, *Battle of Bennington*, 24–25.
41. Quoted in Rose, *John Stark: Maverick General*, 121.
42. Account of Thomas Mellon, quoted in Gabriel, *Battle of Bennington*, 72.
43. Stark to Gates, August 23, 1777, in Stark, *Memoir and Official Correspondence of Gen. John Stark*, 130.
44. Journal entry, August 16, 1777, in Wasmus, *Journal of J.F. Wasmus*, 73–74. Wasmus was captured along with many of his comrades.
45. German officer Glitch account of the battle, Commager and Morris, *Spirit of 'Seventy-Six*, 575.
46. Ibid., 575–76.
47. Stark to the Council of New Hampshire, August 18, 1777, in Stark, *Memoir and Correspondence of Gen. John Stark*, 126.
48. Rose, *John Stark: Maverick General*, 121–23; Gabriel, *Battle of Bennington*, 24–26; Morrissey, *Saratoga*, 52; Stark to the Council of New Hampshire, August 18, 1777, in Stark, *Memoir and Official Correspondence of Gen. John Stark*, 127.
49. Breymann's after action report, August 20, 1777, in Major General Riedesel, *Memoirs*, Vol. 1, 256–57.
50. For an examination of Breymann's failure to relieve Baum's detachment, including an analysis of the rate of march, see Gadue, "Fatal Pique," 49–50. See also Burgoyne, STOE, 101.
51. Journal entry, August 24, 1777, in Hadden, *Journal*, 136; unknown officer journal entry for August 15, 1777, in Barker, "The Battles of Saratoga and the Kinderhook Tea Party," 33. Gadue's conclusion is that there was indeed some conflict between the two men, which contributed to Breymann's deliberate advance. Gadue, "Fatal Pique," 44–56; and Ketchum, *Saratoga*, 302. Contemporary observers also criticized the typically slow German movement rate. One British officer wrote long after the war that the "Germans were heavy and tardy in marching, and, as usual, were loaded with accoutrements that prevented those exertions which such an expedition required." Stedman, *History of the Origin, Progress, and Termination of the American War*, 330–31; and Barker, "Braunschweigers, Hessians and Tories," 29.
52. Thomas Mellen account, quoted in Gabriel, *Battle of Bennington*, 61.
53. Stark to the Council of New Hampshire, August 19, 1777, in Stark, *Memoir and Correspondence of Gen. John Stark*, 127–28.

54. Bense journal entry, August 16, 1777, in Doblin and Lynn, "A Brunswick Grenadier with Burgoyne," 431–32.
55. After failing in his mission to relieve Baum, Breymann wrote in his after-action report that the "loss of the two cannon pains me most." The loss of an artillery piece—let alone two—would have been a mortifying episode for an eighteenth-century military commander, but it still was not as bad as failing to complete a mission that led to the loss of almost one thousand men. Breymann to Burgoyne, August 20, 1777, in Major General Riedesel, *Memoirs,* 258.
56. Thomas Mellen account, quoted in Gabriel, *Battle of Bennington,* 61.
57. Stark to Gates, August 23, 1777, in Stark, *Memoir and Correspondence of Gen. John Stark,* 131.
58. Stark to the Council of New Hampshire, August 19, 1777, ibid., 127–28; Breymann after-action report, August 20, 1777, in Major General Riedesel, *Memoirs,* 257–58; Morrissey, *Saratoga,* 52–53; Gabriel, *Battle of Bennington,* 26–28; and Rose, *John Stark: Maverick General,* 122–23.
59. Burgoyne general order to the army, August 17, 1777, in Burgoyne, *Orderly Book,* 76–77.
60. Casualty figures for the Battle of Bennington are from Morrissey, *Saratoga,* 22, 25–26, 53. Some key personnel did escape, including Captain Fraser, whose independent company had to be reorganized from other units after the battle. See Schnitzer, "Organization of the Army from Canada," 4n.
61. Burgoyne's army arrived at Skenesborough on July 10; it took three weeks to move the army to Fort Edward; it took another two and a half weeks to move the army to Fort Miller, where it arrived on August 11; the army delayed at Fort Miller for four and a half weeks until crossing the Hudson on September 13. Thus, Burgoyne's army took a little over nine weeks to cover about 37 miles, averaging slightly more than half a mile per day. See also Michael R. Barbieri, "Bennington Fatally Delays Burgoyne," *Journal of the American Revolution.* June 11, 2013. http://allthingsliberty.com/2013/06/bennington-fatally-delays-burgoyne/.
62. Burgoyne to Riedesel, August 25, 1777, in Major General Riedesel, *Memoirs,* 272.
63. Burgoyne to Germain (Private), August 20, 1777, in DAR, Vol. 14: 165.
64. Burgoyne to Germain, August 20, 1777, DAR, Vol. 14: 162–65. Burgoyne was probably hoping that more survivors from Breymann's and Baum's commands would make their way back to the army.
65. Burgoyne to Germain (Private), August 20, 1777, in DAR, Vol. 14: 165–67.
66. Ibid.
67. Ibid.
68. Ibid.
69. Clinton to Burgoyne, August 10, 1777 (with marginal notes in Clinton's hand); Cortland Skinner to William Shirreff, August 10, 1777; and Clinton to Edward Harvey, August 18, 1777, in HCP. See also Hargrove, *General John Burgoyne,* 171. It was very difficult for Clinton and Burgoyne to exchange messages. To successfully get a note through American lines, the two generals sent several intrepid messengers on different routes and even with these precautions, some information simply never got through. If a courier was caught, he was often summarily executed as a spy. To keep critical information out of enemy hands, one of Clinton's favorite techniques was the so-called "Cardano System," also called a mask system. The sender would write a letter with seemingly innocuous or even misleading content. The recipient then would lay a prearranged "mask" over the letter, revealing the actual message within the message. The August 10, 1777, letter from Clinton to Burgoyne was one of these "mask letters." For the spycraft used by Clinton and Burgoyne during this campaign, see John A. Nagy, *Invisible Ink: Spycraft of the American Revolution* (Yardley, PA: Westholm, 2010), 3 and 105–10; and Alexander Rose, *Washington's Spies: The Story of America's First Spy Ring* (New York: Random House, 2006), 56–58
70. Burgoyne to Germain (Private), August 20, 1777, in DAR, Vol. 14: 167.

71. Anton Adolph Heinrich Du Roi (attrib.) journal entries, August 19, 23, and September 1, 1777, in Doblin, *Specht Journal*, 69, 71, and 74; journal entries, August 19 and 28, in Digby, *British Invasion from the North*, 253–55 and 256–57; Napier journal entry, August 29, 1777, in Bradford, "Napier's Journal," 311; and unknown British officer journal entry for August 28, 177, in Stanley, *For Want of a Horse*, 139.
72. Journal entry, August 30, 1777, in Thacher, *Military Journal*, 112.
73. Stark to the Council of New Hampshire, August 18, 1777, in Stark, *Memoir and Official Correspondence of Gen. John Stark*, 128.
74. Journal entry, August 19, 1777, in Digby, *British Invasion from the North*, 256.
75. Journal entry, August 22, 1777, in ibid. See Anton Adolph Heinrich Du Roi (attrib.) journal entry, August 27, in Doblin, *Specht Journal*, 72, also Barker, "Battles of Saratoga and Kinderhook Tea Party," 34.
76. Schuyler to Hancock, August 18, 1777, in Stark, *Memoir and Official Correspondence of Gen. John Stark*, 129. The next day Schuyler sent a like letter to Washington, Schuyler to Washington, August 19, 1777, in GWP, Vol. 11: 7–8.
77. John Adams to Abigail Adams, August 21, 1777, in LDC, Vol. 7: 521.
78. Richard Henry Lee to Jefferson, August 25, 1777, in Julian P. Boyd, ed., *The Papers of Thomas Jefferson*, Vol. 2, 1777 to 18 June 1778 (Princeton, NJ: Princeton University Press, 1950), 29–30.
79. *Pennsylvania Evening Post*, September 4, 1777, in Moore, *Diary of the American Revolution from Newspapers and Original Documents*, Vol. 1, 479–81.
80. Walpole to the Countess of Ossory, September 29, 1777, in Cunningham, *Letters of Horace Walpole, Earl of Orford*, Vol. 6, 489.
81. Germain to William Knox, October 31, 1777, in Commager and Morris, *Spirit of 'Seventy-Six*, 580.
82. Germain to Carleton, March 26, 1777, in DAR, Vol. 14: 56.
83. Howe to Germain, August 30, 1777, in GGP. See also Colonial Office General Precis for 1777–1778, Colonial Office Papers, CO5/253.
84. Howe to Henry Clinton, August 31, 1777, in HCP. See also Muenchhausen diary entry, August 28, 1777, Muenchhausen, *At Howe's Side*, 26. John Peebles diary entry, September 1, 1777, in *John Peebles' American War: The Diary of a Scottish Grenadier, 1776–1782*, ed. Ira Gruber (Mechanicsburg, PA: Stackpole Books, 1998), 129.

CHAPTER 17

1. On August 20, 1777, the day after Gates arrived at Northern Army headquarters, Washington mildly rebuked him for his tardy arrival and the fact that he had yet to receive any updates. He clearly expected Gates to have arrived at least a week earlier than he did. Washington to Gates, August 20, 1777, in GWP, Vol. 11: 12.
2. Hancock to Gates, August 14, 1777, in HGP, Reel 5.
3. Nelson, *Horatio Gates*, 106.
4. Ibid., 107; Gerlach, *Proud Patriot*, 302–303; Wilkinson, *Memoirs of My Own Time*, Vol. 1, 222; and Alan Cate, *Founding Fighters: The Battlefield Leaders Who Made American Independence* (Westport, CT: Praeger Security International, 2006), 56.
5. Journal entry, August 30, 1777, in Thacher, *A Military Journal*, 113.
6. Officers of Genl Nixon's Brigade to Gates, August 23, 1777, in HGP, Vol. 5.
7. Journal entry. August 19, 1777, Henry Dearborn, *Revolutionary War Journals of Henry Dearborn, 1775–1783*, ed. Lloyd A. Brown and Howard H. Peckham (New York: De Capo Press, 1971), 102.
8. Gates to Stark, August 19, 1777, in HGP, Reel 5. See also Gates to Arnold, August 19, 1777; Gates to Goose Van Schaick, August 19, 1777; and Gates to George Clinton, August 20, 1777, all from HGP, Reel 5.
9. Benjamin Lincoln to Gates, August 20, 1777; and Stark to Gates, August 22, 1777, HGP, Reel 5.

10. Benjamin Lincoln to Gates, August 23, 1777, in ibid. Lincoln's intelligence was confirmed by a British deserter interrogated by General Glover: a British regiment was at Fort George, a "Hessian" regiment at Fort Edward, the main body of about six thousand camped at Fort Miller, and the enemy had built a bridge across the river at Saratoga covered by a "Flying Army" [Fraser's advanced corps]. Glover to Gates, August 26, 1777, in ibid.
11. Gates to Hancock, August 20, 1777, in ibid.
12. Gates to Jonathan Trumbull Sr., August 24, 1777, in ibid.
13. Ketchum, *Saratoga*, 351; and Rossie, *Politics of Command*, 168.
14. Washington to Daniel Morgan, August 16, 1777, in GWP, Vol. 10: 641. Washington was reluctant to lose Morgan and told Hancock the next day that he had made the decision "contrary to my wishes but from the necessity of the case." Washington to Hancock, August 17, 1777, in ibid., 649. Congress also passed a resolution with the same recommendation, but the commander-in-chief made the decision independent of the congressional resolution. See Resolves of Congress, August 16, 1777, in JCC, Vol. 8: 649. Gates had also not been idle in helping reinforce the Northern Army. Upon his congressional appointment to the command, like Washington, he wrote to all the states concerned urging them to raise and send militia to join the army as soon as possible. Hancock to Gates, August 6, 1777; Gates to the President of the Assembly of the State of New York, August 6, 1777; and Gates to Jonathan Trumbull Sr., August 6, 1777, in HGP, Reel 4.
15. Washington to George Clinton, August 16, 1777, in GWP, Vol. 10: 636, and George Clinton to Gates, August 21, 1777, in ibid., Vol. 11: 39n.
16. Congressional resolution of August 23, 1777, in JCC, Vol. 8: 668. See also Washington to Hancock, August 21, 1777, in GWP, Vol. 11: 23; and Hancock to Washington, August 23, 1777, in ibid., 54.
17. Gates to Washington, August 22, 1777, in GWP, Vol. 11: 38. Alexander Hamilton replied to Gates on August 29. Howe had already landed his army at Head of Elk and Washington was busy preparing to face him. Hamilton, surely echoing Washington's thoughts, wrote that since "the Eastern States can be no longer under any apprehension of a visit from Mr. Howe . . . we may hope our Northern Army will now derive a decisive superiority over the enemy, from the full exertion of the whole force of those states." Hamilton to Gates, August 29, 1777, ibid., 40n.
18. Gates to Washington, August 28, 1777, in GWP, Vol. 11: 84. This was the last letter Gates wrote to the commander-in-chief for more than a month. Washington to Gates, September 1, 1777, and Washington to Hugh Hughes, September 1, 1777, ibid., 107–8. His next letter to Washington was written on October 5, 1777, more than two weeks after the September 19 Battle of Freeman's Farm.
19. Gates to Daniel Morgan, August 29, 1777, in HGP, Reel 5; Henry Dearborn journal entries for September 11 and 12, 1777, in Dearborn, *Journals*, 104–5; Dearborn to Wilkinson, December 20, 1815, *Bulletin of the Fort Ticonderoga Museum*, 5; Samuel Armstrong diary entry for September 13, 1777, Samuel Armstrong, "From Saratoga to Valley Forge: The Diary of Lt. Samuel Armstrong," ed. Joseph Lee Boyle, *Pennsylvania Magazine of History and Biography* 121 (July 1997): 244; and Eric Schnitzer, "A Review of the Organization of the Corps of Light Infantry, Northern Department, August–November 1777" (Stillwater, NY: Saratoga National Historical Park, October 2009), 1–5. The ad hoc Corps of Light Infantry, which numbered about three hundred men (although Schnitzer suggests that the number was probably closer to 375), was under the command of Major (later lieutenant colonel) Henry Dearborn. Dearborn's Light Infantry and Morgan's Provisional Corps of Riflemen comprised the army's Advanced Guard.
20. Don Higginbotham, "Daniel Morgan: Guerrilla Fighter," Billias, *George Washington's Generals and Opponents*, Vol. 1, 293.
21. Ibid., 292–99.
22. Ibid., 299; Milsop, *Continental Infantryman*, 23; and Elting, *Battles of Saratoga*, 86. Like the rifles carried by the German Jäger units, the loading procedure for a muzzle-loading

Pennsylvania rifle took much longer because it required extra steps and the ball had to be laboriously rammed down the barrel to catch the rifled grooves that imparted spin to the projectile giving the weapon its great accuracy and range.

23. Gates to Stark, September 10, 1777; Stark to Benjamin Lincoln, September 6, 1777; Stark to Lincoln, September 7, 1777; Benjamin Lincoln to Gates, September 8, 1777; Stark to Gates, September 9, 1777; and Gates to Lincoln, September 10, 1777, all in HGP, Reel 5.
24. Gates to Hancock, September 10, 1777, in HGP, Reel 5. Stark's brigade of about eight hundred men arrived at Stillwater on September 12 followed by their commander on the 14th. Three days later, on the eve of the first battle of Saratoga, they returned to New Hampshire. Because of their short enlistment, the New Hampshire Committee of Safety had raised more men to replace them, but the replacements did not arrive in time to fight in the battle, but they did play a major role in Burgoyne's eventual capitulation. See Ketchum, *Saratoga*, 353; Baldwin journal entry for September 12 and 14, 1777, in Baldwin, *Revolutionary Journal of Col. Jeduthan Baldwin*, 119; and Thomas Blake journal entry for September 11, 1777, Frederick Kidder, *History of the First New Hampshire Regiment in the War of the Revolution* (Albany, NY: Joel Munsell, 1868), 33.
25. Kosciuszko quoted in William Dunlop, *History of the New Netherlands, Province of New York, and State of New York, to the Adoption of the Federal Constitution* (New York: Carter and Thorp, 1940), 117. See also Storozynski, *Peasant Prince*, 33; and Wilkinson, *Memoirs*, 232.
26. Quoted in Nelson, *Horatio Gates*, 112.
27. Varick to Schuyler, September 15, 1777, in Schuyler Papers, DLAR, Film 659, Reel 9.
28. Kosciuszko quoted in Dunlop, *History of the New Netherlands*, 118. See also Storozynski, *Peasant Prince*, 33; and Wilkinson, *Memoirs*, 232. Wilkinson claimed credit for picking Bemis Heights in his memoirs, but Kosciuszko, with his engineer's eye for terrain, was the man responsible for choosing the site and placing the American units into position.
29. Varick to Schuyler, September 13, 1777, in Schuyler Papers, Film 659, Reel 9, DLAR and Henry Livingston to Schuyler, September 11, 1777, in ibid.
30. Journal entry, September 13, 1777, in Dearborn, *Journals*, 105.
31. Gates to the Chairman of the Several Committees West of the Connecticut River, September 17, 1777, and George Clinton to Gates, September 18, 1777, in HGP, Reel 5. Gates's pleas were successful, but the militia reinforcements would not arrive before the first battle of Saratoga on September 19. See also Gates to Hancock, September 22, 1777, in ibid.
32. Gates to Hancock, September 15, 1777, in ibid. In this letter Gates also noted that he was in constant communication with Lincoln, who was harassing the British left flank, including operations against enemy outposts. Gates's last update to Washington was written on August 28, yet he wrote several times to Hancock before he corresponded with his commander-in-chief again.
33. Glatthaar and Martin, *Forgotten Allies*, 176–83. The Oneida and Tuscarora Indians played a small but important role during the short time they stayed with Gates's army. They gathered intelligence and captured enemy prisoners. Both American and British observers praised their conduct in the closing phases of the Saratoga campaign because of their humane treatment of the captives. Ibid., 180. See also Dearborn to Wilkinson, December 20, 1815, in *Bulletin of the Fort Ticonderoga Museum*, 7.
34. Journal entry, September 6, 1777, in Digby, *British Invasion from the North*, 266. See also unnamed German officer's journal entry for September 11, 1777, Barker, "Battles of Saratoga and the Kinderhook Tea Party," 34.
35. Riedesel, *Memoirs*, 136.
36. Journal entry, September 10, 1777, in Digby, *British Invasion from the North*, 266–67.
37. Journal entry, September 11, 1777, in Hadden, *Journal*, 143. See also STOE, 21.
38. Burgoyne general order for September 12, 1777, in Burgoyne, *Burgoyne's Orderly Book*, 99–100.

39. Unnamed officer's journal entry, September 13, 1777, in Stanley, *For Want of a Horse*, 143. Some historians have incorrectly claimed that this move across the Hudson and the breaking up of the bridge over the Batten Kill was irrevocable. What was done could be undone if Burgoyne had the resources to fall back, rebuild the bridges, and secure his route.
40. Frederike Charlotte Riedesel, *Letters and Journals Relating to the War of the American Revolution, and the Capture of the German Troops at Saratoga, William L. Stone, trans.* (Albany, NY: Joel Munsell, 1867), 91 and 113.
41. Anton Adolph Heinrich Du Roi (attrib.) journal entry, September 15, 1777, in Doblin, *Specht Journal*, 77.
42. Journal entry, September 13, 1777, in Digby, *British Invasion from the North*, 267. Most of the army except for a large part of Riedesel's left wing crossed the Hudson on September 13. All the army had crossed to the west bank by the 15th. See unnamed German officer's journal entry, September 13 and 15, 1777, in Barker, "Battles of Saratoga and the Kinderhook Tea Party," 34.
43. Burgoyne general order for September 14, 1777, in Burgoyne, *Orderly Book*, 105.
44. Journal entry, September 15, 1777, in Hadden, *Journal*, 150.
45. On September 15, 1777, personnel returns for British units in Burgoyne's army indicate that 13.5 percent of the soldiers were not fit and present for duty due to illness. Kopperman, "Numbers Game," 264.
46. Hargrove, *General John Burgoyne*, 179–80; and Burgoyne general order for September 15, 1777, in Burgoyne, *Orderly Book*, 106–7.
47. Journal entry, September 16, 1777, in Digby, *British Invasion from the North*, 269.
48. John Money testimony in STOE, 61; and Harrington testimony, in ibid., 68.
49. Ibid.; journal entry, September 15, 1777, in Hadden, *Journal*, 152; Burgoyne general order for September 16, 1777, in Burgoyne, *Burgoyne's Orderly Book*, 109–12; Burgoyne to Germain, October 20, 1777, in DAR, Vol. 14, 229; and Henry Livingston to Schuyler, September 16, 1777, in Schuyler Papers, DLAR, Film 659, Reel 9.
50. Burgoyne general order for September 18, 1777, in Burgoyne, *Orderly Book*, 113. See also journal entry for September 18, in Hadden, *Journal*, 160, and journal entry for September 18, 1777, in Digby, *British Invasion from the North*, 269–70.
51. Anton Adolph Heinrich Du Roi (attrib.) journal entry, September 18, 1777, in Doblin, *Specht Journal*, 78.
52. Wilkinson, *Memoirs of My Own Life*, Vol. 1, 235; Burgoyne to Germain, October 20, 1777, in DAR, Vol. 14, 229; and journal entry, September 18, 1777, in Baldwin, *Revolutionary Journal*, 120.
53. Lincoln to Gates, September 12, 1777; Lincoln to Gates, September 14, 1777; Gates to Lincoln, September 17, 1777; John Brown to Gates, September 18, 1777; all in HGP, Reel 5; Henry Watson Powell to Carleton, September 18, 1777, DAR, Vol. 14: 185–86; John R. Elting, *The Battles of Saratoga* (Monmouth Beach, NJ: Philip Freneau Press, 1977), 89; Bruce M. Venter, "Behind Enemy Lines: Americans Attack Burgoyne's Supply Lines," *Patriots of the American Revolution* 4, no. 3 (May/June 2011): 12–18; Morrissey, *Saratoga*, 57–58; and Mattern, *Benjamin Lincoln*, 46–47.
54. Gates to Lincoln, September 19, 1777 and Lincoln to Gates, September 20, 1777, HGP, Reel 5.
55. Two letters written the same day, Richard Varick to Schuyler, September 13, 1777, in Schuyler Papers, DLAR, Film 659, Reel 9.
56. Jjournal entry, September 17, and Gates's General Order for September 17, in Thacher, *Military Journal*, 116.
57. Henry Livingston to Schuyler, September 15, 1777, in Schuyler Papers, DLAR, Film 659, Reel 9. Gates also inherited James Wilkinson from Schuyler's staff, but Wilkinson liked and respected both commanders, at least at this point. Wilkinson, *Memoirs of My Own Times*, Vol. 1, 222.

58. Varick to Schuyler, September 16, 1777, in Schuyler Papers, DLAR, Film 659, Reel 9. When Schuyler was relieved of command, Livingston and Varick both refused to join Gates's staff and instead worked for Arnold as temporary staff officers. This upset Gates, who thought correctly that the two men would only work against him. See Nelson, *General Horatio Gates*, 125.

CHAPTER 18

1. Harrington testimony, Burgoyne, STOE, 69.
2. This type of operation today is called a movement to contact.
3. Burgoyne personally questioned Major Robert Kingston two years after the battle during the House of Commons inquiry and asked, "Did you conceive that the chief purpose of that movement [on September 19] was to obtain a knowledge of the left of the enemy's position, and if expedient to attack them there?" Kingston answered, "I understood it was." Kingston testimony, in Burgoyne, STOE, 106.
4. Burgoyne to Germain, October 20, 1777, DAR, Vol. 14: 229–30; Elting, *Battles of Saratoga*, 50–51; Morrissey, *Saratoga*, 59; Schnitzer, "Tactics of the Battles of Saratoga," 41–43; and journal entry, September 19, 1777, in Digby, *British Invasion from the North*, 271–72.
5. Burgoyne to Germain, October 20, 1777, DAR, Vol. 14: 229–30; Elting, *Battles of Saratoga*, 50–51; Morrissey, *Saratoga*, 59; Schnitzer, "Tactics of the Battles of Saratoga," 41–43; Anton Adolph Heinrich Du Roi (attrib.) journal entry, September 19, 1777, in Doblin, *Specht Journal*, 79; and journal entry, September 19, 1777, in Hadden, *Journal*, 161–62
6. Arnold to Gates, October 1, 1777, in HGP, Reel 5; Nelson, *Horatio Gates*, 115; and Martin, *Benedict Arnold*, 374–81.
7. Elting, *Battles of Saratoga*, 50.
8. The description of the American positions is taken from walking the ground and examining contemporary and modern maps.
9. Gates to Hancock, September 22, 1777, HGP, Reel 5. Gates did not write a similar report to Washington. See also Wilkinson, *Memoir of My Own Times*, Vol. 1, 236; and Schnitzer, "The Tactics of the Battles of Saratoga," 45.
10. The description of the terrain is taken from walking the ground and examining contemporary and modern maps.
11. Ibid.
12. Schnitzer, "Tactics of the Battles of Saratoga," 46–48; Morrissey, *Saratoga*, 59; journal entry, September 19, 1777, in Digby, *British Invasion from the North*, 272; and journal entry, September 19, 1777, in Hadden, *Journal*, 162–63. Burgoyne testified to the House of Commons two years after the battle to the effectiveness of Morgan's riflemen. Burgoyne "review of the evidence," in Burgoyne, STOE, 163.
13. Schnitzer, "Tactics of the Battles of Saratoga," 48–49; journal entry, September 19, 1777, in Henry Dearborn, *Journals*, 106; and ournal entry, September 19, 1777, in Digby, *British Invasion from the North*, 272.
14. Wilkinson, *Memoirs*, Vol. 1, 238. As one of Gates's key staff officers, Wilkinson was undoubtedly present at many of the key events during the Saratoga campaign, and thus his account cannot be ignored. However, his memoirs must be used with caution.
15. Schnitzer, "Tactics of the Battles of Saratoga," 48–49; journal entry, September 19, 1777, in Henry Dearborn, *Journals*, 106; and journal entry, September 19, 1777, in Digby, *British Invasion from the North*, 272.
16. Journal entry, September 19, 1777, in Hadden, *Journal*, 163. Strictly speaking, Hadden was mistaken. The main army had briefly exchanged rounds with the Americans during the siege of Fort Ticonderoga in early July.
17. Major Forbes's testimony, in Burgoyne, STOE, 82.
18. Blake journal entry, September 19, 1777, in Kidder, *History of the 1st New Hampshire Regiment*, 34; journal entry, September 19, 1777, in Hadden, *Journal*, 164; journal entry, September 19, 1777, in Dearborn, *Journals*, 106; journal entry, September 19, 1777, in Digby, *British Invasion from the North*, 273; Schnitzer, "Tactics of the Battles of Saratoga,"

49; Morrissey, *Saratoga*, 59; and Burgoyne to Germain, October 20, 1777, DAR, Vol. 14: 230.

19. A lively historical debate began almost immediately after the battle ended on whether Arnold actually fought in the Battle of Freeman's Farm. There are very few first-person accounts of the battle that mention his physical presence, and most of them were written years after the war. Neither Wilkinson, Dearborn, Colonel Philip van Cortlandt of the 2nd New York Regiment, nor two officers from the 8th Massachusetts Regiment mention Arnold in their accounts of the battle, nor do any of the British eyewitnesses. Van Cortlandt noted in his account of the battle that the engagement was largely "conducted by the Colonels." Given the available evidence, it is likely that he was near the field at the very start of the battle, and was able to witness units going into action, as verified by his September 20 general order that he had observed too many officers leading from the front and getting themselves killed and wounded. But for most of the day, he concentrated his efforts on feeding units into the fray and moving between the American fortifications and the southern and western edge of the field where he could observe as much of the field as possible. This was a very important responsibility. For excellent analyses of this debate, and two convincing cases for Arnold's battlefield absence at Freeman's Farm, see Schnitzer, "Tactics of the Battles of Saratoga," 53; Luzader, *Saratoga*, 382–93; and Wayne Lynch, "Debating Arnold's Role at Freeman's Farm," *Journal of the American Revolution* (September 12, 2013). https://allthingsliberty.com/2013/09/debating-arnolds-role-freemans-farm/ See also Wilkinson, *Memoirs*, Vol. 1, 238–39; journal entry, September 19, 1777, in Dearborn, *Journals*, 106–7; diary entry, September 19, 1777, in Samuel Armstrong, "From Saratoga to Valley Forge: The Diary of Lt. Samuel Armstrong," 245; Philip van Cortlandt, *The Revolutionary War Memoir and Selected Correspondence of Philip van Cortlandt*, ed. Jacob Judd (Tarrytown, NY: Sleepy Hollow Restorations, 1976), 47; Maria Campbell, ed., *Revolutionary Service and Civil Life of General William Hull: Prepared from His Manuscripts* (New York: Appleton, 1848), 92–96; "Recollections of Captain E. Wakefield of the American Army," in Commager and Morris, *Spirit of 'Seventy-Six*, 581; Elting *Battles of Saratoga*, 81n; and Martin, *Benedict Arnold*, 379–80.
20. "Refusing" a flank acts to protect the rest of the line from a flank attack.
21. Journal entry, September 19, 1777, in Hadden, *Journal*, 165.
22. Journal entry, September 19, 1777, in Digby, *British Invasion from the North*, 272.
23. Schnitzer, "Tactics of the Battles of Saratoga," 50–51; Elting, *Battles of Saratoga*, 52; journal entry, September 19, 1777, in Hadden, *Journal*, 165–66; Blake journal entry, September 19, 1777, in Kidder, *History of the 1st New Hampshire Regiment*, 34; Campbell, *Life of General William Hull*, 94–95; unknown British officer journal entry, September 19, 1777, in Stanley, *For Want of a Horse*, 148; Major General Riedesel, *Memoirs*, 147; journal entry, September 23, 1777, in Thacher, *Military Journal*, 117; and Cubbison, *The Artillery Never Gained More Honour*, 112. Lieutenant Blake of the 1st New Hampshire Regiment claimed in his journal that "In this engagement the enemy had two field pieces in the field, which we took three or four times, but as it was in the woods, they were not removed."
24. Corporal Roger Lamb quoted in Mercer, "The 9th (East Norfolk) Regiment of Foot," 57.
25. Journal entry, September 19, 1777, in Dearborn, *Journals*, 106.
26. Schnitzer, "Tactics of the Battles of Saratoga," 50–51; Elting, *Battles of Saratoga*, 52–53; and Morrissey, *Saratoga*, 59–61;
27. Anton Adolph Heinrich Du Roi (attrib.) journal entry, September 19, 1777, in Doblin, *Specht Journal*, 80. Burgoyne also ordered Riedesel to "make the best arrangements for covering the artillery, the baggage the bateaux and for giving the left wing the necessary security." Ibid.
28. Anton Adolph Heinrich Du Roi (attrib.) journal entry, September 19, 1777, in Doblin, *Specht Journal*, 80.
29. Unknown German officer diary entry, September 19, 1777, in Barker, "Battles of Saratoga and Kinderhook Tea Party," 35. The eighteenth-century artillery pieces that equipped Burgoyne's army could fire two major types of ammunition: round shot and

case shot. Solid shot is a round, solid metal projectile that would typically be used against enemy formations, entrenchments, and other stationary targets. Case shot consisted of a canister filled with iron balls that was an effective anti-personnel round. The range of the light 6-pounder gun at Saratoga—the most conspicuous type on that battlefield—was about 800 yards for round shot and 300 yards for case shot. Other rounds included shell and grapeshot, but Burgoyne's artillerymen were only supplied with round and case shot during the campaign. For basic artillery information, see Elting, *Battles of Saratoga*, 87; and Eric Schnitzer email to the author, March 27, 2017.

30. Kingston testimony, in Burgoyne, STOE, 104.
31. Schnitzer, "Tactics of the Battles of Saratoga," 51–53; Elting, *Battles of Saratoga*, 53–55; Morrissey, *Saratoga*, 60–61; Pausch, *Journal*, 136–40; journal entry, September 19, 1777, in Hadden, *Journal*, 166; Anton Adolph Heinrich Du Roi (attrib.) journal entry, September 19, 1777, in Doblin, *Specht Journal*, 80; and Major General Riedesel, *Memoirs*, 149–50.
32. Pausch journal entry for September 19, 1777, in Pausch, *Journal*, 143; and unknown British officer journal entry, September 19, 1777, in Stanley, *For Want of a Horse*, 148–49.
33. Journal entry for September 19, 1777, in Digby, *British Invasion from the North*, 274.
34. Unknown German officer diary entry, September 19, 1777, in Barker, "Battles of Saratoga and Kinderhook Tea Party," 35.
35. Anton Adolph Heinrich Du Roi (attrib.) journal entry, September 19, 1777, in Doblin, *Specht Journal*, 81.
36. Lamb, *Memoir of His Own Life*, 192.
37. The casualty figures are best estimates based on often questionable British and American records, and are taken from Morrissey, *Saratoga*, 72n, and Elting, *Battle of Saratoga*, 54–55. The British figures probably do not include Loyalist casualties, so they are on the low side.
38. Lamb, *Memoir of His Own Life*, 192.
39. Burgoyne's medical resources were inadequate to support his army, and with the casualties incurred during the battle of Freeman's Farm, it was overwhelmed. Kopperman, "The Numbers Game," 274. Even if a wounded soldier survived the night and made it to the hospital, the mortality rate was high. One German officer wrote after the battle that "[t]here are daily about twenty or more deaths." journal entry, September 19, 1777, Pausch, *Journal*, 143.
40. Burgoyne to Germain, October 20, 1777, in DAR, Vol. 14, 231.
41. Journal entry, September 19, 1777, in Digby, *British Invasion from the North*, 274.
42. Unknown German officer diary entry, September 19, 1777, in Barker, "Battles of Saratoga and Kinderhook Tea Party," 35.
43. Balcarres testimony, in Burgoyne, STOE, 42.
44. Harrington testimony, in ibid., 70.
45. Burgoyne "Review of the Evidence," in Burgoyne, STOE, 167.
46. Burgoyne General Order for September 21, 1777, in Burgoyne, *Orderly Book*, 115–16.
47. For an excellent analysis of the relative experience levels of the American and British soldiers on the Freeman's farm battlefield, see Schnitzer, "Tactics of the Battles of Saratoga," 57.
48. Roger Lamb, *An Original and Authentic Journal of Occurrences during the Late American War from its Commencement to the Year 1783* (Dublin: Wilkinson and Courtney, 1809), 161.
49. Arnold was particularly upset at the deaths of lieutenant colonels Andrew Colburn of the 3rd New Hampshire Regiment and Winborn Adams of the 2nd New Hampshire Regiment. Arnold General Order dated September 20, 1777, quoted in Elting, *Battles of Saratoga*, 54. The death of Adams and Colburn led to Dearborn's promotion to lieutenant colonel after the September 19 battle. Dearborn to Wilkinson, December 20, 1815, *Bulletin of the Fort Ticonderoga Museum*, 7.
50. Dearborn journal entry for September 19, 1777, in Dearborn, *Journals*, 106–7.

51. Gates to Hancock, September 22, 1777, in HGP, Reel 5. Gates did not write a similar note to the commander-in-chief, and would not write Washington until October 5, 1777, and then only in response to Washington's request to send Morgan and his riflemen back to the main army, if they could be spared. Thus, the American commander-in-chief never received an official report on the Battle of Freeman's Farm.
52. Some historians have even suggested cowardice. Elting, author of a good tactical study of Saratoga, provides just one example of the unfair attacks on Gates and his role during the fighting. Elting, *Battles of Saratoga*, 51–55. See also Morrissey, *Saratoga*, 59. In addition to historian accounts, Gates's reputation was not enhanced by the slanderous accounts of the general and campaign written by Varick and Livingston, who were both supporters of Schuyler and Arnold, and bitter critics of the army commander. In addition, Gates's disputes with Washington, their mutual dislike for one another, and the subsequent Battle of Camden further tarnished his reputation.
53. Journal entry, September 20, 1777, in Digby, *British Invasion from the North*, 275 and 275n; Hargrove, *John Burgoyne*, 184; and Burgoyne General Order for September 20, 1777, in Burgoyne, *Orderly Book*, 114.
54. Varick to Schuyler, September 19, 1777, in Schuyler Papers, DLAR, Film 659, Reel 9.
55. Gates general orders issued September 22, 1777, Wilkinson, *Memoirs*, Vol. 1, 254.
56. Ibid.
57. Ketchum, *Saratoga*, 385–86; and Eric Schnitzer email to the author, March 27, 2017.
58. Varick to Schuyler, September 22, 1777, in Schuyler Papers, Film 659, Reel 9, DLAR.
59. Varick to Schuyler, September 22, 1777, in ibid.
60. Arnold to Gates, September 22, 1777, in HGP, Reel 5.
61. Ibid.
62. Wilkinson, *Memoirs*, Vol. 1, 254.
63. Gates to Arnold, September 23, 1777, in ibid., 257.
64. Arnold to Gates, September 23, 1777, in ibid., 257.
65. Gates to Arnold, September 23, 1777, in ibid., 258.
66. Henry Livingston to Schuyler, September 23, 1777, in Schuyler Papers, Film 659, Reel 9, DLAR.
67. The cannon salute was heard clearly by the British and German soldiers manning Burgoyne's lines only one mile away. Journal entry, September 21, 1777, in Digby, *British Invasion from the North*, 276; and Anton Adolph Heinrich Du Roi (attrib.) journal entry, September 21, 1777, in Doblin, *Specht Journal*, 82.
68. Gates to Lincoln, September 22, 1777, in HGP, Reel 5.
69. Matthew Visscher to Gates, September 22, 1777, in Schuyler Papers, Film 659, Reel 9, DLAR.
70. Journal entry, September 24, 1777, in Dearborn, *Journals*, 107; journal entry, September 24, 1777, in Baldwin, *Revolutionary Journal*, 121; Mattern, *Benjamin Lincoln*, 47; and Blake journal entry, September 24, 1777, in Kidder, *History of the First New Hampshire*, 36. Almost every American first-person account tells of numerous British and German deserters coming into the camp of Gates's army in the days after the Battle of Freeman's Farm. On September 23 a representative from the Massachusetts Bay Council wrote Gates to tell him that they were pushing militia to the Northern Army as fast as they could from Berkshire, Hampshire, Worcester, and Middlesex counties. Jerimiah Powell to Gates, September 23, 1777, in HGP, Reel 5. At the same time, Burgoyne's British and German soldiers were well aware of the situation regarding the relative strengths of the two armies. One British officer wrote on September 21 that they "heard the Enemy's Numbers were continually increasing." Unknown British staff officer journal entry, September 21, 1777, in Stanley, *For Want of a Horse*, 149. Lieutenant Digby confided to his journal that rumors of an American retreat were "not thought very probable by their receiving so large reinforcements daily to their camp." Journal entry, September 23, 1777, in Digby, *British Invasion from the North*, 280.
71. Gates to Elizabeth Gates, September 22, 1777, in HGP, Reel 5.

72. Henry Livingston to Schuyler, September 24, 1777, in Schuyler Papers, Film 659, Reel 9, DLAR. Richard Varick also reported to Schuyler on the 24th, "They are not on speaking terms." Varick to Schuyler, September 24, 1777, ibid. See also Martin, *Benedict Arnold*, 390.
73. Once Lincoln arrived, Gates assigned him command of the right wing and he also replaced Arnold as Gates's second in command on September 25. Arnold retained command of the left wing. See Schnitzer, "Organization of the Army of the United States under Command of Major General Horatio Gates at Bemis Heights," 1–4 and 4n.
74. Henry Livingston to Schuyler, September 25, 1777, in Schuyler Papers, Film 659, Reel 9, DLAR.
75. Varick to Schuyler, September 25, 1777, in ibid.
76. Henry Livingston to Schuyler, September 26, 1777, in ibid. For an excellent discussion on the ill-fated attempt to mediate the dispute between the two generals, see Martin, *Benedict Arnold*, 390–91.
77. Henry Livingston to Schuyler, September 26, 1777, in Schuyler Papers, Film 659, Reel 9, DLAR.
78. Arnold to Gates, September 27, 1777, in HGP, Reel 5.
79. Gates to Arnold, September 28, 1777, in ibid.
80. Lincoln's biographer does not mention any role in resolving the row. See Mattern, *Benjamin Lincoln*, 47–48.
81. Arnold to Gates, October 1, 1777, in HGP, Reel 5.

CHAPTER 19

1. Howe to Clinton, July 30, 1777, in HCP.
2. Willcox, *Portrait of a General*, 175–77.
3. Clinton to Burgoyne, September 10, 1777, in HCP (this letter is dated September 10, but Clinton referred to it later as his September 11 letter, which was probably the day it was sent); and Burgoyne to Germain, October 20, 1777, in DAR, Vol. 14: 231. Surgeon Thacher described the numerous enemy messengers who tried to make their way through American lines: "Messengers or persons in the character of spies, are frequently suspected of passing from one British commander to the other." Journal entry, October 1, 1777, in Thacher, *Military Journal*, 119.
4. Burgoyne to Clinton, September 21, 1777, in HCP. This was one of the encrypted "mask letters" between the two generals. A worried Burgoyne sent yet another "mask letter" to Clinton two days later with essentially the same content. Burgoyne to Clinton, September 23, 1777, ibid.
5. Burgoyne's "narrative," in Burgoyne, STOE, 24.
6. Clinton to Howe, September 27, 1777, in HCP.
7. The composition of Clinton's expedition and the description of the two forts and the surrounding geography is taken from in-person, on-site explorations, various maps, and Morrissey, *Saratoga*, 68–69; Noah Andre Trudeau, "Thunder on the Hudson," *Military History Quarterly* 20 (Summer 2008): 58–59; and James M. Johnson, "A Warm Reception in the Hudson Highlands," in *Key to the Northern Country: The Hudson River in the American Revolution*, ed. James M. Johnson, Christopher Pryslopski, and Andrew Villani (Albany: State University of New York Press, 2013), 211–13.
8. Clinton to Howe, October 9, 1777, in DAR, Vol. 14: 198.
9. Ibid.; Trudeau, "Thunder on the Hudson," 59–60; Morrissey, *Saratoga*, 69–71; Clinton, *The American Rebellion*, 75–77; Johnson, "A Warm Reception in the Hudson Highlands," 214; and William Hotham to Richard Howe, October 9, 1777, in DAR, Vol. 14: 200.
10. Burgoyne to Clinton, September 28, 1777, in HCP.
11. Clinton secretary's memorandum of the conversation between Sir Henry Clinton and Captain Scott, October 9, 1777, in HCP.
12. Clinton, *The American Rebellion*, 83.

13. Clinton secretary's memorandum of the conversation between Clinton and Scott, October 5, 1777, in DAR, Vol. 14: 191. Clinton sent copies of both written messages and memos to Howe, who forwarded them on to Germain. Howe was astounded that Burgoyne implied that some of the responsibility for his problems lay with him, because "I positively mentioned [to Burgoyne] that no direct assistance could be given by the southern army." Howe to Germain, October 22, 1777, ibid., 240.
14. Clinton, *The American Rebellion*, 74.
15. Eric Schnitzer email to the author, March 27, 2017.
16. Clinton to Burgoyne, October 6, 1777, in HCP.
17. Clinton to Howe, October 9, 1777, DAR, Vol. 14: 198; and William Hotham to Richard Howe, October 9, 1777, ibid., 200–201. Sir Henry Clinton's order of battle for the attack on the Hudson Highland forts and troop numbers for both sides is taken from Morrissey, *Saratoga*, 23–24 and 68–69.
18. Clinton to Howe, October 9, 1777, in HCP; William Hotham to Richard Howe, October 9, 1777, in DAR, Vol. 14: 201; Trudeau, "Thunder on the Hudson," 60–61; Clinton, *The American Rebellion*, 76–77; and Morrissey, *Saratoga*, 69 and 71.
19. Clinton to Howe, October 9, 1777, in DAR, Vol. 14: 198.
20. Ibid., 199.
21. Casualty figures are from Trudeau, "Thunder on the Hudson," 62. See also Morrissey, *Saratoga*, 69, 72, and 72n; and British Amy returns dated October 7, 1777, in HCP.
22. Clinton to Burgoyne, October 8, 1777, in HCP.
23. Clinton to Burgoyne, October 9, 1777, ibid.
24. Transcript of verbal message in ibid.
25. Material in the HCP; Nagy, *Invisible Ink*, 109–10; Rose, *Washington's Spies*, 57–58; journal entry, October 14, 1777, in Thatcher, *Military Journal*, 126–27; and Willcox, *Portrait of a General*, 184. There are many conflicting sources on Taylor's rank, and most claim he was a captain; however, British records confirm that he was a private and not an officer. Hoping to save his life, however, Taylor claimed the higher rank. His attempted ruse did not work. Eric Schnitzer email to the author, March 27, 2017. Burgoyne finally received word on October 16 that Clinton had captured the Hudson Highlands forts ten days earlier, but by then it was too late. He surrendered to Gates the next day.
26. Clinton to sisters-in-law Martha and Elizabeth Carter, October 13, 1777, in HCP. See also Clinton, *The American Rebellion*, 79.
27. After Burgoyne surrendered on October 17, Gates wrote a scathing letter to Clinton denouncing Vaughan's despicable and wonton act of destruction. Furthermore, given Clinton's failure to control his subordinate, if Sir Henry condoned such behavior, Gates threatened that if captured, "you, sir, may not always be exempted from the calamities of war." Gates to Clinton, October 31, 1777, in HCP.
28. Excerpts from the October 23, 1777, edition of the *New York Packet* and the October 29, 1777, edition of the *Pennsylvania Ledger*, Moore, *Diary of the American Revolution from Newspapers and Original Documents*, Vol. 1, 510 and 510n.
29. Vaughan to Clinton, October 19, 1777, in HCP. In this letter Vaughan also informed Clinton that it was impossible to send or receive messages from the northern army; and that he could proceed no farther up the river. See also Willcox, *Portrait of a General*, 187–88.
30. Howe, *Narrative of Lieutenant General Sir William Howe*, 19, 21, and 61; Washington to Hancock, September 23, 1777, in GWP, Vol. 11: 301–302; Taaffe, *Philadelphia Campaign*, 63–80 and 88–90; and Clement, *Philadelphia, 1777: Taking the Capital*, 36–85.
31. Washington to Gates, September 24, 1777, in GWP, Vol. 11: 310–11.
32. Gates to Washington, October 5, 1777, ibid., 392–93.
33. Hamilton to Gouverneur Morris, July 6, 1777, in AHP, Vol. 1: 281–82.
34. Howe, *Narrative of Lieutenant General Sir William Howe*, 19, 21, and 61; Taaffe, *Philadelphia Campaign*, 93–107; and Clement, *Philadelphia, 1777: Taking the Capital*, 36–85.
35. Howe to Clinton, October 9, 1777, in HCP.

36. Clinton, *The American Rebellion*, 80.
37. Howe ordered the destruction of the forts later in the month. Howe to Clinton, October 25, 1777, in HCP.
38. After the war, Sir Henry Clinton worked twelve years to produce his account of the war. In it he placed the blame firmly on Howe for Burgoyne's defeat. Clinton, *The American Rebellion*, 82–84.
39. Clinton to James Robertson, October 18, 1777, in HCP. See also Trudeau, "Thunder on the Hudson," 63; and Willcox, *Portrait of a General*, 188–89. Howe's capture of Philadelphia was widely seen, at least at first, as a great victory in Great Britain, but some saw it differently. Diplomat Hugh Elliot, after hearing of Burgoyne's surrender at Saratoga, noted perceptively that "Howe's situation is I think more embarrassing than Burgoyne's, a decisive victory is the only one worth pursuing. . . . Howe's conduct hitherto gives good hopes, but Washington's caution on the other hand was very troubling and bodes ill." Hugh Elliot to William Eden, January 7, 1778, in William Eden, 1st Baron Auckland Papers, British Library; Add Mss 34414, Reel 2, DLAR.

CHAPTER 20

1. Journal entry, September 23, 1777, in Digby, *British Invasion from the North*, 279.
2. Harrington testimony, in Burgoyne, STOE, 71; journal entries, September 22 and 23, 1777, in Digby, *British Invasion from the North*, 278–80; Anton Adolph Heinrich Du Roi (attrib.) journal entries, September 23–29, 1777, in Doblin, *Specht Journal*, 83–85; and unnamed officer journal entry, September 21–29, 1777, in Barker, "Battles of Saratoga and Kinderhook Tea Party," 35.
3. Journal entry, September 26, in Digby, *British Invasion from the North*, 281.
4. Unnamed officer journal entry, September 21, 1777, in Barker, "Battles of Saratoga and Kinderhook Tea Party," 35.
5. These incorrect names have been used by almost every historian for decades; however, they are not strictly correct. The Saratoga National Battlefield Park is in the process of changing the names on park signage and literature to the British Light Infantry Redoubt and Breymann's Fortified Camp. Eric Schnitzer email to the author, March 27, 2017.
6. German soldier quoted in Schnitzer, "Tactics of the Battles of Saratoga," 58. For descriptions of the redoubts, see ibid., and Dean R. Snow, "The British Fortifications," in *The Saratoga Campaign: Uncovering an Embattled Landscape*, ed. William R. Griswold and Donald W. Linebaugh (Hanover, NH: University Press of New England, 2016), 83–84 and 96–97.
7. Schnitzer, "Tactics of the Battle of Saratoga," 58. See also Snow, "The British Fortifications," 91–94.
8. Schnitzer, "Tactics of the Battle of Saratoga," 58.
9. The description of the two redoubts is from ibid., 58–59, and Snow, "The British Fortifications," 93.
10. Lamb, *Memoir of His Own Life*, 199.
11. Unnamed officer journal entry, September 21, 1777, in Barker, "Battles of Saratoga and Kinderhook Tea Party," 35.
12. Journal entry, September 28, 1777, in Digby, *British Invasion from the North*, 284. See also Burgoyne's General Orders for September 27 and 29, 1777, in Burgoyne, *Orderly Books*, 120–21 and 123.
13. Unnamed officer journal entry, October 3, 1777, in Barker, "Battles of Saratoga and Kinderhook Tea Party," 35–36.
14. Ibid.
15. Anton Adolph Heinrich Du Roi (attrib.) journal entry, October 2, 1777, in Doblin, *Specht Journal*, 85.
16. Burgoyne to Germain, October 20, 1777, in DAR, Vol. 14: 231.
17. Unknown German officer journal entry, October 3, 1777, in Barker, "Battles of Saratoga and the Kinderhook Tea Party," 36.

18. Burgoyne General Order for October 3, 1777, in Burgoyne, *Orderly Book*, 125. Because the three messengers sent by Clinton never made it through American lines, Burgoyne did not learn of Sir Henry's success in the Highlands until October 16. Balcarres testimony, in Burgoyne, STOE, 53.
19. Journal entry, September 23, 1777, in Digby, *British Invasion from the North*, 280.
20. Fox, "Corporal Fox's Memoir of Service," 22–23. Lord Harrington agreed with Burgoyne's statement that he "was in hourly expectation of his [Clinton's] attacking the highlands, and his opinion that his success there must dislodge the enemy." Harrington testimony, in Burgoyne, STOE, 71. Captain John Money testified that many of the army's officers "said that if they had retreated without risking an action, at the time Sir Henry Clinton was coming up the North River, the army would never have forgiven him [General Burgoyne]." John Money testimony, in Burgoyne, STOE, 62.
21. Anton Adolph Heinrich Du Roi (attrib.) journal entry, October 6, 1777, in Doblin, *Specht Journal*, 87.
22. Journal entry, September 23, 1777, in Digby, *British Invasion from the North*, 279–80.
23. Gates to Burgoyne, September 25, 1777; Burgoyne to Gates, September 27, 1777; and Burgoyne to Gates, October 2, 1777, in HGP, 5.
24. Graymont, *Iroquois in the American Revolution*, 149.
25. John Nixon to William Heath, October 1, 1777, in William Heath Papers, Reel 6, DLAR. See also John Greaton to Heath, October 5, 1777, ibid.
26. Gates to Matthew Visscher, October 4, 1777, in HGP, Reel 5.
27. Duane to George Clinton, October 3, 1777, in LDC, Vol. 8: 47.
28. Minutes of Congressional Resolutions from October 4, 1777, in JCC, Vol. 9: 770–72.
29. Committee on Foreign Affairs to the American Commissioners at Paris, October 6, 1777, in LDC, Vol. 8: 62.
30. Gates to George Clinton, October 4, 1777, in HGP, Reel 5.
31. Gates to Hancock, October 5, 1777, ibid.
32. Gates to Hancock, October 4, 1777, ibid.
33. Gates to Washington, October 5, 1777, in GWP, Vol. 11: 392–93.
34. Lieutenant Friedrich Christian Cleve diary entry, October 6, 1777, quoted in Eric H. Schnitzer, "What's His Motivation?: Analyzing the Purpose of Burgoyne's 7 October Reconnaissance Force" (Stillwater, NY: Saratoga National Historical Park, October 2009), 4; and Burgoyne General Orders for October 6, 1777, in *Burgoyne's Orderly Book*, 128.
35. Cleve diary entries for September 30 and October 2, 4, and 6, 1777, quoted in Schnitzer, "What's His Motivation," 5–6.
36. Burgoyne to Germain, October 20, 1777, in DAR, Vol. 14: 231–32; and Burgoyne testimony, in Burgoyne, STOE, 166.
37. Anton Adolph Heinrich Du Roi (attrib.) journal entry, October 7, 1777, in Doblin, *Specht Journal*, 89–90. The exact mission of the force dispatched on October 7 has been the subject of some dispute. Some have argued that the intent was wholly offensive and that the force was to attack Gates's left flank, but this makes little sense given the available eyewitness reports, memoirs, and the apparent size and composition of the force. Burgoyne did not intend to attack Gates or even to bring on a major battle. Schnitzer, "What's His Motivation," 10. See also Morrissey, *Saratoga*, 73; and Schnitzer, "Tactics of the Battles of Saratoga," 59–60.
38. Schnitzer, "Tactics of the Battles of Saratoga," 60.
39. Burgoyne to Germain, October 20, 1777, in DAR, Vol. 14: 232; Schnitzer, "What's His Motivation," 12n; and Morrissey, *Saratoga*, 73.
40. Journal entry, October 7, 1777, in Digby, *British Invasion from the North*, 286–87. See also Burgoyne to Germain, October 20, 1777, in DAR, Vol. 14: 232; and F. C. Riedesel, *Letters and Journals*, 116.
41. Schnitzer, "Tactics of the Battles of Saratoga," 60–62; Morrissey, *Saratoga*, 73–75; and Elting, *Battles of Saratoga*, 60. Captain Fraser's men, despite their advantageous position on the very flank of the American defenses, accomplished very little and soon had to

withdraw. Had Burgoyne been able to continue his effort to get close enough to gather useable intelligence of Gates's defenses, the hill would have been valuable to facilitate his movements on the 8th. But Burgoyne soon had his hands full and could offer no support to Fraser.

42. Schnitzer, "Tactics of the Battles of Saratoga," 60–62; Morrissey, *Saratoga*, 73–75; and Elting, *Battles of Saratoga*, 60.
43. Schnitzer, "Tactics of the Battles of Saratoga," 62; Elting, *Battles of Saratoga*, 60; and Pausch, *Journal*, 165.
44. Journal entry, October 6 and 7, 1777, in Dearborn, *Journals*, 108. See also diary entry, October 6, 1777, in Armstrong, "Diary of Lt. Samuel Armstrong," 247. Armstrong was a lieutenant in the 8th Massachusetts Regiment, but in early September he and twelve men from the regiment were detailed to join then-Major Henry Dearborn's light infantry.
45. Wilkinson, *Memoirs*, Vol. 1, 267.
46. Ibid., 267–68, and 273.
47. Dearborn to Wilkinson, December 20, 1815, in *Bulletin of the Fort Ticonderoga Museum*, 7. Dearborn and Brooks contradict Wilkinson's account. Wilkinson's actions at this battle as outlined in his memoirs were clearly actually Arnold's. It was Arnold who prompted Gates to order out Morgan, Dearborn, and General Poor's units, all under Arnold's command. These were not the actions of someone in the proverbial doghouse. I am indebted to the chief historian of the Saratoga National Historical Park for pointing out these contradictions. Eric Schnitzer emails to the author on August 26 and September 3, 2018.
48. Francis Bowen, *Life of Benjamin Lincoln, Major General of the Army of the Revolution*, incorporated in Jared Sparks, *The Library of American Biography, 2nd Series*, Vol. 13 (Boston: Little and Brown, 1847), 260.
49. Oliver Wolcott to Jonathan Trumbull, October 10, 1777, in "Trumbull Papers," transcripts published in *Collections of the Massachusetts Historical Society, 7th Series*, Vol. 2 (Boston: Massachusetts Historical Society, 1902), 159.
50. John Brooks, "Colonel Brooks and Captain Bancroft," *Proceedings of the Massachusetts Historical Society, 1855–1858* (Boston, 1859), 271.
51. Wilkinson, *Memoirs*, Vol. 1, 273. Many historians have more or less repeated this story, or versions of it, including Ketchum, *Saratoga*, 394–95; Nelson, *Gates*, 135–36; Elting, *Saratoga*, 60–61; Nickerson, *The Turning Point*, 362; Luzader, *Saratoga*, 282–85; and Martin, *Benedict Arnold*, 395–96. New evidence points to a much different story. The best discussion of Arnold's role at the Battle of Bemis Heights before the newly discovered evidence came to light is Wayne Lynch, "Arnold in Command at Bemis Heights?" *Journal of the American Revolution* (November 14, 2013). https://allthingsliberty.com/2013/11/arnold-command-bemis-heights/
52. The reasons for Arnold's and Gates's reconciliation, a reconciliation that took place sometime between October 1 and 7, are not known. Whatever happened, Arnold and Gates were working well together during the Battle of Bemis Heights with no lingering hints of discord or bad feelings. Numerous historians have argued that Gates had relieved Arnold of his command sometime between September 19 and October 7, but there is no evidence of what would have been a major event and would have been published in the army's general orders. Plus, Arnold would have been even more outraged than he actually was late in September, if he had been formally relieved. It has made a great story, but it did not happen.
53. Schnitzer, "Tactics of the Battles of Saratoga," 62–63; Morrissey, *Saratoga*, 74–77; Elting, *Battles of Saratoga*, 61; Thomas Blake journal entry, October 7, 1777, in Kidder, *History of the First New Hampshire Regiment*, 36; journal entry for October 7, 1777, in Dearborn, *Journals*, 108; Van Cortlandt, *Revolutionary War Memoir of Philip van Cortlandt*, 48; John Glover to William Heath, October 9, 1777, in Heath Papers, Reel 6, DLAR; and Nathaniel Bacheller to his wife, October 9, 1777, copy in the collection of the Saratoga National Historical Park. Wilkinson's account, and thus the accounts of most historians, indicates that the American forces were deployed brigade by brigade on October 7, but

evidence suggests that Gates instead deployed them in a piecemeal fashion just as he had on September 19. On October 7, Gates sent Morgan and Dearborn around Burgoyne's right and two, or more likely three, of Poor's three New Hampshire regiments against the enemy's left. This was almost identical to the initial deployment of American forces on September 19, 1777. I am indebted to Eric Schnitzer, chief historian at the Saratoga National Battlefield, for helping clarify the deployment of American troops on October 7, 1777. Email exchange between the author and Eric Schnitzer, March 10, 12, and 16, 2017.

54. Captain Thomas Blomefield testimony, in Burgoyne, STOE, 92.
55. Email from Eric Schnitzer to the author, March 16, 2017.
56. Friedrich Wilhelm von Geismar to his father, October 20, 1777, in Helga Boie, trans., "From Proud War Hero to Humble Prisoner: A Letter from Captain von Geismar to his Father," *Hessians: Journal of Johannes Schwalm Historical Association* 6 (1997): 60.
57. Journal entry, October 7, 1777, in Pausch, *Journal*, 166–67.
58. Pausch, *Journal*, 167n; and Kidder, *History of the First New Hampshire*, 22.
59. Journal entry, October 7, 1777, in Pausch, *Journal*, 167. See also Roger Lamb journal entry, October 7, 1777, in Lamb, *Journal of Occurrences*, 163.
60. Burgoyne to Germain, October 20, 1777, DAR, Vol. 14: 232. See also journal entry, October 7, 1777, in Dearborn, *Journals*, 108.
61. Schnitzer, "Tactics of the Battles of Saratoga," 64; Morrissey, *Saratoga*, 74–77; and Elting, *Battles of Saratoga*, 61.
62. Nathaniel Bacheller to his wife, October 9, 1777, Saratoga National Historical Park. The original of the previously unknown Bacheller letter was discovered for sale on eBay by the Saratoga National Battlefield staff in January 2016. The staff made a copy and it was transcribed by Chief Historian Eric Schnitzer on January 28, 2016.
63. Ibid. The most reasonable assessment of the evidence suggests that Scammell's regiment was the last of Poor's first three New Hampshire units to be sent into battle on October 7, or it was on the left of the brigade as they deployed to attack Burgoyne's left flank. Either way, Gates was concerned about the potential of friendly fire from Morgan's men. The rest of Poor's brigade—the New York regiments and Connecticut militia—went in later.
64. Ibid. Bacheller's eyewitness account provides proof that Gates exerted active command and control over the Battle of Bemis Heights and that Arnold and Gates had reconciled at least to the point of being able to work with each other, and perhaps beyond that. This important piece of evidence, from a known reliable source, changes the standard account of the second battle of Saratoga, and especially Gates's part in it. The fact that Wilkinson and Gates had a serious falling out in the months after Burgoyne's surrender further calls into question the veracity of some of Wilkinson's claims about the Arnold-Gates feud and Gates's conduct of the battles.
65. Oliver Wolcott to Jonathan Trumbull, October 10, 1777, in "Trumbull Papers," 159.
66. Journal entry, October 7, 1777, in Pausch, *Journal*, 170–71.
67. Burgoyne to Germain, October 20, 1777, in DAR, Vol. 14: 232.
68. The standard account is that Simon Fraser was shot by Timothy Murphy, one of Morgan's men, from a distance of up to a quarter mile, which would have made it an incredible feat of marksmanship, even for an elite rifleman. Various versions of this story have been repeated by historians over the years, often without any attribution. The truth is that we just do not know who shot Fraser late on October 7, 1777. It might well have been a rifleman, or it could have been a regular Continental soldier, or a militiaman who fired the fatal shot. It could even have been a friendly fire incident. Hugh T. Harrington and Jim Jordan, "The Other Mystery Shot of the American Revolution: Did Timothy Murphy Kill British Brigadier General Simon Fraser at Saratoga?" *Journal of Military History* 74 (October 2010): 1037–45.
69. Journal entry, October 7, 1777, in Digby, *British Invasion from the North*, 287–88.
70. Ibid., 288.

71. Schnitzer, "Tactics of the Battles of Saratoga," 64–65; Morrissey, *Saratoga*, 74–75, 77–78; Elting, *Battles of Saratoga*, 62; Martin, *Benedict Arnold*, 396–97; Lamb journal entry, October 7, 1777, in *Journal of Occurrences*, 163; journal entry, October 7, 1777, in Digby, *British Invasion from the North*, 287–88; and Burgoyne to Germain, October 20, 1777, in DAR, Vol. 14: 232–33.
72. Schnitzer, "Tactics of the Battles of Saratoga," 64–65; Morrissey, *Saratoga*, 74–75, 77–78; Elting, *Battles of Saratoga*, 62; and Martin, *Benedict Arnold*, 396–97.
73. Quoted in Schnitzer, "Tactics of the Battles of Saratoga," 65.
74. Dearborn to Wilkinson, December 20, 1815, *Bulletin of the Fort Ticonderoga Museum*, 9; Martin, *Benedict Arnold*, 400; journal entry, October 7, 1777, in Dearborn, *Journals*, 108–9; and Gates to Hancock, October 12, 1777, in HGP, Reel 5.
75. Samuel Armstrong diary entry, October 7, 1777, Armstrong, "From Saratoga to Valley Forge," 248.
76. Ibid.
77. Burgoyne's army suffered 278 killed in action on October 7, and the Americans lost more than 30 killed in action. Casualty figures taken from Morrissey, *Saratoga*, 80.
78. Burgoyne to Germain, October 20, 1777, in DAR, Vol. 14: 233.
79. Lincoln quoted in Mattern, *Benjamin Lincoln*, 48.
80. Lincoln quoted in Elting, *Battles of Saratoga*, 63.
81. Journal entry for October 8, 1777, in Digby, *British Invasion from the North*, 292.
82. Elting, *Battles of Saratoga*, 63; and Mattern, *Benjamin Lincoln*, 49. The troops that fired on Lincoln may well have been Hessen-Hanau soldiers, but the evidence is not clear.
83. Journal entry, October 8, 1777, in Digby, *British Invasion from the North*, 293.
84. Frederike Riedesel, *Baroness von Riedesel and the American Revolution: Journal and Correspondence of a Tour of Duty, 1776–1783*, edited and translated by Marvin L. Brown, Jr. (Chapel Hill: University of North Carolina Press, 1965), 51–52.
85. Ibid., 52, and journal entry, October 8, 1777, in Digby, *British Invasion from the North*, 293.
86. F. C. Riedesel, *Journal and Correspondence of a Tour of Duty*, 53.

CHAPTER 21

1. Journal entry, October 8, 1777, in Digby, *British Invasion from the North*, 295–96.
2. Unknown German officer journal entry, October 9, 1777, in Barker, "Battles of Saratoga and the Kinderhook Tea Party," 37. See also Balcarres testimony, in Burgoyne, STOE, 43.
3. F. C. Riedesel, *Letters and Journals*, 123.
4. Anton Adolph Heinrich Du Roi (attrib.) journal entry, October 8–9, 1777, in Doblin, *Specht Journal*, 93.
5. Burgoyne "review of the evidence," in Burgoyne, STOE, 170.
6. Anton Adolph Heinrich Du Roi (attrib.) journal entry, October 8–9, 1777, in Doblin, *Specht Journal*, 93.
7. Burgoyne "review of the evidence," in Burgoyne, STOE, 170–74, and Dearborn to Wilkinson, December 20, 1815, in *Bulletin of the Fort Ticonderoga Museum*, 11. Major Acland recovered and was extremely grateful to his captors for their kind treatment.
8. Unknown German officer journal entry, October 9, 1777, in Barker, "Battles of Saratoga and the Kinderhook Tea Party," 37.
9. Balcarres testimony, in Burgoyne, STOE, 43–44 and 170; diary entry, October 9, 1777, in Armstrong, "From Saratoga to Valley Forge," 250; Anton Adolph Heinrich Du Roi (attrib.) journal entry, October 8–9, 1777, in Doblin, *Specht Journal*, 92–93; Gates to Hancock, October 12, 1777, in HGP, Reel 5; Burgoyne to Germain, October 20, 1777, in DAR, Vol. 14: 233; Blake journal entry, October 8–9, 1777, in Kidder, *History of the Forts New Hampshire Regiment*, 37; journal entry, October 9–10, 1777, in Dearborn, *Journals*, 110; Morrissey, *Saratoga*, 81–82; and Elting, *Battles of Saratoga*, 63–64.
10. Doblin, *Specht Journal*, 95. Unlike the British, the Germans were unable to dig in due to the hard ground.
11. Gates to Hancock, October 12, 1777, in HGP, Reel 5.

12. Burgoyne to German, October 20, 1777, in DAR, Vol. 14: 233; and Kingston testimony, in Burgoyne, STOE, 108–9.
13. Morrissey, *Saratoga*, 82–84; Elting, *Battles of Saratoga*, 65; Dearborn to Wilkinson, December 20, 1815, in *Bulletin of the Fort Ticonderoga Museum*, 11; and Matthew Kirk and Justin Divirgilio, "The Retreat to Victory Woods," in *The Saratoga Campaign: Uncovering an Embattled Landscape*, ed. William A. Griswold and Donald W. Linebaugh (Hanover, NH: University Press of New England, 2016), 150–51.
14. Morrissey, *Saratoga*, 82–84; Elting, *Battles of Saratoga*, 65; and Kirk and Divirgilio, "The Retreat to Victory Woods,", 150–51.
15. Journal entry, October 10, 1777, in Digby, *British Invasion from the North*, 302.
16. Journal entry, October 11 and 12, 1777, in ibid., 304.
17. Roger Lamb journal entry, October 11, 1777, in Lamb, *Journal of Occurrences*, 166.
18. Gates to Hancock, October 12, 1777, in HGP, Reel 5.
19. Roger Lamb journal entry, October 11, 1777, in Lamb, *Journal of Occurrences*, 166.
20. Ibid.
21. "Minutes of a council of war held on the Heights of Saratoga, October 12th, 1777," in DAR, Vol. 14: 212–14.
22. Ibid. Riedesel claimed later that he held out for the immediate night retreat, and he was furious that Burgoyne canceled the breakout, arguing that on October 12, "*the retreat was possible.*" Major General Riedesel, *Memoirs*, 178.
23. Burgoyne to Germain, October 20, 1777, in DAR, Vol. 14: 234.
24. Gates to Hancock, October 12, 1777, in HGP, Reel 5.
25. Other than his perfunctory October 5 reply to Washington's request for Morgan's riflemen, Gates had not sent a meaningful report to Washington in over almost six weeks.
26. Anton Adolph Heinrich Du Roi (attrib.) journal entry. October 13, 1777, in Doblin, *Specht Journal*, 96.
27. Bayley reported on October 14 that he had occupied Fort Edward with twenty-two hundred men, all in good "health and high spirits," and that he would intercept any of Burgoyne's units passing through the area to reach Fort George. Bayley to Gates, October 14, 1777, in HGP, Reel 5. See also Harrington testimony, in Burgoyne, STOE, 74.
28. Anton Adolph Heinrich Du Roi (attrib.) journal entry, October 13, 1777, in Doblin, *Specht Journal*, 96–97.
29. Journal entry, October 13, 1777, in Digby, *British Invasion from the North*, 305.
30. "Minutes and proceedings of a council of war consisting of all the general officers and field-officers and captains commanding corps on the Heights of Saratoga, October 13th 1777," in DAR, Vol. 14: 214. See also Major General Riedesel, *Memoirs*, 180; and Balcarres testimony, in Burgoyne, STOE, 44.
31. Phillips to Henry Clinton, October 25, 1777, in HCP; and Kingston testimony, in Burgoyne, STOE, 109–10.
32. Burgoyne to Gates, October 13, 1777, in HGP, Reel 5.
33. Wilkinson, *Memoirss*, Vol. 1, 299–300. Wilkinson's central role in the surrender negotiations is verified by several other sources including Thacher, *Military Journal*, 130.
34. Burgoyne message to Gates, October 14, 1777, in Digby, *British Invasion from the North*, 306–7; Wilkinson, *Memoirss*, Vol. 1, 302; and HGP, Reel 5.
35. Wilkinson, *Memoirss*, Vol. 1, 302; and Gates to Burgoyne, October 14, 1777, in HGP, Reel 5.
36. Burgoyne to Gates, October 14, 1777, in HGP, 5.
37. Burgoyne to Gates, preliminary articles, October 14, 1777, in ibid.
38. Riedesel journal entry for October 15, 1777, Major General Riedesel, *Memoirs, and Letters*, 182.
39. Ibid. See also Proposed Articles of Convention, October 14 and 15, 1777, in HGP, Reel 5.
40. Putnam to Gates, October 11, 1777, Jonathan Trumbull to Gates, October 11, 1777, George Clinton to Gates, October 11, 1777, Putnam to Gates, October 13, 1777, John M. Scott to Gates, October 15, 1777, in ibid.

41. Putnam immediately informed Washington that Burgoyne had surrendered and only found out later that the news was premature. Gates to Putnam, and Gates to George Clinton, October 15, 1777, in HGP, Reel 5.
42. James Craig to James Wilkinson, October 15, 1777, ibid; Burgoyne to Gates, October 15, 1777, in ibid; and Wilkinson, *Memoirs of My Own Times*, Vol. 1, 310–11. See also Nelson, *Horatio Gates*, 140; and Hargrove, *General John Burgoyne*, 200–201.
43. Journal entry, October 16, 1777, in Major General Riedesel, *Memoirs*, 183.
44. Burgoyne to Gates, October 16, 1777, in HGP, Reel 5.
45. Wilkinson to Burgoyne, October 16, 1777, in Wilkinson, *Memoirs*, Vol. 1, 313.
46. Journal entry, October 16, 1777, Riedesel, *Memoirs*, 184. See also Nelson, *Horatio Gates*, 141; and Hargrove, *General John Burgoyne*, 201.
47. William Phillips to Henry Clinton, October 25, 1777, in HCP.
48. Captain von Geismar to his father, October 20, 1777, in Boie, "From Proud War Hero to Humble Prisoner," 61; and Major General Riedesel, *Memoirss*, 188. Some British colors were not surrendered either. Corporal Lamb of the 9th Regiment reported that his regimental colors were sewed into the lining of a mattress and the commander later presented them to the king. Mercer, "The 9th (East Norfolk) Regiment of Foot," 58.
49. Major General Riedesel, *Memoirs*, 187.
50. Journal entry, October 17, 1777, in Digby, *British Invasion from the North*, 319.
51. Articles of Convention, October 16, 1777, in HGP, Reel 5.
52. Burgoyne, May 26, 1778, speech to the House of Commons, in Burgoyne, *The Substance of General Burgoyne's Speeches*, 31.
53. Digby, journal entry for October 17, 1777, in Digby, *British Invasion from the North*, 317.
54. Napier journal entry, October 17, 1777, in Bradford, "Napier's Journal," 328.
55. Journal entry, October 17, 1777, in Digby, *British Invasion from the North*, 317–19.
56. Ibid., 321–23.
57. Wilkinson, *Memoirs*, Vol. 1, 321.
58. Anton Adolph Heinrich Du Roi (attrib.) journal entry, October 13, 1777, in Doblin, *Specht Journal*, 102; and Ketchum, *Saratoga*, 429.
59. Nelson, *General Horatio Gates*, 143.
60. F.C. Riedesel, *Letters and Journals*, 134–35.
61. Journal entry, October 17, 1777, in Digby, *British Invasion from the North*, 320. See also Scott Stull, Michael Rogers, and Len Tantillo, "The Surrender and Aftermath of the Battles," in *The Saratoga Campaign: Uncovering an Embattled Landscape*, ed. William A. Griswold and Donald W. Linebaugh (Lebanon, NH: University Press of New England, 2016), 168.
62. Anton Adolph Heinrich Du Roi (attrib.) journal entry, October 17, 1777, in Doblin, *Specht Journal*, 101.
63. Gates general orders for the army, October 17, 1777, in Daniel Morgan Papers, Film 568, Reel 2, DLAR.
64. Journal entry, October 17, 1777, in Bradford, "Napier's Journal," 324. See also journal entry, October 17, 1777, in Digby, *British Invasion from the North*, 324; and Anton Adolph Heinrich Du Roi (attrib.) journal entry, October 17, 1777, in Doblin, *Specht Journal*, 101–2.
65. Captain von Geismar to his father, October 20, 1777, in Boie, "From Proud War Hero to Humble Prisoner," 61.
66. Journal entry, October 18, 1777, in Thacher, *Military Journal*, 131.
67. Journal entry, October 17, 1777, in Dearborn, *Journals*, 111.
68. John Nixon to William Heath, October 22, 1777, in Heath Papers, Reel 6, DLAR.
69. Stull, et al., "The Surrender and Aftermath of the Battles," 167.
70. Anton Adolph Heinrich Du Roi (attrib.) journal entry, October 17, 1777, in Doblin, *Specht Journal*, 101.
71. Morrissey, *Saratoga*, 84–87.
72. Gates to Hancock, October 18, 1777, in HGP, Reel 5.

73. Ibid.
74. Gates to President of the Massachusetts Council, October 19, 1777, in ibid.
75. George Clinton to Gates and Poor to Gates, both October 25, 1777, in ibid., Reel 6.
76. Gates to Elizabeth Gates, October 20, 1777, in ibid., Reel 6.
77. Burgoyne to Germain, October 20, 1777, in DAR, Vol. 14: 228–36.
78. Burgoyne to Germain, October 20, 1777, in DAR, Vol. 14: 228–36. Clinton was upset when he learned that Burgoyne had complained that Sir Henry had promised to attack the Hudson Highlands in ten days. Clinton to William Phillips, December 11, 1777, in HCP.
79. Burgoyne to Germain, October 20, 1777, in DAR, Vol. 14: 228–36.
80. Ibid.
81. Riedesel memorandum, May 8, 1778, in Major General Riedesel, *Memoirs*, 209.
82. Burgoyne to Richard Burton Phillipson, October 20, 1777, in Montagu, *Private Papers of John, Earl of Sandwich*, Vol. 1, 306–10.
83. Burgoyne, May 26, 1778, speech to the House of Commons, in Burgoyne, *The Substance of General Burgoyne's Speeches*, 9–10.
84. Burgoyne to Henry Clinton, October 25, 1777, in HCP.
85. General Orders, October 18, 1777, in GWP, Vol. 11: 541.
86. Washington to Hancock, October 18, 1777, in ibid., 545.
87. John Adams to Abigail Adams, October 24, 1777, in LDC, Vol. 8: 170. See also Hancock to Washington, October 25, 1777, in ibid., 181.
88. Stirling inherited his title through the Scottish aristocracy and was one of Washington's most capable generals. Thomas Fleming, *Washington's Secret War: The Hidden History of Valley Forge* (New York: Harper Collins, 2005), 90; Chernow, *Washington*, 317–18; and Lord Stirling to Washington, November 3, 1777, in GWP, Vol. 12: 111n.
89. John Adams to Abigail Adams, October 28, 1777, in LDC, Vol. 8: 205.
90. Richard Henry Lee to Patrick Henry, October 28, 1777, in ibid., 208.
91. Charles Thomson to Washington, October 31, 1777, in GWP, Vol. 12: 71; and Nelson, *Horatio Gates*, 144. Note, on the same date, Howe's army in Philadelphia learned of Burgoyne's surrender. ournal entry, October 31, 1777, in Muenchhausen, *At Howe's Side*, 42; and diary entry, November 2, 1777, in Peebles, *John Peebles' American War*, 147.
92. Richard Henry Lee and James Lovell to American Commissioners at Paris, October 31, 1777, in LDC, Vol. 8: 216.
93. Wilkinson address to Congress, November 3, 1777, in HGP, Reel 5.
94. Resolutions of Congress, November 4, 1777, in Ford, *Journals of Congress*, Vol. 9, 861–62.
95. Laurens to Gates, November 5, 1777, in HGP, Reel 5.
96. *Boston Gazette* edition of October 23, 1777, in Moore, *Diary of the American Revolution*, Vol. 1, 513–14.
97. Eliphalet Dyer to Gates, November 5, 1777, in LDC, Vol. 8: 234.
98. James Lovell to Gates, November 5, 1777, ibid, 238.
99. Benjamin Rush to John Adams, October 21, 1777, in Taylor, *Papers of John Adams*, Vol. 5, 316–17.
100. Henry Powell to Germain, November 8 and 9, 1777, in DAR, Vol. 14: 253–54; and Cubbison, *The Artillery Never Gained More Honour*, 138–41.

CHAPTER 22

1. Simms, *Three Victories and a Defeat*, 610. This chapter is adapted with permission from Kevin J. Weddle, "'A Change of Both Men and Measures': British Reassessment of Military Strategy after Saratoga, 1777–1778," *Journal of Military History* 77, no. 3 (July 2013): 837–65.
2. Paul Langford, *A Polite and Commercial People: England, 1727–1783* (London: Guild Publishing, 1989), 541–42.
3. Hugh Percy, 2nd Duke of Northumberland to Sir Henry Clinton, December 8, 1777, in HCP.

4. William Cobbett, *Parliamentary History of England,* Vol. 19 (London: T. C. Hansard, 1806–1820), 354.
5. King George III, November 20, 1777, Cobbett, *Parliamentary History of England,* Vol. 19, 354–56.
6. Chatham speech in the Lords, Cobbett, *Parliamentary History,* Vol. 19, 363–67. See also Jeremy Black, *Pitt the Elder* (Cambridge: Cambridge University Press, 1992).
7. Mackesy, *War for America,* 147.
8. Unknown agent to William Eden, November 30, 1777, in Auckland Papers, British Library; Add Mss 34414, Reel 2, DLAR.
9. Journal entry, December 2, 1777, in Walpole, *Journal of the Reign of King George the Third,* Vol. 2, 170.
10. Germain, December 3, 1777, in Cobbett, *Parliamentary History,* Vol. 19, 533–34.
11. Ibid., 537–38.
12. Ibid., 540.
13. Ibid., 541.
14. Ibid., 486.
15. Sandwich was a capable administrator who played a major role in the strategic reassessment in early 1778. N. A. M Rodger, *The Insatiable Earl: A Life of John Montagu, 4th Earl of Sandwich* (New York: W. W. Norton, 1994).
16. Howe to Germain, October 22, 1777 (received December 1, 1777), in GGP.
17. Germain to Howe, February 4, 1778 (received March 27, 1778), in ibid.
18. Carleton to Germain, October 16, 1777, and November 6, 1777, in DAR, Vol. 14: 217–19 and 247–48.
19. Cobbett, *Parliamentary History,* Vol. 19, 612–13.
20. General Sir Frederick Haldimand replaced Carleton and Admiral John Gambier relieved Lord Howe. Germain to the Lords of the Admiralty, April 12, 1778, in Colonial Office Papers, CO5/254, DLAR; and Sandwich to Gambier, April 13, 1778, in Montagu, *The Private Papers of John, Earl of Sandwich,* 292–93.
21. Howe to Germain, November 20, 1777 (received January 17, 1778), in GGP. By the end of the Philadelphia campaign, Howe had essentially stopped using any initiative. He wrote to Germain on January 17, 1778, that he was at a loss on what to do next "without the knowledge of His Majesty's pleasure." This was an odd admission from a commander-in-chief. Howe to Germain, January 17, 1778, in ibid.
22. King to North, December 4, 1777, in W. Bodham Dunne, ed., *The Correspondence of King George the Third with Lord North, 1763–1783,* Vol. 2 (New York: De Capo Press, 1971), 92.
23. J. C. Long, *Lord Jeffrey Amherst: A Soldier to the King* (New York: Macmillan, 1933).
24. Taffe, *Philadelphia Campaign*; and Clement, *Philadelphia, 1777.*
25. Sandwich to North, December 7, 1777, in John Montagu, *The Private Papers of John, Earl of Sandwich, First Lord of the Admiralty, 1771–1782,* Vol. 1, ed. G. R. Barnes and J. H. Owens (London: Navy Records Society, 1932), 327–35.
26. All quotes are taken from Sandwich to North, December 7, 1777, in ibid., 327–35. See also Rodger, *The Insatiable Earl,* 237; and Montagu, *Private Papers of John, Earl of Sandwich,* 337–39.
27. Spencer to North, unknown date, but probably late December 1777 or early January 1778, in Auckland Papers, BL, Add Mss 34414, Reel 2, DLAR.
28. Spencer to Eden, January 8, 1778, ibid.
29. George III to North, January 13, 1778, in Donne, *The Correspondence of King George the Third,* Vol. 2, 118–19. Piers Mackesy argues that after Saratoga "the King recognized that the political object of the war had to be lowered." Although he is correct that the Carlisle Commission was authorized to give the Americans almost anything except independence, full independence remained non-negotiable. Piers Mackesy, *The War for America, 1775–1783* (Lincoln: University of Nebraska Press, 1993), 159.

30. George III to North, January 13, 1778, in Donne, *Correspondence of King George the Third*, Vol. 2, 118–19. Before March 1778, when he was appointed general in chief, Amherst was a trusted advisor outside the formal chain of command.
31. Cabinet Minutes, January 17, 1778, in Fortescue, *The Correspondence of King George the Third*, Vol. 4, 20–21. See also North to George III, January 18, 1778, in ibid., 21.
32. For the origins of the so-called "Southern Strategy," see Mackesy, *War for America*, 157; and Black, "British Military Strategy," 62–63, 67.
33. George III to North, January 31, 1778, Donne, *Correspondence of King George the Third*, Vol. 2, 125–26; and George III to North, February 2, 1778, ibid., 129.
34. Cobbett, *Parliamentary History*, Vol. 19, 762–67.
35. Ibid., 767.
36. Ibid., 769, 771–72, 774, 775, and 803.
37. Mackesy, *War for America, 1775–1783*, 159. For a good discussion of the Carlisle Peace Commission, see Chris Tudda, "'A Messiah that Will Never Come': A New Look at Saratoga, Independence, and Revolutionary War Diplomacy," *Diplomatic History* 32 (November 2008): 779–810.
38. George III to North, February 5, 1778, in Donne, *The Correspondence of King George the Third*, Vol. 2, 133.
39. North to Sandwich, March 2, 1778, and Sandwich to North, March 6, 1778, in Monatagu, *Private Papers of John, Earl of Sandwich*, 347, 349–52.
40. Germain to Clinton, March 8, 1777, in GGP. For the Southern Strategy and British assumptions of the degree of Loyalist sentiment in the South, see David K. Wilson, *The Southern Strategy: Britain's Conquest of South Carolina and Georgia, 1775–1780* (Columbia: University of South Carolina Press, 2005), 59–64; and John Shy, *A People Numerous and Armed: Reflections on the Military Struggle for American Independence* (New York: Oxford University Press, 1976), 185.
41. George III to North, March 13, 1778, in Donne, *The Correspondence of King George the Third*, Vol. 2, 148.
42. George III to North, March 3, 1778, in ibid., 142–43.
43. George III to North, March 17, 1778, in ibid., 152–53.
44. "Considerations with Regard to the Invasion, and Defence of Ireland in Case of a Rupture with France," March 27, 1778, in Pelham Papers, 33118, fo. 33, British Library.
45. North to George III, March 25, 1778, in Fortescue, *Correspondence of King George the Third*, Vol. 4, 77–78.
46. North to George III, March 15, 1778, in Fortescue, *Correspondence of King George the Third*, Vol. 4, 56–57.
47. George III to North, March 15, 1778, in ibid., 57–58.
48. The king and North continued their correspondence over North's status as prime minister for several days. George III to North, March 16, 1778, in Donne, *The Correspondence of King George the Third*, 149–50; North to George III, March 16, 1778, in Fortescue, *Correspondence of King George the Third*, Vol. 4, 59; George III to North, March 16, 1778,in ibid., 59–60; North to George III, March 16, 1778,in ibid., 60–61; North to George III, March 21, 1778, in ibid., 70–72; George III to North, March 21, 1778, in ibid., 72; Weymouth to George III, March 30, 1778,in ibid., 86–87; North to George III, April 1, 1778,in ibid., 92; and George III to North, April 8, 1778, in ibid., 100–101.
49. "Lord Amherst's Idea about Change of War in America," a memorandum in the papers of Lord Sandwich, no date, but probably in mid- to late March 1778, in Montagu, *The Private Papers of John, Earl of Sandwich*, 361–65. See Mackesy, *The War for America*, 185 for a discussion of the king's consideration and rejection of a total evacuation of America in early 1778.
50. Cabinet Meeting Notes for March 14, 1778 (attendees included North, Germain, Amherst, Sandwich, Weymouth, and Suffolk), in Montagu, *The Private Papers of John, Earl of Sandwich*, 361; Cabinet Meeting Notes for March 18, 1778 (attendees included North,

Germain, Sandwich, Amherst, and Weymouth), in ibid., 363–64. See also Mackesy, *The War for America*, 184–85.

51. "Secret Instructions for General Sir Henry Clinton," March 21, 1778, in Colonial Office Papers, DLAR.
52. Germain to Clinton, March 21, 1778, in Colonial Office Papers, DLAR. Three weeks later, Germain sent instructions for the defense of Canada to the new commander, General Sir Frederick Haldimand. See Germain to Haldimand, April 16, 1778, ibid. Clinton received both sets of instructions on May 9, 1778, the day after he arrived in Philadelphia to assume his new role as commander-in-chief. Clinton, *The American Rebellion*, 86.
53. Mackesy, *The War for America*, 183.
54. With the French entry into the war, the imbalance between British ends and means was significant and pointed to strategic failure. Holcomb, "Managing Strategic Risk," 67.
55. For a short time during this period the king reconsidered American independence, but this was not pursued. King to North, March 27, 1778 in Donne, *Correspondence of King George the Third*, Vol. 2, 161 and Mackasy, *War for America*, 187–88.
56. Clausewitz, *On War*, 92.
57. Laurens to Gates, June 17, 1778, in Commager and Morris, *Spirit of 'Seventy-Six*, 697–98.
58. George III to North, August 12, 1778, in Bonamy Dobree, ed., *The Letters of King George III* (New York: Funk and Wagnalls, 1935), 125. The Carlisle Commission had little chances of success no matter what they offered the Americans. Not only was independence not on the table after Saratoga, but the evacuation of Philadelphia by British forces occurred almost simultaneously with the commission's arrival in America, further undercutting their mission. See Willcox, "British Strategy in America, 1778," 106.
59. Colin Gray, *Schools for Strategy: Teaching Strategy for 21st Century Conflict* (Carlisle, PA: Strategic Studies Institute, November 2009), 3.

CHAPTER 23

1. Washington to Benjamin Lincoln, October 26, 1777, in GWP, Vol. 12: 19.
2. Washington to Israel Putnam, October 26, 1777, in ibid., 21.
3. Washington to Richard Henry Lee, October 28, 1777, in ibid., 41.
4. Washington to Gates, October 30, 1777, in GWP, Vol. 12: 59–60.
5. Washington to Hamilton, October 30, 1777, in ibid., 60–61.
6. Gates to Washington, November 2, 1777, in ibid., 93.
7. Gates's biographer and other historians forgive his failure to keep Washington informed and pass it off as a mere breach of protocol, since the Northern Department commander "was directly under orders from Congress." However, on August 23, 1777, Congress reaffirmed that Washington was "the commander-in-chief of all the continental land forces within the United States." This included the Northern Department. Nelson, *Horatio Gates*, 145–46; and Congressional Resolution of August 23, 1777, in JCC, Vol. 8: 668.
8. Gates to Washington, November 2, 1777, in GWP, Vol. 12: 93.
9. Alexander Hamilton to Gates, November 5, 1777, in AHP, Vol. 1: 352.
10. Alexander Hamilton to Washington, November 6, 1777, in ibid., 353–54.
11. Ron Chernow, *Alexander Hamilton* (New York: Penguin Press, 2004), 102.
12. Gates to Washington, November 7, 1777, in GWP, Vol. 12: 154–55 and 155n.
13. Howe, *Narrative of Lieutenant General Sir William Howe*, 19, 21, and 61; Taaffe, *Philadelphia Campaign*, 93–107; and Clement, *Philadelphia, 1777: Taking the Capital*, 36–85.
14. Washington to William Heath, November 13, 1777, in GWP, Vol. 12: 238–40. Both American and British governments accused the other of not living up to the letter and spirit of the Saratoga Convention, which ensured that Burgoyne's army never made it home until the end of the war.
15. Fleming, *Washington's Secret War*, 100; Thomas Mifflin to Gates, November 17, 1777, in HGP, Reel 6; and Anthony Wayne to Gates, November 21, 1777, in ibid.
16. Stirling to Washington, November 3, 1777, in GWP, Vol. 12: 111n.

17. Washington to Richard Henry Lee, October 16, 1777, in ibid., Vol. 11: 529.
18. Washington to Thomas Conway, November 5, 1777, in ibid, Vol. 12: 129.
19. Thomas Conway to Washington, November 5, 1777, in ibid., Vol. 12: 130–31.
20. Thomas Mifflin to Gates, November 28, 1777, in HGP, Reel 6; and Fleming, *Washington's Secret War*, 118.
21. Fleming, *Washington's Secret War*, 118.
22. Gates to Washington, December 8, 1777, in GWP, Vol. 12: 577.
23. Gates to Henry Laurens, December 8, 1777, in ibid., 577n.
24. Lovell to Gates, November 27, 1777, in HGP, Reel 6.
25. Chernow, *Washington*, 319–20; and Fleming, *Washington's Secret War*, 119–22.
26. Washington to Gates, January 4, 1778, in GWP, Vol. 13: 138–40; and Fleming, *Washington's Secret War*, 148.
27. Gates to Washington, January 23, 1777, in GWP, Vol. 13: 319–22.
28. Washington to Gates, February 9, 1777, in GWP, Vol. 13: 484–87.
29. Gates to Washington, February 19, 1777, in ibid., 590.
30. Washington to Gates, February 24, 1778, in ibid., 654–55.
31. Chernow, *George Washington*, 320.
32. Washington to Patrick Henry, March 28, 1778, in GWP, Vol. 14: 336–37.
33. Quoted in Chernow, *George Washington*, 322.
34. Ibid., 321–22. Whether or not the so-called "Conway Cabal" was really an organized attempt to oust Washington is an open historical debate. Thomas Fleming argues that there was a conspiracy to bring down the commander-in-chief. Fleming, *Washington's Secret War*, 118. Ron Chernow suggests that it was something less and called it instead a "loosely organized network of foes"; *Washington*, 320. Gates's biographer argues that he was basically an innocent bystander to the apparent intrigue by others; Nelson, *Horatio Gates*, 157–85. The author is convinced that if Gates was not an active conspirator, he was at least an ambitious opportunist who saw in his success and Washington's setbacks a chance for advancement. Washington was right to be wary of him.
35. "The American Commissioners: A Public Announcement," December 4, 1777, in William B. Willcox, ed., *The Papers of Benjamin Franklin*, Vol. 25, October 1, 1777, through February 28, 1778 (New Haven, CT: Yale University Press, 1986), 234–36. See also Herring, *From Colony to Superpower*, 20–21.
36. Vergennes to Noailles, December 6, 1777, no. 1760, in Stevens, *Stevens's Facsimiles of Manuscripts*, Vol. 19. Heinonline.org. Most historians agree that the American victory at Saratoga was the decisive factor in convincing France to openly intervene in the war, but Richard W. Van Alstyne, *Empire and Independence: The International History of the American Revolution* (New York: John Wiley and Sons, 1967); Jonathan R. Dull, *The French Navy and American Independence: A Study in Arms and Diplomacy, 1774–1787* (Princeton, NJ: Princeton University Press, 1975); and Tudda, "'A Messiah that Will Never Come': A New Look at Saratoga, Independence, and Revolutionary War Diplomacy," *Diplomatic History* 32 (November 2008):: 779–810, argue that it was not all that important. However, without Burgoyne's surrender, it is doubtful that the circumstances that Vergennes was looking for would ever have come together. It is clear to the author that the victory at Saratoga, if not sufficient, was necessary to secure open French support and ultimate victory.
37. Journal entry, December 6, 1777, in Richard Henry Lee, *Life of Arthur Lee, LL.D.* (Boston: Wells and Lilly, 1829), 111–12 and 357–58.
38. Statement by Vergennes marked "approved" by Louis XVI, December 6, 1777, no. 1762, Stevens, *Stevens's Facsimiles of Manuscripts*, Vol. 20. Heinonline.org
39. "Memorial to Count Vergennes," December 8, 1777, in Lee, *Life of Arthur Lee*, 111–12 and 358; and American Commissioners to Vergennes, December 8, 1777, Willcox, *Papers of Benjamin Franklin*, Vol. 25, 260–62, 261n.
40. Pierre Beaumarchais to Vergennes, December 11, 1777, no. 1768, ibid., Vol. 20. Heinonline.org. The phrase "ce moment accomplit tout" translates to "this moment accomplishes everything" or "this is the decisive moment."

41. Vergennes to Armand Marc, Count of Montmorin de Saint Herem, December 11, 1777, no. 1769, Stevens, *Stevens's Facsimiles of Manuscripts*, Vol. 20. Heinonline.org. Montmorin would later replace Vergennes and lose his life during the French Revolution.
42. Journal entry, December 12, 1777, in Lee, *Life of Arthur Lee*, 360–61.
43. American Commissioners at Paris to the Committee on Foreign Affairs, December 18, 1777, in Willcox, *Papers of Benjamin Franklin*, Vol. 25, 305–309.
44. Arthur Lee to Samuel Adams, December 18, 1777, in Lee, *Life of Arthur Lee*, 114–15.
45. Ketchum, *Saratoga*, 446; Paul Wentworth to William Eden, January 7, 1778, in Willcox, *Papers of Benjamin Franklin*, Vol. 25, 435–40; and Ferling, *Almost a Miracle*, 262. See also Stormont to Thomas Thynne, 3rd Viscount Weymouth, December 6, 1777, no. 1759, in Stevens, *Stevens's Facsimiles of Manuscripts*, Vol. 19. Heinonline.org
46. American Commissioners at Paris to the Committee on Foreign Affairs, December 18, 1777, in Willcox, *Papers of Benjamin Franklin*, Vol. 25, 305–309.
47. Ibid.
48. Ibid.; Spain entered the war in 1779.
49. Vergennes to Noailles, December 20, 1777, no. 1789, in Stevens, *Stevens's Facsimiles of Manuscripts*, Vol. 20. Heinonline.org. See also Herring, *From Colony to Superpower*, 21.
50. Resolves of Congress, November 22, 1777, in JCC, Vol. 9: 952.
51. Lee to Samuel Adams, December 19, 1777, in Lee, *Life of Arthur Lee*, 116.
52. Jacobus Van Zandt (alias, George Lupton) to William Eden, December 31, 1777, in Auckland Papers, BL Add MSS 34415, Reel 2, DLAR.
53. Willcox, *Papers of Benjamin Franklin*, Vol. 25, 336n.
54. Narrative of Conrad Gérard, Secretary to Vergennes, of a conference with the American commissioners, January 9, 1777, in Commager and Morris, *Spirit of 'Seventy-Six*, 682–85.
55. Ferling, *Almost a Miracle*, 263.
56. Journal entry, January 27, 1778, in Lee, *Life of Arthur Lee*, 386–91.
57. Herring, *From Colony to Superpower*, 20–22.
58. Ferling, *Almost a Miracle* 262–63; Herring, *From Colony to Superpower*, 20–21; Ketchum, *Saratoga*, 446–47; Nickerson, *Turning Point*, 412; and American Commissioners at Paris to the Committee on Foreign Affairs, February 28, 1778, Willcox, *Papers of Benjamin Franklin*, Vol. 25, 726–29.
59. Quoted in Ketchum, *Saratoga*, 447. Lee recorded that the king said, "Je serai, bien aide que le congress soit assure de mon amitié." Journal entry, March 20, 1778, in Lee, *Life of Arthur Lee*, 403. See also Ferling, *Almost a Miracle*, 263; and Nickerson, *Turning Point*, 411–12.
60. Benjamin Franklin and Silaxs Deane to the President of Congress, February 8, 1778, in Willcox, *Papers of Benjamin Franklin*, Vol. 25, 634–35.
61. Resolves of Congress, May 4, 1777, in JCC, Vol. 11: 457–58.
62. Samuel Chase to Thomas Johnson, May 3, 1778, in LDC, Vol. 9: 572.
63. Jonathan Bayard Smith to Thomas Warton, May 3, 1778, in ibid., 592.
64. Thomas Burke to Richard Caswell, May 5, 1778, in ibid., 601.
65. Richard Henry Lee to Thomas Jefferson, May 3, 1778, in Boyd, *Papers of Thomas Jefferson*, Vol. 2, 176–77.
66. Richard Henry Lee to George Washington, May 6, 1778, in GWP, Vol. 15: 62–64.
67. Oliver Wolcott to Laura Wolcott, May 9, 1778, in LDC, Vol. 9: 632.
68. Washington to William Heath, May 5, 1778, in GWP, Vol. 15: 42–43.
69. Stoker and Jones, "Colonial Military Strategy," 17–18 and 29–30.

CONCLUSION

1. Hamilton to the New York Committee of Correspondence, April 5, 1777, in AHP, Vol. 1: 220.
2. Hamilton to Gouverneur Morris, July 6, 1777, in ibid., 282.
3. In his long, multi-page memorandum, Burgoyne covered the "junction with General Howe by sea" option in a few sentences, and he essentially dismissed the proposal by

observing that "I do not conceive any expedition from the sea can be so formidable to the enemy or so effectual to close the war as an invasion from Canada by Ticonderoga." Burgoyne, "Thoughts for Conducting the War from the Side of Canada," in DAR, Vol. 14: 46. Burgoyne later complained that Germain did not consider this option, which given his original rejection of the course of action himself, was highly disingenuous. Burgoyne was as committed to the Lake Champlain-Ticonderoga-Hudson River campaign as were the king and Germain. Burgoyne, STOE, 4

4. I am indebted to David Hackett Fischer for the idea of "exercising" the mind as a way of "strengthening" grip.
5. For a discussion of the key characteristics of senior-level leadership, see Stephen J. Gerras, ed., *Strategic Leadership Primer*, 3rd ed. (Carlisle, PA: Department of Command, Leadership and Management, US Army War College, 2019), 48–54.
6. Quoted in Boatner, *Encyclopedia of the American Revolution*, 526.
7. Hugh Elliot to William Eden, January 7, 1778, in Auckland Papers, British Library, Add MSS 34415, Reel 2, DLAR.
8. Fraser to John Robinson, July 13, 1777, in "General Fraser's Account of Burgoyne's Campaign," 142.
9. Quoted in Theodore Thayer, *Nathanael Greene: Strategist of the American Revolution* (New York: Twayne, 1960), 214.
10. Journal entry, October 17, 1777, in Digby, *British Invasion from the North*, 321.
11. Journal entry, October 17, 1777, in Thacher, *Military Journal*, 131.

APPENDIX A

1. Billias, "John Burgoyne," 178–81; O'Shaughnessy, *Men Who Lost America*, 159–62; and Hargrove, *John Burgoyne*, 221–65.
2. Boatner, *Encyclopedia of the American Revolution*, 960–61.
3. Ibid., 933–34.
4. Jones, "Sir William Howe," 62–63; O'Shaughnessy, *Men Who Lost America*, 121; and Boatner, *Encyclopedia of the American Revolution*, 524–25.
5. Willcox, "Sir Henry Clinton: Paralysis of Command," 84–99; O'Shaughnessy, *Men Who Lost America*, 211–46; and Boatner, *Encyclopedia of the American Revolution*, 239–40.
6. Smith, "Sir Guy Carleton," 128–35; and Boatner, *Encyclopedia of the American Revolution*, 183.
7. O'Shaughnessy, *Men Who Lost America*, 198–203; and Boatner, *Encyclopedia of the American Revolution*, 423.
8. Hamilton to James Duane, September 6, 1780, in AHP, Vol. 2: 420–21.
9. Nelson, *Horatio Gates*, 186–295, and Billias, "Horatio Gates," 98–104.
10. Gerlach, *Proud Patriot*, 335–520; Pell, "Philip Schuyler," 69–75; and Boatner, *Encyclopedia of the American Revolution*, 992–93.
11. Chernow, *George Washington*, 347–817; and Boatner, *Encyclopedia of the American Revolution*, 1167–69.
12. Smith, *Life and Public Survives of Arthur St. Clair*, Vol. 1, 97–256; and Boatner, *Encyclopedia of the American Revolution*, 956–57.
13. Martin, *Benedict Arnold*, 403–32; Wallace, "Benedict Arnold," 183–88; and Boatner, *Encyclopedia of the American Revolution*, 28–30.
14. Mattern, *Benjamin Lincoln*, 56–218; Clifford K. Shipton, "Benjamin Lincoln: Old Reliable"; Billias, *George Washington's Generals and Opponents*, Vol. 1, 197–209; and Boatner, *Encyclopedia of the American Revolution*, 636–37.
15. Rose, *John Stark*, 135–66; and Boatner, *Encyclopedia of the American Revolution*, 1053.
16. Higginbotham, "Daniel Morgan," 303–13; and Boatner, *Encyclopedia of the American Revolution*, 736–37.
17. Boatner, *Encyclopedia of the American Revolution*, 411; and Ranzan and Hollis, *Hero of Fort Schuyler*, 90–230.

APPENDIX D

1. Sources vary widely on the orders of battle for this campaign, but Morrissey's and Schnitzer's works are the most reliable. The British order of battle for Burgoyne's main army at the beginning of the campaign is mainly from Morrissey, *Saratoga, 1777*, 19–21; and Eric Schnitzer, "Organization of the Army from Canada Commanded by Lieutenant General John Burgoyne—September 19 to October 7," 1–5. See also Hadden, *Journal*, 44–46; and Anton Adolph Heinrich Du Roi (attrib.) diary entry, May 15, in Doblin, *Specht Journal*, 42. The order of battle changed somewhat by the time of the two battles of Saratoga because of sickness, wounds, and battle losses, and is taken from Morrissey, *Saratoga*, 19–21; Schnitzer, "Organization of the Army from Canada," 1–5; Elting, *Battles of Saratoga*, 89; and Burgoyne, STOE, li. With the exception of artillery, in which Burgoyne enjoyed a distinct superiority, he was slightly outnumbered by the rebels on September 19, but with the influx of American reinforcements and his September 19 losses, the British were heavily outnumbered on October 7, 1777, and after.
2. Note that the number includes all ranks and the strength listed here is total assigned at the end of June 1777, not the number fit for duty, which was less. Digby noted in his journal that the strength of the army fit for duty was closer to about 6,900 men on June 29. Baxter, *British Invasion from the North*, 201. As of July 1, 1777, Burgoyne had 6,740 British and German infantrymen available for duty. The above organization changed slightly because of losses and garrison duties by the time the army crossed the Hudson River in early September. British returns, including sick, dated July 1, 1777, from Burgoyne, STOE, Appendix l; and Paul Kopperman, "The Numbers Game: Health Issues in the Army that Burgoyne Led to Saratoga," *New York History* 88 (Summer 2007): 261. The record shows that Burgoyne had 4,067 British officers and men and 3,016 German officers and men. This return did not include Canadians, Indians, and artillerymen. It also states that the total number of Indians never exceeded 500 warriors, which more or less agreed with Carleton's May 21, 1777, letter to Germain.
3. Morrissey, *Saratoga, 1777*, 24. The actual makeup of the three brigades at Ticonderoga is uncertain due to the confusion surrounding the evacuation of the fort on July 6, 1777. Morrissey's numbers (4,553 present and fit for duty and about 800 sick or otherwise absent) match fairly closely the last official return of the troops at the fort recorded on June 28, 1777, which indicated a total of 4,072 officers and men present for duty. See St. Clair, *Court Martial*, 10–11.
4. Order of battle for the Battle of Hubbardton from Morrissey, *Saratoga, 1777*, 22 and 25.
5. The British order of battle for Brigadier General St. Leger's force at the beginning of his expedition down the Mohawk River is from Morrissey, *Saratoga, 1777*, 23.
6. Ketchum, *Saratoga*, 332.
7. Battle of Bennington British order of battle is from Morrissey, *Saratoga*, 22.
8. The American order of battle for the Battle of Bennington is taken from Morrissey, *Saratoga*, 25–26. Morrissey does not include in his order of battle Colonel Simonds's Massachusetts militia regiment.
9. Breymann's order of battle taken from ibid., 22.
10. The American order of battle for the two Saratoga engagements is taken from Morrissey, *Saratoga*, 26–29; Eric Schnitzer, "Organization of the Army of the United States under Command of Major General Horatio Gates at Bemis Heights, 19 September 1777" (Stillwater, NY: Saratoga National Historical Park, January 2013), 1–3; Eric Schnitzer, "Organization of the Army of the United States under Command of Major General Horatio Gates at Bemis Heights, 7 October 1777" (Stillwater, NY: Saratoga National Historical Park, January 2013), 1–4 and 4n; Schnitzer, "A Review of the Organization of the Corps of Light Infantry," 1–5; and Elting, *The Battles of Saratoga*, 89–91.
11. Numbers of troops and units comprising Burgoyne's October 7, 1777, reconnaissance in force is from Schnitzer, "What's His Motivation," 8–9.

BIBLIOGRAPHY

PRIMARY SOURCES

Army Heritage and Education Center
Horatio Gates Papers

British Library
Auckland Papers
Pelham Papers

Clements Library, University of Michigan
Henry Clinton Papers
George Germain Papers

David Library of the American Revolution
Admiralty Papers
Auckland Papers (British Library)
Colonial Office Papers
Sir Jeffrey Amherst Papers
Haldimand Papers (British Library)
Samuel Benjamin Papers
Benjamin Lincoln Papers
Daniel Morgan Papers
Arthur St. Clair Papers
Philip Schuyler Papers
War Office Papers

Princeton University Library
Jonathan Trumbull Jr. Letter in the Andre de Coppet Collection

Newspapers
London Gazette
The Independent Chronicle (Boston)
The Pennsylvania Packet
Providence Gazette and Country Journal

PUBLISHED PRIMARY SOURCES

Adams, John. *Papers of John Adams.* Edited by Robert J. Taylor. Cambridge, MA: Belknap Press of Harvard University Press, 1983.

Anburey, Thomas. *Travels Through the Interior Parts of America, In a Series of Letters.* London: William Lane, 1789.

Anonymous. "Fort Ticonderoga—A Short History." *Bulletin of the Fort Ticonderoga Museum* 7 (July 1945): 26–28.

Anonymous. "Philip Skene of Skenesboro." *Bulletin of the Fort Ticonderoga Museum* 6 (January 1943): 159–69.

Armstrong, Samuel. "From Saratoga to Valley Forge: The Diary of Lt. Samuel Armstrong." Edited by Joseph Lee Boyle. *Pennsylvania Magazine of History and Biography* 121:3 (July 1997): 237–70.

Baldwin, Colonel Jeduthan. *The Revolutionary Journal of Col. Jeduthan Baldwin, 1775–1778.* Edited by Thomas Williams Baldwin. Bangor, ME: Printed for the DeBurians, 1906.

Barker, G. F. Russell, ed. *Horace Walpole: Memoirs of the Reign of King George the Third.* New York: G.P. Putnam's Sons, 1894.

Barker, Thomas M. "Braunscheigers, Hessians and Tories in the Battle of Bennington (16 August 1777): The American 'Revolution' as a Civil War." *Hessians: Journal of the Johannes Schwalm Historical Association* 10 (2007): 13–39.

Barker, Thomas M. "Braunscheigers, Hessians and Tories in the Battle of Bennington (16 August 1777) Part Two: the sequel." *Hessians: Journal of the Johannes Schwalm Historical Association* 11 (2008): 55–64.

Barker, Thomas M. "The Battles of Saratoga and the Kinderhook Tea Party: The Campaign Diary of a Junior Officer of Baron Riedesel's Musketeer Regiment in the 1777 British Invasion of New York." *Hessians: Journal of the Johannes Schwalm Historical Association* 9 (2006): 25–48.

Barker, Thomas M. "The British Invasion of New York as Seen by a Braunschweig Subaltern at Fort Ticonderoga: Some Frank Thoughts about the Campaign of Lieutenant General John Burgoyne in 1777." *Hessians: Journal of the Johannes Schwalm Historical Association* 7 (2001): 1–11.

Barker, Thomas M., and Jeffery Slade. "On the Eve of Burgoyne's Capitulation at Old Saratoga: Maps of the Emplacement of British, German and Rebel American Forces." *Hessians: Journal of the Johannes Schwalm Historical Association* 8 (2005): 1–27.

Becker, John P. *The Sexagenary: Or, Reminiscences of the Revolution.* Albany, NY: J. Munsell, 1866.

Boie, Helga, trans. Annotated by Donald M. Londahl-Schmidt. "From Proud War Hero to Humble Prisoner: A Letter from Captain Von Geismar to His Father." *Hessians: Journal of the Johannes Schwalm Historical Association* 6.1 (1997): 60–62.

Brooks, John. "Colonel Brooks and Colonel Bancroft." In *Proceedings of the Massachusetts Historical Society, 1855–1858*, 271–77. Boston: Massachusetts Historical Society, 1859.

Brown, Lloyd A., and Howard H. Peckham, eds. *Revolutionary War Journals of Henry Dearborn, 1775–1783.* New York: De Capo, 1971.

Burgoyne, John. *Orderly Book of Lieutenant-General John Burgoyne, from his Entry into the State of New York until his Surrender at Saratoga, 16th Oct. 1777.* Edited by E. B. O'Callaghan. Albany, NY: J. Munsell, 1860.

Burgoyne, John. *A State of the Expedition from Canada as Laid before the House of Commons by Lieutenant-General Burgoyne.* 2nd Ed. London: J. Almon, 1780.

Burgoyne, John. *The Substance of General Burgoyne's Speeches: On Mr. Vyner's Motion, on the 26th of May; and upon Mr. Hartley's Motion, on the 28th of May, 1778. With an Appendix, Containing General Washington's Letter to General Burgoyne. &c.* London: J. Almon, 1778.

Burke, Edmund. *The Correspondence of Edmund Burke.* Vol. 3. Edited by George H. Guttridge. Chicago: University of Chicago Press, 1961.

Burnett, Edmund C., ed. *Letters of Members of the Continental Congress.* 8 vols. Washington, DC: Carnegie Institution, 1921–1936.

Campbell, Maria Hull. *Revolutionary Services and Civil Life of General William Hull, Prepared from His Manuscript.* New York: E. F. Campbell, 1848.

Chipman, Daniel. *Memoir of Colonel Seth Warner.* Middlebury, VT: L. W. Clark, 1848.

Clinton, Henry. *The American Rebellion: Sir Henry Clinton's Narrative of His Campaigns, 1775–1782, with an Appendix of Original Documents.* Edited by William B. Willcox. New Haven, CT: Yale University Press, 1958.

Cobbett, William. *Parliamentary History of England.* 36 vols. London: T. C. Hansard, 1806–20.

Colbrath, William. *Days of Siege: A Journal of the Siege of Fort Stanwix in 1777.* Edited by Larry Lowenthal. Fort Washington, PA: Eastern National, 1983.

Commager, Henry Steele, and Richard B. Morris, eds. *The Spirit of 'Seventy-Six: The Story of the American Revolution as Told by the Participants.* New York: Bonanza Books, 1983.

Connecticut Historical Society. *Orderly Book and Journals Kept by Connecticut Men While Taking Part in the American Revolution. 1775–1778.* Hartford, CT: The Connecticut Society, 1899.

Davies, K.G. ed. *Documents of the American Revolution: Colonial Office Series.* 21 vols. Dublin: Irish University Press, 1972–1981.

Dearborn, Henry. "A Narrative of the Saratoga Campaign, Boston, December 20th, 1815: Letter to James Wilkinson, Dec 20, 1815, from Boston." *Bulletin of the Fort Ticonderoga Museum* 1.5 (January 1929): 2–12.

Digby, William. *Journal, 1776–1777.* In *The British Invasion from the North, the Campaigns of Generals Carlton and Burgoyne from Canada, 1776–1777.* Introductory chapter and notes from James Phinney Baxter. Albany, NY: Joel Munsell's Sons, 1887.

Doblin, Helga. "A Brunswick General with Burgoyne: The Journal of Johann Bense, 1776–1783." *New York History* 66.4 (October 1985).

Doblin, Helga, trans. *The Specht Journal: A Military Journal of the Burgoyne Campaign.* Westport, CT: Greenwood Press, 1995.

Ford, Chauncey, ed. *Journals of the Continental Congress, 1774–1789.* 34 vols. Washington, DC: Library of Congress, 1904–1937.

Fox, George,. "Corporal Fox's Memoir of Service, 1766–1783: Quebec, Saratoga, and the Convention Army." Edited by J. A. Houlding and G. Kenneth Gates. Originally published in *Journal for the Society for Army Historical Research* 68.275 (Autumn 1990).

Fraser, Simon. "General Fraser's Account of Burgoyne's Campaign on Lake Champlain and the Battle of Hubbardton." *Proceedings of the Vermont Historical Society.* 4(1898): 139–47.

Fraser, Simon. "Examination of a Spy from Ticonderoga, June 16, 1777." *The Bulletin of the Fort Ticonderoga Museum.* 10.3 (1959): 240–45.

Gansevoort, Peter. *Hero of Fort Schuyler: Selected Revolutionary War Correspondence of Brigadier General Peter Gansevoort, Jr.* Edited by David Ranzan and Matthew J. Hollis. Jefferson, NC: McFarland & Company, 2014.

George III. *The Correspondence of King George the Third from 1760 to December 1783.* Edited by J. W. Fortescue, 6 vols., London: Macmillan, 1927–28.

George III. *The Correspondence of King George the Third with Lord North, 1768 to 1783.* Vol. 2. Edited by W. Bodham Donne. New York: De Capo Press, 1971.

George III. *The Letters of King George III.* Edited by Bonamy Dobree. New York: Funk and Wagnalls, 1935.

Graham, James. *The Life of Daniel Morgan, of the Virginia Line of the Army of the United States, with Portions of his Correspondence, Compiled from Authentic Sources.* New York: Derby and Jackson, 1856.

Gruber, Ira, ed. *John Peebles' American War: The Diary of a Scottish Grenadier, 1776–1782.* Mechanicsburg, PA: Stackpole Books, 1998.

Hadden, James M. *Hadden's Journal and Orderly Books: A Journal Kept in Canada and upon Burgoyne's Campaign in 1776 and 1777 by Lieut. James M. Hadden.* With an explanatory chapter and notes by Horatio Rogers. Albany, NY.: Joel Munsell's Sons, 1884. With a new introduction and preface by George Athan Billias, Boston: Gregg Press, 1972.

Hamilton, Alexander. *The Papers of Alexander Hamilton, Volume I: 1768–1778.* Edited by Harold C. Syrett. New York: Columbia University Press, 1961.

Howe, William. *The Narrative of Lieutenant General Sir William Howe: In a Committee of the House of Commons, on the 29th of April 1779, relative to His Conduct, During His Late Command of the King's Troops in North America: To Which are Added, Some Observations Upon a Pamphlet, entitled, Letters to a Nobleman.* London: H. Baldwin, 1780.

Jefferson, Thomas. *The Papers of Thomas Jefferson.* Edited by Julian P. Boyd. Vols. 1–2. Princeton, NJ: Princeton University Press, 1950.

Kidder, Frederic. *History of the First New Hampshire Regiment in the War of the Revolution.* Includes Lieutenant Thomas Blake's journal. Reprint of the 1868 edition. Hampton, NH: Peter E. Randall, 1973.

Kingsley, Ronald F. "German Auxiliaries Project: The Incursion to Mount Independence, the Burgoyne Campaign, July 1777. Part II: Then Advance Against Mount Independence." *Hessians: Journal of the Johannes Schwalm Historical Association* 9 (2006): 53–73.

Kingsley, Ronald F., Harvey Alexander, and Eric Schnitzer. "German Auxiliaries Project: The Incursion to Mount Independence, the Burgoyne Campaign, July 1777. Part I: An Investigation of the Landing and Encampment." *Hessians: Journal of the Johannes Schwalm Historical Association* 8 (2005): 28–41.

Kulikoff, Allan, ed. *American Archives: Documents of the American Revolutionary Period, 1774–1776.* DeKalb: Northern Illinois University Libraries. http:// amarch.lib.niu.edLu/islandora/ object/niu-amarch%3A104112

Lamb, Roger. *Memoir of His Own Life by R. Lamb.* Dublin: J. Jones, 1811.

Lamb, Roger. *An Original and Authentic Journal of Occurrences during the Late American War from its Commencement to the Year 1783.* Dublin: Wilkinson and Courtney, 1809.

Lee, Richard Henry. *Life of Arthur Lee, LL.D.* Boston: Wells and Lilly, 1829.

Montagu, John. *The Private Papers of John, Earl of Sandwich, First Lord of the Admiralty, 1771–1782.* 4 vols. Edited by G. R. Barnes and J. H. Owens. London: Navy Records Society, 1932.

Muenchhausen, Friederich von. *At Howe's Side: The Diary of General William Howe's Aide de Camp, Captain Friederich von Muenchhausen.* Translated by Ernst Kipping. Edited by Samuel Smith. Monmouth Beach, NJ: Philip Freneau Press, 1974.

Napier, Francis. "Lord Francis Napier's Journal of the Burgoyne Campaign." *Maryland Historical Magazine* 57 (December 1962): 285–333. Magazine edited by S. Sydney Bradford.

Pausch, Georg. *Journal of Captain Pausch, Chief of the Hanau Artillery During the Burgoyne Campaign.* Translated by William L. Stone. Albany, NY: Joel Munsell's Sons, 1886.

Pettengill, Ray W., trans. and ed. *Letters from America, 1776–1779: Being Letters of Brunswick, Hessian, and Waldeck Officers with the British Armies During the Revolution.* New York: Houghton, Mifflin, 1924.

Powell, H. Watson. "Letters to Sir Guy Carlton, Sept 18–30, 1777." *Bulletin of the Fort Ticonderoga Museum* 7 (July 1945): 26–28.

Putnam, Israel. *General Orders Issued by Major General Israel Putnam, when in Command of the Highland, in the Summer and Fall of 1777.* Edited by Worthington Chauncey Ford. Brooklyn, NY: Historical Printing Club, 1893. More recent edition with a new introduction and preface by George Athan Billias. Boston: Gregg Press, 1972.

Retzer, Henry J., trans. "Journal of the Hessen-Hanau Erbpriz Infantry Regiment: Kept by 2nd Lieutenant Carl August Sartorius, Regimental Quartermaster." *Hessians: Journal of the Johannes Schwalm Historical Association* 6 (1999): 26–35.

Retzer, Henry J., trans. "Journal of the Hessen-Hanau Infantry Regiment Erbprinz—June to August 1777, Kept by Chaplain Philipp Theobald." *Hessians: Journal of the Johannes Schwalm Historical Association* 7 (2001): 40–42.

Riedesel, Frederike Charlotte Luise. *Baroness von Riedesel and the American Revolution; Journal and Correspondence of a Tour of Duty, 1776–1783.* Translated and edited by Marvin L. Brown Jr. Chapel Hill: University of North Carolina Press, 1965.

Riedesel, Frederike Charlotte Luise. *Letters and Journals relating to the War of American Independence and the capture of the German Troops at Saratoga.* Edited by Claus Reuter. Canada: Canadian Museum of Applied History, n.d.

Riedesel, Major General Friedrich A. Von. *Memoirs, and Letters and Journals, of Major General Riedesel During his Residence in America.* Edited by Max von Eelking. Translated by William L. Stone. Albany, NY: J. Munsell, 1868.

St. Clair, Arthur. *The Life and Public Services of Arthur St. Clair, with His Correspondence and Other Papers.* Edited by William Henry Smith. Cincinnati, OH: Robert Clarke, 1882.

St. Clair, Arthur. *Proceedings of a General Court Martial Held at White Plains, in the State of New York by Order of his Excellency George Washington, Commander in Chief of the Army of the United States of America, for the Trial of Major General St. Clair, August 25, 1778. Major General Lincoln, President.* New York-Historical Society Collections, Publication Fund Series, vol. 13, 1880.

Schuyler, Philip. *Proceedings of a General Court Martial Held at Major General Lincoln's Quarters near Quaker-Hill, in the State of New York, by Order of Excellency George Washington, Commander in Chief of the Army of the United States of America, for the Trail of Major General Schuyler, October 1, 1778. Major General Lincoln, President.* New-York Historical Society Collections, Publication Fund Series, Vol. 2, 1879.

Scudder, William. *The Journal of William Scudder, an Officer in the Late New-York Line.* New York: n.p., 1794.

Smith, Paul H., ed. *Letters of Delegates to Congress, 1774–1789.* 24 vols. Washington, DC: Library of Congress, 1976–2000.

Sparks, Jared, ed. *The Diplomatic Correspondence of the American Revolution.* Boston: N. Hale and Gray and Bowen, 1829–1830.

Stanley, Lt. Col. George F. G., ed. *For Want of a Horse: Being a Journal of the Campaigns Against the Americans in 1776 and 1777 Conducted from Canada, by an Officer Who Served with Lt. Gen. Burgoyne.* Sackville, New Brunswick: Tribune Press, 1961.

Stark, Caleb, ed. *Memoir and Official Correspondence of Gen. John Stark.* Concord, NH: G. Parker Lyon, 1860.

Stedman, Charles. *The History of the Origin, Progress, and Termination of the American War.* London: Privately Printed, 1794.

Stevens, Benjamin Franklin, ed., trans. *Facsimiles of Manuscripts in European Archives Relating to America, 1773–1783.* 25 vols. London: Malby & Sons, 1889–1895.

Stone, William L., trans. *Letters of Brunswick and Hessian Officers During the American Revolution.* Albany, NY: Joel Munsell's Sons, 1891.

Thacher, James. *A Military Journal During the American Revolutionary War from 1775–1783.* Boston: Richardson and Lord, 1823.

Walpole, Horace. *Journal of the Reign of King George the Third, from the Year 1771–1783.* Edited by John Doran. 4 vols. London: Bentley, 1859.

Walpole, Horace. *The Letters of Horace Walpole, Earl of Orford.* Edited by Peter Cunningham. London: R. Bentley, 1857.

Walpole, Horace. *The Letters of Horace Walpole, Fourth Earl of Orford, 1777–1779,* Vol. 10. Edited by Paget Toynbee. Oxford: Clarendon Press, 1854.

Washington, George. *The Papers of George Washington: Revolutionary War Series.* Vols. 1, 5, 8–12. Edited by Frank E. Grizzard Jr., Philander D. Chase, Edward Lengel, and David Hoth. Charlottesville: University Press of Virginia, 1985–2002.

Washington, George. *This Glorious Struggle: George Washington's Revolutionary War Letters.* Edited by Edward Lengel. New York: Harper Collins, 2007.

Wasmus, J. F. *An Eyewitness Account of the American Revolution and New England Life: The Journal of J. F. Wasmus, German Company Surgeon, 1776–1783.* Translated by Helga Doblin and edited by Mary C. Lynn. Westport, CT: Greenwood Press, 1990.

Wharton, Francis, ed. *The Revolutionary Diplomatic Correspondence of the United States.* 6 vols. Washington, DC: US Government Printing Office, 1889.

Wilkinson, James. *Memoirs of My Own Times.* Vol. 1. Philadelphia: Abraham Small, 1816.

Willett, William M., ed. *A Narrative of the Military Actions of Colonel Marinus Willett, Taken Chiefly from His Own Manuscript.* New York: G.C.H. Carville, 1831.

SECONDARY SOURCES

Andrlik, Todd. *Reporting the Revolutionary War.* Naperville, IL: Sourcebooks, 2012.

Ascoli, Peter M. "The French Press and the American Revolution: The Battle of Saratoga." *Proceedings of the Fifth Annual Meeting of the Western Society for French History, 10–12 November 1977*: 46–55. Edited by Joyce Duncan Falk. Santa Barbara, CA: Western Society for French History, 1978.

Barbieri, Michael R. "Bennington Fatally Delays Burgoyne." *Journal of the American Revolution.* June 11, 2013. https://allthingsliberty.com/2013/06/bennington-fatally-delays-burgoyne/

Barbieri, Michael R. "Mount Independence: 'The Most Intact Revolutionary War Site in America.'" *Journal of the American Revolution.* May 5, 2016. https://allthingsliberty.com/2016/05/mount-independence-the-most-intact-revolutionary-war-site-in-america/

Barbieri, Michael R. ". . . They Will Not Trouble Us Here this Summer": An Account of some Incidents that Took Place on 17 June 1777 near Fort Ticonderoga." *Bulletin of the Fort Ticonderoga Museum* 16.3 (2000): 253–71.

Bartholomees, J. Boone, ed. *U.S. Army War College Guide to National Security Issues, Volume I: Theory of War and Strategy.* Carlisle, PA: Strategic Studies Institute, June 2012.

Berleth, Richard. *Bloody Mohawk: The French and Indian War & American Revolution on New York's Frontier.* Hensonville, NY: Black Dome Press, 2009.

Bickham, Troy. *Making Headlines: The American Revolution as Seen Through the British Press.* DeKalb: Northern Illinois University Press, 2009.

Billias, George Athan, ed. *George Washington's Generals and Opponents, Their Exploits and Leadership.* 2 Vols. New York: Da Capo Press, 1994.

Billias, George Athan. "Horatio Gates: Professional Soldier." In *George Washington's Generals and Opponents, Their Exploits and Leadership.* Vol. 1, 79–108. Edited by George Anthan Billias. New York: Da Capo Press, 1994.

Billias, George Athan. "John Burgoyne: Ambitious General." In *George Washington's Generals and Opponents, Their Exploits and Leadership.* Vol. 2, 142–92. Edited by George Anthan Billias. New York: Da Capo Press, 1994.

Bird, Harrison. *March to Saratoga: General Burgoyne and the American Campaign, 1777.* New York: Oxford University Press, 1963.

Black, Jeremy. "British Military Strategy." In *Strategy in the American War of Independence: A Global Approach,* 58–72. Edited by Donald Stoker, Kenneth J. Hagan, and Michael T. McMaster. London: Routledge, 2010.

Black, Jeremy. *George III: America's Last King.* New Haven, CT: Yale, 2006.

Black, Jeremy. *Pitt the Elder.* Cambridge: Cambridge University Press, 1992.

Black, Jeremy. "Rethinking the Revolutionary War." *MHQ: Quarterly Journal of Military History* 17 (Spring 2005): 42–51.

Boatner, Mark Mayo, III. *Encyclopedia of the American Revolution.* Mechanicsburg, PA: Stackpole Books, 1994.

Boehlert, Paul A. *The Battle of Oriskany and General Nicholas Herkimer: Revolution in the Mohawk Valley.* Charleston, SC: History Press, 2013.

Bowler, R. Arthur. *Logistics and the Failure of the British Army in America, 1775–1783.* Princeton, NJ: Princeton University Press, 1975.

Brandt, Clare. *The Man in the Mirror: A Life of Benedict Arnold.* New York: Random House, 1994.

Brown, Gerald S. "The Court Martial of Lord George Sackville, Whipping Boy of the Revolutionary War." *William and Mary Quarterly* 9, no. 3 (July 1952): 317–37.

Brumwell, Stephen. *Turncoat: Benedict Arnold and the Crisis of American Liberty.* New Haven, CT: Yale University Press, 2018.

Calloway, Colin G. *The American Revolution in Indian Country: Crisis and Diversity in Native American Communities.* New York: Cambridge University Press, 1995.

Calloway, Colin G. *The Scratch of a Pen: 1763 and the Transformation of North America.* New York: Oxford University Press, 2006.

Cate, Alan C. *Founding Fighters: The Battlefield Leaders Who Made American Independence.* Westport, CT: Praeger Security International, 2006.

Chartrand, René. *American War of Independence Commanders.* Oxford: Osprey, 2003.

Chartrand, René. *Ticonderoga, 1758: Montcalm's Victory Against all Odds.* Oxford: Osprey, 2000.

Chernow, Ron. *Alexander Hamilton.* New York: Penguin Press, 2004.

Chernow, Ron. *Washington: A Life.* New York: Penguin Press, 2010.

Clausewitz, Carl von. *On War.* Edited and translated by Michael Howard and Peter Paret. Princeton, NJ: Princeton University Press, 1984.

Clement, Justin. *Philadelphia, 1777: Taking the Capital.* Oxford: Osprey, 2007.

Cohen, Eliot. *Conquered into Liberty: Two Centuries of Battles along the Great Warpath that Made the American Way of War.* New York: Free Press, 2011.

Cohen, Sheldon S. *British Supporters of the American Revolution, 1775–1783: The Role of the "Middling Level" Activists.* Rochester, NY: Boydell Press, 2004.

Conway, Stephen. "British Mobilization in the War of American Independence." *Historical Research* 72 (February 1999): 58–76.

Conway, Stephen. "From Fellow-Nationals to Foreigners: British Perceptions of the Americans, circa 1739–1783." *William and Mary Quarterly* 59, no. 1 (January 2002): 65–101.

Conway, Stephen. "To Subdue America: British Military Officers and the Conduct of the Revolutionary War." *William and Mary Quarterly* 43, no. 3 (July 1986): 381–407.

Corbett, Theodore. *No Turning Point: The Saratoga Campaign in Perspective.* Norman: University of Oklahoma Press, 2012.

Crary, Catherine S. *The Price of Loyalty: Tory Writings from the Revolutionary Era.* New York: McGraw-Hill, 1973.

Cubbison, Douglas R. *The American Northern Army in 1776: The Ruin and Reconstruction of the Continental Force.* Jefferson, NC: McFarland, 2010.

Cubbison, Douglas R. *"The Artillery Never Gained More Honour": The British Artillery in the 1776 Valcour Island and 1777 Saratoga Campaigns.* Fleischmanns, NY: Purple Mountain Press, 2007.

Cubbison, Douglas R. ed. *Burgoyne and the Saratoga Campaign: His Papers.* Norman, OK: Arthur H. Clark Company, 2012.

Cubbison, Douglas R. "Catastrophe on Lake Champlain, July 6, 1777." *American Revolution* (July/August 2012): 12–18.

de Fonblanque, Edward Barrington. *Political and Military Episodes in the Latter Half of the Eighteenth Century Derived from the Life and Correspondence of the Right Hon. John Burgoyne, General, Statesman, Dramatist.* London: Macmillan, 1876.

Duling, Ennis. "Thomas Anburey at the Battle of Hubbardton: How a Fraudulent Source Misled Historians." *Vermont History* 78, no. 1 (Winter/Spring 2010): 1–14.

Dull, Jonathan R. *A Diplomatic History of the American Revolution.* New Haven, CT: Yale University Press, 1985.

Dull, Jonathan R. *The French Navy and American Independence: A Study in Arms and Diplomacy, 1774–1787.* Princeton, NJ: Princeton University Press, 1975.

Dunlop, William. *History of the New Netherlands, Province of New York, and State of New York, to the Adoption of the Federal Constitution.* New York: Carter and Thorp, 1940.

Elting, John R. *The Battles of Saratoga.* Monmouth Beach, NJ: Philip Freneau Press, 1977.

Engels, Jeremy, and Greg Goodale. "'Our Battle Cry Will Be: Remember Jenny McCrea!': A Precis on the Rhetoric of Revenge." *American Quarterly* 61 (March 2009): 93–112.

Erickson, Edward J. *Gallipoli: Command Under Fire.* New York: Osprey, 2015.

Ferling, John. *Almost a Miracle: The American Victory in the War of Independence.* New York: Oxford University Press, 2007.

Fischer, David Hackett. *Paul Revere's Ride.* New York: Oxford University Press, 1994.

Fischer, David Hackett. *Washington's Crossing.* New York: Oxford University Press, 2004.

Fleming, Thomas. *Washington's Secret War.* New York: Smithsonian Books, 2005.

Gabriel, Michael P. *The Battle of Bennington: Soldiers and Civilians.* Charleston, SC: History Press, 2012.

Gadue, Michael R. "'Fatal Pique': The Failure of LTC Breymann to Relieve LTC Baum at Bennington, August 16, 1777, A Case of Braunschweig Dishonor?" *Hessians: Journal of the Johannes Schwalm Historical Association* 12 (2009): 44–56.

George, M. Dorothy. *London Life in the Eighteenth Century.* New York: Penguin, 1966.

Gerlach, Don R. *Proud Patriot: Philip Schuyler and the War of Independence, 1775–1783.* Syracuse, NY: Syracuse University Press, 1987.

Gerras, Stephen J. *Strategic Leadership Primer.* 3rd Ed. Carlisle Barracks, PA: Department of Command, Leadership, and Management, US Army War College, 2010.

Glatthaar, Joseph T., and James Kirby Martin. *Forgotten Allies: The Oneida Indians and the American Revolution.* New York: Hill and Wang, 2006.

Graymont, Barbara. *The Iroquois in the American Revolution.* Syracuse, NY: Syracuse University Press, 1975.

Grenier, John. *The First Way of War.* New York: Cambridge University Press, 2005.

Griswold, William A., and Donald W. Linebaugh, eds. *The Saratoga Campaign: Uncovering an Embattled Landscape.* Hanover, NH: University Press of New England, 2016.

Griswold, William A., and Donald W. Linebaugh. "The River Overlook Fortifications on Bemis Heights." In *The Saratoga Campaign: Uncovering an Embattled Landscape,* 105–26. Edited by William A. Griswold and Donald W. Linebaugh. Hanover, NH: University Press of New England, 2016.

Gruber, Ira D. *The Howe Brothers and the American Revolution.* New York: Athenaeum, 1972.

Hargrove, Richard J., Jr. *General John Burgoyne.* Newark: University of Delaware Press, 1983.

Harrington, Hugh T., and Jim Jordan. "The Other Mystery Shot of the American Revolution: Did Timothy Murphy Kill British Brigadier General Simon Fraser at Saratoga?" *Journal of Military History* 74 (October 2010): 1037–45.

Hart, Stephen Ashley. *Colossal Cracks: Montgomery's 21st Army Group in Northwest Europe, 1944–45.* Mechanicsburg, PA: Stackpole Books, 2007.

Herring, George. *From Colony to Superpower: U.S. Foreign Relations since 1776.* New York: Oxford University Press, 2008.

Hibbert, Christopher. *Redcoats and Rebels: The American Revolution Through British Eyes.* New York: Norton, 2002.

Higginbotham, Don. *George Washington and the American Military Tradition.* Athens: University of Georgia Press, 1987.

Higginbotham, Don. *George Washington Reconsidered.* Charlottesville: University of Virginia Press, 2001.

Holcomb, James. "Managing Strategic Risk". In *U.S. Army War College Guide to National Security Issues, Volume I: Theory of War and Strategy,* 67–77. Edited by J. Boone Bartholomees. Carlisle, PA: Strategic Studies Institute, June 2012.

Huddleson, Francis J. *Gentleman Johnny Burgoyne: Misadventures of an English General in the Revolution.* New York: Sun Dial Press, 1939.

Johnson, James M., Christopher Pryslopski, and Andrew Villani, eds. *Key to the Northern Country: The Hudson River Valley in the American Revolution.* Albany: State University of New York Press, 2013.

Joint Staff. *Joint Publication (JP) 1-02: Department of Defense Dictionary of Military and Associated Terms.* Washington, DC: The Joint Staff, April 2010.

Joint Staff. *Joint Publication (JP) 3.0: Joint Operations.* Washington, DC: The Joint Staff, August 11, 2011.

Joint Staff. *Joint Publication (JP) 5.0: Joint Operational Planning.* Washington, DC: Department of Defense, August 11, 2011.

Jones, Maldwyn A. "Sir William Howe: Conventional Strategist." In *George Washington's Generals and Opponents, Their Exploits and Leadership.* Vol. 2, 39–72. Edited by George Anthan Billias. New York: Da Capo Press, 1994.

Ketchum, Richard M. *Decisive Day: The Battle of Bunker Hill.* New York: Holt McDougal, 1999.

Ketchum, Richard M. *Saratoga: Turning Point of America's Revolutionary War.* New York: Henry Holt, 1997.

Kirk, Matthew, and Justin Divirgilio. "The Retreat to Victory Woods." In *The Saratoga Campaign: Uncovering an Embattled Landscape,* 145–62. Edited by William A. Griswold and Donald W. Linebaugh. Hanover, NH: University Press of New England, 2016.

Kopperman, Paul, "The Numbers Game: Health Issues in the Army That Burgoyne Led to Saratoga." *New York History* 88 (Summer 2007): 255–85.

Koster, John. "Jane McCrea, Remembered as a Victim of American Indian Brutality, May Have Died Under Different Circumstances." *Military History* 17 (June 2000): 12–16.

Langford, Paul. *A Polite and Commercial People: England, 1727–1783*. New York: Guild Publishing, 1989.
Laramie, Mike. "The Last Invasion of Canada." *Military History Matters* (August 2019): 40–46.
Linebaugh, Donald W. "Commemorating and Preserving an Embattled Landscape." In *The Saratoga Campaign: Uncovering an Embattled Landscape*, 229–58. Edited by William A. Griswold and Donald W. Linebaugh. Hanover, NH: University Press of New England, 2016.
Linklater, Andro. *An Artist in Treason: The Extraordinary Double Life of General James Wilkinson*. New York: Walker and Company, 2009.
Lombardi, Ben. "Assumptions and Grand Strategy." *Parameters* (Spring 2011): 29–40.
Lutnick, Solomon. "The American Victory at Saratoga: A View from the British Press." *New York History* 44, no. 2 (April 1963): 103–27.
Luzader, John F. "The Coming Revolutionary War Battles at Saratoga." In *The Saratoga Campaign: Uncovering an Embattled Landscape*, 1–38. Edited by William A. Griswold and Donald W. Linebaugh. Hanover, NH: University Press of New England, 2016.
Luzader, John F. *Fort Stanwix: Construction and Military History*. Washington, DC: National Park Service, 1976. https://www.nps.gov/parkhistory/online_books/fost/history/history.htm
Luzader, John F. *Saratoga: A Military History of the Decisive Campaign of the American Revolution*. New York: Savas Beatie, LLC, 2008.
Lynch, Wayne. "Arnold in Command at Bemis Heights." *Journal of the American Revolution*. November 14, 2013. http://allthingsliberty.com/2013/11/arnold-command-bemis-heights/
Lynch, Wayne. "Debating Arnold's Role at Freeman's Farm." *Journal of the American Revolution*. September 12, 2013. http://allthingsliberty.com/2013/09/debating-arnolds-role-freemans-farm/
Mackesy, Piers. *The Coward of Minden: The Affair of Lord George Sackville*. New York: St. Martin's Press, 1979.
Mackesy, Piers. *The War for America, 1775–1783*. Lincoln: University of Nebraska Press, 1993.
Magnet, Myron. "When George Washington Became Great: Those Were the Times that Tried Men's Souls." *City Journal*. Winter 2012. http://www.city-journal.org/html/whengeorge-washington-became-great-13458.html
Mahan, Alfred Thayer. "Major Operations of the Royal Navy, 1762–1783." In *The Royal Navy: A History from the Earliest Times to the Present*. Vol. 3. William Laird Clowes, ed. London: Sampson Low, Marston and Company, 1898.
Martin, James Kirby. "Benedict Arnold: The Hero Before the Traitor." *History Net*. February 16, 2016. http://www.historynet.com/benedict-arnold-the-hero-before-the-traitor.htm
Martin, James Kirby. *Benedict Arnold, Revolutionary Hero: An American Warrior Reconsidered*. New York: New York University Press, 2000.
Mattern, David B. *Benjamin Lincoln and the American Revolution*. Columbia: University of South Carolina Press, 1995.
May, Robin. *The British Army in North America, 1775–1783*. Reading, UK: Osprey, 1974.
Mercer, Patrick. "The 9th (East Norfolk) Regiment of Foot, Saratoga, 19 September & 7 October 1777" *Military History Monthly*. February 2017: 55-56.
Middlekauff, Robert. *The Glorious Cause: The American Revolution, 1763–1789*. New York: Oxford University Press, 2005.
Milsop, John. *Continental Infantrymen of the American Revolution*. Oxford: Osprey, 2004.
Mintz, Max M. *The Generals of Saratoga: John Burgoyne & Horatio Gates*. New Haven, CT: Yale University Press, 1990.
Monk, Will. "The Myth of 'Granny Gates.'" *Journal of the American Revolution*. October 2, 2014. http://allthingsliberty.com/2014/10/the-myth-of-granny-gates/
Moore, Frank. *Diary of the American Revolution from Newspapers and Original Documents*. 2 vols. New York: Charles Scribner, 1860.
Morgan, Ron R. "Arthur St. Clair's Decision to Abandon Fort Ticonderoga and Mount Independence." *Journal of the American Revolution*. May 16, 2016. https://allthingsliberty.

com/2016/05/arthur-st-clairs-decision-to-abandon-fort-ticonderoga-and-mount-independence/#_ednref37

Morgan, Ron R. "'Shamefully Abandoning the posts of Ticonderoga and Mount Independence, in His Charge': The Court Martial of Major General Arthur St. Clair and the Verdict of History." Mount Independence Coalition, 2013. http://035a6a2.netsolhost.com/wordpress1/historical-articles/reconsidering-the-retreat-from-mount-independence/

Morrissey, Brendan. *Saratoga, 1777: Turning Point of the Revolution.* Oxford: Osprey, 2000.

Nagy, John A. "British Spy Plot to Capture Fort Ticonderoga in 1777." *Journal of the American Revolution.* February 19, 2014. http://allthingsliberty.com/2014/02/british-spy-plot-to-capture-fort-ticonderoga-in-1777/

Nagy, John A. *Invisible Ink: Spycraft of the American Revolution.* Yardley, PA: Westholm, 2010.

Nelson, Paul David. *General Horatio Gates.* Baton Rouge: Louisiana University Press, 1976.

Nelson, Paul David. *General Sir Guy Carleton, Lord Dorchester: Soldier-Statesman of Early British Canada.* Cranbury, NJ: Fairleigh Dickinson University Press, 2000.

Nester, William R. *The Frontier War for Independence.* Mechanicsburg, PA: Stackpole Books, 2004.

Nickerson, Hoffman. *The Turning Point of the Revolution, or Burgoyne in America.* Boston: Houghton Mifflin, 1928.

Norman, Geoffrey. "Big Win at Saratoga: The 1777 British Surrender was the Revolution's Turning Point." *Military History* (October 2007): 26–35.

O'Shaughnessy, Andrew Jackson. *The Men Who Lost America: British Leadership, the American Revolution, and the Fate of Empire.* New Haven, CT: Yale University Press, 2013.

O'Toole, Fintan. *White Savage: William Johnson and the Invention of America.* New York: Farrar, Straus & Giroux, 2005.

Pell, John H. G. "Philip Schuyler: The General as Aristocrat." InIn *George Washington's Generals and Opponents, Their Exploits and Leadership.* Vol. 1, 54–78. Edited by George Anthan Billias. New York: Da Capo Press, 1994.

Rauser, Amelia. "Hair, Authenticity, and Self-Made Macaroni." *Eighteenth-Century Studies* 38, no. 1 (2004): 101–17.

Reid, Stuart. *British Redcoat, 1740–1793.* London: Osprey, 1998.

Reid, Stuart. *Redcoat Officer, 1740–1815.* Oxford: Osprey, 2002.

Rodger, N.A.M. *The Insatiable Earl: A Life of John Montagu, Fourth Earl of Sandwich, 1718–1792.* New York: W.W. Norton and Company, 1993.

Rose, Alexander. *Washington's Spies: The Story of America's First Spy Ring.* New York: Random House, 2006.

Rose, Ben Z. *John Stark: Maverick General.* Barrington, NH: Bisson & Barcelona, 2007.

Rossie, Jonathan Gregory. *The Politics of Command in the American Revolution.* Syracuse, NY: Syracuse University Press, 1975.

Schnitzer, Eric H. "Organization of the Army from Canada Commanded by Lieutenant-General John Burgoyne—September 19 to October 7, 1777." Stillwater, NY: Saratoga National Military Park. January 2013.

Schnitzer, Eric H. "Organization of the Army of the United States under the Command of Major General Horatio Gates at Bemis Heights 19 September 1777." Stillwater, NY: Saratoga National Military Park. January 2013.

Schnitzer, Eric H. "Organization of the Army of the United States under the Command of Major General Horatio Gates at Bemis Heights 7 October 1777." Stillwater, NY: Saratoga National Military Park. January 2013.

Schnitzer, Eric H. "A Review of the Organization of the Corps of Light Infantry, Northern Department, August–November 1777." Stillwater, NY: Saratoga National Military Park. October 2009.

Schnitzer, Eric H. "The Tactics of the Battles of Saratoga." In *The Saratoga Campaign: Uncovering an Embattled Landscape,* 39–79. Edited by William A. Griswold and Donald W. Linebaugh. Hanover, NH: University Press of New England, 2016.

Schnitzer, Eric H. "What's His Motivation: Analyzing the Purpose of Burgoyne's 7 October 1777 Reconnaissance Force." Stillwater, NY: Saratoga National Military Park. October 2009.

Shipton, Clifford K. "Benjamin Lincoln: Old Reliable." In *George Washington's Generals and Opponents, Their Exploits and Leadership.* Vol. 1, 193–211. Edited by George Anthan Billias. New York: Da Capo Press, 1994.

Shy, John W. *A People Numerous and Armed: Reflections on the Military Struggle for American Independence.* New York: Oxford University Press, 1976.

Simms, Brendan. *Three Victories and a Defeat: The Rise and Fall of the First British Empire.* New York: Basic Books, 2007.

Smith, Paul H. "Sir Guy Carleton: Soldier-Statesman." In *George Washington's Generals and Opponents, Their Exploits and Leadership.* Vol. 2: 103–41. Edited by George Anthan Billias. New York: Da Capo Press, 1994.

Snow, Dean R. "The British Fortifications." In *The Saratoga Campaign: Uncovering an Embattled Landscape,* 81–104. Edited by William A. Griswold and Donald W. Linebaugh. Hanover, NH: University Press of New England, 2016.

Sparks, Jared. *The Library of American Biography.* 2nd Series, Vol. 13. Boston: Little and Brown, 1847.

Spring, Matthew H. *With Zeal and with Bayonets Only: The British Army on Campaign in North America, 1775–1783.* Norman: University of Oklahoma Press, 2008.

Starbuck, David R. "The American Fortifications." In *The Saratoga Campaign: Uncovering an Embattled Landscape,*. 127–44. Edited by William A. Griswold and Donald W. Linebaugh. Hanover, NH: University Press of New England, 2016.

Starbuck, David R. *The Great Warpath: British Army Military Sites from Albany to Crown Point.* Hanover, NH: University Press of New England, 1999.

Starbuck, David R. "The Schuyler House." In *The Saratoga Campaign: Uncovering an Embattled Landscape,* 179–93. Edited by William A. Griswold, and Donald W. Linebaugh. Hanover, NH: University Press of New England, 2016.

Stewart, Richard W., ed. *American Military History, Vol. 1: The United States Army and the Forging of a Nation, 1775–1917.* Washington, DC: Center of American History, 2005.

Stoker, Donald, Kenneth J. Hagan, and Michael T. McMaster, eds. *Strategy in the American War of Independence: A Global Approach.* London: Routledge, 2010.

Storozynski, Alex. *Peasant Prince: Thaddeus Kosciuszko and the Age of Revolution.* New York: St. Martin's Press. 2009.

Stull, Scott, Michael Rogers, and Len Tantillo. "The Surrender and Aftermath of the Battles." In *The Saratoga Campaign: Uncovering an Embattled Landscape,* 163–77. Edited by William A. Griswold and Donald W. Linebaugh, Hanover, NH: University Press of New England, 2016.

Taaffe, Stephen R. *The Philadelphia Campaign, 1777–1778.* Lawrence: University Press of Kansas, 2003.

Thayer, Theodore. *Nathanael Greene: Strategist of the American Revolution.* New York: Twayne, 1960.

Tomlin, Gregory M. "Valcour Island: Setting the Conditions for Victory at Saratoga." In *Key to the Northern Country: The Hudson River Valley in the American Revolution,* 269–84. Edited by James M. Johnson, Christopher Pryslopski, and Andrew Villani. Albany: State University of New York Press, 2013.

Trudeau, Noah Andre. "Thunder on the Hudson." *Military History Quarterly* 20 (Summer 2008): 56–63.

Tudda, Chris. "'A Messiah that Will Never Come': A New Look at Saratoga, Independence, and Revolutionary War Diplomacy." *Diplomatic History* 32 (November 2008): 779–810.

Valentine, Alan. *Lord George Germain.* Oxford: Oxford University Press, 1962.

Valosin, Christine. "The Saratoga Battles in Fifty Artifacts." In *The Saratoga Campaign: Uncovering an Embattled Landscape,* 195–228. Edited by William A. Griswold and Donald W. Linebaugh. Hanover, NH: University Press of New England, 2016.

Van Alstyne, Richard W. *Empire and Independence: The International History of the American Revolution.* New York: Wiley, 1965.

Van Alstyne, Richard W. "Europe, the Rockingham Whigs and the War for American Independence." *Huntington Library Quarterly* 25 (1961–62): 1–28.

Van Alstyne, Richard W. "Great Britain, the War for Independence, and the 'Gathering Storm' in Europe." *Huntington Library Quarterly* 24.4 (August 1964): 311–46.

Venter, Bruce M. *The Battle of Hubbardton: The Rear Guard Action That Saved America.* Charleston, SC: History Press, 2015.

Venter, Bruce M. "Behind Enemy Lines: Americans Attack Burgoyne's Supply Lines." *Patriot s of the American Revolution* 4, no. 3 (May/June 2011): 12–18

Walker, Paul K. *Engineers of Independence: A Documentary History of the Army Engineers in the American Revolution, 1775–1783.* Washington, DC: Historical Division, U.S. Army Corps of Engineers, 1977.

Wallace, Willard M. "Benedict Arnold: Traitorous Patriot." In *George Washington's Generals and Opponents, Their Exploits and Leadership.* Vol. 1, 163–92. Edited by George Anthan Billias. New York: Da Capo Press, 1994.

Watt, Gavin K. *Rebellion in the Mohawk Valley: The St. Leger Expedition of 1777.* Toronto: Dundurn, 2002.

Weddle, Kevin J. "'A Change of Both Men and Measures': British Reassessment of Military Strategy after Saratoga, 1777–1778." *Journal of Military History* 77, no. 3 (July 2013): 837–65.

Whiteley, Peter. *Lord North: The Prime Minister Who Lost America.* London: Hambleton & London, 2006.

Willcox, William B. "British Strategy in America, 1778." *Journal of Modern History* 19 (June 1947): 97–121.

Willcox, William B. *Portrait of a General: Sir Henry Clinton in the War of Independence.* New York: Knopf, 1964.

Willcox, William B. "Sir Henry Clinton: Paralysis of Command." In *George Washington's Generals and Opponents, Their Exploits and Leadership.* Vol. 2, 73–102. Edited by George Anthan Billias. New York: Da Capo Press, 1994.

Willcox, William B. "Too Many Cooks: British Planning Before Saratoga." *Journal of British Studies* 2, no. 1 (November 1962): 56–90.

Willcox, William B. "Why Did the British Lose the American Revolution?" *Michigan Alumnus Review* 62 (1956): 317–24.

Williams, Glenn F. *Year of the Hangman: George Washington's Campaign against the Iroquois.* Yardley, PA: Westholme, 2005.

Williams, John. *The Battle of Hubbardton: The American Rebels Stem the Tide.* Montpelier: Vermont Division for Historical Preservation, 1988.

Wilson, Barry K. *Benedict Arnold: A Traitor in Our Midst.* Montreal: McGill-Queen's University Press, 2001.

Wright, Robert K., Jr. *The Continental Army.* Washington, DC: Center of Military History, 2006.

Yarger, Harry R. *Strategic Theory for the 21st Century: The Little Book on Big Strategy.* Carlisle, PA: Strategic Studies Institute, February 2006.

Yarger, Harry R. *Strategy and the National Security Professional.* Westport, CT: Praeger, 2008.

Yarger, Harry R. "Toward a Theory of Strategy: Art Lykke and the U.S. Army War College Strategy Model." In *U.S. Army War College Guide to National Security Issues, Volume I: Theory of War and Strategy,* 45–51. Edited by J. Boone Bartholomees. Carlisle, PA: Strategic Studies Institute, June 2012.

Zlatich, Marko. *General Washington's Army, Part 1: 1775–1778.* London: Osprey, 1994.

INDEX

Note: Page numbers in *italics* denote maps.